The Editor

JOHN P. HARRINGTON is Dean of the School of Humanities and Social Sciences at Rensselaer Polytechnic Institute. He is the author of *The Life of the Neighborhood Playhouse on Grand Street*, *The Irish Play on the New York Stage*, *The Irish Beckett: Irish Contexts of Samuel Beckett's Work*, and *The English Traveler in Ireland*. He has published many articles on a wide range of topics in Irish literature.

A NORTON CRITICAL EDITION

MODERN AND CONTEMPORARY IRISH DRAMA

Cathleen Ni Houlihan • The Pot of Broth • At the
Hawk's Well • Purgatory • Spreading the News •
The Rising of the Moon • Riders to the Sea • The
Playboy of the Western World • John Bull's Other
Island • Juno and the Paycock • Krapp's Last Tape •
Translations • The Weir • By the Bog of Cats

BACKGROUNDS AND CRITICISM

Second Edition

Edited by

JOHN P. HARRINGTON

RENSSELAER POLYTECHNIC INSTITUTE

W. W. NORTON & COMPANY

New York • London

W. W. Norton & Company has been independent since its founding in 1923, when William Warder Norton and Mary D. Herter Norton first published lectures delivered at the People's Institute, the adult education division of New York City's Cooper Union. The firm soon expanded its program beyond the Institute, publishing books by celebrated academics from America and abroad. By mid-century, the two major pillars of Norton's publishing program—trade books and college texts—were firmly established. In the 1950s, the Norton family transferred control of the company to its employees, and today—with a staff of four hundred and a comparable number of trade, college, and professional titles published each year—W. W. Norton & Company stands as the largest and oldest publishing house owned wholly by its employees.

This title is printed on permanent paper containing
30 percent post-consumer waste recycled fiber.

The text of this book is composed in Fairfield Medium
with the display set in Bernhard Modern.
Book design by Antonina Krass.
Composition by PennSet, Inc.
Manufacturing by the Courier Companies—Westford division.
Production manager: Eric Pier-Hocking.

Library of Congress Cataloging-in-Publication data
Modern and contemporary Irish drama / edited by John P. Harrington. —
2nd ed.
    p.   cm. — (A Norton critical edition)
    Rev. ed. of : Modern Irish drama / edited by John P. Harrington. 1st ed.
c1991.
    Includes bibliographical references.
            ISBN 978-0-393-93243-0
    1. English drama—Irish authors.   2. English drama—Irish authors—
History and criticism.   3. English drama—20th century—History and
criticism.   4. English drama—20th century.   5. Ireland—In literature.
6. Ireland—Drama.   I. Harrington, John P.   II. Modern Irish drama.
PR8869.M63   2009
822'.910809415—dc20

                                                          2008044745

W. W. Norton & Company, Inc., 500 Fifth Avenue, New York, NY 10110-0017
wwnorton.com

W. W. Norton & Company Ltd., Castle House,
75/76 Wells Street, London W1T 3QT

                6   7   8   9   0

Contents

Introduction

In 1897, modern Irish drama as we know it was defined in provocative and unresolved ways by William Butler Yeats, Lady Augusta Gregory, and Edward Martyn in a declaration of intentions for a national dramatic movement for Ireland. The crucial text was composed at Duras House, the country residence of Lady Gregory's French friend Florimand Comte de Basterot, near Lady Gregory's own western Ireland estate, Coole Park, which was near Edward Martyn's estate, Tillyra Castle, and Yeats's future summer home, Thoor Ballylee. The text is reproduced in Lady Gregory's memoir *Our Irish Theatre*:

> We propose to have performed in Dublin, in the spring of every year certain Celtic and Irish plays, which whatever be their degree of excellence will be written with a high ambition, and so to build up a Celtic and Irish school of dramatic literature. We hope to find in Ireland an uncorrupted and imaginative audience trained to listen by its passion for oratory, and believe that our desire to bring upon the stage the deeper thoughts and emotions of Ireland will ensure for us a tolerant welcome, and that freedom to experiment which is not found in theatres of England, and without which no new movement in art or literature can succeed. We will show that Ireland is not the home of buffoonery and of easy sentiment, as it has been represented, but the home of an ancient idealism.

Some local context for this statement is provided in the selection from Lady Gregory's book reprinted in this volume on page [401]. The more general context can be sketched here as introduction to this collection of modern and contemporary Irish plays. All of these plays relate, in assent or in dissent, willingly or unwillingly, and directly or indirectly, to the thesis of this prospectus. The earliest of the plays in this volume is *Cathleen Ni Houlihan*, once attributed to William Butler Yeats as author and now known to be a collaboration of him and Lady Gregory. The most recent is Marina Carr's *By the Bog of Cats* from 1998. The body of work that they and the other plays in this volume represent is Irish theater of the twentieth century. In the course of that century, Ireland itself was transformed from a colony administered by England into an indepen-

dent republic with the fastest-growing and most international economy in Europe. These plays are in part a representation of that
transformation and the cultural history of that century.

The idea of a national drama, which is not at all specific to Ireland, is to represent the theater's audience on its stage ("to bring
upon the stage the deeper thoughts and emotions of Ireland") and
at the same time to elevate that audience (to perform plays written
"with a high ambition"). Thus national drama has a complex relation to its audience: to reflect the audience as it is, and simultaneously to improve it. Both roles are presumptuous. The first
presumes the authority to identify the nation, an exercise of radical
reduction and selection in even so small a country as Ireland. The
authors of the prospectus for an Irish drama on summer holiday on
landed estates, for example, were obviously not representative of
the people of the nation. The exercise of defining a "school of dramatic literature" entails evaluating segments of a national society
and determining which will occupy center stage as the authorized
emblem of nation, or as "the real Ireland." Early in the century, especially in the works of John Millington Synge, the rural peasantry
prevailed as "the real Ireland," and by mid-century, in the face of
modernization that was both reluctant and relentless, this identification of "the real Ireland" hardened into an increasingly irrelevant
convention whereby, many complained, Irish plays were ranked by
measure of "PQ," or peasant quality, rather than ambition or exper-
imentation as forecast by the founders. Audiences, however, were
increasingly content and even proud of the convention as emblem
of the distinctiveness of their culture. In identification of a "real
Ireland," empiricism was rarely the preferred tool. Roger McHugh,
a contributor to the Abbey Theatre in a variety of roles, recalled
how he defended Sean O'Casey's *The Plough and the Stars* before
an audience outraged by one character because, they argued, there
were no prostitutes in Dublin, and how he, McHugh, was that
evening solicited by prostitutes on his way home. The real Ireland,
then, could be fictionalized by dramatists or by audiences alike.

The second original role forecast for the national drama, improving the audience, presumes to identify the people's proper aspirations and to require their enrollment, by attendance, in an
improving program. The historical record indicates that the Irish
audience was generally quite happy with its current aspirations and
so preferred self-congratulatory drama over any "new movement in
art or literature." Further, its "passion for oratory" evidently trained
the "uncorrupted and imaginative audience" in speaking as well as
in listening, for modern Irish drama is notable for obstreperous objections to the images of the Irish people presented to the Irish
people by Irish playwrights. "What is the meaning of this rubbish?"

asked one notable, enraged objector, Frank Hugh O'Donnell, of the first Yeats contribution in 1899 to the Celtic and Irish school of dramatic literature promised by the founders. "How will it help the national cause? How is it to help any cause at all?" The same questions were asked at mid-century. At that time, plays, now much-maligned, prevailed that were, if not wholly self-congratulatory, certainly manageable in their demands. Then it was the playwrights who were discontent. In 1958, in only the second of the annual Dublin Theatre Festivals, O'Casey had a follow-up bout when the Catholic church, acting on behalf of its parishioners, objected to immorality in *The Drums of Father Ned*: O'Casey simply withdrew his play, and in this action he was followed by producers of a dramatization of James Joyce's *Ulysses* and by Samuel Beckett, who banned all of his plays in Ireland "so long as such conditions prevail." In sufficient ire, then, the audience can walk away and the playwrights can close their own plays.

Early in the century, the audience was displeased, and especially so by Synge, and halted performance of his work. In the face of that opposition, the founders of the theater movement were proud to be improvers of the audience. Mid-century guardians of the national theater were content with the role of representing the audience. By end of century, neither role seemed sufficient. The founding intentions for the institution of national drama were rendered obsolete once the audience was no longer national, but international, and the framework of institutional intentions was no longer distinguishing Ireland from England but representing Ireland in an increasingly globalized context both economic and cultural. At the centenary celebration of the Abbey Theatre in 2004, the Irish critic Fintan O'Toole described the prospectus of 1897 as essentially a rebuttal to the globalization of its time, the reach of British empire, and asked, "how does that motivation continue to exist and to mean something in a society which has now become actually very comfortably globalized in many ways?"

In Ireland in 1897 the focus was on national independence. To this national focus, drama was a significant contribution, though a problematic one. It could please, as with *Cathleen Ni Houlihan*, and it could infuriate, as with *The Playboy of the Western World*. Nationalism, one of the principal factors in modern history, is organization and agitation to establish or to preserve a government that reflects its constituency. Nationalism takes shape in the wake of colonialism, a prior factor in history, in which single imperialist states amassed global territories and administered them with policies that reflected home base more than local population. Ireland was claimed by England as long ago as 1141, and it was with considerable difficulty maintained as a barely manageable colony by

Elizabeth I in 1601 and by successive monarchs. The persistent, contrary Irish agitation for self-rule entered a modern phase in the nineteenth century, when the modern nation states began to emerge from and to replace empire throughout the world. In Ireland, the Young Ireland movement addressed its people in the literary medium of patriotic poems and ballads, a medium that, like theater, demands group performance. Some argue that the Irish independence movement concluded in 1922, with the establishment of the Irish Free State of twenty-six counties; others argue that it continues today, when the island is partitioned into an autonomous Irish Republic and a smaller Northern Ireland territory of six counties that continues to be administered by Britain.

As the Yeats/Gregory/Martyn prospectus for an Irish national drama dates from 1897, and as Irish playwrights continue to address the issue of self-determination and continuing civil strife today, nationalism is the informing focus of modern Irish drama in this century. There are exceptions and counter-traditions, such as those represented by Samuel Beckett. And Nationalism is a focus, but not a position: drama helps articulate both arguments and counterarguments; the drama is national but not nationalist. Bernard Shaw noted this in a 1913 essay on nationalism written about ten years after *John Bull's Other Island* and its preface: "The modern Irish theatre began with the *Cathleen Ni Houlihan* of Mr. Yeats and Lady Gregory's *Rising of the Moon*, in which the old patriotism stirred and wrung its victims; but when the theatre thus established called on Young Ireland to write plays and found a national school of drama, the immediate result was a string of plays of Irish life—and very true to life they were—in which heroines proclaimed that they were sick of Ireland and [be]rated their Nationalist husbands for sacrificing all the realities of life to senseless Fenian maunderings." Such was the outcome of the Yeats/Martyn/Gregory call for a "Celtic and Irish school of dramatic literature." The result was not a common set of unimpeachable axioms. It was an extended and ongoing critique with many points of comparison connecting the earliest to the latest of the plays in this volume. For example, the theme of "strangers in the house" informs *Cathleen Ni Houlihan* no less than *The Weir* or *By the Bog of Cats*.

Political nationalism is a pragmatic program in which a native population or spokespeople for a native population organize formidable resistance to outside, colonial government. Though he was not one, a political pragmatist might well ask Frank Hugh O'Donnell's question: How will it help the cause? In *Juno and the Paycock* Sean O'Casey gives a particularly chilling portrait of political nationalists, members of the Irish Republican Army, assassinating one of their own, Johnny Boyle, as a matter of praxis: elimination of a suspected informer. Cultural nationalism, generally a corollary movement, is an aesthetic program to organize for a native population a sustaining image of itself, its uniqueness, and its dignity, all contrary to the subordinate and submissive identity nurtured by external, foreign administration. Much of the thrust of cultural nationalism is rescue of a dignified indigenous culture previously submerged by the powerful colonial culture: in the Irish context, this found expression in the concept of "the hidden Ireland," which movements for cultural rebirth, like a national dramatic movement, can recover. Thus a national drama often focuses on local culture as yet unspoiled by the influence of foreign colonialism, as in Synge's *Riders to the Sea,* or, better yet, in plays written and performed in Irish Gaelic, like Douglas Hyde's *Casadh an tSugain (The Twisting of the Rope).* Thus a national literary movement, like Ireland's at the turn of the century, is termed a "revival": restoration of a culture temporarily marginalized by outsiders to its proper, central place. A key component of this effort is reinterpretation of local history from a native perspective. In this collection, *Cathleen Ni Houlihan* and *Translations* are historical dramas that restore Irish dignity to historical episodes previously regarded most often and most "officially" from a British perspective.

Cultural nationalism, however, is not as pragmatic or didactic as political nationalism, and that accounts for drama's lack of unanimity. The background material on the Irish Dramatic Movement in this volume offers simultaneous and quite contrary views on founding priorities from Gregory, John Eglinton, Yeats, and Frank Fay that might be termed respectively as the pragmatic, the modernist, the artistic, and the nationalist ways forward. Lady Gregory, despite the prospectus of an Irish National Theatre, admits buffoonery in depiction of folk culture in *Spreading the News.* Shaw depicts Irish nationalism as a clever scam in *John Bull's Other Island.* Further, political nationalists, seeking unanimity, could and did argue that the dramatists establishing images of folk culture were not of it. Yeats, Gregory, and Martyn, who presumed to tell the people who they were and who they should be, were landed gentry or, in Yeats's case, at least of such pretension. Colm Tóibín, in his essay on the collaboration of Yeats and Lady Gregory, comments on their "aristocratic qualities." Yeats's own poems frequently acknowledge both the distance of the shapers of Irish culture of his time from "the people" and also the nobility of their contribution to the cause. Synge, authorized dramatist of peasant culture, could be termed an urban, professorial linguist with equal enthusiasms for Gaelic folk culture and the very latest in Parisian intellectual fashion. Thus the landmark early plays of Irish national drama could plausibly be viewed, as they have been by some, as an invented folk culture that

served the needs of artists and intellectuals. The notable theater riots in Dublin over Synge and O'Casey plays were audience counterarguments that the plays in question were neither useful nor
accurate. Playwrights often responded without challenging that
point. In his autobiography, Yeats wrote that the national drama,
and in particular the Abbey Theatre that epitomizes it, "will fail to
do its full work because there is no accepted authority to explain
why the more difficult pleasure is the nobler pleasure. The fascination of the National Movement for me in my youth was, I think,
that it seemed to promise such authority." Hence his work, for example *At the Hawk's Well*, took an aesthetic route not followed by
others and might be termed the Irish dramatic movement that was
not. His own "Introduction to My Plays" concedes that the audience demanded comedy, not his exercises in music and movement
on stage. Contemporary Irish playwrights such as Conor McPherson and Marina Carr, whose lives have more closely resembled
those of their audiences, have succeeded in drawing theatergoers to
plays that are both comedies and difficult pleasures.

The theatergoer in Dublin at the turn of the century might well
have wondered if the playwrights even considered the value of entertainment. Though the comic mode was an element of modern Irish drama from its beginning, the national drama scarcely
matched the popular draw of other theater fare already well-
established in Dublin. Dublin was in fact the site of the first licensed English theater outside London: it was established by a new
Lord Deputy of Ireland, Thomas Wentworth, and opened in 1637
on Werburgh Street near the center of colonial administration at
Dublin Castle. There the estimable dramatist and resident playwright James Shirley wrote *St. Patrick for Ireland* (1639), generally
considered the first play with Irish subject matter. After the restoration of Stuart monarchy reopened theaters briefly closed by Puritan
government, Dublin was notable for the Smock Alley Theatre and
for a series of playwrights, Irish by birth or association, critical
to English drama: William Congreve, George Farquhar, Richard
Steele, Oliver Goldsmith, Richard Brinsley Sheridan, and others.
These, like Oscar Wilde and Bernard Shaw in a later period, gravi-
tated to London, to its dramatic traditions and innovations, and to
its English audiences. Dublin theater functioned as a provincial
theater, or a straw-hat circuit theater, trying out productions that
hoped to reach London or wringing last earnings from productions
already closed in London. By the late nineteenth century Dublin
houses offered light operas, melodramas, the "well-made" plays of
curtain solutions, and musical variety shows. This was entertainment indeed. Robert Hogan and James Kilroy's *The Irish Literary
Theatre* lists offerings in the late 1890s that included the musical

comedies *The Skirt Dancer* and *A Greek Slave,* respectable British dramas such as Arthur Wing Pinero's *The Second Mrs. Tanqueray,* and a musical card with Virto, "the Man of Many Instruments"; Werner and Rieder, "Duettists and Swiss Warblers"; *and* the Eight Eldorados. Some of this could be done with an Irish angle: there was the light opera *Lily of Killarney* or the drama *An Irish Gentleman.* There were as well the Irish melodramas of Dion Boucicault, such as *Arrah-na-Pogue* and *The Colleen Bawn:* these were and are thought to have more than purely melodramatic value. But all this Irish material was done with an eye to export, usually to London, though Boucicault went to New York. Hence the "Irish" quality— conspicuous drunkenness, clownishness, and sentimentality—was exaggerated for recognition by a foreign audience, and the result was a caricature known as "the stage Irishman." One of the interesting points of comparisons on Irish theater at the beginning and at the end of the twentieth century is that the Irish playwright may now, as before, look toward export and the London audience. Conor McPherson, in particular, has opened many of his works in London, where he believes levels of artistic support and audience interest exceed those of Dublin.

The syndrome of theater looking abroad before it looked to home audiences was the condition the Irish Literary Theatre hoped to offset by resolving "to build up a Celtic and Irish school of dramatic literature" in Dublin. The prospectus written by Yeats, Martyn, and Lady Gregory resulted most immediately in productions in 1899 intended to add to this functioning Dublin theatrical scene artistic idealism and native culture. The project operated in conjunction with an Irish literary revival in all genres: poetry, fiction, criticism, new histories, and translation from and into Irish Gaelic. Because drama is fundamentally a group event, involving authors, production personnel, and an audience, Irish drama took a critical public role in this revival. The dramatic movement, in particular, took on the role of the Young Ireland movement of the mid-nineteenth century. The Young Ireland movement had hoped to catalyze nationalistic unity with ballads. It lost influence when political nationalism, particularly agitation over ownership known as the land wars, was more influential than cultural nationalism. In 1890 the political movement for Home Rule, or parliamentary autonomy, collapsed with the fortunes of its charismatic leader, Charles Stewart Parnell. With political nationalism in eclipse, cultural nationalism could and did regain its influence. Yeats organized a London Irish Literary Society in 1891 and a National Literary Society in Dublin in 1892. The conception of a national drama in Dublin benefited from the local literary revival, and participants in the Irish Literary Theatre usually had sidelines in other genres. However, the dramatic move-

ment also benefited immensely from external models, a foreign influence that, though distinctly not English, was to engender its own
complications. In 1850 Ole Bull had established a national theater
in Norway, to which Henrik Ibsen, especially when young, contributed plays based on Norwegian life, history, and cultural traditions. The later, better-known Ibsen plays had direct impact on the
Irish Literary Theatre, especially through Martyn, for whom Ibsen
was a model, and Yeats, for whom Ibsen's social drama was a perfect example of how not to proceed. Other Continental models, to
be taken for positive and negative instruction, included Andre
Antoine, who founded Théâtre Libre in Paris in 1887, and Otto
Brahm, who founded the Freie Buhne in Berlin in 1889. In addition, Richard Wagner's Bayreuth theater festival was a great personal influence on some of the founding participants of the Irish
Literary Theatre.

All these factors, local and Continental, nationalistic and aesthetic, came to bear on the first, formative production of the Irish
Literary Theatre in May 1899: Yeats's *The Countess Cathleen* and
Martyn's *The Heather Field*. The first represented the theater of art,
of aesthetics, initially bound up in Yeats's own emerging philosophy
of drama. The second represented the theater of praxis, of social
drama, immediately descended from Ibsen. The organizing force
joining them was Lady Gregory, assuming a managerial role that
would continue. The result was general clamor. The Yeats play, for
its personification of a feminine Ireland bartering immortality
for food, was denounced as heresy by the keepers of a distinctly
Catholic public morality of "Irish Ireland." Police protection was
required for performance, and newspapers were filled with letters
from those outraged by the play's representation of Ireland. The
Martyn play, for its extended consideration of agricultural ethics,
was denounced as pedestrian by keepers of literary standards, and
reviews decried its mechanical exhaustion of a predictable liberal
thesis. At issue was both the accuracy of the representation of Ireland on the stage and the formulation of Ireland's proper ambition:
the central conflict in nationalism between the pragmatic and the
aesthetic. Martyn saw no benefit in alienating the audience or,
most important, the Catholic Church; he saw the benefit of addressing the audience on its own terms, with its own problems, and
with realistic resolutions. Yeats instead took the course of a drama
that would be "remote, spiritual, and ideal."

All participants in that general clamor of 1899, however critical,
were active participants in a debate about a drama with national
pretensions and so about the nation itself. This same debate, sustained by Lady Gregory and successors under auspices of the national theater, the Abbey, and the dissenting competitors it inspired,

has continued throughout the history of modern Irish drama represented in this volume, both in the dramatic texts themselves and in
the critical texts they have provoked. The most noteworthy public
clamors followed the plays of Synge and O'Casey, but the work of
Shaw, Beckett, and Friel, especially, also demanded, on public performance, a public response to dramatic provocation. McPherson's
and Carr's works have been received as evidence of profound
changes in Irish society at the end of the twentieth century and
have fueled discussions of those changes. What joins all these plays
is not the birthplace of the authors but their collective contemplation of Ireland's identity. These plays dwell on shared national symbols, such as Cathleen Ni Houlihan or the Shan Van Vocht; events,
such as the 1798 rising; political movements, such as Home Rule
or civil rights in Northern Ireland; and emblematic places, such as
the political landmark Kilmainham Jail or the mythic West of Ireland. The importance of the iconic places is reaffirmed at end of
century in the fairy forts of *The Weir*, the desolate landscape of *By
the Bog of Cats*, and by the work of many other playwrights of the
same generation, all of whom also emphasize the pressures on
these traditional places of the forces of modernity and globalization. In response to this common framework, these plays offer plu-
ral commentaries. The history of modern and contemporary Irish
drama is notable for shifting allegiances to self or to place, to the
individual or to the collective obligation, to liberatory aesthetics or
to unifying themes, to tradition or to counter-tradition, and most of
these shifts are of degrees rather than mutually exclusive opposi-
tions. At issue throughout is the relation between individual writer
and national state, a relation that binds even in dissent. "The first
duty of a writer," the Irish playwright Brendan Behan wrote, "is to
let his Fatherland down, otherwise he is no writer." Since drama is
by definition a performance before an audience, the role of the audience, apart from enjoying the pleasures of performance, is to as-
sess that relation of self to state, an action that gives theater its
civic function and creates the social roles of a national theater.

While the history of modern and contemporary Irish drama has
continuing themes, it is not uniform. In earlier periods, such as
Restoration and Victorian, Irish playwrights flourished without
choosing Ireland as their subject. The modern period was frequently described as a "Renaissance," or a rebirth, with an analogy
of Ireland's recovery of its hidden past with the European Renaissance recovery of its classical heritage. Many, including Lionel Pilkington in this volume, date a second renaissance to fundamental
changes in mid-century Ireland that were reflected in its drama.
The chronology in this volume notes many of the important social
changes in Ireland in the 1950s: the Industrial Development Act

that opened the economy to foreign investment; the creation and growth of the Irish Tourist Board and the Aer Lingus airline; the rise of border disputes; the entry into the United Nations and the rejection of membership in the European Union. All document a time of changes in the national social context, which was becoming, and not without resistence or regret, less insular and more international. This social change was reflected especially well in two early plays by writers of lasting importance and influence: Tom Murphy's *A Whistle in the Dark*, which opened in London in 1961, and Brian Friel's *Philadelphia, Here I Come!*, which opened in the Dublin Theatre Festival in 1964 and soon moved to Broadway in New York City. Both of these were powerfully imaginative dramatizations of immigration, and in that subject the intertwined forces of international relations, including those with Great Britain, and economic development, with its requirements for external partners.

Many date another great social change in Ireland and so in its drama in the 1990s. That decade was one of great national loss: ongoing scandals of abuses of power by clergy of the Catholic Church and by members of the main political parties, and so both of the main pillars of civic society in Ireland. At the same time, there was great gain: the Irish economy exploded into a remarkable period of growth. The only precedents were recent changes of great magnitude in counties called "Asian Tigers" for remarkable economic growth, and so Ireland became the "Celtic Tiger." References in the bibliography to this volume provide data on this extraordinary transformation of a country that earlier in the century aspired to only a modest agricultural economy. The social effect of simultaneous cultural loss and profit was complex. The social historian Terence Brown has written, "In the boom years the alleged misdoings of some of the few who found themselves before the tribunals [i.e. under investigation] paled before a success story that drew the attention of the world." The loss may have paled before the profit that created a consumer society far wealthier than it had ever expected to be. But it did not disappear. Some of the conflicted nature of the contemporary Irish cultural situation can be seen in the forces of change meeting the habits and satisfactions of tradition in *The Weir*, *By the Bog of Cats*, and the work of the many Irish contemporaries of Conor McPherson and Marina Carr: whatever may have paled, the prolific production of drama in Ireland has not. Conor McPherson has described discussing with others the idea that "Irish playwrights prove so popular because our country is in a state of flux. There's an energy created by writers trying to figure out what's going on." Of that discussion, he added, "I have to say I don't know if that's true."

Those comments are characteristic of a period of great change and great uncertainty. In that context, recent Irish drama has returned in theater to the sense of the supernatural that was characteristic of the earliest years of modern Irish drama, and the plays have also revised that sense. *Cathleen Ni Houlihan*'s "woman from beyond the world" or the ghost rider in *Riders to the Sea* introduce the supernatural as fact and a practice of oral culture and the folk identity of the hidden society to be restored in the renaissance of modern Irish drama. Contemporary Irish drama introduces the supernatural as matter of ambiguity: the possibility of ghosts in *The Weir* and *By the Bog of Cats* is characteristic of other work by Conor McPherson and Marina Carr and also other contemporary playwrights. This is an exciting area of literary practice that has been described by Freud as the "uncanny," or the German word *unheimlich*, which is mentioned in Antoinette Quinn's essay on *Cathleen ni Houlihan* in this collection. Freud's essay on this subject lists English synonyms for "uncanny" such as "uncomfortable" and "uneasy" and only secondarily to synonyms such as "haunted." The uncanny is, however, distinct from the fantastic, where the supernatural or inexplicable is certain. The uncanny is not specific to Ireland: it has many versions in folk tales, Gothic traditions, and the work of such writers as Baudelaire and Poe. Nor is it specific to Freud: it is an important tool of analysis for the literary theorist Tzvetan Todorov in his work on the fantastic as a literary genre. However, the uncanny is also a powerful stage representation of uncertainty, and especially uncertainty expressed through ordinary and familiar situations. In contemporary Irish drama, the forces of change, including erosion of authority and economic boom, are dramatized in relation to the habits and desires of traditional and eroding ways of life and the proximity of that life to the supernatural. The result, however, is unsettling rather than resolute. Echoing McPherson's uncertainty, Marina Carr, on being asked in an interview, "Do you reckon there are ghosts, spirits of those departed, around us?" replied, with a crucial qualification, "I think they're probably around us all."

Modern and contemporary Irish drama is an excellent subject for the study of Irish literature and culture and, because of its great works of the twentieth century, an excellent subject for the study of drama. Because of the complex forces of historical and contemporary Ireland, and the remarkable degrees of difference between Ireland in 1899 and 1999, modern and contemporary Irish drama is also an excellent subject for the study of cultural change. It is possible to wonder whether Irish drama as we know it will continue. It emerged through difference, especially the difference between Ireland and the predominating culture of English empire at the beginning of the twentieth century, and it is possible that in the twenty-first century those differences will be eclipsed by prevailing similarities of countries in a globalized society. In this history, modern Irish drama did not exist until the twentieth century; before then, the forces of nationality that created it did not exist. Those forces also may not exist in the twenty-first century. Writing of fiction rather than drama, but in terms that certainly apply, the Irish critic Declan Kiberd has hypothesized that "it is just possible that 'Irish Writing' will, in the next five or six decades, be subsumed back into the general fiction category from which it so recently and so precariously emerged." It is possible that in the future Irish playwrights will be known for producing drama rather than "Irish drama," and it is very likely that many playwrights would welcome that freedom. In that case, the twentieth-century Irish drama would remain as important a subject for study because of its unique complex of cultural forces with quite powerful work, like the combination of specific forces and powerful work that continues to sustain Shakespearean theater or classical tragedy as subjects for study. More likely, because contemporary work has drawn so heavily on earlier work through recurring concepts like iconic places or themes like the supernatural, and because the drama completed in that process has been so powerful and provocative, the history of modern and contemporary drama will continue to evolve through new permutations in degrees of those shifting allegiances to self or to place, to the individual or to the collective obligation, to the relation of the individual to society, and above all to the nature of cultural change.

JOHN P. HARRINGTON
Rensselaer Polytechnic Institute

THE TEXTS OF
THE PLAYS

W. B. YEATS AND LADY GREGORY

Cathleen Ni Houlihan[†]

Persons in the Play

PETER GILLANE
MICHAEL GILLANE, *his son, going to be married*
PATRICK GILLANE, *a lad of twelve, Michael's brother*
BRIDGET GILLANE, *Peter's wife*
DELIA CAHEL, *engaged to Michael*
THE POOR OLD WOMAN
NEIGHBOURS

Interior of a cottage close to Killala, in 1798.[1] BRIDGET *is standing at a table undoing a parcel.* PETER *is sitting at one side of the fire,* PATRICK *at the other.*

PETER.   What is the sound I hear?
PATRICK.   I don't hear anything. [*He listens.*] I hear it now. It's like cheering. [*He goes to the window and looks out.*] I wonder what they are cheering about. I don't see anybody.
PETER.   It might be a hurling.[2]
PATRICK.   There's no hurling to-day. It must be down in the town the cheering is.
BRIDGET.   I suppose the boys must be having some sport of their own. Come over here, Peter, and look at Michael's wedding clothes.
PETER [*shifts his chair to table*].   Those are grand clothes, indeed.
BRIDGET.   You hadn't clothes like that when you married me, and no coat to put on of a Sunday more than any other day.
PETER.   That is true, indeed. We never thought a son of our own would be wearing a suit of that sort for his wedding, or have so good a place to bring a wife to.
PATRICK [*who is still at the window*].   There's an old woman coming down the road. I don't know is it here she is coming.

---

† From *The Collected Plays of W. B. Yeats*, rev. ed. (New York: Macmillan, 1953).
1. Site, in western Ireland, and date, on August 22, of the landing of a French force supporting Irish rebellion against British control; the French and the Irish alike surrendered to the British on September 8.
2. Game, somewhat like field hockey, with origins in Celtic Ireland.

BRIDGET.   It will be a neighbour coming to hear about Michael's wedding. Can you see who it is?

PATRICK.   I think it is a stranger, but she's not coming to the house. She's turned into the gap that goes down where Maurteen and his sons are shearing sheep. [*He turns towards* BRIDGET.] Do you remember what Winny of the Cross-Roads was saying the other night about the strange woman that goes through the country whatever time there's war or trouble coming?

BRIDGET.   Don't be bothering us about Winny's talk, but go and open the door for your brother. I hear him coming up the path.

PETER.   I hope he has brought Delia's fortune with him safe, for fear the people might go back on the bargain and I after making it. Trouble enough I had making it.

[PATRICK *opens the door and* MICHAEL *comes in.*]

BRIDGET.   What kept you, Michael? We were looking out for you this long time.

MICHAEL.   I went round by the priest's house to bid him be ready to marry us to-morrow.

BRIDGET.   Did he say anything?

MICHAEL.   He said it was a very nice match, and that he was never better pleased to marry any two in his parish than myself and Delia Cahel.

PETER.   Have you got the fortune, Michael?

MICHAEL.   Here it is.

[MICHAEL *puts bag on table and goes over and leans against chimney-jamb.* BRIDGET, *who has been all this time examining the clothes, pulling the seams and trying the lining of the pockets, etc., puts the clothes on the dresser.*]

PETER [*getting up and taking the bag in his hand and turning out the money*].   Yes, I made the bargain well for you, Michael. Old John Cahel would sooner have kept a share of this a while longer. 'Let me keep the half of it until the first boy is born,' says he. 'You will not,' says I. 'Whether there is or is not a boy, the whole hundred pounds must be in Michael's hands before he brings your daughter to the house.' The wife spoke to him then, and he gave in at the end.

BRIDGET.   You seem well pleased to be handling the money, Peter.

PETER.   Indeed, I wish I had had the luck to get a hundred pounds, or twenty pounds itself, with the wife I married.

BRIDGET.   Well, if I didn't bring much I didn't get much. What had you the day I married you but a flock of hens and you feeding them, and a few lambs and you driving them to the market at Ballina? [*She is vexed and bangs a jug on the dresser.*] If I brought no fortune I worked it out in my bones, laying down the baby, Michael that is standing there now, on a stook of straw, while I dug the potatoes, and never asking big dresses or anything but to be working.

PETER.   That is true, indeed. [*He pats her arm.*]

BRIDGET.   Leave me alone now till I ready the house for the woman that is to come into it.

PETER.   You are the best woman in Ireland, but money is good, too. [*He begins handling the money again and sits down.*] I never thought to see so much money within my four walls. We can do great things now we have it. We can take the ten acres of land we have the chance of since Jamsie Dempsey died, and stock it. We will go to the fair at Ballina to buy the stock. Did Delia ask any of the money for her own use, Michael?

MICHAEL.   She did not, indeed. She did not seem to take much notice of it, or to look at it at all.

BRIDGET.   That's no wonder. Why would she look at it when she had yourself to look at, a fine, strong young man? It is proud she must be to get you; a good steady boy that will make use of the money, and not be running through it or spending it on drink like another.

PETER.   It's likely Michael himself was not thinking much of the fortune either, but of what sort the girl was to look at.

MICHAEL [*coming over towards the table*].   Well, you would like a nice comely girl to be beside you, and to go walking with you. The fortune only lasts for a while, but the woman will be there always.

PATRICK [*turning round from the window*].   They are cheering again down in the town. Maybe they are landing horses from Enniscrone. They do be cheering when the horses take the water well.

MICHAEL.   There are no horses in it. Where would they be going and no fair at hand? Go down to the town, Patrick, and see what is going on.

PATRICK [*opens the door to go out, but stops for a moment on the threshold*].   Will Delia remember, do you think, to bring the greyhound pup she promised me when she would be coming to the house?

MICHAEL.   She will surely.

[PATRICK *goes out, leaving the door open.*]

PETER.   It will be Patrick's turn next to be looking for a fortune, but he won't find it so easy to get it and he with no place of his own.

BRIDGET.   I do be thinking sometimes, now things are going so well with us, and the Cahels such a good back to us in the district, and Delia's own uncle a priest, we might be put in the way of making Patrick a priest some day, and he so good at his books.

PETER.   Time enough, time enough. You have always your head full of plans, Bridget.

BRIDGET.   We will be well able to give him learning, and not to send him tramping the country like a poor scholar that lives on charity.

MICHAEL.   They're not done cheering yet. [*He goes over to the door and stands there for a moment, putting up his hand to shade his eyes.*]

BRIDGET.   Do you see anything?

MICHAEL.   I see an old woman coming up the path.

BRIDGET.   Who is it, I wonder? It must be the strange woman Patrick saw a while ago.

MICHAEL.   I don't think it's one of the neighbours anyway, but she has her cloak over her face.

BRIDGET.   It might be some poor woman heard we were making ready for the wedding and came to look for her share.

PETER.   I may as well put the money out of sight. There is no use leaving it out for every stranger to look at.

[*He goes over to a large box in the corner, opens it and puts the bag in and fumbles at the lock.*]

MICHAEL.   There she is father!

[*An* OLD WOMAN *passes the window slowly. She looks at* MICHAEL *as she passes.*]

I'd sooner a stranger not to come to the house the night before my wedding.

BRIDGET.   Open the door, Michael; don't keep the poor woman waiting.

[*The* OLD WOMAN *comes in.* MICHAEL *stands aside to make way for her.*]

OLD WOMAN.   God save all here!

PETER.   God save you kindly!

OLD WOMAN.   You have good shelter here.

PETER.   You are welcome to whatever shelter we have.

BRIDGET.   Sit down there by the fire and welcome.

OLD WOMAN [*warming her hands*].   There is a hard wind outside.

[MICHAEL *watches her curiously from the door.* PETER *comes over to the table.*]

PETER.   Have you travelled far to-day?

OLD WOMAN.   I have travelled far, very far; there are few have travelled so far as myself, and there's many a one that doesn't make me welcome. There was one that had strong sons I thought were friends of mine, but they were shearing their sheep, and they wouldn't listen to me.

PETER.   It's a pity indeed for any person to have no place of their own.

OLD WOMAN.   That's true for you indeed, and it's long I'm on the roads since I first went wandering.

BRIDGET.   It is a wonder you are not worn out with so much wandering.

OLD WOMAN.   Sometimes my feet are tired and my hands are quiet, but there is no quiet in my heart. When the people see me quiet, they think old age has come on me and that all the stir has gone out of me. But when the trouble is on me I must be talking to my friends.

BRIDGET.   What was it put you wandering?

OLD WOMAN.   Too many strangers in the house.

BRIDGET.   Indeed you look as if you'd had your share of trouble.

OLD WOMAN.   I have had trouble indeed.

BRIDGET.   What was it put the trouble on you?

OLD WOMAN.   My land that was taken from me.

PETER.   Was it much land they took from you?

OLD WOMAN.   My four beautiful green fields.[3]

PETER [aside to BRIDGET].   Do you think could she be the widow Casey that was put out of her holding at Kilglass a while ago?

BRIDGET.   She is not. I saw the widow Casey one time at the market in Ballina, a stout fresh woman.

PETER [to OLD WOMAN].   Did you hear a noise of cheering, and you coming up the hill?

OLD WOMAN.   I thought I heard the noise I used to hear when my friends came to visit me. [She begins singing half to herself.]

> I will go cry with the woman,
> For yellow-haired Donough is dead,
> With a hempen rope for a neckcloth,
> And a white cloth on his head,—[4]

MICHAEL [coming from the door].   What is it that you are singing, ma'am?

OLD WOMAN.   Singing I am about a man I knew one time, yellow-haired Donough that was hanged in Galway.[5] [She goes on singing, much louder.]

> I am come to cry with you, woman,
> My hair is unwound and unbound;
> I remember him ploughing his field,
> Turning up the red side of the ground,
> And building his barn on the hill
> With the good mortared stone;
> O! we'd have pulled down the gallows
> Had it happened in Enniscrone!

MICHAEL.   What was it brought him to his death?

OLD WOMAN.   He died for love of me: many a man has died for love of me.

3. The island of Ireland's traditional division is into four provinces: Ulster, Munster, Leinster, and Connacht.

4. In a 1904 note Yeats identified music of this original lyric as "an old Irish air" and the music for the two original lyrics below as airs heard in a dream by a member of the original cast.

5. A translation titled in English "A Lament for Fair-Haired Donough that was Hanged in Galway" appeared in Lady Gregory's *The Kiltartan Poetry Book* (1919).

PETER [*aside to* BRIDGET].   Her trouble has put her wits astray.

MICHAEL.   Is it long since that song was made? Is it long since he got his death?

OLD WOMAN.   Not long, not long. But there were others that died for love of me a long time ago.

MICHAEL.   Were they neighbours of your own, ma'am?

OLD WOMAN.   Come here beside me and I'll tell you about them.

[MICHAEL *sits down beside her on the hearth.*]

There was a red man of the O'Donnells from the north, and a man of the O'Sullivans from the south, and there was one Brian that lost his life at Clontarf by the sea,[6] and there were a great many in the west, some that died hundreds of years ago, and there are some that will die to-morrow.

MICHAEL.   Is it in the west that men will die to-morrow?

OLD WOMAN.   Come nearer, nearer to me.

BRIDGET.   Is she right, do you think? Or is she a woman from beyond the world?

PETER.   She doesn't know well what she's talking about, with the want and the trouble she has gone through.

BRIDGET.   The poor thing, we should treat her well.

PETER.   Give her a drink of milk and a bit of the oaten cake.

BRIDGET.   Maybe we should give her something along with that, to bring her on her way. A few pence or a shilling itself, and we with so much money in the house.

PETER.   Indeed I'd not begrudge it to her if we had it to spare, but if we go running through what we have, we'll soon have to break the hundred pounds, and that would be a pity.

BRIDGET.   Shame on you, Peter. Give her the shilling and your blessing with it, or our own luck will go from us.

[PETER *goes to the box and takes out a shilling.*]

BRIDGET [*to the* OLD WOMAN].   Will you have a drink of milk, ma'am?

OLD WOMAN.   It is not food or drink that I want.

PETER [*offering the shilling*].   Here is something for you.

OLD WOMAN.   This is not what I want. It is not silver I want.

PETER.   What is it you would be asking for?

OLD WOMAN.   If anyone would give me help he must give me himself, he must give me all.

[PETER *goes over to the table staring at the shilling in his hand in a bewildered way, and stands whispering to* BRIDGET.]

MICHAEL.   Have you no one to care you in your age, ma'am?

OLD WOMAN.   I have not. With all the lovers that brought me their love I never set out the bed for any.

6. Red Hugh O'Donnell (1571–1602), Donal O'Sullivan Beare (c. 1560–1618), and Brian Boru (926–1014).

MICHAEL. Are you lonely going the roads, ma'am?

OLD WOMAN. I have my thoughts and I have my hopes.

MICHAEL. What hopes have you to hold to?

OLD WOMAN. The hope of getting my beautiful fields back again; the hope of putting the strangers out of my house.

MICHAEL. What way will you do that, ma'am?

OLD WOMAN. I have good friends that will help me. They are gathering to help me now. I am not afraid. If they are put down to-day they will get the upper hand to-morrow. [*She gets up.*] I must be going to meet my friends. They are coming to help me and I must be there to welcome them. I must call the neighbours together to welcome them.

MICHAEL. I will go with you.

BRIDGET. It is not her friends you have to go and welcome, Michael; it is the girl coming into the house you have to welcome. You have plenty to do; it is food and drink you have to bring to the house. The woman that is coming home is not coming with empty hands; you would not have an empty house before her. [*To the* OLD WOMAN.] Maybe you don't know, ma'am, that my son is going to be married to-morrow.

OLD WOMAN. It is not a man going to his marriage that I look to for help.

PETER [*to* BRIDGET]. Who is she, do you think, at all?

BRIDGET. You did not tell us your name yet, ma'am.

OLD WOMAN. Some call me the Poor Old Woman, and there are some that call me Cathleen, the daughter of Houlihan.

PETER. I think I knew some one of that name, once. Who was it, I wonder? It must have been some one I knew when I was a boy. No, no; I remember, I heard it in a song.

OLD WOMAN [*who is standing in the doorway*]. They are wondering that there were songs made for me; there have been many songs made for me. I heard one on the wind this morning. [*Sings.*]

> Do not make a great keening
> When the graves have been dug to-morrow.
> Do not call the white-scarfed riders
> To the burying that shall be to-morrow.
> Do not spread food to call strangers
> To the wakes that shall be to-morrow;
> Do not give money for prayers
> For the dead that shall die to-morrow. . . .

They will have no need of prayers, they will have no need of prayers.

MICHAEL. I do not know what that song means, but tell me something I can do for you.

PETER. Come over to me, Michael.

MICHAEL. Hush, father, listen to her.

OLD WOMAN. It is a hard service they take that help me. Many that are red-cheeked now will be pale-cheeked; many that have

been free to walk the hills and the bogs and the rushes will be
sent to walk hard streets in far countries; many a good plan will
be broken; many that have gathered money will not stay to spend
it; many a child will be born and there will be no father at its
christening to give it a name. They that have red cheeks will have
pale cheeks for my sake, and for all that, they will think they are
well paid. [*She goes out; her voice is heard outside singing.*]

> They shall be remembered for ever,
> They shall be alive for ever,
> They shall be speaking for ever,
> The people shall hear them for ever.

BRIDGET [*to* PETER].   Look at him, Peter; he has the look of a man
that has got the touch. [*Raising her voice*] Look here, Michael, at
the wedding clothes. Such grand clothes as these are! You have a
right to fit them on now; it would be a pity to-morrow if they did
not fit. The boys would be laughing at you. Take them, Michael,
and go into the room and fit them on. [*She puts them on his
arm.*]

MICHAEL.   What wedding are you talking of? What clothes will I
be wearing to-morrow?

BRIDGET.   These are the clothes you are going to wear when you
marry Delia Cahel to-morrow.

MICHAEL.   I had forgotten that. [*He looks at the clothes and turns
towards the inner room, but stops at the sound of cheering outside.*]

PETER.   There is the shouting come to our own door. What is it
has happened?

> [*Neighbours come crowding in,* PATRICK *and* DELIA *with
> them.*]

PATRICK.   There are ships in the Bay; the French are landing at
Killala!

> [PETER *takes his pipe from his mouth and his hat off, and
> stands up. The clothes slip from* MICHAEL's *arm.*]

DELIA.   Michael!

> [*He takes no notice.*]

Michael!

> [*He turns towards her.*]

Why do you look at me like a stranger?

> [*She drops his arm.* BRIDGET *goes over towards her.*]

PATRICK.   The boys are all hurrying down the hillside to join the
French.

DELIA.   Michael won't be going to join the French.

BRIDGET [*to* PETER].   Tell him not to go, Peter.

PETER.   It's no use. He doesn't hear a word we're saying.
BRIDGET.   Try and coax him over to the fire.
DELIA.   Michael, Michael! You won't leave me! You won't join the French, and we going to be married!

[*She puts her arms about him, he turns towards her as if about to yield.*]

OLD WOMAN's *voice outside.*

They shall be speaking for ever,
The people shall hear them for ever.

[MICHAEL *breaks away from* DELIA, *stands for a second at the door, then rushes out, following the* OLD WOMAN's *voice.* BRIDGET *takes* DELIA, *who is crying silently, into her arms.*]

PETER [*to* PATRICK, *laying a hand on his arm*].   Did you see an old woman going down the path?
PATRICK.   I did not, but I saw a young girl, and she had the walk of a queen.

W. B. YEATS AND LADY GREGORY

The Pot of Broth

Persons in the Play

JOHN CONEELY, *an elderly man*
SIBBY CONEELY, *a young or middle-aged woman*
A TRAMP

A cottage kitchen. Fire on the hearth; table with cabbage, onions, a plate of meal, etc. Half-open door. A TRAMP *enters, looks about.*

TRAMP.   What sort are the people of this house, I wonder? Was it a good place for me to come to look for my dinner, I wonder? What's in that big pot? [*Lifts cover.*] Nothing at all! What's in the little pot? [*Lifts cover.*] Nothing at all! What's in that bottle, I wonder? [*Takes it up excitedly and tastes.*] Milk! milk in a bottle! I wonder they wouldn't afford a tin can to milk the cow into! Not much chance for a poor man to make a living here. What's in that chest? [*Kneels and tries to lift cover.*] Locked! [*Smells at the keyhole.*] There's a good smell—there must be a still not far off.

> [*Gets up and sits on chest. A noise heard outside, shouts, footsteps, and loud frightened cackling.*]

TRAMP.   What in the earthly world is going on outside? Any one would think it was the Fiannta-h-Eireann[1] at their hunting!
SIBBY'S VOICE.   Stop the gap, let you stop the gap, John. Stop that old schemer of a hen flying up on the thatch like as if she was an eagle!
JOHN'S VOICE.   What can I do, Sibby? I all to had my hand upon her when she flew away!
SIBBY'S VOICE.   She's out into the garden! Follow after her! She has the wide world before her now.
TRAMP.   Sibby he called her. I wonder is it Sibby Coneely's house I am in? If that's so it's a bad chance I have of going out heavier than I came in. I often heard of her, a regular slave-driver that

---

1. The Fianna of Ireland were pre-modern historical groups of hunter-warriors who appear in the Fenian cycle of epic Irish poems and whose name has frequently been adopted by nationalist organizations.

would starve the rats. A niggard with her eyes on kippeens,[2] that would skin a flea for its hide! It was the bad luck of the world brought me here, and not a house or a village between this and Tubber. And it isn't much I have left to bring me on there. [*Begins emptying out his pockets on the chest.*] There's my pipe and not a grain to fill it with! There's my handkerchief I got at the coronation dinner! There's my knife and nothing left of it but the handle. [*Shakes his pocket out.*] And there's a crust of the last dinner I got, and the last I'm likely to get till to-morrow. That's all I have in the world unless the stone I picked up to pelt at that yelping dog a while ago. [*Takes stone out of pocket and tosses it up and down.*] In the time long ago I usen't to have much trouble to find a dinner, getting over the old women and getting round the young ones! I remember the time I met the old minister on the path and sold him his own flock of turkeys. My wits used to fill my stomach then, but I'm afraid they're going from me now with all the hardship I went through. [*Cackling heard again and cries.*]

SIBBY'S *voice*.   Catch her, she's round the bush! Put your hands in the nettles, don't be daunted!

[*A choked cackle and prolonged screech.*]

TRAMP.   There's a dinner for somebody anyway. That it may be for myself! How will I come round her, I wonder? There is no more pity in her heart than there's a soul in a dog. If all the saints were standing barefoot before her she'd bid them to call another day. It's myself I have to trust to now, and my share of talk. [*Looks at the stone.*] I know what I'll do, I know what the tinker did with a stone, and I'm as good a man as he is anyway. [*He jumps up and waves the stone over his head.*] Now, Sibby! If I don't do it one way I'll do it another. My wits against the world!

> There's broth in the pot for you, old man,
> There's broth in the pot for you, old man,
> There's cabbage for me
>   And broth for you,
> And beef for Jack the journeyman.
>
> I wish you were dead, my gay old man,
> I wish you were dead, my gay old man,
>   I wish you were dead
>   And a stone at your head,
> So as I'd marry poor Jack the journeyman.

JOHN'S *voice* [*outside*].   Bring it in, bring it in, Sibby. You'll be late with the priest's dinner.

SIBBY'S *voice*.   Can't you wait a minute till I'll draw it?

[*Enter* JOHN.]

2. Twigs for burning.

JOHN.   I didn't know there was any one in the house.

TRAMP.   It's only this minute I came in, tired with the length of the road I am, and fasting since morning.

JOHN [*begins groping among the pots and pans*].   I'll see can I find anything here for you . . . I don't see much . . . Maybe there's something in the chest.

> [*He takes key from a hiding-place at back of hearth, opens chest, takes out bottle, takes out a ham-bone and is cutting a bit from it when* SIBBY *enters, carrying chicken by the neck.* JOHN *drops the ham-bone on a bench.*]

SIBBY.   Hurry now, John, after all the time you have wasted. Why didn't you steal up on the old hen that time she was scratching in the dust?

JOHN.   Sure I thought one of the chickens would be the tenderest.

SIBBY.   Cock you up with tenderness! All the expense I'm put to! My grand hen I've been feeding these five years! Wouldn't that have been enough to part with? Indeed I wouldn't have thought of parting with her itself, but she had got tired of laying since Easter.

JOHN.   Well, I thought we ought to give his Reverence something that would have a little good in it.

SIBBY.   What does the age of it matter? A hen's a hen when it's on the table. [*Sitting down to pluck chicken.*] Why couldn't the Kernans have given the priest his dinner the way they always do? What did it matter their mother's brother to have died? It is an excuse they had made up to put the expense of the dinner on me.

JOHN.   Well, I hope you have a good bit of bacon to put in the pot along with the chicken.

SIBBY.   Let me alone. The taste of meat on the knife is all that high-up people like the clergy care for, nice genteel people, no way greedy like potato-diggers or harvest men.

JOHN.   Well, I never saw the man, gentle or simple, wouldn't be glad of his fill of bacon and he hungry.

SIBBY.   Let me alone, I'll show the Kernans what I can do. I have what is better than bacon, a nice bit of a ham I am keeping in the chest this good while, thinking we might want it for company. [*She catches sight of* TRAMP *and calls out.*] Who is there? A beggarman, is it? Then you may quit this house if you please. We have nothing for you. [*She gets up and opens the door.*]

TRAMP [*comes forward*].   It is a mistake you are making, ma'am, it is not asking anything I am. It is giving I am more used to. I was never in a house yet but there would be a welcome for me in it again.

SIBBY.   Well, you have the appearance of a beggar, and if it isn't begging you are, what way do you make your living?

TRAMP.   If I was a beggar, ma'am, it is to common people I would be going and not to a nice grand woman like yourself, that is only used to be talking with high-up noble people.

SIBBY.   Well, what is it you are asking? If it's a bit to eat you want,
  I can't give it to you, for I have company coming that will clear
  all before them.
TRAMP.   Is it me ask anything to eat? [*Holds up stone.*] I have here
  what is better than beef and mutton, and currant cakes and sacks
  of flour.
SIBBY.   What is it at all?
TRAMP [*mysteriously*].   Those that gave it to me wouldn't like me to
  tell that.
SIBBY [*to* JOHN].   Do you think is he a man that has friends among
  the Sidhe?[3]
JOHN.   Your mind is always running on the Sidhe since the time
  they made John Molloy find buried gold on the bridge of Limerick. I see nothing in it but a stone.
TRAMP.   What can you see in it, you that never saw what it can do?
JOHN.   What is it it can do?
TRAMP.   It can do many things, and what it's going to do now is to
  make me a drop of broth for my dinner.
SIBBY.   I'd like to have a stone that could make broth.
TRAMP.   No one in the world but myself has one, ma'am, and no
  other stone in the world has the same power, for it has enchantment on it. All I'll ask of you now, ma'am, is the loan of a pot
  with a drop of boiling water in it.
SIBBY.   You're welcome to that much. John, fill the small pot with
  water.

    [JOHN *fills the pot from a kettle.*]

TRAMP [*putting in stone*].   There now, that's all I have to do but to
  put it on the fire to boil, and it's a grand pot of broth will be before me then.
SIBBY.   And is that all you have to put in it?
TRAMP.   Nothing at all but that—only, maybe, a bit of an herb for
  fear the enchantment might slip away from it. You wouldn't have
  a bit of Slanlus[4] in the house, ma'am, that was cut with a black-
  handled knife?
SIBBY.   No, indeed, I have none of that in the house.
TRAMP.   Or a bit of the Fearavan that was picked when the wind
  was from the north?
SIBBY.   No, indeed, I'm sorry there's none.
TRAMP.   Or a sprig of the Athair-talav, the father of herbs?
JOHN.   There's plenty of it by the hedge. I'll go out and get it for
  you.
TRAMP.   O, don't mind taking so much trouble; those leaves beside
  me will do well enough. [*He takes a couple of good handfuls of the
  cabbage and onions and puts them in.*]

3. Fairies (pronounced *shee*).
4. Like "Fearavan" and "Athair-talav" below, "Slanlus" is an herb associated with curative
   properties.

SIBBY.   But where at all did you get the stone?

TRAMP.   Well, this is how it happened. I was out one time, and a grand greyhound with me, and it followed a hare, and I went after it. And I came up at last to the edge of a gravel pit where there were a few withered furzy bushes, and there was my fine hound sitting up, and it shivering, and a little old man sitting before it, and he taking off a hareskin coat. [*Looking round at the ham-bone.*] Give me the loan of a kippeen to stir the pot with. . . . [*He takes the ham-bone and puts it into the pot.*]

JOHN.   Oh! the ham-bone!

TRAMP.   I didn't say a ham-bone, I said a hareskin coat.

SIBBY.   Hold your tongue, John, if it's deaf you are getting.

TRAMP [*stirring the pot with the ham-bone*].   Well, as I was telling you, he was sitting up, and one time I thought he was as small as a nut, and the next minute I thought his head to be in the stars. Frightened I was.

SIBBY.   No wonder, no wonder at all in that.

TRAMP.   He took the little stone then—that stone I have with me—out of the side pocket of his coat, and he showed it to me. 'Call off your dog', says he, 'and I'll give you that stone, and if ever you want a good drop of broth or a bit of stirabout, or a drop of poteen[5] itself, all you have to do is to put it down in a pot with a drop of water and stir it awhile, and you'll have the thing you were wanting ready before you.'

SIBBY.   Poteen! Would it make that?

TRAMP.   It would, ma'am; and wine, the same as the Clare Militia uses.

SIBBY.   Let me see what does it look like now. [*Is bending forward.*]

TRAMP.   Don't look at it for your life, ma'am. It might bring bad luck on any one that would look at it, and it boiling. I must put a cover on the pot, or I must colour the water some way. Give me a handful of that meal.

[SIBBY *holds out a plate of meal and he puts in a handful or two.*]

JOHN.   Well, he is a gifted man!

SIBBY.   It would be a great comfort to have a stone like that. [*She has finished plucking the chicken which lies in her lap.*]

TRAMP.   And there's another thing it does, ma'am, since it came into Catholic hands. If you put it into a pot of a Friday[6] with a bit of the whitest meat in Ireland in it, it would turn it as black as black.

SIBBY.   That is no less than a miracle. I must tell Father John about that.

TRAMP.   But to put a bit of meat with it any other day of the week, it would do it no harm at all, but good. Look here now, ma'am,

5. Porridge and distilled liquor.
6. Traditionally a day of abstinence from meat.

I'll put that nice little hen you have in your lap in the pot for a minute till you'll see. [*Takes it and puts it in.*]

JOHN [*sarcastically*].   It's a good job this is not a Friday!

SIBBY.   Keep yourself quiet, John, and don't be interrupting the talk or you'll get a knock on the head like the King of Lochlann's grandmother.[7]

JOHN.   Go on, go on, I'll say no more.

TRAMP.   If I'm passing this way some time of a Friday, I'll bring a nice bit of mutton, or the breast of a turkey, and you'll see how it will be no better in two minutes than a fistful of bog mould.

SIBBY [*getting up*].   Let me take the chicken out now.

TRAMP.   Stop till I'll help you, ma'am, you might scald your hand. I'll show it to you in a minute as white as your own skin, where the lily and the rose are fighting for mastery. Did you ever hear what the boys in your own parish were singing after you being married from them—such of them that had any voice at all and not choked with crying, or senseless with the drop of drink they took to comfort them and to keep their wits from going, with the loss of you?

[SIBBY *sits down again complacently.*]

SIBBY.   Did they do that indeed?

TRAMP.   They did, ma'am, this is what they used to be singing:

> Philomel, I've listened oft
> To thy lay, near weeping willow—

No, that's not it—it's a queer thing the memory is—

'Twas at the dance at Dermody's that first I caught a sight of her.

No, that's not it either—ah, now I have it.

> My Paistin Finn is my sole desire,
> And I am shrunken to skin and bone.[8]

SIBBY.   Why would they call me Paistin?

TRAMP.   And why wouldn't they? Would you wish them to put your right name in a song, and your man ready to knock the brains of any man will as much as look your side of the road?

SIBBY.   Well, maybe so.

TRAMP.   I was standing by the man that made the song, and he writing it with an old bit of a carpenter's pencil, and the tears running down—

> My Paistin Finn is my sole desire,
> And I am shrunken to skin and bone,
> For all my heart has had for its hire
> Is what I can whistle alone and alone.
>   *Oro, oro!*
> *To-morrow night I will break down the door.*

7. Emer, grandmother of Lochlann of Drumshee in Scottish cycles of Gaelic verse.
8. See Yeats's poem "Two Songs Rewritten for the Tune's Sake."

[SIBBY *takes a fork and rises to take out the chicken.* TRAMP *puts his hand to stop her and goes on.*]

> What is the good of a man and he
> Alone and alone with a speckled shin?
> I would that I drank with my love on my knee,
> Between two barrels at the inn.
> > *Oro, oro!*
> *To-morrow night I will break down the door.*

[SIBBY *half rises again.* TRAMP *puts his hand upon her hand.*]

TRAMP.   Wait now till you hear the end [*sings*]:

> Alone and alone nine nights I lay
> Between two bushes under the rain;
> I thought to have whistled her down that way,
> I whistled and whistled and whistled in vain.
> > *Oro, oro!*
> *To-morrow night I will break down the door.*

[*He repeats the verse,* SIBBY *singing too and beating time with fork.*]

SIBBY [*to* JOHN].   I always knew I was too good for you! [*She goes on humming.*]

JOHN.   Well, he has the poor woman bewitched.

SIBBY [*suddenly coming to her wits*].   Did you take the chicken out yet?

TRAMP [*taking it out and giving it a good squeeze into the pot*].   I did, ma'am. Look at it there. [*He takes it and lays it on table.*]

JOHN.   How is the broth getting on?

TRAMP [*tasting it with a spoon*].   It's grand. It's always grand.

SIBBY.   Give me a taste of it.

TRAMP [*takes the pot off and slips the ham-bone behind him*].   Give me some vessel till I'll give this sky-woman a taste of it.

[JOHN *gives him an egg-cup which he fills and gives to* SIBBY. JOHN *gives him a mug, and he fills this for himself, pouring it back and forward from the mug to a bowl that is on the table, and drinking gulps now and again.* SIBBY *blows at hers and smells it.*]

SIBBY.   There's a good smell on it anyway. [*Tasting.*] It's lovely. O, I'd give the world and all to have the stone that made that!

TRAMP.   The world and all wouldn't buy it, ma'am. If I was inclined to sell it the Lord Lieutenant would have given me Dublin Castle[9] and all that's in it long ago.

SIBBY.   O, couldn't we coax it out of you any way at all?

TRAMP [*drinking more soup*].   The whole world wouldn't coax it out of me except maybe for one thing . . . [*looks depressed*]. Now

---

9. Seat of British government in Dublin.

I think of it, there's only one reason I might think of parting with
it at all.

SIBBY [*eagerly*].   What reason is that?

TRAMP.   It's a misfortune that overtakes me, ma'am, every time I
make an attempt to keep a pot of my own to boil it in, and I don't
like to be always under a compliment to the neighbours, asking
the loan of one. But whatever way it is, I never can keep a pot
with me. I had a right to ask one of the little man that gave me the
stone. The last one I bought got the bottom burned out of it one
night I was giving a hand to a friend that keeps a still, and the one
before that I hid under a bush one time I was going into Ennis for
the night, and some boys in the town dreamed about it and went
looking for treasure in it, and they found nothing but eggshells,
but they brought it away for all that. And another one . . .

SIBBY.   Give me the loan of the stone itself, and I'll engage I'll keep
a pot for it. . . . Wait now till I'll make some offer to you. . . .

TRAMP [*aside*].   I'd best not be stopping to bargain, the priest
might be coming in on me. [*Gets up.*] Well, ma'am, I'm sorry I
can't oblige you. [*Goes to door, shades his eyes and looks out, turns
suddenly.*] I have no time to lose, ma'am, I'm off. [*Comes to table
and takes his hat.*] Well, ma'am, what offer will you make?

JOHN.   You might as well leave it for a day on trial first.

TRAMP [*to* JOHN].   I think it likely I'll not be passing this way again.
[*To* SIBBY] Well, now, ma'am, as you were so kind, and for the
sake of the good treatment you gave me, I'll ask nothing at all for
it. Here it is for you and welcome, and that you may live long to
use it! But I'll just take a little bit in my bag that'll do for my supper, for fear I mightn't be in Tubber before night. [*He takes up
the chicken.*] And you won't begrudge me a drop of whisky when
you can make plenty for yourself from this out. [*Takes the bottle.*]

JOHN.   You deserve it, you deserve it indeed. You are a very gifted
man. Don't forget the kippeen!

TRAMP.   It's here! [*Slaps his pocket and exit.* JOHN *follows him.*]

SIBBY [*looking at the stone in her hand*].   Broth of the best, stirabout, poteen, wine itself, he said! And the people that will be
coming to see the miracle! I'll be as rich as Biddy Early before I
die!

[JOHN *comes back.*]

SIBBY.   Where were you, John?

JOHN.   I just went out to shake him by the hand. He's a very gifted
man.

SIBBY.   He is so indeed.

JOHN.   And the priest's at the top of the boreen[1] coming for his
dinner. Maybe you'd best put the stone in the pot again.

THE END

1. Path.

W. B. YEATS

At the Hawk's Well[†]

Persons in the Play

THREE MUSICIANS *(their faces made up to resemble masks)*
THE GUARDIAN OF THE WELL *(with face made up to resemble a mask)*
AN OLD MAN *(wearing a mask)*
A YOUNG MAN *(wearing a mask)*

Time—the Irish Heroic Age

The stage is any bare space before a wall against which stands a patterned screen. A drum and a gong and a zither have been laid close to the screen before the play begins. If necessary, they can be carried in, after the audience is seated, by the FIRST MUSICIAN, *who also can attend to the lights if there is any special lighting. We had two lanterns upon posts—designed by Mr. Dulac[1]—at the outer corners of the stage, but they did not give enough light, and we found it better to play by the light of a large chandelier. Indeed, I think, so far as my present experience goes, that the most effective lighting is the lighting we are most accustomed to in our rooms. These masked players seem stranger when there is no mechanical means of separating them from us. The* FIRST MUSICIAN *carries with him a folded black cloth and goes to the centre of the stage towards the front and stands motionless, the folded cloth hanging from between his hands. The two other* MUSICIANS *enter and, after standing a moment at either side of the stage, go towards him and slowly unfold the cloth, singing as they do so:*

> I call to the eye of the mind
> A well long choked up and dry
> And boughs long stripped by the wind,
> And I call to the mind's eye
> Pallor of an ivory face,
> Its lofty dissolute air,
> A man climbing up to a place
> The salt sea wind has swept bare.

[†] From *The Collected Plays of W. B. Yeats*, rev. ed. (New York: Macmillan, 1953).
1. Edmund Dulac (see Foster, p. 435 of this Norton Critical Edition).

20

As they unfold the cloth, they go backward a little so that the stretched cloth and the wall make a triangle with the FIRST MUSICIAN *at the apex supporting the centre of the cloth. On the black cloth is a gold pattern suggesting a hawk. The* SECOND *and* THIRD MUSICIANS *now slowly fold up the cloth again, pacing with a rhythmic movement of the arms towards the* FIRST MUSICIAN *and singing:*

> What were his life soon done!
> Would he lose by that or win?
> A mother that saw her son
> Doubled over a speckled shin,
> Cross-grained with ninety years,
> Would cry, 'How little worth
> Were all my hopes and fears
> And the hard pain of his birth!'

The words 'a speckled shin' are familiar to readers of Irish legendary stories in descriptions of old men bent double over the fire. While the cloth has been spread out, the GUARDIAN OF THE WELL *has entered and is now crouching upon the ground. She is entirely covered by a black cloak; beside her lies a square blue cloth to represent a well. The three* MUSICIANS *have taken their places against the wall beside their instruments of music; they will accompany the movements of the players with gong or drum or zither.*

FIRST MUSICIAN [*singing*].
> The boughs of the hazel shake,
> The sun goes down in the west.

SECOND MUSICIAN [*singing*].
> The heart would be always awake,
> The heart would turn to its rest.

[*They now go to one side of the stage rolling up the cloth.*]

FIRST MUSICIAN [*speaking*].   Night falls;
> The mountain-side grows dark;
> The withered leaves of the hazel
> Half choke the dry bed of the well;
> The guardian of the well is sitting
> Upon the old grey stone at its side,
> Worn out from raking its dry bed,
> Worn out from gathering up the leaves.
> Her heavy eyes
> Know nothing, or but look upon stone.
> The wind that blows out of the sea
> Turns over the heaped-up leaves at her side;
> They rustle and diminish.

SECOND MUSICIAN.   I am afraid of this place.

BOTH MUSICIANS [*singing*].
> 'Why should I sleep?' the heart cries,
> 'For the wind, the salt wind, the sea wind,

Is beating a cloud through the skies;
I would wander always like the wind.'

[*An* OLD MAN *enters through the audience.*]

FIRST MUSICIAN [*speaking*].   That old man climbs up hither,
Who has been watching by his well
These fifty years.
He is all doubled up with age;
The old thorn-trees are doubled so
Among the rocks where he is climbing.

[*The* OLD MAN *stands for a moment motionless by the side of
the stage with bowed head. He lifts his head at the sound of a
drumtop. He goes towards the front of the stage moving to the
taps of the drum. He crouches and moves his hands as if making a fire. His movements, like those of the other persons of
the play, suggest a marionette.*]

FIRST MUSICIAN [*speaking*].   He has made a little heap of leaves;
He lays the dry sticks on the leaves
And, shivering with cold, he has taken up
The fire-stick and socket from its hole.
He whirls it round to get a flame;
And now the dry sticks take the fire,
And now the fire leaps up and shines
Upon the hazels and the empty well.
MUSICIANS [*singing*].
'O wind, O salt wind, O sea wind!'
Cries the heart, 'it is time to sleep;
Why wander and nothing to find?
Better grow old and sleep.'
OLD MAN [*speaking*].   Why don't you speak to me? Why don't you say:
'Are you not weary gathering those sticks?
Are not your fingers cold?' You have not one word,
While yesterday you spoke three times. You said:
'The well is full of hazel leaves.' You said:
'The wind is from the west.' And after that:
'If there is rain it's likely there'll be mud.'
To-day you are as stupid as a fish,
No, worse, worse, being less lively and as dumb. [*He goes nearer.*]
Your eyes are dazed and heavy. If the Sidhe[2]
Must have a guardian to clean out the well
And drive the cattle off, they might choose somebody
That can be pleasant and companionable
Once in the day. Why do you stare like that?
You had that glassy look about the eyes
Last time it happened. Do you know anything?
It is enough to drive an old man crazy

2. Fairies (pronounced *shee*).

To look all day upon these broken rocks,
And ragged thorns, and that one stupid face,
And speak and get no answer.

YOUNG MAN [*who has entered through the audience during the last
speech*].   Then speak to me,
For youth is not more patient than old age;
And though I have trod the rocks for half a day
I cannot find what I am looking for.

OLD MAN.   Who speaks?
Who comes so suddenly into this place
Where nothing thrives? If I may judge by the gold
On head and feet and glittering in your coat,
You are not of those who hate the living world.

YOUNG MAN.   I am named Cuchulain,[3] I am Sualtim's son.

OLD MAN.   I have never heard that name.

YOUNG MAN.   It is not unknown.
I have an ancient house beyond the sea.

OLD MAN.   What mischief brings you hither?—you are like those
Who are crazy for the shedding of men's blood,
And for the love of women.

YOUNG MAN.   A rumour has led me,
A story told over the wine towards dawn.
I rose from table, found a boat, spread sail,
And with a lucky wind under the sail
Crossed waves that have seemed charmed, and found this shore.

OLD MAN.   There is no house to sack among these hills
Nor beautiful woman to be carried off.

YOUNG MAN.   You should be native here, for that rough tongue
Matches the barbarous spot. You can, it may be,
Lead me to what I seek, a well wherein
Three hazels drop their nuts and withered leaves,
And where a solitary girl keeps watch
Among grey boulders. He who drinks, they say,
Of that miraculous water lives for ever.

OLD MAN.   And are there not before your eyes at the instant
Grey boulders and a solitary girl
And three stripped hazels?

YOUNG MAN.   But there is no well.

OLD MAN.   Can you see nothing yonder?

YOUNG MAN.   I but see
A hollow among stones half-full of leaves.

OLD MAN.   And do you think so great a gift is found
By no more toil than spreading out a sail,
And climbing a steep hill? O, folly of youth,
Why should that hollow place fill up for you,
That will not fill for me? I have lain in wait

---

3. Heroic figure from the Ulster Cycle of epic Irish poetry and a recurring figure in Yeats's
work.

For more than fifty years, to find it empty,
Or but to find the stupid wind of the sea
Drive round the perishable leaves.

YOUNG MAN.   So it seems
There is some moment when the water fills it.

OLD MAN.   A secret moment that the holy shades
That dance upon the desolate mountain know,
And not a living man, and when it comes
The water has scarce plashed before it is gone.

YOUNG MAN.   I will stand here and wait. Why should the luck
Of Sualtim's son desert him now? For never
Have I had long to wait for anything.

OLD MAN.   No! Go from this accursed place! This place
Belongs to me, that girl there, and those others,
Deceivers of men.

YOUNG MAN.   And who are you who rail
Upon those dancers that all others bless?

OLD MAN.   One whom the dancers cheat. I came like you
When young in body and in mind, and blown
By what had seemed to me a lucky sail.
The well was dry, I sat upon its edge,
I waited the miraculous flood, I waited
While the years passed and withered me away.
I have snared the birds for food and eaten grass
And drunk the rain, and neither in dark nor shine
Wandered too far away to have heard the plash,
And yet the dancers have deceived me. Thrice
I have awakened from a sudden sleep
To find the stones were wet.

YOUNG MAN.   My luck is strong,
It will not leave me waiting, nor will they
That dance among the stones put me asleep;
If I grow drowsy I can pierce my foot.

OLD MAN.   No, do not pierce it, for the foot is tender,
It feels pain much. But find your sail again
And leave the well to me, for it belongs
To all that's old and withered.

YOUNG MAN.   No, I stay.

[*The* GUARDIAN OF THE WELL *gives the cry of the hawk.*]

There is that bird again.

OLD MAN.   There is no bird.

YOUNG MAN.   It sounded like the sudden cry of a hawk,
But there's no wing in sight. As I came hither
A great grey hawk swept down out of the sky,
And though I have good hawks, the best in the world
I had fancied, I have not seen its like. It flew
As though it would have torn me with its beak,
Or blinded me, smiting with that great wing.

I had to draw my sword to drive it off,
And after that it flew from rock to rock.
I pelted it with stones, a good half-hour,
And just before I had turned the big rock there
And seen this place, it seemed to vanish away.
Could I but find a means to bring it down
I'd hood it.

OLD MAN.   The Woman of the Sidhe herself,
The mountain witch, the unappeasable shadow.
She is always flitting upon this mountain-side,
To allure or to destroy. When she has shown
Herself to the fierce women of the hills
Under that shape they offer sacrifice
And arm for battle. There falls a curse
On all who have gazed in her unmoistened eyes;
So get you gone while you have that proud step
And confident voice, for not a man alive
Has so much luck that he can play with it.
Those that have long to live should fear her most,
The old are cursed already. That curse may be
Never to win a woman's love and keep it;
Or always to mix hatred in the love;
Or it may be that she will kill your children,
That you will find them, their throats torn and bloody,
Or you will be so maddened that you kill them
With your own hand.

YOUNG MAN.   Have you been set down there
To threaten all who come, and scare them off?
You seem as dried up as the leaves and sticks,
As though you had no part in life.

[*The* GUARDIAN OF THE WELL *gives hawk cry again.*]

                              That cry!
There is that cry again. That woman made it,
But why does she cry out as the hawk cries?

OLD MAN.   It was her mouth, and yet not she, that cried.
It was that shadow cried behind her mouth;
And now I know why she has been so stupid
All the day through, and had such heavy eyes.
Look at her shivering now, the terrible life
Is slipping through her veins. She is possessed.
Who knows whom she will murder or betray
Before she awakes in ignorance of it all,
And gathers up the leaves? But they'll be wet;
The water will have come and gone again;
That shivering is the sign. O, get you gone,
At any moment now I shall hear it bubble.
If you are good you will leave it. I am old,
And if I do not drink it now, will never;

I have been watching all my life and maybe
Only a little cupful will bubble up.
YOUNG MAN.   I'll take it in my hands. We shall both drink,
And even if there are but a few drops,
Share them.
OLD MAN.   But swear that I may drink the first;
The young are greedy, and if you drink the first
You'll drink it all. Ah, you have looked at her;
She has felt your gaze and turned her eyes on us;
I cannot bear her eyes, they are not of this world,
Nor moist, nor faltering; they are no girl's eyes.

> [*He covers his head. The* GUARDIAN OF THE WELL *throws off
> her cloak and rises. Her dress under the cloak suggests a
> hawk.*]

YOUNG MAN.   Why do you fix those eyes of a hawk upon me?
I am not afraid of you, bird, woman, or witch.

> [*He goes to the side of the well, which the* GUARDIAN OF THE
> WELL *has left.*]

Do what you will, I shall not leave this place
Till I have grown immortal like yourself.

> [*He has sat down; the* GUARDIAN OF THE WELL *has begun to
> dance, moving like a hawk. The* OLD MAN *sleeps. The dance
> goes on for some time.*]

FIRST MUSICIAN [*singing or half-singing*].
                    O God, protect me
                    From a horrible deathless body
                    Sliding through the veins of a sudden.

> [*The dance goes on for some time. The* YOUNG MAN *rises
> slowly.*]

FIRST MUSICIAN [*speaking*].   The madness has laid hold upon him
now,
For he grows pale and staggers to his feet. [*The dance goes on.*]
YOUNG MAN.   Run where you will,
Grey bird, you shall be perched upon my wrist.
Some were called queens and yet have been perched there. [*The
dance goes on.*]
FIRST MUSICIAN [*speaking*].   I have heard water plash; it comes, it
comes;
Look where it glitters. He has heard the plash;
Look, he has turned his head.

> [*The* GUARDIAN OF THE WELL *has gone out. The* YOUNG MAN
> *drops his spear as if in a dream and goes out.*]

MUSICIANS [*singing*].

He has lost what may not be found
Till men heap his burial-mound
And all the history ends.
He might have lived at his ease,
An old dog's head on his knees,
Among his children and friends.

[*The* OLD MAN *creeps up to the well.*]

OLD MAN.   The accursed shadows have deluded me,
   The stones are dark and yet the well is empty;
   The water flowed and emptied while I slept.
   You have deluded me my whole life through,
   Accursed dancers, you have stolen my life.
   That there should be such evil in a shadow!
YOUNG MAN [*entering*].   She has fled from me and hidden in the
   rocks.
OLD MAN.   She has but led you from the fountain. Look!
   Though stones and leaves are dark where it has flowed,
   There's not a drop to drink.

[*The* MUSICIANS *cry* 'Aoife!'⁴ 'Aoife!' *and strike gong.*]

YOUNG MAN.   What are those cries?
   What is that sound that runs along the hill?
   Who are they that beat a sword upon a shield?
OLD MAN.   She has roused up the fierce women of the hills,
   Aoife, and all her troop, to take your life,
   And never till you are lying in the earth
   Can you know rest.
YOUNG MAN.   The clash of arms again!
OLD MAN.   O, do not go! The mountain is accursed;
   Stay with me, I have nothing more to lose,
   I do not now deceive you.
YOUNG MAN.   I will face them.

[*He goes out, no longer as if in a dream, but shouldering his
spear and calling:*]

He comes! Cuchulain, son of Sualtim, comes!

[*The* MUSICIANS *stand up; one goes to centre with folded
cloth. The others unfold it. While they do so they sing. During
the singing, and while hidden by the cloth, the* OLD MAN *goes
out. When the play is performed with Mr. Dulac's music, the*
MUSICIANS *do not rise or unfold the cloth till after they have
sung the words* 'a bitter life'.]

[*Songs for the unfolding and folding of the cloth*]

___

4. Mythological warrior-queen.

Come to me, human faces,
Familiar memories;
I have found hateful eyes
Among the desolate places,
Unfaltering, unmoistened eyes.

Folly alone I cherish,
I choose it for my share;
Being but a mouthful of air,
I am content to perish;
I am but a mouthful of sweet air.

O lamentable shadows,
Obscurity of strife!
I choose a pleasant life
Among indolent meadows;
Wisdom must live a bitter life.

[*They then fold up the cloth, singing.*]

'The man that I praise',
Cries out the empty well,
'Lives all his days
Where a hand on the bell
Can call the milch cows
To the comfortable door of his house.
Who but an idiot would praise
Dry stones in a well?'
'The man that I praise',
Cries out the leafless tree,
'Has married and stays
By an old hearth, and he
On naught has set store
But children and dogs on the floor.
Who but an idiot would praise
A withered tree?'

[*They go out.*]

THE END

W. B. YEATS

Purgatory[†]

Persons in the Play

A BOY
AN OLD MAN

SCENE.—*A ruined house and a bare tree in the background.*

BOY.   Half-door, hall door,
   Hither and thither day and night,
   Hill or hollow, shouldering this pack,
   Hearing you talk.
OLD MAN.   Study that house.
   I think about its jokes and stories;
   I try to remember what the butler
   Said to a drunken gamekeeper
   In mid-October, but I cannot.
   If I cannot, none living can.
   Where are the jokes and stories of a house,
   Its threshold gone to patch a pig-sty?
BOY.   So you have come this path before?
OLD MAN.   The moonlight falls upon the path,
   The shadow of a cloud upon the house,
   And that's symbolical; study that tree,
   What is it like?
BOY.   A silly old man.
OLD MAN.   It's like—no matter what it's like.
   I saw it a year ago stripped bare as now,
   So I chose a better trade.
   I saw it fifty years ago
   Before the thunderbolt had riven it,
   Green leaves, ripe leaves, leaves thick as butter,
   Fat, greasy life. Stand there and look,
   Because there is somebody in that house.

[*The* BOY *puts down pack and stands in the doorway.*]

BOY.   There's nobody here.
OLD MAN.   There's somebody there.
BOY.   The floor is gone, the windows gone,
  And where there should be roof there's sky,
  And here's a bit of an egg-shell thrown
  Out of a jackdaw's nest.
OLD MAN.   But there are some
  That do not care what's gone, what's left:
  The souls in Purgatory that come back
  To habitations and familiar spots.
BOY.   Your wits are out again.
OLD MAN.   Re-live
  Their transgressions, and that not once
  But many times; they know at last
  The consequence of those transgressions
  Whether upon others or upon themselves;
  Upon others, others may bring help,
  For when the consequence is at an end
  The dream must end; if upon themselves,
  There is no help but in themselves
  And in the mercy of God.
BOY.   I have had enough!
  Talk to the jackdaws, if talk you must.
OLD MAN.   Stop! Sit there upon that stone.
  That is the house where I was born.
BOY.   The big old house that was burnt down?
OLD MAN.   My mother that was your grand-dam owned it,
  This scenery and this countryside,
  Kennel and stable, horse and hound—
  She had a horse at the Curragh,[1] and there met
  My father, a groom in a training stable,
  Looked at him and married him.
  Her mother never spoke to her again,
  And she did right.
BOY.   What's right and wrong?
  My grand-dad got the girl and the money.
OLD MAN.   Looked at him and married him,
  And he squandered everything she had.
  She never knew the worst, because
  She died in giving birth to me,
  But now she knows it all, being dead.
  Great people lived and died in this house;
  Magistrates, colonels, members of Parliament,
  Captains and Governors, and long ago
  Men that had fought at Aughrim and the Boyne.[2]

1. Center for Irish horse racing in county Kildare.
2. The conquest of Ireland by William of Orange included crucial victories over the Irish at
   the Boyne River on July 1, 1690, and at Aughrim on July 12, 1691.

Some that had gone on Government work
To London or to India came home to die,
Or came from London every spring
To look at the may-blossom in the park.
They had loved the trees that he cut down
To pay what he had lost at cards
Or spent on horses, drink and women;
Had loved the house, had loved all
The intricate passages of the house,
But he killed the house; to kill a house
Where great men grew up, married, died,
I here declare a capital offence.
BOY.   My God, but you had luck! Grand clothes,
And maybe a grand horse to ride.
OLD MAN.   That he might keep me upon his level
He never sent me to school, but some
Half-loved me for my half of her:
A gamekeeper's wife taught me to read,
A Catholic curate[3] taught me Latin.
There were old books and books made fine
By eighteenth-century French binding, books
Modern and ancient, books by the ton.
BOY.   What education have you given me?
OLD MAN.   I gave the education that befits
A bastard that a pedlar got
Upon a tinker's[4] daughter in a ditch.
When I had come to sixteen years old
My father burned down the house when drunk.
BOY.   But that is my age, sixteen years old,
At the Puck Fair.[5]
OLD MAN.   And everything was burnt;
Books, library, all were burnt.
BOY.   Is what I have heard upon the road the truth,
That you killed him in the burning house?
OLD MAN.   There's nobody here but our two selves?
BOY.   Nobody, Father.
OLD MAN.   I stuck him with a knife,
That knife that cuts my dinner now,
And after that I left him in the fire.
They dragged him out, somebody saw
The knife-wound but could not be certain
Because the body was all black and charred.
Then some that were his drunken friends
Swore they would put me upon trial,
Spoke of quarrels, a threat I had made.

3. Priest.
4. An itinerant peddler's.
5. August festival in county Kerry notable for folk traditions, including the crowning as
   king of a goat, and for attendance by tinkers.

The gamekeeper gave me some old clothes,
I ran away, worked here and there
Till I became a pedlar on the roads,
No good trade, but good enough
Because I am my father's son,
Because of what I did or may do.
Listen to the hoof-beats! Listen, listen!
BOY.   I cannot hear a sound
OLD MAN.   Beat! Beat!
This night is the anniversary
Of my mother's wedding night,
Or of the night wherein I was begotten.
My father is riding from the public-house,[6]
A whiskey-bottle under his arm.

[*A window is lit showing a young girl.*]

Look at the window; she stands there
Listening, the servants are all in bed,
She is alone, he has stayed late
Bragging and drinking in the public-house.
BOY.   There's nothing but an empty gap in the wall.
You have made it up. No, you are mad!
You are getting madder every day.
OLD MAN.   It's louder now because he rides
Upon a gravelled avenue
All grass to-day. The hoof-beat stops,
He has gone to the other side of the house,
Gone to the stable, put the horse up.
She has gone down to open the door.
This night she is no better than her man
And does not mind that he is half drunk,
She is mad about him. They mount the stairs,
She brings him into her own chamber.
And that is the marriage-chamber now.
The window is dimly lit again.

Do not let him touch you! It is not true
That drunken men cannot beget,
And if he touch he must beget
And you must bear his murderer.
Deaf! Both deaf! If I should throw
A stick or a stone they would not hear;
And that's a proof my wits are out.
But there's a problem: she must live
Through everything in exact detail,
Driven to it by remorse, and yet

6. Tavern, or, in short form, pub.

Can she renew the sexual act
And find no pleasure in it, and if not,
If pleasure and remorse must both be there,
Which is the greater?
                         I lack schooling.
Go fetch Tertullian;[7] he and I
Will ravel all that problem out
Whilst those two lie upon the mattress
Begetting me.
                    Come back! Come back!
And so you thought to slip away,
My bag of money between your fingers,
And that I could not talk and see!
You have been rummaging in the pack.

> [*The light in the window has faded out.*]

BOY.   You never gave me my right share.
OLD MAN.   And had I given it, young as you are,
   You would have spent it upon drink.
BOY.   What if I did? I had a right
   To get it and spend it as I chose.
OLD MAN.   Give me that bag and no more words.
BOY.   I will not.
OLD MAN.   I will break your fingers.

> [*They struggle for the bag. In the struggle it drops, scattering the money. The* OLD MAN *staggers but does not fall. They stand looking at each other. The window is lit up. A man is seen pouring whiskey into a glass.*]

BOY.   What if I killed you? You killed my grand-dad,
   Because you were young and he was old.
   Now I am young and you are old.
OLD MAN.   [*staring at window*].   Better-looking, those sixteen
   years—
BOY.   What are you muttering?
OLD MAN.   Younger—and yet
   She should have known he was not her kind.
BOY.   What are you saying? Out with it! [OLD MAN *points to win-
   dow.*]
   My God! The window is lit up
   And somebody stands there, although
   The floorboards are all burnt away.
OLD MAN.   The window is lit up because my father
   Has come to find a glass for his whiskey.
   He leans there like some tired beast.
BOY.   A dead, living, murdered man!
OLD MAN.   'Then the bride-sleep fell upon Adam':

---

7. Latin rhetorician and early Christian theologian (c. 160–240).

Where did I read those words?[8]
                              And yet
There's nothing leaning in the window
But the impression upon my mother's mind;
Being dead she is alone in her remorse.
BOY.   A body that was a bundle of old bones
Before I was born. Horrible! Horrible!

    [*He covers his eyes.*]

OLD MAN.   That beast there would know nothing, being nothing,
If I should kill a man under the window
He would not even turn his head.

    [*He stabs the* BOY.]

My father and my son on the same jack-knife!
That finishes—there—there—there—

    [*He stabs again and again. The window grows dark.*]

'Hush-a-bye baby, thy father's a knight,
Thy mother a lady, lovely and bright.'[9]
No, that is something that I read in a book,
And if I sing it must be to my mother,
And I lack rhyme.

    [*The stage has grown dark except where the tree stands in white light.*]

                Study that tree.
It stands there like a purified soul,
All cold, sweet, glistening light.
Dear mother, the window is dark again,
But you are in the light because
I finished all that consequence.
I killed that lad because had he grown up
He would have stuck a woman's fancy,
Begot, and passed pollution on.
I am a wretched foul old man
And therefore harmless. When I have stuck
This old jack-knife into a sod
And pulled it out all bright again,
And picked up all the money that he dropped,
I'll to a distant place, and there
Tell my old jokes among new men.

    [*He cleans the knife and begins to pick up money.*]

Hoof-beats! Dear God,
How quickly it returns—beat—beat—!

8. In "Eden Bower," by Dante Gabriel Rossetti (1828–82), English poet.
9. "Lullaby of an Infant Chief," by Sir Walter Scott (1771–1832).

Her mind cannot hold up that dream.
Twice a murderer and all for nothing,
And she must animate that dead night
Not once but many times!
                    O God,
Release my mother's soul from its dream!
Mankind can do no more. Appease
The misery of the living and the remorse of the dead.

LADY GREGORY

Spreading the News[†]

Persons

BARTLEY FALLON

MRS. FALLON

JACK SMITH

SHAWN EARLY

TIM CASEY

JAMES RYAN

MRS. TARPEY

MRS. TULLY

A POLICEMAN (JO MULDOON)

A REMOVABLE MAGISTRATE[1]

SCENE. *The outskirts of a Fair. An Apple Stall.* MRS. TARPEY *sitting at it.* MAGISTRATE *and* POLICEMAN *enter.*

MAGISTRATE. So that is the Fair Green. Cattle and sheep and mud. No system. What a repulsive sight!

POLICEMAN. That is so, indeed.

MAGISTRATE. I suppose there is as good deal of disorder in this place?

POLICEMAN. There is.

MAGISTRATE. Common assault?

POLICEMAN. It's common enough.

MAGISTRATE. Agrarian crime, no doubt?

POLICEMAN. That is so.

MAGISTRATE. Boycotting? Maiming of cattle? Firing into houses?

POLICEMAN. There was one time, and there might be again.

MAGISTRATE. That is bad. Does it go any farther than that?

POLICEMAN. Far enough, indeed.

MAGISTRATE. Homicide, then! This district has been shamefully neglected! I will change all that. When I was in the Andaman Is-

---

† From *The Collected Plays of Lady Gregory,* Coole Edition, published by Oxford University Press and Colin Smythe Limited.

1. An appointed, rather than elected, magistrate subject to removal from office; in Ireland, where most common, often called a "Removable."

lands,[2] my system never failed. Yes, yes, I will change all that. What has that woman on her stall?

POLICEMAN.   Apples mostly—and sweets.

MAGISTRATE.   Just see if there are any unlicensed goods underneath—spirits or the like. We had evasions of the salt tax in the Andaman Islands.

POLICEMAN [sniffing cautiously and upsetting a heap of apples].   I see no spirits here—or salt.

MAGISTRATE [to MRS. TARPEY].   Do you know this town well, my good woman?

MRS. TARPEY. [holding out some apples].   A penny the half-dozen, your honor.

POLICEMAN [shouting].   The gentleman is asking do you know the town! He's the new magistrate!

MRS. TARPEY [rising and ducking].   Do I know the town? I do, to be sure.

MAGISTRATE [shouting].   What is its chief business?

MRS. TARPEY.   Business, is it? What business would the people here have but to be minding one another's business?

MAGISTRATE.   I mean what trade have they?

MRS. TARPEY.   Not a trade. No trade at all but to be talking.

MAGISTRATE.   I shall learn nothing here.

[JAMES RYAN comes in, pipe in mouth. Seeing MAGISTRATE he retreats quickly, taking pipe from mouth.]

MAGISTRATE.   The smoke from that man's pipe had a greenish look; he may be growing unlicensed tobacco at home. I wish I had brought my telescope to this district. Come to the post-office, I will telegraph for it. I found it very useful in the Andaman Islands.

[MAGISTRATE and POLICEMAN go out left.]

MRS. TARPEY.   Bad luck to Jo Muldoon, knocking my apples this way and that way. [Begins arranging them.] Showing off he was to the new magistrate.

[Enter BARTLEY FALLON and MRS. FALLON.]

BARTLEY.   Indeed it's a poor country and a scarce country to be living in. But I'm thinking if I went to America it's long ago the day I'd be dead!

MRS. FALLON.   So you might, indeed. [She puts her basket on a barrel and begins putting parcels in it, taking them from under her cloak.]

BARTLEY.   And it's a great expense for a poor man to be buried in America.

MRS. FALLON.   Never fear, Bartley Fallon, but I'll give you a good burying the day you'll die.

2. An archipelago of more than two hundred islands in the Bay of Bengal that served as a British penal colony from 1858 to 1942.

BARTLEY.   Maybe it's yourself will be buried in the graveyard of
Cloonmara before me, Mary Fallon, and I myself that will be dying unbeknownst some night, and no one a-near me. And the cat
itself may be gone straying through the country, and the mice
squealing over the quilt.

MRS. FALLON.   Leave off talking of dying. It might be twenty years
you'll be living yet.

BARTLEY [*with a deep sigh*].   I'm thinking if I'll be living at the end
of twenty years, it's a very old man I'll be then!

MRS. TARPEY [*turns and sees them*].   Good morrow, Bartley Fallon;
good morrow, Mrs. Fallon. Well, Bartley, you'll find no cause for
complaining to-day; they are all saying it was a good fair.

BARTLEY [*raising his voice*].   It was not a good fair, Mrs. Tarpey. It
was a scattered sort of a fair. If we didn't expect more, we got
less. That's the way with me always; whatever I have to sell goes
down and whatever I have to buy goes up. If there's ever any misfortune coming to this world, it's on myself in pitches, like a flock
of crows on seed potatoes.

MRS. FALLON.   Leave off talking of misfortunes, and listen to Jack
Smith that is coming the way, and he singing.

[*Voice of* JACK SMITH *heard singing.*]

> I thought, my first love,
>   There'd be but one house between you and me,
> And I thought I would find
>   Yourself coaxing my child on your knee.
> Over the tide
>   I would leap with the leap of a swan,
> Till I came to the side
>   Of the wife of the Red-haired man!

[JACK SMITH *comes in; he is a red-haired man, and is carrying
a hayfork.*]

MRS. TARPEY.   That should be a good song if I had my hearing.

MRS. FALLON [*shouting*].   It's "The Red-haired Man's Wife."

MRS. TARPEY.   I know it well. That's the song that has a skin on it!
[*She turns her back to them and goes on arranging her apples.*]

MRS. FALLON.   Where's herself, Jack Smith?

JACK SMITH.   She was delayed with her washing; bleaching the
clothes on the hedge she is, and she daren't leave them, with all
the tinkers that do be passing to the fair. It isn't to the fair I came
myself, but up to the Five Acre Meadow I'm going, where I have
a contract for the hay. We'll get a share of it into tramps to-day.
[*He lays down hayfork and lights his pipe.*]

BARTLEY.   You will not get it into tramps to-day. The rain will be
down on it by evening, and on myself too. It's seldom I ever
started on a journey but the rain would come down on me before
I'd find any place of shelter.

JACK SMITH.   If it didn't itself, Bartley, it is my belief you would carry a leaky pail on your head in place of a hat, the way you'd not be without some cause of complaining.

[*A voice heard:* God on, now, go on that o' that. Go on I say.]

JACK SMITH.   Look at that young mare of Pat Ryan's that is backing into Shaughnessy's bullocks with the dint of the crowd! Don't be daunted, Pat, I'll give you a hand with her. [*He goes out, leaving his hayfork.*]

MRS. FALLON.   It's time for ourselves to be going home. I have all I bought put in the basket. Look at there, Jack Smith's hayfork he left after him! He'll be wanting it. [*Calls.*] Jack Smith! Jack Smith!—He's gone through the crowd—hurry after him, Bartley, he'll be wanting it.

BARTLEY.   I'll do that. This is no safe place to be leaving it. [*He takes up fork awkwardly and upsets the basket.*] Look at that now! If there is any basket in the fair upset, it must be our own basket! [*He goes out to right.*]

MRS. FALLON.   Get out of that! It is your own fault, it is. Talk of misfortunes and misfortunes will come. Glory be! Look at my new eggcups rolling in every part—and my two pound of sugar with the paper broke—

MRS. TARPEY [*turning from stall*].   God help us, Mrs. Fallon, what happened your basket?

MRS. FALLON.   It's himself that knocked it down, bad manners to him. [*Putting things up.*] My grand sugar that's destroyed, and he'll not drink his tea without it. I had best go back to the shop for more, much good may it do him!

[*Enter* TIM CASEY.]

TIM CASEY.   Where is Bartley Fallon, Mrs. Fallon? I want a word with him before he'll leave the fair. I was afraid he might have gone home by this, for he's a temperate man.

MRS. FALLON.   I wish he did go home! It'd be best for me if he went home straight from the fair green, or if he never came with me at all? Where is he, is it? He's gone up the road [*jerks elbow*] following Jack Smith with a hayfork. [*She goes out to left.*]

TIM CASEY.   Following Jack Smith with a hayfork! Did ever any one hear the like of that. [*Shouts*]. Did you hear that news, Mrs. Tarpey?

MRS. TARPEY.   I heard no news at all.

TIM CASEY.   Some dispute I suppose it was that rose between Jack Smith and Bartley Fallon, and it seems Jack made off, and Bartley is following him with a hayfork!

MRS. TARPEY.   Is he now? Well, that was quick work! It's not ten minutes since the two of them were here, Bartley going home and Jack going to the Five Acre Meadow; and I had my apples to settle up, that Jo Muldoon of the police had scattered, and when I looked round again Jack Smith was gone, and Bartley Fallon was gone, and Mrs. Fallon's basket upset, and all in it strewed

upon the ground—the tea here—the two pound of sugar there—
the eggcups there—Look, now, what a great hardship the deafness puts upon me, that I didn't hear the commencement of the
fight! Wait till I tell James Ryan that I see below; he is a neighbour of Bartley's, it would be a pity if he wouldn't hear the news!

[*She goes out. Enter* SHAWN EARLY *and* MRS. TULLEY.]

TIM CASEY.   Listen, Shawn Early! Listen, Mrs. Tully, to the news!
Jack Smith and Bartley Fallon had a falling out, and Jack
knocked Mrs. Fallon's basket into the road, and Bartley made an
attack on him with a hayfork, and away with Jack, and Bartley after him. Look at the sugar here yet on the road!

SHAWN EARLY.   Do you tell me so? Well, that's a queer thing, and
Bartley Fallon so quiet a man!

MRS. TULLY.   I wouldn't wonder at all. I would never think well of
a man that would have that sort of a mouldering look. It's likely
he has overtaken Jack by this.

[*Enter* JAMES RYAN *and* MRS. TARPEY.]

JAMES RYAN.   That is great news Mrs. Tarpey was telling me! I suppose that's what brought the police and the magistrate up this
way. I was wondering to see them in it a while ago.

SHAWN EARLY.   The police after them? Bartley Fallon must have in-
jured Jack so. They wouldn't meddle in a fight that was only for
show!

MRS. TULLY.   Why wouldn't he injure him? There was many a man
killed with no more of a weapon than a hayfork.

JAMES RYAN.   Wait till I run north as far as Kelly's bar to spread the
news! [*He goes out.*]

TIM CASEY.   I'll go tell Jack Smith's first cousin that is standing
there south of the church after selling his lambs. [*Goes out.*]

MRS. TULLY.   I'll go telling a few of the neighbours I see beyond to
the west. [*Goes out.*]

SHAWN EARLY.   I'll give word of it beyond at the east of the green.

[*Is going out when* MRS. TARPEY *seizes hold of him.*]

MRS. TARPEY.   Stop a minute, Shawn Early, and tell me did you see
red Jack Smith's wife, Kitty Keary, in any place?

SHAWN EARLY.   I did. At her own house she was, drying clothes on
the hedge as I passed.

MRS. TARPEY.   What did you say she was doing?

SHAWN EARLY [*breaking away*].   Laying out a sheet on the hedge.
[*He goes.*]

MRS. TARPEY.   Laying out a sheet for the dead! The Lord have
mercy on us! Jack Smith dead, and his wife laying out a sheet for
his burying! [*Calls out.*] Why didn't you tell me that before,
Shawn Early? Isn't the deafness the great hardship? Half the
world might be dead without me knowing of it or getting word of
it all! [*She sits down and rocks herself.*] O my poor Jack Smith! To

be going to his work so nice and so hearty, and to be left stretched on the ground in the light of the day!

[*Enter* TIM CASEY.]

TIM CASEY.   What is it, Mrs. Tarpey? What happened since?

MRS. TARPEY.   O my poor Jack Smith!

TIM CASEY.   Did Bartley overtake him?

MRS. TARPEY.   O the poor man!

TIM CASEY.   Is it killed he is?

MRS. TARPEY.   Stretched on the Five Acre Meadow!

TIM CASEY.   The Lord have mercy on us! Is that a fact?

MRS. TARPEY.   Without the rites of the Church or a ha'porth!

TIM CASEY.   Who was telling you?

MRS. TARPEY.   And the wife laying out a sheet for his corpse. [*Sits up and wipes her eyes.*] I suppose they'll wake him the same as another?

[*Enter* MRS. TULLY, SHAWN EARLY, *and* JAMES RYAN.]

MRS. TULLY.   There is great talk about this work in every quarter of the fair.

MRS. TARPEY.   Ochone![3] cold and dead. And myself maybe the last he was speaking to!

JAMES RYAN.   The Lord save us! Is it dead he is?

TIM CASEY.   Dead surely, and the wife getting provision for the wake.

SHAWN EARLY.   Well, now, hadn't Bartley Fallon great venom in him?

MRS. TULLY.   You may be sure he had some cause. Why would he have made an end of him if he had not? [*To* MRS. TARPEY, *raising her voice.*] What was it rose the dispute at all, Mrs. Tarpey?

MRS. TARPEY.   Not a one of me knows. The last I saw of them, Jack Smith was standing there, and Bartley Fallon was standing there, quiet and easy, and he listening to "The Red-haired Man's Wife."

MRS. TULLY.   Do you hear that, Tim Casey? Do you hear that, Shawn Early and James Ryan? Bartley Fallon was there this morning listening to red Jack Smith's wife, Kitty Keary that was! Listening to her and whispering with her! It was she started the fight so!

SHAWN EARLY.   She must have followed him from her own house. It is likely some person roused him.

TIM CASEY.   I never knew, before, Bartley Fallon was great with Jack Smith's wife.

MRS. TULLY.   How would you know it? Sure it's not in the streets they would be calling it. If Mrs. Fallon didn't know of it, and if I that have the next house to them didn't know of it, and if Jack Smith himself didn't know of it, it is not likely you would know of it, Tim Casey.

3. An expression of lamentation.

SHAWN EARLY. Let Bartley Fallon take charge of her from this out so, and let him provide for her. It is little pity she will get from any person in this parish.

TIM CASEY. How can he take charge of her?[4] Sure he has a wife of his own. Sure you don't think he'd turn souper and marry her in a Protestant church?

JAMES RYAN. It would be easy for him to marry her if he brought her to America.

SHAWN EARLY. With or without Kitty Keary, believe me it is for America he's making at this minute. I saw the new magistrate and Jo Muldoon of the police going into the post-office as I came up—there was hurry on them—you may be sure it was to telegraph they went, the way he'll be stopped in the docks at Queenstown!

MRS. TULLY. It's like Kitty Keary is gone with him, and not minding a sheet or a wake at all. The poor man, to be deserted by his own wife, and the breath hardly gone out yet from his body that is lying bloody in the field!

[*Enter* MRS. FALLON.]

MRS. FALLON. What is it the whole of the town is talking about? And what is it you yourselves are talking about? Is it about my man Bartley Fallon you are talking? Is it lies about him you are telling, saying that he went killing Jack Smith? My grief that ever he came into this place at all!

JAMES RYAN. Be easy now, Mrs. Fallon. Sure there is no one at all in the whole fair but is sorry for you!

MRS. FALLON. Sorry for me, is it? Why would any one be sorry for me? Let you be sorry for yourselves, and that there may be shame on you for ever and at the day of judgment, for the words you are saying and the lies you are telling to take away the character of my poor man, and to take the good name off of him, and to drive him to destruction! That is what you are doing!

SHAWN EARLY. Take comfort now, Mrs. Fallon. The police are not so smart as they think. Sure he might give them the slip yet, the same as Lynchehaun.[5]

MRS. TULLY. If they do get him, and if they do put a rope around his neck, there is no one can say he does not deserve it!

MRS. FALLON. Is that what you are saying, Bridget Tully, and is that what you think? I tell you it's too much talk you have, making yourself out to be such a great one, and to be running down every respectable person! A rope, is it? It isn't much of a rope was needed to tie up your own furniture the day you came into Martin Tully's house, and you never bringing as much as a blanket, or a penny, or a suit of clothes with you and I myself bringing sev-

4. Reference to Catholics, in famine, who converted in exchange for soup offered by Protestant evangelists.
5. A famous outlaw whose story also influenced J. M. Synge's *Playboy*.

enty pounds and two feather beds. And now you are stiffer than a
woman would have a hundred pounds! It is too much talk the
whole of you have. A rope is it? I tell you the whole of this town
is full of liars and schemers that would hang you up for half a
glass of whiskey. [*Turning to go.*] People they are you wouldn't
believe as much as daylight from without you'd get up to have a
look at it yourself. Killing Jack Smith indeed! Where are you at
all, Bartley, till I bring you out of this? My nice quiet little man!
My decent comrade! He that is as kind and as harmless as an innocent beast of the field! He'll be doing no harm at all if he'll
shed the blood of some of you after this day's work! That much
would be no harm at all. [*Calls out.*] Bartley! Bartley Fallon!
Where are you? [*Going out.*] Did any one see Bartley Fallon?

[*All turn to look after her.*]

JAMES RYAN.   It is hard for her to believe any such a thing, God
help her!

[*Enter* BARTLEY FALLON *from right, carrying hayfork.*]

BARTLEY.   It is what I often said to myself, if there is ever any misfortune coming to this world it is on myself it is sure to come!

[*All turn round and face him.*]

To be going about with this fork and to find no one to take it, and
no place to leave it down, and I wanting to be gone out of this—
Is that you, Shawn Early? [*Holds out fork.*] It's well I met you.
You have no call to be leaving the fair for a while the way I have,
and how can I go till I'm rid of this fork? Will you take it and
keep it until such time as Jack Smith—

SHAWN EARLY [*backing*].   I will not take it, Bartley Fallon, I'm very
thankful to you!

BARTLEY [*turning to apple stall*].   Look at it now, Mrs. Tarpey, it
was here I got it; let me thrust it in under the stall. It will lie
there safe enough, and no one will take notice of it until such
time as Jack Smith—

MRS. TARPEY.   Take your fork out of that! Is it to put trouble on me
and to destroy me you want? putting it there for the police to be
rooting it out maybe. [*Thrusts him back.*]

BARTLEY.   That is a very unneighbourly thing for you to do, Mrs.
Tarpey. Hadn't I enough care on me with that fork before this,
running up and down with it like the swinging of a clock, and
afeard to lay it down in any place! I wish I never touched it or
meddled with it at all!

JAMES RYAN.   It is a pity, indeed, you ever did.

BARTLEY.   Will you yourself take it, James Ryan? You were always a
neighbourly man.

JAMES RYAN [*backing*].   There is many a thing I would do for you,
Bartley Fallon, but I won't do that!

SHAWN EARLY.   I tell you there is no man will give you any help or any encouragement for this day's work. If it was something agrarian now—

BARTLEY.   If no one at all will take it, maybe it's best to give it up to the police.

TIM CASEY.   There'd be a welcome for it with them surely! [*Laughter.*]

MRS. TULLY.   And it is to the police Kitty Keary herself will be brought.

MRS. TARPEY [*rocking to and fro*].   I wonder now who will take the expense of the wake for poor Jack Smith?

BARTLEY.   The wake for Jack Smith!

TIM CASEY.   Why wouldn't he get a wake as well as another? Would you begrudge him that much?

BARTLEY.   Red Jack Smith dead! Who was telling you?

SHAWN EARLY.   The whole town knows of it by this.

BARTLEY.   Do they say what way did he die?

JAMES RYAN.   You don't know that yourself, I suppose, Bartley Fallon? You don't know he was followed and that he was laid dead with a stab of a hayfork?

BARTLEY.   The stab of a hayfork!

SHAWN EARLY.   You don't know, I suppose, that the body was found in the Five Acre Meadow?

BARTLEY.   The Five Acre Meadow!

TIM CASEY.   It is likely you don't know that the police are after the man that did it?

BARTLEY.   The man that did it!

MRS. TULLY.   You don't know, maybe, that he was made away with for the sake of Kitty Keary, his wife?

BARTLEY.   Kitty Keary, his wife! [*Sits down bewildered.*]

MRS. TULLY.   And what have you to say now, Bartley Fallon?

BARTLEY [*crossing himself*].   I to bring that fork here, and to find that news before me! It is much if I can ever stir from this place at all, or reach as far as the road!

TIM CASEY.   Look, boys, at the new magistrate, and Jo Muldoon along with him! It's best for us to quit this.

SHAWN EARLY.   That is so. It is best not to be mixed in this business at all.

JAMES RYAN.   Bad as he is, I wouldn't like to be an informer against any man.

[*All hurry away except* MRS. TARPEY, *who remains behind her stall. Enter* MAGISTRATE *and* POLICEMAN.]

MAGISTRATE.   I knew the district was in a bad state, but I did not expect to be confronted with a murder at the first fair I came to.

POLICEMAN.   I am sure you did not, indeed.

MAGISTRATE.   It was well I had not gone home. I caught a few words here and there that roused my suspicions.

POLICEMAN.   So they would, too.

MAGISTRATE.   You heard the same story from everyone you asked?

POLICEMAN.   The same story—or if it was not altogether the same, anyway it was no less than the first story.

MAGISTRATE.   What is that man doing? He is sitting alone with a hayfork. He has a guilty look. The murder was done with a hayfork!

POLICEMAN [*in a whisper*].   That's the very man they say did the act; Bartley Fallon himself!

MAGISTRATE.   He must have found escape difficult—he is trying to brazen it out. A convict in the Andaman Islands tried the same game, but he could not escape my system! Stand aside—Don't go far—have the handcuffs ready. [*He walks up to Bartley, folds his arms, and stands before him.*] Here, my man, do you know anything of John Smith?

BARTLEY.   Of John Smith! Who is he, now?

POLICEMAN.   Jack Smith, sir—Red Jack Smith!

MAGISTRATE [*coming a step nearer and tapping him on the shoulder*].   Where is Jack Smith?

BARTLEY [*with a deep sigh, and shaking his head slowly*].   Where is he, indeed?

MAGISTRATE.   What have you to tell?

BARTLEY.   It is where he was this morning, standing in this spot, singing his share of songs—no, but lighting his pipe—scraping a match on the sole of his shoes—

MAGISTRATE.   I ask you, for the third time, where is he?

BARTLEY.   I wouldn't like to say that. It is a great mystery, and it is hard to say of any man, did he earn hatred or love.

MAGISTRATE.   Tell me all you know.

BARTLEY.   All that I know—Well, there are the three estates; there is Limbo, and there is Purgatory, and there is—

MAGISTRATE.   Nonsense! This is trifling! Get to the point.

BARTLEY.   Maybe you don't hold with the clergy so? That is the teaching of the clergy. Maybe you hold with the old people. It is what they do be saying, that the shadow goes wandering, and the soul is tired, and the body is taking a rest—The shadow! [*Starts up.*] I was nearly sure I saw Jack Smith not ten minutes ago at the corner of the forge, and I lost him again—Was it his ghost I saw, do you think?

MAGISTRATE [*to* POLICEMAN].   Conscience-struck! He will confess all now!

BARTLEY.   His ghost to come before me! It is likely it was on account of the fork! I to have it and he to have no way to defend himself the time he met with his death!

MAGISTRATE [*to* POLICEMAN].   I must note down his words. [*Takes out notebook. To* BARTLEY.] I warn you that your words are being noted.

BARTLEY.   If I had ha' run faster in the beginning, this terror would not be on me at the latter end! Maybe he will cast it up against me at the day of judgment—I wouldn't wonder at all at that.

MAGISTRATE [*writing*].   At the day of judgment—

BARTLEY.   It was soon for his ghost to appear to me—is it coming after me always by day it will be, and stripping the clothes off in the night time?—I wouldn't wonder at all at that, being as I am an unfortunate man!

MAGISTRATE [*sternly*].   Tell me this truly. What was the motive of this crime?

BARTLEY.   The motive, is it?

MAGISTRATE.   Yes; the motive; the cause.

BARTLEY.   I'd sooner not say that.

MAGISTRATE.   You had better tell me truly. Was it money?

BARTLEY.   Not at all! What did poor Jack Smith ever have in his pockets unless it might be his hands that would be in them?

MAGISTRATE.   Any dispute about land?

BARTLEY [*indignantly*].   Not at all! He never was a grabber or grabbed from any one!

MAGISTRATE.   You will find it better for you if you tell me at once.

BARTLEY.   I tell you I wouldn't for the whole world wish to say what it was—it is a thing I would not like to be talking about.

MAGISTRATE.   There is no use in hiding it. It will be discovered in the end.

BARTLEY.   Well, I suppose it will, seeing that mostly everybody knows it before. Whisper here now. I will tell no lie; where would be the use?

[*Puts his hand to his mouth, and* MAGISTRATE *stoops.*]

Don't be putting the blame on the parish, for such as thing was never done in the parish before—it was done for the sake of Kitty Keary, Jack Smith's wife.

MAGISTRATE [*to policeman*].   Put on the handcuffs. we have been saved some trouble. I knew he would confess if taken in the right way.

[POLICEMAN *puts on handcuffs.*]

BARTLEY.   Handcuffs now! Glory be! I always said, if there was ever any misfortune coming to this place it was on myself it would fall. I to be in handcuffs! There's no wonder at all in that.

[*Enter* MRS. FALLON, *followed by the rest. She is looking back at them as she speaks.*]

MRS. FALLON.   Telling lies the whole of the people of his town are; telling lies, telling lies as fast as a dog will trot! Speaking against my poor respectable man! Saying he made an end of Jack Smith! My decent comrade! There is no better man and no kinder man in the whole of the five parishes! It's little annoyance he ever gave to any one! [*Turns and sees him.*] What in the earthly world do I see before me? Bartley Fallon in charge of the police! Handcuffs on him! O Bartley, what did you do at all at all?

BARTLEY.   O Mary, there has a great misfortune come upon me! It is what I always said, that if there is ever any misfortune—

MRS. FALLON. What did he do at all, or is it bewitched I am?

MAGISTRATE. This man has been arrested on a charge of murder.

MRS. FALLON. Whose charge is that? Don't believe them! They are all liars in this place! Give me back my man!

MAGISTRATE. It is natural you should take his part, but you have no cause of complaint against your neighbors. He has been arrested for the murder of John Smith, on his own confession.

MRS. FALLON. The saints of heaven protect us! And what did he want killing Jack Smith?

MAGISTRATE. It is best you should know all. He did it on account of a love affair with the murdered man's wife.

MRS. FALLON. [*sitting down*]. With Jack Smith's wife! With Kitty Keary!—Ochone, the traitor!

THE CROWD. A great shame, indeed. He is a traitor indeed.

MRS. TULLY. To America he was bringing her, Mrs. Fallon.

BARTLEY. What are you saying, Mary? I tell you—

MRS. FALLON. Don't say a word! I won't listen to any word you'll say! [*Stops her ears.*] O, isn't he the treacherous villain? Ohone go deo![6]

BARTLEY. Be quiet till I speak! Listen to what I say!

MRS. FALLON. Sitting beside me on the ass car coming to the town, so quiet and so respectable, and treachery like that in his heart!

BARTLEY. Is it your wits you have lost or is it I myself that have lost my wits?

MRS. FALLON. And it's hard I earned you, slaving—and you grumbling, and sighing, and coughing, and discontented, and the priest wore out anointing you, with all the times you threatened to die!

BARTLEY. Let you be quiet till I tell you!

MRS. FALLON. You to bring such a disgrace into the parish. A thing that was never heard of before!

BARTLEY. Will you shut your mouth and hear me speaking?

MRS. FALLON. And if it was for any sort of a fine handsome woman, but for a little fistful of a woman like Kitty Keary, that's not four feet high hardly, and not three teeth in her head unless she got new ones! May God reward you, Bartley Fallon, for the black treachery in your heart and the wickedness in your mind, and the red blood of poor Jack Smith that is wet upon your hand!

[*Voice of* JACK SMITH *heard singing.*]

> The sea shall be dry,
>   The earth under mourning and ban!
> Then loud shall he cry
>   For the wife of the red-haired man!

BARTLEY. It's Jack Smith's voice—I never knew a ghost to sing before—

6. Irish gaelic expression of anguish.

It is after myself and the fork he is coming! [*Goes back.*]

    [*Enter* JACK SMITH.]

Let one of you give him the fork and I will be clear of him now and for eternity!

MRS. TARPEY.   The Lord have mercy on us! Red Jack Smith! The man that was going to be waked!

JAMES RYAN.   Is it back from the grave you are come?

SHAWN EARLY.   Is it alive you are, or is it dead you are?

TIM CASEY.   Is it yourself at all that's in it?

MRS. TULLY.   Is it letting on you were to be dead?

MRS. FALLON.   Dead or alive, let you stop Kitty Keary, your wife, from bringing my man away with her to America!

JACK SMITH.   It is what I think, the wits are gone astray on the whole of you. What would my wife want bringing Bartley Fallon to America?

MRS. FALLON.   To leave yourself, and to get quit of you she wants, Jack Smith, and to bring him away from myself. That's what the two of them had settled together.

JACK SMITH.   I'll break the head of any man that says that! Who is it says it? [*To* TIM CASEY.] Was it you said it? [*To* SHAWN EARLY.] Was it you?

ALL TOGETHER [*backing and shaking their heads*].   It wasn't I said it!

JACK SMITH.   Tell me the name of any man that said it!

ALL TOGETHER [*pointing to Bartley*].   It was *him* that said it!

JACK SMITH.   Let me at him till I break his head!

    [BARTLEY *backs in terror. Neighbours hold* JACK SMITH *back.*]

JACK SMITH. [*trying to free himself*].   Let me at him! Isn't he the pleasant sort of a scarecrow for any woman to be crossing the ocean with! It's back from the docks of New York he'd be turned [*trying to rush at him again*], with a lie in his mouth and treachery in his heart, and another man's wife by his side, and he passing her off as his own! Let me at him can't you.

    [*Makes another rush, but is held back.*]

MAGISTRATE [*pointing to* JACK SMITH].   Policeman, put the handcuffs on this man. I see it all now. A case of false impersonation, a conspiracy to defeat the ends of justice. There was a case in the Andaman Islands, a murderer of the Mopsa tribe, a religious enthusiast—

POLICEMAN.   So he might be, too.

MAGISTRATE.   We must take both these men to the scene of the murder. We must confront them with the body of the real Jack Smith.

JACK SMITH.   I'll break the head of any man that will find my dead body!

MAGISTRATE.   I'll call more help from the barracks. [*Blows* POLICE-MAN's *whistle.*]

BARTLEY.   It is what I am thinking, if myself and Jack Smith are put together in the one cell for the night, the handcuffs will be taken off him, and his hands will be free, and murder will be done that time surely!

MAGISTRATE.   Come on!

[*They turn to the right.*][7]

7. *The earliest printings of this play left the last word to Mrs. Tarpey.* "The two of them in charge now, and a great hoop of people going by from the fair. Come up here the whole of you! It would be a pity you to be passing, and I not be spreading the news!" [*Oxford UP note.*]

LADY GREGORY

The Rising of the Moon[†]

Persons

SERGEANT
POLICEMAN X
POLICEMAN B
A RAGGED MAN

SCENE. *Side of a quay in a seaport town. Some posts and chains. A large barrel. Enter three* POLICEMEN. *Moonlight.*

> [SERGEANT, *who is older than the others, crosses the stage to right and looks down steps. The others put down a pastepot and unroll a bundle of placards.*]

POLICEMAN B.   I think this would be a good place to put up a notice. [*He points to barrel.*]

POLICEMAN X.   Better ask him. [*Calls to* SERGEANT.] Will this be a good place for a placard?

> [*No answer.*]

POLICEMAN B.   Will we put up a notice here on the barrel?

> [*No answer.*]

SERGEANT.   There's a flight of steps here that leads to the water. This is a place that should be minded well. If he got down here, his friends might have a boat to meet him; they might send it in here from outside.

POLICEMAN B.   Would the barrel be a good place to put a notice up?

SERGEANT.   It might; you can put it there.

> [*They paste the notice up.*]

SERGEANT [*reading it*].   Dark hair—dark eyes, smooth face, height five feet five—there's not much to take hold of in that—It's a pity I had no chance of seeing him before he broke out of gaol. They

† From *The Collected Plays of Lady Gregory*, Coole Edition, published by Oxford University Press and Colin Smythe Limited.

say he's a wonder, that it's he makes all the plans for the whole organization. There isn't another man in Ireland would have broken gaol the way he did. He must have some friends among the gaolers.

POLICEMAN B.   A hundred pounds is little enough for the Government to offer for him. You may be sure any man in the force that takes him will get promotion.

SERGEANT.   I'll mind this place myself. I wouldn't wonder at all if he came this way. He might come slipping along there [*points to side of quay*], and his friends might be waiting for him there [*points down steps*], and once he got away it's little chance we'd have of finding him; it's maybe under a load of kelp he'd be in a fishing boat, and not one to help a married man that wants it to the reward.

POLICEMAN X.   And if we get him itself, nothing but abuse on our heads for it from the people, and maybe from our own relations.

SERGEANT.   Well, we have to do our duty in the force. Haven't we the whole country depending on us to keep law and order? It's those that are down would be up and those that are up would be down, if it wasn't for us. Well, hurry on, you have plenty of other places to placard yet, and come back here then to me. You can take the lantern. Don't be too long now. It's very lonesome here with nothing but the moon.

POLICEMAN B.   It's a pity we can't stop with you. The Government should have brought more police into the town, with *him* in gaol, and at assize[1] time too. Well, good luck to your watch.

[*They go out.*]

SERGEANT [*walks up and down once or twice and looks at placard*]. A hundred pounds and promotion sure. There must be a great deal of spending in a hundred pounds. It's a pity some honest man not to be better of that.

[A RAGGED MAN *appears at left and tries to slip past.* SERGEANT *suddenly turns.*]

SERGEANT.   Where are you going?

MAN.   I'm a poor ballad-singer, your honor. I thought to sell some of these [*holds out bundle of ballads*] to the sailors. [*He goes on.*]

SERGEANT.   Stop! Didn't I tell you to stop? You can't go on there.

MAN.   Oh, very well. It's a hard thing to be poor. All the world's against the poor!

SERGEANT.   Who are you?

MAN.   You'd be as wise as myself if I told you, but I don't mind. I'm one Jimmy Walsh, a ballad-singer.

SERGEANT.   Jimmy Walsh? I don't know that name.

MAN.   Ah, sure, they know it well enough in Ennis. Were you ever in Ennis, sergeant?

1. Periodical legal proceedings.

SERGEANT.   What brought you here?

MAN.   Sure, it's to the assizes I came, thinking I might make a few shillings here or there. It's in the one train with the judges I came.

SERGEANT.   Well, if you came so far, you may as well go farther, for you'll walk out of this.

MAN.   I will, I will; I'll just go on where I was going. [*Goes toward steps.*]

SERGEANT.   Come back from those steps; no one has leave to pass down them to-night.

MAN.   I'll just sit on the top of the steps till I see will some sailor buy a ballad off me that would give me my supper. They do be late going back to the ship. It's often I saw them in Cork carried down the quay in a hand-cart.

SERGEANT.   Move on, I tell you. I won't have any one lingering about the quay to-night.

MAN.   Well, I'll go. It's the poor have the hard life! Maybe yourself might like one, sergeant. Here's a good sheet now. [*Turns one over.*] "Content and a Pipe"—that's not much. "The Peeler and the Goat"—you wouldn't like that. "Johnny Hart"—that's a lovely song.

SERGEANT.   Move on.

MAN.   Ah, wait till you hear it. [*Sings.*]

There was a rich farmer's daughter lived near the town of Ross;
She courted a Highland soldier, his name was Johnny Hart;
Says the mother to her daughter, "I'll go distracted mad
If you marry that Highland soldier dressed up in Highland plaid."

SERGEANT.   Stop that noise.

[MAN *wraps up his ballads and shuffles towards the steps.*]

SERGEANT.   Where are you going?

MAN.   Sure you told me to be going, and I am going.

SERGEANT.   Don't be a fool. I didn't tell you to go that way; I told you to go back to the town.

MAN.   Back to the town, is it?

SERGEANT [*taking him by the shoulder and shoving him before him*].   Here, I'll show you the way. Be off with you. What are you stopping for?

MAN [*who has been keeping his eye on the notice, points to it*].   I think I know what you're waiting for, sergeant.

SERGEANT.   What's that to you?

MAN.   And I know well the man you're waiting for—I know him well—I'll be going. [*He shuffles on.*]

SERGEANT.   You know him? Come back here. What sort is he?

MAN.   Come back is it, sergeant? Do you want to have me killed?

SERGEANT.   Why do you say that?

MAN.   Never mind. I'm going. I wouldn't be in your shoes if the reward was ten times as much. [*Goes on off stage to left.*] Not if it was ten times as much.

SERGEANT [*rushing after him*].   Come back here, come back.
[*Drags him back.*] What sort is he? Where did you see him?

MAN.   I saw him in my own place, in the County Clare. I tell you
you wouldn't like to be looking at him. You'd be afraid to be in
the one place with him. There isn't a weapon he doesn't know
the use of, and as to strength, his muscles are as hard as that
board. [*Slaps barrel.*]

SERGEANT.   Is he as bad as that?

MAN.   He is then.

SERGEANT.   Do you tell me so?

MAN.   There was a poor man in our place, a sergeant from Bally-
vaughan.—It was with a lump of stone he did it.

SERGEANT.   I never heard of that.

MAN.   And you wouldn't, sergeant. It's not everything that happens gets into the papers. And there was a policeman in plain
clothes, too . . . It is in Limerick he was. . . . It was after the time
of the attack on the police barrack in Kilmallock. . . . Moonlight
. . . just like this . . . waterside. . . . Nothing was known for
certain.

SERGEANT.   Do you say so? It's a terrible county to belong to.

MAN.   That's so, indeed! You might be standing there, looking out
that way, thinking you saw him coming up this side of the quay
[*points*], and he might be coming up this other side [*points*], and
he'd be on you before you knew where you were.

SERGEANT.   It's a whole troop of police they ought to put here to
stop a man like that.

MAN.   But if you'd like me to stop with you, I could be looking
down this side. I could be sitting up here on this barrel.

SERGEANT.   And you know him well, too?

MAN.   I'd know him a mile off, sergeant.

SERGEANT.   But you wouldn't want to share the reward?

MAN.   Is it a poor man like me, that has to be going the roads and
singing in fairs, to have the name on him that he took a reward?
but you don't want me. I'll be safer in the town.

SERGEANT.   Well, you can stop.

MAN [*getting up on barrel*].   All right, sergeant, I wonder, now,
you're tired out, sergeant, walking up and down the way you are.

SERGEANT.   If I'm tired I'm used to it.

MAN.   You might have hard work before you to-night yet. Take it
easy while you can. There's plenty of room up here on the barrel,
and you see farther when you're higher up.

SERGEANT.   Maybe so. [*Gets up beside him on barrel, facing right.*]

[*They sit back to back, looking different ways.*]

You made me feel a bit queer with the way you talked.

MAN.   Give me a match, sergeant [*he gives it and* MAN *lights pipe*];
take a draw yourself? It'll quiet you. Wait now till I give you a
light, but you needn't turn round. Don't take your eye off the
quay for the life of you.

SERGEANT.   Never fear, I won't. [*Lights pipe.*]

[*They both smoke.*]

Indeed it's a hard thing to be in the force, out at night and no thanks for it, for all the danger we're in. And it's little we get but abuse from the people, and no choice but to obey our orders, and never asked when a man is sent into danger, if you are a married man with a family.

MAN [*sings*].

As through the hills I walked to view the hills and shamrock plain,
I stood awhile where nature smiles to view the rocks and streams,
On a matron fair I fixed my eyes beneath a fertile vale,
And she sang her song it was on the wrong of poor old Granuaile.[2]

SERGEANT.   Stop that; that's no song to be singing in these times.

MAN.   Ah, sergeant, I was only singing to keep my heart up. It sinks when I think of him. To think of us two sitting here, and he creeping up the quay, maybe, to get to us.

SERGEANT.   Are you keeping a good lookout?

MAN.   I am; and for no reward too. Amn't I the fool man? But when I saw a man in trouble, I never could help trying to get him out of it. What's that? Did something hit me? [*Rubs his heart.*]

SERGEANT [*patting him on the shoulder*].   You will get your reward in heaven.

MAN.   I know that, I know that, sergeant, but life is precious.

SERGEANT.   Well, you can sing if it gives you more courage.

MAN [*sings*].

Her head was bare, her hands and feet with iron bands were
    bound,
Her pensive strain and plaintive wail mingles with the evening
    gale,
And the song she sang with mournful air, I am old Granuaile.
Her lips so sweet that monarchs kissed . . .

SERGEANT.   That's not it. . . . "Her gown she wore was stained with gore." . . . That's it—you missed that.

MAN.   You're right, sergeant, so it is; I missed it. [*Repeats line.*] But to think of a man like you knowing a song like that.

SERGEANT.   There's many a thing a man might know and might not have any wish for.

MANA.   Now, I daresay, sergeant, in your youth, you used to be sitting up on a wall, the way you are sitting up on this barrel now, and the other lads beside you, and you singing "Granuaile"? . . .

SERGEANT.   I did then.

MAN.   And the "Shan Van Vocht"?[3] . . .

2. In "The Song of Old Granuaile," a female figure epitomizes injustice to Ireland, like Cathleen Ni Houlihan.
3. Song of another poor old woman, personification of Ireland, foretelling the coming of the French to aid Irish rebellion.

SERGEANT. I did then.

MAN. And the "Green on the Cape"?

SERGEANT. That was one of them.

MAN. And maybe the man you are watching for to-night used to be sitting on the wall, when he was young, and singing those same songs. . . . It's a queer world. . . .

SERGEANT. Whisht! . . . I think I see something coming. . . . It's only a dog.

MAN. And isn't it a queer world? . . . Maybe it's one of the boys you used to be singing with that time you will be arresting to-day or to-morrow, and sending into the dock. . . .

SERGEANT. That's true indeed.

MAN. And maybe one night, after you had been singing, if the other boys had told you some plan they had, some plan to free the country, you might have joined with them . . . and maybe it is you might be in trouble now.

SERGEANT. Well, who knows but I might? I had a great spirit in those days.

MAN. It's a queer world, sergeant, and it's little any mother knows when she sees her child creeping on the floor what might happen to it before it has gone through its life, or who will be who in the end.

SERGEANT. That's a queer thought now, and a true thought. Wait now till I think it out. . . . If it wasn't for the sense I have, and for my wife and family, and for me joining the force the time I did, it might be myself now would be after breaking gaol and hiding in the dark, and it might be him that's hiding in the dark and that got out of gaol would be sitting up here where I am on this barrel. . . . And it might be myself would be creeping up trying to make my escape from himself, and it might be himself would be keeping the law, and myself would be breaking it, and myself would be trying to put a bullet in his head, or to take up a lump of stone the way you said he did . . . no, that myself did. . . . Oh! [*Gasps. After a pause*] What's that? [*Grasps man's arm.*]

MAN [*jumps off barrel and listens, looking out over water*]. It's nothing, sergeant.

SERGEANT. I thought it might be a boat. I had a notion there might be friends of his coming about the quays with a boat.

MAN. Sergeant, I am thinking it was with the people you were, and not with the law you were, when you were a young man.

SERGEANT. Well, if I was foolish then, that time's gone.

MAN. Maybe, sergeant, it comes into your head sometimes, in spite of your belt and your tunic, that it might have been as well for you to have followed Granuaile.

SERGEANT. It's no business of yours what I think.

MAN. Maybe, sergeant, you'll be on the side of the country yet.

SERGEANT [*gets off barrel*]. Don't talk to me like that. I have my duties and I know them. [*Looks round.*] That was a boat; I hear the oars. [*Goes to the steps and looks down.*]

MAN [*sings*].

> O, then, tell me, Shawn O'Farrell,
>> Where the gathering is to be.
> In the old spot by the river
>> Right well known to you and me!

SERGEANT.   Stop that! Stop that, I tell you!
MAN [*sings louder*].

> One word more, for signal token,
>> Whistle up the marching tune,
> With your pike upon your shoulder,
>> At the Rising of the Moon.[4]

SERGEANT.   If you don't stop that, I'll arrest you.

  [*A whistle from below answers, repeating the air.*]

SERGEANT.   That's a signal. [*Stands between him and steps.*] You
must not pass this way . . . Step farther back. . . . Who are you?
You are no ballad-singer.
MAN.   You needn't ask who I am; that placard will tell you. [*Points
to placard.*]
SERGEANT.   You are the man I am looking for.
MAN [*takes off hat and wig*].

  [SERGEANT *seizes them.*]

I am. There's a hundred pounds on my head. There is a friend of
mine below in a boat. He knows a safe place to bring me to.
SERGEANT [*looking still at hat and wig*].   It's a pity! It's a pity. You
deceived me. You deceived me well.
MAN.   I am a friend of Granuaile. There is a hundred pounds on
my head.
SERGEANT.   It's a pity, it's a pity!
MAN.   Will you let me pass, or must I make you let me?
SERGEANT.   I am in the force. I will not let you pass.
MAN.   I thought to do it with my tongue. [*Puts hand in breast.*]
What is that?

  [*Voice of* POLICEMAN X *outside*: Here, this is where we left
  him.]

SERGEANT.   It's my comrades coming.
MAN.   You won't betray me . . . the friend of Granuaile. [*Slips be-
hind barrel.*]
Voice of POLICEMAN B.   That was the last of the placards.
POLICEMAN X [*as they come in*].   If he makes his escape it won't be
unknown he'll make it.

  [SERGEANT *puts hat and wig behind his back.*]

---

4. Verses from the nationalist ballad "The Rising of the Moon."

POLICEMAN B.   Did any one come this way?

SERGEANT [*after a pause*].   No one.

POLICEMAN B.   No one at all?

SERGEANT.   No one at all.

POLICEMAN B.   We had no orders to go back to the station; we can stop along with you.

SERGEANT.   I don't want you. There is nothing for you to do here.

POLICEMAN B.   You bade us to come back here and keep watch with you.

SERGEANT.   I'd sooner be alone. Would any man come this way and you making all that talk? It is better the place to be quiet.

POLICEMAN B.   Well, we'll leave you the lantern anyhow.

[*Hands it to him.*]

SERGEANT.   I don't want it. Bring it with you.

POLICEMAN B.   You might want it. There are clouds coming up and you have the darkness of the night before you yet. I'll leave it over here on the barrel. [*Goes to barrel.*]

SERGEANT.   Bring it with you I tell you. No more talk.

POLICEMAN B.   Well, I thought it might be a comfort to you. I often think when I have it in my hand and can be flashing it about into every dark corner [*doing so*] that it's the same as being beside the fire at home, and the bits of bogwood blazing up now and again. [*Flashes it about, now on the barrel, now on* SERGEANT.]

SERGEANT [*furious*].   Be off the two of you, yourselves and your lantern!

[*They go out.* MAN *comes from behind barrel. He and* SERGEANT *stand looking at one another.*]

SERGEANT.   What are you waiting for?

MAN.   For my hat, of course, and my wig. You wouldn't wish me to get my death of cold?

[SERGEANT *gives them.*]

MAN [*going towards steps*].   Well, good-night, comrade, and thank you. You did me a good turn to-night, and I'm obliged to you. Maybe I'll be able to do as much for you when the small rise up and the big fall down . . . when we all change places at the rising [*waves his hand and disappears*] of the Moon.

SERGEANT [*turning his back to audience and reading placard*].   A hundred pounds reward! A hundred pounds! [*turns towards audience.*] I wonder, now, am I as great a fool as I think I am?

J. M. SYNGE

Riders to the Sea[†]

Persons in the Play

MAURYA, *an old woman*
BARTLEY, *her son*
CATHLEEN, *her daughter*
NORA, *a younger daughter*
MEN *and* WOMEN

SCENE. *An Island off the West of Ireland.*

> [*Cottage kitchen, with nets, oil-skins, spinning wheel, some new boards standing by the wall, etc.* CATHLEEN, *a girl of about twenty, finishes kneading cake, and puts it down in the pot-oven by the fire; then wipes her hands, and begins to spin at the wheel.* NORA, *a young girl, puts her head in at the door.*]

NORA [*in a low voice*]. Where is she?
CATHLEEN. She's lying down, God help her, and may be sleeping, if she's able.

> [NORA *comes in softly, and takes a bundle from under her shawl.*]

CATHLEEN [*spinning the wheel rapidly*]. What is it you have?
NORA. The young priest is after bringing them. It's a shirt and a plain stocking were got off a drowned man in Donegal.

> [CATHLEEN *stops her wheel with a sudden movement, and leans out to listen.*]

NORA. We're to find out if it's Michael's they are, some time her-self will be down looking at the sea.
CATHLEEN. How would they be Michael's, Nora. How would he go the length of that way to the far north?
NORA. The young priest says he's known the like of it. "If it's Michael's they are," says he, "you can tell herself he's got a clean burial by the grace of God, and if they're not his, let no one say a

---

† From *The Complete Plays of John M. Synge* (New York: Random House, 1935), Vintage Books edition.

58

word about them, for she'll be getting her death," says he, "with crying and lamenting."

[*The door which* NORA *half closed is blown open by a gust of wind.*]

CATHLEEN [*looking out anxiously*].   Did you ask him would he stop Bartley going this day with the horses to the Galway fair?[1]

NORA.   "I won't stop him," says he, "but let you not be afraid. Herself does be saying prayers half through the night, and the Almighty God won't leave her destitute," says he, "with no son living."

CATHLEEN.   Is the sea bad by the white rocks, Nora?

NORA.   Middling bad, God help us. There's a great roaring in the west, and it's worse it'll be getting when the tide's turned to the wind. [*She goes over to the table with the bundle.*] Shall I open it now?

CATHLEEN.   Maybe she'd wake up on us, and come in before we'd done. [*Coming to the table.*] It's a long time we'll be, and the two of us crying.

NORA [*goes to the inner door and listens*].   She's moving about on the bed. She'll be coming in a minute.

CATHLEEN.   Give me the ladder, and I'll put them up in the turf-loft, the way she won't know of them at all, and maybe when the tide turns she'll be going down to see would he be floating from the east.

[*They put the ladder against the gable of the chimney;* CATHLEEN *goes up a few steps and hides the bundle in the turf-loft.* MAURYA *comes from the inner room.*]

MAURYA [*looking up at Cathleen and speaking querulously*].   Isn't it turf enough you have for this day and evening?

CATHLEEN.   There's a cake baking at the fire for a short space [*throwing down the turf*] and Bartley will want it when the tide turns if he goes to Connemara.[2]

[NORA *picks up the turf and puts it round the pot-oven.*]

MAURYA [*sitting down on a stool at the fire*].   He won't go this day with the wind rising from the south and west. He won't go this day, for the young priest will stop him surely.

NORA.   He'll not stop him, mother, and I heard Eamon Simon and Stephen Pheety and Colum Shawn saying he would go.

MAURYA.   Where is he itself?

NORA.   He went down to see would there be another boat sailing in the week, and I'm thinking it won't be long till he's here now, for the tide's turning at the green head, and the hooker's tacking from the east.

1. Going to the mainland.
2. Nearest mainland point on the route to Galway.

CATHLEEN.   I hear some one passing the big stones.

NORA [*looking out*].   He's coming now, and he in a hurry.

BARTLEY [*comes in and looks round the room. Speaking sadly and quietly*].   Where is the bit of new rope, Cathleen, was bought in Connemara?

CATHLEEN [*coming down*].   Give it to him, Nora; it's on a nail by the white boards. I hung it up this morning, for the pig with the black feet was eating it.

NORA [*giving him a rope*].   Is that it, Bartley?

MAURYA.   You'd do right to leave that rope, Bartley, hanging by the boards.

   [BARTLEY *takes the rope.*]

It will be wanting in this place, I'm telling you, if Michael is washed up to-morrow morning, or the next morning, or any morning in the week, for it's a deep grave we'll make him by the grace of God.

BARTLEY [*beginning to work with the rope*].   I've no halter the way I can ride down on the mare, and I must go now quickly. This is the one boat going for two weeks or beyond it, and the fair will be a good fair for horses I heard them saying below.

MAURYA.   It's a hard thing they'll be saying below if the body is washed up and there's no man in it to make the coffin, and I after giving a big price for the finest white boards you'd find in Connemara. [*She looks round at the boards.*]

BARTLEY.   How would it be washed up, and we after looking each day for nine days, and a strong wind blowing a while back from the west and south?

MAURYA.   If it wasn't found itself, that wind is raising the sea, and there was a star up against the moon, and it rising in the night. If it was a hundred horses, or a thousand horses you had itself, what is the price of a thousand horses against a son where there is one son only?

BARTLEY [*working at the halter, to* CATHLEEN].   Let you go down each day, and see the sheep aren't jumping in on the rye, and if the jobber comes you can sell the pig with the black feet if there is a good price going.

MAURYA.   How would the like of her get a good price for a pig?

BARTLEY [*to* CATHLEEN].   If the west wind holds with the last bit of the moon let you and Nora get up weed enough for another cock for the kelp. It's hard set we'll be from this day with no one in it but one man to work.

MAURYA.   It's hard set we'll be surely the day you're drown'd with the rest. What way will I live and the girls with me, and I an old woman looking for the grave?

   [BARTLEY *lays down the halter, takes off his old coat, and puts on a newer one of the same flannel.*]

BARTLEY [*to* NORA].   Is she coming to the pier?

NORA [*looking out*].   She's passing the green head and letting fall her sails.

BARTLEY [*getting his purse and tobacco*].   I'll have half an hour to go down, and you'll see me coming again in two days, or in three days, or maybe in four days if the wind is bad.

MAURYA [*turning round to the fire, and putting her shawl over her head*].   Isn't it a hard and cruel man won't hear a word from an old woman, and she holding him from the sea?

CATHLEEN.   It's the life of a young man to be going on the sea, and who would listen to an old woman with one thing and she saying it over?

BARTLEY [*taking the halter*].   I must go now quickly. I'll ride down on the red mare, and the gray pony 'll run behind me. . . . The blessing of God on you. [*He goes out.*]

MAURYA [*crying out as he is in the door*].   He's gone now, God spare us, and we'll not see him again. He's gone now, and when the black night is falling I'll have no son left me in the world.

CATHLEEN.   Why wouldn't you give him your blessing and he looking round in the door? Isn't it sorrow enough is on every one in this house without your sending him out with an unlucky word behind him, and a hard word in his ear?

[MAURYA *takes up the tongs and begins raking the fire aimlessly without looking round.*]

NORA [*turning towards her*].   You're taking away the turf from the cake.

CATHLEEN [*crying out*].   The Son of God forgive us, Nora, we're after forgetting his bit of bread. [*She comes over to the fire.*]

NORA.   And it's destroyed he'll be going till dark night, and he after eating nothing since the sun went up.

CATHLEEN [*turning the cake out of the oven*].   It's destroyed he'll be, surely. There's no sense left on any person in a house where an old woman will be talking for ever.

[MAURYA *sways herself on her stool.*]

CATHLEEN [*cutting off some of the bread and rolling it in a cloth; to* MAURYA].   Let you go down now to the spring well and give him this and he passing. You'll see him when the dark word will be broken, and you can say "God speed you," the way he'll be easy in his mind.

MAURYA [*taking the bread*].   Will I be in it as soon as himself?

CATHLEEN.   If you go now quickly.

MAURYA [*standing up unsteadily*].   It's hard set I am to walk.

CATHLEEN [*looking at her anxiously*].   Give her the stick, Nora, or maybe she'll slip on the big stones.

NORA.   What stick?

CATHLEEN.   The stick Michael brought from Connemara.

MAURYA [*taking a stick* NORA *gives her*].   In the big world the old people do be leaving things after them for their sons and children, but in this place it is the young men do be leaving things behind for them that do be old. [*She goes out slowly.*]

[NORA *goes over to the ladder.*]

CATHLEEN.   Wait, Nora, maybe she'd turn back quickly. She's that sorry, God help her, you wouldn't know the thing she'd do.

NORA.   Is she gone round by the bush?

CATHLEEN [*looking out*].   She gone now. Throw it down quickly, for the Lord knows when she'll be out of it again.

NORA [*getting the bundle from the loft*].   The young priest said he'd be passing to-morrow, and we might go down and speak to him below if it's Michael's they are surely.

CATHLEEN [*taking the bundle*].   Did he say what way they were found?

NORA [*coming down*].   "There were two men," says he, "and they rowing round with poteen[3] before the cocks crowed, and the oar of one of them caught the body, and they passing the black cliffs of the north."

CATHLEEN [*trying to open the bundle*].   Give me a knife, Nora, the string's perished with the salt water, and there's a black knot on it you wouldn't loosen in a week.

NORA [*giving her a knife*].   I've heard tell it was a long way to Donegal.

CATHLEEN [*cutting the string*].   It is surely. There was a man in here a while ago—the man sold us that knife—and he said if you set off walking from the rocks beyond, it would be seven days you'd be in Donegal.

NORA.   And what time would a man take, and he floating?

[CATHLEEN *opens the bundle and takes out a bit of a stocking. They look at them eagerly.*]

CATHLEEN [*in a low voice*].   The Lord spare us, Nora! Isn't it a queer hard thing to say if it's his they are surely?

NORA.   I'll get his shirt off the hook the way we can put the one flannel on the other. [*She looks through some clothes hanging in the corner.*] It's not with them, Cathleen, and where will it be?

CATHLEEN.   I'm thinking Bartley put it on him in the morning, for his own shirt was heavy with the salt in it [*pointing to the corner*]. There's a bit of a sleeve was of the same stuff. Give me that and it will do.

[NORA *brings it to her and they compare the flannel.*]

CATHLEEN.   It's the same stuff, Nora; but if it is itself aren't there great rolls of it in the shops of Galway, and isn't it many another man may have a shirt of it as well as Michael himself?

NORA [*who has taken up the stocking and counted the stitches, crying*

3. Home-distilled spirits.

out].   It's Michael, Cathleen, it's Michael; God spare his soul, and what will herself say when she hears this story, and Bartley on the sea?

CATHLEEN [*taking the stocking*].   It's a plain stocking.

NORA.   It's the second one of the third pair I knitted, and I put up three score stitches, and I dropped four of them.

CATHLEEN [*counts the stitches*].   It's that number is in it [*crying out*]. Ah, Nora, isn't it a bitter thing to think of him floating that way to the far north, and no one to keen him[4] but the black hags that do be flying on the sea?

NORA [*swinging herself round, and throwing out her arms on the clothes*].   And isn't it a pitiful thing when there is nothing left of a man who was a great rower and fisher, but a bit of an old shirt and a plain stocking?

CATHLEEN [*after an instant*].   Tell me is herself coming, Nora? I hear a little sound on the path.

NORA [*looking out*].   She is, Cathleen. She's coming up to the door.

CATHLEEN.   Put these things away before she'll come in. Maybe it's easier she'll be after giving her blessing to Bartley, and we won't let on we've heard anything the time he's on the sea.

NORA [*helping* CATHLEEN *to close the bundle*].   We'll put them here in the corner.

[*They put them into a hole in the chimney corner.* CATHLEEN *goes back to the spinning-wheel.*]

NORA.   Will she see it was crying I was?

CATHLEEN.   Keep your back to the door the way the light'll not be on you.

[NORA *sits down at the chimney corner, with her back to the door.* MAURYA *comes in very slowly, without looking at the girls, and goes over to her stool at the other side of the fire. The cloth with the bread is still in her hand. The girls look at each other, and* NORA *points to the bundle of bread.*]

CATHLEEN [*after spinning for a moment*].   You didn't give him his bit of bread?

[MAURYA *begins to keen softly, without turning round.*]

CATHLEEN.   Did you see him riding down?

[MAURYA *goes on keening.*]

CATHLEEN [*a little impatiently*].   God forgive you; isn't it a better thing to raise your voice and tell what you seen, than to be making lamentation for a thing that's done? Did you see Bartley, I'm saying to you.

MAURYA [*with a weak voice*].   My heart's broken from this day.

---

4. To mourn by keening, or moaning and wailing, as at the end of the play.

CATHLEEN [*as before*].   Did you see Bartley?

MAURYA.   I seen the fearfulest thing.

CATHLEEN [*leaves her wheel and looks out*].   God forgive you; he's
riding the mare now over the green head, and the gray pony behind him.

MAURYA [*starts, so that her shawl falls back from her head and shows
her white tossed hair. With a frightened voice*].   The gray pony
behind him.

CATHLEEN [*coming to the fire*].   What is it ails you, at all?

MAURYA [*speaking very slowly*].   I've seen the fearfulest thing any
person has seen, since the day Bride Dara seen the dead man
with the child in his arms.

CATHLEEN AND NORA.   Uah.

  [*They crouch down in front of the old woman at the fire.*]

NORA.   Tell us what it is you seen.

MAURYA.   I went down to the spring well, and I stood there saying
a prayer to myself. Then Bartley came along, and he riding on
the red mare with the gray pony behind him. [*She puts up her
hands, as if to hide something from her eyes.*] The Son of God
spare us, Nora!

CATHLEEN.   What is it you seen.

MAURYA.   I seen Michael himself.

CATHLEEN [*speaking softly*].   You did not, mother; It wasn't Michael you seen, for his body is after being found in the far north,
and he's got a clean burial by the grace of God.

MAURYA [*a little defiantly*].   I'm after seeing him this day, and he
riding and galloping. Bartley came first on the red mare; and I
tried to say "God speed you," but something choked the words in
my throat. He went by quickly; and "the blessing of God on you,"
says he, and I could say nothing. I looked up then, and I crying,
at the gray pony, and there was Michael upon it—with fine
clothes on him, and new shoes on his feet.

CATHLEEN [*begins to keen*].   It's destroyed we are from this day. It's
destroyed, surely.

NORA.   Didn't the young priest say the Almighty God wouldn't
leave her destitute with no son living?

MAURYA [*in a low voice, but clearly*].   It's little the like of him
knows of the sea. . . . Bartley will be lost now, and let you call in
Eamon and make me a good coffin out of the white boards, for I
won't live after them. I've had a husband, and a husband's father,
and six sons in this house—six fine men, though it was a hard
birth I had with every one of them and they coming to the
world—and some of them were found and some of them were
not found, but they're gone now the lot of them. . . . There were
Stephen, and Shawn, were lost in the great wind, and found after
in the Bay of Gregory of the Golden Mouth, and carried up the
two of them on the one plank, and in by that door.

[*She pauses for a moment, the girls start as if they heard something through the door that is half open behind them.*]

NORA [*in a whisper*].   Did you hear that, Cathleen? Did you hear a noise in the north-east?

CATHLEEN [*in a whisper*].   There's some one after crying out by the seashore.

MAURYA [*continues without hearing anything*].   There was Sheamus and his father, and his own father again were lost in a dark night, and not a stick or sign was seen of them when the sun went up. There was Patch after was drowned out of a curagh[5] that turned over. I was sitting here with Bartley, and he a baby, lying on my two knees, and I seen two women; and three women and four women coming in, and they crossing themselves, and not saying a word. I looked out then, and there were men coming after them, and they holding a thing in the half of a red sail, and water dripping out of it—it was a dry day, Nora—and leaving a track to the door.

[*She pauses again with her hand stretched out towards the door. It opens softly and old* WOMEN *begin to come in, crossing themselves on the threshold, and kneeling down in front of the stage with red petticoats over their heads.*]

MAURYA [*half in a dream, to* CATHLEEN].   Is it Patch or Michael, or what is it at all?

CATHLEEN.   Michael is after being found in the far north, and when he is found there how could he be here in this place?

MAURYA.   There does be a power of young men floating round in the sea, and what way would they know if it was Michael they had, or another man like him, for when a man is nine days in the sea, and the wind blowing, it's hard set his own mother would be to say what man was it.

CATHLEEN.   It's Michael, God spare him, for they're after sending us a bit of his clothes from the far north.

[*She reaches out and hands* MAURYA *the clothes that belonged to* MICHAEL. MAURYA *stands up slowly and takes them in her hands.* NORA *looks out.*]

NORA.   They're carrying a thing among them and there's water dripping out of it and leaving a track by the big stones.

CATHLEEN [*in a whisper to the* WOMEN *who have come in*].   Is it Bartley it is?

ONE OF THE WOMEN.   It is surely, God rest his soul.

[*Two younger* WOMEN *come in and pull out the table. Then* MEN *carry in the body of* BARTLEY, *laid on a plank, with a bit of a sail over it, and lay it on the table.*]

5. A frail boat of traditional construction, wood-frame and canvas shell, rowed in the open sea.

CATHLEEN [*to the women, as they are doing so*]. What way was he drowned?

ONE OF THE WOMEN. The gray pony knocked him into the sea, and he was washed out where there is a great surf on the white rocks.

[MAURYA *has gone over and knelt down at the head of the table. The* WOMEN *are keening softly and swaying themselves with a slow movement.* CATHLEEN *and* NORA *kneel at the other end of the table. The* MEN *kneel near the door.*]

MAURYA [*raising her head and speaking as if she did not see the people around her*]. They're all gone now, and there isn't anything more the sea can do to me. . . . I'll have no call now to be up crying and praying when the wind breaks from the south, and you can hear the surf is in the east, and the surf is in the west, making a great stir with the two noises, and they hitting one on the other. I'll have no call now to be going down and getting Holy Water in the dark nights after Samhain,[6] and I won't care what way the sea is when the other women will be keening. [*To* NORA.] Give me the Holy Water, Nora, there's a small sup still on the dresser.

[NORA *gives it to her.*]

MAURYA [*drops* MICHAEL'S *clothes across* BARTLEY'S *feet, and sprinkles the Holy Water over him*]. It isn't that I haven't prayed for you, Bartley, to the Almighty God. It isn't that I haven't said prayers in the dark night till you wouldn't know what I'd be saying; but it's a great rest I'll have now, and it's time surely. It's a great rest I'll have now, and great sleeping in the long nights after Samhain, if it's only a bit of wet flour we do have to eat, and maybe a fish that would be stinking.

[*She kneels down again, crossing herself, and saying prayers under her breath.*]

CATHLEEN [*to an* OLD MAN]. Maybe yourself and Eamon would make a coffin when the sun rises. We have fine white boards herself bought, God help her, thinking Michael would be found, and I have a new cake you can eat while you'll be working.

THE OLD MAN [*looking at the boards*]. Are there nails with them?

CATHLEEN. There are not, Colum; we didn't think of the nails.

ANOTHER MAN. It's a great wonder she wouldn't think of the nails, and all the coffins she's seen made already.

CATHLEEN. It's getting old she is, and broken.

[MAURYA *stands up again very slowly and spreads out the pieces of Michael's clothes beside the body, sprinkling them with the last of the Holy Water.*]

NORA [*in a whisper to* CATHLEEN]. She's quiet now and easy; but the day Michael was drowned you could hear her crying out from

6. All Saints' Day, November 1.

this to the spring well. It's fonder she was of Michael, and would any one have thought that?

CATHLEEN [*slowly and clearly*].   An old woman will be soon tired with anything she will do, and isn't it nine days herself is after crying and keening, and making great sorrow in the house?

MAURYA [*puts the empty cup mouth downwards on the table, and lays her hands together on* BARTLEY'S *feet*].   They're all together this time, and the end is come. May the Almighty God have mercy on Bartley's soul, and on Michael's soul, and on the souls of Sheamus and Patch, and Stephen and Shawn [*bending her head*]; and may He have mercy on my soul, Nora, and on the soul of every one is left living in the world.

> [*She pauses, and the keen rises a little more loudly from the women, then sinks away.*]

MAURYA [*continuing*].   Michael has a clean burial in the far north, by the grace of the Almighty God. Bartley will have a fine coffin out of the white boards, and a deep grave surely. What more can we want than that? No man at all can be living for ever, and we must be satisfied.

> [*She kneels down again and the curtain falls slowly.*]

J. M. SYNGE

The Playboy of the
Western World[†]

Persons in the Play

CHRISTOPHER MAHON
OLD MAHON, *his father, a squatter*[1]
MICHAEL JAMES FLAHERTY, *called* MICHAEL JAMES, *a publican*
MARGARET FLAHERTY, *called* PEGEEN MIKE, *his daughter*
WIDOW QUIN, *a woman of about thirty*
SHAWN KEOGH, *her cousin, a young farmer*
PHILLY CULLEN *and* JIMMY FARRELL, *small farmers*
SARA TANSEY, SUSAN BRADY, *and* HONOR BLAKE, *village girls*
A BELLMAN
SOME PEASANTS

The action takes place near a village, on a wild coast of Mayo. The first Act passes on an evening of autumn, the other two Acts on the following day.

Act 1

SCENE. *Country public-house or shebeen, very rough and untidy. There is a sort of counter on the right with shelves, holding many bottles and jugs, just seen above it. Empty barrels stand near the counter. At back, a little to left of counter, there is a door into the open air, then, more to the left, there is a settle with shelves above it, with more jugs, and a table beneath a window. At the left there is a large open fire-place, with turf fire, and a small door into inner room.* PEGEEN, *a wild-looking but fine girl, of about twenty, is writing at table. She is dressed in the usual peasant dress.*

PEGEEN [*slowly as she writes*].   Six yards of stuff for to make a yellow gown. A pair of lace boots with lengthy heels on them and

---

† From *The Complete Plays of John M. Synge* (New York: Random House, 1935), Vintage Books edition.
1. A settler without legal title, which was often unavailable in unsurveyed rural districts.

brassy eyes. A hat is suited for a wedding-day. A fine tooth comb. To be sent with three barrels of porter in Jimmy Farrell's creel cart on the evening of the coming Fair to Mister Michael James Flaherty. With the best compliments of this season. Margaret Flaherty.

SHAWN KEOGH [*a fat and fair young man comes in as she signs, looks round awkwardly, when he sees she is alone*]. Where's himself?

PEGEEN [*without looking at him*]. He's coming. [*She directs the letter.*] To Mister Sheamus Mulroy, Wine and Spirit Dealer, Castlebar.

SHAWN [*uneasily*]. I didn't see him on the road.

PEGEEN. How would you see him [*licks stamp and puts it on letter*] and it dark night this half hour gone by?

SHAWN [*turning towards the door again*]. I stood a while outside wondering would I have a right to pass on or to walk in and see you, Pegeen Mike [*comes to fire*], and I could hear the cows breathing, and sighing in the stillness of the air, and not a step moving any place from this gate to the bridge.

PEGEEN [*putting letter in envelope*]. It's above at the cross-roads he is, meeting Philly Cullen; and a couple more are going along with him to Kate Cassidy's wake.

SHAWN [*looking at her blankly*]. And he's going that length in the dark night?

PEGEEN [*impatiently*]. He is surely, and leaving me lonesome on the scruff of the hill. [*She gets up and puts envelope on dresser, then winds clock.*] Isn't it long the nights are now, Shawn Keogh, to be leaving a poor girl with her own self counting the hours to the dawn of day?

SHAWN [*with awkward humour*]. If it is, when we're wedded in a short while you'll have no call to complain, for I've little will to be walking off to wakes or weddings in the darkness of the night.

PEGEEN [*with rather scornful good humour*]. You're making might certain, Shaneen,[2] that I'll wed you now.

SHAWN. Aren't we after making a good bargain, the way we're only waiting these days on Father Reilly's dispensation from the bishops, or the Court of Rome.

PEGEEN [*looking at him teasingly, washing up at dresser*]. It's a wonder, Shaneen, the Holy Father'd be taking notice of the likes of you; for if I was him I wouldn't bother with this place where you'll meet none but Red Linahan, has a squint in his eye, and Patcheen is lame in his heel, or the mad Mulrannies were driven from California and they lost in their wits. We're a queer lot these times to go troubling the Holy Father on his sacred seat.

SHAWN [*scandalized*]. If we are, we're as good this place as another, maybe, and as good these times as we were for ever.

PEGEEN [*with scorn*]. As good, is it? Where now will you meet the

---

2. The *-een* suffix is an Irish diminutive, as in "Pegeen" or, later, "priesteen"; it may be used endearingly or contemptuously.

like of Daneen Sullivan knocked the eye from a peeler,[3] or Marcus Quin, God rest him, got six months for maiming ewes, and he a great warrant to tell stories of old Ireland till he'd have the old women shedding down tears about their feet. Where will you find the like of them, I'm saying?

SHAWN [timidly]. If you don't, it's a good job, maybe; for [with peculiar emphasis on the words] Father Reilly has small conceit to have that kind walking around and talking to the girls.

PEGEEN [impatiently, throwing water from basin out of the door]. Stop tormenting me with Father Reilly [imitating his voice] when I'm asking only what way I'll pass these twelve hours of dark, and not take my death with the fear. [Looking out of door.]

SHAWN [timidly]. Would I fetch you the Widow Quin, maybe?

PEGEEN. Is it the like of that murderer? You'll not, surely.

SHAWN [going to her, soothingly]. Then I'm thinking himself will stop along with you when he sees you taking on, for it'll be a long nighttime with great darkness, and I'm after feeling a kind of fellow above in the furzy ditch, groaning wicked like a maddening dog, the way it's good cause you have, maybe, to be fearing now.

PEGEEN [turning on him sharply]. What's that? Is it a man you seen?

SHAWN [retreating]. I couldn't see him at all; but I heard him groaning out, and breaking his heart. It should have been a young man from his words speaking.

PEGEEN [going after him]. And you never went near to see was he hurted or what ailed him at all?

SHAWN. I did not, Pegeen Mike. It was a dark, lonesome place to be hearing the like of him.

PEGEEN. Well, you're a daring fellow, and if they find his corpse stretched above in the dews of dawn, what'll you say then to the peelers, or the Justice of the Peace?

SHAWN [thunderstruck]. I wasn't thinking of that. For the love of God, Pegeen Mike, don't let on I was speaking of him, don't tell your father and the men is coming above; for if they heard that story, they'd have great blabbing this night at the wake.

PEGEEN. I'll maybe tell them, and I'll maybe not.

SHAWN. They are coming at the door. Will you whisht, I'm saying?

PEGEEN. Whisht yourself.

[She goes behind counter. MICHAEL JAMES, fat jovial publican, comes in followed by PHILLY CULLEN, who is thin and mistrusting, and JIMMY FARRELL, who is fat and amorous, about forty-five.]

MEN [together]. God bless you. The blessing of God on this place.

PEGEEN. God bless you kindly.

---

3. Policeman, a term originally applied to a member of the Royal Irish Constabulary force established by Robert Peel (1788–1850), chief secretary for Ireland (1812–18) and later prime minister.

MICHAEL [*to men who go to the counter*].   Sit down now, and take
your rest. [*Crosses to* SHAWN *at the fire.*] And how is it you are,
Shawn Keogh? Are you coming over the sands to Kate Cassidy's
wake?

SHAWN.   I am not, Michael James. I'm going home the short cut to
my bed.

PEGEEN [*speaking across the counter*].   He's right too, and have you
no shame, Michael James, to be quitting off for the whole night,
and leaving myself lonesome in the shop?

MICHAEL [*good-humouredly*].   Isn't it the same whether I go for the
whole night or a part only? and I'm thinking it's a queer daughter
you are if you'd have me crossing backward through the Stooks
of the Dead Women,[4] with a drop taken.

PEGEEN.   If I am a queer daughter, it's a queer father'd be leaving
me lonesome these twelve hours of dark, and I piling the turf
with the dogs barking, and the calves mooing, and my own teeth
rattling with the fear.

JIMMY [*flatteringly*].   What is there to hurt you, and you a fine,
hardy girl would knock the head of any two men in the place?

PEGEEN [*working herself up*].   Isn't there the harvest boys with
their tongues red for drink, and the ten tinkers is camped in the
east glen, and the thousand militia—bad cess[5] to them!—walking
idle through the land. There's lots surely to hurt me, and I won't
stop alone in it, let himself do what he will.

MICHAEL.   If you're afeard, let Shawn Keogh stop along with you.
It's the will of God, I'm thinking, himself should be seeing to you
now.

[*They all turn on* SHAWN.]

SHAWN [*in horrified confusion*].   I would and welcome, Michael
James, but I'm afeard of Father Reilly; and what at all would the
Holy Father and the Cardinals of Rome be saying if they heard I
did the like of that?

MICHAEL [*with contempt*].   God help you! Can't you sit in by the
hearth with the light lit and herself beyond in the room? You'll do
that surely, for I've heard tell there's a queer fellow above, going
mad or getting his death, maybe, in the gripe of the ditch,[6] so
she'd be safer this night with a person here.

SHAWN [*with plaintive despair*].   I'm afeard of Father Reilly, I'm
saying. Let you not be tempting me, and we near married itself.

PHILLY [*with cold contempt*].   Lock him in the west room. He'll
stay then and have no sin to be telling to the priest.

MICHAEL [*to* SHAWN, *getting between him and the door*].   Go up
now.

---

4. Shoreline rock formation named for a ship disaster and described in Synge's *Wicklow,
West Kerry, and Connemara*.
5. Expression meaning "bad luck" derived from the practice of tax assessment of the Irish
for provision of British military forces.
6. Trench at the edge of a hedge.

SHAWN [*at the top of his voice*].   Don't stop me, Michael James. Let
me out of the door, I'm saying, for the love of the Almighty God.
Let me out [*trying to dodge past him*]. Let me out of it, and may
God grant you His indulgence in the hour of need.

MICHAEL [*loudly*].   Stop your noising, and sit down by the hearth.
[*Gives him a push and goes to counter laughing.*]

SHAWN [*turning back, wringing his hands*].   Oh, Father Reilly
and the saints of God, where will I hide myself to-day? Oh, St.
Joseph and St. Patrick and St. Brigid, and St. James, have mercy
on me now! [SHAWN *turns round, sees door clear, and makes a rush
for it.*]

MICHAEL [*catching him by the coat-tail*].   You'd be going, is it?

SHAWN [*screaming*].   Leave me go, Michael James, leave me go,
you old Pagan, leave me go, or I'll get the curse of the priests on
you, and of the scarlet-coated bishops of the courts of Rome.

> [*With a sudden movement he pulls himself out of his coat,
> and disappears out of the door, leaving his coat in* MICHAEL'S
> *hands.*]

MICHAEL [*turning round, and holding up coat*].   Well, there's the
coat of a Christian man. Oh, there's sainted glory this day in the
lonesome west; and by the will of God I've got you a decent man,
Pegeen, you'll have no call to be spying after if you've a score of
young girls, maybe, weeding in your fields.

PEGEEN [*taking up the defence of her property*].   What right have
you to be making game of a poor fellow for minding the priest,
when it's your own the fault is, not paying a penny pot-boy
to stand along with me and give me courage in the doing of
my work? [*She snaps the coat away from him, and goes behind
counter with it.*]

MICHAEL [*taken aback*].   Where would I get a pot-boy? Would
you have me send the bellman screaming in the streets of Castlebar?

SHAWN [*opening the door a chink and putting in his head, in a small
voice*].   Michael James!

MICHAEL [*imitating him*].   What ails you?

SHAWN.   The queer dying fellow's beyond looking over the ditch.
He's come up, I'm thinking, stealing your hens. [*Looks over his
shoulder.*] God help me, he's following me now [*he runs into
room*], and if he's heard what I said, he'll be having my life, and I
going home lonesome in the darkness of the night.

> [*For a perceptible moment they watch the door with curiosity.
> Some one coughs outside. Then* CHRISTY MAHON, *a slight
> young man, comes in very tired and frightened and dirty.*]

CHRISTY [*in a small voice*].   God save all here!

MEN.   God save you kindly.

CHRISTY [*going to the counter*].   I'd trouble you for a glass of
porter, woman of the house. [*He puts down coin.*]

PEGEEN [*serving him*].   You're one of the tinkers,⁷ young fellow, is beyond camped in the glen?

CHRISTY.   I am not; but I'm destroyed walking.

MICHAEL [*patronizingly*].   Let you come up then to the fire. You're looking famished with the cold.

CHRISTY.   God reward you. [*He takes up his glass and goes a little way across to the left, then stops and looks about him.*] Is it often the police do be coming into this place, master of the house?

MICHAEL.   If you'd come in better hours, you'd have seen "Licensed for the sale of Beer and Spirits, to be consumed on the premises," written in white letters above the door, and what would the polis want spying on me, and not a decent house within four miles, the way every living Christian is a bona fide,⁸ saving one widow alone?

CHRISTY [*with relief*].   It's a safe house, so. [*He goes over to the fire, sighing and moaning. Then he sits down, putting his glass beside him and begins gnawing a turnip, too miserable to feel the others staring at him with curiosity.*]

MICHAEL [*going after him*].   Is it yourself is fearing the polis? You're wanting, maybe?

CHRISTY.   There's many wanting.

MICHAEL.   Many surely, with the broken harvest and the ended wars.⁹ [*He picks up some stockings, etc., that are near the fire, and carries them away furtively.*] It should be larceny, I'm thinking?

CHRISTY [*dolefully*].   I had it in my mind it was a different word and a bigger.

PEGEEN.   There's a queer lad. Were you never slapped in school, young fellow, that you don't know the name of your deed?

CHRISTY [*bashfully*].   I'm slow at learning, a middling scholar only.

MICHAEL.   If you're a dunce itself, you'd have a right to know that larceny's robbing and stealing. Is it for the like of that you're wanting?

CHRISTY [*with a flash of family pride*].   And I the son of a strong farmer [*with a sudden qualm*], God rest his soul, could have bought up the whole of your old house a while since, from the butt of his tailpocket, and not have missed the weight of it gone.

MICHAEL [*impressed*].   If it's not stealing, it's maybe something big.

CHRISTY [*flattered*].   Aye; it's maybe something big.

JIMMY.   He's a wicked-looking young fellow. Maybe he followed after a young woman on a lonesome night.

CHRISTY [*shocked*].   Oh, the saints forbid, mister; I was all times a decent lad.

PHILLY [*turning on* JIMMY].   You're a silly man, Jimmy Farrell. He said his father was a farmer a while since, and there's himself

---

7. Itinerant peddlers.
8. A real traveler and so permitted to purchase spirits after closing time of licensed pubs.
9. The Land Wars, at peak in the 1880s, to nationalize ownership of land and so protect tenant farmers from eviction.

74   J. M. Synge

now in a poor state. Maybe the land was grabbed from him, and
he did what any decent man would do.

MICHAEL [*to* CHRISTY, *mysteriously*].   Was it baliffs?

CHRISTY.   The divil a one.

MICHAEL.   Agents?

CHRISTY.   The divil a one.

MICHAEL.   Landlords?

CHRISTY [*peevishly*].   Ah, not at all, I'm saying. You'd see the like of
them stories on any little paper of a Munster town. But I'm not
calling to mind any person, gentle, simple, judge or jury, did the
like of me.

[*They all drew nearer with delighted curiosity.*]

PHILLY.   Well, that lad's a puzzle-the-world.

JIMMY.   He'd beat Dan Davies' circus, or the holy missioners making sermons on the villainy of man. Try him again, Philly.

PHILLY.   Did you strike golden guineas out of solder, young fellow,
or shilling coins itself?

CHRISTY.   I did not, mister, not sixpence nor a farthing coin.

JIMMY.   Did you marry three wives maybe? I'm told there's a sprinkling have done that among the holy Luthers of the preaching
north.

CHRISTY [*shyly*].   I never married with one, let alone with a couple
or three.

PHILLY.   Maybe he went fighting for the Boers, the like of the man
beyond, was judged to be hanged, quartered and drawn. Were
you off east, young fellow, fighting bloody wars for Kruger and
the freedom of the Boers?[1]

CHRISTY.   I never left my own parish till Tuesday was a week.

PEGEEN [*coming from counter*].   He's done nothing, so. [*To*
CHRISTY.] If you didn't commit murder or a bad, nasty thing, or
false coining, or robbery, or butchery, or the like of them, there
isn't anything that would be worth your troubling for to run from
now. You did nothing at all.

CHRISTY [*his feelings hurt*].   That's an unkindly thing to be saying
to a poor orphaned traveller, has a prison behind him, and hanging before, and hell's gap gaping below.

PEGEEN [*with a sign to the men to be quiet*].   You're only saying it.
You did nothing at all. A soft lad the like of you wouldn't slit the
windpipe of a screeching sow.

CHRISTY [*offended*].   You're not speaking the truth.

PEGEEN [*in mock rage*].   Not speaking the truth, is it? Would you
have me knock the head of you with the butt of the broom?

CHRISTY [*twisting round on her with a sharp cry of horror*].   Don't
strike me. I killed my poor father, Tuesday was a week, for doing
the like of that.

1. Paul Kruger, president of the South African Republic established by Boers, Dutch settlers, and suppressed by the British in the Boer War (1899–1902).

PEGEEN [*with blank amazement*].   Is it killed your father?

CHRISTY [*subsiding*].   With the help of God I did surely, and that the Holy Immaculate Mother may intercede for his soul.

PHILLY [*retreating with* JIMMY].   There's a daring fellow.

JIMMY.   Oh, glory be to God!

MICHAEL [*with great respect*].   That was a hanging crime, mister honey. You should have had good reason for doing the like of that.

CHRISTY [*in a very reasonable tone*].   He was a dirty man, God forgive him, and he getting old and crusty, the way I couldn't put up with him at all.

PEGEEN.   And you shot him dead?

CHRISTY [*shaking his head*].   I never used weapons. I've no license, and I'm a law-fearing man.

MICHAEL.   It was with a hilted knife maybe? I'm told, in the big world it's bloody knives they use.

CHRISTY [*loudly, scandalized*].   Do you take me for a slaughter-boy?

PEGEEN.   You never hanged him, the way Jimmy Farrell hanged his dog from the license, and had it screeching and wriggling three hours at the butt of a string, and himself swearing it was a dead dog, and the peelers swearing it had life?

CHRISTY.   I did not then. I just riz the loy[2] and let fall the edge of it on the ridge of his skull, and he went down at my feet like an empty sack, and never let a grunt or groan from him at all.

MICHAEL [*making a sign to* PEGEEN *to fill* CHRISTY'S *glass*].   And what way weren't you hanged, mister? Did you bury him then?

CHRISTY [*considering*].   Aye. I buried him then. Wasn't I digging spuds in the field?

MICHAEL.   And the peelers never followed after you the eleven days that you're out?

CHRISTY [*shaking his head*].   Never a none of them, and I walking forward facing hog, dog, or divil on the highway of the road.

PHILLY [*nodding wisely*].   It's only with a common week-day kind of a murderer them lads would be trusting their carcase, and that man should be a great terror when his temper's roused.

MICHAEL.   He should then. [*To* CHRISTY.] And where was it, mister honey, that you did the deed?

CHRISTY [*looking at him with suspicion*].   Oh, a distant place, master of the house, a windy corner of high, distant hills.

PHILLY [*nodding with approval*].   He's a close man, and he's right, surely.

PEGEEN.   That'd be a lad with the sense of Solomon to have for a pot-boy, Michael James, if it's the truth you're seeking one at all.

PHILLY.   The peelers is fearing him, and if you'd that lad in the house there isn't one of them would come smelling around if the dogs itself were lapping poteen[3] from the dung-pit of the yard.

2. Small spade, usually used for digging potatoes.
3. Home-distilled spirits.

JIMMY. Bravery's a treasure in a lonesome place, and a lad would kill his father, I'm thinking, would face a foxy divil with a pitchpike on the flags of hell.

PEGEEN. It's the truth they're saying, and if I'd that lad in the house, I wouldn't be fearing the looséd kharki[4] cut-throats, or the walking dead.

CHRISTY [swelling with surprise and triumph]. Well, glory be to God!

MICHAEL [with deference]. Would you think well to stop here and be pot-boy, mister honey, if we gave you good wages, and didn't destroy you with the weight of work?

SHAWN [coming forward uneasily]. That'd be a queer kind to bring into a decent quiet household with the like of Pegeen Mike.

PEGEEN [very sharply]. Will you whisht? Who's speaking to you?

SHAWN [retreating]. A bloody-handed murderer the like of . . .

PEGEEN [snapping at him]. Whisht I am saying; we'll take no fooling from your like at all. [To CHRISTY with a honeyed voice.] And you, young fellow, you'd have a right to stop, I'm thinking, for we'd do our all and utmost to content your needs.

CHRISTY [overcome with wonder]. And I'd be safe in this place from the searching law?

MICHAEL. You would, surely. If they're not fearing you, itself, the peelers in this place is decent droughty[5] poor fellows, wouldn't touch a cur dog and not give warning in the dead of night.

PEGEEN [very kindly and persuasively]. Let you stop a short while anyhow. Aren't you destroyed walking with your feet in bleeding blisters, and your whole skin needing washing like a Wicklow sheep.

CHRISTY [looking round with satisfaction]. It's a nice room, and if it's not humbugging me you are, I'm thinking that I'll surely stay.

JIMMY [jumps up]. Now, by the grace of God, herself will be safe this night, with a man killed his father holding danger from the door, and let you come on, Michael James, or they'll have the best stuff drunk at the wake.

MICHAEL [going to the door with MEN]. And begging your pardon, mister, what name will we call you, for we'd like to know?

CHRISTY. Christopher Mahon.

MICHAEL. Well, God bless you, Christy, and a good rest till we meet again when the sun'll be rising to the noon of day.

CHRISTY. God bless you all.

MEN. God bless you.

[They go out except SHAWN, who lingers at door.]

SHAWN [to PEGEEN]. Are you wanting me to stop along with you and keep you from harm?

PEGEEN [gruffly]. Didn't you say you were fearing Father Reilly?

4. Khaki, tan cotton associated with the British field uniform.
5. Thirsty.

SHAWN.   There'd be no harm staying now, I'm thinking, and himself in it too.

PEGEEN.   You wouldn't stay when there was need for you, and let you step off nimble this time when there's none.

SHAWN.   Didn't I say it was Father Reilly . . .

PEGEEN.   Go on, then, to Father Reilly [*in a jeering tone*], and let him put you in the holy brotherhoods, and leave that lad to me.

SHAWN.   If I meet the Widow Quin . . .

PEGEEN.   Go on, I'm saying, and don't be waking this place with your noise. [*She hustles him out and bolts the door.*] That lad would wear the spirits from the saints of peace.

> [*Bustles about, then takes off her apron and pins it up in the window as a blind.* CHRISTY *watching her timidly. Then she comes to him and speaks with bland good-humour.*]

Let you stretch out now by the fire, young fellow. You should be destroyed travelling.

CHRISTY [*shyly again, drawing off his boots*].   I'm tired, surely, walking wild eleven days, and waking fearful in the night. [*He holds up one of his feet, feeling his blisters, and looking at them with compassion.*]

PEGEEN [*standing beside him, watching him with delight*].   You should have had great people in your family, I'm thinking, with the little, small feet you have, and you with a kind of a quality name, the like of what you'd find on the great powers and potentates of France and Spain.

CHRISTY [*with pride*].   We were great surely, with wide and windy acres of rich Munster land.

PEGEEN.   Wasn't I telling you, and you a fine, handsome young fellow with a noble brow?

CHRISTY [*with a flash of delighted surprise*].   Is it me?

PEGEEN.   Aye, Did you never hear that from the young girls where you come from in the west or south?

CHRISTY [*with venom*].   I did not then. Oh, they're bloody liars in the naked parish where I grew a man.

PEGEEN.   If they are itself, you've heard it these days, I'm thinking, and you walking the world telling out your story to young girls or old.

CHRISTY.   I've told my story no place till this night, Pegeen Mike, and it's foolish I was here, maybe, to be talking free, but you're decent people, I'm thinking, and yourself a kindly woman, the way I wasn't fearing you at all.

PEGEEN [*filling a sack with straw*].   You've said the like of that, maybe, in every cot and cabin where you've met a young girl on your way.

CHRISTY [*going over to her, gradually raising his voice*].   I've said it nowhere till this night, I'm telling you, for I've seen none the like of you the eleven long days I am walking the world, looking over a low ditch or a high ditch on my north or my south, into stony

scattered fields, or scribes of bog, where you'd see young, limber
girls, and fine prancing women making laughter with the men.

PEGEEN.   If you weren't destroyed travelling, you'd have as much
talk and streeleen,[6] I'm thinking, as Owen Roe O'Sullivan or the
poets of the Dingle Bay, and I've heard all times it's the poets are
your like, fine fiery fellows with great rages when their temper's
roused.

CHRISTY [*drawing a little nearer to her*].   You've a power of rings,
God bless you, and would there be any offence if I was asking are
you single now?

PEGEEN.   What would I want wedding so young?

CHRISTY [*with relief*].   We're alike, so.

PEGEEN [*she puts sack on settle and beats it up*].   I never killed my
father. I'd be afeard to do that, except I was the like of yourself
with blind rages tearing me within, for I'm thinking you should
have had great tussling when the end was come.

CHRISTY [*expanding with delight at the first confidential talk he has
ever had with a woman*].   We had not then. It was a hard woman
was come over the hill, and if he was always a crusty kind when
he'd a hard woman setting him on, not the divil himself or his
four fathers could put up with him at all.

PEGEEN [*with curiosity*].   And isn't it a great wonder that one
wasn't fearing you?

CHRISTY [*very confidentially*].   Up to the day I killed my father,
there wasn't a person in Ireland knew the kind I was, and I there
drinking, waking, eating, sleeping, a quiet, simple poor fellow
with no man giving me heed.

PEGEEN [*getting a quilt out of the cupboard and putting it on the
sack*].   It was the girls were giving you heed maybe, and I'm
thinking it's most conceit you'd have to be gaming with their like.

CHRISTY [*shaking his head, with simplicity*].   Not the girls itself,
and I won't tell you a lie. There wasn't anyone heeding me in that
place saving only the dumb beasts of the field. [*He sits down at
fire.*]

PEGEEN [*with disappointment*].   And I thinking you should have
been living the like of a king of Norway or the Eastern world.
[*She comes and sits beside him after placing bread and mug of
milk on the table.*]

CHRISTY [*laughing piteously*].   The like of a king, is it? And I after
toiling, moiling, digging, dodging from the dawn till dusk with
never a sight of joy or sport saving only when I'd be abroad in the
dark night poaching rabbits on hills, for I was a devil to poach,
God forgive me, [*very naïvely*] and I near got six months for going
with a dung fork and stabbing a fish.

PEGEEN.   And it's that you'd call sport, is it, to be abroad in the
darkness with yourself alone?

6. Wandering, like Owen Roe O'Sullivan (1748–84), poet and scholar of county Kerry and
its Dingle peninsula.

CHRISTY.   I did, God help me, and there I'd be as happy as the sunshine of St. Martin's Day,[7] watching the light passing the north or
the patches of fog, till I'd hear a rabbit starting to screech and I'd
go running in the furze. Then when I'd my full share I'd come
walking down where you'd see the ducks and geese stretched
sleeping on the highway of the road, and before I'd pass the
dunghill, I'd hear himself snoring out, a loud lonesome snore
he'd be making all times, the while he was sleeping, and he a
man 'd be raging all times, the while he was waking, like a gaudy
officer you'd hear cursing and damning and swearing oaths.

PEGEEN.   Providence and Mercy, spare us all!

CHRISTY.   It's that you'd say surely if you seen him and he after
drinking for weeks, rising up in the red dawn, or before it maybe,
and going out into the yard as naked as an ash tree in the moon
of May, and shying clods against the viságe of the stars till he'd
put the fear of death into the banbhs[8] and the screeching sows.

PEGEEN.   I'd be well-nigh afeard of that lad myself, I'm thinking.
And there was no one in it but the two of you alone?

CHRISTY.   The divil a one, though he'd sons and daughters walking
all great states and territories of the world, and not a one of
them, to this day, but would say their seven curses on him, and
the rousing up to let a cough or sneeze, maybe, in the deadness
of the night.

PEGEEN [*nodding her head*].   Well, you should have been a queer
lot. I never cursed my father the like of that, though I'm twenty
and more years of age.

CHRISTY.   Then you'd have cursed mine, I'm telling you, and he a
man never gave peace to any, saving when he'd get two months or
three, or be locked in the asylums for battering peelers or as-
saulting men [*with depression*] the way it was a bitter life he led
me till I did up a Tuesday and halve his skull.

PEGEEN [*putting her hand on his shoulder*].   Well, you'll have peace
in this place, Christy Mahon, and none to trouble you, and it's
near time a fine lad like you should have your good share of the
earth.

CHRISTY.   It's the time surely, and I a seemly fellow with great
strength in me and bravery of . . .

        [*Someone knocks.*]

CHRISTY [*clinging to* PEGEEN].   Oh, glory! it's late for knocking, and
this last while I'm in terror of the peelers, and the walking dead.

        [*Knocking again.*]

PEGEEN.   Who's there?
VOICE [*outside*].   Me.

7. November 11, a festival day, Martinmas, before St. Martin's Lent, a period of penitence
extending through Christmas.
8. Piglets.

PEGEEN. Who's me?

VOICE. The Widow Quin.

PEGEEN [*jumping up and giving him the bread and milk*]. Go on now with your supper, and let on to be sleepy, for if she found you were such a warrant to talk, she'd be stringing gabble till the dawn of day.

[*He takes bread and sits shyly with his back to the door.*]

PEGEEN [*opening door, with temper*]. What ails you, or what is it you're wanting at this hour of the night?

WIDOW QUIN [*coming in a step and peering at* CHRISTY]. I'm after meeting Shawn Keogh and Father Reilly below, who told me of your curiosity man, and they fearing by this time he was maybe roaring, romping on your hands with drink.

PEGEEN [*pointing to* CHRISTY]. Look now is he roaring, and he stretched away drowsy with his supper and his mug of milk. Walk down and tell that to Father Reilly and to Shaneen Keogh.

WIDOW QUIN [*coming forward*]. I'll not see them again, for I've their word to lead that lad forward for to lodge with me.

PEGEEN [*in blank amazement*]. This night, is it?

WIDOW QUIN [*going over*]. This night. "It isn't fitting," says the priesteen, "to have his likeness lodging with an orphaned girl." [*To* CHRISTY.] God save you, mister!

CHRISTY [*shyly*]. God save you kindly.

WIDOW QUIN [*looking at him with half-amazed curiosity*]. Well, aren't you a little smiling fellow? It should have been great and bitter torments did rouse your spirits to a deed of blood.

CHRISTY [*doubtfully*]. It should, maybe.

WIDOW QUIN. It's more than "maybe" I'm saying, and it'd soften my heart to see you sitting so simple with your cup and cake, and you fitter to be saying your catechism than slaying your da.

PEGEEN [*at counter, washing glasses*]. There's talking when any'd see he's fit to be holding his head high with the wonders of the world. Walk on from this, for I'll not have him tormented and he destroyed travelling since Tuesday was a week.

WIDOW QUIN [*peaceably*]. We'll be walking surely when his supper's done, and you'll find we're great company, young fellow, when it's of the like of you and me you'd hear the penny poets singing in an August Fair.

CHRISTY [*innocently*]. Did you kill your father?

PEGEEN [*contemptuously*]. She did not. She hit himself with a worn pick, and the rusted poison did corrode his blood the way he never overed it, and died after. That was a sneaky kind of murder did win small glory with the boys itself. [*She crosses to* CHRISTY'*s left.*]

WIDOW QUIN [*with good-humour*]. If it didn't, maybe all knows a widow woman has buried her children and destroyed her man is a wiser comrade for a young lad than a girl, the like of you, who'd

go helter-skeltering after any man would let you a wink upon the
road.

PEGEEN [*breaking out into wild rage*].   And you'll say that, Widow
Quin, and you gasping with the rage you had racing the hill beyond to look on his face.

WIDOW QUIN [*laughing derisively*].   Me, is it? Well, Father Reilly
has cuteness to divide you now. [*She pulls* CHRISTY *up.*] There's
great temptation in a man did slay his da, and we'd best be going,
young fellow; so rise up and come with me.

PEGEEN [*seizing his arm*].   He'll not stir. He's pot-boy in this place,
and I'll not have him stolen off and kidnabbed while himself's
abroad.

WIDOW QUIN.   It'd be a crazy pot-boy'd lodge him in the shebeen
where he works by day, so you'd have a right to come on, young
fellow, till you see my little houseen, a perch off on the rising hill.

PEGEEN.   Wait till morning, Christy Mahon. Wait till you lay eyes
on her leaky thatch is growing more pasture for her buck goat
than her square of fields, and she without a tramp itself to keep
in order her place at all.

WIDOW QUIN.   When you see me contriving in my little gardens,
Christy Mahon, you'll swear the Lord God formed me to be living
lone, and that there isn't my match in Mayo for thatching, or
mowing, or shearing a sheep.

PEGEEN [*with noisy scorn*].   It's true the Lord God formed you to
contrive indeed. Doesn't the world know you reared a black lamb
at your own breast, so that the Lord Bishop of Connaught felt
the elements of a Christian, and he eating it after in a kidney
stew? Doesn't the world know you've been seen shaving the foxy
skipper from France for a threepenny bit and a sop of grass tobacco would wring the liver from a mountain goat you'd meet
leaping the hills?

WIDOW QUIN [*with amusement*].   Do you hear her now, young fellow? Do you hear the way she'll be rating at your own self when
a week is by?

PEGEEN [*to* CHRISTY].   Don't heed her. Tell her to go into her pigsty
and not plague us here.

WIDOW QUIN.   I'm going; but he'll come with me.

PEGEEN [*shaking him*].   Are you dumb, young fellow?

CHRISTY [*timidly, to* WIDOW QUIN].   God increase you; but I'm pot-
boy in his place, and it's here I'd liefer[9] stay.

PEGEEN [*triumphantly*].   Now you have heard him, and go on from
this.

WIDOW QUIN [*looking round the room*].   It's lonesome this hour
crossing the hill, and if he won't come along with me, I'd have a
right maybe to stop this night with yourselves. Let me stretch out
on the settle, Pegeen Mike; and himself can lie by the hearth.

9. Willingly, gladly.

PEGEEN [*short and fiercely*].   Faith, I won't. Quit off or I will send you now.

WIDOW QUIN [*gathering her shawl up*].   Well, it's a terror to be aged a score. [*To* CHRISTY.] God bless you now, young fellow, and let you be wary, or there's right torment will await you here if you go romancing with her like, and she waiting only, as they bade me say, on a sheepskin parchment to be wed with Shawn Keogh of Killakeen.

CHRISTY [*going to* PEGEEN *as she bolts the door*].   What's that she's after saying?

PEGEEN.   Lies and blather, you've no call to mind. Well, isn't Shawn Keogh an impudent fellow to send up spying on me? Wait till I lay hands on him. Let him wait, I'm saying.

CHRISTY.   And you're not wedding him at all?

PEGEEN.   I wouldn't wed him if a bishop came walking for to join us here.

CHRISTY.   That God in glory may be thanked for that.

PEGEEN.   There's your bed now. I've put a quilt upon you I'm after quilting a while since with my own two hands, and you'd best stretch out now for your sleep, and may God give you a good rest till I call you in the morning when the cocks will crow.

CHRISTY [*as she goes to inner room*].   May God and Mary and St. Patrick bless you and reward you, for your kindly talk.

[*She shuts the door behind her. He settles his bed slowly, feeling the quilt with immense satisfaction.*]

Well, it's a clean bed and soft with it, and it's great luck and company I've won me in the end of time—two fine women fighting for the likes of me—till I'm thinking this night wasn't I a foolish fellow not to kill my father in the years gone by.

Act 2

SCENE, *as before. Brilliant morning light.* CHRISTY, *looking bright and cheerful, is cleaning a girl's boots.*

CHRISTY [*to himself, counting jugs on dresser*].   Half a hundred beyond. Ten there. A score that's above. Eighty jugs. Six cups and a broken one. Two plates. A power of glasses. Bottles, a schoolmaster'd be hard set to count, and enough in them, I'm thinking, to drunken all the wealth and wisdom of the County Clare. [*He puts down the boot carefully.*] There's her boots now, nice and decent for her evening use, and isn't it grand brushes she has? [*He puts them down and goes by degrees to the looking-glass.*] Well, this'd be a fine place to be my whole life talking out with swearing Christians, in place of my old dogs and cat, and I stalking around, smoking my pipe and drinking my fill, and never a day's work but drawing a cork an odd time, or wiping a glass, or rinsing out a shiny tumbler for a decent man. [*He takes the looking-glass from the wall and puts it on the back of a chair; then sits down in front of it and begins washing his face.*] Didn't I know rightly I was handsome, though it was the divil's own mirror we had beyond, would twist a squint across an angel's brow; and I'll be growing fine from this day, the way I'll have a soft lovely skin on me and won't be the like of the clumsy young fellows do be ploughing all times in the earth and dung. [*He starts.*] Is she coming again? [*He looks out.*] Stranger girls. God help me, where'll I hide myself away and my long neck naked to the world? [*He looks out.*] I'd best go to the room maybe till I'm dressed again.

[*He gathers up his coat and the looking-glass, and runs into the inner room. The door is pushed open, and* SUSAN BRADY *looks in, and knocks on door.*]

SUSAN.   There's nobody in it. [*Knocks again.*]
NELLY [*pushing her in and following her, with* HONOR BLAKE *and* SARA TANSEY]. It'd be early for them both to be out walking the hill.
SUSAN.   I'm thinking Shawn Keogh was making game of us and there's no such man in it at all.
HONOR [*pointing to straw and quilt*].   Look at that. He's been sleeping there in the night. Well, it'll be a hard case if he's gone off now, the way we'll never set our eyes on a man killed his father, and we after rising early and destroying ourselves running fast on the hill.
NELLY.   Are you thinking them's his boots?
SARA [*taking them up*].   If they are, there should be his father's track on them. Did you never read in the papers the way murdered men do bleed and drip?
SUSAN.   Is that blood there, Sara Tansey?
SARA [*smelling it*].   That's bog water, I'm thinking, but it's his own they are surely, for I never seen the like of them for whity mud, and red mud, and turf on them, and the fine sands of the sea. That man's been walking, I'm telling you. [*She goes down right, putting on one of his boots.*]
SUSAN [*going to window*].   Maybe he's stolen off to Belmullet with the boots of Michael James, and you'd have a right so to follow after him, Sara Tansey, and you the one yoked the ass cart and drove ten miles to set your eyes on the man bit the yellow lady's nostril on the northern shore. [*She looks out.*]
SARA [*running to window with one boot on*].   Don't be talking, and we fooled to-day. [*Putting on other boot.*] There's a pair do fit me well, and I'll be keeping them for walking to the priest, when you'd be ashamed this place, going up winter and summer with nothing worth while to confess at all.
HONOR [*who has been listening at the door*].   Whisht! there's someone inside the room. [*She pushes door a chink open.*] It's a man.

[SARA *kicks off boots and puts them where they were. They all stand in a line looking through chink.*]

SARA.   I'll call him. Mister! Mister!

> [*He puts in his head.*]

Is Pegeen within?

CHRISTY [*coming in as meek as a mouse, with the looking-glass held
  behind his back*].   She's above on the cnucean,[1] seeking the
  nanny goats, the way she'd have a sup of goat's milk for to colour
  my tea.

SARA.   And asking your pardon, is it you's the man killed his father?

CHRISTY   [*sidling toward the nail where the glass was hanging*].   I
  am, God help me!

SARA [*taking eggs she has brought*].   Then my thousand welcomes
  to you, and I've run up with a brace of duck's eggs for your food
  to-day. Pegeen's ducks is no use, but these are the real rich sort.
  Hold out your hand and you'll see it's no lie I'm telling you.

CHRISTY [*coming forward shyly, and holding out his left hand*].
  They're a great and weighty size.

SUSAN.   And I run up with a pat of butter, for it'd be a poor thing
  to have you eating your spuds dry, and you after running a great
  way since you did destroy your da.

CHRISTY.   Thank you kindly.

HONOR.   And I brought you a little cut of cake, for you should have
  a thin stomach on you, and you that length walking the world.

NELLY.   And I brought you a little laying pullet—boiled and all she
  is—was crushed at the fall of night by the curate's car. Feel the
  fat of that breast, mister.

CHRISTY.   It's bursting, surely. [*He feels it with the back of his hand,
  in which he holds the presents.*]

SARA.   Will you pinch it? Is your right hand too sacred for to use at
  all? [*She slips round behind him.*] It's a glass he has. Well, I never
  seen to this day a man with a looking-glass held to his back.
  Them that kills their fathers is a vain lot surely.

> [GIRLS *giggle.*]

CHRISTY [*smiling innocently and piling presents on glass*].   I'm very
  thankful to you all to-day . . .

WIDOW QUIN [*coming in quickly, at door*].   Sara Tansey, Susan
  Brady, Honor Blake! What in glory has you here at this hour of
  day?

GIRLS [*giggling*].   That's the man killed his father.

WIDOW QUIN [*coming to them*].   I know well it's the man; and I'm
  after putting him down in the sports below for racing, leaping,
  pitching, and the Lord knows what.

SARA [*exuberantly*].   That's right, Widow Quin. I'll bet my dowry
  that he'll lick the world.

WIDOW QUIN.   If you will, you'd have a right to have him fresh and

---

1. Small hill.

nourished in place of nursing a feast. [*Taking presents.*] Are you fasting or fed, young fellow?

CHRISTY.   Fasting, if you please.

WIDOW QUIN [*loudly*].   Well, you're the lot. Stir up now and give him his breakfast. [*To* CHRISTY.] Come here to me [*she puts him on bench beside her while the girls make tea and get his breakfast*] and let you tell us your story before Pegeen will come, in place of grinning your ears off like the moon of May.

CHRISTY [*beginning to be pleased*].   It's a long story; you'd be destroyed listening.

WIDOW QUIN.   Don't be letting on to be shy, a fine, gamey, treacherous lad the like of you. Was it in your house beyond you cracked his skull?

CHRISTY [*shy but flattered*].   It was not. We were digging spuds in his cold, sloping, stony, divil's patch of a field.

WIDOW QUIN.   And you went asking money of him, or making talk of getting a wife would drive him from his farm?

CHRISTY.   I did not, then; but there I was, digging and digging, and "You squinting idiot," says he, "let you walk down now and tell the priest you'll wed the Widow Casey in a score of days."

WIDOW QUIN.   And what kind was she?

CHRISTY [*with horror*].   A walking terror from beyond the hills, and she two score and five years, and two hundredweights and five pounds in the weighing scales, with a limping leg on her, and a blinded eye, and she a woman of noted misbehaviour with the old and young.

GIRLS [*clustering round him, serving him*].   Glory be.

WIDOW QUIN.   And what did he want driving you to wed with her? [*She takes a bit of the chicken.*]

CHRISTY [*eating with growing satisfaction*].   He was letting on I was wanting a protector from the harshness of the world, and he without a thought the whole while but how he'd have her hut to live in and her gold to drink.

WIDOW QUIN.   There's maybe worse than a dry hearth and a widow woman and your glass at night. So you hit him then?

CHRISTY [*getting almost excited*].   I did not. "I won't wed her," says I, "when all know she did suckle me for six weeks when I came into the world, and she a hag this day with a tongue on her has the crows and seabirds scattered, the way they wouldn't cast a shadow on her garden with the dread of her curse."

WIDOW QUIN [*teasingly*].   That one should be right company.

SARA [*eagerly*].   Don't mind her. Did you kill him then?

CHRISTY.   "She's too good for the like of you," says he, "and go on now or I'll flatten you out like a crawling beast has passed under a dray." "You will not if I can help it," says I. "Go on," says he, "or I'll have the divil making garters of your limbs to-night." "You will not if I can help it," says I. [*He sits up, brandishing his mug.*]

SARA.   You were right surely.

CHRISTY [*impressively*].   With that the sun came out between the

cloud and the hill, and it shining green in my face. "God have
mercy on your soul," says he, lifting a scythe; "or on your own,"
says I, raising the loy.

SUSAN.   That's a grand story.

HONOR.   He tells it lovely.

CHRISTY [*flattered and confident, waving bone*].   He gave a drive
with the scythe, and I gave a lep to the east. Then I turned
around with my back to the north, and I hit a blow on the ridge
of his skull, laid him stretched out, and he split to the knob of his
gullet. [*He raises the chicken bone to his Adam's apple.*]

GIRLS [*together*].   Well, you're a marvel! Oh, God bless you! You're
the lad surely!

SUSAN.   I'm thinking the Lord God sent him this road to make a
second husband to the Widow Quin, and she with a great yearning to be wedded, though all dread her here. Lift him on her
knee, Sara Tansey.

WIDOW QUIN.   Don't tease him.

SARA [*going over to dresser and counter very quickly, and getting two
glasses and porter*].   You're heroes surely, and let you drink a supeen with your arms linked like the outlandish lovers in the
sailor's song.

   [*She links their arms and gives them the glasses.*]

There now. Drink a health to the wonders of the western world,
the pirates, preachers, poteen-makers, with the jobbing jockies;
parching peelers, and the juries fill their stomachs selling judg-
ments of the English law. [*Brandishing the bottle.*]

WIDOW QUIN.   That's a right toast, Sara Tansey. Now Christy.

   [*They drink with their arms linked, he drinking with his left
   hand, she with her right. As they are drinking,* PEGEEN MIKE
   *comes in with a milk can and stands aghast. They all spring
   away from* CHRISTY. *He goes down left.* WIDOW QUIN *remains
   seated.*]

PEGEEN [*angrily, to* SARA].   What is it you're wanting?

SARA [*twisting her apron*].   An ounce of tobacco.

PEGEEN.   Have you tuppence?

SARA.   I've forgotten my purse.

PEGEEN.   Then you'd best be getting it and not fooling us here. [*To
the* WIDOW QUIN, *with more elaborate scorn.*] And what is it you're
wanting, Widow Quin?

WIDOW QUIN [*insolently*].   A penn'orth of starch.

PEGEEN [*breaking out*].   And you without a white shift or a shirt in
your whole family since the drying of the flood. I've no starch for
the like of you, and let you walk on now to Killamuck.

WIDOW QUIN [*turning to* CHRISTY, *as she goes out with the girls*].
Well, you're mighty huffy this day, Pegeen Mike, and, you young
fellow, let you not forget the sports and racing when the noon is
by.

[*They go out.*]

PEGEEN [*imperiously*].   Fling out that rubbish and put them cups away.

[CHRISTY *tidies away in great haste.*]

Shove in the bench by the wall.

[*He does so.*]

And hang that glass on the nail. What disturbed it at all?

CHRISTY [*very meekly*].   I was making myself decent only, and this a fine country for young lovely girls.

PEGEEN [*sharply*].   Whisht your talking of girls. [*Goes to counter— right.*]

CHRISTY.   Wouldn't any wish to be decent in a place . . .

PEGEEN.   Whisht I'm saying.

CHRISTY [*looks at her face for a moment with great misgivings, then as a last effort, takes up a loy, and goes towards her, with feigned assurance*].   It was with a loy the like of that I killed my father.

PEGEEN [*still sharply*].   You've told me that story six times since the dawn of day.

CHRISTY [*reproachfully*].   It's a queer thing you wouldn't care to be hearing it and them girls after walking four miles to be listening to me now.

PEGEEN [*turning round astonished*].   Four miles.

CHRISTY [*apologetically*].   Didn't himself say there were only four bonafides living in the place?

PEGEEN.   It's bona fides by the road they are, but that lot came over the river lepping the stones. It's not three perches when you go like that, and I was down this morning looking on the papers the post-boy does have in his bag. [*With meaning and emphasis.*] For there was great news this day, Christopher Mahon. [*She goes into room left.*]

CHRISTY [*suspiciously*].   Is it news of my murder?

PEGEEN [*inside*].   Murder, indeed.

CHRISTY [*loudly*].   A murdered da?

PEGEEN [*coming in again and crossing right*].   There was not, but a story filled half a page of the hanging of a man. Ah, that should be a fearful end, young fellow, and it worst of all for a man who destroyed his da, for the like of him would get small mercies, and when it's dead he is, they'd put him in a narrow grave, with cheap sacking wrapping him round, and pour down quicklime on his head, the way you'd see a woman pouring any frish-frash from a cup.

CHRISTY [*very miserably*].   Oh, God help me. Are you thinking I'm safe? You were saying at the fall of night, I was shut of jeopardy and I here with yourselves.

PEGEEN [*severely*].   You'll be shut of jeopardy no place if you go talking with a pack of wild girls the like of them do be walking abroad with the peelers, talking whispers at the fall of night.

CHRISTY [*with terror*].   And you're thinking they'd tell?

PEGEEN [*with mock sympathy*].   Who knows, God help you.

CHRISTY [*loudly*].   What joy would they have to bring hanging to the likes of me?

PEGEEN.   It's queer joys they have, and who knows the thing they'd do, if it'd make the green stones cry itself to think of you swaying and swiggling at the butt of a rope, and you with a fine, stout neck, God bless you! the way you'd be a half an hour, in great anguish, getting your death.

CHRISTY [*getting his boots and putting them on*].   If there's that terror of them, it'd be best, maybe, I went on wandering like Esau or Cain and Abel on the sides of Neifin or the Erris plain.[2]

PEGEEN [*beginning to play with him*].   It would, maybe, for I've heard the Circuit Judges this place is a heartless crew.

CHRISTY [*bitterly*].   It's more than Judges this place is a heartless crew. [*Looking up at her.*] And isn't it a poor thing to be starting again and I a lonesome fellow will be looking out on women and girls the way the needy fallen spirits do be looking on the Lord?

PEGEEN.   What call have you to be that lonesome when there's poor girls walking Mayo in their thousands now?

CHRISTY [*grimly*].   It's well you know what call I have. It's well you know it's a lonesome thing to be passing small towns with the lights shining sideways when the night is down, or going in strange places with a dog noising before you and a dog noising behind, or drawn to the cities where you'd hear a voice kissing and talking deep love in every shadow of the ditch, and you passing on with an empty, hungry stomach failing from your heart.

PEGEEN.   I'm thinking you're an odd man, Christy Mahon. The oddest walking fellow I ever set my eyes on to this hour to-day.

CHRISTY.   What would any be but odd men and they living lonesome in the world?

PEGEEN.   I'm not odd, and I'm my whole life with my father only.

CHRISTY [*with infinite admiration*].   How would a lovely handsome woman the like of you be lonesome when all men should be thronging around to hear the sweetness of your voice, and the little infant children should be pestering your steps I'm thinking, and you walking the roads.

PEGEEN.   I'm hard set to know what way a coaxing fellow the like of yourself should be lonesome either.

CHRISTY.   Coaxing?

PEGEEN.   Would you have me think a man never talked with the girls would have the words you've spoken today? It's only letting on you are to be lonesome, the way you'd get around me now.

CHRISTY.   I wish to God I was letting on; but I was lonesome all times, and born lonesome, I'm thinking, as the moon of dawn. [*Going to door.*]

2. Christy conflates biblical figures with Irish place names.

PEGEEN [*puzzled by his talk*].   Well, it's a story I'm not understanding at all why you'd be worse than another, Christy Mahon, and you a fine lad with the great savagery to destroy your da.

CHRISTY.   It's little I'm understanding myself, saving only that my heart's scalded this day, and I going off stretching out the earth between us, the way I'll not be waking near you another dawn of the year till the two of us do arise to hope or judgment with the saints of God, and now I'd best be going with my wattle in my hand, for hanging is a poor thing [*turning to go*], and it's little welcome only is left me in this house to-day.

PEGEEN [*sharply*].   Christy!

[*He turns round.*]

Come here to me.

[*He goes towards her.*]

Lay down that switch and throw some sods on the fire. You're potboy in this place, and I'll not have you mitch off from us now.

CHRISTY.   You were saying I'd be hanged if I stay.

PEGEEN [*quite kindly at last*].   I'm after going down and reading the fearful crimes of Ireland for two weeks or three, and there wasn't a word of your murder. [*Getting up and going over to the counter.*] They've likely not found the body. You're safe so with ourselves.

CHRISTY [*astonished, slowly*].   It's making game of me you were [*following her with fearful joy*], and I can stay so, working at your side, and I not lonesome from this mortal day.

PEGEEN.   What's to hinder you from staying, except the widow woman or the young girls would inveigle you off?

CHRISTY [*with rapture*].   And I'll have your words from this day filling my ears, and that look is come upon you meeting my two eyes, and I watching you loafing around in the warm sun, or rinsing your ankles when the night is come.

PEGEEN [*kindly, but a little embarrassed*].   I'm thinking you'll be a loyal young lad to have working around, and if you vexed me a while since with your leaguing with the girls, I wouldn't give a thraneen[3] for a lad hadn't a mighty spirit in him and a gamey heart.

[SHAWN KEOGH *runs in carrying a cleeve*[4] *on his back, followed by the* WIDOW QUIN.]

SHAWN [*to* PEGEEN].   I was passing below, and I seen your mountainy sheep eating cabbages in Jimmy's field. Run up or they'll be bursting surely.

PEGEEN.   Oh, God mend them! [*She puts a shawl over her head and runs out.*]

3. Thread, song, scrap.
4. Basket.

CHRISTY [*looking from one to the other. Still in high spirits*].   I'd best go to her aid maybe. I'm handy with ewes.

WIDOW QUIN [*closing the door*].   She can do that much, and there is Shaneen has long speeches for to tell you now. [*She sits down with an amused smile.*]

SHAWN [*taking something from his pocket and offering it to* CHRISTY]. Do you see that, mister?

CHRISTY [*looking at it*].   The half of a ticket to the Western States!

SHAWN [*trembling with anxiety*].   I'll give it to you and my new hat [*pulling it out of hamper*]; and my breeches with the double seat [*pulling it off*]; and my new coat is woven from the blackest shearings for three miles around [*giving him the coat*]; I'll give you the whole of them, and my blessing, and the blessing of Father Reilly itself, maybe, if you'll quit from this and leave us in the peace we had till last night at the fall of dark.

CHRISTY [*with a new arrogance*].   And for what is it you're wanting to get shut of me?

SHAWN [*looking to the* WIDOW *for help*].   I'm a poor scholar with middling faculties to coin a lie, so I'll tell you the truth, Christy Mahon. I'm wedding with Pegeen beyond, and I don't think well of having a clever fearless man the like of you dwelling in her house.

CHRISTY [*almost pugnaciously*].   And you'd be using bribery for to banish me?

SHAWN [*in an imploring voice*].   Let you not take it badly, mister honey, isn't beyond the best place for you where you'll have golden chains and shiny coats and you riding upon hunters with the ladies of the land. [*He makes an eager sign to the* WIDOW QUIN *to come to help him.*]

WIDOW QUIN [*coming over*].   It's true for him, and you'd best quit off and not have that poor girl setting her mind on you, for there's Shaneen thinks she wouldn't suit you though all is saying that she'll wed you now.

[CHRISTY *beams with delight.*]

SHAWN [*in terrified earnest*].   She wouldn't suit you, and she with the divil's own temper the way you'd be strangling one another in a score of days. [*He makes the movement of strangling with his hands.*] It's the like of me only that she's fit for, a quiet simple fellow wouldn't raise a hand upon her if she scratched itself.

WIDOW QUIN [*putting* SHAWN'S *hat on* CHRISTY].   Fit them clothes on you anyhow, young fellow, and he'd maybe loan them to you for the sports. [*Pushing him towards inner door.*] Fit them on and you can give your answer when you have them tried.

CHRISTY [*beaming, delighted with the clothes*].   I will then. I'd like herself to see me in them tweeds and hat. [*He goes into room and shuts the door.*]

SHAWN [*in great anxiety*].   He'd like herself to see them. He'll not leave us, Widow Quin. He's a score of divils in him the way it's well nigh certain he will wed Pegeen.

WIDOW QUIN [*jeering*].   It's true all girls are fond of courage and do hate the like of you.

SHAWN [*walking about in desperation*].   Oh, Widow Quin, what'll I be doing now? I'd inform again him, but he'd burst from Kilmainham[5] and he'd be sure and certain to destroy me. If I wasn't so God-fearing, I'd near have courage to come behind him and run a pike into his side. Oh, it's a hard case to be an orphan and not to have your father that you're used to, and you'd easy kill and make yourself a hero in the sight of all. [*Coming up to her.*] Oh, Widow Quin, will you find me some contrivance when I've promised you a ewe?

WIDOW QUIN.   A ewe's a small thing, but what would you give me if I did wed him and did save you so?

SHAWN [*with astonishment*].   You?

WIDOW QUIN.   Aye. Would you give me the red cow you have and the mountainy ram, and the right of way across your rye path, and a load of dung at Michaelmas,[6] and turbary[7] upon the western hill?

SHAWN [*radiant with hope*].   I would surely, and I'd give you the wedding-ring I have, and the loan of a new suit, the way you'd have him decent on the wedding-day. I'd give you two kids for your dinner, and a gallon of poteen, and I'd call the piper on the long car to your wedding from Crossmolina or from Ballina. I'd give you . . .

WIDOW QUIN.   That'll do so, and let you whisht, for he's coming now again.

[CHRISTY *comes in very natty in the new clothes.* WIDOW QUIN *goes to him admiringly.*]

WIDOW QUIN.   If you seen yourself now, I'm thinking you'd be too proud to speak to us at all, and it'd be a pity surely to have your like sailing from Mayo to the Western World.

CHRISTY [*as proud as a peacock*].   I'm not going. If this is a poor place itself, I'll make myself contented to be lodging here.

[WIDOW QUIN *makes a sign to* SHAWN *to leave them.*]

SHAWN.   Well, I'm going measuring the race-course while the tide is low, so I'll leave you the garments and my blessing for the sports today. God bless you! [*He wriggles out.*]

WIDOW QUIN [*admiring* CHRISTY].   Well, you're mighty spruce, young fellow. Sit down now while you're quiet till you talk with me.

---

5. Jail in Dublin.
6. Feast of St. Michael, September 29.
7. Right to cut turf, for fuel, on another's property.

CHRISTY [*swaggering*].   I'm going abroad on the hillside for to seek
Pegeen.

WIDOW QUIN.   You'll have time and plenty for to seek Pegeen, and
you heard me saying at the fall of night the two of us should be
great company.

CHRISTY.   From this out I'll have no want of company when all
sorts is bringing me their food and clothing [*he swaggers to the
door, tightening his belt*], the way they'd set their eyes upon a gallant orphan cleft his father with one blow to the breeches belt.
[*He opens door, then staggers back.*] Saints of glory! Holy angels
from the throne of light!

WIDOW QUIN [*going over*].   What ails you?

CHRISTY.   It's the walking spirit of my murdered da?

WIDOW QUIN [*looking out*].   Is it that tramper?

CHRISTY [*wildly*].   Where'll I hide my poor body from that ghost of
hell?

> [*The door is pushed open, and old* MAHON *appears on thresh-
> old.* CHRISTY *darts in behind door.*]

WIDOW QUIN [*in great amusement*].   God save you, my poor man.

MAHON [*gruffly*].   Did you see a young lad passing this way in the
early morning or the fall of night?

WIDOW QUIN.   You're a queer kind to walk in not saluting at all.

MAHON.   Did you see the young lad?

WIDOW QUIN [*stiffly*].   What kind was he?

MAHON.   An ugly young streeler with a murderous gob[8] on him,
and a little switch in his hand. I met a tramper seen him coming
this way at the fall of night.

WIDOW QUIN.   There's harvest hundreds do be passing these days
for the Sligo boat. For what is it you're wanting him, my poor
man?

MAHON.   I want to destroy him for breaking the head on me with
the clout of a loy. [*He takes off a big hat, and shows his head in a
mass of bandages and plaster, with some pride.*] It was he did that,
and amn't I a great wonder to think I've traced him ten days with
that rent in my crown?

WIDOW QUIN [*taking his head in both hands and examining it with
extreme delight*].   That was a great blow. And who hit you? A
robber maybe?

MAHON.   It was my own son hit me, and he the divil a robber, or
anything else, but a dirty, stuttering lout.

WIDOW QUIN [*letting go his skull and wiping her hands in her apron*].
You'd best be wary of a mortified scalp, I think they call it, lepping around with that wound in the splendour of the sun. It was
a bad blow surely, and you should have vexed him fearful to make
him strike that gash in his da.

MAHON.   Is it me?

8. That is, a worthless youth with a foul mouth.

WIDOW QUIN [*amusing herself*].   Aye. And isn't it a great shame when the old and hardened do torment the young?

MAHON [*raging*].   Torment him is it? And I after holding out with the patience of a martyred saint till there's nothing but destruction on, and I'm driven out in my old age with none to aid me.

WIDOW QUIN [*greatly amused*].   It's a sacred wonder the way that wickedness will spoil a man.

MAHON.   My wickedness, is it? Amn't I after saying it is himself has me destroyed, and he a liar on walls, a talker of folly, a man you'd see stretched the half of the day in the brown ferns with his belly to the sun.

WIDOW QUIN.   Not working at all?

MAHON.   The divil a work, or if he did itself, you'd see him raising up a haystack like the stalk of a rush, or driving our last cow till he broke her leg at the hip, and when he wasn't at that he'd be fooling over little birds he had—finches and felts[9]—or making mugs at his own self in the bit of a glass we had hung on the wall.

WIDOW QUIN [*looking at* CHRISTY].   What way was he so foolish? It was running wild after the girls may be?

MAHON [*with a shout of derision*].   Running wild, is it? If he seen a red petticoat coming swinging over the hill, he'd be off to hide in the sticks, and you'd see him shooting out his sheep's eyes between the little twigs and the leaves, and his two ears rising like a hare looking out through a gap. Girls, indeed!

WIDOW QUIN.   It was drink maybe?

MAHON.   And he a poor fellow would get drunk on the smell of a pint. He'd a queer rotten stomach, I'm telling you, and when I gave him three pulls from my pipe a while since, he was taken with contortions till I had to send him in the ass cart to the females' nurse.

WIDOW QUIN [*clasping her hands*].   Well, I never till this day heard tell of a man the like of that!

MAHON.   I'd take a mighty oath you didn't surely, and wasn't he the laughing joke of every female woman where four baronies meet, the way the girls would stop their weeding if they seen him coming the road to let a roar at him, and call him the looney of Mahon's.

WIDOW QUIN.   I'd give the world and all to see the like of him. What kind was he?

MAHON.   A small low fellow.

WIDOW QUIN.   And dark?

MAHON.   Dark and dirty.

WIDOW QUIN [considering].   I'm thinking I seen him.

MAHON [*eagerly*].   An ugly young blackguard.

WIDOW QUIN.   A hideous, fearful villain, and the spit of you.

MAHON.   What way is he fled?

9. Thrushes.

WIDOW QUIN.   Gone over the hills to catch a coasting steamer to the north or south.

MAHON.   Could I pull up on him now?

WIDOW QUIN.   If you'll cross the sands below where the tide is out, you'll be in it as soon as himself, for he had to go round ten miles by the top of the bay. [*She points to the door.*] Strike down by the head beyond and then follow on the roadway to the north and east.

[MAHON *goes abruptly.*]

WIDOW QUIN [*shouting after him*].   Let you give him a good vengeance when you come up with him, but don't put yourself in the power of the law, for it'd be a poor thing to see a judge in his black cap reading out his sentence on a civil warrior the like of you. [*She swings the door to and looks at* CHRISTY, *who is cowering in terror, for a moment, then she bursts into a laugh.*]

WIDOW QUIN.   Well, you're the walking Playboy of the Western World, and that's the poor man you had divided to his breeches belt.

CHRISTY [*looking out: then, to her*].   What'll Pegeen say when she hears that story? What'll she be saying to me now?

WIDOW QUIN.   She'll knock the head of you, I'm thinking, and drive you from the door. God help her to be taking you for a wonder, and you a little schemer making up the story you destroyed your da.

CHRISTY [*turning to the door, nearly speechless with rage, half to himself*].   To be letting on he was dead, and coming back to his life, and following after me like an old weazel tracing a rat, and coming in here laying desolation between my own self and the fine women of Ireland, and he a kind of carcase that you'd fling upon the sea . . .

WIDOW QUIN [*more soberly*].   There's talking for a man's one only son.

CHRISTY [*breaking out*].   His one son, is it? May I meet him with one tooth and it aching, and one eye to be seeing seven and seventy divils in the twists of the road, and one old timber leg on him to limp into the scalding grave. [*Looking out.*] There he is now crossing the strands, and that the Lord God would send a high wave to wash him from the world.

WIDOW QUIN [*scandalized*].   Have you no shame? [*Putting her hand on his shoulder and turning him round.*] What ails you? Near crying, is it?

CHRISTY [*in despair and grief*].   Amn't I after seeing the love-light of the star of knowledge shining from her brow, and hearing words would put you thinking on the holy Brigid speaking to the infant saints, and now she'll be turning again, and speaking hard words to me, like an old woman with a spavindy ass she'd have, urging on a hill.

WIDOW QUIN.   There's poetry talk for a girl you'd see itching and scratching, and she with a stale stink of poteen on her from selling in the shop.

CHRISTY [*impatiently*].   It's her like is fitted to be handling merchandise in the heavens above, and what'll I be doing now, I ask you, and I a kind of wonder was jilted by the heavens when a day was by.

[*There is a distant noise of girls' voices.* WIDOW QUIN *looks from window and comes to him, hurriedly.*]

WIDOW QUIN.   You'll be doing like myself, I'm thinking, when I did destroy my man, for I'm above many's the day, odd times in great spirits, abroad in the sunshine, darning a stocking or stitching a shift; and odd times again looking out on the schooners, hookers, trawlers is sailing the sea, and I thinking on the gallant hairy fellows are drifting beyond, and myself long years living alone.

CHRISTY [*interested*].   You're like me, so.

WIDOW QUIN.   I am your like, and it's for that I'm taking a fancy to you, and I with my little houseen above where there'd be myself to tend you, and none to ask were you a murderer or what at all.

CHRISTY.   And what would I be doing if I left Pegeen?

WIDOW QUIN.   I've nice jobs you could be doing, gathering shells to make a whitewash for our hut within, building up a little goosehouse, or stretching a new skin on an old currach I have, and if my hut is far from all sides, it's there you'll meet the wisest old men, I tell you, at the corner of my wheel, and it's there yourself and me will have great times whispering and hugging. . . .

VOICES [*outside, calling far away*].   Christy! Christy Mahon! Christy!

CHRISTY.   Is it Pegeen Mike?

WIDOW QUIN.   It's the young girls, I'm thinking, coming to bring you to the sports below, and what is it you'll have me to tell them now?

CHRISTY.   Aid me for to win Pegeen. It's herself only that I'm seeking now.

[WIDOW QUIN *gets up and goes to window.*]

Aid me for to win her, and I'll be asking God to stretch a hand to you in the hour of death, and lead you short cuts through the Meadows of Ease, and up the floor of Heaven to the Footstool of the Virgin's Son.

WIDOW QUIN.   There's praying.

VOICES [*nearer*].   Christy! Christy Mahon!

CHRISTY [*with agitation*].   They're coming. Will you swear to aid and save me for the love of Christ?

WIDOW QUIN [*looks at him for a moment*].   If I aid you, will you swear to give me a right of way I want, and a mountainy ram, and a load of dung at Michaelmas, the time that you'll be master here?

CHRISTY.   I will, by the elements and stars of night.

WIDOW QUIN.   Then we'll not say a word of the old fellow, the way
Pegeen won't know your story till the end of time.

CHRISTY.   And if he chances to return again?

WIDOW QUIN.   We'll swear he's a maniac and not your da. I could
take an oath I seen him raving on the sands to-day.

[*Girls run in.*]

SUSAN.   Come on to the sports below. Pegeen says you're to come.

SARA TANSEY.   The lepping's beginning, and we've a jockey's suit to
fit upon you for the mule race on the sands below.

HONOR.   Come on, will you?

CHRISTY.   I will then if Pegeen's beyond.

SARA TANSEY.   She's in the boreen[1] making game of Shaneen
Keogh.

CHRISTY.   Then I'll be going to her now.

[*He runs out followed by the girls.*]

WIDOW QUIN.   Well, if the worst comes in the end of all, it'll be
great game to see there's none to pity him but a widow woman,
the like of me, has buried her children and destroyed her man.
[*She goes out.*]

Act 3

SCENE, *as before. Later in the day.* JIMMY *comes in, slightly drunk.*

JIMMY [*calls*].   Pegeen! [*Crosses to inner door.*] Pegeen Mike!
[*Comes back again into the room.*] Pegeen!

[PHILLY *comes in in the same state.*]

[*To* PHILLY.] Did you see herself?

PHILLY.   I did not; but I sent Shawn Keogh with the ass cart for to
bear him home. [*Trying cupboards which are locked.*] Well, isn't
he a nasty man to get into such staggers at a morning wake? and
isn't herself the divil's daughter for locking, and she so fussy after
that young gaffer, you might take your death with drought and
none to heed you?

JIMMY.   It's little wonder she'd be fussy, and he after bringing
bankrupt ruin on the roulette man, and the trick-o'-the-loop
man, and breaking the nose of the cockshot-man, and winning
all in the sports below, racing, lepping, dancing, and the Lord
knows what! He's right luck, I'm telling you.

PHILLY.   If he has, he'll be rightly hobbled yet, and he not able to
say ten words without making a brag of the way he killed his father, and the great blow he hit with the loy.

JIMMY.   A man can't hang by his own informing, and his father
should be rotten by now.

1. Small path.

[OLD MAHON *passes window slowly.*]

PHILLY.   Supposing a man's digging spuds in that field with a long spade, and supposing he flings up the two halves of that skull, what'll be said then in the papers and the courts of law?

JIMMY.   They'd say it was an old Dane, maybe, was drowned in the flood.

[OLD MAHON *comes in and sits down near door listening.*]

Did you never hear tell of the skulls they have in the city of Dublin, ranged out like blue jugs in a cabin of Connaught?[2]

PHILLY.   And you believe that?

JIMMY [*pugnaciously*].   Didn't a lad see them and he after coming from harvesting in the Liverpool boat? "They have them there," says he, "making a show of the great people there was one time walking the world. White skulls and black skulls and yellow skulls, and some with full teeth, and some haven't only but one."

PHILLY.   It was no lie, maybe, for when I was a young lad there was a graveyard beyond the house with the remnants of a man who had thighs as long as your arm. He was a horrid man, I'm telling you, and there was many a fine Sunday I'd put him together for fun, and he with shiny bones, you wouldn't meet the like of these days in the cities of the world.

MAHON [*getting up*].   You wouldn't, is it? Lay your eyes on that skull, and tell me where and when there was another the like of it, is splintered only from the blow of a loy.

PHILLY.   Glory be to God! And who hit you at all?

MAHON [*triumphantly*].   It was my own son hit me. Would you believe that?

JIMMY.   Well, there's wonders hidden in the heart of man!

PHILLY [*suspiciously*].   And what way was it done?

MAHON [*wandering about the room*].   I'm after walking hundreds and long scores of miles, winning clean beds and the fill of my belly four times in the day, and I doing nothing but telling stories of that naked truth. [*He comes to them a little aggressively.*] Give me a supeen[3] and I'll tell you now.

[WIDOW QUIN *comes in and stands aghast behind him. He is facing* JIMMY *and* PHILLY, *who are on the left.*]

JIMMY.   Ask herself beyond. She's the stuff hidden in her shawl.

WIDOW QUIN [*coming to* MAHON *quickly*]. You here, is it? You didn't go far at all?

MAHON.   I seen the coasting steamer passing, and I got a drought upon me and a cramping leg, so I said, "The divil go along with him," and turned again. [*Looking under her shawl.*] And let you give me a supeen, for I'm destroyed travelling since Tuesday was a week.

2. Danish Vikings settled Dublin c. 850, but never penetrated Connacht in the west of Ireland.
3. Small drink.

WIDOW QUIN [*getting a glass, in a cajoling tone*].   Sit down then by
the fire and take your ease for a space. You've a right to be destroyed indeed, with your walking, and fighting, and facing the
sun [*giving him poteen from a stone jar she has brought in*]. There
now is a drink for you, and may it be to your happiness and
length of life.

MAHON [*taking glass greedily and sitting down by fire*].   God increase you!

WIDOW QUIN [*taking men to the right stealthily*].   Do you know
what? That man's raving from his wound to-day, for I met him a
while since telling a rambling tale of a tinker had him destroyed.
Then he heard of Christy's deed, and he up and says it was his
son had cracked his skull. O isn't madness a fright, for he'll go
killing someone yet, and he thinking it's the man has struck him
so?

JIMMY [*entirely convinced*].   It's a fright, surely. I knew a party was
kicked in the head by a red mare, and he went killing horses a
great while, till he eat the insides of a clock and died after.

PHILLY [*with suspicion*].   Did he see Christy?

WIDOW QUIN.   He didn't. [*With a warning gesture.*] Let you not be
putting him in mind of him, or you'll be likely summoned if
there's murder done. [*Looking round at* MAHON.] Whisht! He's listening. Wait now till you hear me taking him easy and unravel-
ling all. [*She goes to* MAHON.] And what way are you feeling,
mister? Are you in contentment now?

MAHON [*slightly emotional from his drink*].   I'm poorly only, for it's
a hard story the way I'm left to-day, when it was I did tend him
from his hour of birth, and he a dunce never reached his second
book, the way he'd come from school, many's the day, with his
legs lamed under him, and he blackened with his beatings like a
tinker's ass. It's a hard story, I'm saying, the way some do have
their next and nighest raising up a hand of murder on them, and
some is lonesome getting their death with lamentation in the
dead of night.

WIDOW QUIN [*not knowing what to say*].   To hear you talking so
quiet, who'd know you were the same fellow we seen pass to-day?

MAHON.   I'm the same surely. The wrack and ruin of three score
years; and it's a terror to live that length, I tell you, and to have
your sons going to the dogs against you, and you wore out scolding them, and skelping them, and God knows what.

PHILLY [*to* JIMMY].   He's not raving. [*To* WIDOW QUIN.] Will you ask
him what kind was his son?

WIDOW QUIN [*to* MAHON, *with a peculiar look*].   Was your son that
hit you a lad of one year and a score maybe, a great hand at racing and lepping and licking the world?

MAHON [*turning on her with a roar of rage*].   Didn't you hear me
say he was the fool of men, the way from this out he'll know the
orphan's lot with old and young making game of him and they
swearing, raging, kicking at him like a mangy cur.

[*A great burst of cheering outside, some way off.*]

MAHON [*putting his hands to his ears*].   What in the name of God do they want roaring below?

WIDOW QUIN [*with the shade of a smile*].   They're cheering a young lad, the champion Playboy of the Western World.

[*More cheering.*]

MAHON [*going to window*].   It'd split my heart to hear them, and I with pulses in my brain-pan for a week gone by. Is it racing they are?

JIMMY [*looking from door*].   It is then. They are mounting him for the mule race will be run upon the sands. That's the playboy on the winkered[4] mule.

MAHON [*puzzled*].   That lad, is it? If you said it was a fool he was, I'd have laid a mighty oath he was the likeness of my wandering son [*uneasily, putting his hand to his head*]. Faith, I'm thinking I'll go walking for to view the race.

WIDOW QUIN [*stopping him, sharply*].   You will not. You'd best take the road to Belmullet, and not be dilly-dallying in this place where there isn't a spot you could sleep.

PHILLY [*coming forward*].   Don't mind her. Mount there on the bench and you'll have a view of the whole. They're hurrying before the tide will rise, and it'd be near over if you went down the pathway through the crags below.

MAHON [*mounts on bench*, WIDOW QUIN *beside him*].   That's a right view again the edge of the sea. They're coming now from the point. He's leading. Who is he at all?

WIDOW QUIN.   He's the champion of the world, I tell you, and there isn't a hop'orth isn't falling lucky to his hands to-day.

PHILLY [*looking out, interested in the race*].   Look at that. They're pressing him now.

JIMMY.   He'll win it yet.

PHILLY.   Take your time, Jimmy Farrell. It's too soon to say.

WIDOW QUIN [*shouting*].   Watch him taking the gate. There's riding.

JIMMY [*cheering*].   More power to the young lad!

MAHON.   He's passing the third.

JIMMY.   He'll lick them yet!

WIDOW QUIN.   He'd lick them if he was running races with a score itself.

MAHON.   Look at the mule he has, kicking the stars.

WIDOW QUIN.   There was a lep! [*Catching hold of* MAHON *in her excitement.*] He's fallen! He's mounted again! Faith, he's passing them all!

JIMMY.   Look at him skelping[5] her!

4. Wearing a harness with blinders.
5. Whipping.

PHILLY.   And the mountain girls hooshing him on!

JIMMY.   It's the last turn! The post's cleared for them now!

MAHON.   Look at the narrow place. He'll be into the bogs! [*With a yell.*] Good rider! He's through it again!

JIMMY.   He neck and neck!

MAHON.   Good boy to him! Flames, but he's in!

[*Great cheering, in which all join.*]

MAHON [*with hesitation*].   What's that? They're raising him up. They're coming this way. [*With a roar of rage and astonishment.*] It's Christy! by the stars of God! I'd know his way of spitting and he astride the moon.

[*He jumps down and makes for the door, but* WIDOW QUIN *catches him and pulls him back.*]

WIDOW QUIN.   Stay quiet, will you. That's not your son. [*To* JIMMY.] Stop him, or you'll get a month for the abetting of manslaughter and be fined as well.

JIMMY.   I'll hold him.

MAHON [*struggling*].   Let me out! Let me out, the lot of you! till I have my vengeance on his head to-day.

WIDOW QUIN [*shaking him, vehemently*].   That's not your son. That's a man is going to make a marriage with the daughter of this house, a place with fine trade, with a license, and with poteen too.

MAHON [*amazed*].   That man marrying a decent and a moneyed girl! Is it mad yous are? Is it in a crazy-house for females that I'm landed now?

WIDOW QUIN.   It's mad yourself is with the blow upon your head. That lad is the wonder of the Western World.

MAHON.   I seen it's my son.

WIDOW QUIN.   You seen that you're mad.

[*Cheering outside.*]

Do you hear them cheering him in the zig-zags of the road? Aren't you after saying that your son's a fool, and how would they be cheering a true idiot born?

MAHON [*getting distressed*].   It's maybe out of reason that that man's himself.

[*Cheering again.*]

There's none surely will go cheering him. Oh, I'm raving with a madness that would fright the world! [*He sits down with his hand to his head.*] There was one time I seen ten scarlet divils letting on they'd cork my spirit in a gallon can; and one time I seen rats as big as badgers sucking the life blood from the butt of my lug;[6]

6. My earlobe.

but I never till this day confused that dribbling idiot with a likely man. I'm destroyed surely.

WIDOW QUIN.   And who'd wonder when it's your brain-pan that is gaping now?

MAHON.   Then the blight of the sacred drought upon myself and him, for I never went mad to this day, and I not three weeks with the Limerick girls drinking myself silly, and parlatic from the dusk to dawn. [*To* WIDOW QUIN, *suddenly.*] Is my visage astray?

WIDOW QUIN.   It is then. You're a sniggering maniac, a child could see.

MAHON [*getting up more cheerfully*].   Then I'd best be going to the union[7] beyond, and there'll be a welcome before me, I tell you [*with great pride*], and I a terrible and fearful case, the way that there I was one time, screeching in a straitened waistcoat, with seven doctors writing out my sayings in a printed book. Would you believe that?

WIDOW QUIN.   If you're a wonder itself, you'd best be hasty, for them lads caught a maniac one time and pelted the poor creature till he ran out, raving and foaming, and was drowned in the sea.

MAHON [*with philosophy*].   It's true mankind is the divil when your head's astray. Let me out now and I'll slip down the boreen, and not see them so.

WIDOW QUIN [*showing him out*].   That's it. Run to the right, and not a one will see.

[*He runs off.*]

PHILLY [*wisely*].   You're at some gaming, Widow Quin; but I'll walk after him and give him his dinner and a time to rest, and I'll see then if he's raving or as sane as you.

WIDOW QUIN [*annoyed*].   If you go near that lad, let you be wary of your head, I'm saying. Didn't you hear him telling he was crazed at times?

PHILLY.   I heard him telling a power; and I'm thinking we'll have right sport, before night will fall. [*He goes out.*]

JIMMY.   Well, Philly's a conceited and foolish man. How could that madman have his senses and his brain-pan slit? I'll go after them and see him turn on Philly now.

[*He goes;* WIDOW QUIN *hides poteen behind counter. Then hubbub outside.*]

VOICES.   There you are! Good jumper! Grand lepper! Darlint boy! He's the racer! Bear him on, will you!

[CHRISTY *comes in, in Jockey's dress, with* PEGEEN MIKE, SARA, *and other* GIRLS, *and* MEN.]

PEGEEN [*to crowd*].   Go on now and don't destroy him and he

_____
7. Public-assistance workhouse.

drenching with sweat. Go along, I'm saying, and have your tug-of-warring till he's dried his skin.

CROWD.   Here's his prizes! A bagpipes! A fiddle was played by a poet in the years gone by! A flat and three-thorned blackthorn[8] would lick the scholars out of Dublin town!

CHRISTY [*taking prizes from the* MEN].   Thank you kindly, the lot of you. But you'd say it was little only I did this day if you'd seen me a while since striking my one single blow.

TOWN CRIER [*outside, ringing a bell*].   Take notice, last event of this day! Tug-of-warring on the green below! Come on, the lot of you! Great achievements for all Mayo men!

PEGEEN.   Go on, and leave him for to rest and dry. Go on, I tell you, for he'll do no more.

  [*She hustles crowd out;* WIDOW QUIN *following them.*]

MEN [*going*].   Come on then. Good luck for the while!

PEGEEN [*radiantly, wiping his face with her shawl*].   Well, you're the lad, and you'll have great times from this out when you could win that wealth of prizes, and you sweating in the heat of noon!

CHRISTY [*looking at her with delight*].   I'll have great times if I win the crowning prize I'm seeking now, and that's your promise that you'll wed me in a fortnight, when our banns is called.

PEGEEN [*backing away from him*].   You've right daring to go ask me that, when all knows you'll be starting to some girl in your own townland, when your father's rotten in four months, or five.

CHRISTY [*indignantly*].   Starting from you, is it? [*He follows her*]. I will not, then, and when the airs is warming in four months, or five, it's then yourself and me should be pacing Neifin in the dews of night, the times sweet smells do be rising, and you'd see a little shiny new moon, maybe, sinking on the hills.

PEGEEN [*looking at him playfully*].   And it's that kind of a poacher's love you'd make, Christy Mahon, on the sides of Neifin, when the night is down?

CHRISTY.   It's little you'll think if my love's a poacher's, or an earl's itself, when you'll feel my two hands stretched around you, and I squeezing kisses on your puckered lips, till I'd feel a kind of pity for the Lord God is all ages sitting lonesome in his golden chair.

PEGEEN.   That'll be right fun, Christy Mahon, and any girl would walk her heart out before she'd meet a young man was your like for eloquence, or talk, at all.

CHRISTY [*encouraged*].   Let you wait, to hear me talking, till we're astray in Erris, when Good Friday's by, drinking a sup from a well, and making mighty kisses with our wetted mouths, or gaming in a gap or sunshine, with yourself stretched back unto your necklace, in the flowers of the earth.

PEGEEN [*in a lower voice, moved by his tone*].   I'd be nice so, is it?

CHRISTY [*with rapture*].   If the mitred bishops seen you that time,

---

8. Walking cane or shilelagh.

they'd be the like of the holy prophets, I'm thinking, do be straining the bars of Paradise to lay eyes on the Lady Helen of Troy,
and she abroad, pacing back and forward, with a nosegay in her
golden shawl.

PEGEEN [*with real tenderness*].   And what is it I have, Christy Mahon, to make me fitting entertainment for the like of you, that
has such poet's talking, and such bravery of heart?

CHRISTY [*in a low voice*].   Isn't there the light of seven heavens in
your heart alone, the way you'll be an angel's lamp to me from
this out, and I abroad in the darkness, spearing salmons in the
Owen, or the Carrowmore?

PEGEEN.   If I was your wife, I'd be along with you those nights,
Christy Mahon, the way you'd see I was a great hand at coaxing
bailiffs,[9] or coining funny nick-names for the stars of night.

CHRISTY.   You, is it? Taking your death in the hailstones, or in the
fogs of dawn.

PEGEEN.   Yourself and me would shelter easy in a narrow bush,
[*with a qualm of dread*] but we're only talking, maybe, for this
would be a poor, thatched place to hold a fine lad is the like of
you.

CHRISTY [*putting his arm round her*].   If I wasn't a good Christian,
it's on my naked knees I'd be saying my prayers and paters to
every jack-straw you have roofing your head, and every stony peb-
ble is paving the laneway to your door.

PEGEEN [*radiantly*].   If that's the truth, I'll be burning candles
from this out to the miracles of God that have brought you from
the south to-day, and I, with my gowns bought ready, the way
that I can wed you, and not wait at all.

CHRISTY.   It's miracles, and that's the truth. Me there toiling a long
while, and walking a long while, not knowing at all I was drawing
all times nearer to this holy day.

PEGEEN.   And myself, a girl, was tempted often to go sailing the
seas till I'd marry a Jew-man, with ten kegs of gold, and I not
knowing at all there was the like of you drawing nearer, like the
stars of God.

CHRISTY.   And to think I'm long years hearing women talking that
talk, to all bloody fools, and this the first time I've heard the like
of your voice talking sweetly for my own delight.

PEGEEN.   And to think it's me is talking sweetly, Christy Mahon,
and I the fright of seven townlands for my biting tongue. Well,
the heart's a wonder; and, I'm thinking, there won't be our like in
Mayo, for gallant lovers, from this hour, to-day.

[*Drunken singing is heard outside.*]

There's my father coming from the wake, and when he's had his
sleep we'll tell him, for he's peaceful then.

[*They separate.*]

9. A legal officer serving court papers; more formally, an "enforcement agent."

MICHAEL [*singing outside.*]

> The jailor and the turnkey
> They quickly ran us down,
> And brought us back as prisoners
> Once more to Cavan town.

[*He comes in supported by* SHAWN.]

> There we lay bewailing
> All in a prison bound. . . .

[*He sees* CHRISTY. *Goes and shakes him drunkenly by the hand, while* PEGEEN *and* SHAWN *talk on the left.*]

MICHAEL [*to* CHRISTY].   The blessing of God and the holy angels on your head, young fellow. I hear tell you're after winning all in the sports below; and wasn't it a shame I didn't bear you along with me to Kate Cassidy's wake, a fine, stout lad, the like of you, for you'd never see the match of it for flows of drink, the way when we sunk her bones at noonday in her narrow grave, there were five men, aye, and six men, stretched out retching speechless on the holy stones.

CHRISTY [*uneasily, watching* PEGEEN].   Is that the truth?

MICHAEL.   It is then, and aren't you a louty schemer to go burying your poor father unbeknownst when you'd a right to throw him on the crupper of a Kerry mule and drive him westwards, like holy Joseph in the days gone by, the way we could have given him a decent burial, and not have him rotting beyond, and not a Christian drinking a smart drop to the glory of his soul?

CHRISTY [*gruffly*].   It's well enough he's lying, for the likes of him.

MICHAEL [*slapping him on the back*].   Well, aren't you a hardened slayer? It'll be a poor thing for the household man where you go sniffing for a female wife; and [*pointing to* SHAWN] look beyond at that shy and decent Christian I have chosen for my daughter's hand, and I after getting the gilded dispensation this day for to wed them now.

CHRISTY.   And you'll be wedding them this day, is it?

MICHAEL [*drawing himself up*].   Aye. Are you thinking, if I'm drunk itself, I'd leave my daughter living single with a little frisky rascal is the like of you?

PEGEEN [*breaking away from* SHAWN].   Is it the truth the dispensation's come?

MICHAEL [*triumphantly*].   Father Reilly's after reading it in gallous[1] Latin, and "It's come in the nick of time," says he; "so I'll wed them in a hurry, dreading that young gaffer who'd capsize the stars."

---

1. Grand, powerful, or impressive.

PEGEEN [*fiercely*].   He's missed his nick of time, for it's that lad, Christy Mahon, that I'm wedding now.

MICHAEL [*loudly with horror*].   You'd be making him a son to me, and he wet and crusted with his father's blood?

PEGEEN.   Aye. Wouldn't it be a bitter thing for a girl to go marrying the like of Shaneen, and he a middling kind of a scarecrow, with no savagery or fine words in him at all?

MICHAEL [*gasping and sinking on a chair*].   Oh, aren't you a heathen daughter to go shaking the fat of my heart, and I swamped and drownded with the weight of drink? Would you have them turning on me the way that I'd be roaring to the dawn of day with the wind upon my heart? Have you not a word to aid me, Shaneen? Are you not jealous at all?

SHANEEN [*in great misery*].   I'd be afeard to be jealous of a man did slay his da.

PEGEEN.   Well, it'd be a poor thing to go marrying your like. I'm seeing there's a world of peril for an orphan girl, and isn't it a great blessing I didn't wed you, before himself came walking from the west or south?

SHAWN.   It's a queer story you'd go picking a dirty tramp up from the highways of the world.

PEGEEN [*playfully*].   And you think you're a likely beau to go straying along with, the shiny Sundays of the opening year, when it's sooner on a bullock's liver you'd put a poor girl thinking than on the lily or the rose?

SHAWN.   And have you no mind of my weight of passion, and the holy dispensation, and the drift of heifers I am giving, and the golden ring?

PEGEEN.   I'm thinking you're too fine for the like of me, Shawn Keogh of Killakeen, and let you go off till you'd find a radiant lady with droves of bullocks on the plains of Meath, and herself bedizened in the diamond jewelleries of Paraoh's ma. That'd be your match, Shaneen. So God save you now! [*She retreats behind* CHRISTY.]

SHAWN.   Won't you hear me telling you . . . ?

CHRISTY [*with ferocity*].   Take yourself from this, young fellow, or I'll maybe add a murder to my deeds to-day.

MICHAEL [*springing up with a shriek*].   Murder is it? Is it mad yous are? Would you go making murder in this place, and it piled with poteen for our drink tonight? Go on to the foreshore if it's fighting you want, where the rising tide will wash all traces from the memory of man.

[*Pushing* SHAWN *towards* CHRISTY.]

SHAWN [*shaking himself free, and getting behind* MICHAEL].   I'll not fight him, Michael James. I'd liefer live a bachelor, simmering in passions to the end of time, than face a leaping savage the like of him has descended from the Lord knows where. Strike him your-

self, Michael James, or you'll lose my drift of heifers and my blue
bull from Sneem.

MICHAEL.   Is it me fight him, when it's father-slaying he's bred to
now? [*Pushing* SHAWN.] Go on you fool and fight him now.

SHAWN [*coming forward a little*].   Will I strike him with my hand?

MICHAEL.   Take the loy is on your western side.

SHAWN.   I'd be afeard of the gallows if I struck him with that.

CHRISTY [*taking up the loy*].   Then I'll make you face the gallows or
quit off from this.

> [SHAWN *flies out of the door.*]

CHRISTY.   Well, fine weather be after him, [*going to* MICHAEL, *coax-
ingly*] and I'm thinking you wouldn't wish to have that quaking
blackguard in your house at all. Let you give us your blessing and
hear her swear her faith to me, for I'm mounted on the springtide
of the stars of luck, the way it'll be good for any to have me in the
house.

PEGEEN [*at the other side of* MICHAEL].   Bless us now, for I swear to
God I'll wed him, and I'll not renege.

MICHAEL [*standing up in the centre, holding on to both of them*].
It's the will of God, I'm thinking, that all should win an easy or a
cruel end, and it's the will of God that all should rear up lengthy
families for the nurture of the earth. What's a single man, I ask
you, eating a bit in one house and drinking a sup in another, and
he with no place of his own, like an old braying jackass strayed
upon the rocks? [*To* CHRISTY.] It's many would be in dread to
bring your like into their house for to end them, maybe, with a
sudden end; but I'm a decent man of Ireland, and I liefer face
the grave untimely and I seeing a score of grandsons growing up
little gallant swearers by the name of God, than go peopling my
bedside with puny weeds the like of what you'd breed, I'm thinking, out of Shaneen Keogh. [*He joins their hands.*] A daring fellow is the jewel of the world, and a man did split his father's
middle with a single clout, should have the bravery of ten, so may
God and Mary and St. Patrick bless you, and increase you from
this mortal day.

CHRISTY *and* PEGEEN.   Amen, O Lord!

> [*Hubbub outside.*]

> [OLD MAHON *rushes in, followed by all the crowd, and* WIDOW
> QUIN. *He makes a rush at* CHRISTY, *knocks him down, and be-
> gins to beat him.*]

PEGEEN [*dragging back his arm*].   Stop that, will you. Who are you
at all?

MAHON.   His father, God forgive me!

PEGEEN [*drawing back*].   Is it rose from the dead?

MAHON.   Do you think I look so easy quenched with the tap of a
loy? [*Beats* CHRISTY *again.*]

PEGEEN [*glaring at* CHRISTY].   And it's lies you told, letting on you had him slitted, and you nothing at all.

CHRISTY [*catching* MAHON's *stick*].   He's not my father. He's a raving maniac would scare the world. [*Pointing to* WIDOW QUIN.] Herself knows it is true.

CROWD.   You're fooling Pegeen! The Widow Quin seen him this day, and you likely knew! You're a liar!

CHRISTY [*dumbfounded*].   It's himself was a liar, lying stretched out with an open head on him, letting on he was dead.

MAHON.   Weren't you off racing the hills before I got my breath with the start I had seeing you turn on me at all?

PEGEEN.   And to think of the coaxing glory we had given him, and he after doing nothing but hitting a soft blow and chasing northward in a sweat of fear. Quit off from this.

CHRISTY [*piteously*].   You've seen my doings this day, and let you save me from the old man; for why would you be in such a scorch of haste to spur me to destruction now?

PEGEEN.   It's there your treachery is spurring me, till I'm hard set to think you're the one I'm after lacing in my heart-strings half-an-hour gone by. [*To* MAHON.] Take him on from this, for I think bad the world should see me raging for a Munster liar, and the fool of men.

MAHON.   Rise up now to retribution, and come on with me.

CROWD [*jeeringly*].   There's the playboy! There's the lad thought he'd rule the roost in Mayo. Slate him now, mister.

CHRISTY [*getting up in shy terror*].   What is it drives you to torment me here, when I'd asked the thunders of the might of God to blast me if I ever did hurt to any saving only that one single blow.

MAHON [*loudly*].   If you didn't, you're a poor good-for-nothing, and isn't it by the like of you the sins of the whole world are committed.

CHRISTY [*raising his hands*].   In the name of the Almighty God. . . .

MAHON.   Leave troubling the Lord God. Would you have him sending down droughts, and fevers, and the old hen and the cholera morbus?[2]

CHRISTY [*to* WIDOW QUIN].   Will you come between us and protect me now?

WIDOW QUIN.   I've tried a lot, God help me, and my share is done.

CHRISTY [*looking round in desperation*].   And I must go back into my torment is it, or run off like a vagabond straying through the Unions with the dusts of August making mudstains in the gullet of my throat, or the winds of March blowing on me till I'd take an oath I felt them making whistles of my ribs within?

SARA.   Ask Pegeen to aid you. Her like does often change.

CHRISTY.   I will not then, for there's torment in the splendour of her like, and she a girl any moon of midnight would take pride to meet, facing southwards on the heaths of Keel. But what did I

---

2. Gastroenteritis, rather than classic, contagious cholera.

want crawling forward to scorch my understanding at her flaming brow?

PEGEEN [*to* MAHON, *vehemently, fearing she will break into tears*]. Take him on from this or I'll set the young lads to destroy him here.

MAHON [*going to him, shaking his stick*].   Come on now if you wouldn't have the company to see you skelped.

PEGEEN [*half laughing, through her tears*].   That's it, now the world will see him pandied, and he an ugly liar was playing off the hero, and the fright of men.

CHRISTY [*to* MAHON, *very sharply*].   Leave me go!

CROWD.   That's it. Now Christy. If them two set fighting, it will lick the world.

MAHON [*making a grab at* CHRISTY].   Come here to me.

CHRISTY [*more threateningly*].   Leave me go, I'm saying.

MAHON.   I will maybe, when your legs is limping, and your back is blue.

CROWD.   Keep it up, the two of you. I'll back the old one. Now the playboy.

CHRISTY [*in low and intense voice*].   Shut your yelling, for if you're after making a mighty man of me this day by the power of a lie, you're setting me now to think if it's a poor thing to be lonesome, it's worse maybe to go mixing with the fools of earth.

[MAHON *makes a movement towards him.*]

CHRISTY [*almost shouting*].   Keep off . . . lest I do show a blow unto the lot of you would set the guardian angels winking in the clouds above. [*He swings round with a sudden rapid movement and picks up a loy.*]

CROWD [*half frightened, half amused*].   He's going mad! Mind yourselves! Run from the idiot!

CHRISTY.   If I am an idiot, I'm after hearing my voice this day saying words would raise the topknot on a poet in a merchant's town. I've won your racing, and your lepping, and . . .

MAHON.   Shut your gullet and come on with me.

CHRISTY.   I'm going, but I'll stretch you first.

[*He runs at* OLD MAHON *with the loy, chases him out of the door, followed by crowd and* WIDOW QUIN. *There is a great noise outside, then a yell, and dead silence for a moment.* CHRISTY *comes in, half dazed, and goes to fire.*]

WIDOW QUIN [*coming in, hurriedly, and going to him*].   They're turning again you. Come on, or you'll be hanged, indeed.

CHRISTY.   I'm thinking, from this out, Pegeen'll be giving me praises the same as in the hours gone by.

WIDOW QUIN [*impatiently*].   Come by the back-door. I'd think bad to have you stifled on the gallows tree.

CHRISTY [*indignantly*].   I will not, then. What good'd be my lifetime, if I left Pegeen?

WIDOW QUIN.   Come on, and you'll be no worse than you were last night; and you with a double murder this time to be telling to the girls.

CHRISTY.   I'll not leave Pegeen Mike.

WIDOW QUIN [*impatiently*].   Isn't there the match of her in every parish public, from Binghamstown unto the plain of Meath? Come on, I tell you, and I'll find you finer sweethearts at each waning moon.

CHRISTY.   It's Pegeen I'm seeking only, and what'd I care if you brought me a drift of chosen females, standing in their shifts it-self, maybe, from this place to the Eastern World?

SARA [*runs in, pulling off one of her petticoats*].   They're going to hang him. [*Holding out petticoat and shawl.*] Fit these upon him, and let him run off to the east.

WIDOW QUIN.   He's raving now; but we'll fit them on him, and I'll take him, in the ferry, to the Achill boat.

CHRISTY [*struggling feebly*].   Leave me go, will you? when I'm thinking of my luck to-day, for she will wed me surely, and I a proven hero in the end of all.

[*They try to fasten petticoat around him.*]

WIDOW QUIN.   Take his left hand, and we'll pull him now. Come on, young fellow.

CHRISTY [*suddenly starting up*].   You'll be taking me from her? You're jealous, is it, of her wedding me? Go on from this. [*He snatches up a stool, and threatens them with it.*]

WIDOW QUIN [*going*].   It's in the mad-house they should put him, not in jail, at all. We'll go by the back-door, to call the doctor, and we'll save him so.

[*She goes out, with* SARA, *through inner room.* MEN *crowd in the doorway.* CHRISTY *sits down again by the fire.*]

MICHAEL [*in a terrified whisper*].   Is the old lad killed surely?

PHILLY.   I'm after feeling the last gasps quitting his heart.

[*They peer in at* CHRISTY.]

MICHAEL [*with a rope*].   Look at the way he is. Twist a hangman's knot on it, and slip it over his head, while he's not minding at all.

PHILLY.   Let you take it, Shaneen. You're the soberest of all that's here.

SHAWN.   Is it me to go near him, and he the wickedest and worst with me? Let you take it, Pegeen Mike.

PEGEEN.   Come on, so.

[*She goes forward with the others, and they drop the double hitch over his head.*]

CHRISTY.   What ails you?

SHAWN [*triumphantly, as they pull the rope tight on his arms*]. Come on to the peelers, till they stretch you now.

CHRISTY.   Me!

MICHAEL.   If we took pity on you, the Lord God would, maybe,
bring us ruin from the law to-day, so you'd best come easy, for
hanging is an easy and a speedy end.

CHRISTY.   I'll not stir. [*To* PEGEEN.] And what is it you'll say to me,
and I after doing it this time in the face of all?

PEGEEN.   I'll say, a strange man is a marvel, with his mighty talk;
but what's a squabble in your back-yard, and the blow of a loy,
have taught me that there's a great gap between a gallous story
and a dirty deed.[3] [*To* MEN.] Take him on from this, or the lot of
us will be likely put on trial for his deed to-day.

CHRISTY [*with horror in his voice*].   And it's yourself will send me
off, to have a horny-fingered hangman hitching his bloody slip-
knots at the butt of my ear.

MEN [*pulling rope*].   Come on, will you?

[*He is pulled down on the floor.*]

CHRISTY [*twisting his legs round the table*].   Cut the rope, Pegeen,
and I'll quit the lot of you, and live from this out, like the madmen of Keel, eating muck and green weeds, on the faces of the
cliffs.

PEGEEN.   And leave us to hang, is it, for a saucy liar, the like of
you? [*To* MEN.] Take him on, out from this.

SHAWN.   Pull a twist on his neck, and squeeze him so.

PHILLY.   Twist yourself. Sure he cannot hurt you if you keep your
distance from his teeth alone.

SHAWN.   I'm afeard of him. [*To* PEGEEN.] Lift a lighted sod, will
you, and scorch his leg.

PEGEEN [*blowing the fire, with a bellows*].   Leave go now, young
fellow, or I'll scorch your shins.

CHRISTY.   You're blowing for to torture me. [*His voice rising and
growing stronger.*] That's your kind, is it? Then let the lot of you
be wary, for, if I've to face the gallows, I'll have a gay march
down, I tell you, and shed the blood of some of you before I die.

SHAWN [*in terror*].   Keep a good hold, Philly. Be wary, for the love
of God. For I'm thinking he would liefest wreak his pains on me.

CHRISTY [*almost gaily*].   If I do lay my hands on you, it's the way
you'll be at the fall of night, hanging as a scarecrow for the fowls
of hell. Ah, you'll have a gallous jaunt I'm saying, coaching out
through Limbo with my father's ghost.

SHAWN [*to* PEGEEN].   Make haste, will you? Oh, isn't he a holy terror, and isn't it true for Father Reilly, that all drink's a curse that
has the lot of you so shaky and uncertain now?

CHRISTY.   If I can wring a neck among you, I'll have a royal judgment looking on the trembling jury in the courts of law. And
won't there be crying out in Mayo the day I'm stretched upon the

---

3. Between a grand tale and actual fact.

rope with ladies in their silks and satins snivelling in their lacy kerchiefs, and they rhyming songs and ballads on the terror of my fate? [*He squirms round on the floor and bites* SHAWN's *leg.*]

SHAWN [*shrieking*].   My leg's bit on me. He's the like of a mad dog, I'm thinking, the way that I will surely die.

CHRISTY [*delighted with himself*].   You will then, the way you can shake out hell's flags of welcome for my coming in two weeks or three, for I'm thinking Satan hasn't many have killed their da in Kerry, and in Mayo too.

> [OLD MAHON *comes in behind on all fours and looks on unnoticed.*]

MEN [*to* PEGEEN].   Bring the sod, will you?

PEGEEN [*coming over*].   God help him so. [*Burns his leg.*]

CHRISTY [*kicking and screaming*].   O, glory be to God!

> [*He kicks loose from the table, and they all drag him towards the door.*]

JIMMY [*seeing* OLD MAHON].   Will you look what's come in?

> [*They all drop* CHRISTY *and run left.*]

CHRISTY [*scrambling on his knees face to face with* OLD MAHON]. Are you coming to be killed a third time, or what ails you now?

MAHON.   For what is it they have you tied?

CHRISTY.   They're taking me to the peelers to have me hanged for slaying you.

MICHAEL [*apologetically*].   It is the will of God that all should guard their little cabins from the treachery of law, and what would my daughter be doing if I was ruined or was hanged itself?

MAHON [*grimly, loosening* CHRISTY].   It's little I care if you put a bag on her back, and went picking cockles till the hour of death; but my son and myself will be going our own way, and we'll have great times from this out telling stories of the villainy of Mayo, and the fools is here. [*To* CHRISTY, *who is freed.*] Come on now.

CHRISTY.   Go with you, is it? I will then, like a gallant captain with his heathen slave. Go on now and I'll see you from this day stewing my oatmeal and washing my spuds, for I'm master of all fights from now. [*Pushing* MAHON.] Go on, I'm saying.

MAHON.   Is it me?

CHRISTY.   Not a word out of you. Go on from this.

MAHON [*walking out and looking back at* CHRISTY *over his shoulder*]. Glory be to God! [*With a broad smile.*] I am crazy again! [*Goes.*]

CHRISTY.   Ten thousand blessings upon all that's here, for you've turned me a likely gaffer in the end of all, the way I'll go romancing through a romping lifetime from this hour to the dawning of the judgment day. [*He goes out.*]

MICHAEL.   By the will of God, we'll have peace now for our drinks. Will you draw the porter, Pegeen?

SHAWN [*going up to her*].   It's a miracle Father Reilly can wed us in the end of all, and we'll have none to trouble us when his vicious bite is healed.

PEGEEN [*hitting him a box on the ear*].   Quit my sight. [*Putting her shawl over her head and breaking out into wild lamentations.*] Oh my grief, I've lost him surely. I've lost the only Playboy of the Western World.

BERNARD SHAW

John Bull's Other Island[†]

Characters

BROADBENT
LARRY DOYLE
TIM HAFFIGAN
HODSON
PETER KEEGAN
PATSY FARRELL
FATHER DEMPSEY
CORNEY DOYLE
BARNEY DORAN
MATTHEW HAFFIGAN
AUNT JUDY
NORA

PERIOD—*The Present. London and Ireland*

ACT ONE *Office of Broadbent and Doyle, Civil Engineers, Great George Street, Westminster*

ACT TWO *Scene 1: Roscullen Hill*
Scene 2: The Round Tower

ACT THREE—*The Grass Plot before Corney Doyle's House*

ACT FOUR *Scene 1: The Parlor at Corney Doyle's*
Scene 2: Roscullen Hill

Act 1

Great George Street, Westminster, is the address of Doyle and Broadbent, civil engineers. On the threshold one reads that the firm con-

sists of MR LAURENCE DOYLE *and* MR THOMAS BROADBENT, *and that their rooms are on the first floor. Most of these rooms are private; for the partners, being bachelors and bosom friends, live there; and the door marked Private, next the clerk's office, is their domestic sitting room as well as their reception room for clients. Let me describe it briefly from the point of view of a sparrow on the window sill. The outer door is in the opposite wall, close to the right hand corner. Between this door and the left hand corner is a hatstand and a table consisting of large drawing boards on trestles, with plans, rolls of tracing paper, mathematical instruments, and other draughtsman's accessories on it. In the left hand wall is the fireplace, and the door of an inner room between the fireplace and our observant sparrow. Against the right hand wall is a filing cabinet, with a cupboard on it, and, nearer, a tall office desk and stool for one person. In the middle of the room a large double writing table is set across, with a chair at each end for the two partners. It is a room which no woman would tolerate, smelling of tobacco, and much in need of repapering, repainting, and recarpeting; but this is the effect of bachelor untidiness and indifference, not want of means; for nothing that* DOYLE *and* BROADBENT *themselves have purchased is cheap; nor is anything they want lacking. On the walls hang a large map of South America, a pictorial advertisement of a steamship company, an impressive portrait of Gladstone, and several caricatures of Mr Balfour as a rabbit and Mr Chamberlain as a fox by Francis Carruthers Gould.*[1]

At twenty minutes to five o'clock on a summer afternoon in 1904, the room is empty. Presently the outer door is opened, and a VALET *comes in laden with a large Gladstone bag and a strap of rugs. He carries them into the inner room. He is a respectable valet, old enough to have lost all alacrity and acquired an air of putting up patiently with a great deal of trouble and indifferent health. The luggage belongs to* BROADBENT, *who enters after the valet. He pulls off his overcoat and hangs it with his hat on the stand. Then he comes to the writing table and looks through the letters waiting there for him. He is a robust, full-blooded, energetic man in the prime of life, sometimes eager and credulous, sometimes shrewd and roguish, sometimes portentously solemn, sometimes jolly and impetuous, always buoyant and irresistible, mostly likeable, and enormously absurd in his most earnest moments. He bursts open his letters with his thumb, and glances through them, flinging the envelopes about the floor with reckless untidiness whilst he talks to the valet.*

BROADBENT [*calling*].　　Hodson.

HODSON [*in the bedroom*].　　Yes sir.

---

1. W. E. Gladstone (1809–98), liberal prime minister associated with Home Rule for Ireland; Arthur James Balfour (1848–1930), conservative statesman, chief secretary for Ireland, associated with authoritarian British presence in Ireland; Joseph Chamberlain (1836–1914), MP from Birmingham opposed to Home Rule and involved in negotiation of Irish policies and treaties; Francis Carruthers Gould (1844–1925), caricaturist.

BROADBENT.   Don't unpack. Just take out the things I've worn; and put in clean things.

HODSON [*appearing at the bedroom door*].   Yes sir. [*He turns to go back into the bedroom.*]

BROADBENT.   And look here!

[HODSON *turns again.*]

Do you remember where I put my revolver?

HODSON.   Revolver, sir! Yes sir. Mr Doyle uses it as a paper-weight, sir, when he's drawing.

BROADBENT.   Well, I want it packed. Theres a packet of cartridges somewhere, I think. Find it and pack it as well.

HODSON.   Yes sir.

BROADBENT.   By the way, pack your own traps too. I shall take you with me this time.

HODSON [*hesitant*].   Is it a dangerous part youre going to, sir? Should I be expected to carry a revolver, sir?

BROADBENT.   Perhaps it might be as well. I'm going to Ireland.

HODSON [*reassured*].   Yes, sir.

BROADBENT.   You don't feel nervous about it, I suppose?

HODSON.   Not at all, sir. I'll risk it, sir.

BROADBENT.   Ever been in Ireland?

HODSON.   No sir. I understand it's a very wet climate, sir. I'd better pack your india-rubber overalls.

BROADBENT.   Do. Wheres Mr Doyle?

HODSON.   I'm expecting him at five, sir. He went out after lunch.

BROADBENT.   Anybody been looking for me?

HODSON.   A person giving the name of Haffigan has called twice today, sir.

BROADBENT.   Oh, I'm sorry. Why didn't he wait? I told him to wait if I wasnt in.

HODSON.   Well sir, I didnt know you expected him; so I thought it best to—to—not to encourage him, sir.

BROADBENT.   Oh, he's all right. He's an Irishman, and not very particular about his appearance.

HODSON.   Yes sir: I noticed that he was rather Irish.

BROADBENT.   If he calls again let him come up.

HODSON.   I think I saw him waiting about, sir, when you drove up. Shall I fetch him, sir?

BROADBENT.   Do, Hodson.

HODSON.   Yes sir. [*He makes for the outer door.*]

BROADBENT.   He'll want tea. Let us have some.

HODSON [*stopping*].   I shouldnt think he drank tea, sir.

BROADBENT.   Well, bring whatever you think he'd like.

HODSON.   Yes sir.

[*An electric bell rings.*]

Here he is, sir. Saw you arrive, sir.

BROADBENT.   Right. Shew him in.

[HODSON *goes out.* BROADBENT *gets through the rest of his letters before* HODSON *returns with the visitor.*]

HODSON.   Mr Affigan.

[HAFFIGAN *is a stunted, shortnecked, smallheaded man of about 30, with a small bullet head, a red nose, and furtive eyes. He is dressed in seedy black, almost clerically, and might be a tenth-rate schoolmaster ruined by drink. He hastens to shake* BROADBENT's *hand with a show of reckless geniality and high spirits, helped out by a rollicking stage brogue. This is perhaps a comfort to himself, as he is secretly pursued by the horrors of incipient delirium tremens.*]

HAFFIGAN.   Tim Haffigan, sir, at your service. The top o the mornin to you, Misther Broadbent.

BROADBENT [*delighted with his Irish visitor*].   Good afternoon, Mr Haffigan.

TIM.   An is it the afthernoon it is already? Begorra, what I call the mornin is all the time a man fasts afther breakfast.

BROADBENT.   Havnt you lunched?

TIM.   Divil a lunch!

BROADBENT.   I'm sorry I couldnt get back from Brighton in time to offer you some; but—

TIM.   Not a word, sir, not a word. Sure itll do tomorrow. Besides, I'm Irish, sir: a poor aither, but a powerful dhrinker.

BROADBENT.   I was just about to ring for tea when you came. Sit down, Mr Haffigan.

TIM.   Tay is a good dhrink if your nerves can stand it. Mine cant.

[HAFFIGAN *sits down at the writing table, with his back to the filing cabinet.* BROADBENT *sits opposite him.* HODSON *enters empty-handed; takes two glasses, a siphon, and a tantalus from the cupboard; places them before* BROADBENT *on the writing table; looks ruthlessly at* HAFFIGAN, *who cannot meet his eye; and retires.*]

BROADBENT.   Try a whisky and soda.

TIM [*sobered*].   There you touch the national wakeness, sir. [*Piously.*] Not that I share it meself. Ive seen too much of the mischief of it.

BROADBENT [*pouring the whisky*].   Say when.

TIM.   Not too sthrong.

[BROADBENT *stops and looks inquiringly at him*].

Say half-an-half.

[BROADBENT, *somewhat startled by this demand, pours a little more, and again stops and looks*].

Just a dhrain more: the lower half o the tumbler doesnt hold a fair half. Thankya.

BROADBENT [*laughing*].   You Irishmen certainly do know how to drink. [*Pouring some whisky for himself.*] Not thats my poor English idea of a whisky and soda.

TIM.   An a very good idea it is too. Dhrink is the curse o me unhappy counthry. I take it meself because Ive a wake heart and a poor digestion; but in principle I'm a tee-toatler.

BROADBENT [*suddenly solemn and strenuous*].   So am I, of course. I'm a Local Optionist[2] to the backbone. You have no idea, Mr Haffigan, of the ruin that is wrought in this country by the unholy alliance of the publicans, the bishops, the Tories, and The Times. We must close the public-houses at all costs. [*He drinks.*]

TIM.   Sure I know. It's awful, [*He drinks.*] I see youre a good Liberal like meself, sir.

BROADBENT.   I am a lover of liberty, like every true Englishman, Mr Haffigan. My name is Broadbent. If my name were Breitstein, and I had a hooked nose and a house in Park Lane, I should carry a Union Jack handkerchief and a penny trumpet, and tax the food of the people to support the Navy League, and clamor for the destruction of the last remnants of national liberty—

TIM.   Not another word. Shake hands.

BROADBENT.   But I should like to explain—

TIM.   Sure I know every word youre goin to say before yev said it. *I* know the sort o man yar. An so youre thinkin o comin to Ireland for a bit?

BROADBENT.   Where else can I go? I am an Englishman and a Liberal; and now that South Africa has been enslaved and destroyed, there is no country left to me to take an interest in but Ireland. Mind; I dont say that an Englishman has not other duties. He has a duty to Finland and a duty to Macedonia. But what sane man can deny that an Englishman's first duty is his duty to Ireland? Unfortunately, we have politicians here more unscrupulous than Bobrikoff,[3] more bloodthirsty than Abdul the Damned;[4] and it is under their heel that Ireland is now writhing.

TIM.   Faith, theyve reckoned up with poor oul Bobrikoff anyhow.

BROADBENT.   Not that I defend assassination: God forbid! However strongly we may feel that the unfortunate and patriotic young man who avenged the wrongs of Finland on the Russian tyrant was perfectly right from his own point of view, yet every civilized man must regard murder with abhorrence. Not even in defence of Free Trade would I lift my hand against a political opponent, however richly he might deserve it.

TIM.   I'm sure you wouldnt; and I honor you for it. Youre goin to Ireland, then, out o sympathy: is it?

BROADBENT.   I'm going to develop an estate there for the Land De-

2. Advocate of community right to permit or prohibit alcoholic beverages.
3. Nikolay Bobrikov (1839–1904), dictatorial Russian administrator of Finnish territory.
4. Abdul-Hamid II (1842–1918), despot ruler of the Ottoman Empire.

velopment Syndicate, in which I am interested. I am convinced
that all it needs to make it pay is to handle it properly, as estates
are handled in England. You know the English plan, Mr Haffigan, dont you?

TIM.   Bedad I do, sir. Take all you can out of Ireland and spend it
in England: thats it.

BROADBENT [*not quite liking this*].   My plan, sir, will be to take a
little money out of England and spend it in Ireland.

TIM.   More power to your elbow! an may your shadda never be
less! for youre the broth of a boy intirely. An how can I help you?
Command me to the last dhrop o me blood.

BROADBENT.   Have you ever heard of Garden City?[5]

TIM [*doubtfully*].   D'ye mane Heavn?

BROADBENT.   Heaven! No: it's near Hitchin. If you can spare half
an hour I'll go into it with you.

TIM.   I tell you hwat. Gimme a prospectus. Lemmy take it home
and reflect on it.

BROADBENT.   Youre quite right: I will. [*He gives him a copy of
Ebenezer Howard's book,[6] and several pamphlets.*] You understand
that the map of the city—the circular construction—is only a
suggestion.

TIM.   I'll make a careful note o that [*looking dazedly at the map*].

BROADBENT.   What I say is, why not start a Garden City in Ireland?

TIM [*with enthusiasm*].   Thats just what was on the tip o me
tongue to ask you. Why not? [*Defiantly*]. Tell me why not.

BROADBENT.   There are difficulties. I shall overcome them; but
there are difficulties. When I first arrive in Ireland I shall be
hated as an Englishman. As a Protestant, I shall be denounced
from every altar. My life may be in danger. Well, I am prepared to
face that.

TIM.   Never fear, sir. We know how to respict a brave innimy.

BROADBENT.   What I really dread is misunderstanding. I think you
could help me to avoid that. When I heard you speak the other
evening in Bermondsey at the meeting of the National League,[7] I
saw at once that you were— You wont mind my speaking frankly?

TIM.   Tell me all me faults as man to man. I can stand anything
but flatthery.

BROADBENT.   May I put it this way? that I saw at once that you are
a thorough Irishman, with all the faults and all the qualities of
your race: rash and improvident but brave and goodnatured; not
likely to succeed in business on your own account perhaps, but
eloquent, humorous, a lover of freedom, and a true follower of
that great Englishman Gladstone.

TIM.   Spare me blushes. I mustnt sit here to be praised to me face.

5. Urban planning movement founded in 1898 by Ebenezer Howard in England.
6. *Tomorrow: A Peaceful Path to Real Reform* (1898).
7. Organization, founded in 1882, for the return of Irish land to Irish ownership.

But I confess to the goodnature: it's an Irish wakeness. I'd share me last shillin with a friend.

BROADBENT.   I feel sure you would. Mr Haffigan.

TIM [*impulsively*].   Damn it! call me Tim. A man that talks about Ireland as you do may call me anything. Gimmy a howlt o that whisky bottle [*he replenishes*].

BROADBENT [*smiling indulgently*].   Well, Tim, will you come with me and help to break the ice between me and your warmhearted, impulsive countrymen?

TIM.   Will I come to Madagascar or Cochin China[8] wid you? Bedad I'll come to the North Pole wid you if yll pay me fare; for the divil a shillin I have to buy a third class ticket.

BROADBENT.   Ive not forgotten that, Tim. We must put that little matter on a solid English footing, though the rest can be as Irish as you please. You must come as my—my—well, I hardly know what to call it. If we call you my agent, theyll shoot you. If we call you a bailiff, theyll duck you in the horsepond. I have a secretary already; and—

TIM.   Then we'll call him the Home Secretary and me the Irish Secretary. Eh?

BROADBENT [*laughing industriously*].   Capital. Your Irish wit has settled the first difficulty. Now about your salary—

TIM.   A salary, is it? Sure I'd do it for nothin, only me cloes ud disgrace you; and I'd be dhriven to borra money from your friends: a thing thats agin me nacher. But I wont take a penny more than a hundherd a year. [*He looks with restless cunning at* BROADBENT, *trying to guess how far he may go.*]

BROADBENT.   If that will satisfy you—

TIM [*more than reassured*].   Why shouldnt it satisfy me? A hundherd a year is twelve pound a month, isnt it?

BROADBENT.   No. Eight pound six and eightpence.

TIM.   Oh murdher! An I'll have to sind five timmy poor oul mother in Ireland. But no matther: I said a hundherd; and what I said I'll stick to, if I have to starve for it.

BROADBENT [*with business caution*].   Well, let us say twelve pounds for the first month. Afterwards, we shall see how we get on.

TIM.   Youre a gentleman, sir. Whin me mother turns up her toes, you shall take the five pounds off; for your expinses must be kep down wid a sthrong hand; an— [*He is interrupted by the arrival of* BROADBENT'*s partner*].

[MR LAURENCE DOYLE *is a man of 36, with cold grey eyes, strained nose, fine fastidious lips, critical brows, clever head, rather refined and goodlooking on the whole, but with a suggestion of thin-skinnedness and dissatisfaction that contrasts strongly with* BROADBENT'*s eupeptic jollity.*

8.   Historic region of Southeast Asia subject to colonialism.

He comes in as a man at home there, but on seeing the
stranger shrinks at once, and is about to withdraw when
BROADBENT *reassures him. He then comes forward to the*
table, between the two others.]

DOYLE [*retreating*].   Youre engaged.

BROADBENT.   Not at all, not at all. Come in. [*To* TIM.] This gentleman is a friend who lives with me here: my partner, Mr DOYLE.
[*To* DOYLE.] This is a new Irish friend of mine, Mr Tim Haffigan.

TIM [*rising with effusion*].   Sure it's meself thats proud to meet any
friend o Misther Broadbent's. The top o the mornin to you, sir!
Me heart goes out teeye both. It's not often I meet two such
splendid speciments iv the Anglo-Saxon race.

BROADBENT [*chuckling*].   Wrong for once, Tim. My friend Mr
Doyle is a countryman of yours.

[TIM *is noticeably dashed by this announcement. He draws in*
his horns at once, and scowls suspiciously at DOYLE *under a*
vanishing mask of goodfellowship: cringing a little, too, in
mere nerveless fear of him.]

DOYLE [*with cool disgust*].   Good evening. [*He retires to the fire-*
place, and says to BROADBENT *in a tone which conveys the strongest*
possible hint to HAFFIGAN *that he is unwelcome.*] Will you soon be
disengaged?

TIM [*his brogue decaying into a common would-be genteel accent*
with an unexpected strain of Glasgow in it]. I must be going. Avn-
mpoartnt engeegement in the west end.

BROADBENT [*rising*].   It's settled, then, that you come with me.

TIM.   Ashll be verra pleased to accompany ye, sir.

BROADBENT.   But how soon? Can you start tonight? from Paddington? We go by Milford Haven.

TIM [*hesitating*].   Well—A'm afraid—A

[DOYLE *goes abruptly into the bedroom, slamming the door*
and shattering the last remnant of TIM's *nerve. The poor*
wretch saves himself from bursting into tears by plunging
again into his role of daredevil Irishman. He rushes to BROAD-
BENT; *plucks at his sleeve with trembling fingers; and pours*
forth his entreaty with all the brogue he can muster, subduing
his voice lest DOYLE *should hear and return.*]

Misther Broadbent: dont humiliate me before a fella counthry-
man. Look here: me cloes is up the spout. Gimmy a fypoun-
note—I'll pay ya nex Choosda whin me ship comes home—or
you can stop it out of me month's sallery. I'll be on the platform
at Paddnton punctial an ready. Gimmy it quick, before he comes
back. You wont mind me axin, will ye?

BROADBENT.   Not at all. I was about to offer you an advance for
travelling expenses. [*He gives him a bank note*].

TIM [*pocketing it*].   Thank you. I'll be there half an hour before the
thrain starts.

[LARRY *is heard at the bedroom door, returning.*]

Whisht: he's comin back. Goodbye an God bless ye. [*He hurries out almost crying, the £5 note and all the drink it means to him being too much for his empty stomach and overstrained nerves.*]

DOYLE [*returning*].   Where the devil did you pick up that seedy swindler? What was he doing here? [*He goes up to the table where the plans are, and makes a note on one of them, referring to his pocket book as he does so.*]

BROADBENT.   There you go! Why are you so down on every Irishman you meet, especially if he's a bit shabby? poor devil! Surely a fellow-countryman may pass you the top of the morning without offence, even if his coat is a bit shiny at the seams.

DOYLE [*contemptuously*].   The top of the morning! Did he call you the broth of a boy? [*He comes to the writing table.*]

BROADBENT [*triumphantly*].   Yes.

DOYLE.   And wished you more power to your elbow?

BROADBENT.   He did.

DOYLE.   And that your shadow might never be less?

BROADBENT.   Certainly.

DOYLE [*taking up the depleted whisky bottle and shaking his head at it*].   And he got about half a pint of whisky out of you.

BROADBENT.   It did him no harm. He never turned a hair.

DOYLE.   How much money did he borrow?

BROADBENT.   It was not borrowing exactly. He shewed a very honorable spirit about money. I believe he would share his last shilling with a friend.

DOYLE.   No doubt he would share his friend's last shilling if his friend was fool enough to let him. How much did he touch you for?

BROADBENT.   Oh, nothing. An advance on his salary—for travelling expenses.

DOYLE.   Salary! In Heaven's name, what for?

BROADBENT.   For being my Home Secretary, as he very wittily called it.

DOYLE.   I dont see the joke.

BROADBENT.   You can spoil any joke by being cold blooded about it. I saw it all right when he said it. It was something—something really very amusing—about the Home Secretary and the Irish Secretary. At all events, he's evidently the very man to take with me to Ireland to break the ice for me. He can gain the confidence of the people there, and make them friendly to me, Eh? [*He seats himself on the office stool, and tilts it back so that the edge of the standing desk supports his back and prevents his toppling over.*]

DOYLE.   A nice introduction, by George! Do you suppose the whole population of Ireland consists of drunken begging letter writers, or that even if it did, they would accept one another as references?

BROADBENT.   Pooh! nonsense! he's only an Irishman. Besides, you
dont seriously suppose that Haffigan can humbug me, do you?

DOYLE.   No: he's too lazy to take the trouble. All he has to do is to
sit there and drink your whisky while you humbug yourself. However, we neednt argue about Haffigan, for two reasons. First,
with your money in his pocket he will never reach Paddington:
there are too many public houses on the way. Second, he's not an
Irishman at all.

BROADBENT.   Not an Irishman! [*He is so amazed by the statement
that he straightens himself and brings the stool bolt upright.*]

DOYLE.   Born in Glasgow. Never was in Ireland in his life. I know
all about him.

BROADBENT.   But he spoke—he behaved just like an Irishman.

DOYLE.   Like an Irishman!! Man alive, dont you know that all this
top-o-the-morning and broth-of-a-boy and more-power-to-your-
elbow business is got up in England to fool you, like the Albert
Hall concerts of Irish music? No Irishman ever talks like that in
Ireland, or ever did, or ever will. But when a thoroughly worthless Irishman comes to England, and finds the whole place full of
romantic duffers like you, who will let him loaf and drink and
sponge and brag as long as he flatters your sense of moral superiority by playing the fool and degrading himself and his country,
he soon learns the antics that take you in. He picks them up at
the theatre or the music hall. Haffigan learnt the rudiments from
his father, who came from my part of Ireland. I knew his uncles,
Matt and Andy Haffigan of Rosscullen.

BROADBENT [*still incredulous*].   But his brogue?

DOYLE.   His brogue! A fat lot you know about brogues! Ive heard
you call a Dublin accent that you could hang your hat on, a
brogue. Heaven help you! you dont know the difference between
Connemara and Rathmines.[9] [*With violent irritation.*] Oh, damn
Tim Haffigan! lets drop the subject: he's not worth wrangling
about.

BROADBENT.   Whats wrong with you today, Larry? Why are you so
bitter?

> [DOYLE *looks at him perplexedly; comes slowly to the writing
> table; and sits down at the end next to the fireplace before re-
> plying.*]

DOYLE.   Well: your letter completely upset me, for one thing.

BROADBENT.   Why?

LARRY.   Your foreclosing this Rosscullen mortgage and turning
poor Nick Lestrange out of house and home has rather taken me
aback; for I liked the old rascal when I was a boy and had the run
of his park to play in. I was brought up on the property.

BROADBENT.   But he wouldnt pay the interest. I had to foreclose
on behalf of the Syndicate. So now I'm off to Rosscullen to look

---

9. The difference between a wild, western, rural district and a Dublin suburb.

after the property myself. [*He sits down at the writing table oppo-site* LARRY, *and adds, casually, but with an anxious glance at his partner.*] Youre coming with me, of course?

DOYLE [*rising nervously and recommencing his restless movements*]. Thats it. Thats what I dread. Thats what has upset me.

BROADBENT.   But dont you want to see your country again after 18 years absence? to see your people? to be in the old home again? to—

DOYLE [*interrupting him very impatiently*].   Yes, yes: I know all that as well as you do.

BROADBENT.   Oh well, of course [*with a shrug*] if you take it in that way, I'm sorry.

DOYLE.   Never you mind my temper: it's not meant for you, as you ought to know by this time. [*He sits down again, a little ashamed of his petulance; reflects a moment bitterly; then bursts out*] I have an instinct against going back to Ireland: an instinct so strong that I'd rather go with you to the South Pole than to Rosscullen.

BROADBENT.   What! Here you are, belonging to a nation with the strongest patriotism! the most inveterate homing instinct in the world! and you pretend youd rather go anywhere than back to Ireland. You dont suppose I believe you, do you? In your heart—

DOYLE.   Never mind my heart: an Irishman's heart is nothing but his imagination. How many of all those millions that have left Ireland have ever come back or wanted to come back? But whats the use of talking to you? Three verses of twaddle about the Irish emigrant "sitting on the stile, Mary," or three hours of Irish patri-otism in Bermondsey or the Scotland Division of Liverpool, go further with you than all the facts that stare you in the face. Why, man alive, look at me! You know the way I nag, and worry, and carp, and cavil, and disparage, and am never satisfied and never quiet, and try the patience of my best friends.

BROADBENT.   Oh, come, Larry! do yourself justice. Youre very amusing and agreeable to strangers.

DOYLE.   Yes, to strangers. Perhaps if I was a bit stiffer to strangers, and a bit easier at home, like an Englishman, I'd be better com-pany for you.

BROADBENT.   We get on well enough. Of course you have the melancholy of the Keltic race—

DOYLE [*bounding out of his chair*].   Good God!!!

BROADBENT [*slyly*].   —and also its habit of using strong language when theres nothing the matter.

DOYLE.   Nothing the matter! When people talk about the Celtic race, I feel as if I could burn down London. That sort of rot does more harm than ten Coercion Acts.[1] Do you suppose a man need be a Celt to feel melancholy in Rosscullen? Why, man, Ireland was peopled just as England was; and its breed was crossed by just the same invaders.

_____

1. Introductions of martial law to suppress rebellion.

BROADBENT.   True. All the capable people in Ireland are of English extraction. It has often struck me as a most remarkable circumstance that the only party in parliament which shews the genuine old English character and spirit is the Irish party. Look at its independence, its determination, its defiance of bad Governments, its sympathy with oppressed nationalities all the world over! How English!

DOYLE.   Not to mention the solemnity with which it talks old-fashioned nonsense which it knows perfectly well to be a century behind the times. Thats English, if you like.

BROADBENT.   No, Larry, no. You are thinking of the modern hybrids that now monopolize England. Hypocrites, humbugs, Germans, Jews, Yankees, foreigners, Park Laners, cosmopolitan riffraff. Dont call them English. They dont belong to the dear old island, but to their confounded new empire; and by George! theyre worthy of it; and I wish them joy of it.

DOYLE [unmoved by this outburst].   There! You feel better now, dont you?

BROADBENT [defiantly].   I do. Much better.

DOYLE.   My dear Tom, you only need a touch of the Irish climate to be as big a fool as I am myself. If all my Irish blood were poured into your veins, you wouldnt turn a hair of your constitution and character. Go and marry the most English English-woman you can find, and then bring up your son in Rosscullen; and that son's character will be so like mine and so unlike yours that everybody will accuse me of being his father. [With sudden anguish.] Rosscullen! oh, good Lord, Rosscullen! The dullness! the hopelessness! the ignorance! the bigotry!

BROADBENT [matter-of-factly].   The usual thing in the country, Larry. Just the same here.

DOYLE [hastily].   No, no: the climate is different. Here, if the life is dull, you can be dull too, and no great harm done. [Going off into a passionate dream.] But your wits cant thicken in that soft moist air, on those white springy roads, in those misty rushes and brown bogs, on those hillsides of granite rocks and magenta heather. Youve no such colors in the sky, no such lure in the distances, no such sadness in the evenings. Oh, the dreaming! the dreaming! the torturing, heartscalding, never satisfying dreaming, dreaming, dreaming, dreaming! [Savagely.] No debauchery that ever coarsened and brutalized an Englishman can take the worth and usefulness out of him like that dreaming. An Irishman's imagination never lets him alone, never convinces him, never satisfies him; but it makes him that he cant face reality nor deal with it nor handle it nor conquer it: he can only sneer at them that do, and [bitterly, at BROADBENT] be "agreeable to strangers," like a good-for-nothing woman on the streets. [Gabbling at BROADBENT across the table.] It's all dreaming, all imagination. He cant be religious. The inspired Churchman that teaches him the sanctity of life and the importance of conduct is sent away empty; while the poor village priest that gives him a miracle or a sentimental story of a saint, has cathedrals built for him out of the pennies of the poor. He cant be intelligently political; he dreams of what the Shan Van Vocht said in ninetyeight.[2] If you want to interest him in Ireland youve got to call the unfortunate island Kathleen in Hoolihan and pretend shes a little old woman. It saves thinking. It saves working. It saves everything except imagination, imagination, imagination; and imagination's such a torture that you cant bear it without whisky. [*With fierce shivering self-contempt.*] At last you get that you can bear nothing real at all: youd rather starve than cook a meal; youd rather go shabby and dirty than set your mind to take care of your clothes and wash yourself; you nag and squabble at home because your wife isnt an angel, and she despises you because youre not a hero; and you hate the whole lot round you because theyre only poor slovenly useless devils like yourself. [*Dropping his voice like a man making some shameful confidence.*] And all the while there goes on a horrible, senseless, mischievous laughter. When youre young, you exchange drinks with other young men; and you exchange vile stories with them; and as youre too futile to be able to help or cheer them, you chaff and sneer and taunt them for not doing the things you darent do yourself. And all the time you laugh! laugh! laugh! eternal derision, eternal envy, eternal folly, eternal fouling and staining and degrading, until, when you come at last to a country where men take a question seriously and give a serious answer to it, you deride them for having no sense of humor, and plume yourself on your own worthlessness as if it made you better than them.

BROADBENT [*roused to intense earnestness by* DOYLE's *eloquence*]. Never despair, Larry. There are great possibilities for Ireland. Home Rule[3] will work wonders under English guidance.

DOYLE [*pulled up short, his face twitching with a reluctant smile*]. Tom, why do you select my most tragic moments for your most irresistible strokes of humor?

BROADBENT.   Humor! I was perfectly serious. What do you mean? Do you doubt my seriousness about Home Rule?

DOYLE.   I am sure you are serious, Tom, about the English guidance.

BROADBENT [*quite reassured*].   Of course I am. Our guidance is the important thing. We English must place our capacity for government without stint at the service of nations who are less fortunately endowed in that respect; so as to allow them to develop in perfect freedom to the English level of self-government, you know. You understand me?

DOYLE.   Perfectly. And Rosscullen will understand you too.

---

2. The Shan Van Vocht, personification of Ireland as an old woman foretelling the arrival of the French to aid Irish rebellion.
3. Local government for Ireland by restoration of the Irish parliament.

BROADBENT [*cheerfully*].   Of course it will. So thats all right. [*He pulls up his chair and settles himself comfortably to lecture* DOYLE]. Now, Larry, Ive listened carefully to all youve said about Ireland; and I can see nothing whatever to prevent your coming with me. What does it all come to? Simply that you were only a young fellow when you were in Ireland. Youll find all that chaffing and drinking and not knowing what to be at in Peckham just the same as in Donnybrook. You looked at Ireland with a boy's eyes and saw only boyish things. Come back with me and look at it with a man's; and get a better opinion of your country.

DOYLE.   I daresay youre partly right in that: at all events I know very well that if I had been the son of a laborer instead of the son of a country landagent, I should have struck more grit than I did. Unfortunately I'm not going back to visit the Irish nation, but to visit my father and Aunt Judy and Nora Reilly and Father Dempsey and the rest of them.

BROADBENT.   Well, why not? Theyll be delighted to see you, now that England has made a man of you.

DOYLE [*struck by this*].   Ah! you hit the mark there, Tom, with true British inspiration.

BROADBENT.   Common sense, you mean.

DOYLE [*quickly*].   No I dont: youve no more common sense than a gander. No Englishman has any common sense, or ever had, or ever will have. Youre going on a sentimental expedition for perfectly ridiculous reasons, with your head full of political nonsense that would not take in any ordinarily intelligent donkey; but you can hit me in the eye with the simple truth about myself and my father.

BROADBENT [*amazed*].   I never mentioned your father.

DOYLE [*not heeding the interruption*].   There he is in Rosscullen, a landagent who's always been in a small way because he's a Catholic, and the landlords are mostly Protestants. What with land courts reducing rents and Land Purchase Acts turning big estates into little holdings, he'd be a beggar if he hadnt taken to collecting the new purchase instalments instead of the old rents. I doubt if he's been further from home than Athenmullet for twenty years. And here am I, made a man of, as you say, by England.

BROADBENT [*apologetically*].   I assure you I never meant—

DOYLE.   Oh, dont apologize: it's quite true. I daresay Ive learnt something in America and a few other remote and inferior spots; but in the main it is by living with you and working in double harness with you that I have learnt to live in a real world and not in an imaginary one. I owe more to you than to any Irishman.

BROADBENT [*shaking his head with a twinkle in his eye*].   Very friendly of you, Larry, old man, but all blarney. I like blarney; but it's rot, all the same.

DOYLE.   No it's not. I should never have done anything without you; though I never stop wondering at that blessed old head of yours with all its ideas in watertight compartments, and all the compartments warranted impervious to anything it doesnt suit you to understand.

BROADBENT [*invincible*].   Unmitigated rot, Larry, I assure you.

DOYLE.   Well, at any rate you will admit that all my friends are either Englishmen or men of the big world that belongs to the big Powers. All the serious part of my life has been lived in that atmosphere: all the serious part of my work has been done with men of that sort. Just think of me as I am now going back to Rosscullen! to that hell of littleness and monotony! How am I to get on with a little country landagent that ekes out his 5 per cent with a little farming and a scrap of house property in the nearest country town? What am I to say to him? What is he to say to me?

BROADBENT [*scandalized*].   But youre father and son, man!

DOYLE.   What difference does that make? What would you say if I proposed a visit to your father?

BROADBENT [*with filial rectitude*].   I always made a point of going to see my father regularly until his mind gave way.

DOYLE [*concerned*].   He has gone mad? You never told me.

BROADBENT.   He has joined the Tariff Reform League.[4] He would never have done that if his mind had not been weakened. [*Beginning to declaim.*] He has fallen a victim to the arts of a political charlatan who—

DOYLE [*interrupting him*].   You mean that you keep clear of your father because he differs from you about Free Trade, and you dont want to quarrel with him. Well, think of me and my father! He's a Nationalist and a Separatist. I'm a metallurgical chemist turned civil engineer. Now whatever else metallurgical chemistry may be, it's not national. It's international. And my business and yours as civil engineers is to join countries, not to separate them. The one real political conviction that our business has rubbed into us is that frontiers are hindrances and flags confounded nuisances.

BROADBENT [*still smarting under Mr Chamberlain's[5] economic heresy*].   Only when there is a protective tariff—

DOYLE [*firmly*].   Now look here, Tom: you want to get in a speech on Free Trade; and youre not going to do it: I wont stand it. My father wants to make St George's Channel a frontier and hoist a green flag on College Green; and I want to bring Galway within 3 hours of Colchester and 24 of New York. I want Ireland to be the brains and imagination of a big Commonwealth, not a Robinson Crusoe island. Then theres the religious difficulty. My Catholicism is the Catholicism of Charlemagne or Dante, qualified by a great deal of modern science and folklore which Father

---

4. An organization for the abolition of all protective tariffs; a conservative position, associated below with Joseph Chamberlain, and antithetical to the liberal position, associated below with Broadbent, of tariffs as beneficial economic control.

5. Joseph Chamberlain (1836–1914), proponent of tax reform in response to international trade.

Dempsey would call the ravings of an Atheist. Well, my father's Catholicism is the Catholicism of Father Dempsey.

BROADBENT [*shrewdly*].   I dont want to interrupt you, Larry; but you know this is all gammon.[6] These differences exist in all families; but the members rub on together all right. [*Suddenly relapsing into portentousness.*] Of course there are some questions which touch the very foundations of morals; and on these I grant you even the closest relationships cannot excuse any compromise or laxity. For instance—

DOYLE [*impatiently springing up and walking about*].   For instance, Home Rule, South Africa, Free Trade, and putting the Church schools on the Education Rate. Well, I should differ from my father on every one of them, probably, just as I differ from you about them.

BROADBENT.   Yes; but you are an Irishman; and these things are not serious to you as they are to an Englishman.

DOYLE.   What! not even Home Rule!

BROADBENT [*steadfastly*].   Not even Home Rule. We owe Home Rule not to the Irish, but to our English Gladstone.[7] No, Larry: I cant help thinking that theres something behind all this.

DOYLE [*hotly*].   What is there behind it? Do you think I'm humbugging you?

BROADBENT.   Dont fly out, old chap. I only thought—

DOYLE.   What did you think?

BROADBENT.   Well, a moment ago I caught a name which is new to me: a Miss Nora Reilly, I think.

[DOYLE *stops dead and stares at him with something like awe.*]

I don't wish to be impertinent, as you know, Larry; but are you sure she has nothing to do with your reluctance to come to Ireland with me?

DOYLE [*sitting down again, vanquished*].   Thomas Broadbent: I surrender. The poor silly-clever Irishman takes off his hat to God's Englishman. The man who could in all seriousness make that recent remark of yours about Home Rule and Gladstone must be simply the champion idiot of all the world. Yet the man who could in the very next sentence sweep away all my special pleading and go straight to the heart of my motives must be a man of genius. But that the idiot and the genius should be the same man! how is that possible? [*Springing to his feet.*] By Jove, I see it all now. I'll write an article about it, and send it to Nature.

BROADBENT [*staring at him*].   What on earth—

DOYLE.   It's quite simple. You know that a caterpillar—

BROADBENT.   A caterpillar!!!

DOYLE.   Yes, a caterpillar. Now give your mind to what I am going

6. Irrelevant and distracting chat.
7. William Ewart Gladstone (1809–1898), British Liberal Party Prime Minister.

to say; for it's a new and important scientific theory of the English national character. A caterpillar—

BROADBENT.   Look here, Larry: dont be an ass.

DOYLE [*insisting*].   I say a caterpillar and I mean a caterpillar. Youll understand presently. A caterpillar

[BROADBENT *mutters a slight protest, but does not press it.*]

when it gets into a tree, instinctively makes itself look exactly like a leaf; so that both its enemies and its prey may mistake it for one and think it not worth bothering about.

BROADBENT.   Whats that got to do with our English national character?

DOYLE.   I'll tell you. The world is as full of fools as a tree is full of leaves. Well, the Englishman does what the caterpillar does. He instinctively makes himself look like a fool, and eats up all the real fools at his ease while his enemies let him alone and laugh at him for being a fool like the rest. Oh, nature is cunning! cunning! [*He sits down, lost in contemplation of his word-picture.*]

BROADBENT [*with hearty admiration*].   Now you know, Larry, that would never have occurred to me. You Irish people are amazingly clever. Of course it's all tommy rot; but it's so brilliant, you know! How the dickens do you think of such things! You really must write an article about it: theyll pay you something for it. If Nature wont have it, I can get it into Engineering for you: I know the editor.

DOYLE.   Lets get back to business. I'd better tell you about Nora Reilly.

BROADBENT.   No: never mind. I shouldnt have alluded to her.

DOYLE.   I'd rather. Nora has a fortune.

BROADBENT [*keenly interested*].   Eh? How much?

DOYLE.   Forty per annum.

BROADBENT.   Forty thousand?

DOYLE.   No, forty. Forty pounds.

BROADBENT [*much dashed*].   Thats what you call a fortune in Rosscullen, is it?

DOYLE.   A girl with a dowry of five pounds calls it a fortune in Rosscullen. Whats more, £40 a year is a fortune there; and Nora Reilly enjoys a good deal of social consideration as an heiress on the strength of it. It has helped my father's household through many a tight place. My father was her father's agent. She came on a visit to us when he died, and has lived with us ever since.

BROADBENT [*attentively, beginning to suspect* LARRY *of misconduct with* NORA, *and resolving to get to the bottom of it*].   Since when? I mean how old were you when she came?

DOYLE.   I was seventeen. So was she: if she'd been older she'd have had more sense than to stay with us. We were together for 18 months before I went up to Dublin to study. When I went home for Christmas and Easter, she was there. I suppose it used to be something of an event for her, though of course I never thought of that then.

BROADBENT.   Were you at all hard hit?

DOYLE.   Not really. I had only two ideas at that time: first, to learn to do something; and then to get out of Ireland and have a chance of doing it. She didnt count. I was romantic about her, just as I was romantic about Byron's heroines or the old Round Tower of Rosscullen;[8] but she didnt count any more than they did. Ive never crossed St George's Channel since for her sake—never even landed at Queenstown and come back to London through Ireland.

BROADBENT.   But did you ever say anything that would justify her in waiting for you?

DOYLE.   No, never. But she is waiting for me.

BROADBENT.   How do you know?

DOYLE.   She writes to me—on her birthday. She used to write on mine, and send me little things as presents; but I stopped that by pretending that it was no use when I was travelling, as they got lost in the foreign post-offices. [*He pronounces post-offices with the stress on offices, instead of post.*]

BROADBENT.   You answer the letters?

DOYLE.   Not very punctually. But they get acknowledged at one time or another.

BROADBENT.   How do you feel when you see her handwriting?

DOYLE.   Uneasy. I'd give £50 to escape a letter.

BROADBENT [*looking grave, and throwing himself back in his chair to intimate that the cross-examination is over, and the result very damaging to the witness*].   Hm!

DOYLE.   What d'ye mean by Hm!

BROADBENT.   Of course I know that the moral code is different in Ireland. But in England it's not considered fair to trifle with a woman's affections.

DOYLE.   You mean that an Englishman would get engaged to another woman and return Nora her letters and presents with a letter to say he was unworthy of her and wished her every happiness?

BROADBENT.   Well, even that would set the poor girl's mind at rest.

DOYLE.   Would it? I wonder! One thing I can tell you; and that is that Nora would wait until she died of old age sooner than ask my intentions or condescend to hint at the possibility of my having any. You dont know what Irish pride is. England may have knocked a good deal of it out of me; but she's never been in England; and if I had to choose between wounding that delicacy in her and hitting her in the face, I'd hit her in the face without a moment's hesitation.

BROADBENT [*who has been nursing his knee and reflecting, apparently rather agreeably*].   You know, all this sounds rather inter-

---

8. Ninth-century round towers, built by monastic societies, found throughout Ireland; as emblems of inspiration, they can be associated with the work of the Romantic poets such as Lord Byron (1788–1824).

esting. Theres the Irish charm about it. Thats the worst of you: the Irish charm doesnt exist for you.

DOYLE.   Oh yes it does. But it's the charm of a dream. Live in contact with dreams and you will get something of their charm: live in contact with facts and you will get something of their brutality. I wish I could find a country to live in where the facts were not brutal and the dreams not unreal.

BROADBENT [*changing his attitude and responding to* DOYLE's *earnestness with deep conviction: his elbows on the table and his hands clenched*].   Dont despair, Larry, old boy: things may look black; but there will be a great change after the next election.

DOYLE [*jumping up*].   Oh, get out, you idiot!

BROADBENT [*rising also, not a bit snubbed*].   Ha! ha! you may laugh; but we shall see. However, dont let us argue about that. Come now! you ask my advice about Miss Reilly?

DOYLE [*reddening*].   No I dont. Damn your advice! [*Softening.*] Lets have it, all the same.

BROADBENT.   Well, everything you tell me about her impresses me favorably. She seems to have the feelings of a lady; and though we must face the fact that in England her income would hardly maintain her in the lower middle class—

DOYLE [*interrupting*].   Now look here, Tom. That reminds me. When you go to Ireland, just drop talking about the middle class and bragging of belonging to it. In Ireland youre either a gentleman or youre not. If you want to be particularly offensive to Nora, you can call her a Papist; but if you call her a middle-class woman, Heaven help you!

BROADBENT [*irrepressible*].   Never fear. Youre all descended from the ancient kings: I know that. [*Complacently.*] I'm not so tactless as you think, my boy. [*Earnest again.*] I expect to find Miss Reilly a perfect lady; and I strongly advise you to come and have another look at her before you make up your mind about her. By the way, have you a photograph of her?

DOYLE.   Her photographs stopped at twenty-five.

BROADBENT [*saddened*].   Ah yes, I suppose so. [*With feeling, severely.*] Larry: youve treated that poor girl disgracefully.

DOYLE.   By George, if she only knew that two men were talking about her like this—!

BROADBENT.   She wouldnt like it, would she! Of course not. We ought to be ashamed of ourselves, Larry. [*More and more carried away by his new fancy*]. You know, I have a sort of presentiment that Miss Reilly is a very superior woman.

DOYLE [*staring hard at him*].   Oh! you have, have you?

BROADBENT.   Yes I have. There is something very touching about the history of this beautiful girl.

DOYLE.   Beau—! Oho! Heres a chance for Nora! and for me! [*Calling.*] Hodson.

HODSON [*appearing at the bedroom door*].   Did you call, sir?

DOYLE.   Pack for me too. I'm going to Ireland with Mr Broadbent.

HODSON.   Right, sir. [*He retires into the bedroom*].

BROADBENT [*clapping* DOYLE *on the shoulder*].   Thank you, old chap. Thank you.

Act 2

Rosscullen. Westward a hillside of granite rock and heather slopes upward across the prospect from south to north. A huge stone stands on it in a naturally impossible place, as if it had been tossed up there by a giant. Over the brow, in the desolate valley beyond, is a round tower. A lonely white high road trending away westward past the tower loses itself at the foot of the far mountains. It is evening; and there are great breadths of silken green in the Irish sky. The sun is setting.

A MAN *with the face of a young saint, yet with white hair and perhaps 50 years on his back, is standing near the stone in a trance of intense melancholy, looking over the hills as if by mere intensity of gaze he could pierce the glories of the sunset and see into the streets of heaven. He is dressed in black, and is rather more clerical in appearance than most English curates are nowadays; but he does not wear the collar and waistcoat of a parish priest. He is roused from his trance by the chirp of an insect from a tuft of grass in a crevice of the stone. His face relaxes: he turns quietly, and gravely takes off his hat to the tuft, addressing the insect in a brogue which is the jocular assumption of a gentleman and not in the natural speech of a peasant.*

THE MAN.   An is that yourself, Misther Grasshopper? I hope I see you well this fine evenin.

THE GRASSHOPPER [*prompt and shrill in answer*].   X.X.

THE MAN [*encouragingly*].   Thats right. I suppose now youve come out to make yourself miserable be admyerin the sunset?

THE GRASSHOPPER [*sadly*].   X.X.

THE MAN.   Aye, youre a true Irish grasshopper.

THE GRASSHOPPER [*loudly*].   X.X.X.

THE MAN.   Three cheers for ould Ireland, is it? That helps you to face out the misery and the poverty and the torment, doesnt it?

THE GRASSHOPPER [*plaintively*].   X.X.

THE MAN.   Ah, it's no use, me poor little friend. If you could jump as far as a kangaroo you couldn't jump away from your own heart an its punishment. You can only look at Heaven from here: you cant reach it. There! [*pointing with his stick to the sunset*] thats the gate o glory, isnt it?

THE GRASSHOPPER [*assenting*].   X.X.

THE MAN.   Sure its the wise grasshopper yar to know that. But tell me this, Misther Unworldly Wiseman:[9] why does the sight of

9. Ironic allusion to the allegory of John Bunyan (1628–88), *Pilgrim's Progress* (1678), in which a solitary wanderer named Christian encounters the character Worldly Wiseman from the town of Carnal Policy.

Heaven wring your heart an mine as the sight of holy wather wrings the heart o the divil? What wickedness have you done to bring that curse on you? Here! where are you jumpin to? Wheres your manners to go skyrocketin like that out o the box in the middle o your confession? [*He threatens it with his stick.*]

THE GRASSHOPPER [*penitently*]. X.

THE MAN [*lowering the stick*].   I accept your apology; but dont do it again. And now tell me one thing before I let you go home to bed. Which would you say this counthry was: hell or purgatory?

THE GRASSHOPPER. X.

THE MAN.   Hell! Faith I'm afraid youre right. I wondher what you and me did when we were alive to get sent here.

THE GRASSHOPPER [*shrilly*]. X.X.

THE MAN [*nodding*].   Well, as you say, it's a delicate subject; and I wont press it on you. Now off widja.

THE GRASSHOPPER. X.X. [*It springs away*].

THE MAN [*waving his stick*].   God speed you!

> [*He walks away past the stone towards the brow of the hill. Immediately a young* LABORER, *his face distorted with terror, slips round from behind the stone.*]

THE LABORER [*crossing himself repeatedly*].   Oh glory be to God! glory be to God! Oh Holy Mother an all the saints! Oh murdher! murdher! [*Beside himself, calling.*] Fadher Keegan! Fadher Keegan!

THE MAN [*turning*].   Who's there? Whats that?

> [*He comes back and finds the* LABORER, *who clasps his knees.*]

Patsy Farrell! What are you doing here?

PATSY.   Oh for the love o God dont lave me here wi dhe grasshopper. I hard it spakin to you. Dont let it do me any harm, Father darlint.

KEEGAN.   Get up, you foolish man, get up. Are you afraid of a poor insect because I pretended it was talking to me?

PATSY.   Oh, it was no pretendin, Fadher dear. Didnt it give three cheers n say it was a divil out o hell? Oh say youll see me safe home, Fadher; n put a blessin on me or somethin. [*He moans with terror.*]

KEEGAN.   What were you doin there, Patsy, listnin? Were you spyin on me?

PATSY.   No, Fadher: on me oath an soul I wasnt: I was waitn to meet Master Larry n carry his luggage from the car; n I fell asleep on the grass; n you woke me talkin to the grasshopper; n I hard its wicked little voice. Oh, d'ye think I'll die before the year's out, Fadher?

KEEGAN.   For shame, Patsy! Is that your religion, to be afraid of a little deeshy grasshopper? Suppose it was a divil, what call have you to fear it? If I could ketch it, I'd make you take it home widja in your hat for a penance.

PATSY.   Sure, if you wont let it harm me, I'm not afraid, your river-
ence. [*He gets up, a little reassured. He is a callow, flaxen polled,
smoothfaced, downy chinned lad, fully grown but not yet fully
filled out, with blue eyes and an instinctively acquired air of helplessness and silliness, indicating, not his real character, but a cunning developed by his constant dread of a hostile dominance,
which he habitually tries to disarm and tempt into unmasking by
pretending to be a much greater fool than he really is. Englishmen
think him half-witted, which is exactly what he intends them to
think. He is clad in corduroy trousers, unbuttoned waistcoat, and
coarse blue striped shirt.*]

KEEGAN [*admonitorily*].   Patsy: what did I tell you about callin me
Father Keegan an your reverence? What did Father Dempsey tell
you about it?

PATSY.   Yis, Fadher.

KEEGAN.   Father!

PATSY [*desperately*].   Arra, hwat am I to call you? Fadher Dempsey
sez youre not a priest; n we all know youre not a man; n how do
we now what ud happen to us if we shewed any disrespect to
you? N sure they say wanse a priest always a priest.

KEEGAN [*sternly*].   It's not for the like of you, Patsy, to go behind
the instruction of your parish priest and set yourself up to judge
whether your Church is right or wrong.

PATSY.   Sure I know that, sir.

KEEGAN.   The Church let me be its priest as long as it thought me
fit for its work. When it took away my papers it meant you to
know that I was only a poor madman, unfit and unworthy to take
charge of the souls of the people.

PATSY.   But wasnt it only because you knew more Latn than Father
Dempsey that he was jealous of you?

KEEGAN [*scolding him to keep himself from smiling*].   How dar you,
Patsy Farrell, put your own wicked little spites and foolishnesses
into the heart of your priest? For two pins I'd tell him what you
just said.

PATSY [*coaxing*].   Sure you wouldnt—

KEEGAN.   Wouldnt I? God forgive you! youre little better than a
heathen.

PATSY.   Deedn I am, Fadher: it's me bruddher the tinsmith in
Dublin youre thinkin of. Sure he had to be a freethinker when he
larnt a thrade and went to live in the town.

KEEGAN.   Well, he'll get to Heaven before you if youre not careful,
Patsy. And now you listen to me, once and for all. Youll talk to me
and pray for me by the name of Pether Keegan, so you will. And
when youre angry and tempted to lift your hand agen the donkey
or stamp your foot on the little grasshopper, remember that the
donkey's Pether Keegan's brother, and the grasshopper Pether
Keegan's friend. And when youre tempted to throw a stone at a
sinner or a curse at a beggar, remember that Pether Keegan is a
worse sinner and a worse beggar, and keep the stone and the

curse for him the next time you meet him. Now say God bless you, Pether, to me before I go, just to practise you a bit.

PATSY.   Sure it wouldnt be right, Fadher. I cant—

KEEGAN.   Yes you can. Now out with it; or I'll put this stick into your hand an make you hit me with it.

PATSY [*throwing himself on his knees in an ecstasy of adoration*]. Sure it's your blessin I want, Fadher Keegan. I'll have no luck widhout it.

KEEGAN [*shocked*].   Get up out o that, man. Dont kneel to me: I'm not a saint.

PATSY [*with intense conviction*].   On in throth yar, sir.

> [*The grasshopper chirps.* PATSY, *terrified, clutches at* KEEGAN's *hands.*]

Dont set it on me, Fadher: I'll do anythin you bid me.

KEEGAN [*pulling him up*].   You bosthoon, you! Dont you see that it only whistled to tell me Miss Reilly's comin? There! Look at her and pull yourself together for shame. Off widja to the road: youll be late for the car if you dont make haste [*bustling him down the hill*]. I can see the dust of it in the gap already.

PATSY.   The Lord save us! [*He goes down the hill towards the road like a haunted man.*]

> [NORA REILLY *comes down the hill. A slight weak woman in a pretty muslin print gown (her best), she is a figure commonplace enough to Irish eyes; but on the inhabitants of fatter-fed, crowded, hustling and bustling modern countries she makes a very different impression. The absence of any symptoms of coarseness or hardness or appetite in her, her comparative delicacy of manner and sensibility of apprehension, her fine hands and frail figure, her novel accent, with the caressing plaintive Irish melody of her speech, give her a charm which is all the more effective because, being untravelled, she is unconscious of it, and never dreams of deliberately dramatizing and exploiting it, as the Irishwomen in England do. For* TOM BROADBENT *therefore, an attractive woman, whom he would even call ethereal. To* LARRY DOYLE, *an everyday woman fit only for the eighteenth century, helpless, useless, almost sexless, an invalid without the excuse of disease, an incarnation of everything in Ireland that drove him out of it. These judgments have little value and no finality; but they are the judgments on which her fate hangs just at present.* KEEGAN *touches his hat to her: he does not take it off.*]

NORA.   Mr Keegan: I want to speak to you a minute if you dont mind.

KEEGAN [*dropping the broad Irish vernacular of his speech to* PATSY]. An hour if you like, Miss Reilly: youre always welcome. Shall we sit down?

NORA.   Thank you. [*They sit on the heather. She is shy and anxious;*

but she comes to the point promptly because she can think of noth-
ing else.] They say you did a gradle[1] o travelling at one time.

KEEGAN.   Well, you see I'm not a Mnooth man [*he means that he
was not a student at Maynooth College*][2] When I was young I admired the older generation of priests that had been educated in
Salamanca. So when I felt sure of my vocation I went to Salamanca. Then I walked from Salamanca to Rome, an sted in a
monastery there for a year. My pilgrimage to Rome taught me
that walking is a better way of travelling than the train; so I
walked from Rome to the Sorbonne in Paris; and I wish I could
have walked from Paris to Oxford; for I was very sick on the sea.
After a year of Oxford I had to walk to Jerusalem to walk the Oxford feeling off me. From Jerusalem I came back to Patmos, and
spent six months at the monastery of Mount Athos. From that I
came to Ireland and settled down as a parish priest until I went
mad.

NORA [*startled*].   Oh dont say that.

KEEGAN.   Why not? Dont you know the story? how I confessed a
black man and gave him absolution? and how he put a spell on
me and drove me mad?

NORA.   How can you talk such nonsense about yourself? For
shame!

KEEGAN.   It's not nonsense at all: it's true—in a way. But never
mind the black man. Now that you know what a travelled man I
am, what can I do for you?

> [*She hesitates and plucks nervously at the heather. He stays
> her hand gently.*]

Dear Miss Nora: dont pluck the little flower. If it was a pretty
baby you wouldn't want to pull its head off and stick it in a vawse
o water to look at. [*The grasshopper chirps:* KEEGAN *turns his head
and addresses it in the vernacular.*] Be aisy, me son: she wont spoil
the swing-swong in your little three. [*To* NORA, *resuming his ur-
bane style.*] You see I'm quite cracked; but never mind: I'm harmless. Now what is it?

NORA [*embarrassed*].   Oh, only idle curiosity. I wanted to know
whether you found Ireland—I mean the country part of Ireland,
of course—very small and backwardlike when you came back to
it from Rome and Oxford and all the great cities.

KEEGAN.   When I went to those great cities I saw wonders I had
never seen in Ireland. But when I came back to Ireland I found
all the wonders there waiting for me. You see they had been there
all the time; but my eyes had never been opened to them. I did
not know what my own house was like, because I had never been
outside it.

1. A great deal.
2. Principal seminary in Ireland.

NORA. D'ye think thats the same with everybody?

KEEGAN. With everybody who has eyes in his soul as well as in his head.

NORA. But really and truly now, werent the people rather disappointing? I should think the girls must have seemed rather coarse and dowdy after the foreign princesses and people? But I suppose a priest wouldnt notice that.

KEEGAN. It's a priest's business to notice everything. I wont tell you all I noticed about women; but I'll tell you this. The more a man knows, and the farther he travels, the more likely he is to marry a country girl afterwards.

NORA [*blushing with delight*]. Youre joking, Mr Keegan: I'm sure yar.

KEEGAN. My way of joking is to tell the truth. It's the funniest joke in the world.

NORA [*incredulous*]. Galong with you!

KEEGAN [*springing up actively*]. Shall we go down to the road and meet the car?

[*She gives him her hand and he helps her up.*]

Patsy Farrell told me you were expecting young Doyle.

NORA [*tossing her chin up at once*]. Oh, I'm not expecting him particularly. It's a wonder he's come back at all. After staying away eighteen years he can harly expect us to be very anxious to see him: can he now?

KEEGAN. Well, not anxious perhaps; but you will be curious to see how much he's changed in all these years.

NORA [*with a sudden bitter flush*]. I suppose thats all that brings him back to look at us, just to see how much weve changed. Well, he can wait and to see me be candlelight: I didn't come out to meet him: I'm going to walk to the Round Tower [*going west across the hill*].

KEEGAN. You couldnt do better this fine evening. [*Gravely.*] I'll tell him where youve gone.

[*She turns as if to forbid him; but the deep understanding in his eyes makes that impossible; and she only looks at him earnestly and goes. He watches her disappear on the other side of the hill; then says*]

Aye, he's come to torment you; and youre driven already to torment him. [*He shakes his head, and goes slowly away across the hill in the opposite direction, lost in thought.*]

[*By this time the car has arrived, and dropped three of its passengers on the high road at the foot of the hill. It is a monster jaunting car, black and dilapidated, one of the last survivors of the public vehicles known to earlier generations as Beeyankiny cars, the Irish having laid violent tongues on the name of their projector, one Bianconi, an enterprising Italian.*]

The three passengers are the parish priest, FATHER DEMPSEY; CORNELIUS DOYLE, LARRY's father; and BROADBENT, all in over-coats and as stiff as only an Irish car could make them.

The priest, stout and fatherly, falls far short of that finest type of countryside pastor which represents the genius of priesthood; but he is equally far above the base type in which a strongminded unscrupulous peasant uses the Church to ex-tort money, power, and privilege. He is a priest neither by vo-cation nor ambition, but because the life suits him. He has boundless authority over his flock, and taxes them stiffly enough to be a rich man. The old Protestant ascendency is now too broken to gall him. On the whole, an easygoing, ami-able, even modest man as long as his dues are paid and his au-thority and dignity fully admitted.

CORNELIUS DOYLE is an elder of the small wiry type, with a hardskinned, rather worried face, clean shaven except for sandy whiskers blanching into a lustreless pale yellow and quite white at the roots. His dress is that of a country-town man of business: that is, an oldish shooting suit, with elastic sided boots quite unconnected with shooting. Feeling shy with BROADBENT, he is hasty, which is his way of trying to appear genial.

BROADBENT, for reasons which will appear later, has no lug-gage except a field glass and a guide book. The other two have left theirs to the unfortunate PATSY FARRELL, who struggles up the hill after them, loaded with a sack of potatoes, a hamper, a fat goose, a colossal salmon, and several paper parcels.

CORNELIUS leads the way up the hill, with BROADBENT at his heels. The priest follows. PATSY lags laboriously behind.]

CORNELIUS.   This is a bit of a climb, Mr Broadbent; but it's shorter than goin round be the road.

BROADBENT [*stopping to examine the great stone*].   Just a moment, Mr Doyle: I want to look at this stone. It must be Finian's die-cast.

CORNELIUS [*in blank bewilderment*].   Hwat?

BROADBENT.   Murray describes it. One of your great national he-roes—I cant pronounce the name—Finian Somebody, I think.

FATHER DEMPSEY [*also perplexed, and rather scandalized*].   Is it Fin McCool you mean?

BROADBENT.   I daresay it is. [*Referring to the guide book.*] Murray says that a huge stone, probably of Druidic origin, is still pointed out as the die cast by Fin in his celebrated match with the devil.

CORNELIUS [*dubiously*].   Jeuce a word I ever heard of it!

FATHER DEMPSEY [*very seriously indeed, and even a little severely*].   Dont believe any such nonsense, sir. There never was any such thing. When people talk to you about Fin McCool and the like, take no notice of them. It's all idle stories and superstition.

BROADBENT [*somewhat indignantly; for to be rebuked by an Irish priest for superstition is more than he can stand*].   You dont suppose I believe it, do you?

FATHER DEMPSEY.   Oh, I thought you did. D'ye see the top of the Roun Tower there? thats an antiquity worth lookin at.

BROADBENT [*deeply interested*].   Have you any theory as to what the Round Towers were for?

FATHER DEMPSEY [*a little offended*].   A theory? Me! [*Theories are connected in his mind with the late Professor Tyndall,*[3] *and with scientific scepticism generally: also perhaps with the view that the Round Towers are phallic symbols.*]

CORNELIUS [*remonstrating*].   Father Dempsey is the priest of the parish, Mr Broadbent. What would he be doing with a theory?

FATHER DEMPSEY [*with gentle emphasis*].   I have a knowledge of what the Roun Towers were, if thats what you mean. They are the forefingers of the early Church, pointing us all to God.

[PATSY, *intolerably overburdened, loses his balance, and sits down involuntarily. His burdens are scattered over the hillside.* CORNELIUS *and* FATHER DEMPSEY *turn furiously on him, leaving* BROADBENT *beaming at the stone and the tower with fatuous interest.*]

CORNELIUS.   Oh, be the hokey, the sammin's broke in two! You schoopid ass, what d'ye mean?

FATHER DEMPSEY.   Are you drunk, Patsy Farrell? Did I tell you to carry that hamper carefully or did I not?

PATSY [*rubbing the back of his head, which has almost dinted a slab of granite*].   Sure me futslipt. Howkn I carry three men's luggage at wanst?

FATHER DEMPSEY.   You were told to leave behind what you couldnt carry, an go back for it.

PATSY.   An whose things was I to lave behind? Hwat would your reverence think if I left your hamper behind in the wet grass; n hwat would the masther say if I left the sammin and the goose be the side o the road for annywan to pick up?

CORNELIUS.   Oh, youve a dale to say for yourself, you butther-fingered omadhaun.[4] Waitll Ant Judy sees the state o that sammin: she'll talk to you. Here! gimmy that birdn that fish there; an take Father Dempsey's hamper to his house for him; n then come back for the rest.

FATHER DEMPSEY.   Do, Patsy, And mind you dont fall down again.

PATSY.   Sure I—

CORNELIUS [*bustling him up the hill*].   Whisht! heres Ant Judy.

[PATSY *goes grumbling in disgrace, with* FATHER DEMPSEY'S *hamper.*]
[AUNT JUDY *comes down the hill, a woman of 50, in no way*

3. John Tyndall (1820–93), professor of natural history and popularizer of science in books and lectures.
4. Fool.

*remarkable, lively and busy without energy or grip, placid
without tranquility, kindly without concern for others: indeed
without much concern for herself: a contented product of a
narrow, stainless life. She wears her hair parted in the middle
and quite smooth, with a flattened bun at the back. Her dress
is a plain brown frock, with a woollen pelerine of black and
aniline mauve over her shoulders, all very trim in honor of the
occasion. She looks round for* LARRY; *is puzzled; then stares incredulously at Broadbent.*]

AUNT JUDY.   Surely to goodness thats not you, Larry!

CORNELIUS.   Arra how could he be Larry, woman alive? Larry's in
no hurry home, it seems. I havnt set eyes on him. This is his
friend, Mr Broadbent. Mr Broadbent: me sister Judy.

AUNT JUDY [*hospitably: going to* BROADBENT *and shaking hands
heartily*].   Mr Broadbent! Fancy me takin you for Larry! Sure we
havnt seen a sight of him for eighteen years, n he ony a lad when
he left us.

BROADBENT.   It's not Larry's fault: he was to have been here before
me. He started in our motor an hour before Mr Doyle arrived, to
meet us at Athenmullet, intending to get here long before me.

AUNT JUDY.   Lord save us! do you think he's had n axidnt?

BROADBENT.   No: he's wired to say he's had a breakdown and will
come on as soon as he can. He expects to be here at about ten.

AUNT JUDY.   There now! Fancy him trustn himself in a motor
and we all expectn him! Just like him! he'd never do anything
like anybody else. Well, what cant be cured must be injoored.
Come on in, all of you. You must be dyin for your tea, Mr Broadbent.

BROADBENT [*with a slight start*].   Oh, I'm afraid it's too late for tea.
[*He looks at his watch.*]

AUNT JUDY.   Not a bit: we never have it airlier than this. I hope
they gave you a good dinner at Athenmullet.

BROADBENT [*trying to conceal his consternation as he realizes that he
is not going to get any dinner after his drive*].   Oh—er—excellent, excellent. By the way, hadnt I better see about a room at the
hotel? [*They stare at him.*]

CORNELIUS.   The hotel!

FATHER DEMPSEY.   Hwat hotel?

AUNT JUDY.   Indeedn youre not goin to a hotel. Youll stay with us.
I'd have put you into Larry's room, ony the boy's pallyass is too
short for you; but we'll make a comfortable bed for you on the
sofa in the parlor.

BROADBENT.   Youre very kind, Miss Doyle; but really I'm ashamed
to give you so much trouble unnecessarily. I shant mind the hotel in the least.

FATHER DEMPSEY.   Man alive! theres no hotel in Rosscullen.

BROADBENT.   No hotel! Why, the driver told me there was the
finest hotel in Ireland here.

[*They regard him joylessly.*]

AUNT JUDY.   Arra would you mind what the like of him would tell you? Sure he'd say hwatever was the least trouble to himself and the pleasantest to you, thinkin you might give him a thruppeny bit for himself or the like.

BROADBENT.   Perhaps theres a public house.

FATHER DEMPSEY [*grimly*].   Theres seventeen.

AUNT JUDY.   Ah then, how could you stay at a public house? theyd have no place to put you even if it was a right place for you to go. Come! is it the sofa youre afraid of? If it is, you can have me own bed. I can sleep with Nora.

BROADBENT.   Not at all, not at all: I should be only too delighted. But to upset your arrangements in this way—

CORNELIUS [*anxious to cut short the discussion, which makes him ashamed of his house; for he guesses* BROADBENT's *standard of comfort a little more accurately than his sister does*].   Thats all right: itll be no trouble at all. Hweres Nora?

AUNT JUDY.   Oh, how do I know? She slipped out a little while ago: I thought she was goin to meet the car.

CORNELIUS [*dissatisfied*].   It's a queer thing of her to run out o the way at such a time.

AUNT JUDY.   Sure she's a queer girl altogether. Come. Come in: come in.

FATHER DEMPSEY.   I'll say good-night, Mr Broadbent. If theres anything I can do for you in this parish, let me know.

[*He shakes hands with* BROADBENT.]

BROADBENT [*effusively cordial*].   Thank you, Father Dempsey. Delighted to have met you, sir.

FATHER DEMPSEY [*passing on to* AUNT JUDY].   Good-night, Miss Doyle.

AUNT JUDY.   Wont you stay to tea?

FATHER DEMPSEY.   Not to-night, thank you kindly: I have business to do at home.

[*He turns to go, and meets* PATSY FARRELL *returning unloaded.*]

Have you left that hamper for me?

PATSY.   Yis, your reverence.

FATHER DEMPSEY.   Thats a good lad [*going*].

PATSY [*to* AUNT JUDY].   Fadher Keegan sez—

FATHER DEMPSEY [*turning sharply on him*].   Whats that you say?

PATSY [*frightened*].   Fadher Keegan—

FATHER DEMPSEY.   How often have you heard me bid you call Mister Keegan in his proper name, the same as I do? Father Keegan indeed! Cant you tell the difference between your priest and any ole madman in a black coat?

PATSY.   Sure I'm afraid he might put a spell on me.

FATHER DEMPSEY [*wrathfully*].   You mind what I tell you or I'll put
a spell on you thatll make you lep. D'ye mind that now? [*He goes
home.*]

> [PATSY *goes down the hill to retrieve the fish, the bird, and the
> sack.*]

AUNT JUDY.   Ah, hwy cant you hold your tongue, Patsy, before Father Dempsey?

PATSY.   Well, hwat was I to do? Father Keegan bid me tell you Miss
Nora was gone to the Roun Tower.

AUNT JUDY.   An hwy couldnt you wait to tell us until Father
Dempsey was gone?

PATSY.   I was afeerd o forgetn it; and then may be he'd a sent the
grasshopper or the little dark looker into me at night to remind
me of it. [*The dark looker is the common grey lizard, which is supposed to walk down the throats of incautious sleepers and cause
them to perish in a slow decline.*]

CORNELIUS.   Yah, you great gaum,[5] you! Widjer grasshoppers and
dark lookers! Here: take up them things and let me hear no more
o your foolish lip.

> [PATSY *obeys.*]

You can take the sammin under your oxther. [*He wedges the
salmon into* PATSY'S *axilla.*]

PATSY.   I can take the goose too, sir. Put it on me back n gimmy
the neck of it in me mouth.

> [CORNELIUS *is about to comply thoughtlessly.*]

AUNT JUDY [*feeling that* BROADBENT'S *presence demands special punc-
tiliousness.*]   For shame, Patsy! to offer to take the goose in your
mouth that we have to eat after you! The masterll bring it in for
you.

PATSY.   Arra what would a dead goose care for me mouth? [*He
takes his load up the hill.*]

CORNELIUS.   Hwats Nora doin at the Roun Tower?

AUNT JUDY.   Oh, the Lord knows! Romancin, I suppose. Praps she
thinks Larry would go there to look for her and see her safe
home.

BROADBENT.   Miss Reilly must not be left to wait and walk home
alone at night. Shall I go for her?

AUNT JUDY [*contemptuously*].   Arra hwat ud happen to her? Hurry
in now, Corny. Come, Mr Broadbent: I left the tea on the hob to
draw; and itll be black if we dont go in an drink it.

> [*They go up the hill. It is dusk by this time.*
>
>   BROADBENT *does not fare so badly after all at* AUNT JUDY'S
> *board. He gets not only tea and bread-and-butter, but more
> mutton chops than he has ever conceived it possible to eat at*

5. Buffoon.

one sitting. There is also a most filling substance called potato cake. Hardly have his fears of being starved been replaced by his first misgiving that he is eating too much and will be sorry for it tomorrow, when his appetite is revived by the production of a bottle of illicitly distilled whisky, called potcheen, which he has read and dreamed of (he calls it pottine) and is now at last to taste. His goodhumor rises almost to excitement before CORNELIUS *shews signs of sleepiness. The contrast between* AUNT JUDY'S *table service and that of the south and east coast hotels at which he spends his Fridays-to-Tuesdays when he is in London, seems to him delightfully Irish. The almost total atrophy of any sense of enjoyment in* CORNELIUS, *or even any desire for it or toleration of the possibility of life being something better than a round of sordid worries, relieved by tobacco, punch, fine mornings, and petty successes in buying and selling, passes with his guest as the whimsical affectation of a shrewd Irish humorist and incorrigible spendthrift.* AUNT JUDY *seems to him an incarnate joke. The likelihood that the joke will pall after a month or so, and is probably not apparent at any time to born Rossculleners, or that he himself unconsciously entertains* AUNT JUDY *by his fantastic English personality and English mispronunciations, does not occur to him for a moment. In the end he is so charmed, and so loth to go to bed and perhaps dream of prosaic England, that he insists on going out to smoke a cigar and look for* NORA REILLY *at the Round Tower. Not that any special insistence is needed; for the English inhibitive instinct does not seem to exist in Rosscullen. Just as* NORA'S *liking to miss a meal and stay out at the Round Tower is accepted as a sufficient reason for her doing it, and for the family going to bed and leaving the door open for her, so* BROADBENT'S *whim to go out for a late stroll provokes neither hospitable remonstrance nor surprise. Indeed* AUNT JUDY *wants to get rid of him whilst she makes a bed for him on the sofa. So off he goes, full fed, happy and enthusiastic, to explore the valley by moonlight.*

The Round Tower stands about half an Irish mile from Rosscullen, some fifty yards south of the road on a knoll with a circle of wild greensward on it. The road once ran over this knoll; but modern engineering has tempered the level to the Beeyankiny car by carrying the road partly round the knoll and partly through a cutting; so that the way from the road to the tower is a footpath up the embankment through furze and brambles.

On the edge of this slope, at the top of the path, NORA *is straining her eyes in the moonlight, watching for* LARRY. *At last she gives it up with a sob of impatience, and retreats to the hoary foot of the tower, where she sits down discouraged and cries a little. Then she settles herself resignedly to wait, and hums a song—not an Irish melody, but a hackneyed English drawing room ballad of the season before last—until some slight noise suggests a footstep, when she springs up eagerly and runs to the edge of the slope again. Some moments of silence and suspense follow, broken by unmistakable footsteps. She gives a little gasp as she sees a man approaching.*]

NORA.   Is that you, Larry? [*Frightened a little.*] Who's that?

[BROADBENT's *voice from below on the path:* Dont be alarmed.]

NORA.   Oh, what an English accent youve got!

BROADBENT [*rising into view*].   I must introduce myself—

NORA [*violently startled, retreating*].   It's not you! Who are you? What do you want?

BROADBENT [*advancing*].   I'm really so sorry to have alarmed you, Miss Reilly. My name is Broadbent. Larry's friend, you know.

NORA [*chilled*].   And has Mr Doyle not come with you?

BROADBENT.   No. Ive come instead. I hope I am not unwelcome.

NORA [*deeply mortified*].   I'm sorry Mr Doyle should have given you the trouble, I'm sure.

BROADBENT.   You see, as a stranger and an Englishman, I thought it would be interesting to see the Round Tower by moonlight.

NORA.   Oh, you came to see the tower. I thought— [*confused, trying to recover her manners*]. Oh, of course. I was so startled. It's a beautiful night, isn't it?

BROADBENT.   Lovely. I must explain why Larry has not come himself.

NORA.   Why should he come? He's seen the tower often enough: it's no attraction to him. [*Genteelly.*] An what do you think of Ireland, Mr Broadbent? Have you ever been here before?

BROADBENT.   Never.

NORA.   An how do you like it?

BROADBENT [*suddenly betraying a condition of extreme sentimentality*].   I can hardly trust myself to say how much I like it. The magic of this Irish scene, and—I really dont want to be personal, Miss Reilly; but the charm of your Irish voice—

NORA [*quite accustomed to gallantry, and attaching no seriousness whatever to it*].   Oh, get along with you, Mr Broadbent! Youre breaking your heart about me already, I daresay, after seeing me for two minutes in the dark.

BROADBENT.   The voice is just as beautiful in the dark, you know. Besides, Ive heard a great deal about you from Larry.

NORA [*with bitter indifference*].   Have you now? Well, thats a great honor, I'm sure.

BROADBENT.   I have looked forward to meeting you more than to anything else in Ireland.

NORA [*ironically*]. Dear me! did you now?

BROADBENT.   I did really. I wish you had taken half as much interest in me.

NORA.   Oh, I was dying to see you, of course. I daresay you can imagine the sensation an Englishman like you would make among us poor Irish people.

BROADBENT.   Ah, now youre chaffing me, Miss Reilly: you know you are. You mustnt chaff me. I'm very much in earnest about Ireland and everything Irish. I'm very much in earnest about you and about Larry.

NORA.   Larry has nothing to do with me, Mr Broadbent.

BROADBENT.   If I really thought that, Miss Reilly, I should—well, I should let myself feel that charm of which I spoke just now more deeply than I—than I—

NORA.   Is it making love to me you are?

BROADBENT [*scared and much upset*].   On my word I believe I am, Miss Reilly. If you say that to me again I shant answer for myself: all the harps of Ireland are in your voice.

[*She laughs at him. He suddenly loses his head and seizes her arms, to her great indignation.*]

Stop laughing: do you hear! I am in earnest: in English earnest. When I say a thing like that to a woman, I mean it. [*Releasing her and trying to recover his ordinary manner in spite of his bewildering emotion.*] I beg your pardon.

NORA.   How dare you touch me?

BROADBENT.   There are not many things I would not dare for you. That does not sound right perhaps; but I really— [*He stops and passes his hand over his forehead, rather lost.*]

NORA.   I think you ought to be ashamed. I think if you were a gentleman, and me alone with you in this place at night, you would die rather than do such a thing.

BROADBENT.   You mean that it's an act of treachery to Larry?

NORA.   Deed I dont. What has Larry to do with it? It's an act of disrespect and rudeness to me: it shews what you take me for. You can go your way now; and I'll go mine. Goodnight, Mr Broadbent.

BROADBENT.   No, please, Miss Reilly. One moment. Listen to me. I'm serious: I'm desperately serious. Tell me that I'm interfering with Larry; and I'll go straight from this spot back to London and never see you again. Thats on my honor: I will. Am I interfering with him?

NORA [*answering in spite of herself in a sudden spring of bitterness*]. I should think you ought to know better than me whether youre interfering with him. Youve seen him oftener than I have. You know him better than I do, by this time. Youve come to me quicker than he has, havnt you?

BROADBENT.   I'm bound to tell you, Miss Reilly, that Larry has not arrived in Rosscullen yet. He meant to get here before me; but his car broke down; and he may not arrive until to-morrow.

NORA [*her face lighting up*].   Is that the truth?

BROADBENT.   Yes: thats the truth.

[*She gives a sigh of relief.*]

Youre glad of that?

NORA [*up in arms at once*].   Glad indeed! Why should I be glad? As
weve waited eighteen years for him we can afford to wait a day
longer, I should think.

BROADBENT.   If you really feel like that about him, there may be a
chance for another man yet. Eh?

NORA [*deeply offended*].   I suppose people are different in England,
Mr Broadbent; so perhaps you dont mean any harm. In Ireland
nobody'd mind what a man'd say in fun, nor take advantage of
what a woman might say in answer to it. If a woman couldnt talk
to a man for two minutes at their first meeting without being
treated the way youre treating me, no decent woman would ever
talk to a man at all.

BROADBENT.   I dont understand that. I dont admit that. I am sincere; and my intentions are perfectly honorable. I think you will
accept the fact that I'm an Englishman as a guarantee that I am
not a man to act hastily or romantically; though I confess that
your voice had such an extraordinary effect on me just now when
you asked me so quaintly whether I was making love to you—

NORA [*flushing*].   I never thought—

BROADBENT [*quickly*].   Of course you didnt: I'm not so stupid as
that. But I couldnt bear your laughing at the feeling it gave me.
You— [*again struggling with a surge of emotion*] you dont know
what I— [*he chokes for a moment and then blurts out with unnatural steadiness*] Will you be my wife?

NORA [*promptly*].   Deed I wont. The idea! [*Looking at him more
carefully.*] Arra, come home, Mr Broadbent; and get your senses
back again. I think youre not accustomed to potcheen punch in
the evening after your tea.

BROADBENT [*horrified*].   Do you mean to say that I—I—I—my
God! that I appear drunk to you, Miss Reilly?

NORA [*compassionately*].   How many tumblers had you?

BROADBENT [*helplessly*].   Two.

NORA.   The flavor of the turf prevented you noticing the strength
of it. Youd better come home to bed.

BROADBENT [*fearfully agitated*].   But this is such a horrible doubt
to put into my mind—to—to—For Heaven's sake, Miss Reilly, am
I really drunk?

NORA [*soothingly*].   Youll be able to judge better in the morning.
Come on now back with me, an think no more about it.

> [*She takes his arm with motherly solicitude and urges him
> gently towards the path.*]

BROADBENT [*yielding in despair*].   I must be drunk: frightfully
drunk; for your voice drove me out of my senses— [*he stumbles
over a stone*]. No: on my word, on my most sacred word of honor,
Miss Reilly, I tripped over that stone. It was an accident: it was
indeed.

NORA. Yes, of course it was. Just take my arm, Mr Broadbent, while we're goin down the path to the road. Youll be all right then.

BROADBENT [*submissively taking it*]. I cant sufficiently apologize, Miss Reilly, or express my sense of your kindness when I am in such a disgusting state. How could I be such a bea— [*he trips again*] damn the heather! my foot caught in it.

NORA. Steady now, steady. Come along: come.

[*He is led down to the road in the character of a convicted drunkard. To him there is something divine in the sympathetic indulgence she substitutes for the angry disgust with which one of his own countrywomen would resent his supposed condition. And he has no suspicion of the fact, or of her ignorance of it, that when an Englishman is sentimental he behaves very much as an Irishman does when he is drunk.*]

Act 3

Next morning BROADBENT *and* LARRY *are sitting at the ends of a breakfast table in the middle of a small grass plot before* CORNELIUS DOYLE's *house. They have finished their meal, and are buried in newspapers. Most of the crockery is crowded upon a large square black tray of japanned metal. The teapot is of brown delft ware. There is no silver; and the butter, on a dinner plate, is en bloc. The background to this breakfast is the house, a small white slated building, accessible by a half-glazed door. A person coming out into the garden by this door would find the table straight in front of him, and a gate leading to the road half way down the garden on his right; or, if he turned sharp to his left, he could pass round the end of the house through an unkempt shrubbery. The mutilated remnant of a huge plaster statue, nearly dissolved by the rains of a century, and vaguely resembling a majestic female in Roman draperies, with a wreath in her hand, stands neglected amid the laurels. Such statues, though apparently works of art, grow naturally in Irish gardens. Their germination is a mystery to the oldest inhabitants, to whose means and tastes they are totally foreign.*

There is a rustic bench, much soiled by the birds, and decorticated and split by the weather, near the little gate. At the opposite side, a basket lies unmolested because it might as well be there as anywhere else. An empty chair at the table was lately occupied by CORNELIUS, *who has finished his breakfast and gone in to the room in which he receives rents and keeps his books and cash, known in the household as "the office." This chair, like the two occupied by* LARRY *and* BROADBENT, *has a mahogany frame and is upholstered in black horsehair.*

LARRY *rises and goes off through the shrubbery with his newspaper.* HODSON *comes in through the garden gate, disconsolate.* BROADBENT, *who sits facing the gate, augurs the worst from his expression.*

BROADBENT.   Have you been to the village?

HODSON.   No use, sir. We'll have to get everything from London by parcel post.

BROADBENT.   I hope they made you comfortable last night.

HODSON.   I was no worse than you were on that sofa, sir. One expects to rough it here, sir.

BROADBENT.   We shall have to look out for some other arrangement. [*Cheering up irrepressibly.*] Still, it's no end of a joke. How do you like the Irish, Hodson?

HODSON.   Well, sir, theyre all right anywhere but in their own country. Ive known lots of em in England, and generally liked em. But here, sir, I seem simply to hate em. The feeling come over me the moment we landed at Cork, sir. It's no use my pretendin, sir: I cant bear em. My mind rises up agin their ways, somehow: they rub me the wrong way all over.

BROADBENT.   Oh, their faults are on the surface: at heart they are one of the finest races on earth.

> [HODSON *turns away, without affecting to respond to his enthusiasm.*]

By the way, Hodson—

HODSON [*turning*].   Yes, sir.

BROADBENT.   Did you notice anything about me last night when I came in with that lady?

HODSON [*surprised*].   No, sir.

BROADBENT.   Not any—er—? You may speak frankly.

HODSON.   I didnt notice nothing, sir. What sort of thing did you mean, sir?

BROADBENT.   Well—er—er—well, to put it plainly, was I drunk?

HODSON [*amazed*].   No, sir.

BROADBENT.   Quite sure?

HODSON.   Well, I should a said rather the opposite, sir. Usually when youve been enjoying yourself, youre a bit hearty like. Last night you seemed rather low, if anything.

BROADBENT.   I certainly have no headache. Did you try the pottine, Hodson?

HODSON.   I just took a mouthful, sir. It tasted of peat: oh! something horrid, sir. The people here call peat turf. Potcheen and strong porter is what they like, sir. I'm sure I dont know how they can stand it. Give me beer, I say.

BROADBENT.   By the way, you told me I couldnt have porridge for breakfast; but Mr Doyle had some.

HODSON.   Yes, sir. Very sorry, sir. They call it stirabout, sir: thats how it was. They know no better, sir.

BROADBENT.   All right: I'll have some tomorrow.

> [HODSON *goes to the house. When he opens the door he finds* NORA *and* AUNT JUDY *on the threshold. He stands aside to let them pass, with the air of a well trained servant oppressed by heavy trials. Then he goes in.* BROADBENT *rises.* AUNT JUDY *goes*

to the table and collects the plates and cups on the tray. NORA *goes to the back of the rustic seat and looks out at the gate with the air of a woman accustomed to having nothing to do.* LARRY *returns from the shrubbery.*]

BROADBENT.   Good morning, Miss Doyle.

AUNT JUDY [*thinking it absurdly late in the day for such a salutation*]. Oh, good morning. [*Before moving his plate.*] Have you done?

BROADBENT.   Quite, thank you. You must excuse us for not waiting for you. The country air tempted us to get up early.

AUNT JUDY.   N d'ye call this airly, God help you?

LARRY.   Aunt Judy probably breakfasted about half past six.

AUNT JUDY.   Whisht, you! draggin the parlor chairs out into the gardn n givin Mr Broadbent his death over his meals out here in the cold air. [*To* BROADBENT.] Why d'ye put up with his foolishness, Mr Broadbent?

BROADBENT.   I assure you I like the open air.

AUNT JUDY.   Ah galong! How can you like whats not natural? I hope you slept well.

NORA.   Did anything wake yup with a thump at three o'clock? I thought the house was falling. But then I'm a very light sleeper.

LARRY.   I seem to recollect that one of the legs of the sofa in the parlor had a way of coming out unexpectedly eighteen years ago. Was that it, Tom?

BROADBENT [*hastily*].   Oh, it doesnt matter: I was not hurt—at least—er—

AUNT JUDY.   Oh now what a shame! An I told Patsy Farrll to put a nail in it.

BROADBENT.   He did, Miss Doyle. There was a nail, certainly.

AUNT JUDY.   Dear oh dear!

[*An oldish peasant farmer, small, leathery, peat-faced, with a deep voice and a surliness that is meant to be aggressive, and is in effect pathetic—the voice of a man of hard life and many sorrows—comes in at the gate. He is old enough to have perhaps worn a long tailed frieze coat and knee breeches in his time; but now he is dressed respectably in a black frock coat, tall hat, and pollard colored trousers; and his face is as clean as washing can make it, though that is not saying much, as the habit is recently acquired and not yet congenial.*]

THE NEW-COMER [*at the gate*].   God save all here! [*He comes a little way into the garden.*]

LARRY [*patronizingly, speaking across the garden to him*].   Is that yourself, Matt Haffigan? Do you remember me?

MATTHEW [*intentionally rude and blunt*].   No. Who are you?

NORA.   Oh, I'm sure you remember him, Mr Haffigan.

MATTHEW [*grudgingly admitting it*].   I suppose he'll be young Larry Doyle that was.

LARRY.   Yes.

MATTHEW [*to* LARRY].   I hear you done well in America.

LARRY.   Fairly well.

MATTHEW.   I suppose you saw me brother Andy out dhere.

LARRY.   No. It's such a big place that looking for a man there is like looking for a needle in a bundle of hay. They tell me he's a great man out there.

MATTHEW.   So he is, God be praised. Wheres your father?

AUNT JUDY.   He's inside, in the office, Mr Haffigan, with Barney Doran and Father Dempsey.

> [MATTHEW, *without wasting further words on the company, goes curtly into the house.*]

LARRY [*staring after him*].   Is anything wrong with old Matt?

NORA.   No. He's the same as ever. Why?

LARRY.   He's not the same to me. He used to be very civil to Masther Larry: a deal too civil, I used to think. Now he's as surly and stand-off as a bear.

AUNT JUDY.   Oh sure he's bought his farm in the Land Purchase. He's independent now.

NORA.   It's made a great change, Larry. Youd harly know the old tenants now. Youd think it was a liberty to speak t'dhem—some o dhem.

> [*She goes to the table, and helps to take off the cloth, which she and* AUNT JUDY *fold up between them.*]

AUNT JUDY.   I wonder what he wants to see Corny for. He hasnt been here since he paid the last of his old rent; and then he as good as threw it in Corny's face, I thought.

LARRY.   No wonder! Of course they all hated us like the devil. Ugh! [*Moodily.*] Ive seen them in that office, telling my father what a fine boy I was, and plastering him with compliments, with your honor here and your honor there, when all the time their fingers were itching to be at his throat.

AUNT JUDY.   Deedn why should they want to hurt poor Corny? It was he that got Matt the lease of his farm, and stood up for him as an industrious decent man.

BROADBENT.   Was he industrious? Thats remarkable, you know, in an Irishman.

LARRY.   Industrious! That man's industry used to make me sick, even as a boy. I tell you, an Irish peasant's industry is not human: it's worse than the industry of a coral insect. An Englishman has some sense about working: he never does more than he can help—and hard enough to get him to do that without scamping it; but an Irishman will work as if he'd die the moment he stopped. That man Matthew Haffigan and his brother Andy made a farm out of a patch of stones on the hillside: cleared it and dug it with their own naked hands and bought their first spade out of their first crop of potatoes. Talk of making two blades of wheat grow where one grew before! those two men made a whole field of wheat grow where not even a furze bush had ever got its head up between the stones.

BROADBENT.   That was magnificent, you know. Only a great race is capable of producing such men.

LARRY.   Such fools, you mean! What good was it to them? The moment theyd done it, the landlord put a rent of £5 a year on them, and turned them out because they coudnt pay it.

AUNT JUDY.   Why coudnt they pay as well as Billy Byrne that took it after them?

LARRY [angrily].   You know very well that Billy Byrne never paid it. He only offered it to get possession. He never paid it.

AUNT JUDY.   That was because Andy Haffigan hurt him with a brick so that he was never the same again. Andy had to run away to America for it.

BROADBENT [glowing with indignation].   Who can blame him, Miss Doyle? Who can blame him?

LARRY [impatiently].   Oh, rubbish! whats the good of the man thats starved out of a farm murdering the man thats starved into it? Would you have done such a thing!

BROADBENT.   Yes. I—I—I—I— [stammering with fury] I should have shot the confounded landlord, and wrung the neck of the damned agent, and blown the farm up with dynamite, and Dublin Castle[6] along with it.

LARRY.   Oh yes: youd have done great things; and a fat lot of good youd have got out of it, too! Thats an Englishman all over! make bad laws and give away all the land, and then, when your economic incompetence produces its natural and inevitable results, get virtuously indignant and kill the people that carry out your laws.

AUNT JUDY.   Sure never mind him, Mr Broadbent. It doesnt matter, anyhow, because theres harly any landlords left; and therll soon be none at all.

LARRY.   On the contrary, therll soon be nothing else; and the Lord help Ireland then!

AUNT JUDY.   Ah, youre never satisfied, Larry. [To NORA.] Come on, alanna, an make the paste for the pie. We can leave them to their talk. They dont want us. [She takes up the tray and goes into the house.]

BROADBENT [rising and gallantly protesting].   Oh, Miss Doyle! Really, really—

[NORA, following AUNT JUDY with the rolled-up cloth in her hands, looks at him and strikes him dumb. He watches her until she disappears; then comes to LARRY and addresses him with sudden intensity.]

BROADBENT.   Larry.

LARRY.   What is it?

6. Norman structure, at the time of the play the seat of British administration of Ireland.

152 BERNARD SHAW

BROADBENT. I got drunk last night, and proposed to Miss Reilly.

LARRY. You hwat??? [*He screams with laughter in the falsetto Irish register unused for that purpose in England.*]

BROADBENT. What are you laughing at?

LARRY [*stopping dead*]. I dont know. Thats the sort of thing an Irishman laughs at. Has she accepted you?

BROADBENT. I shall never forget that with the chivalry of her nation, though I was utterly at her mercy, she refused me.

LARRY. That was extremely improvident of her. [*Beginning to reflect.*] But look here: when were you drunk? You were sober enough when you came back from the Round Tower with her.

BROADBENT. No, Larry, I was drunk, I am sorry to say. I had two tumblers of punch. She had to lead me home. You must have noticed it.

LARRY. I did not.

BROADBENT. She did.

LARRY. May I ask how long it took you to come to business? You can hardly have known her for more than a couple of hours.

BROADBENT. I am afraid it was hardly a couple of minutes. She was not here when I arrived; and I saw her for the first time at the tower.

LARRY. Well, you are a nice infant to be let loose in this country! Fancy the potcheen going to your head like that!

BROADBENT. Not to my head, I think. I have no headache; and I could speak distinctly. No: potcheen goes to the heart, not to the head. What ought I to do?

LARRY. Nothing. What need you do?

BROADBENT. There is rather a delicate moral question involved. The point is, was I drunk enough not to be morally responsible for my proposal? Or was I sober enough to be bound to repeat it now that I am undoubtedly sober?

LARRY. I should see a little more of her before deciding.

BROADBENT. No, no. That would not be right. That would not be fair. I am either under a moral obligation or I am not. I wish I knew how drunk I was.

LARRY. Well, you were evidently in a state of blithering sentimentality, anyhow.

BROADBENT. That is true, Larry: I admit it. Her voice has a most extraordinary effect on me. That Irish voice!

LARRY [*sympathetically*]. Yes, I know. When I first went to London I very nearly proposed to walk out with a waitress in an Aerated Bread shop because her Whitechapel accent was so distinguished, so quaintly touching, so pretty—

BROADBENT [*angrily*]. Miss Reilly is not a waitress, is she?

LARRY. Oh, come! The waitress was a very nice girl.

BROADBENT. You think every Englishwoman an angel. You really have coarse tastes in that way, Larry. Miss Reilly is one of the finer types: a type rare in England, except perhaps in the best of the aristocracy.

LARRY.   Aristocracy be blowed! Do you know what Nora eats?

BROADBENT.   Eats! what do you mean?

LARRY.   Breakfast: tea and bread-and-butter, with an occasional rasher, and an egg on special occasions: say on her birthday. Dinner in the middle of the day, one course and nothing else. In the evening, tea and bread-and-butter again. You compare her with your Englishwomen who wolf down from three to five meat meals a day; and naturally you find her a sylph. The difference is not a difference of type: it's the difference between the woman who eats not wisely but too well, and the woman who eats not wisely but too little.

BROADBENT [*furious*].   Larry: you—you—you disgust me. You are a damned fool. [*He sits down angrily on the rustic seat, which sustains the shock with difficulty.*]

LARRY.   Steady! stead-eee! [*He laughs and seats himself on the table.*]

> [CORNELIUS DOYLE, FATHER DEMPSEY, BARNEY DORAN, *and* MATTHEW HAFFIGAN *come from the house.* DORAN *is a stout bodied, short armed, roundheaded, red haired man on the verge of middle age, of sanguine temperament, with an enormous capacity for derisive, obscene, blasphemous, or merely cruel and senseless fun, and a violent and impetuous intolerance of other temperaments and other opinions, all this representing energy and capacity wasted and demoralized by want of sufficient training and social pressure to force it into beneficent activity and build a character with it; for* BARNEY *is by no means either stupid or weak. He is recklessly untidy as to his person; but the worst effects of his neglect are mitigated by a powdering of flour and mill dust; and his unbrushed clothes, made of a fashionable tailor's sackcloth, were evidently chosen regardless of expense for the sake of their appearance.*
>
> MATTHEW HAFFIGAN, *ill at ease, coasts the garden shyly on the shrubbery side until he anchors near the basket, where he feels least in the way. The priest comes to the table and slaps* LARRY *on the shoulder.* LARRY, *turning quickly, and recognizing* FATHER DEMPSEY, *alights from the table and shakes the priest's hand warmly.* DORAN *comes down the garden between* FATHER DEMPSEY *and* MATT; *and* CORNELIUS, *on the other side of the table, turns to* BROADBENT, *who rises genially.*]

CORNELIUS.   I think we all met las night.

DORAN.   I hadnt that pleasure.

CORNELIUS.   To be sure, Barney: I forgot. [*To* BROADBENT, *introducing* BARNEY.] Mr Doran. He owns that fine mill you noticed from the car.

BROADBENT [*delighted with them all*].   Most happy, Mr Doran. Very pleased indeed.

> [DORAN, *not quite sure whether he is being courted or patronized, nods independently.*]

DORAN.   Hows yourself, Larry?

LARRY.   Finely, thank you. No need to ask you.

[DORAN *grins; and they shake hands.*]

CORNELIUS.   Give Father Dempsey a chair, Larry.

[MATTHEW HAFFIGAN *runs to the nearest end of the table and takes the chair from it, placing it near the basket; but* LARRY *has already taken the chair from the other end and placed it in front of the table.* FATHER DEMPSEY *accepts that more central position.*]

CORNELIUS.   Sit down, Barney, will you; and you, Matt.

[DORAN *takes the chair* MATT *is still offering to the priest; and poor* MATTHEW, *outfaced by the miller, humbly turns the basket upside down and sits on it.* CORNELIUS *brings his own breakfast chair from the table and sits down on* FATHER DEMPSEY's *right.* BROADBENT *resumes his seat on the rustic bench.* LARRY *crosses to the bench and is about to sit down beside him when* BROADBENT *holds him off nervously.*]

BROADBENT.   Do you think it will bear two, Larry?

LARRY.   Perhaps not. Dont move. I'll stand [*He posts himself behind the bench.*]

[*They are all now seated, except* LARRY; *and the session assumes a portentous air, as if something important were coming.*]

CORNELIUS.   Praps youll explain, Father Dempsey.

FATHER DEMPSEY.   No, no: go on, you: the Church has no politics.

CORNELIUS.   Were yever thinkin o goin into parliament at all, Larry?

LARRY.   Me!

FATHER DEMPSEY [*encouragingly*].   Yes, you. Hwy not?

LARRY.   I'm afraid my ideas would not be popular enough.

CORNELIUS.   I dont know that. Do you, Barney?

DORAN.   Theres too much blatherumskite in Irish politics: a dale too much.

LARRY.   But what about your present member? Is he going to retire?

CORNELIUS.   No: I dont know that he is.

LARRY [*interrogatively*].   Well? then?

MATTHEW [*breaking out with surly bitterness*].   Weve had enough of his foolish talk agen lanlords. Hwat call has he to talk about the lan, that never was outside of a city office in his life?

CORNELIUS.   We're tired of him. He doesn't know hwere to stop. Every man cant own land; and some men must own it to employ them. It was all very well when solid men like Doran an Matt were kep from ownin land. But hwat man in his senses ever wanted to give land to Patsy Farrll an dhe like o him?

BROADBENT.   But surely Irish landlordism was accountable for what Mr Haffigan suffered.

MATTHEW.   Never mind hwat I suffered. I know what I suffered ad-hout you tellin me. But did I ever ask for more dhan the farm I made wid me own hans? tell me that, Corny Doyle, and you that knows. Was I fit for the responsibility or was I not? [*Snarling angrily at* CORNELIUS.] Am I to be compared to Patsy Farrll, that doesnt harly know his right hand from his left? What did he ever suffer, I'd like to know?

CORNELIUS.   Thats just what I say. I wasnt comparin you to your disadvantage.

MATTHEW [*implacable*].   Then hwat did you mane be talkin about givin him lan?

DORAN.   Aisy, Matt, aisy. Youre like a bear with a sore back.

MATTHEW [*trembling with rage*].   An who are you, to offer to taitch me manners?

FATHER DEMPSEY [*admonitorily*].   Now, now, now, Matt! none o dhat. How often have I told you youre too ready to take offence where none is meant? You dont understand: Corny Doyle is saying just what you want to have said. [*To* CORNELIUS.] Go on, Mr Doyle; and never mind him.

MATTHEW [*rising*].   Well, if me lan is to be given to Patsy and his like, I'm goin oura dhis. I—

DORAN [*with violent impatience*].   Arra who's goin to give your lan to Patsy, yowl fool ye?

FATHER DEMPSEY.   Aisy, Barney, aisy. [*Sternly, to* MATT.] I told you, Matthew Haffigan, that Corny Doyle was sayin nothin against you. I'm sorry your priest's word is not good enough for you. I'll go, sooner than stay to make you commit a sin against the Church. Good morning, gentlemen.

[*He rises. They all rise, except* BROADBENT.]

DORAN [*to* MATT].   There Sarve you dam well right, you cantanker-ous oul noodle.

MATTHEW [*appalled*].   Dont say dhat, Fadher Dempsey. I never had a thought agen you or the Holy Church. I know I'm a bit hasty when I think about the lan. I ax your pardon for it.

FATHER DEMPSEY [*resuming his seat with dignified reserve*].   Very well: I'll overlook it this time.

[*He sits down. The others sit down, except* MATTHEW. FATHER DEMPSEY, *about to ask* CORNY *to proceed, remembers* MATTHEW *and turns to him, giving him just a crumb of graciousness.*]

Sit down, Matt.

[MATTHEW, *crushed, sits down in disgrace, and is silent, his eyes shifting piteously from one speaker to another in an intensely mistrustful effort to understand them.*]

Go on, Mr Doyle. We can make allowances. Go on.

156 BERNARD SHAW

CORNELIUS. Well, you see how it is, Larry. Round about here, weve got the land at last; and we want no more Goverment meddlin. We want a new class o man in parliament: one dhat knows dhat the farmer's the real backbone o the country, n doesnt care a snap of his fingers for the shoutn o the riff-raff in the towns, or for the foolishness of the laborers.

DORAN. Aye; an dhat can afford to live in London and pay his own way until Home Rule comes, instead o wantin subscriptions and the like.

FATHER DEMPSEY. Yes: thats a good point, Barney. When too much money goes to politics, it's the Church that has to starve for it. A member of parliament ought to be a help to the Church instead of a burden on it.

LARRY. Heres a chance for you, Tom. What do you say?

BROADBENT [deprecatory, but important and smiling]. Oh, I have no claim whatever to the seat. Besides, I'm a Saxon.

DORAN. A hwat?

BROADBENT. A Saxon. An Englishman.

DORAN. An Englishman. Bedad I never heard it called dhat before.

MATTHEW [cunningly]. If I might make so bould, Fadher, I woudnt say but an English Prodestn mightnt have a more indepindent mind about the lan, an be less afeerd to spake out about it, dhan an Irish Catholic.

CORNELIUS. But sure Larry's as good as English: arnt you, Larry?

LARRY. You may put me out of your head, father, once for all.

CORNELIUS. Arra why?

LARRY. I have strong opinions which wouldnt suit you.

DORAN [rallying him blatantly]. Is it still Larry the bould Fenian?

LARRY. No: the bold Fenian is now an older and possibly foolisher man.

CORNELIUS. Hwat does it matter to us hwat your opinions are? You know that your father's bought his place here, just the same as Matt's farm n Barney's mill. All we ask now is to be let alone. Youve nothin against that, have you?

LARRY. Certainly I have. I dont believe in letting anybody or anything alone.

CORNELIUS [losing his temper]. Arra what d'ye mean, you young fool? Here Ive got you the offer of a good seat in parliament; n you think yourself mighty smart to stand there and talk foolishness to me. Will you take it or leave it?

LARRY. Very well: I'll take it with pleasure if youll give it to me.

CORNELIUS [subsiding sulkily]. Well, why couldnt you say so at once? It's a good job youve made up your mind at last.

DORAN [suspiciously]. Stop a bit; stop a bit.

MATTHEW [writhing between his dissatisfaction and his fear of the priest]. It's not because he's your son that he's to get the sate. Fadher Dempsey: wouldnt you think well to ask him what he manes about the lan?

LARRY [*coming down on* MATT *promptly*].   I'll tell you, Matt. I always thought it was a stupid, lazy, good-for-nothing sort of thing to leave the land in the hands of the old landlords without calling them to a strict account for the use they made of it, and the condition of the people on it. I could see for myself that they thought of nothing but what they could get out of it to spend in England; and that they mortgaged and mortgaged until hardly one of them owned his own property or could have afforded to keep it up decently if he'd wanted to. But I tell you plump and plain, Matt, that if anybody thinks things will be any better now that the land is handed over to a lot of little men like you, without calling you to account either, theyre mistaken.

MATTHEW [*sullenly*].   What call have you to look down on me? I suppose you think youre everybody because your father was a land agent.

LARRY.   What call have you to look down on Patsy Farrell? I suppose you think youre everybody because you own a few fields.

MATTHEW.   Was Patsy Farrll ever ever ill used as I was ill used? tell me dhat.

LARRY.   He will be, if ever he gets into your power as you were in the power of your old landlord. Do you think, because youre poor and ignorant and half-crazy with toiling and moiling morning noon and night, that youll be any less greedy and oppressive to them that have no land at all than old Nick Lestrange, who was an educated travelled gentleman that would not have been tempted as hard by a hundred pounds as youd be by five shillings? Nick was too high above Patsy Farrell to be jealous of him; but you, that are only one little step above him, would die sooner than let him come up that step; and well you know it.

MATTHEW [*black with rage, in a low growl*].   Lemmy oura dhis.

[*He tries to rise; but* DORAN *catches his coat and drags him down again.*]

I'm goin, I say. [*Raising his voice.*] Leggo me coat, Barney Doran.

DORAN.   Sit down, yowl omadhaun, you. [*Whispering.*] Dont you want to stay an vote agen him?

FATHER DEMPSEY [*holding up his finger*].   Matt!

[MATT *subsides.*]

Now, now, now! come, come! Hwats all dhis about Patsy Farrll? Hwy need you fall out about him?

LARRY.   Because it was by using Patsy's poverty to undersell England in the markets of the world that we drove England to ruin Ireland. And she'll ruin us again the moment we lift our heads from the dust if we trade in cheap labor; and serve us right too! If I get into parliament, I'll try to get an Act to prevent any of you from giving Patsy less than a pound a week [*they all start, hardly able to believe their ears*] or working him harder than youd work a horse that cost you fifty guineas.

DORAN.   Hwat!!!

CORNELIUS [*aghast*].   A pound a—God save us! the boy's mad.

> [MATTHEW, *feeling that here is something quite beyond his powers, turns openmouthed to the priest, as if looking for nothing less than the summary excommunication of* LARRY.]

LARRY.   How is the man to marry and live a decent life on less?

FATHER DEMPSEY.   Man alive, hwere have you been living all these years? and hwat have you been dreaming of? Why, some o dhese honest men here cant make that much out o the land for dhemselves, much less give it to a laborer.

LARRY [*now thoroughly roused*].   Then let them make room for those who can. Is Ireland never to have a chance? First she was given to the rich; and now that they have gorged on her flesh, her bones are to be flung to the poor, that can do nothing but suck the marrow out of her. If we cant have men of honor own the land, lets have men of ability. If we cant have men with ability, let us at least have men with capital. Anybody's better than Matt, who has neither honor, nor ability, nor capital, nor anything but mere brute labor and greed in him, Heaven help him!

DORAN.   Well, we're not all foostherin oul doddherers like Matt. [*Pleasantly, to the subject of this description.*] Are we, Matt?

LARRY.   For modern industrial purposes you might just as well be, Barney. Youre all children: the big world that I belong to has gone past you and left you. Anyhow, we Irishmen were never made to be farmers; and we'll never do any good at it. We're like the Jews: the Almighty gave us brains, and bid us farm them, and leave the clay and the worms alone.

FATHER DEMPSEY [*with gentle irony*].   Oh! is it Jews you want to make of us? I must catechize you a bit meself, I think. The next thing youll be proposing is to repeal the disestablishment of the so-called Irish Church.[7]

LARRY.   Yes: why not?

> [*Sensation.*]

MATTHEW [*rancorously*].   He's a turncoat.

LARRY.   St Peter, the rock on which our Church was built, was crucified head downwards for being a turncoat.

FATHER DEMPSEY [*with a quiet authoritative dignity which checks* DORAN, *who is on the point of breaking out*].   Thats true. You hold your tongue as befits your ignorance, Matthew Haffigan; and trust your priest to deal with this young man. Now, Larry Doyle, whatever the blessed St Peter was crucified for, it was not for being a Prodestan. Are you one?

LARRY.   No. I am a Catholic intelligent enough to see that the

---

7. The Church of Ireland, Protestant and Anglican; in 1869 it was disestablished, or stripped of a privileged connection with government.

Protestants are never more dangerous to us than when they are free from all alliances with the State. The so-called Irish Church is stronger today than ever it was.

MATTHEW.   Fadher Dempsey: will you tell him dhat me mother's ant was shot and kilt dead in the sthreet o Rosscullen be a soljer in the tithe war?[8] [*Frantically.*] He wants to put the tithes on us again. He—

LARRY [*interrupting him with overbearing contempt*].   Put the tithes on you again! Did the tithes ever come off you? Was your land any dearer when you paid the tithe to the parson than it was when you paid the same money to Nick Lestrange as rent, and he handed it over to the Church Sustentation Fund? Will you always be duped by Acts of Parliament that change nothing but the necktie of the man that picks your pocket? I'll tell you what I'd do with you, Matt Haffigan: I'd make you pay tithes to your own Church. I want the Catholic Church established in Ireland: thats what I want. Do you think that I, brought up to regard myself as the son of a great and holy Church, can bear to see her begging her bread from the ignorance and superstition of men like you? I would have her as high above worldly want as I would have her above worldly pride or ambition. Aye; and I would have Ireland compete with Rome itself for the chair of St Peter and the citadel of the Church; for Rome, in spite of all the blood of the martyrs, is pagan at heart to this day, while in Ireland the people is the Church and the Church the people.

FATHER DEMPSEY [*startled, but not at all displeased*].   Whisht, man! youre worse than mad Pether Keegan himself.

BROADBENT [*who has listened in the greatest astonishment*].   You amaze me, Larry. Who would have thought of your coming out like this! [*Solemnly.*] But much as I appreciate your really brilliant eloquence, I implore you not to desert the great Liberal principle of Disestablishment.[9]

LARRY.   I am not a Liberal: Heaven forbid! A disestablished Church is the worst tyranny a nation can groan under.

BROADBENT [*making a wry face*].   Dont be paradoxical, Larry. It really gives me a pain in my stomach.

LARRY.   Youll soon find out the truth of it here. Look at Father Dempsey! he is disestablished: he has nothing to hope or fear from the State; and the result is that he's the most powerful man in Rosscullen. The member for Rosscullen would shake in his shoes if Father Dempsey looked crooked at him.

> [FATHER DEMPSEY *smiles, by no means averse to this acknowledgment of his authority.*]

Look at yourself! you would defy the established Archbishop of Canterbury ten times a day; but catch you daring to say a word

8. Conflicts in the 1830s over mandatory Catholic contributions to the Anglican Church.
9. Separation of a single church from official national establishment above others.

that would shock a Nonconformist! not you. The Conservative party today is the only one thats not priestridden—excuse the expression, Father

[FATHER DEMPSEY *nods tolerantly*].

—because it's the only one that has established its Church and can prevent a clergyman becoming a bishop if he's not a Statesman as well as a Churchman.

[*He stops. They stare at him dumbfounded, and leave it to the priest to answer him.*]

FATHER DEMPSEY [*judicially*].   Young man; youll not be the member for Roscullen; but dheres more in your head than the comb will take out.

LARRY.   I'm sorry to disappoint you, father; but I told you it would be no use. And now I think the candidate had better retire and leave you to discuss his successor.

[*He takes a newspaper from the table and goes away through the shrubbery amid dead silence, all turning to watch him until he passes out of sight round the corner of the house.*]

DORAN [*dazed*].   Hwat sort of a fella is he at all at all?

FATHER DEMPSEY.   He's a clever lad: dheres the making of a man in him yet.

MATTHEW [*in consternation*].   D'ye mane to say dhat yll put him into parliament to bring back Nick Lesthrange on me, and to put tithes on me, and to rob me for the like o Patsy Farrll, because he's Corny Doyle's son?

DORAN [*brutally*].   Arra hould your whist: who's goin to send him into parliament? Maybe youd like us to send you dhere to thrate dhem to a little o your anxiety about dhat dirty little podato patch o yours.

MATTHEW [*plaintively*].   Am I to be towld dhis afther all me sufferins?

DORAN.   Och, I'm tired o your sufferins. Weve been hearin nothin else ever since we was childher but sufferins. Hwen it wasnt yours it was somebody else's; and hwen it was nobody else's it was ould Irelan's. How the divil are we to live on wan anodher's sufferins?

FATHER DEMPSEY.   Thats a thrue word, Barney Doran; only your tongue's a little too familiar wi dhe divil. [*To* MATT.] If youd think a little more o the sufferins of the blessed saints, Matt, an a little less o your own, youd find the way shorter from your farm to heaven.

[MATT *is about to reply.*]

Dhere now! dhats enough! we know you mean well; an I'm not angry with you.

BROADBENT.   Surely, Mr Haffigan, you can see the simple explanation of all this. My friend Larry Doyle is a most brilliant speaker; but he's a Tory: an ingrained old-fashioned Tory.

CORNELIUS.   N how d'ye make dhat out, if I might ask you, Mr Broadbent?

BROADBENT [*collecting himself for a political deliverance*].   Well, you know, Mr Doyle, theres a strong dash of Toryism in the Irish character. Larry himself says that the great Duke of Wellington[1] was the most typical Irishman that ever lived. Of course thats an absurd paradox; but still theres a great deal of truth in it. Now I am a Liberal. You know the great principles of the Liberal Party. Peace—

FATHER DEMPSEY [*piously*].   Hear! hear!

BROADBENT [*encouraged*].   Thank you. Retrenchment— [*he waits for further applause*].

MATTHEW [*timidly*].   What might rethrenchment mane now?

BROADBENT.   It means an immense reduction in the burden of the rates and taxes.

MATTHEW [*respectfully approving*].   Dhats right. Dhats right, sir.

BROADBENT [*perfunctorily*].   And, of course, Reform.

CORNELIUS
FATHER DEMPSEY } [*conventionally*].   Of course.
DORAN

MATTHEW [*still suspicious*].   Hwat does Reform mane, sir? Does it mane altherin annythin dhats as it is now?

BROADBENT [*impressively*].   It means, Mr Haffigan, maintaining those reforms which have already been conferred on humanity by the Liberal Party, and trusting for future developments to the free activity of a free people on the basis of those reforms.

DORAN.   Dhats right. No more meddlin. We're all right now: all we want is to be let alone.

CORNELIUS.   Hwat about Home Rule?

BROADBENT [*rising so as to address them more imposingly*].   I really cannot tell you what I feel about Home Rule without using the language of hyperbole.

DORAN.   Savin Fadher Dempsey's presence, eh?

BROADBENT [*not understanding him*].   Quite so—er—oh yes. All I can say is that as an Englishman I blush for the Union.[2] It is the blackest stain on our national history. I look forward to the time—and it cannot be far distant, gentlemen, because Humanity is looking forward to it too, and insisting on it with no uncertain voice—I look forward to the time when an Irish legislature shall arise once more on the emerald pasture of College Green, and the Union Jack—that detestable symbol of a decadent Imperialism—be replaced by a flag as green as the island over which it waves: a flag on which we shall ask for England only a modest

---

1. Arthur Wellesley, First Duke of Wellington (1769–1852), British military leader born in Ireland.
2. The Act of Union, absorption of the Irish parliament by the British parliament on January 1, 1801.

quartering in memory of our great party and of the immortal
name of our grand old leader.

DORAN [*enthusiastically*].   Dhats the style, begob! [*He smites his
knee, and winks at* MATT.]

MATTHEW.   More power to you, sir!

BROADBENT.   I shall leave you now, gentlemen, to your delibera-
tions. I should like to have enlarged on the services rendered by
the Liberal Party to the religious faith of the great majority of the
people of Ireland; but I shall content myself with saying that in
my opinion you should choose no representative who—no matter
what his personal creed may be—is not an ardent supporter of
freedom of conscience, and is not prepared to prove it by contributions, as lavish as his means will allow, to the great and beneficent work which you, Father Dempsey

[FATHER DEMPSEY *bows*],

are doing for the people of Rosscullen. Nor should the lighter,
but still most important question of the sports of the people be
forgotten. The local cricket club—

CORNELIUS.   The hwat!

DORAN.   Nobody plays bat n ball here, if dhats what you mane.

BROADBENT.   Well, let us say quoits. I saw two men, I think, last
night—but after all, these are questions of detail. The main thing
is that your candidate, whoever he may be, shall be a man of some
means, able to help the locality instead of burdening it. And if he
were a countryman of my own, the moral effect on the House of
Commons would be immense! tremendous! Pardon my saying
these few words: nobody feels their impertinence more than I do.
Good morning, gentlemen. [*He turns impressively to the gate, and
trots away, congratulating himself, with a little twist of his head and
cock of his eye, on having done a good stroke of political business.*]

HAFFIGAN [*awestruck*].   Good morning, sir.

THE REST.   Good morning. [*They watch him vacantly until he is out
of earshot.*]

CORNELIUS.   Hwat d'ye think, Father Dempsey?

FATHER DEMPSEY [*indulgently*].   Well, he hasnt much sense, God
help him; but for the matter o that, neether has our present
member.

DORAN.   Arra musha he's good enough for parliament: what is
there to do there but gas a bit, an chivy the Government, an vote
wi dh Irish party?

CORNELIUS [*ruminatively*].   He's the queerest Englishman I ever
met. When he opened the paper dhis mornin the first thing he
saw was that an English expedition had been bet in a battle in
Inja somewhere; an he was as pleased as Punch! Larry told him
that if he'd been alive when the news o Waterloo[3] came, he'd a

3. Defeat of Napoleon on June 18, 1815, by the British commanded by the Dublin-born
duke of Wellington (1769–1852).

died o grief over it. Bedad I dont think he's quite right in his head.

DORAN.   Divil a matther if he has plenty o money. He'll do for us right enough.

MATTHEW [*deeply impressed by* BROADBENT, *and unable to understand their levity concerning him*].   Did you mind what he said about rethrenchment? That was very good, I thought.

FATHER DEMPSEY.   You might find out from Larry, Corny, what his means are. God forgive us all! it's poor work spoiling the Egyptians, though we have good warrant for it; so I'd like to know how much spoil there is before I commit meself.

[*He rises. They all rise respectfully.*]

CORNELIUS [*ruefully*].   I'd set me mind on Larry himself for the seat; but I suppose it cant be helped.

FATHER DEMPSEY [*consoling him*].   Well, the boy's young yet; an he had a head on him. Goodbye, all. [*He goes out through the gate.*]

DORAN.   I must be goin, too. [*He directs* CORNELIUS's *attention to what is passing in the road.*] Look at me bould Englishman shaking hans wid Fadher Dempsey for all the world like a candidate on election day. And look at Fadher Dempsey givin him a squeeze an a wink as much as to say It's all right, me boy. You watch him shakin hans with me too: he's waitn for me. I'll tell him he's as good as elected. [*He goes, chuckling mischievously.*]

CORNELIUS.   Come in with me, Matt. I think I'll sell you the pig after all. Come in an wet the bargain.

MATTHEW [*instantly dropping into the old whine of the tenant*].   I'm afeerd I can't afford the price, sir. [*He follows* CORNELIUS *into the house.*]

[LARRY, *newspaper still in hand, comes back through the shrubbery.* BROADBENT *returns through the gate.*]

LARRY.   Well? What has happened?

BROADBENT [*hugely self-satisfied*].   I think Ive done the trick this time. I just gave them a bit of straight talk; and it went home. They were greatly impressed: everyone of those men believes in me and will vote for me when the question of selecting a candidate comes up. After all, whatever you say, Larry, they like an Englishman. They feel they can trust him, I suppose.

LARRY.   Oh! theyve transferred the honor to you, have they?

BROADBENT [*complacently*].   Well, it was a pretty obvious move, I should think. You know, these fellows have plenty of shrewdness in spite of their Irish oddity.

[HODSON *comes from the house.* LARRY *sits in* DORAN's *chair and reads.*]

Oh, by the way, Hodson—

HODSON [*coming between* BROADBENT *and* LARRY].   Yes, sir?

BROADBENT.   I want you to be rather particular as to how you treat the people here.

HODSON.   I havnt treated any of em yet, sir. If I was to accept all the treats they offer me I shouldnt be able to stand at this present moment, sir.

BROADBENT.   Oh well, dont be too stand-offish, you know, Hodson. I should like you to be popular. If it costs anything I'll make it up to you. It doesnt matter if you get a bit upset at first: theyll like you all the better for it.

HODSON.   I'm sure youre very kind, sir; but it dont seem to matter to me whether they like me or not. I'm not going to stand for parliament here, sir.

BROADBENT.   Well, I am. Now do you understand?

HODSON [waking up at once].   Oh, I beg your pardon, sir, I'm sure. I understand, sir.

CORNELIUS [appearing at the house door with MATT].   Patsy'll drive the pig over this evenin, Matt. Goodbye.

> [He goes back into the house. MATT makes for the gate. BROAD-
> BENT stops him. HODSON, pained by the derelict basket, picks
> it up and carries it away behind the house.]

BROADBENT [beaming candidatorially].   I must thank you very particularly, Mr Haffigan, for your support this morning. I value it because I know that the real heart of a nation is the class you represent, the yeomanry.

MATTHEW [aghast].   The yeomanry!!!

LARRY [looking up from his paper].   Take care, Tom! In Rosscullen a yeoman means a sort of Orange Bashi-Bazouk.[4] In England, Matt, they call a freehold farmer a yeoman.

MATTHEW [huffily].   I dont need to be insthructed be you, Larry Doyle. Some people think no one knows anythin but dhemselves. [To BROADBENT, deferentially.] Of course I know a gentleman like you would not compare me to the yeomanry. Me own granfather was flogged in the sthreets of Athenmullet be them when they put a gun in the thatch of his house an then went and found it there, bad cess to them!

BROADBENT [with sympathetic interest].   Then you are not the first martyr of your family, Mr. Haffigan?

MATTHEW.   They turned me out o the farm I made out of the stones o Little Rosscullen hill wid me own hans.

BROADBENT.   I have heard about it; and my blood still boils at the thought. [Calling.] Hodson—

HODSON [behind the corner of the house].   Yes, sir. [He hurries forward.]

BROADBENT.   Hodson: this gentleman's sufferings should make every Englishman think. It is want of thought rather than want of heart that allows such iniquities to disgrace society.

---

4. Protestant mercenary soldier.

HODSON [*prosaically*].   Yes, sir.

MATTHEW.   Well, I'll be goin. Good mornin to you kindly, sir.

BROADBENT.   You have some distance to go, Mr Haffigan: will you allow me to drive you home?

MATTHEW.   Oh sure it'd be throublin your honor.

BROADBENT.   I insist: it will give me the greatest pleasure, I assure you. My car is in the stable: I can get it round in five minutes.

MATTHEW.   Well, sir, if you wouldnt mind, we could bring the pig Ive just bought from Corny—

BROADBENT [*with enthusiasm*].   Certainly, Mr Haffigan: it will be quite delightful to drive with a pig in the car: I shall feel quite like an Irishman. Hodson: stay with Mr Haffigan; and give him a hand with the pig if necessary. Come, Larry; and help me. [*He rushes away through the shrubbery.*]

LARRY [*throwing the paper ill-humoredly on the chair*].   Look here, Tom! here, I saw! counfound it!— [*he runs after him*].

MATTHEW [*glowering disdainfully at* HODSON, *and sitting down on* CORNELIUS's *chair as an act of social self-assertion*].   N are you the valley?

HODSON.   The valley? Oh, I follow you: yes: I'm Mr Broadbent's valet.

MATTHEW.   Ye have an aisy time of it: you look purty sleek. [*With suppressed ferocity.*] Look at me! Do *I* look sleek?

HODSON [*sadly*].   I wish I ad your ealth: you look as ard as nails. I suffer from an excess of uric acid.

MATTHEW.   Musha what sort o disease is zhouragassid? Didjever suffer from injustice and starvation? Dhats the Irish disease. It's aisy for you to talk o sufferin, an you livin on the fat o the land wid money wrung from us.

HODSON [*suddenly dropping the well-spoken valet, and breaking out in his native cockney*].   Wots wrong with you, aold chep? Ez ennybody been doin ennythink to you?

MATTHEW.   Anythin timmy! Didnt your English masther say that the blood biled in him to hear the way they put a rint on me for the farm I made wid me own hans, and turned me out of it to give it to Billy Byrne?

HODSON.   Ow, Tom Broadbent's blad boils pretty easy over ennything that eppens aht of his aown cantry. Downt you be tiken in by my aowl men, Peddy.

MATTHEW [*indignantly*].   Paddy yourself! How dar you call me Paddy?

HODSON [*unmoved*].   You jast keep your air on and listen to me. You Awrish people are too well off: thets wots the metter with you. [*With sudden passion.*] You talk of your rotten little fawm cause you mide it by chackin a few stowns dahn a ill! Well, wot prawce maw grenfawther, Oi should lawk to knaow, that fitted up a fust clawss shop and built ap a fust clawss dripery business in Landon by sixty years work, and then was chacked aht of it on is ed at the end of is lease withaht a penny for his goodwill. You talk of evictions! you that cawnt be moved until youve ran ap ighteen months rent. Oi once ran ap four weeks in Lembeth wen Oi was aht of a job in winter. They took the door off its inges and the winder aht of its seshes on me, and gev maw wawf pnoomownia. Oi'm a widower nah. [*Between his teeth.*] Gawd! when Oi think of the things we Englishmen as to pat ap with, and eah you Awrish ahlin abaht your silly little grievances, and see the wy you mike it worse for haz by the rotten wiges youll cam over and tike and the rotten plices youll sleep in, I jast feel that I could tike the aowl bloomin British awland and mike you a present of it, jast to let you fawnd aht wot reel awdship's lawk.

MATTHEW [*starting up, more in scandalized incredulity than in anger*].   D'ye have the face to set up England agen Ireland for injustices an wrongs an disthress an sufferin?

HODSON [*with intense disgust and contempt*].   Ow, chack it, Paddy. Cheese it. You danno wot awdship is owver eah: all you knaow is ah to ahl abaht it. You tike the biscuit at thet, you do. Oi'm a Owm Ruler, Oi em. Do you knaow woy?

MATTHEW [*equally contemptuous*].   D'ye know, yourself?

HODSON.   Yus Oido. It's because Oi want a little attention pide to my aown cantry; and thetll never be as long as your cheps are ollerin at Wesminister as if nowbody mettered but your own bloomin selves. Send em beck to ell or C'naught, as good aowld English Cramwell[5] said. I'm jast sick of Awrland. Let it gow. Cat the caible. Mike it a present to Germany to keep the aowl Kyzer[6] busy for a wawl; and give poor aowld England a chawnce: thets wot Oi sy.

MATTHEW [*full of scorn for a man so ignorant as to be unable to pronounce the word Connaught, which practically rhymes with bonnet in Ireland, though in* HODSON'S *dialect it rhymes with untaught*].   Take care we dont cut the cable ourselves some day, bad scran[7] to you! An tell me dhis: have yanny Coercion Acs in England? Have yanny Removable magisthruts?[8] Have you Dublin Castle to suppress every newspaper dhat takes the part o your own counthry?

HODSON.   We can beyive ahrselves withaht sich things.

MATTHEW.   Bedad youre right. It'd ony be waste o time to muzzle a sheep. Here! wheres me pig? God forgimmy for talkin to a poor ignorant craycher like you!

HODSON [*grinning with good-humored malice, too convinced of his own superiority to feel his withers wrung*].   Your pig'll ev a rare

5. Oliver Cromwell (1599–1658) brutally conquered Ireland in 1649 and transferred Irish landholders to the west, thus condemning them "to Hell or Connacht."
6. Kaiser Wilhelm (1859–1941), king of Prussia, emperor of Germany, and antagonist of Britain until abdication after World War I.
7. Bad luck.
8. Appointed magistrates subject to removal from office and so, in Ireland, eager to please colonial authorities.

doin in that car, Peddy. Forty mawl an ahr dahn that rocky line
will strawk it pretty pink, you bet.

MATTHEW [*scornfully*].   Hwy cant you tell a raisonable lie when
youre about it? What horse can go forty mile an hour?

HODSON.   Orse! Wy, you silly aowl rotter, it's not a orse: it's a mow-
tor. Do you spowse Tom Broadbent ud gow himself to fetch a
orse?

MATTHEW [*in consternation*].   Holy Moses! dont tell me it's the ingine he wants to take me on.

HODSON.   Wot else?

MATTHEW.   Your sowl to Morris Kelly! why didnt you tell me that
before? The divil an ingine he'll get me on this day. [*His ear
catches an approaching teuf-teuf.*] Oh murdher! It's comin afther
me: I hear the puff-puff of it.

> [*He runs away through the gate, much to* HODSON's *amuse-
> ment. The noise of the motor ceases; and* HODSON, *anticipat-
> ing* BROADBENT's *return, throws off the cockney and
> recomposes himself as a valet.* BROADBENT *and* LARRY *come
> through the shrubbery* HODSON *moves aside to the gate.*]

BROADBENT.   Where is Mr Haffigan? Has he gone for the pig?

HODSON.   Bolted, sir? Afraid of the motor, sir.

BROADBENT [*much disappointed*].   Oh, thats very tiresome. Did he
leave any message?

HODSON.   He was in too great a hurry, sir. Started to run home, sir,
and left his pig behind him.

BROADBENT [*eagerly*].   Left the pig! Then it's all right. The pig's the
thing: the pig will win over every Irish heart to me. We'll take the
pig home to Haffigan's farm in the motor: it will have a tremendous effect. Hodson!

HODSON.   Yes, sir?

BROADBENT.   Do you think you could collect a crowd to see the
motor?

HODSON.   Well, I'll try, sir.

BROADBENT.   Thank you, Hodson: do.

> [HODSON *goes out through the gate.*]

LARRY [*desperately*].   Once more, Tom, will you listen to me?

BROADBENT.   Rubbish! I tell you it will be all right.

LARRY.   Only this morning you confessed how surprised you were
to find that the people here shewed no sense of humor.

BROADBENT [*suddenly very solemn*].   Yes: their sense of humor is in
abeyance: I noticed it the moment we landed. Think of that in a
country where every man is a born humorist! Think of what it
means! [*Impressively.*] Larry: we are in the presence of a great national grief.

LARRY.   Whats to grieve them?

BROADBENT.   I divined it, Larry: I saw it in their faces. Ireland has

never smiled since her hopes were buried in the grave of Gladstone.

LARRY.   Oh, whats the use of talking to such a man? Now look
here, Tom. Be serious for a moment if you can.

BROADBENT [*stupent*].   Serious! I!!!

LARRY.   Yes, you. You say the Irish sense of humor is in abeyance.
Well, if you drive through Rosscullen in a motor car with Haffigan's pig, it wont stay in abeyance. Now I warn you.

BROADBENT [*breezily*].   Why, so much the better! I shall enjoy the
joke myself more than any of them. [*Shouting.*] Hallo, Patsy Farrell, where are you?

PATSY [*appearing in the shrubbery*].   Here I am, your honor.

BROADBENT.   Go and catch the pig and put into the car: we're going to take it to Mr Haffigan's. [*He gives* LARRY *a slap on the
shoulders that sends him staggering off through the gate, and follows him buoyantly, exclaiming*] Come on, you old croaker! I'll
shew you how to win an Irish seat.

PATSY [*meditatively*].   Bedad, if dhat pig gets a howlt o the handle
o the machine— [*He shakes his head ominously and drifts away to
the pigsty.*]

Act 4

The parlor in CORNELIUS DOYLE's *house. It communicates with the
garden by a half glazed door. The fireplace is at the other side of the
room, opposite the door and windows, the architect not having been
sensitive to draughts. The table, rescued from the garden, is in the
middle; and at it sits* KEEGAN, *the central figure in a rather crowded
apartment.* NORA, *sitting with her back to the fire at the end of the
table, is playing backgammon across its corner with him, on his left
hand.* AUNT JUDY, *a little further back, sits facing the fire knitting,
with her feet on the fender. A little to* KEEGAN's *right, in front of the
table, and almost sitting on it, is* BARNEY DORAN. *Half a dozen friends
of his, all men, are between him and the open door, supported by others outside. In the corner behind them is the sofa, of mahogany and
horsehair, made up as a bed for* BROADBENT. *Against the wall behind*
KEEGAN *stands a mahogany sideboard. A door leading to the interior
of the house is near the fireplace, behind* AUNT JUDY. *There are chairs
against the wall, one at each end of the sideboard.* KEEGAN's *hat is on
the one nearest the inner door; and his stick is leaning against it. A
third chair, also against the wall, is near the garden door.*

*There is a strong contrast of emotional atmosphere between the two
sides of the room.* KEEGAN *is extraordinarily stern: no game of
backgammon could possibly make a man's face so grim.* AUNT JUDY *is
quietly busy.* NORA *is trying to ignore* DORAN *and attend to her game.*

On the other hand DORAN *is reeling in an ecstasy of mischievous
mirth which has infected all his friends. They are screaming with
laughter, doubled up, leaning on the furniture and against the walls,
shouting, screeching, crying.*

AUNT JUDY [*as the noise lulls for a moment*].   Arra hold your noise, Barney. What is there to laugh at?

DORAN.   It got its fut into the little hweel— [*he is overcome afresh; and the rest collapse again*].

AUNT JUDY.   Ah, have some sense: youre like a parcel o childher. Nora: hit him a thump on the back: he'll have a fit.

DORAN [*with squeezed eyes, exsufflicate with cachinnation*].   Frens, he sez to dhem outside Doolan's: I'm takin the gintleman that pays the rint for a dhrive.

AUNT JUDY.   Who did he mean be that?

DORAN.   They call a pig that in England. Thats their notion of a joke.

AUNT JUDY.   Musha God help them if they can joke no better than that!

DORAN [*with renewed symptoms*].   Thin—

AUNT JUDY.   Ah now dont be tellin it all over and settin yourself off again, Barney.

NORA.   Youve told us three times, Mr Doran.

DORAN.   Well but whin I think of it—!

AUNT JUDY.   Then dont think of it, alanna.

DORAN.   Dhere was Patsy Farrll in the back sate wi dhe pig between his knees, n me bould English boyoh in front at the machinery, n Larry Doyle in the road startin the injine wid a bed winch. At the first puff of it the pig lep out of its skin and bled Patsy's nose wi dhe ring in its snout.

[*Roars of laughter:* KEEGAN *glares at them*].

Before Broadbint knew hwere he was, the pig was up his back and over into his lap; and bedad the poor baste did credit to Corny's thrainin of it; for it put in the fourth speed wid its right crubeen as if it was enthered for the Gordn Bennett.[9]

NORA [*reproachfully*].   And Larry in front of it and all! It's nothin to laugh at, Mr Doran.

DORAN.   Bedad, Miss Reilly, Larry cleared six yards sideways at wan jump if he cleared an inch; and he'd a cleared seven if Doolan's granmother hadnt cotch him in her apern widout intindin to.

[*Immense merriment.*]

AUNT JUDY.   Ah, for shame, Barney! the poor old woman! An she was hurt before, too, when she slipped on the stairs.

DORAN.   Bedad, maam, she's hurt behind now; for Larry bouled her over like a skittle.

[*General delight at this typical stroke of Irish Rabelaisianism.*[1]]

---

9 Annual international automobile race.
1. Coarsely true, as per the French writer François Rabelais (1494–1553).

NORA.　It's well Mr Doyle wasnt killed.

DORAN.　Faith it wasnt o Larry we were thinkin jus dhen, wi dhe pig takin the main sthreet o Rosscullen on market day at a mile a minnit. Dh ony thing Broadbint could get at wi dhe pig in front of him was a fut brake; n the pig's tail was undher dhat; so that whin he thought he was putn non the brake he was ony squeezin the life out of the pig's tail. The more he put the brake on the more the pig squealed n the fasther he dhruv.

AUNT JUDY.　Why couldnt he throw the pig out into the road?

DORAN.　Sure he couldnt stand up to it, because he was spanchelled-like between his seat and dhat thing like a wheel on top of a stick between his knees.

AUNT JUDY.　Lord have mercy on us!

NORA.　I dont know how you can laugh. Do you, Mr Keegan?

KEEGAN [grimly].　Why not? There is danger, destruction, torment! What more do we need to make us merry? Go on, Barney: the last drops of joy are not squeezed from the story yet. Tell us again how our brother was torn asunder.

DORAN [puzzled].　Whose bruddher?

KEEGAN.　Mine.

NORA.　He means the pig, Mr Doran. You know his way.

DORAN [rising gallantly to the occasion].　Bedad I'm sorry for your poor bruddher, Misther Keegan; but I recommend you to try him wid a couple of fried eggs for your breakfast tomorrow. It was a case of Excelsior wi dhat ambitious baste; for not content wid jumpin from the back seat into the front wan, he jumped from the front wan into the road in front of the car. And—

KEEGAN.　And everybody laughed!

NORA.　Dont go over that again, please, Mr Doran.

DORAN.　Faith be the time the car went over the poor pig dhere was little left for me or anywan else to go over except wid a knife an fork.

AUNT JUDY.　Why didnt Mr Broadbent stop the car when the pig was gone?

DORAN.　Stop the car! He might as well ha thried to stop a mad bull. First it went wan way an made fireworks o Molly Ryan's crockery stall, an dhen it slewed round an ripped ten fut o wall out o the corner o the pound. [With enormous enjoyment.] Begob, it just tore the town in two and sent the whole dam market to blazes.

[NORA offended, rises.]

KEEGAN [indignantly].　Sir!

DORAN [quickly].　Savin your presence, Miss Reilly, and Misther Keegan's. Dhere! I wont say anuddher word.

NORA.　I'm surprised at you, Mr Doran. [She sits down again.]

DORAN [reflectively].　He has the divil's own luck, that Englishman, annyway; for hwen they picked him up he hadnt a scratch on him, barrn hwat the pig did to his cloes. Patsy had two fingers out of jynt; but the smith pulled them sthraight for him. Oh, you never heard such a hullaballoo as there was. There was Molly cryin Me chaney, me beautyful chaney! n oul Matt shoutin Me pig, me pig! n the polus takin the number o the car, n not a man in the town able to speak for laughin—

KEEGAN [*with intense emphasis*].   It is hell: it is hell. Nowhere else coud such a scene be a burst of happiness for the people.

> [CORNELIUS *comes in hastily from the garden, pushing his way through the little crowd.*]

CORNELIUS.   Whisht your laughin, boys! Here he is. [*He puts his hat on the sideboard, and goes to the fireplace, where he posts himself with his back to the chimneypiece.*]

AUNT JUDY.   Remember your behavior, now.

> [*Everybody becomes silent, solemn, concerned, sympathetic.* BROADBENT *enters, soiled and disordered as to his motoring coat: immensely important and serious as to himself. He makes his way to the end of the table nearest the garden door, whilst* LARRY, *who accompanies him, throws his motoring coat on the sofa bed, and sits down, watching the proceedings.*]

BROADBENT [*taking off his leather cap with dignity and placing it on the table*].   I hope you have not been anxious about me.

AUNT JUDY.   Deedn we have, Mr Broadbent. It's a mercy you werent killed.

DORAN.   Kilt! It's a mercy dheres two bones of you left houldin together. How dijjescape at all at all? Well, I never thought I'd be so glad to see you safe and sound again. Not a man in the town would say less.

> [*Murmurs of kindly assent.*]

Wont you come down to Doolan's and have a dhrop o brandy to take the shock off?

BROADBENT.   Youre all really too kind; but the shock has quite passed off.

DORAN [*jovially*].   Never mind. Come along all the same and tell us about it over a frenly glass.

BROADBENT.   May I say how deeply I feel the kindness with which I have been overwhelmed since my accident? I can truthfully declare that I am glad it happened, because it has brought out the kindness and sympathy of the Irish character to an extent I had no conception of.

SEVERAL { Oh, sure youre welcome!
PRESENT. { Sure it's only natural.
         { Sure you might have been kilt.

> [*A young man, feeling that he must laugh or burst, hurries out.* BARNEY *puts an iron constraint on his features.*]

BROADBENT.   All I can say is that I wish I could drink the health of everyone of you.

DORAN.   Dhen come an do it.

BROADBENT [*very solemnly*].   No: I am a teetotaller.

AUNT JUDY [*incredulously*].   Arra since when?

BROADBENT.   Since this morning, Miss Doyle. I have had a lesson [*he looks at* NORA *significantly*] that I shall not forget. It may be that total abstinence has already saved my life; for I was astonished at the steadiness of my nerves when death stared me in the face today. So I will ask you to excuse me. [*He collects himself for a speech.*] Gentlemen: I hope the gravity of the peril through which we have all passed—for I know that the danger to the bystanders was as great as to the occupants of the car—will prove an earnest of closer and more serious relations between us in the future. We have had a somewhat agitating day: a valuable and innocent animal has lost its life: a public building has been wrecked: an aged and infirm lady has suffered an impact for which I feel personally responsible, though my old friend Mr Laurence Doyle unfortunately incurred the first effects of her very natural resentment. I greatly regret the damage to Mr Patrick Farrell's fingers; and I have of course taken care that he shall not suffer pecuniarily by his mishap.

> [*Murmurs of admiration at his magnanimity, and* A Voice "Youre a gentleman, sir".]

I am glad to say that Patsy took it like an Irishman, and, far from expressing any vindictive feeling, declared his willingness to break all his fingers and toes for me on the same terms.

> [*Subdued applause, and* "More power to Patsy!"]

Gentlemen: I felt at home in Ireland from the first.

> [*Rising excitement among his hearers.*]

In every Irish breast I have found that spirit of liberty,

> [*A cheery voice* "Hear Hear."]

that instinctive mistrust of the Government,

> [*A small pious voice, with intense expression,* "God bless you, sir!"]

that love of independence [*A defiant voice,* "Thats it! Independence!"], that indignant sympathy with the cause of oppressed nationalities abroad

> [*A threatening growl from all: the ground-swell of patriotic passion.*]

and with the resolute assertion of personal rights at home, which is all but extinct in my own country. If it were legally possible I should become a naturalized Irishman; and if ever it be my good fortune to represent an Irish constituency in parliament, it shall be my first care to introduce a Bill legalizing such an operation. I believe a large secton of the Liberal party would avail themselves of it.

[*Momentary scepticism.*]

I do.

[*Convulsive cheering.*]

Gentlemen: I have said enough.

[*Cries of* "Go on."]

No: I have as yet no right to address you at all on political subjects; and we must not abuse the warmhearted Irish hospitality of Miss Doyle by turning her sitting room into a public meeting.

DORAN [*energetically*].   Three cheers for Tom Broadbent, the future member for Rosscullen!

AUNT JUDY [*waving a half knitted sock*].   Hip hip hurray!

[*The cheers are given with great heartiness, as it is by this time, for the more humorous spirits present, a question of vociferation of internal rupture.*]

BROADBENT.   Thank you from the bottom of my heart, friends.

NORA [*whispering to* DORAN].   Take them away, Mr Doran.

[*They shake hands.*]

Good evenin, Miss Doyle.

[*General handshaking,* BROADBENT *shaking hands with everybody effusively. He accompanies them to the garden and can be heard outside saying Goodnight in every inflexion known to parliamentary candidates.* NORA, AUNT JUDY, KEEGAN, LARRY, *and* CORNELIUS *are left in the parlor.* LARRY *goes to the threshold and watches the scene in the garden.*]

NORA.   It's a shame to make game of him like that. He's a gradle more good in him than Barney Doran.

CORNELIUS.   It's all up with his candidature. He'll be laughed out o the town.

LARRY [*turning quickly from the doorway*].   Oh no he wont: he's not an Irishman. He'll never know theyre laughing at him; and while theyre laughing he'll win the seat.

CORNELIUS.   But he cant prevent the story getting about.

LARRY.   He wont want to. He'll tell it himself as one of the most providential episodes in the history of England and Ireland.

AUNT JUDY.   Sure he wouldn't make a fool of himself like that.

LARRY.   Are you sure he's such a fool after all, Aunt Judy? Suppose you had a vote! which would you rather give it to? the man that told the story of Haffigan's pig Barney Doran's way or Broadbent's way?

AUNT JUDY.   Faith I wouldnt give it to a man at all. It's a few women they want in parliament to stop their foolish blather.

BROADBENT [*bustling into the room, and taking off his damaged motoring overcoat, which he puts down on the sofa*]. Well, thats over. I must apologize for making a speech, Miss Doyle; but they like it, you know. Everything helps in electioneering.

[LARRY *takes the chair near the door; draws it near the table; and sits astride it, with his elbows folded on the back.*]

AUNT JUDY. I'd no notion you were such an orator, Mr Broadbent.

BROADBENT. Oh, it's only a knack. One picks it up on the platform. It stokes up their enthusiasm.

AUNT JUDY. Oh, I forgot. Youve not met Mr Keegan. Let me introjoosha.

BROADBENT [*shaking hands effusively*]. Most happy to meet you, Mr Keegan. I have heard of you, though I have not had the pleasure of shaking your hand before. And now may I ask you—for I value no man's opinion more—what you think of my chances here.

KEEGAN [*coldly*]. Your chances, sir, are excellent. You will get into parliament.

BROADBENT [*delighted*]. I hope so. I think so. [*Fluctuating.*] You really think so? You are sure you are not allowing your enthusiasm for our principles to get the better of your judgment?

KEEGAN. I have no enthusiasm for your principles, sir. You will get into parliament because you want to get into it enough to be prepared to take the necessary steps to induce the people to vote for you. That is how people usually get into that fantastic assembly.

BROADBENT [*puzzled*]. Of course. [*Pause.*] Quite so. [*Pause.*] Er— yes. [*Buoyant again.*] I think they will vote for me. Eh? Yes?

AUNT JUDY. Arra why shouldnt they? Look at the people they do vote for!

BROADBENT [*encouraged*]. Thats true: thats very true. When I see the windbags, the carpet-baggers, the charlatans, the—the—the fools and ignoramuses who corrupt the multitude by their wealth, or seduce them by spouting balderdash to them, I cannot help thinking that an Englishman with no humbug about him, who will talk straight common sense and take his stand on the solid ground of principle and public duty, must win his way with men of all classes.

KEEGAN [*quietly*]. Sir: there was a time, in my ignorant youth, when I should have called you a hypocrite.

BROADBENT [*reddening*]. A hypocrite!

NORA [*hastily.*] Oh I'm sure you dont think anything of the sort, Mr Keegan.

BROADBENT [*emphatically*]. Thank you, Miss Reilly: thank you.

CORNELIUS [*gloomily*]. We all have to stretch it a bit in politics: hwats the use o pretendin we dont?

BROADBENT [*stiffly*]. I hope I have said or done nothing that calls for any such observation, Mr Doyle. If there is a vice I detest—or against which my whole public life has been a protest—it is the vice of hypocrisy. I would almost rather be inconsistent than insincere.

KEEGAN.   Do not be offended, sir: I know that you are quite sincere. There is a saying in the Scripture which runs—so far as the memory of an oldish man can carry the words—Let not the right side of your brain know what the left side doeth. I learnt at Oxford that this is the secret of the Englishman's strange power of making the best of both worlds.

BROADBENT.   Surely the text refers to our right and left hands. I am somewhat surprised to hear a member of your Church quote so essentially Protestant a document as the Bible; but at least you might quote it accurately.

LARRY.   Tom: with the best intentions youre making an ass of yourself. You dont understand Mr Keegan's peculiar vein of humor.

BROADBENT [*instantly recovering his confidence*].   Ah! it was only your delightful Irish humor, Mr Keegan. Of course, of course. How stupid of me! I'm so sorry. [*He pats* KEEGAN *consolingly on the back.*] John Bull's wits are still slow, you see. Besides, calling me a hypocrite was too big a joke to swallow all at once, you know.

KEEGAN.   You must also allow for the fact that I am mad.

NORA.   Ah, dont talk like that, Mr Keegan.

BROADBENT [*encouragingly*].   Not at all, not at all. Only a whimsical Irishman, eh?

LARRY.   Are you really mad, Mr Keegan?

AUNT JUDY [*shocked*].   Oh, Larry, how could you ask him such a thing?

LARRY.   I dont think Mr Keegan minds. [*To* KEEGAN.] Whats the true version of the story of that black man you confessed on his deathbed?

KEEGAN.   What story have you heard about that?

LARRY.   I am informed that when the devil came for the black heathen, he took off your head and turned it three times round before putting it on again; and that your head's been turned ever since.

NORA [*reproachfully*].   Larry!

KEEGAN [*blandly*].   That is not quite what occurred. [*He collects himself for a serious utterance: they attend involuntarily.*] I heard that a black man was dying, and that the people were afraid to go near him. When I went to the place I found an elderly Hindoo, who told me one of those tales of unmerited misfortune, of cruel ill luck, of relentless persecution by destiny, which sometimes wither the commonplaces of consolation on the lips of a priest. But this man did not complain of his misfortunes. They were brought upon him, he said, by sins committed in a former existence. Then, without a word of comfort from me, he died with a cleareyed resignation that my most earnest exhortations have rarely produced in a Christian, and left me sitting there by his bedside with the mystery of this world suddenly revealed to me.

BROADBENT.   That is a remarkable tribute to the liberty of conscience enjoyed by the subjects of our Indian Empire.

LARRY.   No doubt; but may we venture to ask what is the mystery
of this world?

KEEGAN.   This world, sir, is very clearly a place of torment and
penance, a place where the fool flourishes and the good and wise
are hated and persecuted, a place where men and women torture
one another in the name of love; where children are scourged
and enslaved in the name of parental duty and education; where
the weak in body are poisoned and mutilated in the name of
healing, and the weak in character are put to the horrible torture
of imprisonment, not for hours but for years, in the name of justice. It is a place where the hardest toil is a welcome refuge from
the horror and tedium of pleasure, and where charity and good
works are done only for hire to ransom the souls of the spoiler
and the sybarite. Now, sir, there is only one place of horror and
torment known to my religion; and that place is hell. Therefore it
is plain to me that this earth of ours must be hell, and that we
are all here, as the Indian, revealed to me—perhaps he was sent
to reveal it to me—to expiate crimes committed by us in as former existence.

AUNT JUDY [awestruck].   Heaven save us, what a thing to say!

CORNELIUS [sighing].   It's a queer world: thats certain.

BROADBENT.   Your idea is a very clever one, Mr Keegan: really most
brilliant: I should never have thought of it. But it seems to me—
if I may say so—that you are overlooking the fact that, of the
evils you describe, some are absolutely necessary for the preser-
vation of society, and others are encouraged only when the Tories
are in office.

LARRY.   I expect you were a Tory in a former existence; and that is
why you are here.

BROADBENT [with conviction].   Never, Larry, never. But leaving politics out of the question, I find the world quite good enough for
me: rather a jolly place, in fact.

KEEGAN [looking at him with quiet wonder].   You are satisfied?

BROADBENT.   As a reasonable man, yes. I see no evils in the
world—except, of course, natural evils—that cannot be remedied
by freedom, self-government, and English institutions. I think so,
not because I am an Englishman, but as a matter of common
sense.

KEEGAN.   You feel at home in the world, then?

BROADBENT.   Of course. Dont you?

KEEGAN [from the very depths of his nature].   No.

BROADBENT [breezily].   Try phosphorus pills. I always take them
when my brain is overworked. I'll give you the address in Oxford
Street.

KEEGAN [enigmatically: rising].   Miss Doyle: my wandering fit has
come on me: will you excuse me?

AUNT JUDY.   To be sure: you know you can come in n nout as you like.

KEEGAN.   We can finish the game some other time, Miss Reilly. [*He goes for his hat and stick.*]

NORA.   No: I'm out with you [*she disarranges the pieces and rises.*] I was too wicked in a former existence to play backgammon with a good man like you.

AUNT JUDY [*whispering to her*].   Whisht, whisht, child! Dont set him back on that again.

KEEGAN [*to* NORA].   When I look at you, I think that perhaps Ireland is only purgatory, after all. [*He passes on to the garden door.*]

NORA.   Galong with you!

BROADBENT [*whispering to Cornelius*].   Has he a vote?

CORNELIUS [*nodding*].   Yes. An theres lotsle vote the way he tells them.

KEEGAN [*at the garden door, with gentle gravity*].   Good evening, Mr Broadbent. You have set me thinking. Thank you.

BROADBENT [*delighted, hurrying across to him to shake hands*].   No, really? You find that contact with English ideas is stimulating, eh?

KEEGAN.   I am never tired of hearing you talk, Mr Broadbent.

BROADBENT [*modestly remonstrating*].   Oh come! come!

KEEGAN.   Yes, I assure you. You are an extremely interesting man. [*He goes out.*]

BROADBENT [*enthusiastically*].   What a nice chap! What an intelligent, broadminded character, considering his cloth! By the way, I'd better have a wash. [*He takes up his coat and cap, and leaves the room through the inner door.*]

[NORA *returns to her chair and shuts up the backgammon board.*]

AUNT JUDY.   Keegan's very queer today. He has his mad fit on him.

CORNELIUS [*worried and bitter*].   I wouldn't say but he's right after all. It's a contrairy world. [*To* LARRY.] Why would you be such a fool as to let Broadbent take the seat in parliament from you?

LARRY [*glancing at* NORA].   He will take more than that from me before he's done here.

CORNELIUS.   I wish he'd never set foot in my house, bad luck to his fat face! D'ye think he'd lend me £300 on the farm, Larry? When I'm so hard up, it seems a waste o money not to mortgage it now it's me own.

LARRY.   *I* can lend you £300 on it.

CORNELIUS.   No, no; I wasnt putn in for that. When I die and leave you the farm I should like to be able to feel that it was all me own, and not half yours to start with. Now I'll take me oath Barney Doarn's going to ask Broadbent to lend him £500 on the mill to put in a new hweel; for the old one'll harly hol together. An Haffigan cant sleep with covetn that corner o land at the foot of his medda that belongs to Doolan. He'll have to mortgage to buy it. I may as well be first as last. D'ye think Broadbent'd len me a little?

LARRY.   I'm quite sure he will.

CORNELIUS.   Is he as ready as that? Would he len me five hunderd, d'ye think?

LARRY.   He'll lend you more than the landll ever be worth to you; so for Heaven's sake be prudent.

CORNELIUS [*judicially*].   All right, all right, me son: I'll be careful. I'm goin into the office for a bit. [*He withdraws through the inner door, obviously to prepare his application to* BROADBENT.]

AUNT JUDY [*indignantly*].   As if he hadnt seen enough o borryin when he was an agent without beginning borryin himself! [*She rises.*] I'll borry him, so I will. [*She puts her knitting on the table and follows him out, with a resolute air that bodes trouble for* COR-NELIUS.]

> [LARRY *and* NORA *are left together for the first time since his arrival. She looks at him with a smile that perishes as she sees him aimlessly rocking his chair, and reflecting, evidently not about her, with his lips pursed as if he were whistling. With a catch in her throat she takes up* AUNT JUDY's *knitting, and makes a pretence of going on with it.*]

NORA.   I suppose it didnt seem very long to you.

LARRY [*starting*].   Eh? What didnt?

NORA.   The eighteen years youve been away.

LARRY.   Oh, that! No: it seems hardly more than a week. I've been so busy—had so little time to think.

NORA.   Ive had nothin else to do but think.

LARRY.   That was very bad for you. Why didnt you give it up? Why did you stay here?

NORA.   Because nobody sent for me to go anywhere else, I sup-pose. Thats why.

LARRY.   Yes: one does stick frightfully in the same place, unless some external force comes and routs one out.

> [*He yawns slightly; but as she looks up quickly at him, he pulls himself together and rises with an air of waking up and setting to work cheerfully to make himself agreeable.*]

And how have you been all this time?

NORA.   Quite well, thank you.

LARRY.   Thats right. [*Suddenly finding that he has nothing else to say, and being ill at ease in consequence, he strolls about the room humming distractedly.*]

NORA [*struggling with her tears*].   Is that all you have to say to me, Larry?

LARRY.   Well, what is there to say? You see, we know each other so well.

NORA [*a little consoled*].   Yes: of course we do.

[*He does not reply.*]

I wonder you came back at all.

LARRY.   I couldnt help it.

[*She looks up affectionately.*]

Tom made me.

[*She looks down again quickly to conceal the effect of this blow. He whistles another stave; then resumes.*]

I had a sort of dread of returning to Ireland. I felt somehow that my luck would turn if I came back. And now here I am, none the worse.

NORA.   Praps it's a little dull for you.

LARRY.   No: I havnt exhausted the interest of strolling about the old places and remembering and romancing about them.

NORA [*hopefully*].   Oh! You do remember the places, then?

LARRY.   Of course. They have associations.

NORA [*not doubting that the associations are with her*].   I suppose so.

LARRY.   M'yes. I can remember particular spots where I had long fits of thinking about the countries I meant to get to when I escaped from Ireland. America and London, and sometimes Rome and the east.

NORA [*deeply mortified*].   Was that all you used to be thinking about?

LARRY.   Well, there was precious little else to think about here, my dear Nora, except sometimes at sunset, when one got maudlin and called Ireland Erin, and imagined one was remembering the days of old, and so forth. [*He whistles Let Erin Remember.*]

NORA.   Did jever get a letter I wrote you last February?

LARRY.   Oh yes; and I really intended to answer it. But I havnt had a moment; and I knew you wouldn't mind. You see, I am so afraid of boring you by writing about affairs you dont understand and people you dont know! And yet what else have I to write about? I begin a letter; and then I tear it up again. The fact is, fond as we are of one another, Nora, we have so little in common—I mean of course the things one can put in a letter—that correspondence is apt to become the hardest of hard work.

NORA.   Yes: it's hard for me to know anything about you if you never tell me anything.

LARRY [*pettishly*].   Nora: a man cant sit down and write his life day by day when he's tired enough with having lived it.

NORA.   I'm not blaming you.

LARRY [*looking at her with some concern*].   You seem rather out of spirits. [*Going closer to her, anxiously and tenderly.*] You havnt got neuralgia, have you?

NORA.   No.

LARRY [*reassured*].   I get a touch of it sometimes when I am below par. [*Absently, again strolling about.*] Yes, yes. [*He gazes through the doorway at the Irish landscape, and sings, almost unconsciously, but very expressively, an air from Offenbach's Whittington.*][2]

Though sum-mer smiles on here for e-ver, And though full sweet the charm may be, Tell Eng-land I'll for-get her ne-ver,

[NORA, *who has been at first touched by the tenderness of his singing, puts down her knitting at this very unexpected sentiment, and stares at him. He continues until the melody soars out of his range, when he trails off into whistling Let Erin Remember.*]

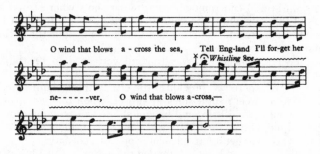

O wind that blows a-cross the sea, Tell Eng-land I'll for-get her ne------ver, O wind that blows a-cross,—

I'm afraid I'm boring you, Nora, though youre too kind to say so.

NORA.   Are you wanting to get back to England already?

LARRY.   Not at all. Not at all.

NORA.   Thats a queer song to sing to me if youre not.

LARRY.   The song! Oh, it doesnt mean anything: it's by a German Jew, like most English patriotic sentiment. Never mind me, my dear: go on with your work; and dont let me bore you.

NORA [*bitterly*].   Rosscullen isnt such a lively place that I am likely to be bored by you at our first talk together after eighteen years, though you dont seem to have much to say to me after all.

LARRY.   Eighteen years is a devilish long time, Nora. Now if it had been eighteen minutes, or even eighteen months, we should be able to pick up the interrupted thread, and chatter like two mag-

---

2. Jacques Offenbach (1819–80); "Whittington and His Cat" (1874), operetta based on a folktale.

pies. But as it is, I have simply nothing to say; and you seem to have less.

NORA.   I— [*her tears choke her; but she keeps up appearances desperately*].

LARRY [*quite unconscious of his cruelty*].   In a week or so we shall be quite old friends again. Meanwhile, as I feel that I am not making myself particularly entertaining, I'll take myself off. Tell Tom Ive gone for a stroll over the hill.

NORA.   You seem very fond of Tom, as you call him.

LARRY [*the triviality going suddenly out of his voice*].   Yes: I'm fond of Tom.

NORA.   Oh, well, dont let me keep you from him.

LARRY.   I know quite well that my departure will be a relief. Rather a failure, this first meeting after eighteen years, eh? Well, never mind: these great sentimental events always are failures; and now the worst of it's over anyhow. [*He goes out through the garden door.*]

> [NORA, *left alone, struggles wildly to save herself from breaking down, and then drops her face on the table and gives way to a convulsion of crying. Her sobs shake her so that she can hear nothing; and she has no suspicion that she is no longer alone until her head and breast are raised by* BROADBENT, *who, returning newly washed and combed through the inner door, has seen her condition, first with surprise and concern, and then with an emotional disturbance that quite upsets him.*]

BROADBENT.   Miss Reilly. Miss Reilly. Whats the matter? Dont cry: I cant stand it: you musnt cry.

> [*She makes a choked effort to speak, so painful that he continues with impulsive sympathy.*]

No: dont try to speak: it's all right now. Have your cry out: never mind me: trust me. [*Gathering her to him, and babbling consolatorily.*] Cry on my chest: the only really comfortable place for a woman to cry is a man's chest: a real man, a real friend. A good broad chest, eh? not less than forty-two inches—no: dont fuss: never mind the conventions: we're two friends, arnt we? Come now, come, come! It's all right and comfortable and happy now, isnt it?

NORA [*through her tears*].   Let me go. I want me handkerchief.

BROADBENT [*holding her with one arm and producing a large silk handkerchief from his breast pocket*].   Heres a handkerchief. Let me [*he dabs her tears dry with it*]. Never mind your own: it's too small: it's one of those wretched little cambric handkerchiefs—

NORA [*sobbing*].   Indeed it's a common cotton one.

BROADBENT.   Of course it's a common cotton one—silly little cotton one—not good enough for the dear eyes of Nora Cryna—

NORA [*spluttering into a hysterical laugh and clutching him convul-*

sively with her fingers while she tries to stifle her laughter against his collar bone].   Oh dont make me laugh: please dont make me laugh.

BROADBENT [*terrified*].   I didnt mean to, on my soul. What is it? What is it?

NORA.   Nora Creena, Nora Creena.

BROADBENT [*patting her*].   Yes, yes, of course, Nora Creena, Nora acushla[3] [*he makes cush rhyme to plush*]—

NORA.   Acushla [*she makes cush rhyme to bush*].

BROADBENT.   Oh, confound the language! Nora darling—my Nora—the Nora I love—

NORA [*shocked into propriety*].   You musnt talk like that to me.

BROADBENT [*suddenly becoming prodigiously solemn and letting her go*].   No, of course not. I dont mean it. At least I do mean it; but I know it's premature. I had no right to take advantage of your being a little upset; but I lost my self-control for a moment.

NORA [*wondering at him*].   I think youre a very kindhearted man, Mr Broadbent; but you seem to me to have no self-control at all [*she turns her face away with a keen pang of shame and adds*] no more than myself.

BROADBENT [*resolutely*].   Oh yes, I have: you should see me when I am really roused: then I have TREMENDOUS self-control. Remember: we have been alone together only once before; and then, I regret to say, I was in a disgusting state.

NORA.   Ah no, Mr Broadbent: you wernt disgusting.

BROADBENT [*mercilessly*].   Yes I was: nothing can excuse it: perfectly beastly. It must have made a most unfavorable impression on you.

NORA.   Oh, sure it's all right. Say no more about that.

BROADBENT.   I must, Miss Reilly: it is my duty. I shall not detain you long. May I ask you to sit down.

[*He indicates her chair with oppressive solemnity. She sits down wondering. He then, with the same portentous gravity, places a chair for himself near her; sits down; and proceeds to explain.*]

First, Miss Reilly, may I say that I have tasted nothing of an alcoholic nature today.

NORA.   It doesnt seem to make as much difference in you as it would in an Irishman, somehow.

BROADBENT.   Perhaps not. Perhaps not. I never quite lose myself.

NORA [*consolingly*].   Well, anyhow, youre all right now.

BROADBENT [*fervently*].   Thank you, Miss Reilly: I am. Now we shall get along. [*Tenderly, lowering his voice.*] Nora: I was in earnest last night.

[NORA *moves as if to rise.*]

3. Gaelic endearment: Nora of my heart.

No: one moment. You must not think I am going to press you for an answer before you have known me for 24 hours. I am a reasonable man, I hope; and I am prepared to wait as long as you like, provided you will give me some small assurance that the answer will not be unfavorable.

NORA.   How could I go back from it if I did? I sometimes think youre not quite right in your head, Mr Broadbent, you say such funny things.

BROADBENT.   Yes: I know I have a strong sense of humor which sometimes makes people doubt whether I am quite serious. That is why I have always thought I should like to marry an Irishwoman. She would always understand my jokes. For instance, you would understand them, eh?

NORA [*uneasily*].   Mr Broadbent: I couldnt.

BROADBENT [*soothingly*].   Wait: let me break this to you gently, Miss Reilly: hear me out. I daresay you have noticed that in speaking to you I have been putting a very strong constraint on myself, so as to avoid wounding your delicacy by too abrupt an avowal of my feelings. Well, I feel now that the time has come to be open, to be frank, to be explicit. Miss Reilly: you have inspired in me a very strong attachment. Perhaps, with a woman's intuition, you have already guessed that.

NORA [*rising distractedly*].   Why do you talk to me in that unfeeling nonsensical way?

BROADBENT [*rising also, much astonished*].   Unfeeling! Nonsensical!

NORA.   Dont you know that you have said things to me that no man ought to say unless—unless— [*she suddenly breaks down again and hides her face on the table as before*]. Oh, go away from me: I wont get married at all: what is it but heartbreak and disappointment?

BROADBENT [*developing the most formidable symptoms of rage and grief*].   Do you mean to say that you are going to refuse me: that you dont care for me?

NORA [*looking at him in consternation*].   Oh, dont take it to heart, Mr Br—

BROADBENT [*flushed and almost choking*].   I dont want to be petted and blarneyed. [*With childish rage.*] I love you. I want you for my wife. [*In despair*] I cant help your refusing. I'm helpless: I can do nothing. You have no right to ruin my whole life. You— [*a hysterical convulsion stops him*].

NORA [*almost awestruck*].   Youre not going to cry, are you? I never thought a man could cry. Dont.

BROADBENT.   I'm not crying. I—I—I leave that sort of thing to your damned sentimental Irishmen. You think I have no feeling because I am a plain unemotional Englishman, with no powers of expression.

NORA.   I dont think you know the sort of man you are at all. Whatever may be the matter with you, it's not want of feeling.

BROADBENT [*hurt and petulant*].   It's you who have no feeling.
Youre as heartless as Larry.

NORA.   What do you expect me to do? Is it to throw meself at your
head the minute the word is out o your mouth?

BROADBENT [*striking his silly head with his fists*].   Oh, what a fool!
what a brute I am! It's only your Irish delicacy: of course, of
course. You mean Yes. Eh? What? Yes? yes? yes?

NORA.   I think you might understand that though I might choose
to be an old maid, I could never marry anybody but you now.

BROADBENT [*clasping her violently to his breast, with a crow of immense relief and triumph*].   Ah, thats right, thats right: thats
magnificent. I knew you would see what a first-rate thing this will
be for both of us.

NORA [*incommoded and not at all enraptured by his ardor*].   Youre
dreadfully strong, an a gradle too free with your strength. An I
never thought o whether it'd be a good thing for us or not. But
when you found me here that time, I let you be kind to me, and
cried in your arms, because I was too wretched to think of anything but the comfort of it. An how could I let any other man
touch me after that?

BROADBENT [*moved*].   Now thats very nice of you, Nora: thats
really most delicately womanly. [*He kisses her hand chivalrously.*]

NORA [*looking earnestly and a little doubtfully at him*].   Surely if
you let one woman cry on you like that youd never let another
touch you.

BROADBENT [*conscientiously*].   One should not. One ought not, my
dear girl. But the honest truth is, if a chap is at all a pleasant sort
of chap, his chest becomes a fortification that has to stand many
assaults: at least it is so in England.

NORA [*curtly, much disgusted*].   Then youd better marry an Englishwoman.

BROADBENT [*making a wry face*].   No, no: the Englishwoman is too
prosaic for my taste, too material, too much of the animated
beefsteak about her. The ideal is what I like. Now Larry's taste is
just the opposite: he likes em solid and bouncing and rather keen
about him. It's a very convenient difference; for weve never been
in love with the same woman.

NORA.   An d'ye mean to tell me to me face that youve ever been in
love before?

BROADBENT.   Lord! yes.

NORA.   I'm not your first love!

BROADBENT.   First love is only a little foolishness and a lot of curiosity: no really self-respecting woman would take advantage of
it. No, my dear Nora: Ive done with all that long ago. Love affairs
always end in rows. We're not going to have any rows: we're going
to have a solid four-square home: man and wife: comfort and
common sense. And plenty of affection, eh [*he puts his arm
round her with confident proprietorship*]?

NORA [*coldly, trying to get away*].   I dont want any other woman's leavings.

BROADBENT [*holding her*].   Nobody asked you to, maam. I never asked any woman to marry me before.

NORA [*severely*].   Then why didnt you if youre an honorable man?

BROADBENT.   Well, to tell you the truth, they were mostly married already. But never mind! there was nothing wrong. Come! dont take a mean advantage of me. After all, you must have had a fancy or two yourself, eh?

NORA [*conscience-stricken*].   Yes. I suppose Ive no right to be particular.

BROADBENT [*humbly*].   I know I'm not good enough for you, Nora. But no man is, you know, when the woman is a really nice woman.

NORA.   Oh, I'm no better than yourself. I may as well tell you about it.

BROADBENT.   No, no: lets have no telling: much better not. *I* shant tell you anything: dont you tell me anything. Perfect confidence in one another and no tellings: thats the way to avoid rows.

NORA.   Dont think it was anything I need be ashamed of.

BROADBENT.   I dont.

NORA.   It was only that I'd never known anybody else that I could care for; and I was foolish enough once to think that Larry—

BROADBENT [*disposing of the idea at once*].   Larry! Oh, that wouldnt have done at all, not at all. You dont know Larry as I do, my dear. He has absolutely no capacity for enjoyment: he couldnt make any woman happy. He's as clever as beblowed; but life's too earthly for him: he doesnt really care for anything or anybody.

NORA.   Ive found that out.

BROADBENT.   Of course you have. No, my dear: take my word for it, youre jolly well out of that. There! [*swinging her round against his breast*] thats much more comfortable for you.

NORA [*with Irish peevishness*].   Ah, you mustnt go on like that. I dont like it.

BROADBENT [*unabashed*].   Youll acquire the taste by degrees. You mustnt mind me: it's an absolute necessity of my nature that I should have somebody to hug occasionally. Besides, it's food for you: itll plump out your muscles and make em elastic and set up your figure.

NORA.   Well, I'm sure! if this is English manners! Arnt you ashamed to talk about such things?

BROADBENT [*in the highest feather*].   Not a bit. By George, Nora, it's a tremendous thing to be able to enjoy oneself. Lets go off for a walk out of this stuffy little room. I want the open air to expand in, Come along. Co-o-ome along.

[*He puts her arm into his and sweeps her out into the garden as an equinoctial gale might sweep a dry leaf.*

Later in the evening, the grasshopper is again enjoying the sunset by the great stone on the hill; but this time he enjoys neither the stimulus of KEEGAN's *conversation nor the pleasure of terrifying* PATSY FARRELL. *He is alone until* NORA *and* BROADBENT *come up the hill arm in arm.* BROADBENT *is still breezy and confident; but she has her head averted from him and is almost in tears.*]

BROADBENT [*stopping to snuff up the hillside air*]. Ah! I like this spot. I like this view. This would be a jolly good place for a hotel and a golf links. Friday to Tuesday, railway ticket and hotel all inclusive. I tell you, Nora, I'm going to develop this place. [*Looking at her.*] Hallo! Whats the matter? Tired?

NORA [*unable to restrain her tears*].   I'm ashamed out o me life.

BROADBENT [*astonished*].   Ashamed! What of?

NORA.   Oh, how could you drag me all round the place like that, telling everybody that we're going to be married, and introjoocing me to the lowest of the low, and letting them shake hans with me, and encouraging them to make free with us? I little thought I should live to be shaken hans with be Doolan in broad daylight in the public street of Rosscullen.

BROADBENT.   But, my dear, Doolan's a publican: a most influential man. By the way, I asked him if his wife would be at home tomorrow. He said she would; so you must take the motor car round and call on her.

NORA [*aghast*].   Is it me call on Doolan's wife!

BROADBENT.   Yes, of course: call on all their wives. We must get a copy of the register and a supply of canvassing cards. No use calling on people who havnt votes. Youll be a great success as a canvasser, Nora: they call you the heiress; and theyll be flattered no end by your calling, especially as youve never cheapened yourself by speaking to them before—have you?

NORA [*indignantly*].   Not likely, indeed.

BROADBENT.   Well, we musnt be stiff and stand-off, you know. We must be thoroughly democratic, and patronize everybody without distinction of class. I tell you I'm a jolly lucky man, Nora Cryna. I get engaged to the most delightful woman in Ireland; and it turns out that I couldnt have done a smarter stroke of electioneering.

NORA.   An would you let me demean meself like that, just to get yourself into parliament?

BROADBENT [*buoyantly*].   Aha! Wait til you find out what an exciting game electioneering is: youll be mad to get me in. Besides, youd like people to say that Tom Broadbent's wife had been the making of him? that she got him into parliament? into the Cabinet, perhaps, eh?

NORA.   God knows I dont grudge you me money! But to lower meself to the level of common people—

BROADBENT.   To a member's wife, Nora, nobody is common provided he's on the register. Come, my dear! it's all right: do you think I'd let you do it if it wasnt? The best people do it. Everybody does it.

NORA [*who has been bitting her lip and looking over the hill, disconsolate and unconvinced*]. Well, praps you know best what they do in England. They must have very little respect for themselves. I think I'll go in now. I see Larry and Mr Keegan coming up the hill; and I'm not fit to talk to them.

BROADBENT. Just wait and say something nice to Keegan. They tell me he controls nearly as many votes as Father Dempsey himself.

NORA. You little know Peter Keegan. He'd see through me as if I was a pane o glass.

BROADBENT. Oh, he wont like it any the less for that. What really flatters a man is that you think him worth flattering. Not that I would flatter any man: dont think that. I'll just go and meet him.

[*He goes down the hill with the eager forward look of a man about to greet a valued acquaintance.* NORA *dries her eyes, and turns to go as* LARRY *strolls up the hill to her.*]

LARRY.   Nora.

[*She turns and looks at him hardly, without a word. He continues anxiously, in his most conciliatory tone.*]

When I left you that time, I was just as wretched as you. I didnt rightly know what I wanted to say; and my tongue kept clacking to cover the loss I was at. Well, Ive been thinking ever since; and now I know what I ought to have said. Ive come back to say it.

NORA.   Youve come too late, then. You thought eighteen years was not long enough, and that you might keep me waiting a day longer. Well, you were mistaken. I'm engaged to your friend Mr Broadbent; and I'm done with you.

LARRY [*naïvely*].   But that was the very thing I was going to advise you to do.

NORA [*involuntarily*].   Oh you brute! to tell me that to me face!

LARRY [*nervously relapsing into his most Irish manner*].   Nora, dear, dont you understand that I'm an Irishman, and he's an Englishman. He wants you; and he grabs you. *I* want you; and I quarrel with you and have to go on wanting you.

NORA.   So you may. Youd better go back to England to the animated beefsteaks youre so fond of.

LARRY [*amazed*].   Nora! [*Guessing where she got the metaphor.*] He's been talking about me, I see. Well, never mind: we must be friends, you and I. I dont want his marriage to you to be his divorce from me.

NORA.   You care more for him than you ever did for me.

LARRY [*with curt sincerity*].   Yes of course I do: why should I tell you lies about it? Nora Reilly was a person of very little consequence to me or anyone else outside this miserable little hole. But Mrs Tom Broadbent will be a person of very considerable consequence indeed. Play your new part well, and there will be no more neglect, no more loneliness, no more idle regrettings and vain-hopings in the evenings by the Round Tower, but real life and real work and real cares and real joys among real people: solid English life in London, the very centre of the world. You will find your work cut out for you keeping Tom's house and entertaining Tom's friends and getting Tom into parliament; but it will be worth the effort.

NORA.   You talk as if I was under an obligation to him for marrying me.

LARRY.   I talk as I think. Youve made a very good match, let me tell you.

NORA.   Indeed! Well, some people might say he's not done so badly himself.

LARRY.   If you mean that you will be a treasure to him, he thinks so now; and you can keep him thinking so if you like.

NORA.   I wasnt thinking o meself at all.

LARRY.   Were you thinking of your money, Nora?

NORA.   I didnt say so.

LARRY.   Your money will not pay your cook's wages in London.

NORA [*flaming up*].   If thats true—and the more shame for you to throw it in me face if it is true—at all events itll make us independent; for if the worst comes to the worst, we can always come back here an live on it. An if I have to keep his house for him, at all events I can keep you out of it; for Ive done with you; and I wish I'd never seen you. So goodbye to you, Mister Larry Doyle. [*She turns her back on him and goes home.*]

LARRY [*watching her as she goes*].   Goodbye. Goodbye, Oh, thats so Irish! Irish both of us to the backbone: Irish! Irish! Iri—

[BROADBENT *arrives, conversing energetically with* KEEGAN.]

BROADBENT.   Nothing pays like a golfing hotel, if you hold the land instead of the shares, and if the furniture people stand in with you, and if you are a good man of business.

LARRY.   Nora's gone home.

BROADBENT [*with conviction*].   You were right this morning, Larry. I must feed up Nora. She's weak; and it makes her fanciful. Oh, by the way, did I tell you that we're engaged?

LARRY.   She told me herself.

BROADBENT [*complacently*].   She's rather full of it, as you may imagine. Poor Nora! Well, Mr Keegan, as I said, I begin to see my way here. I begin to see my way.

KEEGAN [*with a courteous inclination*].   The conquering Englishman, sir. Within 24 hours of your arrival you have carried off our only heiress, and practically secured the parliamentary seat. And you have promised me that when I come here in the evenings to meditate on my madness; to watch the shadow of the Round Tower lengthening in the sunset; to break my heart uselessly in the curtained gloaming over the dead heart and blinded soul of the island of the saints, you will comfort me with the bustle of a great hotel, and the sight of the little children carrying the golf clubs of your tourists as a preparation for the life to come.

BROADBENT [*quite touched, mutely offering him a cigar to console him, at which he smiles and shakes his head*].   Yes, Mr Keegan: youre quite right. Theres poetry in everything, even [*looking absently into the cigar case*] in the most modern prosaic things, if you know how to extract it [*he extracts a cigar for himself and offers one to* LARRY, *who takes it*]. If I was to be shot for it I couldnt extract it myself; but thats where you come in, you see. [*Roguishly, waking up from his reverie and bustling* KEEGAN *goodhumoredly.*] And then I shall wake you up a bit. Thats where I come in: eh? d'ye see? Eh? eh? [*He pats him very pleasantly on the shoulder, half admiringly, half pityingly.*] Just so, just so. [*Coming back to business.*] By the way, I believe I can do better than a light railway here. There seems to be no question now that the motor boat has come to stay. Well, look at your magnificent river there, going to waste.

KEEGAN [*closing his eyes*].   "Silent, O Moyle, be the roar of thy waters."[4]

BROADBENT.   You know, the roar of a motor boat is quite pretty.

KEEGAN.   Provided it does not drown the Angelus.

BROADBENT [*reassuringly*].   Oh no: it wont do that: not the least danger. You know, a church bell can make a devil of a noise when it likes.

KEEGAN.   You have an answer for everything, sir. But your plans leave one question still unanswered: how to get butter out of a dog's throat.

BROADBENT.   Eh?

KEEGAN.   You cannot build your golf links and hotels in the air. For that you must own our land. And how will you drag our acres from the ferret's grip of Matthew Haffigan? How will you persuade Cornelius Doyle to forgo the pride of being a small landowner? How will Barney Doran's millrace agree with your motor boats? Will Doolan help you to get a license for your hotel?

BROADBENT.   My dear sir: to all intents and purposes the syndicate I represent already owns half Rosscullen. Doolan's is a tied house; and the brewers are in the syndicate. As to Haffigan's farm and Doran's mill and Mr Doyle's place and half a dozen others, they will be mortgaged to me before a month is out.

KEEGAN.   But pardon me, you will not lend them more on their land than the land is worth; so they will be able to pay you the interest.

BROADBENT.   Ah, you are a poet, Mr Keegan, not a man of business.

LARRY.   We will lend everyone of these men half as much again on their land as it is worth, or ever can be worth, to them.

---

4. "The Song of Fionnuala," by Irish poet Thomas Moore (1779–1852).

BROADBENT.   You forget, sir, that we, with our capital, our knowledge, our organization, and may I say our English business
habits, can make or lose ten pounds out of land that Haffigan,
with all his industry, could not make or lose ten shillings out of.
Doran's mill is a superannuated folly: I shall want it for electric
lighting.

LARRY.   What is the use of giving land to such men? they are too
small, too poor, too ignorant, too simpleminded to hold it against
us: you might as well give a dukedom to a crossing sweeper.

BROADBENT.   Yes, Mr Keegan: this place may have an industrial future, or it may have a residential future: I cant tell yet; but it's
not going to be a future in the hands of your Dorans and Haffigans, poor devils!

KEEGAN.   It may have no future at all. Have you thought of that?

BROADBENT.   Oh, I'm not afraid of that. I have faith in Ireland.
Great faith, Mr Keegan.

KEEGAN.   And we have none: only empty enthusiasms and patrio-
tisms, and emptier memories and regrets. Ah yes: you have some
excuse for believing that if there be any future, it will be yours; for
our faith seems dead, and our hearts cold and cowed. An island of
dreamers who wake up in your jails, of critics and cowards whom
you buy and tame for your own service, of bold rogues who help
you to plunder us that they may plunder you afterwards.

BROADBENT [*a little impatient of this unbusinesslike view*].   Yes, yes;
but you know you might say that of any country. The fact is,
there are only two qualities in the world: efficiency and ineffi-
ciency, and only two sorts of people: the efficient and the inefficient. It dont matter whether theyre English or Irish. I shall
collar this place, not because I'm an Englishman and Haffigan
and Co are Irishmen, but because theyre duffers, and I know my
way about.

KEEGAN.   Have you considered what is to become of Haffigan?

LARRY.   Oh, we'll employ him in some capacity or other, and probably pay him more than he makes for himself now.

BROADBENT [*dubiously*].   Do you think so? No no: Haffigan's too
old. It really doesnt pay now to take on men over forty even for
unskilled labor, which I suppose is all Haffigan would be good
for. No: Haffigan had better go to America, or into the Union,[5]
poor old chap! He's worked out, you know: you can see it.

KEEGAN.   Poor lost soul, so cunningly fenced in with invisible bars!

LARRY.   Haffigan doesnt matter much. He'll die presently.

BROADBENT [*shocked*].   Oh come, Larry! Don't be unfeeling. It's
hard on Haffigan. It's always hard on the inefficient.

LARRY.   Pah! what does it matter where an old and broken man
spends his last days, or whether he has a million at the bank or
only the workhouse dole? It's the young men, the able men, that
matter. The real tragedy of Haffigan is the tragedy of his wasted

---

5. Public-assistance workhouse.

youth, his stunted mind, his drudging over his clods and pigs until he has become a clod and a pig himself—until the soul within
him has smouldered into nothing but a dull temper that hurts
himself and all around him. I say let him die, and let us have no
more of his like. And let young Ireland take care that it doesnt
share his fate, instead of making another empty grievance of it.
Let your syndicate come—

BROADBENT.   Your syndicate too, old chap. You have your bit of the
stock.

LARRY.   Yes: mine if you like. Well, our syndicate has no conscience: it has no more regard for your Haffigans and Doolans
and Dorans than it has for a gang of Chinese coolies. It will use
your patriotic blatherskite and balderdash to get parliamentary
powers over you as cynically as it would bait a mousetrap with
toasted cheese. It will plan, and organize, and find capital while
you slave like bees for it and revenge yourselves by paying politicians and penny newspapers out of your small wages to write articles and report speeches against its wickedness and tyranny,
and to crack up your own Irish heroism, just as Haffigan once
paid a witch a penny to put a spell on Billy Byrne's cow. In the
end it will grind the nonsense out of you, and grind strength and
sense into you.

BROADBENT [out of patience].   Why cant you say a simple thing
simply, Larry, without all that Irish exaggeration and talky-talky?
The syndicate is a perfectly respectable body of responsible men
of good position. We'll take Ireland in hand, and by straightforward business habits teach it efficiency and self-help on sound
Liberal principles. You agree with me, Mr Keegan, dont you?

KEEGAN.   Sir: I may even vote for you.

BROADBENT [sincerely moved, shaking his hand warmly].   You shall
never regret it, Mr Keegan: I give you my word for that. I shall
bring money here: I shall raise wages: I shall found public institutions: a library, Polytechnic (undenominational, of course), a
gymnasium, a cricket club, perhaps an art school. I shall make a
Garden city of Rosscullen: the round tower shall be thoroughly
repaired and restored.

KEEGAN.   And our place of torment shall be as clean and orderly as
the cleanest and most orderly place I know in Ireland, which is
our poetically named Mountjoy prison.[6] Well, perhaps I had better vote for an efficient devil that knows his own mind and his
own business than for a foolish patriot who has no mind and no
business.

BROADBENT [stiffly].   Devil is rather a strong expression in that
connexion, Mr Keegan.

KEEGAN.   Not from a man who knows that this world is hell. But
since the word offends you, let me soften it, and compare you
simply to an ass.

6. Prison in Dublin.

[LARRY *whitens with anger.*]

BROADBENT [*reddening*].   An ass!

KEEGAN [*gently*].   You may take it without offence from a madman who calls the ass his brother—and a very honest, useful and faithful brother too. The ass, sir, is the most efficient of beasts, matter-of-fact, hardy, friendly when you treat him as a fellow-creature, stubborn when you abuse him, ridiculous only in love, which sets him braying, and in politics, which move him to roll about in the public road and raise a dust about nothing. Can you deny these qualities and habits in yourself, sir?

BROADBENT [*goodhumoredly*].   Well, yes, I'm afraid I do, you know.

KEEGAN.   Then perhaps you will confess to the ass's one fault.

BROADBENT.   Perhaps so: what is it?

KEEGAN.   That he wastes all his virtues—his efficiency, as you call it—in doing the will of his greedy masters instead of doing the will of Heaven that is in himself. He is efficient in the service of Mammon, mighty in mischief, skilful in ruin, heroic in destruction. But he comes to browse here without knowing that the soil his hoof touches is holy ground. Ireland, sir, for good or evil, is like no other place under heaven; and no man can touch its sod or breathe its air without becoming better or worse. It produces two kinds of men in strange perfection: saints and traitors. It is called the island of the saints; but indeed in these later years it might be more fitly called the island of the traitors; for our harvest of these is the fine flower of the world's crop of infamy. But the day may come when these islands shall live by the quality of their men rather than by the abundance of their minerals; and then we shall see.

LARRY.   Mr Keegan: if you are going to be sentimental about Ireland, I shall bid you good evening. We have had enough of that, and more than enough of cleverly proving that everybody who is not an Irishman is an ass. It is neither good sense nor good manners. It will not stop the syndicate; and it will not interest young Ireland so much as my friend's gospel of efficiency.

BROADBENT.   An, yes, yes: efficiency is the thing. I dont in the least mind your chaff, Mr Keegan; but Larry's right on the main point. The world belongs to the efficient.

KEEGAN [*with polished irony*].   I stand rebuked, gentlemen. But believe me, I do every justice to the efficiency of you and your syndicate. You are both, I am told, thoroughly efficient civil engineers; and I have no doubt the golf links will be a triumph of your art. Mr. Broadbent will get into parliament most efficiently, which is more than St Patrick could do if he were alive now. You may even build the hotel efficiently if you can find enough efficient masons, carpenters, and plumbers, which I rather doubt. [*Dropping his irony, and beginning to fall into the attitude of the priest rebuking sin.*] When the hotel becomes insolvent.

[BROADBENT *takes his cigar out of his mouth, a little taken aback.*]

your English business habits will secure the thorough efficiency of the liquidation. You will recognize the scheme efficiently; you will liquidate its second bankruptcy efficiently;

[BROADBENT *and* LARRY *look quickly at one another; for this, unless the priest is an old financial hand, must be inspiration.*]

you will get rid of its original shareholders efficiently after efficiently ruining them; and you will finally profit very efficiently by getting that hotel for a few shillings on the pound. [*More and more sternly.*] Besides these efficient operations, you will foreclose your mortgages most efficiently [*his rebuking forefinger goes up in spite of himself*]; you will drive Haffigan to America very efficiently; you will find a use for Barney Doran's foul mouth and bullying temper by employing him to slavedrive your laborers very efficiently; and [*low and bitter*] when at last this poor desolate countryside becomes a busy mint in which we shall all slave to make money for you, with our Polytechnic to teach us how to do it efficiently, and our library to fuddle the few imaginations your distilleries will spare, and our repaired Round Tower with admission sixpence, and refreshments and penny-in-the-slot mutoscopes to make it interesting, then no doubt your English and American shareholders will spend all the money we make for them very efficiently in shooting and hunting, in operations for cancer and appendicitis, in gluttony and gambling; and you will devote what they save to fresh land development schemes. For four wicked centuries the world has dreamed this foolish dream of efficiency; and the end is not yet. But the end will come.

BROADBENT [*seriously*]. Too true, Mr Keegan, only too true. And most eloquently put. It reminds me of poor Ruskin: a great man, you know. I sympathize. Believe me, I'm on your side. Dont sneer, Larry: I used to read a lot of Shelley[7] years ago. Let us be faithful to the dreams of our youth [*he wafts a wreath of cigar smoke at large across the hill*].

KEEGAN. Come, Mr Doyle! is this English sentiment so much more efficient than our Irish sentiment, after all? Mr Broadbent spends his life inefficiently admiring the thoughts of great men, and efficiently serving the cupidity of base money hunters. We spend our lives efficiently sneering at him and doing nothing. Which of us has any right to reproach the other?

BROADBENT [*coming down the hill again to* KEEGAN'*s right hand*]. But you know, something must be done.

KEEGAN. Yes: when we cease to do, we cease to live. Well, what shall we do?

7. John Ruskin (1819–1900), art critic and social commentator; Percy Bysshe Shelley (1792–1822), English Romantic poet: both critical of commercial progress.

BROADBENT.   Why, what lies to our hand.

KEEGAN.   Which is the making of golf links and hotels to bring idlers to a country which workers have left in millions because it is a hungry land, a naked land, an ignorant and oppressed land.

BROADBENT.   But, hang it all, the idlers will bring money from England to Ireland!

KEEGAN.   Just as our idlers have for so many generations taken money from Ireland to England. Has that saved England from poverty and degradation more horrible than we have ever dreamed of? When I went to England, sir, I hated England. Now I pity it.

> [BROADBENT *can hardly conceive an Irishman pitying England; but as* LARRY *intervenes angrily, he gives it up and takes to the hill and his cigar again.*]

LARRY.   Much good your pity will do it!

KEEGAN.   In the accounts kept in heaven, Mr Doyle, a heart purified of hatred may be worth more than even a Land Development Syndicate of Anglicized Irishmen and Gladstonized Englishmen.

LARRY.   Oh, in heaven, no doubt. I have never been there. Can you tell me where it is?

KEEGAN.   Could you have told me this morning where hell is? Yet you know now that it is here. Do not despair of finding heaven: it may be no farther off.

LARRY [*ironically*].   On this holy ground, as you call it, eh?

KEEGAN [*with fierce intensity*].   Yes, perhaps, even on this holy ground which such Irishmen as you have turned into a Land of Derision.

BROADBENT [*coming between them*].   Take care! you will be quarrelling presently. Oh, you Irishmen, you Irishmen! Toujours Ballyhooly, eh?

> [LARRY, *with a shrug, half comic, half impatient, turns away up the hill, but presently strolls back on* KEEGAN's *right.* BROADBENT *adds, confidentially to* KEEGAN.]

Stick to the Englishman, Mr Keegan: he has a bad name here; but at least he can forgive you for being an Irishman.

KEEGAN.   Sir: when you speak to me of English and Irish you forget that I am a Catholic. My country is not Ireland nor England, but the whole mighty realm of my Church. For me there are but two countries: heaven and hell; but two conditions of men: salvation and damnation. Standing here between you the Englishman, so clever in your foolishness, and this Irishman, so foolish in his cleverness, I cannot in my ignorance be sure which of you is the more deeply damned; but I should be unfaithful to my calling if I opened the gates of my heart less widely to one than to the other.

LARRY.   In either case it would be an impertinence, Mr Keegan, as your approval is not of the slightest consequence to us. What use do you suppose all this drivel is to men with serious practical business in hand?

BROADBENT.   I dont agree with that, Larry. I think these things cannot be said too often: they keep up the moral tone of the community. As you know, I claim the right to think for myself in religious matters: in fact, I am ready to avow myself a bit of a— of a—well, I dont care who knows it—a bit of a Unitarian; but if the Church of England contained a few men like Mr Keegan, I should certainly join it.

KEEGAN.   You do me too much honor, sir. [*With priestly humility to* LARRY.] Mr. Doyle: I am to blame for having unintentionally set your mind somewhat on edge against me. I beg your pardon.

LARRY [*unimpressed and hostile*].   I didnt stand on ceremony with you: you neednt stand on it with me. Fine manners and fine words are cheap in Ireland: you can keep both for my friend here, who is still imposed on by them. *I* know their value.

KEEGAN.   You mean you dont know their value.

LARRY [*angrily*].   I mean what I say.

KEEGAN [*turning quietly to the Englishman*].   You see, Mr Broadbent, I only make the hearts of my countrymen harder when I preach to them: the gates of hell still prevail against me. I shall wish you good evening. I am better alone, at the Round Tower, dreaming of heaven. [*He goes up the hill.*]

LARRY.   Aye, thats it! there you are! dreaming! dreaming! dreaming! dreaming!

KEEGAN [*halting and turning to them for the last time*].   Every dream is a prophecy: every jest is an earnest in the womb of Time.

BROADBENT [*reflectively*].   Once, when I was a small kid, I dreamt I was in heaven.

> [*They both stare at him.*]

It was a sort of pale blue satin place, with all the pious old ladies in our congregation sitting as if they were at a service; and there was some awful person in the study at the other side of the hall. I didnt enjoy it, you know. What is it like in your dreams?

KEEGAN.   In my dreams it is a country where the State is the Church and the Church the people: three in one and one in three. It is a commonwealth in which work is play and play is life: three in one and one in three. It is a temple in which the priest is the worshipper and the worshipper the worshipped: three in one and one in three. It is a godhead in which all life is human and all humanity divine: three in one and one in three. It is, in short, the dream of a madman. [*He goes away across the hill.*]

BROADBENT [*looking after him affectionately*].   What a regular old Church and State Tory he is! He's a character: he'll be an attraction here. Really almost equal to Ruskin and Carlyle.[8]

---

8. Thomas Carlyle (1795–1881), historian, novelist, and lecturer who was "Tory," or conservative, in opposition to modernization.

LARRY.   Yes; and much good they did with all their talk!

BROADBENT.   Oh tut, tut, Larry! They improved my mind: they raised my tone enormously. I feel sincerely obliged to Keegan: he has made me feel a better man: distinctly better. [*With sincere elevation.*] I feel now as I never did before that I am right in devoting my life to the cause of Ireland. Come along and help me to choose the site for the hotel.

SEAN O'CASEY

Juno and the Paycock[†]

A Tragedy in Three Acts

Characters

'CAPTAIN' JACK BOYLE
JUNE BOYLE, *his wife*
JOHNNY BOYLE }
MARY BOYLE } *their children*
'JOXER' DALY
MRS MAISIE MADIGAN
'NEEDLE' NUGENT, A TAILOR
MRS TANCRED
JERRY DEVINE

*residents in
the tenement*

CHARLES BENTHAM, *a schoolteacher*
AN IRREGULAR MOBILISER
TWO IRREGULARS
A COAL-BLOCK VENDOR
A SEWING-MACHINE MAN
TWO FURNITURE-REMOVAL MEN
TWO NEIGHBOURS

Place and Time

ACT ONE *The living apartment of a two-roomed tenancy of the Boyle family, in a tenement house in Dublin.*

ACT TWO *The same.*

ACT THREE *The same.*

A few days elapse between Acts One and Two, and two months between Acts Two and Three.

† From *Seven Plays by Sean O'Casey*. Reprinted by permission of the Estate of Sean O'Casey and Macnaughton Lord Representation.

198   SEAN O'CASEY

*During Act Three the curtain is lowered for a few minutes to denote
the lapse of one hour. Period of the play, 1922.*[1]

Act 1

*The living-room of a two-room tenancy occupied by the Boyle family
in a tenement house in Dublin. Left, a door leading to another part
of the house; left of door a window looking into the street; at back a
dresser; farther to right at back, a window looking into the back of
the house. Between the window and the dresser is a picture of the
Virgin; below the picture, on a bracket, is a crimson bowl in which a
floating votive light is burning. Farther to the right is a small bed
partly concealed by cretonne hangings strung on a twine. To the right
is the fireplace; near the fireplace is a door leading to the other room.
Beside the fireplace is a box containing coal. On the mantelshelf is an
alarm clock lying on its face. In a corner near the window looking
into the back is a galvanised bath. A table and some chairs. On the
table are breakfast things for one. A teapot is on the hob and a frying-
pan stands inside the fender. There are a few books on the dresser and
one on the table. Leaning against the dresser is a long-handled
shovel—the kind invariably used by labourers when turning concrete
or mixing mortar.* JOHNNY BOYLE *is sitting crouched beside the fire.*
MARY *with her jumper off—it is lying on the back of a chair—is arranging her hair before a tiny mirror perched on the table. Beside the
mirror is stretched out the morning paper, which she looks at when
she isn't gazing into the mirror. She is a well-made and good-looking
girl of twenty-two. Two forces are working in her mind—one, through
the circumstances of her life, pulling her back; the other, through the
influence of books she has read, pushing her forward. The opposing
forces are apparent in her speech and her manners, both of which are
degraded by her environment, and improved by her acquaintance—
slight though it be—with literature. The time is early forenoon.*

MARY [*looking at the paper*].   On a little by-road, out beyant Finglas, he was found.

> [MRS BOYLE[2] *enters by door on right; she has been shopping
> and carries a small parcel in her hand. She is forty-five years
> of age, and twenty years ago she must have been a pretty
> woman; but her face has now assumed that look which ulti-
> mately settles down upon the faces of the women of the
> working-class; a look of listless monotony and harassed anxi-
> ety, blending with an expression of mechanical resistance.*

---

1. The Anglo-Irish Treaty of 1921 granted Ireland some degree of political autonomy; dis-
agreement between those satisfied with the treaty (Free Staters) and those dissatisfied
with it (Republicans, or "Diehards") led to the Irish Civil War, 1922–23.
2. Juno, June Boyle's nickname, was one of the most important ancient roman deities, associated with motherhood, and frequently depicted visually with peacocks.

Were circumstances favourable, she would probably be a handsome, active and clever woman.]

MRS BOYLE.   Isn't he come in yet?

MARY.   No, mother.

MRS BOYLE.   Oh, he'll come in when he likes; struttin' about the town like a paycock with Joxer, I suppose. I hear all about Mrs Tancred's son is in this mornin's paper.

MARY.   The full details are in it this mornin'; seven wounds he had—one enthrin' the neck, with an exit wound beneath the left shoulderblade; another in the left breast penethratin' the heart, an' . . .

JOHNNY [*springing up from the fire*].   Oh, quit readin' for God's sake! Are yous losin' all your feelin's? It'll soon be that none of you'll read anythin' that's not about butcherin'! [*He goes quickly into the room on the left.*]

MARY.   He's gettin' very sensitive, all of a sudden!

MRS BOYLE.   I'll read it myself, Mary, by an' by, when I come home. Everybody's sayin' that he was a Diehard—thanks be to God that Johnny had nothin' to do with him this long time . . . . [*Opening the parcel and taking out some sausages, which she places on a plate.*] Ah, then, if that father o' yours doesn't come in soon for his breakfast, he may go without any; I'll not wait much longer for him.

MARY.   Can't you let him get it himself when he comes in?

MRS BOYLE.   Yes, an' let him bring in Joxer Daly along with him? Ay, that's what he'd like an' that's what he's waitin' for—till he thinks I'm gone to work, an' then sail in with the boul' Joxer, to burn all the coal an' dhrink all the tea in the place, to show them what a good Samaritan he is! But I'll stop here till he comes in, if I have to wait till tomorrow mornin'.

VOICE OF JOHNNY INSIDE.   Mother!

MRS BOYLE.   Yis?

VOICE OF JOHNNY.   Bring us in a dhrink o' wather.

MRS BOYLE.   Bring in that fella a dhrink o' wather, for God's sake, Mary.

MARY.   Isn't he big an' able enough to come out an' get it himself?

MRS BOYLE.   If you weren't well yourself you'd like somebody to bring you in a dhrink o' wather. [*She brings in drink and returns.*] Isn't it terrible to have to be waitin' this way! You'd think he was bringin' twenty poun's a week into the house the way he's going on. He wore out the Health Insurance long ago, he's afther wearin' out the unemployment dole, an', now he's thryin' to wear out me! An' constantly singin', no less, when he ought always to be on his knees offerin' up a Novena for a job!

MARY [*tying a ribbon fillet-wise around her head*].   I don't like this ribbon, Ma; I think I'll wear the green—it looks better than the blue.

MRS BOYLE.   Ah, wear whatever ribbon you like, girl, only don't be
botherin' me. I don't know what a girl on strike wants to be
wearin' a ribbon round her head for, or silk stockin's on her legs
either; it's wearin' them things that make the employers think
they're givin' yous too much money.

MARY.   The hour is past now when we'll ask the employers' permission to wear what we like.

MRS BOYLE.   I don't know why you wanted to walk out for Jennie
Claffey; up to this you never had a good word for her.

MARY.   What's the use of belongin' to a Trades Union if you won't
stand up for your principles? Why did they sack her? It was a
clear case of victimisation. We couldn't let her walk the streets,
could we?

MRS BOYLE.   No, of course yous couldn't—yous wanted to keep her
company. Wan victim wasn't enough. When the employers sacrifice wan victim, the Trades Unions go wan betther be sacrificin' a
hundred.

MARY.   It doesn't matter what you say, Ma—a principle's a principle.

MRS BOYLE.   Yis; an' when I go into oul' Murphy's tomorrow, an' he
gets to know that, instead o' payin' all, I'm goin' to borry more,
what'll he say when I tell him a principle's a principle? What'll
we do if he refuses to give us any more on tick?

MARY.   He daren't refuse—if he does, can't you tell him he's paid?

MRS BOYLE.   It's lookin' as if he was paid, whether he refuses or no.

[JOHNNY *appears at the door on left. He can be plainly seen*
now; he is a thin, delicate fellow, something younger than
MARY. *He has evidently gone through a rough time. His face is*
pale and drawn; there is a tremulous look of indefinite fear in
his eyes. The left sleeve of his coat is empty, and he walks with
a slight halt.]

JOHNNY.   I was lyin' down; I thought yous were gone. Oul' Simon
Mackay is thrampin' about like a horse over me head, an' I can't
sleep with him—they're like thunder-claps in me brain! The
curse o'—God forgive me for goin' to curse!

MRS BOYLE.   There, now; go back an' lie down again an' I'll bring
you in a nice cup o' tay.

JOHNNY.   Tay, tay, tay! You're always thinkin' o' tay. If a man was
dyin', you'd thry to make him swally a cup o' tay! [*He goes back.*]

MRS BOYLE.   I don't know what's goin' to be done with him. The
bullet he got in the hip in Easter Week was bad enough; but the
bomb that shatthered his arm in the fight in O'Connell Street
put the finishin' touch on him. I knew he was makin' a fool of
himself. God knows I went down on me bended knees to him not
to go agen the Free State.[3]

___

3. The Easter rebellion of 1916 launched years of conflict that ended with the Free State
   Treaty (1921), which was opposed by the Republican "Diehards."

MARY.   He stuck to his principles, an', no matter how you may argue, ma, a principle's a principle.

VOICE OF JOHNNY.   Is Mary goin' to stay here?

MARY.   No, I'm not goin' to stay here; you can't expect me to be always at your beck an' call, can you?

VOICE OF JOHNNY.   I won't stop here be meself!

MRS BOYLE.   Amn't I nicely handicapped with the whole o' yous! I don't know what any o' yous ud do without your ma. [*To* JOHNNY.] Your father'll be here in a minute, an' if you want anythin,' he'll get it for you.

JOHNNY.   I hate assin' him for anythin' . . . He hates to be assed to stir. . . . Is the light lightin' before the picture o' the Virgin?

MRS BOYLE.   Yis, yis! The wan inside to St Anthony isn't enough, but he must have another wan to the Virgin here!

> [JERRY DEVINE *enters hastily. He is about twenty-five, well set, active and earnest. He is a type, becoming very common now in the Labour Movement, of a mind knowing enough to make the mass of his associates, who know less, a power, and too little to broaden that power for the benefit of all.* MARY *seizes her jumper and runs hastily into room left.*]

JERRY [*breathless*].   Where's the Captain, Mrs Boyle, where's the Captain?

MRS BOYLE.   You may well ass a body that: he's wherever Joxer Daly is—dhrinkin' in some snug[4] or another.

JERRY.   Father Farrell is just afther stoppin' to tell me to run up an' get him to go to the new job that's goin' on in Rathmines; his cousin is foreman o' the job, an' Father Farrell was speakin' to him about poor Johnny an' his father bein' so idle so long, an' the foreman told Father Farrell to send the Captain up an' he'd give him a start—I wondher where I'd find him?

MRS BOYLE.   You'll find he's ayther in Ryan's or Foley's.

JERRY.   I'll run round to Ryan's—I know it's a great house o' Joxer's. [*He rushes out.*]

MRS BOYLE [*piteously*].   There now, he'll miss that job, or I know for what! If he gets win' o' the word, he'll not come back till evenin', so that it'll be too late. There'll never be any good got out o' him so long as he goes with that shouldher-shruggin' Joxer. I killin' meself workin', an' he sthruttin' about from mornin' till night like a paycock!

> [*The steps of two persons are heard coming up a flight of stairs. They are the footsteps of* CAPTAIN BOYLE *and* JOXER. CAPTAIN BOYLE *is singing in a deep, sonorous, self-honouring voice.*]

THE CAPTAIN.   Sweet Spirit, hear me prayer! Hear . . . oh . . . hear . . . me prayer . . . hear, oh, hear . . . Oh, he . . . ar . . . oh, he . . . ar . . . me . . . pray . . . er!

---

4. Small, comfortable side-room of a pub, or tavern.

JOXER [*outside*]. Ah, that's a darlin' song, a daaarlin' song!

MRS BOYLE [*viciously*]. Sweet spirit hear his prayer! Ah, then, I'll take me solemn affeydavey,[5] it's not for a job he's prayin'! [*She sits down on the bed so that the cretonne hangings hide her from the view of those entering.*]

> [*The* CAPTAIN *comes in. He is a man of about sixty; stout, grey-haired and stocky. His neck is short, and his head looks like a stone ball that one sometimes sees on top of a gate-post. His cheeks, reddish-purple, are puffed out, as if he were always repressing an almost irrepressible ejaculation. On his upper lip is a crisp, tightly cropped moustache; he carries himself with the upper part of his body slightly thrown back, and his stomach slightly thrust forward. His walk is a slow, consequential strut. His clothes are dingy, and he wears a faded seaman's-cap with a glazed peak.*]

BOYLE [*to* JOXER, *who is still outside*]. Come on, come on in, Joxer; she's gone out long ago, man. If there's nothing else to be got, we'll furrage out a cup o' tay, anyway. It's the only bit I get in comfort when she's away. 'Tisn't Juno should be her pet name at all, but Deirdre of the Sorras,[6] for she's always grousin'.

> [JOXER *steps cautiously into the room. He may be younger than the* CAPTAIN *but he looks a lot older. His face is like a bundle of crinkled paper; his eyes have a cunning twinkle; he is spare and loosely built; he has a habit of constantly shrugging his shoulders with a peculiar twitching movement, meant to be ingratiating. His face is invariably ornamented with a grin.*]

JOXER. It's a terrible thing to be tied to a woman that's always grousin'. I don't know how you stick it—it ud put years on me. It's a good job she has to be so ofen away, for [*with a shrug*] when the cat's away, the mice can play!

BOYLE [*with a commanding and complacent gesture*]. Pull over to the fire, Joxer, an' we'll have a cup o' tay in a minute.

JOXER. Ah, a cup o' tay's a darlin' thing, a daaarlin' thing—the cup that cheers but doesn't . . .

> [JOXER'S *rhapsody is cut short by the sight of* MRS BOYLE *coming forward and confronting the two cronies. Both are stupefied.*]

MRS BOYLE [*with sweet irony—poking the fire, and turning her head to glare at* JOXER]. Pull over to the fire, Joxer Daly, an' we'll have a cup o' tay in a minute! Are you sure, now, you wouldn't like an egg?

---

5. Affidavit, sworn statement.
6. Heroine of Celtic mythology sorrowful for doomed flight with a true love from an arranged marriage; a number of modern versions of the story were written during the Irish literary revival.

JOXER.   I can't stop, Mrs Boyle; I'm in a desperate hurry, a desperate hurry.

MRS BOYLE.   Pull over to the fire, Joxer Daly; people is always far more comfortabler here than they are in their own place.

[JOXER *makes hastily for the door.*]

BOYLE [*stirs to follow him; thinks of something to relieve the situation—stops, and says suddenly*]   Joxer!

JOXER [*at door ready to bolt*].   Yis?

BOYLE.   You know the foreman o' that job that's goin' on down in Killesther, don't you, Joxer?

JOXER [*puzzled*].   Foreman—Killesther?

BOYLE [*with a meaning look*].   He's a butty o' yours, isn't he?

JOXER [*the truth dawning on him*].   The foreman at Killesther—oh yis, yis. He's an oul' butty o' mine—oh, he's a darlin' man, a daarlin' man.

BOYLE.   Oh, then, it's a sure thing. It's a pity we didn't go down at breakfast first thing this mornin'—we might ha' been working now; but you didn't know it then.

JOXER [*with a shrug*].   It's better late then never.

BOYLE.   It's nearly time we got a start, anyhow; I'm fed up knockin' round, doin' nothin'. He promised you—gave you the straight tip?

JOXER.   Yis. 'Come down on the blow o' dinner', says he, 'an' I'll start you, an' any friend you like to brin' with you.' 'Ah,' says I, 'you're a darlin' man, a daaarlin' man.'

BOYLE.   Well, it couldn't come at a betther time—we're a long time waitin' for it.

JOXER.   Indeed we were; but it's a long lane that has no turnin'.

BOYLE.   The blow-up for dinner is at one—wait till I see what time it 'tis. [*He goes over to the mantelpiece, and gingerly lifts the clock.*]

MRS BOYLE.   Min' now, how you go on fiddlin' with that clock—you know the least little thing sets it asthray.

BOYLE.   The job couldn't come at a betther time; I'm feelin' in great fettle, Joxer. I'd hardly believe I ever had a pain in me legs, an' last week I was nearly crippled with them.

JOXER.   That's betther an' betther; ah, God never shut wan door but He opened another!

BOYLE.   It's only eleven o'clock; we've lashins o' time. I'll slip on me oul' moleskins afther breakfast, an' we can saunter down at our ayse. [*Putting his hand on the shovel.*] I think, Joxer, we'd betther bring our shovels?

JOXER.   Yis, Captain, yis; it's betther to go fully prepared an' ready for all eventualities. You bring your long-tailed shovel, an' I'll bring me navvy. We mighten' want them, an', then agen, we might: for want of a nail the shoe was lost, for want of a shoe the horse was lost, an' for want of a horse the man was lost—aw, that's a darlin' proverb, a daaarlin' . . .

[*As* JOXER *is finishing his sentence,* MRS BOYLE *approaches the door and* JOXER *retreats hurriedly. She shuts the door with a bang.*]

BOYLE [*suggestively*].   We won't be long pullin' ourselves together agen when I'm working for a few weeks.

[MRS BOYLE *takes no notice.*]

The foreman on the job is an oul' butty o' Joxer's; I have an idea that I know him meself. [*Silence.*] . . . There's a button off the back o' me moleskin trousers. . . . If you leave out a needle an' thread I'll sew it on meself. . . . Thanks be to God, the pains in me legs is gone, anyhow!

MRS BOYLE [*with a burst*].   Look here, Mr Jackie Boyle, them yarns won't go down with Juno. I know you an' Joxer Daly of an oul' date, an' if you think you're able to come it over me with them fairy tales, you're in the wrong shop.

BOYLE [*coughing subduedly to relieve the tenseness of the situation*]. U-u-u-ugh!

MRS BOYLE.   Butty o' Joxer's! Oh, you'll do a lot o' good as long as you continue to be a butty o' Joxer's!

BOYLE.   U-u-u-ugh!

MRS BOYLE.   Shovel! Ah, then, me boyo, you'd do far more work with a knife an' fork than ever you'll do with a shovel! If there was e'er a genuine job goin' you'd be dh'other way about—not able to lift your arms with the pains in your legs! Your poor wife slavin' to keep the bit in your mouth, an' you gallivantin' about all the day like a paycock!

BOYLE.   It ud be betther for a man to be dead, betther for a man to be dead.

MRS BOYLE [*ignoring the interruption*].   Everybody callin' you 'Captain', an' you only wanst on the wather, in an oul' collier from here to Liverpool, when anybody, to listen or look at you, ud take you for a second Christo For Columbus!

BOYLE.   Are you never goin' to give us a rest?

MRS BOYLE.   Oh, you're never tired o' lookin' for a rest.

BOYLE.   D'ye want to dhrive me out o' the house?

MRS BOYLE.   It ud be easier to dhrive you out o' the house than to dhrive you into a job. Here, sit down an' take your breakfast—it may be the last you'll get, for I don't know where the next is goin' to come from.

BOYLE.   If I get this job we'll be all right.

MRS BOYLE.   Did ye see Jerry Devine?

BOYLE [*testily*].   No, I didn't see him.

MRS BOYLE.   No, but you seen Joxer. Well, he was here lookin' for you.

BOYLE.   Well, let him look!

MRS BOYLE.   Oh, indeed, he may well look, for it ud be hard for him to see you, an' you stuck in Ryan's snug.

BOYLE. I wasn't in Ryan's snug—I don't go into Ryan's.

MRS BOYLE. Oh, is there a mad dog there? Well, if you weren't in Ryan's you were in Foley's.

BOYLE. I'm telling you for the last three weeks I haven't tasted a dhrop of intoxicatin' liquor. I wasn't in ayther wan snug or dh'other—I could swear that on a prayer-book—I'm as innocent as the child unborn!

MRS BOYLE. Well, if you'd been in for your breakfast you'd ha' seen him.

BOYLE [*suspiciously*]. What does he want me for?

MRS BOYLE. He'll be back any minute an' then you'll soon know.

BOYLE. I'll dhrop out an' see if I can meet him.

MRS BOYLE. You'll sit down an' take your breakfast, an' let me go to me work, for I'm an hour late already waitin' for you.

BOYLE. You needn't ha' waited, for I'll take no breakfast—I've a little spirit left in me still!

MRS BOYLE. Are you goin' to have your breakfast—yes or no?

BOYLE [*too proud to yield*]. I'll have no breakfast—yous can keep your breakfast. [*Plaintively.*] I'll knock out a bit somewhere, never fear.

MRS BOYLE. Nobody's goin' to coax you—don't think that. [*She vigorously replaces the pan and the sausages in the press.*]

BOYLE. I've a little spirit left in me still.

[JERRY DEVINE *enters hastily.*]

JERRY. Oh, here you are at last! I've been searchin' for you everywhere. The foreman in Foley's told me you hadn't left the snug with Joxer ten minutes before I went in.

MRS BOYLE. An' he swearin' on the holy prayer-book that he wasn't in no snug!

BOYLE [*to* JERRY]. What business is it o' yours whether I was in a snug or no? What do you want to be gallopin' about afther me for? Is a man not allowed to leave his house for a minute without havin' a pack o' spies, pimps an' informers cantherin' at his heels?

JERRY. Oh, you're takin' a wrong view of it, Mr Boyle; I simply was anxious to do you a good turn. I have a message for you from Father Farrell: he says that if you go to the job that's on in Rathmines, an' ask for Foreman Mangan, you'll get a start.

BOYLE. That's all right, but I don't want the motions of me body to be watched the way an ashtronomer ud watch a star. If you're folleyin' Mary aself, you've no pereeogative to be folleyin' me. [*Suddenly catching his thigh.*] U-ugh, I'm afther gettin' a terrible twinge in me right leg!

MRS BOYLE. Oh, it won't be very long now till it travels into your left wan. It's miraculous that whenever he scents a job in front of him, his legs begin to fail him! Then, me bucko, if you lose this chance, you may go an' furrage for yourself!

JERRY. This job'll last for some time too, Captain, an' as soon as the foundations are in, it'll be cushy enough.

BOYLE. Won't it be a climbin' job? How d'ye expect me to be able to go up a ladder with these legs? An', if I get up aself, how am I goin to get down agen?

MRS BOYLE [*viciously*]. Get wan o' the labourers to carry you down in a hod! You can't climb a laddher, but you can skip like a goat into a snug!

JERRY. I wouldn't let myself be let down that easy, Mr Boyle; a little exercise, now, might do you all the good in the world.

BOYLE. It's a docthor you should have been, Devine—maybe you know more about the pains in me legs than meself that has them?

JERRY [*irritated*]. Oh, I know nothin' about the pains in your legs; I've brought the message that Father Farrell gave me, an' that's all I can do.

MRS BOYLE. Here, sit down an' take your breakfast, an' go an' get ready; an' don't be actin' as if you couldn't pull a wing out of a dead bee.

BOYLE. I want no breakfast, I tell you; it ud choke me afther all that's been said. I've a little spirit left in me still.

MRS BOYLE. Well, let's see your spirit, then, an' go in at wanst an' put on your moleskin trousers!

BOYLE [*moving towards the door on left*]. It ud be betther for a man to be dead! U-ugh! There's another twinge in me other leg! Nobody but meself knows the sufferin' I'm goin' through with the pains in these legs o' mine!

[*He goes into the room on left as* MARY *comes out with her hat in her hand.*]

MRS BOYLE. I'll have to push off now, for I'm terrible late already, but I was determined to stay an' hunt that Joxer this time. [*She goes off.*]

JERRY. Are you going out, Mary?

MARY. It looks like it when I'm putting on my hat, doesn't it?

JERRY. The bitther word agen, Mary.

MARY. You won't allow me to be friendly with you; if I thry, you deliberately misundherstand it.

JERRY. I didn't always misundherstand it; you were often delighted to have the arms of Jerry around you.

MARY. If you go on talkin' like this, Jerry Devine, you'll make me hate you!

JERRY. Well, let it be either a weddin' or a wake! Listen, Mary, I'm standin' for the Secretaryship of our Union. There's only one opposin' me; I'm popular with all the men, an' a good speaker—all are sayin' that I'll get elected.

MARY. Well?

JERRY. The job's worth three hundred an' fifty pounds a year, Mary. You an' I could live nice an' cosily on that; it would lift you out o' this place an' . . .

MARY. I haven't time to listen to you now—I have to go.

[*She is going out, when* JERRY *bars the way.*]

JERRY [*appealingly*].   Mary, what's come over you with me for the last few weeks? You hardly speak to me, an' then only a word with a face o' bitherness on it. Have you forgotten, Mary, all the happy evenins that were as sweet as the scented hawthorn that sheltered the sides o' the road as we saunthered through the country?

MARY.   That's all over now. When you get your new job, Jerry, you won't be long findin' a girl far betther than I am for your sweetheart.

JERRY.   Never, never, Mary! No matther what happens, you'll always be the same to me.

MARY.   I must be off; please let me go, Jerry.

JERRY.   I'll go a bit o' the way with you.

MARY.   You needn't, thanks; I want to be by meself.

JERRY [*catching her arm*].   You're goin' to meet another fella; you've clicked with someone else, me lady!

MARY.   That's no concern o' yours, Jerry Devine; let me go!

JERRY.   I saw yous comin' out o' the Cornflower Dance class, an' you hangin' on his arm—a thin, lanky strip of a Micky Dazzler, with a walkin' stick an' gloves!

VOICE OF JOHNNY [*loudly*].   What are you doin' there—pullin' about everything!

VOICE OF BOYLE [*loudly and viciously*].   I'm puttin' on me moleskin trousers!

MARY.   You're hurtin' me arm! Let me go, or I'll scream, an' then you'll have the oul' fella out on top of us!

JERRY.   Don't be so hard on a fella, Mary, don't be so hard.

BOYLE [*appearing at the door*].   What's the meanin' of all this hillabaloo?

MARY.   Let me go, let me go!

BOYLE.   D'ye hear me—what's all this hillabaloo about?

JERRY [*plaintively*].   Will you not give us one kind word, one kind word, Mary?

BOYLE.   D'ye hear me talkin' to yous? What's all this hillabaloo for?

JERRY.   Let me kiss your hand, your little, tiny, white hand!

BOYLE.   Your little, tiny, white hand—are you takin' leave o' your senses, man?

[MARY *breaks away and rushes out.*]

This is a nice goin's on in front of her father!

JERRY.   Ah, dhry up, for God's sake! [*He follows* MARY.]

BOYLE.   Chiselurs[7] don't care a damn now about their parents, they're bringin' their father's grey hairs down with sorra to the grave, an' laughin' at it. Ah, I suppose it's just the same everywhere—the whole worl's in a state o' chassis![8] [*He sits by the fire.*]

7. Youths.
8. Chaos, in Boyle's own malapropism.

Breakfast! Well, they can keep their breakfast for me. Not if they
went down on their bended knees would I take it—I'll show them
I've a little spirit in me still! [*He goes over to the press, takes out a
plate and looks at it.*] Sassige! Well, let her keep her sassige. [*He
returns to the fire, takes up the teapot and gives it a gentle shake.*]
The tea's wet right enough. [*A pause; he rises, goes to the press,
takes out the sausage, puts it on the pan, and puts both on the fire.
He attends the sausage with a fork. Singing*]

When the robins nest agen,
And the flowers are in bloom,
When the Springtime's sunny smile seems to banish all
        sorrow an' gloom;
Then me bonny blue-ey'd lad, if me heart be true till then—
He's promised he'll come back to me,
When the robins nest agen!

[*He lifts his head at the high note, and then drops his eyes to
the pan. Singing*]

When the . . .

[*Steps are heard approaching; he whips the pan off the fire
and puts it under the bed, then sits down at the fire. The door
opens and a bearded man looking in says*]

You don't happen to want a sewin' machine?
BOYLE [*furiously*].   No, I don't want e'er a sewin' machine! [*He returns the pan to the fire, and commences to sing again. Singing*]

When the robins nest asgen,
And the flowers they are in bloom,
He's . . .

[*A thundering knock is heard at the street door.*]

There's a terrible tatheraraa—that's a stranger—that's nobody belongin' to the house.

[*Another loud knock.*]

JOXER [*sticking his head in at the door*].   Did ye hear them tather-
arahs?
BOYLE.   Well, Joxer, I'm not deaf.
JOHNNY [*appearing in his shirt and trousers at the door on left; his
face is anxious and his voice is tremulous*].   Who's that at the
door; who's that at the door? Who gave that knock—d'ye yous
hear me—are yous deaf or dhrunk or what?
BOYLE [*to* JOHNNY].   How the hell do I know who 'tis? Joxer, stick
your head out o' the window an' see.
JOXER.   An' mebbe get a bullet in the kisser? Ah, none o' them
thricks for Joxer! It's betther to be a coward than a corpse!
BOYLE [*looking cautiously out of the window*].   It's a fella in a
thrench coat.

JOHNNY.   Holy Mary, Mother o' God, I . . .

BOYLE.   He's goin' away—he must ha' got tired knockin'.

[JOHNNY *returns to the room on left.*]

BOYLE.   Sit down an' have a cup o' tay, Joxer.

JOXER.   I'm afraid the missus ud pop in on us agen before we'd know where we are. Somethin's tellin' me to go at wanst.

BOYLE.   Don't be superstitious, man; we're Dublin men, an' not boyos that's only afther comin' up from the bog o' Allen[9]—though if she did come in, right enough, we'd be caught like rats in a thrap.

JOXER.   An' you know the sort she is—she wouldn't listen to reason—an' wanse bitten twice shy.

BOYLE [*going over to the window at back*].   If the worst came to the worst, you could dart out here, Joxer; it's only a dhrop of a few feet to the roof of the return room,[1] an' the first minute she goes into dh'other room I'll give you the bend, an' you can slip in an' away.

JOXER [*yielding to the temptation*].   Ah, I won't stop very long anyhow. [*Picking up a book from the table.*] Whose is the buk?

BOYLE.   Aw, one o' Mary's; she's always readin' lately—nothin' but thrash, too. There's one I was lookin' at dh'other day: three stories, *The Doll's House, Ghosts,* an' *The Wild Duck*[2]—buks only fit for chiselurs!

JOXER.   Didja ever rade *Elizabeth,* or *Th' Exile o' Sibayria?* . . . Ah, it's a darlin' story, a daarlin' story!

BOYLE.   You eat your sassige, an' never min' *Th' Exile o' Sibayria.*

[*Both sit down;* BOYLE *fills out tea, pours gravy on* JOXER's *plate, and keeps the sausage for himself.*]

JOXER.   What are you wearin' your moleskin trousers for?

BOYLE.   I have to go to a job, Joxer. Just afther you'd gone, Devine kem runnin' in to tell us that Father Farrell said if I went down to the job that's goin' on in Rathmines I'd get a start.

JOXER.   Be the holy, that's good news!

BOYLE.   How is it good news? I wondher if you were in my condition, would you call it good news?

JOXER.   I thought . . .

BOYLE.   You thought! You think too sudden sometimes, Joxer. D'ye know, I'm hardly able to crawl with the pains in me legs!

JOXER.   Yis, yis; I forgot the pains in your legs. I know you can do nothin' while they're at you.

BOYLE.   You forget; I don't think any of yous realise the state I'm in with the pains in my legs. What ud happen if I had to carry a bag o' cement?

9. Great central bog of Ireland, associated by Boyle with primitive life and premodern society.
1. Building extension.
2. Plays by Norwegian playwright Henrik Ibsen (1828–1906).

JOXER.   Ah, any man havin' the like of them pains id be down an'
out, down an' out.

BOYLE.   I wouldn't mind if he had said it to meself; but, no, oh no,
he rushes in an' shouts it out in front o' Juno, an' you know what
Juno is, Joxer. We all know Devine knows a little more than the
rest of us, but he doesn't act as if he did; he's a good boy, sober,
able to talk an' all that, but still . . .

JOXER.   Oh ay; able to argufy, but still . . .

BOYLE.   If he's runnin' afther Mary, aself, he's not goin' to be runnin' afther me. Captain Boyle's able to take care of himself. Afther all, I'm not gettin' brought up on Virol.[3] I never heard him
usin' a curse; I don't believe he was ever dhrunk in his life—sure
he's not like a Christian at all!

JOXER.   You're afther takin' the word out o' me mouth—afther all, a
Christian's natural, but he's unnatural.

BOYLE.   His oul' fella was just the same—a Wicklow man.

JOXER.   A Wicklow man! That explains the whole thing. I've met
many a Wicklow man in me time, but I never met wan that was
any good.

BOYLE.   'Father Farrell', says he, 'sent me down to tell you.' Father
Farrell! . . . D'ye know, Joxer, I never like to be beholden to any o'
the clergy.

JOXER.   It's dangerous, right enough.

BOYLE.   If they do anything for you, they'd want you to be livin' in
the Chapel . . . I'm goin' to tell you somethin', Joxer, that I
wouldn't tell to anybody else—the clergy always had too much
power over the people in this unfortunate country.

JOXER.   You could sing that if you had an air to it!

BOYLE [becoming enthusiastic].   Didn't they prevent the people in
'47 from seizin' the corn, an' they starvin'; didn't they down Parnell; didn't they say that hell wasn't hot enough nor eternity long
enough to punish the Fenians?[4] We don't forget, we don't forget
them things, Joxer. If they've taken everything else from us, Joxer,
they've left us our memory.

JOXER [emotionally].   For mem'ry's the only friend that grief can
call its own, that grief . . . can . . . call . . . it's own!

BOYLE.   Father Farrell's beginnin' to take a great intherest in Captain Boyle; because of what Johnny did for his country, says he to
me wan day. It's a curious way to reward Johnny be makin' his
poor oul' father work. But that's what the clergy want, Joxer—
work, work, work for me an' you; havin' us mulin' from mornin'
till night, so that they may be in betther fettle when they come

3. Baby food.
4. Corn, or grain, was exported from Ireland during the famine in the years around 1847;
   Charles Stewart Parnell (1846–91), parliamentarian agitator for Home Rule for Ireland
   until undone by the scandal of an extramarital affair; Fenians, or members of the Irish
   Republican Brotherhood, a late nineteenth-century secret society for military overthrow
   of British government.

hoppin' round for their dues! Job! Well, let him give his job to wan of his hymn-singin', prayer-spoutin', craw-thumpin' Confraternity[5] men!

[*The voice of a* COAL-BLOCK VENDOR *is heard chanting in the street.*]

VOICE OF THE COAL VENDOR.   Blocks . . . coal-blocks! Blocks . . . coal-blocks!

JOXER.   God be with the young days when you were steppin' the deck of a manly ship, with the win' blowin' a hurricane through the masts, an' the only sound you'd hear was 'Port your helm!' an' the only answer, 'Port it is, sir!'

BOYLE.   Them was days, Joxer, them was days. Nothin' was too hot or too heavy for me then. Sailin' from the Gulf o' Mexico to the Antanartic Ocean. I seen things, I seen things, Joxer, that no mortal man should speak about that knows his Catechism. Ofen, an' ofen, when I was fixed to the wheel with a marlin-spike, an' the win's blowin' fierce an' the waves lashin' an' lashin', till you'd think every minute was goin' to be your last, an' it blowed—blew is the right word, Joxer, but blowed is what the sailors use. . . .

JOXER.   Aw, it's a darlin' word, a daarlin' word.

BOYLE.   An', as it blowed, I ofen looked up at the sky an' assed meself the question—what is the stars, what is the stars?

VOICE OF THE COAL VENDOR.   Any blocks, coal-blocks; blocks, coal-blocks!

JOXER.   Ah, that's the question, that's the question—what is the stars?

BOYLE.   An' then, I'd have another look, an' I'd ass meself—what is the moon?

JOXER.   Ah, that's the question—what is the moon, what is the moon?

[*Rapid steps are heard coming towards the door.* BOYLE *makes desperate efforts to hide everything;* JOXER *rushes to the window in a frantic effort to get out;* BOYLE *begins to innocently lilt 'Oh, me darlin' Jennie, I will be thrue to thee', when the door is opened, and the black face of the* COAL VENDOR *appears.*]

THE COAL VENDOR.   D'yez want any blocks?

BOYLE [*with a roar*].   No, we don't want any blocks!

JOXER [*coming back with a sigh of relief*].   That's afther puttin' the heart across me—I could ha' sworn it was Juno. I'd betther be goin', Captain; you couldn't tell the minute Juno'd hop in on us.

BOYLE.   Let her hop in; we may as well have it out first as at last. I've made up me mind—I'm not goin' to do only what she damn well likes.

5. The Confraternity of the Sacred Heart.

JOXER. Them sentiments does you credit, Captain; I don't like to say anything as between man an' wife, but I say as a butty, as a butty, Captain, that you've stuck it too long, an' that it's about time you showed a little spunk.

> How can a man die betther than facin' fearful odds,
> For th' ashes of his fathers an' the temples of his gods?[6]

BOYLE. She has her rights—there's no denyin' it, but haven't I me rights too?

JOXER. Of course you have—the sacred rights o' man!

BOYLE. Today, Joxer, there's goin' to be issued a proclamation be me, establishin' an independent Republic, an' Juno'll have to take an oath of allegiance.

JOXER. Be firm, be firm, Captain; the first few minutes'll be the worst: if you gently touch a nettle it'll sting you for your pains; grasp it like a lad of mettle, an' as soft as silk remains!

VOICE OF MRS BOYLE OUTSIDE. Can't stop, Mrs Madigan—I haven't a minute!

JOXER [flying out of the window]. Holy God, here she is!

BOYLE [packing the things away with a rush in the press]. I knew that fella ud stop till she was in on top of us! [He sits down by the fire.]

MRS BOYLE [enters hastily; she is flurried and excited]. Oh, you're in—you must have been only afther comin' in?

BOYLE. No, I never went out.

MRS BOYLE. It's curious, then, you never heard the knockin'. [She puts her coat and hat on bed.]

BOYLE. Knockin'? Of course I heard the knockin'.

MRS BOYLE. An' why didn't you open the door, then? I suppose you were so busy with Joxer that you hadn't time.

BOYLE. I haven't seen Joxer since I seen him before. Joxer! What ud bring Joxer here?

MRS BOYLE. D'ye mean to tell me that the pair of yous wasn't col-login'[7] together here when me back was turned?

BOYLE. What ud we be collogin' together about? I have somethin' else to think of besides collogin' with Joxer. I can swear on all the holy prayer-books . . .

MRS BOYLE. That you weren't in no snug! Go on in at wanst now, an' take off that moleskin trousers o' yours, an' put on a collar an' tie to smarten yourself up a bit. There's a visitor comin' with Mary in a minute, an' he has great news for you.

BOYLE. A job, I suppose; let us get wan first before we start lookin' for another.

MRS BOYLE. That's the thing that's able to put the win' up you. Well, it's no job, but news that'll give you the chance o' your life.

BOYLE. What's all the mysthery about?

6. Thomas Babington Macaulay (1800–59), "Horatius," from *Lays of Ancient Rome* (1842).
7. Conversing.

MRS BOYLE.   G'win an' take off the moleskin trousers when you're told!

[BOYLE *goes into room on left.* MRS BOYLE *tidies up the room, puts the shovel under the bed, and goes to the press.*]

Oh, God bless us, looka the way everything's thrun about! Oh, Joxer was here, Joxer was here!

[MARY *enters with* CHARLIE BENTHAM; *he is a young man of twenty-five, tall, good-looking, with a very high opinion of himself generally. He is dressed in a brown coat, brown knee-breeches, grey stockings, a brown sweater, with a deep blue tie; he carries gloves and a walking-stick.*]

MRS BOYLE [*fussing round*].   Come in, Mr Bentham; sit down, Mr Bentham, in this chair; it's more comfortabler than that, Mr Bentham. Himself'll be here in a minute; he's just takin' off his trousers.

MARY.   Mother!

BENTHAM.   Please don't put yourself to any trouble, Mrs Boyle—I'm quite all right here, thank you.

MRS BOYLE.   An' to think of you knowin' Mary, an' she knowin' the news you had for us, an' wouldn't let on; but it's all the more welcomer now, for we were on our last lap!

VOICE OF JOHNNY INSIDE.   What are you kickin' up all the racket for?

BOYLE [*roughly*].   I'm takin' off me moleskin trousers!

JOHNNY.   Can't you do it, then, without lettin' th' whole house know you're takin' off your trousers? What d'ye want puttin' them on an' takin' them off again?

BOYLE.   Will you let me alone, will you let me alone? Am I never goin' to be done thryin' to please th' whole o' yous?

MRS BOYLE [*to* BENTHAM].   You must excuse th' state o' th' place, Mr Bentham; th' minute I turn me back that man o' mine always makes a litther o' th' place.

BENTHAM.   Don't worry, Mrs Boyle; it's all right, I assure . . .

BOYLE [*inside*].   Where's me braces; where in th' name o' God did I leave me braces? . . . Ay, did you see where I put me braces?

JOHNNY [*inside, calling out*].   Ma, will you come in here an' take da away ou' o' this or he'll dhrive me mad.

MRS BOYLE [*going towards the door*].   Dear, dear, dear, that man'll be lookin' for somethin' on th' day o' Judgement. [*Looking into room and calling to* BOYLE] Look at your braces, man, hangin' round your neck!

BOYLE [*inside*].   Aw, Holy God!

MRS BOYLE [*calling*].   Johnny, Johnny, come out here for a minute.

JOHNNY.   Ah, leave Johnny alone, an' don't be annoyin' him!

MRS BOYLE.   Come on, Johnny, till I inthroduce you to Mr Bentham. [*To* BENTHAM.] My son, Mr Bentham; he's after goin' through the mill. He was only a chiselur of a Boy Scout in Easter

Week, when he got hit in the hip; and his arm was blew off in the fight in O'Connell Street.

[JOHNNY *comes in.*]

Here he is, Mr Bentham; Mr Bentham, Johnny. None can deny he done his bit for Irelan', if that's goin' to do him any good.

JOHNNY [*boastfully*].   I'd do it agen, ma, I'd do it agen; for a principle's a principle.

MRS BOYLE.   Ah, you lost your best principle, me boy, when you lost your arm; them's the only sort o' principles that's any good to a workin' man.

JOHNNY.   Ireland only half free'll never be at peace while she has a son left to pull a trigger.

MRS BOYLE.   To be sure, to be sure—no bread's a lot betther than half a loaf. [*Calling loudly in to* BOYLE.] Will you hurry up there?

[BOYLE *enters in his best trousers, which aren't too good, and looks very uncomfortable in his collar and tie.*]

MRS BOYLE.   This is my husband; Mr Boyle, Mr Bentham.

BENTHAM.   Ah, very glad to know you, Mr Boyle. How are you?

MR BOYLE.   Ah, I'm not too well at all; I suffer terrible with pains in me legs. Juno can tell you there what . . .

MRS BOYLE.   You won't have many pains in your legs when you hear what Mr Bentham has to tell you.

BENTHAM.   Juno! What an interesting name! It reminds one of Homer's glorious story of ancient gods and heroes.

BOYLE.   Yis, doesn't it? You see, Juno was born an' christened in June; I met her in June; we were married in June, an' Johnny was born in June, so wan day I says to her, 'You should ha' been called Juno', an' the name stuck to her ever since.

MRS BOYLE.   Here, we can talk o' them things agen; let Mr Bentham say what he has to say now.

BENTHAM.   Well, Mr Boyle, I suppose you'll remember a Mr Ellison of Santry—he's a relative of yours, I think.

BOYLE [*viciously*].   Is it that prognosticator an' procrastinator! Of course I remember him.

BENTHAM.   Well, he's dead, Mr Boyle . . .

BOYLE.   Sorra many'll go into mournin' for him.

MRS BOYLE.   Wait till you hear what Mr Bentham has to say, an' then, maybe, you'll change your opinion.

BENTHAM.   A week before he died he sent for me to write his will for him. He told me that there were two only that he wished to leave his property to: his second cousin, Michael Finnegan of Santry, and John Boyle, his first cousin, of Dublin.

BOYLE [*excitedly*].   Me, is it me, me?

BENTHAM.   You, Mr Boyle; I'll read a copy of the will that I have here with me, which has been duly filed in the Court of Probate. [*He takes a paper from his pocket and reads.*]

6th February 1922

This is the last Will and Testament of William Ellison, of Santry, in the County of Dublin. I hereby order and wish my property to be sold and divided as follows:

£20 to the St Vincent de Paul Society.

£60 for Masses for the repose of my soul (5s. for each Mass).

The rest of my property to be divided between my first and second cousins.

I hereby appoint Timothy Buckly, of Santry, and Hugh Brierly, of Coolock, to be my Executors.

(SIGNED) WILLIAM ELLISON
HUGH BRIERLY
TIMOTHY BUCKLY
CHARLES BENTHAM, NT[8]

BOYLE [*eagerly*].   An' how much'll be comin' out of it, Mr Bentham?

BENTHAM.   The Executors told me that half of the property would be anything between £1500 and £2000.

MARY.   A fortune, father, a fortune!

JOHNNY.   We'll be able to get out o' this place now, an' go somewhere we're not known.

MRS BOYLE.   You won't have to trouble about a job for awhile, Jack.

BOYLE [*fervently*].   I'll never doubt the goodness o' God agen.

BENTHAM.   I congratulate you, Mr Boyle.

[*They shake hands.*]

BOYLE.   An' now, Mr Bentham, you'll have to have a wet.

BENTHAM.   A wet?

BOYLE.   A wet—a jar—a boul![9]

MRS BOYLE.   Jack, you're speakin' to Mr Bentham, an' not to Joxer.

BOYLE [*solemnly*].   Juno . . . Mary . . . Johnny . . . we'll have to go into mournin' at wanst . . . . I never expected that poor Bill ud die so sudden. . . . Well, we all have to die some day . . . you, Juno, today . . . an' me, maybe, tomorrow. . . . It's sad, but it can't be helped. . . . *Requiescat in pace* . . . or, usin' our oul' tongue like St Patrick or St Bridget, *Guh sayeree jeea ayera!*

MARY.   Oh, father, that's not Rest in Peace; that's God save Ireland.

BOYLE.   U-u-ugh, it's all the same—isn't it a prayer? . . . Juno, I'm done with Joxer; he's nothin' but a prognosticator an' a . . .

JOXER [*climbing angrily through the window and bounding into the room*].   You're done with Joxer, are you? Maybe you thought I'd

---

8. National Teacher, a certification, but not as a lawyer.
9. ""Jar," pint of beer; "boul," or ball, a measure of whiskey.

stop on the roof all the night for you! Joxer out on the roof with the win' blowin' through him was nothin' to you an' your friend with the collar an' tie!

MRS BOYLE.   What in the name o' God brought you out on the roof; what were you doin' there?

JOXER [*ironically*].   I was dhreamin' I was standin' on the bridge of a ship, an' she sailin' the Antartic Ocean, an' it blowed, an' blowed, an' I lookin' up at the sky an' saying', what is the stars, what is the stars?

MRS BOYLE [*opening the door and standing at it*].   Here, get ou' o' this, Joxer Daly; I was always thinkin' you had a slate off.

JOXER [*moving to the door*].   I have to laugh every time I look at the deep-sea sailor; an' a row on a river ud make him sea-sick!

BOYLE.   Get ou' o' this before I take the law into me own hands!

JOXER [*going out*].   Say aw rewaeawr, but not goodbye. Lookin' for work, an' prayin' to God he won't get it! [*He goes.*]

MRS BOYLE.   I'm tired tellin' you what Joxer was; maybe now you see yourself the kind he is.

BOYLE.   He'll never blow the froth off a pint o' mine agen, that's a sure thing. Johnny . . . Mary . . . you're to keep yourselves to yourselves for the future. Juno, I'm done with Joxer. . . . I'm a new man from this out. . . . [*Clasping* MRS BOYLE's *hand, and singing emotionally.*]

> O, me darlin' Juno, I will be thrue to thee;
> Me own, me darlin' Juno, you're all the world to me.

Act 2

The same, but the furniture is more plentiful, and of a vulgar nature. A glaringly upholstered armchair and lounge; cheap pictures and photos everywhere. Every available spot is ornamented with huge vases filled with artificial flowers. Crossed festoons of coloured paper chains stretch from end to end of ceiling. On the table is an old attaché case. It is about six in the evening, and two days after the First Act. BOYLE, *in his shirt-sleeves, is voluptuously stretched on the sofa; he is smoking a clay pipe. He is half asleep. A lamp is lighting on the table. After a few moments' pause the voice of* JOXER *is heard singing softly outside at the door—'Me pipe I'll smoke, as I dhrive me moke— are you there, Mor . . . ee . . . ar . . . i . . . teee!'*

BOYLE [*leaping up, takes a pen in his hand and busies himself with papers*].   Come along, Joxer, me son, come along.

JOXER [*putting his head in*].   Are you be yourself?

BOYLE.   Come on, come on; that doesn't matther; I'm masther now, an' I'm goin' to remain masther.

[JOXER *comes in.*]

JOXER.   How d'ye feel now, as a man o' money?

BOYLE [*solemnly*].   It's a responsibility, Joxer, a great responsibility.

JOXER.   I suppose 'tis now, though you wouldn't think it.

BOYLE.   Joxer, han' me over that attackey case on the table there.

[JOXER *hands the case.*]

Ever since the Will was passed I've run hundreds o' dockyments through me han's—I tell you, you have to keep your wits about you. [*He busies himself with papers.*]

JOXER.   Well, I won't disturb you; I'll dhrop in when . . .

BOYLE [*hastily*].   It's all right, Joxer, this is the last one to be signed today. [*He signs a paper, puts it into the case, which he shuts with a snap, and sits back pompously in the chair.*] Now, Joxer, you want to see me; I'm at your service—what can I do for you, me man?

JOXER.   I've just dhropped in with the three pouns five shillings that Mrs Madigan riz on the blankets an' table for you, an' she says you're to be in no hurry payin' it back.

BOYLE.   She won't be long without it; I expect the first cheque for a couple o' hundhred any day. There's the five bob for yourself—go on, take it, man; it'll not be the last you'll get from the Captain. Now an' agen we have our differ, but we're there together all the time.

JOXER.   Me for you, an' you for me, like the two Musketeers.

BOYLE.   Father Farrell stopped me today an' tole me how glad he was I fell in for the money.

JOXER.   He'll be stoppin' you ofen enough now; I suppose it was 'Mr' Boyle with him?

BOYLE.   He shuk me be the han' . . .

JOXER [*ironically*].   I met with Napper Tandy, an' he shuk me be the han'![1]

BOYLE.   You're seldom asthray, Joxer, but you're wrong shipped this time. What you're sayin' of Father Farrell is very near to blasfeemey. I don't like anyone to talk disrespectful of Father Farrell.

JOXER.   You're takin' me up wrong, Captain; I wouldn't let a word be said agen Father Farrell—the heart o' the rowl, that's what he is; I always said he was a darlin' man, a daarlin' man.

BOYLE.   Comin' up the stairs who did I meet but that bummer, Nugent. 'I seen you talkin' to Father Farrell', says he, with a grin on him. 'He'll be folleyin' you,' says he, 'like a Guardian Angel from this out'—all the time the oul' grin on him, Joxer.

JOXER.   I never seen him yet but he had the oul' grin on him!

BOYLE.   'Mr Nugent,' says I, 'Father Farrell is a man o' the people, an', as far as I know the History o' me country, the priests was always in the van of the fight for Irelan's freedom.'

JOXER [*fervently*].

Who was it led the van, Soggart Aroon?[2]
Since the fight first began, Soggart Aroon?

---

1. Line from the song "The Wearing of the Green" about James Napper Tandy (1740–1803), who attempted to instigate a rebellion in Ireland in 1798.
2. Irish for "dear priest."

BOYLE.   'Who are you tellin'?' says he. 'Didn't they let down the Fenians, an' didn't they do in Parnell? An' now . . .' 'You ought to be
ashamed o' yourself,' says I, interruptin' him, 'not to know the
History o' your country.' An' I left him gawkin' where he was.

JOXER.   Where ignorance's bliss 'tis folly to be wise; I wondher did
he ever read *The Story o' Ireland.*[3]

BOYLE.   Be J. L. Sullivan? Don't you know he didn't.

JOXER.   Ah, it's a darlin' buk, a daarlin' buk!

BOYLE.   You'd betther be goin', now, Joxer; his Majesty, Bentham'll
be here any minute, now.

JOXER.   Be the way things is lookin', it'll be a match between him
an' Mary. She's thrun over Jerry altogether. Well, I hope it will,
for he's a darlin' man.

BOYLE.   I'm glad you think so—I don't. [*Irritably.*] What's darlin'
about him?

JOXER [*nonplussed*].   I only seen him twiced; if you want to know
me, come an' live with me.

BOYLE.   He's too dignified for me—to hear him talk you'd think he
knew as much as a Boney's Oraculum.[4] He's given up his job as
teacher, an' is goin' to become a solicitor in Dublin—he's been
studyin' law. I suppose he thinks I'll set him up, but he's wrong
shipped. An' th' other fella—Jerry's as bad. The two o' them ud
give you a pain in your face, listenin' to them; Jerry believin' in
nothin', an' Bentham believin' in everythin'. One that says all is
God an' no man; an' th' other that says all is man an' no God!

JOXER.   Well, I'll be off now.

BOYLE.   Don't forget to dhrop down afther awhile; we'll have a
quiet jar, an' a song or two.

JOXER.   Never fear.

BOYLE.   An' tell Mrs Madigan that I hope we'll have the pleasure
of her organisation at our little enthertainment.

JOXER.   Righto; we'll come down together. [*He goes out.*]

> [JOHNNY *comes from room on left, and sits down moodily at
> the fire.* BOYLE *looks at him for a few moments, and shakes his
> head. He fills his pipe.*]

VOICE OF MRS BOYLE AT THE DOOR.   Open the door, Jack; this thing
has me nearly kilt with the weight.

> [BOYLE *opens the door.* MRS BOYLE *enters carrying the box of a
> gramophone, followed by* MARY *carrying the horn and some
> parcels.* MRS BOYLE *leaves the box on the table and flops into a
> chair.*]

---

3. Joxer quotes the English poet Thomas Gray (1716–71); he refers to A. M. Sullivan's *The
Story of Ireland* (1883), a nationalist, notoriously romanticized and extremely popular
history; John L. Sullivan was an American prizefighter of Irish descent.
4. A cheap and unreliable compendium of "improving" knowledge.

MRS BOYLE.   Carryin' that from Henry Street was no joke.

BOYLE.   U-u-ugh, that's a grand-lookin' insthrument—how much was it?

MRS BOYLE.   Pound down, an' five to be paid at two shillin's a week.

BOYLE.   That's reasonable enough.

MRS BOYLE.   I'm afraid we're runnin' into too much debt; first the furniture, an' now this.

BOYLE.   The whole lot won't be much out of £2000.

MARY.   I don't know what you wanted a gramophone for—I know Charlie hates them; he says they're destructive of real music.

BOYLE.   Desthructive of music—that fella ud give you a pain in your face. All a gramophone wants is to be properly played; its thrue wondher is only felt when everythin's quiet—what a gramophone wants is dead silence!

MARY.   But, father, Jerry says the same; afther all, you can only appreciate music when your ear is properly trained.

BOYLE.   That's another fella ud give you a pain in your face. Properly thrained! I suppose you couldn't appreciate football unless your fut was properly thrained.

MRS BOYLE [*to* MARY].   Go on in ower that an' dress or Charlie'll be in on you, an' tea nor nothin'll be ready.

[MARY *goes into room left.*]

MRS BOYLE [*arranging table for tea*].   You didn't look at your new gramophone, Johnny?

JOHNNY.   'Tisn't gramophones I'm thinking of.

MRS BOYLE.   An' what is it you're thinkin' of, allanna?[5]

JOHNNY.   Nothin', nothin', nothin'.

MRS BOYLE.   Sure, you must be thinkin' of somethin'; it's yourself that has yourself the way y'are; sleepin' wan night in me sisther's, an' the nex' in your father's brother's—you'll get no rest goin' on that way.

JOHNNY.   I can rest nowhere, nowhere, nowhere.

MRS BOYLE.   Sure, you're not thryin' to rest anywhere.

JOHNNY.   Let me alone, let me alone, let me alone, for God's sake.

[*A knock at street door.*]

MRS BOYLE [*in a flutter*].   Here he is; here's Mr Bentham!

BOYLE.   Well, there's room for him; it's a pity there's not a brass band to play him in.

MRS BOYLE.   We'll han' the tea round, an' not be clusthered round the table, as if we never seen nothin'.

[*Steps are heard approaching, and* MRS BOYLE, *opening the door, allows* BENTHAM *to enter.*]

---

5. Irish *an leanbh*, "O child."

Give your hat an' stick to Jack, there . . . sit down, Mr Bentham
. . . no, not there . . . in th' easy chair be the fire . . . there, that's
betther. Mary'll be out to you in a minute.

BOYLE [*solemnly*].   I seen be the paper this mornin' that Consols[6]
was down half per cent. That's serious, min' you, an' shows the
whole counthry's in a state o' chassis.

MRS BOYLE.   What's Consols, Jack?

BOYLE.   Consols? Oh, Consols is—oh, there's no use tellin' women
what Consols is—th' wouldn't undherstand.

BENTHAM.   It's just as you were saying, Mrs Boyle.

[MARY *enters, charmingly dressed.*]

Oh, good evening, Mary; how pretty you're looking!

MARY [*archly*].   Am I?

BOYLE.   We were just talkin' when you kem in, Mary; I was tellin'
Mr Bentham that the whole counthry's in a state o' chassis.

MARY [*to* BENTHAM].   Would you prefer the green or the blue ribbon round me hair, Charlie?

MRS BOYLE.   Mary, your father's speakin'.

BOYLE [*rapidly*].   I was jus' tellin' Mr Bentham that the whole
country's in a state o' chassis.

MARY.   I'm sure you're frettin', da, whether it is or no.

MRS BOYLE.   With all our churches an' religions, the worl's not a
bit the betther.

BOYLE [*with a commanding gesture*].   Tay!

[MARY *and* MRS BOYLE *dispense the tea.*]

MRS BOYLE.   An' Irelan's takin' a leaf out o' the worl's buk; when we
got the makin' of our own laws I thought we'd never stop to look
behind us, but instead of that we never stopped to look before us!
If the people ud folley up their religion betther there'd be a betther chance for us—what do you think, Mr Bentham?

BENTHAM.   I'm afraid I can't venture to express an opinion on that
point, Mrs Boyle; dogma has no attraction for me.

MRS BOYLE.   I forgot you didn't hold with us: what's this you said
you were?

BENTHAM.   A Theosophist, Mrs Boyle.

MRS BOYLE.   An' what in the name o' God's a Theosophist?

BOYLE.   A Theosophist, Juno, 's a—tell her, Mr Bentham, tell her.

BENTHAM.   It's hard to explain in a few words: Theosophy's
founded on the Vedas, the religious books of the East. Its central
theme is the existence of an all-pervading Spirit—the Life-
Breath. Nothing really exists but this one Universal Life-Breath.
And whatever even seems to exist separately from this Life-
Breath, doesn't really exist at all. It is all vital force in man, in all
animals, and in all vegetation. This Life-Breath is called the
Prawna.

6. Securities traded on the stock market.

MRS BOYLE.   The Prawna! What a comical name.

BOYLE.   Prawna; yis, the Prawna. [*Blowing gently through his lips.*] That's the Prawna!

MRS BOYLE.   Whist, whist, Jack.

BENTHAM.   The happiness of man depends upon his sympathy with this Spirit. Men who have reached a high state of excellence are called Yogi. Some men become Yogi in a short time, it may take others millions of years.

BOYLE.   Yogi! I seen hundhreds of them in the streets o' San Francisco.

BENTHAM.   It is said by these Yogi that if we practise certain mental exercises we would have powers denied to others—for instance, the faculty of seeing things that happen miles and miles away.

MRS BOYLE.   I wouldn't care to meddle with that sort o' belief; it's a very curious religion, altogether.

BOYLE.   What's curious about it? Isn't all religions curious?—if they weren't, you wouldn't get any one to believe them. But religions is passin' away—they've had their day like everything else. Take the real Dublin people, f'rinstance: they know more about Charlie Chaplin an' Tommy Mix[7] than they do about SS. Peter an' Paul!

MRS BOYLE.   You don't believe in ghosts, Mr Bentham?

MARY.   Don't you know he doesn't, mother?

BENTHAM.   I don't know that, Mary. Scientists are beginning to think that what we call ghosts are sometimes seen by persons of a certain nature. They say that sensational actions, such as the killing of a person, demand great energy, and that energy lingers in the place where the action occurred. People may live in the place and see nothing, when someone may come along whose personality has some peculiar connection with the energy of the place, and, in a flash, the person sees the whole affair.

JOHNNY [*rising swiftly, pale and affected*].   What sort o' talk is this to be goin' on with? Is there nothin' betther to be talkin' about but the killin' o' people? My God, isn't it bad enough for these things to happen without talkin' about them! [*He hurriedly goes into the room on left.*]

BENTHAM.   Oh, I'm very sorry, Mrs Boyle; I never thought . . .

MRS BOYLE [*apologetically*].   Never mind, Mr Bentham, he's very touchy.

[*A frightened scream is heard from* JOHNNY *inside.*]

Mother of God, what's that?

[*He rushes out again, his face pale, his lips twitching, his limbs trembling.*]

JOHNNY.   Shut the door, shut the door, quick, for God's sake! Great

7. Film stars.

God, have mercy on me! Blessed Mother o' God, shelter me,
shelter your son!

MRS BOYLE [*catching him in her arms*].   What's wrong with you?
What ails you? Sit down, sit down, here, no the bed . . . there
now . . . there now.

MARY.   Johnny, Johnny, what ails you?

JOHNNY.   I seen him, I seen him . . . kneelin' in front o' the statue
. . . merciful Jesus, have pity on me!

MRS BOYLE [*to* BOYLE].   Get him a glass o' whisky . . . quick, man,
an' don't stand gawkin'.

[BOYLE *gets the whisky.*]

JOHNNY.   Sit here, sit here, mother . . . between me an' the door.

MRS BOYLE.   I'll sit beside you as long as you like, only tell me what
was it came across you at all?

JOHNNY [*after taking some drink*].   I seen him . . . I seen Robbie
Tancred kneelin' down before the statue . . . an' the red light
shinin' on him . . . an' when I went in . . . he turned an' looked at
me . . . an' I seen the woun's bleedin' in his breast. . . . Oh, why
did he look at me like that? . . . it wasn't my fault that he was
done in . . . Mother o' God, keep him away from me!

MRS BOYLE.   There, there, child, you've imagined it all. There was
nothin' there at all—it was the red light you seen, an' the talk we
had put all the rest into your head. Here, dhrink more o' this—
it'll do you good. . . . An', now, stretch yourself down on the bed
for a little. [*To* BOYLE.] Go in, Jack, an' show him it was only in
his own head it was.

BOYLE [*making no move*].   E-e-e-e-eh; it's all nonsense; it was only
a shadda he saw.

MARY.   Mother o' God, he made me heart lep!

BENTHAM.   It was simply due to an overwrought imagination—we
all get that way at times.

MRS BOYLE.   There, dear, lie down in the bed, an' I'll put the quilt
across you . . . e-e-e-eh, that's it . . . you'll be as right as the mail
in a few minutes.

JOHNNY.   Mother, go into the room an' see if the light's lightin' before the statue.

MRS BOYLE [*to* BOYLE].   Jack, run in an' see if the light's lightin' before the statue.

BOYLE [*to* MARY].   Mary, slip in an' see if the light's lightin' before
the statue.

[MARY *hesitates .to go in.*]

BENTHAM.   It's all right; Mary, I'll go. [*He goes into the room; remains for a few moments, and returns.*] Everything's just as it
was—the light burning bravely before the statue.

BOYLE.   Of course; I knew it was all nonsense. [*A knock at the
door. Going to open the door*] E-e-e-e-eh.

[*He opens it, and* JOXER, *followed by* MRS MADIGAN, *enters.*
MRS MADIGAN *is a strong, dapper little woman of about forty-
five; her face is almost always a widespread smile of compla-
cency. She is a woman who, in manner at least, can mourn
with them that mourn, and rejoice with them that do rejoice.
When she is feeling comfortable, she is inclined to be reminiscent; when others say anything, or following a statement made
by herself, she has a habit of putting her head a little to one
side, and nodding it rapidly several times in succession, like a
bird pecking at a hard berry. Indeed, she has a good deal of the
bird in her, but the bird instinct is by no means a melodious
one. She is ignorant, vulgar and forward, but her heart is generous withal. For instance, she would help a neighbour's sick
child; she would probably kill the child, but her intention
would be to cure it; she would be more at home helping a
drayman to lift a fallen horse. She is dressed in a rather soiled
grey dress and a vivid purple blouse; in her hair is a huge
comb, ornamented with huge coloured beads. She enters with
a gliding step, beaming smile and nodding head.* BOYLE *receives them effusively.*]

BOYLE.   Come on in, Mrs Madigan; come on in; I was afraid you
    weren't comin'. . . . [*Slyly.*] There's some people able to dhress,
    ay, Joxer?
JOXER.   Fair as the blossoms that bloom in the May, an' sweet as
    the scent of the new-mown hay. . . . Ah, well she may wear them.
MRS MADIGAN [*looking at* MARY].   I know some as are as sweet as
    the blossoms that bloom in the May—oh, no names, no pack
    dhrill.
BOYLE.   An' now I'll inthroduce the pair o' yous to Mary's intended:
    Mr Bentham, this is Mrs Madigan, an oul' back-parlour neigh-
    bour, that, if she could help it at all, ud never see a body shuk!
BENTHAM [*rising, and tentatively shaking the hand of* MRS MADIGAN].
    I'm sure, it's a great pleasure to know you, Mrs Madigan.
MRS MADIGAN.   An, I'm goin' to tell you, Mr Bentham, you're goin'
    to get as nice a bit o' skirt in Mary, there, as ever you seen in your
    puff. Not like some of the dhressed-up dolls that's knockin' about
    lookin' for men when it's a skelpin[8] they want. I remember, as
    well as I remember yesterday, the day she was born—of a Tues-
    day, the 25th o' June, in the year 1901, at thirty-three minutes
    past wan in the day by Foley's clock, the pub at the corner o' the
    street. A cowld day it was too, for the season o' the year, an' I re-
    member sayin' to Joxer, there, who I met comin' up th' stairs, that
    the new arrival in Boyle's ud grow up a hardy chiselur if it lived,
    an' that she'd be somethin' one o' these days that nobody sus-
    pected, an' so signs on it, here she is today, goin' to be married to
    a young man lookin' as if he'd be fit to commensurate in any po-
    sition in life it ud please God to call him!

8. Spanking.

BOYLE [*effusively*].   Sit down, Mrs Madigan, sit down, me oul'
sport. [*To* BENTHAM.] This is Joxer Daly, Past Chief Ranger of the
Dear Little Shamrock Branch of the Irish National Foresters, an
oul' front-top neighbour, that never despaired, even in the dark-
est days of Ireland's sorra.

JOXER.   *Nil desperandum,* Captain, *nil desperandum.*[9]

BOYLE.   Sit down, Joxer, sit down. The two of us was ofen in a
tight corner.

MRS BOYLE.   Ay, in Foley's snug!

JOXER.   An' we kem out of it flyin', we kem out of it flyin', Captain.

BOYLE.   An' now for a dhrink—I know yous won't refuse an oul'
friend.

MRS MADIGAN [*to* MRS BOYLE].   Is Johnny not well, Mrs. . . .

MRS BOYLE [*warningly*].   S-s-s-sh.

MRS MADIGAN.   Oh, the poor darlin'.

BOYLE.   Well, Mrs Madigan, is it tea or what?

MRS MADIGAN.   Well, speakin' for meself, I jus' had me tea a
minute ago, an' I'm afraid to dhrink any more—I'm never the
same when I dhrink too much tay. Thanks, all the same, Mr
Boyle.

BOYLE.   Well, what about a bottle o' stout or a dhrop o' whisky?

MRS MADIGAN.   A bottle o' stout ud be a little too heavy for me
stummock afther me tay. . . . A-a-ah, I'll thry the ball o' malt.

   [BOYLE *prepares the whisky.*]

There's nothin' like a ball o' malt occasional like—too much of it
isn't good. [*To* BOYLE, *who is adding water.*] Ah, God, Johnny,
don't put too much wather on it! [*She drinks.*] I suppose yous'll
be lavin' this place.

BOYLE.   I'm looking for a place near the sea; I'd like the place that
you might say was me cradle, to be me grave as well. The sea is
always callin' me.

JOXER.   She is callin', callin', callin', in the win' an' on the sea.

BOYLE.   Another dhrop o' whisky, Mrs Madigan?

MRS MADIGAN.   Well, now, it ud be hard to refuse seein' the suspicious times that's in it.

BOYLE [*with a commanding gesture*].   Song! . . . Juno . . . Mary . . .
'Home to our Mountains'!

MRS MADIGAN [*enthusiastically*].   Hear, hear!

JOXER.   Oh, tha's a darlin' song, a daarlin' song!

MARY [*bashfully*].   Ah no, da; I'm not in a singin' humour.

MRS MADIGAN.   Gawn with you, child, an' you only goin' to be mar-
rid; I remember as well as I remember yestherday—it was on a
lovely August evenin', exactly, accordin' to date, fifteen years ago,
come the Tuesday folleyin' the nex' that's comin' on, when me
own man—*the Lord be good to him*—an' me was sittin' shy together in a doty little nook on a counthry road, adjacent to The

---

9. Do not despair.

Stiles.¹ 'That'll scratch your lovely, little white neck', says he, ketchin' hould of a danglin' bramble branch, holdin' clusters of the loveliest flowers you ever seen, an' breakin' if off, so that his arm fell, accidental like, roun' me waist, an' as I felt it tightenin', an tightenin', an' tightenin', I thought me buzzom was every minute goin' to burst out into a roystherin' song about

The little green leaves that were shakin' on the threes,
The gallivantin' buttherflies, an' buzzin' o' the bees!

BOYLE.   Ordher for the song!

MRS BOYLE.   Come on, Mary—we'll do our best.

[MRS BOYLE *and* MARY *stand up, and choosing a suitable position, sing simply* 'Home to our Mountains'. *They bow to the company, and return to their places.*]

BOYLE [*emotionally, at the end of the song*].   'Lull . . . me . . . to . . . rest!'

JOXER [*clapping his hands*].   Bravo, bravo! Darlin' girulls, darlin' girulls!

MRS MADIGAN.   Juno, I never seen you in better form.

BENTHAM.   Very nicely rendered indeed.

MRS MADIGAN.   A noble call, a noble call!

MRS BOYLE.   What about yourself, Mrs Madigan?

[*After some coaxing,* MRS MADIGAN *rises, and in a quavering voice sings the following verse:*]

If I were a blackbird I'd whistle and sing;
I'd follow the ship that my thrue love was in;
An' on the top riggin', I'd there build me nest,
An' at night I would sleep on me Willie's white breast!

[*Becoming husky, amid applause, she sits down.*]

MRS MADIGAN.   Ah, me voice is too husky now, Juno; though I remember the time when Maisie Madigan could sing like a nightingale at matin' time. I remember as well as I remember yesterday, at a party given to celebrate the comin' of the first chiselur to Annie an' Benny Jimeson—who was the barber, yous may remember, in Henrietta Street, that, afther Easter Week, hung out a green, white an' orange pole, an' then, when the Tans² started their jazz dancin', whipped it in agen, an' stuck out a red, white an' blue wan instead, givin' as an excuse that a barber's pole was strictly non-political—singin' 'An' You'll Remember Me' with the top notes quiverin' in a dead hush of pethrified attention, folleyed be a clappin' o' han's that shuk the tumblers on the table, an' capped by Jimeson, the barber, sayin' that it was the

---

1. Place by the northern side of Dublin Bay.
2. The Black and Tans, so-called for uniform colors, a brutal auxiliary police force employed by British authorities, 1920–22.

best rendherin' of 'You'll Remember Me' he ever heard in his
natural!

BOYLE [*peremptorily*].   Ordher for Joxer's song!

JOXER.   Ah no, I couldn't; don't ass me, Captain.

BOYLE.   Joxer's song, Joxer's song—give us wan of your shut-eyed
wans.

JOXER [*settles himself in his chair; takes a drink; clears his throat;
solemnly closes his eyes, and begins to sing in a very querulous
voice*].

> She is far from the lan' where her young hero sleeps,[3]
> An' lovers around her are sighing [*He hesitates.*]
> An' lovers around her are sighin' . . . sighin' . . .
>   sighin' . . . [*A pause.*]

BOYLE [*imitating* JOXER].

And lovers around her are sighing!
What's the use of you thryin' to sing the song if you don't know
it?

MARY.   Thry another one, Mr Daly—maybe you'd be more fortu-
nate.

MRS MADIGAN.   Gawn, Joxer; thry another wan.

JOXER [*starting again*].

> I have heard the mavis singin' his love song to the morn;[4]
> I have seen the dew-dhrop clingin' to the rose jus' newly born;
>   but . . . but . . . [*frantically*] To the rose jus' newly born . . .
>   newly born . . . born.

JOHNNY.   Mother, put on the gramophone, for God's sake, an' stop
Joxer's bawlin'.

BOYLE [*commandingly*].   Gramophone! . . . I hate to see fellas
thryin' to do what they're not able to do. [BOYLE *arranges the
gramophone, and is about to start it, when voices are heard of persons descending the stairs.*]

MRS BOYLE [*warningly*].   Whisht, Jack, don't put it on, don't put it
on yet; this must be poor Mrs Tancred comin' down to go to the
hospital—I forgot all about them bringin' the body to the church
tonight. Open the door, Mary, an' give them a bit o' light.

> [MARY *opens the door, and* MRS TANCRED—*a very old woman,
> obviously shaken by the death of her son—appears, accompa-
> nied by several* NEIGHBOURS. *The first few phrases are spoken
> before they appear.*]

FIRST NEIGHBOUR.   It's a sad journey we're goin' on, but God's
good, an' the Republicans won't be always down.

MRS TANCRED.   Ah, what good is that to me now? Whether they're
up or down—it won't bring me darlin' boy from the grave.

---

3. One of the poet Thomas Moore's *Irish Melodies* (1808).
4. "Mary of Argyle," by Charles Jefferys (1807–65).

MRS BOYLE.   Come in an' have a hot cup o' tay, Mrs Tancred, before you go.

MRS TANCRED.   Ah, I can take nothin' now, Mrs Boyle—I won't be
long afther him.

FIRST NEIGHBOUR.   Still an' all, he died a noble death, an' we'll
bury him like a king.

MRS TANCRED.   An' I'll go on livin' like a pauper. Ah, what's the
pains I suffered bringin' him into the world to carry him to his
cradle, to the pains I'm sufferin' now, carryin' him out o' the
world to bring him to his grave!

MARY.   It would be better for you not to go at all, Mrs Tancred, but
to stay at home beside the fire with some o' the neighbours.

MRS TANCRED.   I seen the first of him, an' I'll see the last of him.

MRS BOYLE.   You'd want a shawl, Mrs Tancred; it's a cowld night,
an' the win's blowin' sharp.

MRS MADIGAN [*rushing out*].   I've a shawl above.

MRS TANCRED.   Me home is gone now; he was me only child, an' to
think that he was lyin' for a whole night stretched out on the side
of a lonely counthry lane, with his head, his darlin' head, that I
often kissed an' fondled, half hidden in the wather of a runnin'
brook. An' I'm told he was the leadher of the ambush where me
nex' door neighbour, Mrs Mannin', lost her Free State soldier
son. An' now here's the two of us oul' women, standin' one on
each side of a scales o' sorra, balanced be the bodies of our two
dead darlin' sons.

[MRS MADIGAN *returns, and wraps a shawl around her.*]

God bless you, Mrs. Madigan. . . . [*She moves slowly towards
the door.*] Mother o' God, Mother o' God, have pity on the pair
of us! . . . O Blessed Virgin, where were you when me darlin'
son was riddled with bullets, when me darlin' son was riddled with bullets! . . . Sacred Heart of the Crucified Jesus, take
away our hearts o' stone . . . an' give us hearts o' flesh![5] . . . Take
away this murdherin' hate . . . an' give us Thine own eternal
love!

[*They pass out of the room.*]

MRS BOYLE [*explanatorily to* BENTHAM].   That was Mrs Tancred of
the two-pair back; her son was found, e'er yesterday, lyin' out
beyant Finglas riddled with bullets. A Diehard he was, be all accounts. He was a nice quiet boy, but lattherly he went to hell,
with his Republic first, an' Republic last an' Republic over all. He
often took tea with us here, in the oul' days, an' Johnny, there, an'
him used to be always together.

JOHNNY.   Am I always to be havin' to tell you that he was no friend
o' mine? I never cared for him, an' he could never stick me. It's

_____

5. Ezekiel 36.26.

not because he was Commandant of the Battalion that I was
Quarther-Masther of, that we were friends.

MRS BOYLE.   He's gone now—the Lord be good to him! God help
his poor oul' creature of a mother, for no matther whose friend or
enemy he was, he was her poor son.

BENTHAM.   The whole thing is terrible, Mrs Boyle; but the only
way to deal with a mad dog is to destroy him.

MRS BOYLE.   An' to think of me forgettin' about him bein' brought
to the church tonight, an' we singin' an' all, but it was well we
hadn't the gramophone goin', anyhow.

BOYLE.   Even if we had aself. We've nothin' to do with these
things, one way or t'other. That's the Government's business, an'
let them do what we're payin' them for doin'.

MRS BOYLE.   I'd like to know how a body's not to mind these
things; look at the way they're afther leavin' the people in this
very house. Hasn't the whole house, nearly, been massacreed?
There's young Dougherty's husband with his leg off; Mrs Travers
that had her son blew up be a mine in Inchegeela, in County
Cork; Mrs Mannin' that lost wan of her sons in an ambush a few
weeks ago, an' now, poor Mrs Tancred's only child gone west with
his body made a collandher of. Sure, if it's not our business, I
don't know whose business it is.

BOYLE.   Here, there, that's enough about them things; they don't
affect us, an' we needn't give a damn. If they want a wake, well,
let them have a wake. When I was a sailor, I was always resigned
to meet with a wathery grave; an' if they want to be soldiers,
well, there's no use o' them squealin' when they meet a soldier's
fate.

JOXER.   Let me like a soldier fall—me breast expandin' to th' ball![6]

MRS BOYLE.   In wan way, she deserves all she got; for lately, she let
th' Diehards make an open house of th' place; an' for th' last couple of months, either when th' sun was risin' or when th' sun was
settin' you had CID[7] men burstin' into your room, assin' you
where were you born, where were you christened, where were
you married, an' where would you be buried!

JOHNNY.   For God's sake, let us have no more o' this talk.

MRS MADIGAN.   What about Mr Boyle's song before we start th'
gramophone?

MARY [getting her hat, and putting it on].   Mother, Charlie and I
are goin' out for a little sthroll.

MRS BOYLE.   All right, darlin'.

BENTHAM [going out with MARY].   We won't be long away, Mrs
Boyle.

MRS MADIGAN.   Gwan, Captain, gwan.

BOYLE.   E-e-e-e-eh, I'd want to have a few more jars in me, before
I'd be in fettle for singin'.

6. From the opera *Maritana* (1845) by W. V. Wallace (1812–65).
7. Criminal Investigation Department.

JOXER.   Give us that poem you writ t'other day. [*To the rest.*] Aw, it's a darlin' poem, a daarlin' poem.

MRS BOYLE.   God bless us, is he startin' to write poetry!

BOYLE [*rising to his feet*].   E-e-e-e-eh. [*He recites in an emotional, consequential manner the following verses.*]

Shawn an' I were friends, sir, to me he was all in all.
His work was very heavy and his wages were very small.
None betther on th' beach as Docker, I'll go bail,
'Tis now I'm feelin' lonely, for today he lies in jail.
He was not what some call pious—seldom at church or prayer;
For the greatest scoundrels I know, sir, goes every Sunday there.
Fond of his pint—well, rather, but hated the Boss by creed
But never refused a copper to comfort a pal in need.

E-e-e-e-eh. [*He sits down.*]

MRS MADIGAN.   Grand, grand; you should folly that up, you should folly that up.

JOXER.   It's a daarlin' poem!

BOYLE [*delightedly*].   E-e-e-e-eh.

JOHNNY.   Are yous goin' to put on th' gramophone tonight, or are yous not?

MRS BOYLE.   Gwan, Jack, put on a record.

MRS MADIGAN.   Gwan, Captain, gwan.

BOYLE.   Well, yous'll want to keep a dead silence.

[*He sets a record, starts the machine, and it begins to play 'If You're Irish Come into the Parlour'. As the tune is in full blare, the door is suddenly opened by a brisk, little bald-headed man, dressed circumspectly in a black suit; he glares fiercely at all in the room; he is 'NEEDLE' NUGENT, a tailor. He carries his hat in his hand.*]

NUGENT [*loudly, above the noise of the gramophone*].   Are yous goin' to have that thing bawlin' an' the funeral of Mrs Tancred's son passin' the house? Have none of yous any respect for the Irish people's National regard for the dead?

[BOYLE *stops the gramophone.*]

MRS BOYLE.   Maybe, Needle Nugent, it's nearly time we had a little less respect for the dead, an' a little more regard for the livin'.

MRS MADIGAN.   We don't want you, Mr Nugent, to teach us what we learned at our mother's knee. You don't look yourself as if you were dyin' of grief; if y'ass Maisie Madigan anything, I'd call you a real thrue Diehard an' live-soft Republican, attendin' Republican funerals in the day, an' stoppin' up half the night makin' suits for the Civic Guards!

[*Persons are heard running down the street, some saying 'Here it is, here it is.'* NUGENT *withdraws, and the rest, except* JOHNNY, *go to the window looking into the street, and look out. Sounds of a crowd coming nearer are heard; portions are singing]*

> To Jesus' Heart all burning
> With fervent love for men,
> My heart with fondest yearning
> Shall raise its joyful strain.
> While ages course along,
> Blest be with loudest song
> The Sacred Heart of Jesus
> By every heart and tongue.

MRS BOYLE.   Here's the hearse, here's the hearse!

BOYLE.   There's t' oul' mother walkin' behin' the coffin.

MRS MADIGAN.   You can hardly see the coffin with the wreaths.

JOXER.   Oh, it's a darlin' funeral, a daarlin' funeral!

MRS MADIGAN.   We'd have a betther view from the street.

BOYLE.   Yes—this place ud give you a crick in your neck.

[*They leave the room, and go down.* JOHNNY *sits moodily by the fire. A* YOUNG MAN *enters; he looks at* JOHNNY *for a moment.*]

YOUNG MAN.   Quarther-Masther Boyle.

JOHNNY [*with a start*].   The Mobiliser!

YOUNG MAN.   You're not at the funeral?

JOHNNY.   I'm not well.

YOUNG MAN.   I'm glad I've found you; you were stoppin' at your aunt's; I called there but you'd gone. I've to give you an ordher to attend a Battalion Staff meetin' the night afther tomorrow.

JOHNNY.   Where?

YOUNG MAN.   I don't know; you're to meet me at the Pillar[8] at eight o'clock; then we're to go to a place I'll be told of tonight; there we'll meet a mothor that'll bring us to the meeting. They think you might be able to know somethin' about them that gave the bend where Commandant Tancred was shelterin'.

JOHNNY.   I'm not goin', then. I know nothing about Tancred.

YOUNG MAN [*at the door*].   You'd better come for you own sake—remember your oath.

JOHNNY [*passionately*].   I won't go! Haven't I done enough for Ireland! I've lost me arm, an' me hip's desthroyed so that I'll never be able to walk right agen! Good God, haven't I done enough for Ireland?

YOUNG MAN.   Boyle, no man can do enough for Ireland! [*He goes.*]

[*Faintly in the distance the crowd is heard saying*]

> Hail, Mary, full of grace, the Lord is with Thee;
> Blessed art Thou amongst women, and blessed [*etc.*]

8. O'Connell Street monument to Admiral Lord Nelson (1758–1805), British naval leader; it was destroyed by the Irish Republican Army in 1966, fiftieth anniversary of Easter Week 1916.

Act 3

*The same as Act Two. It is about half-past six on a November evening;
a bright fire burns in the grate;* MARY, *dressed to go out, is sitting on a
chair by the fire, leaning forward, her hands under her chin, her elbows on her knees. A look of dejection, mingled with uncertain anxiety, is on her face. A lamp, turned low, is lighting on the table. The
votive light under the picture of the Virgin gleams more redly than
ever.* MRS BOYLE *is putting on her hat and coat. It is two months later.*

MRS BOYLE.   An' has Bentham never even written to you since—
not one line for the past month?
MARY [*tonelessly*].   Not even a line, mother.
MRS BOYLE.   That's very curious. . . . What came between the two
of yous at all? To leave you so sudden, an' yous so great together.
. . . To go away t' England, an' not to even leave you his address.
. . . The way he was always bringin' you to dances, I thought he
was mad afther you. Are you sure you said nothin' to him?
MARY.   No, mother—at least nothing that could possibly explain
his givin' me up.
MRS BOYLE.   You know you're a bit hasty at times, Mary, an' say
things you shouldn't say.
MARY.   I never said to him what I shouldn't say, I'm sure of that.
MRS BOYLE.   How are you sure of it?
MARY.   Because I love him with all my heart and soul, mother.
Why, I don't know; I often thought to myself that he wasn't the
man poor Jerry was, but I couldn't help loving him, all the same.
MRS BOYLE.   But you shouldn't be frettin' the way you are; when a
woman loses a man, she never knows what she's afther losin', to
be sure, but, then, she never knows what she's afther gainin', either. You're not the one girl of a month ago—you look like one
pinin' away. It's long ago I had a right to bring you to the doctor,
instead of waitin' till tonight.
MARY.   There's no necessity, really, mother, to go to the doctor;
nothing serious is wrong with me—I'm run down and disappointed, that's all.
MRS BOYLE.   I'll not wait another minute; I don't like the look of
you at all. . . . I'm afraid we made a mistake in throwin' over poor
Jerry. . . . . He'd have been betther for you than that Bentham.
MARY.   Mother, the best man for a woman is the one for whom she
has the most love, and Charlie had it all.
MRS BOYLE.   Well, there's one thing to be said for him—he couldn't
have been thinkin' of the money, or he wouldn't ha' left you . . . it
must ha' been somethin' else.
MARY [*wearily*].   I don't know, mother . . . only I think . . .
MRS BOYLE.   What d'ye think?
MARY.   I imagine . . . he thought . . . we weren't . . . good enough
for him.
MRS BOYLE.   An' what was he himself, only a school teacher?

Though I don't blame him for fightin' shy of people like that Joxer
fella an' that oul' Madigan wan—nice sort o' people for your father to inthroduce to a man like Mr Bentham. You might have
told me all about this before now, Mary; I don't know why you
like to hide everything from your mother; you knew Bentham, an'
I'd ha' known nothin' about it if it hadn't bin for the Will; an' it
was only today, afther long coaxin', that you let out that he's left
you.

MARY.   It would have been useless to tell you—you wouldn't understand.

MRS BOYLE [*hurt*].   Maybe not. . . . Maybe I wouldn't understand.
. . . Well, we'll be off now. [*She goes over to door left, and speaks
to* BOYLE *inside.*] We're goin' now to the doctor's. Are you goin' to
get up this evenin'?

BOYLE [*from inside*].   The pains in me legs is terrible! It's me
should be poppin' off to the doctor instead o' Mary, the way I
feel.

MRS BOYLE.   Sorra mend you! A nice way you were in last night—
carried in in a frog's march,[9] dead to the world. If that's the way
you'll go on when you get the money it'll be the grave for you, an
asylum for me and the Poorhouse for Johnny.

BOYLE.   I thought you were goin'?

MRS BOYLE.   That's what has you as you are—you can't bear to be
spoken to. Knowin' the way we are, up to our ears in debt, it's a
wondher you wouldn't ha' got up to go to th' solicitor's an' see if
we could ha' gotten a little o' the money even.

BOYLE [*shouting*].   I can't be goin' up there night, noon an'
mornin', can I? He can't give the money till he gets it, can he? I
can't get blood out of a turnip, can I?

MRS BOYLE.   It's nearly two months since we heard of the Will, an'
the money seems as far off as ever. . . . I suppose you know we
owe twenty pouns to oul' Murphy?

BOYLE.   I've a faint recollection of you tellin' me that before.

MRS BOYLE.   Well, you'll go over to the shop yourself for the things
in future—I'll face him no more.

BOYLE.   I thought you said you were goin'?

MRS BOYLE.   I'm goin' now; come on, Mary.

BOYLE.   Ey, Juno, ey!

MRS BOYLE.   Well, what d'ye want now?

BOYLE.   Is there e're a bottle o' stout left?

MRS BOYLE.   There's two o' them here still.

BOYLE.   Show us in one o' them an' leave t'other there till I get up.
An' throw us in the paper that's on the table, an' the bottle o'
Sloan's Liniment that's in th' drawer.

MRS BOYLE [*getting the liniment and the stout*].   What paper is it
you want—the *Messenger*?

9. Carried by others face-down, like a prisoner.

BOYLE.   *Messenger!* The *News o' the World!*[1]

[MRS BOYLE *brings in the things asked for, and comes out again.*]

MRS BOYLE [at door].   Mind the candle, now, an' don't burn the house over our heads. I left t'other bottle o' stout on the table.

[*She puts bottle of stout on table. She goes out with* MARY. *A cork is heard popping inside.*]

[*A pause; then outside the door is heard the voice of* JOXER *lilting softly: 'Me pipe I'll smoke, as I dhrive me moke . . . are you . . . there . . . Mor . . . ee . . . ar . . . i . . . tee!' A gentle knock is heard, and after a pause the door opens and* JOXER, *followed by* NUGENT, *enters.*]

JOXER.   Be God, they must be all out; I was thinkin' there was somethin' up when he didn't answer the signal. We seen Juno an' Mary goin', but I didn't see him, an' it's very seldom he escapes me.

NUGENT.   He's not goin' to escape me—he's not goin' to be let go to the fair altogether.

JOXER.   Sure, the house couldn't hould them lately; an' he goin' about like a mastherpiece of the Free State counthry; forgettin' their friends; forgettin' God—wouldn't even lift his hat passin' a chapel! Sure they were bound to get a dhrop! An' you really think there's no money comin' to him afther all?

NUGENT.   Not as much as a red rex, man; I've been a bit anxious this long time over me money, an' I went up to the solicitor's to find out all I could—ah, man, they were goin' to throw me down the stairs. They toul' me that the oul' cock himself had the stairs worn away comin' up afther it, an' they black in the face tellin' him he'd get nothin'. Some way or another that the Will is writ he won't be entitled to get as much as a make!

JOXER.   Ah, I thought there was somethin' curious about the whole thing; I've bin havin' sthrange dhreams for the last couple o' weeks. An' I notice that that Bentham fella doesn't be comin' here now—there must be somethin' on the mat there too. Anyhow, who, in the name o' God, ud leave anythin' to that oul' bummer? Sure it ud be unnatural. An' the way Juno an' him's been throwin' their weight about for the last few months! Ah, him that goes a borrowin' goes a sorrowin'!

NUGENT.   Well, he's not goin' to throw his weight about in the suit I made for him much longer. I'm tellin' you seven pouns aren't to be found growin' on the bushes these days.

JOXER.   An' there isn't hardly a neighbour in the whole street that hasn't lent him money on the strength of what he was goin' to

---

1. *Messenger*, a pious, Catholic, and Irish newspaper; the *News*, a sensational British tabloid.

get, but they're after backing the wrong horse. Wasn't it a mercy o' God that I'd nothin' to give him! The softy I am, you know, I'd ha' lent him me last juice! I must have had somebody's good prayers. Ah, afther all, an honest man's the noblest work o' God!

[boyle *coughs inside.*]

Whisht, damn it, he must be inside in bed.

NUGENT.   Inside o' bed or outside of it, he's goin' to pay me for that suit, or give it back—he'll not climb up my back as easily as he thinks.

JOXER.   Gwan in at wanst, man, an' get it off him, an' don't be a fool.

NUGENT [*going to door left, opening it and looking in*].   Ah, don't disturb yourself, Mr Boyle; I hope you're not sick?

BOYLE.   Th' oul' legs, Mr Nugent, the oul' legs.

NUGENT.   I just called over to see if you could let me have anything off the suit?

BOYLE.   E-e-e-eh, how much is this it is?

NUGENT.   It's the same as it was at the start—seven pouns.

BOYLE.   I'm glad you kem, Mr Nugent; I want a good heavy top-coat—Irish frieze, if you have it. How much would a topcoat like that be, now?

NUGENT.   About six pouns.

BOYLE.   Six pouns—six an' seven, six an' seven is thirteen—that'll be thirteen pounds I'll owe you.

[JOXER *slips the bottle of stout that is on the table into his pocket.* NUGENT *rushes into the room, and returns with suit on his arm; he pauses by the door.*

NUGENT.   You'll owe me no thirteen pouns. Maybe you think you're betther able to owe it than pay it!

BOYLE [*frantically*].   Here, come back to hell ower that—where're you goin' with them clothes o' mine?

NUGENT.   Where am I goin' with them clothes o' yours? Well, I like your damn cheek!

BOYLE.   Here, what am I goin' to dhress meself in when I'm goin' out?

NUGENT.   What do I care what you dhress yourself in! You can put yourself in a bolsther cover,[2] if you like.

[*He goes towards the other door, followed by* JOXER.]

JOXER.   What'll he dhress himself in! Gentleman Jack an' his frieze coat!

[*They go out.*]

BOYLE [*inside*].   Ey, Nugent; ey, Mr Nugent, Mr Nugent! [*After a pause* BOYLE *enters hastily, buttoning the braces of his moleskin*

2. Pillowcase.

trousers; his coat and vest are on his arm; he throws these on a chair and hurries to the door on right.] Ey, Mr Nugent, Mr Nugent!

JOXER [*meeting him at the door*]. What's up, what's wrong, Captain?

BOYLE.   Nugent's been here an' took away me suit—the only things I had to go out in!

JOXER.   Tuk your suit—for God's sake! An' what were you doin' while he was takin' them?

BOYLE.   I was in bed when he stole in like a thief in the night, an' before I knew even what he was thinkin' of, he whipped them from the chair an' was off like a redshank!³

JOXER.   An' what, in the name o' God, did he do that for?

BOYLE.   What did he do it for? How the hell do I know what he done it for?—jealousy an' spite, I suppose.

JOXER.   Did he not say what he done it for?

BOYLE.   Amn't I afther tellin' you that he had them whipped up an' was gone before I could open me mouth?

JOXER.   That was a very sudden thing to do; there mus' be somethin' behin' it. Did he hear anythin', I wondher?

BOYLE.   Did he hear anythin'?—you talk very queer, Joxer—what could he hear?

JOXER.   About you not gettin' the money, in some way or t'other?

BOYLE.   An' what ud prevent me from gettin' th' money?

JOXER.   That's jus' what I was thinkin'—what ud prevent you from gettin' the money—nothin', as far as I can see.

BOYLE [*looking round for bottle of stout, with an exclamation*].   Aw, holy God!

JOXER.   What's up, Jack?

BOYLE.   He must have afther lifted the bottle o' stout that Juno left on the table!

JOXER [*horrified*].   Ah no, ah no; he wouldn't be afther doin' that now.

BOYLE.   An' who done it then? Juno left a bottle o' stout here, an' it's gone—it didn't walk, did it?

JOXER.   Oh, that's shockin'; ah, man's inhumanity to man makes countless thousands mourn!⁴

MRS MADIGAN [*appearing at the door*].   I hope I'm not disturbin' you in any discussion on your forthcomin' legacy—if I may use the word—an' that you'll let me have a barny⁵ for a minute or two with you, Mr Boyle.

BOYLE [*uneasily*].   To be sure, Mrs Madigan—an oul' friend's always welcome.

JOXER.   Come in the evenin', come in th' mornin'; come when your assed, or come without warnin', Mrs Madigan.

---

3. Swift wading bird, and also an archaic, derogatory term for the Irish or Scottish as red-legged because of wearing kilts.
4. From "Man Was Made to Mourn," by Robert Burns (1759–96).
5. Brief word.

BOYLE. Sit down, Mrs Madigan.

MRS MADIGAN [*ominously*]. Th' few words I have to say can be said standin'. Puttin' aside all formularies, I suppose you remember me lendin' you some time ago three pouns that I raised on blankets an' furniture in me uncle's?

BOYLE. I remember it well. I have it recorded in me book—three pouns five shillings from Maisie Madigan, raised on articles pawned; an' item: fourpence, given to make up the price of a pint, on th' principle that no bird ever flew on wan wing; all to be repaid at par, when the ship comes home.

MRS MADIGAN. Well, ever since I shoved in the blankets I've been perishing with th' cowld, an' I've decided, if I'll be too hot in th' next world aself, I'm not goin' to be too cowld in this wan; an' consequently, I want me three pouns if you please.

BOYLE. This is a very sudden demand, Mrs Madigan, an' can't be met; but I'm willin' to give you a receipt in full, in full.

MRS MADIGAN. Come on, out with th' money, an' don't be jack-actin'.

BOYLE. You can't get blood out of a turnip, can you?

MRS MADIGAN [*rushing over and shaking him*]. Gimme me money, y'oul' reprobate, or I'll shake the worth of it out of you!

BOYLE. Ey, houl' on, there; houl' on, there! You'll wait for your money now, me lassie!

MRS MADIGAN [*looking around the room and seeing the gramophone*]. I'll wait for it, will I? Well, I'll not wait long; if I can't get th' cash, I'll get th' worth of it. [*She snatches up the gramophone.*]

BOYLE. Ey, ey, there, wher'r you goin' with that?

MRS MADIGAN. I'm goin' to th' pawn to get me three quid five shillins'; I'll brin' you th' ticket, an' then you can do what you like, me bucko.

BOYLE. You can't touch that, you can't touch that! It's not my property, an' it's not ped for yet!

MRS MADIGAN. So much th' better. It'll be an ayse to me conscience, for I'm takin' what doesn't belong to you. You're not goin' to be swankin' it like a paycock with Maisie Madigan's money— I'll pull some o' th' gorgeous feathers out o' your tail! [*She goes off with the gramophone.*]

BOYLE. What's th' world comin' to at all? I ass you, Joxer Daly, is there any morality left anywhere?

JOXER. I wouldn't ha' believed it, only I see it with me own two eyes. I didn't think Maisie Madigan was that sort of woman; she has either a sup taken, or she's heard somethin'.

BOYLE. Heard somethin'—about what, if it's not any harm to ass you?

JOXER. She must ha' heard some rumour or other that you weren't goin' to get th' money.

BOYLE. Who says I'm not goin' to get th' money?

JOXER. Sure, I don't know—I was only sayin'.

BOYLE. Only sayin' what?

JOXER. Nothin'.

BOYLE. You were goin' to say somethin'—don't be a twisther.

JOXER [*angrily*]. Who's a twisther?

BOYLE. Why don't you speak your mind, then?

JOXER. You never twisted yourself—no, you wouldn't know how!

BOYLE. Did you ever know me to twist; did you ever know me to twist?

JOXER [*fiercely*]. Did you ever do anythin' else! Sure, you can't believe a word that comes out o' your mouth.

BOYLE. Here, get out, ower o' this; I always knew you were a prognosticator an' a procrastinator!

JOXER [*going out as* JOHNNY *comes in*]. The anchor's weighed, farewell, ree . . . mem . . . me. Jacky Boyle, Esquire, infernal rogue an' damned liar.

JOHNNY. Joxer an' you at it agen?—when are you goin' to have a little respect for yourself, an' not be always makin' a show of us all?

BOYLE. Are you goin' to lecture me now?

JOHNNY. Is mother back from the doctor yet, with Mary?

> [MRS BOYLE *enters; it is apparent from the serious look on her face that something has happened. She takes off her hat and coat without a word and puts them by. She then sits down near the fire, and there is a few moments' pause.*]

BOYLE. Well, what did the doctor say about Mary?

MRS BOYLE [*in an earnest manner and with suppressed agitation*]. Sit down here, Jack; I've something to say to you . . . about Mary.

BOYLE [*awed by her manner*]. About . . . Mary?

MRS BOYLE. Close that door there and sit down here.

BOYLE [*closing the door*]. More throuble in our native land, is it? [*He sits down.*] Well, what is it?

MRS BOYLE. It's about Mary.

BOYLE. Well, what about Mary—there's nothin' wrong with her, is there?

MRS BOYLE. I'm sorry to say there's a gradle⁶ wrong with her.

BOYLE. A gradle wrong with her! [*Peevishly.*] First Johnny an' now Mary; is the whole house goin' to become an hospital! It's not consumption, is it?

MRS BOYLE. No . . . it's not consumption . . . it's worse.

JOHNNY. Worse! Well, we'll have to get her into some place ower this, there's no one here to mind her.

MRS BOYLE. We'll all have to mind her now. You might as well know now, Johnny, as another time. [*To* BOYLE.] D'ye know what the doctor said to me about her, Jack?

BOYLE. How ud I know—I wasn't there, was I?

MRS BOYLE. He told me to get her married at wanst.

BOYLE. Married at wanst! An' why did he say the like o' that?

---

6. Great deal.

MRS BOYLE.   Because Mary's goin' to have a baby in a short time.

BOYLE.   Goin' to have a baby!—my God, what'll Bentham say when he hears that?

MRS BOYLE.   Are you blind, man, that you can't see that it was Bentham that has done this wrong to her?

BOYLE [*passionately*].   Then he'll marry her, he'll have to marry her!

MRS BOYLE.   You know he's gone to England, an' God knows where he is now.

BOYLE.   I'll folly him, I'll folly him, an' bring him back, an' make him do her justice. The scoundrel, I might ha' known what he was, with his Yogees an' his Prawna!

MRS BOYLE.   We'll have to keep it quiet till we see what we can do.

BOYLE.   Oh, isn't this a nice thing to come on top o' me, an' the state I'm in! A pretty show I'll be to Joxer an' to that oul' wan, Madigan! Amn't I afther goin' through enough without havin' to go through this!

MRS BOYLE.   What you an' I'll have to go through'll be nothin' to what poor Mary'll have to go through; for you an' me is middlin' old, an' most of our years is spent; but Mary'll have maybe forty years to face an' handle, an' every wan of them'll be tainted with a bitther memory.

BOYLE.   Where is she? Where is she till I tell her off? I'm tellin' you when I'm done with her she'll be a sorry girl!

MRS BOYLE.   I left her in me sister's till I came to speak to you. You'll say nothin' to her, Jack; ever since she left school she's earned her livin', an' your fatherly care never throubled the poor girl.

BOYLE.   Gwan, take her part agen her father! But I'll let you see whether I'll say nothin' to her or no! Her an' her readin'! That's more o' th' blasted nonsense that has the house fallin' on top of us! What did th' likes of her, born in a tenement house, want with readin'? Her readin's afther bringin' her to a nice pass—oh, it's madnin', madnin', madnin'!

MRS BOYLE.   When she comes back say nothin' to her, Jack, or she'll leave this place.

BOYLE.   Leave this place! Ay, she'll leave this place, an' quick too!

MRS BOYLE.   If Mary goes, I'll go with her.

BOYLE.   Well, go with her! Well, go, th' pair o' yous! I lived before I seen yous, an' I can live when yous are gone. Isn't this a nice thing to come rollin' in on top o' me afther all your prayin' to St Anthony an' the Little Flower! An' she's a Child o' Mary, too—I wonder what'll the nuns think of her now? An' it'll be bellows'd all over th' disthrict before you could say Jack Robinson; an' whenever I'm seen they'll whisper, 'That's th' father of Mary Boyle that had th' kid be th' swank she used to go with; d'ye know?' To be sure they'll know—more about it than I will meself!

JOHNNY.   She should be dhriven out o' th' house she's brought disgrace on!

MRS BOYLE.   Hush, you, Johnny. We needn't let it be bellows'd all

over the place; all we've got to do is to leave this place quietly an'
go somewhere where we're not known an' nobody'll be th' wiser.

BOYLE.   You're talkin' like a two-year-oul', woman. Where'll we get
a place ou' o' this—places aren't that easily got.

MRS BOYLE.   But, Jack, when we get the money . . .

BOYLE.   Money—what money?

MRS BOYLE.   Why, oul' Ellison's money, of course.

BOYLE.   There's no money comin' from oul' Ellison, or any one
else. Since you've heard of wan throuble, you might as well hear
of another. There's no money comin' to us at all—the Will's a
wash-out!

MRS BOYLE.   What are you sayin', man—no money?

JOHNNY.   How could it be a wash-out?

BOYLE.   The boyo that's afther doin' it to Mary done it to me as
well. The thick made out the Will wrong; he said in th' Will, only
first cousin an' second cousin, instead of mentionin' our names,
an' now any one that thinks he's a first cousin or second cousin
t'oul Ellison can claim the money as well as me, an' they're
springin' up in hundreds, an' comin' from America an' Australia,
thinkin' to get their whack out of it, while all the time the lawyers
is gobblin' it up, till there's not as much as ud buy a stockin' for
your lovely daughter's baby!

MRS BOYLE.   I don't believe it, I don't believe it, I don't believe it!

JOHNNY.   Why did you say nothin' about this before?

MRS BOYLE.   You're not serious, Jack; you're not serious!

BOYLE.   I'm tellin' you the scholar, Bentham, made a banjax o' th'
Will; instead o' sayin', 'th' rest o' me property to be divided between me first cousin, Jack Boyle, an' me second cousin Mick
Finnegan, o' Santhry', he writ down only, 'me first an' second
cousins', an' the world an' his wife are afther th' property now.

MRS BOYLE.   Now I know why Bentham left poor Mary in th' lurch;
I can see it all now—oh, is there not even a middlin' honest man
left in th' world?

JOHNNY [to BOYLE].   An' you let us run into debt, an' you borreyed
money from everybody to fill yourself with beer! An' now you tell
us the whole thing's a washout! Oh, if it's thrue, I'm done with
you, for you're worse than me sisther Mary!

BOYLE.   You hole your tongue, d'ye hear? I'll not take any lip from
you. Go an' get Bentham if you want satisfaction for all that's afther happenin' us.

JOHNNY.   I won't hole me tongue, I won't hole me tongue! I'll tell
you what I think of you, father an' all as you are . . . you . . .

MRS BOYLE.   Johnny, Johnny, Johnny, for God's sake, be quiet!

JOHNNY.   I'll not be quiet, I'll not be quiet; he's a nice father, isn't
he? is it any wondher Mary went asthray, when . . .

MRS BOYLE.   Johnny, Johnny, for my sake be quiet—for your
mother's sake!

BOYLE.   I'm goin' out now to have a few dhrinks with th' last
few makes I have, an' tell that lassie o' yours not to be here when

I come back; for if I lay me eyes on her, I'll lay me hans on her, an' if I lay me hans on her, I won't be accountable for me actions!

JOHNNY.   Take care somebody doesn't lay his hans on you—y'oul'. . .

MRS BOYLE.   Johnny, Johnny!

BOYLE [*at door, about to go out*].   Oh, a nice son, an' a nicer daughter, I have. [*Calling loudly upstairs.*] Joxer, Joxer, are you there?

JOXER [*from a distance*].   I'm here, More . . . ee . . . aar . . . i . . . tee!

BOYLE.   I'm goin' down to Foley's—are you comin'?

JOXER.   Come with you? With that sweet call me heart is stirred; I'm only waiting for the word, an' I'll be with you, like a bird!

[BOYLE *and* JOXER *pass the door going out.*]

JOHNNY [*throwing himself on the bed*].   I've a nice sisther, an' a nice father, there's no bettin' on it. I wish to God a bullet or a bomb had whipped me ou' o' this long ago! Not one o' yous, have any thought for me!

MRS BOYLE [*with passionate remonstrance*].   If you don't whisht, Johnny, you'll drive me mad. Who has kep' th' home together for the past few years—only me? An' who'll have to bear th' biggest part o' this throuble but me?—but whinin' an' whingin' isn't goin' to do any good.

JOHNNY.   You're to blame yourself for a gradle of it—givin' him his own way in everything, an' never assin' to check him, no matther what he done. Why didn't you look afther th' money? why . . .

[*There is a knock at the door;* MRS BOYLE *opens it;* JOHNNY *rises on his elbow to look and listen; two men enter.*]

FIRST MAN.   We've been sent up be th' Manager of the Hibernian Furnishing Company, Mrs Boyle, to take back the furniture that was got a while ago.

MRS BOYLE.   Yous'll touch nothin' here—how do I know who yous are?

FIRST MAN [*showing a paper*].   There's the ordher, ma'am. [*Reading.*] A chest o' drawers, a table, wan easy an' two ordinary chairs; wan mirror; wan chesterfield divan, an' a wardrobe an' two vases. [*To his comrade.*] Come on, Bill, it's afther knockin-off time already.

JOHNNY.   For God's sake, mother, run down to Foley's an' bring father back, or we'll be left without a stick.

[*The men carry out the table.*]

MRS BOYLE.   What good would it be?—you heard what he said before he went out.

JOHNNY.   Can't you thry? He ought to be here, an' the like of this goin' on.

[MRS BOYLE *puts a shawl around her, as* MARY *enters.*]

MARY.   What's up, mother? I met a man carryin' away the table, an'
everybody's talking about us not gettin' the money after all.

MRS BOYLE.   Everythin's gone wrong, Mary, everythin'. We're not
gettin' a penny out o' the Will, not a penny—I'll tell you all when
I come back; I'm goin' for your father. [*She runs out.*]

JOHNNY [*to* MARY, *who has sat down by the fire*].   It's a wondher
you're not ashamed to show your face here, afther what has happened.

[JERRY *enters slowly; there is a look of earnest hope on his
face. He looks at* MARY *for a few moments.*]

JERRY [*softly*].   Mary! [MARY *does not answer.*] Mary, I want to speak
to you for a few moments, may I? [MARY *remains silent;* JOHNNY
goes slowly into room on left.] Your mother has told me everything, Mary, and I have come to you. . . . I have come to tell you,
Mary, that my love for you is greater and deeper than ever. . . .

MARY [*with a sob*].   Oh, Jerry, Jerry, say no more; all that is over
now; anything like that is impossible now!

JERRY.   Impossible? Why do you talk like that, Mary?

MARY.   After all that has happened.

JERRY.   What does it matter what has happened? We are young
enough to be able to forget all those things. [*He catches her
hand.*] Mary, Mary, I am pleading for your love. With Labour,
Mary, humanity is above everything; we are the Leaders in the
fight for a new life. I want to forget Bentham, I want to forget
that you left me—even for a while.

MARY.   Oh, Jerry, Jerry, you haven't the bitter word of scorn for me
after all.

JERRY [*passionately*].   Scorn! I love you, love you, Mary!

MARY [*rising, and looking him in the eyes*].   Even though . . .

JERRY.   Even though you threw me over for another man; even
though you gave me many a bitter word!

MARY.   Yes, yes, I know; but you love me, even though . . . even
though . . . I'm . . . goin' . . . goin' . . .

[*He looks at her questioningly, and fear gathers in his eyes.*]

Ah, I was thinkin' so. . . . You don't know everything!

JERRY [*poignantly*].   Surely to God, Mary, you don't mean that . . .
that . . . that . . .

MARY.   Now you know all, Jerry; now you know all!

JERRY.   My God, Mary, have you fallen as low as that?

MARY.   Yes, Jerry, as you say, I have fallen as low as that.

JERRY.   I didn't mean it that way, Mary . . . it came on me so sudden, that I didn't mind what I was sayin'. . . . I never expected
this—your mother never told me. . . . I'm sorry . . . God knows,
I'm sorry for you, Mary.

MARY.   Let us say no more, Jerry; I don't blame you for thinkin' it's
terrible. . . . I suppose it is. . . . Everybody'll think the same . . .

it's only as I expected—your humanity is just as narrow as the humanity of the others.

JERRY.   I'm sorry, all the same . . . I shouldn't have troubled you. . . . I wouldn't if I'd known. . . . If I can do anything for you . . . Mary . . . I will. [*He turns to go, and halts at the door.*]

MARY.   Do you remember, Jerry, the verses you read when you gave the lecture in the Socialist Rooms some time ago, on Humanity's Strife with Nature?

JERRY.   The verses—no; I don't remember them.

MARY.   I do. They're runnin' in me head now—

> An' we felt the power that fashion'd
> All the lovely things we saw,
> That created all the murmur
> Of an everlasting law,
> Was a hand of force an' beauty,
> With an eagle's tearin' claw.
>
> Then we saw our globe of beauty
> Was an ugly thing as well,
> A hymn divine whose chorus
> Was an agonisin' yell;
> Like the story of a demon,
> That an angel had to tell;
>
> Like a glowin' picture by a
> Hand unsteady, brought to ruin;
> Like her craters, if their deadness
> Could give life unto the moon;
> Like the agonising horror
> Of a violin out of tune.

[*There is a pause, and* JERRY *goes slowly out.*]

JOHNNY [*returning*].   Is he gone?

MARY.   Yes.

[*The two men re-enter.*]

FIRST MAN.   We can't wait any longer for t'oul' fella—sorry, Miss, but we have to live as well as th' nex' man. [*They carry out some things.*]

JOHNNY.   Oh, isn't this terrible! . . . I suppose you told him everything . . . couldn't you have waited for a few days? . . . he'd have stopped th' takin' of the things, if you'd kep' your mouth shut. Are you burnin' to tell every one of the shame you've brought on us?

MARY [*snatching up her hat and coat.*]   Oh, this is unbearable! [*She rushes out.*]

FIRST MAN [*re-entering*].   We'll take the chest o' drawers next—it's the heaviest.

[*The votive light flickers for a moment, and goes out.*]

JOHNNY [*in a cry of fear*].   Mother o' God, the light's afther goin' out!

FIRST MAN.   You put the win' up me the way you bawled that time. The oil's all gone, that's all.

JOHNNY [*with an agonising cry*].   Mother o' God, there's a shot I'm afther gettin'!

FIRST MAN.   What's wrong with you, man? Is it a fit you're takin'?

JOHNNY.   I'm afther feelin' a pain in me breast, like the tearin' by of a bullet!

FIRST MAN.   He's goin' mad—it's a wondher they'd leave a chap like that here by myself.

> [*Two* IRREGULARS *enter swiftly; they carry revolvers; one goes over to* JOHNNY; *the other covers the two furniture men.*]

FIRST IRREGULAR [*to the men, quietly and incisively*].   Who are you?—what are yous doin' here?—quick!

FIRST MAN.   Removin' furniture that's not paid for.

IRREGULAR.   Get over to the other end of the room an' turn your faces to the wall—quick! [*The two men turn their faces to the wall, with their hands up.*]

SECOND IRREGULAR [*to* JOHNNY].   Come on, Sean Boyle, you're wanted; some of us have a word to say to you.

JOHNNY.   I'm sick, I can't—what do you want with me?

SECOND IRREGULAR.   Come on, come on; we've a distance to go an' haven't much time—come on.

JOHNNY.   I'm an oul' comrade—yous wouldn't shoot an oul' comrade.

SECOND IRREGULAR.   Poor Tancred was an oul' comrade o' yours, but you didn't think o' that when you gave him away to the gang that sent him to his grave. But we've no time to waste; come on—here, Dermot, ketch his arm. [*To* JOHNNY.] Have you your beads?

JOHNNY.   Me beads! Why do you ass me that, why do you ass me that?

SECOND IRREGULAR.   Go on, go on, march!

JOHNNY.   Are yous goin' to do in a comrade?—look at me arm, I lost it for Ireland.

SECOND IRREGULAR.   Commandant Tancred lost his life for Ireland.

JOHNNY.   Sacred Heart of Jesus, have mercy on me! Mother o' God pray for me—be with me now in the agonies o' death! . . . Hail, Mary, full o' grace . . . the Lord is . . . with Thee.

> [*They drag out* JOHNNY BOYLE, *and the curtain falls. When it rises again the most of the furniture is gone.* MARY *and* MRS BOYLE, *one on each side, are sitting in a darkened room, by the fire; it is an hour later.*]

MRS BOYLE.   I'll not wait much longer . . . what did they bring him away in the mothor for? Nugent says he thinks they had guns . . .

is me throubles never goin' to be over? . . . If anything ud happen
to poor Johnny, I think I'd lose me mind. . . . I'll go to the Police
Station, surely they ought to be able to do somethin'.

[*Below is heard the sound of voices.*]

Whisht, is that something? Maybe, it's your father, though when
I left him in Foley's he was hardly able to lift his head. Whisht!

[*A knock at the door, and the voice of* MRS MADIGAN, *speaking
very softly:*]

Mrs Boyle, Mrs Boyle. [MRS BOYLE *opens the door.*] Oh, Mrs
Boyle, God an' His Blessed Mother be with you this night!
MRS BOYLE [*calmly*].   What is it, Mrs Madigan? It's Johnny—some-
thing about Johnny.
MRS MADIGAN.   God send it's not, God send it's not Johnny!
MRS BOYLE.   Don't keep me waitin', Mrs Madigan; I've gone
through so much lately that I feel able for anything.
MRS MADIGAN.   Two polismen below wantin' you.
MRS BOYLE.   Wantin' me; an' why do they want me?
MRS MADIGAN.   Some poor fella's been found, an' they think it's,
it's . . .
MRS BOYLE.   Johnny, Johnny!
MARY [*with her arms round her mother*].   Oh, mother, mother, me
poor, darlin' mother.
MRS BOYLE.   Hush, hush, darlin'; you'll shortly have your own
throuble to bear. [*To* MRS MADIGAN.] An' why do the polis think
it's Johnny, Mrs Madigan?
MRS MADIGAN.   Because one o' the doctors knew him when he was
attendin' with his poor arm.
MRS BOYLE.   Oh, it's thrue, then; it's Johnny, it's me son, me own
son!
MARY.   Oh, it's thrue, it's thrue what Jerry Devine says—there isn't
a God, there isn't a God; if there was He wouldn't let these
things happen!
MRS BOYLE.   Mary, you mustn't say them things. We'll want all the
help we can get from God an' His Blessed Mother now! These
things have nothin' to do with the Will o' God. Ah, what can God
do agen the stupidity o' men!
MRS MADIGAN.   The polis want you to go with them to the hospital
to see the poor body—they're waitin' below.
MRS BOYLE.   We'll go. Come, Mary, an' we'll never come back here
agen. Let your father furrage for himself now; I've done all I
could an' it was all no use—he'll be hopeless till the end of his
days. I've got a little room in me sisther's where we'll stop till
your throuble is over, an' then we'll work together for the sake of
the baby.
MARY.   My poor little child that'll have no father!
MRS BOYLE.   It'll have what's far betther—it'll have two mothers.

A ROUGH VOICE SHOUTING FROM BELOW.   Are yous goin' to keep us
    waitin' for yous all night?

MRS MADIGAN [*going to the door, and shouting down*].   Take your
    hour, there, take your hour! If yous are in such a hurry, skip off,
    then, for nobody wants you here—if they did yous wouldn't be
    found. For you're the same as yous were undher the British Gov-
    ernment—never where yous are wanted! As far as I can see, the
    Polis as Polis, in this city, is Null an' Void!

MRS BOYLE.   We'll go, Mary, we'll go; you to see your poor dead
    brother, an' me to see me poor dead son!

MARY.   I dhread it, mother, I dhread it!

MRS BOYLE.   I forgot, Mary, I forgot; your poor oul' selfish mother
    was only thinkin' of herself. No, no, you mustn't come—it wouldn't
    be good for you. You go on to me sisther's an' I'll face th' ordeal
    meself. Maybe I didn't feel sorry enough for Mrs Tancred when
    her poor son was found as Johnny's been found now—because
    he was a Diehard! Ah, why didn't I remember that then he wasn't
    a Diehard or a Stater, but only a poor dead son! It's well I remem-
    ber all that she said—an' it's my turn to say it now: What was the
    pain I suffered, Johnny, bringin' you into the world to carry you
    to your cradle, to the pains I'll suffer carryin' you out o' the world
    to bring you to your grave! Mother o' God, Mother o' God, have
    pity on us all! Blessed Virgin, where were you when me darlin'
    son was riddled with bullets, when me darlin' son was riddled
    with bullets? Sacred Heart o' Jesus, take away our hearts o' stone,
    and give us hearts o' flesh! Take away this murdherin' hate, an'
    give us Thine own eternal love!

    [*They all go slowly out.*]

    [*There is a pause; then a sound of shuffling steps on the stairs
    outside. The door opens and* BOYLE *and* JOXER, *both of them
    very drunk, enter.*]

BOYLE.   I'm able to go no farther. . . . Two polis, ey . . . what were
    they doin' here, I wondher? . . . Up to no good, anyhow . . . an'
    Juno an' that lovely daughter o' mine with them. [*Taking a six-
    pence from his pocket and looking at it.*] Wan single, solitary tan-
    ner left out of all I borreyed . . . [*He lets it fall.*] The last o' the
    Mohecans. . . . The blinds are down, Joxer, the blinds is down!

JOXER [*walking unsteadily across the room, and anchoring at the
    bed*].   Put all . . . your throubles . . . in your oul' kit-bag . . . an'
    smile . . . smile . . . smile!

BOYLE.   The counthry'll have to steady itself . . . it's goin' . . . to
    hell. . . . Where'r all . . . the chairs . . . gone to . . . steady itself,
    Joxer. . . . Chairs'll . . . have to . . . steady themselves. . . . No
    matther . . . what any one may . . . say. . . . Irelan' sober . . . is Ire-
    lan' . . . free.

JOXER [*stretching himself on the bed*].   Chains . . . an' . . . slaveree
    . . . that's a darlin' motto . . . a daaarlin' . . . motto!

BOYLE. If th' worst comes . . . to th' worse . . . I can join a . . . flyin'
. . . column . . . I done . . . me bit . . . in Easther Week . . . had
no business . . . to . . . be . . . there . . . but Captain Boyle's Captain Boyle!

JOXER. Breathes there a man with soul . . . so . . . de . . . ad . . .
this . . . me . . . o . . . wn, me nat . . . ive I . . . an'!

BOYLE [*subsiding into a sitting posture on the floor*]. Commandant
Kelly died . . . in them . . . arms . . . Joxer. . . . Tell me Volunteer
butties . . . says he . . . that . . . I died for . . . Irelan'!

JOXER. D'jever rade 'Willie . . . Reilly . . . an' His Own . . . Colleen
. . . Bawn?[7] It's a darlin' story, a daarlin' story!

BOYLE. I'm telling you . . . Joxer . . . th' whole worl's . . . in a terr
. . . ible state o' . . . chassis!

---

7. The final lines are a confused series of literary phrases from popular and sentimental
works.

SAMUEL BECKETT

Krapp's Last Tape[†]

A late evening in the future.

KRAPP's *den.*   [*handwritten:* ↗ focus]

Front centre a small table, the two drawers of which open towards audience.   [*handwritten:* keeping himself away from them ↵]

Sitting at the table, facing front, i.e. across from the drawers, a wearish old man: [*handwritten:* → late evening]
KRAPP.

Rusty black narrow trousers too short for him. Rusty black sleeveless waistcoat, four capacious pockets. Heavy silver watch and chain. Grimy white shirt open at neck, no collar. Surprising pair of dirty white boots, size ten at least, very narrow and pointed. [*handwritten:* ↦ clown gone wrong (+ white face, large shoes)]
White face. Purple nose. Disordered grey hair. Unshaven. [*handwritten:* ↗ shows how narrow his world is]
Very near-sighted (but unspectacled). Hard of hearing. Cracked voice. Distinctive intonation.

Laborious walk.

On the table a tape-recorder with microphone and a number of cardboard boxes containing reels of recorded tapes. [*handwritten:* ↗ focus]
Table and immediately adjacent area in strong white light. Rest of stage in darkness.

KRAPP *remains a moment motionless, heaves a great sigh, looks at his watch, fumbles in his pockets, takes out an envelope, puts it back, fumbles, takes out a small bunch of keys, raises it to his eyes, chooses a key, gets up and moves to front of table. He stoops, unlocks first drawer, peers into it, feels about inside it, takes out a reel of tape,*

247

peers at it, puts it back, locks drawer, unlocks second drawer, peers into it, feels about inside it, takes out a large banana, peers at it, locks drawer, puts keys back in his pocket. He turns, advances to edge of stage, halts, strokes banana, peels it, drops skin at his feet, puts end of banana in his mouth and remains motionless, staring vacuously before him. Finally he bites off the end, turns aside and begins pacing to and fro at edge of stage, in the light, i.e. not more than four or five paces either way, meditatively eating banana. He treads on skin, slips, nearly falls, recovers himself, stoops and peers at skin and finally pushes it, still stooping, with his foot over the edge of stage into pit. He resumes his pacing, finishes banana, returns to table, sits down, remains a moment motionless, heaves a great sigh, takes keys from his pockets, raises them to his eyes, chooses key, gets up and moves to front of table, unlocks second drawer, takes out a second large banana, peers at it, locks drawer, puts back keys in his pocket, turns, advances to edge of stage, halts, strokes banana, peels it, tosses skin into pit, puts end of banana in his mouth and remains motionless, staring vacuously before him. Finally he has an idea, puts banana in his waistcoat pocket, the end emerging, and goes with all the speed he can muster backstage into darkness. Ten seconds. Loud pop of cork. Fifteen seconds. He comes back into light carrying an old ledger and sits down at table. He lays ledger on table, wipes his mouth, wipes his hands on the front of his waistcoat, brings them smartly together and rubs them.

KRAPP [*briskly*]. Ah! [*He bends over ledger, turns the pages, finds the entry he wants, reads.*] Box . . . thrree . . . spool . . . five. [*He raises his head and stares front. With relish.*] Spool! [*Pause.*] Spooool! [*Happy smile. Pause. He bends over table, starts peering and poking at the boxes.*] Box . . . thrree . . . thrree . . . four . . . two . . . [*with surprise*] nine! good God! . . . seven . . . ah! the little rascal! [*He takes up box, peers at it.*] Box thrree. [*He lays it on table, opens it and peers at spools inside.*] Spool . . . [*he peers at ledger*] . . . five . . . [*he peers at spools*] . . . five . . . five . . . ah! the little scoundrel! [*He takes out a spool, peers at it.*] Spool five. [*He lays it on table, closes box three, puts it back with the others, takes up the spool.*] Box thrree, spool five. [*He bends over the machine, looks up. With relish.*] Spooool! [*Happy smile. He bends, loads spool on machine, rubs his hands.*] Ah! [*He peers at ledger, reads entry at foot of page.*] Mother at rest at last . . . Hm . . . The black ball . . . [*He raises his head, stares blankly front. Puzzled.*] Black ball? . . . [*He peers again at ledger, reads.*] The dark nurse . . . [*He raises his head, broods, peers again at ledger, reads.*] Slight improvement in bowel condition . . . Hm . . . Memorable . . . what? [*He peers closer.*] Equinox, memorable equinox. [*He raises his head, stares blankly front. Puzzled.*] Memorable equinox? . . . [*Pause. He shrugs his shoulders, peers again at ledger, reads.*] Farewell to— [*he turns the page*] —love.

[*He raises his head, broods, bends over machine, switches on and assumes listening posture, i.e. leaning forward, elbows on table, hand cupping ear towards machine, face front.*]

TAPE [*strong voice, rather pompous, clearly* KRAPP's *at a much earlier time*]. Thirty-nine today, sound as a— [*settling himself more comfortably he knocks one of the boxes off the table, curses, switches off, sweeps boxes and ledger violently to the ground, winds tape back to beginning, switches on, resumes posture*]. Thirty-nine today, sound as a bell, apart from my old weakness, and intellectually I have now every reason to suspect at the . . . [*hesitates*] . . . crest of the wave—or thereabouts. Celebrated the awful occasion, as in recent years, quietly at the Winehouse. Not a soul. Sat before the fire with closed eyes, separating the grain from the husks. Jotted down a few notes, on the back of an envelope. Good to be back in my den, in my old rags. Have just eaten I regret to say three bananas and only with difficulty refrained from a fourth. Fatal things for a man with my condition. [*Vehemently.*] Cut 'em out! [*Pause.*] The new light above my table is a great improvement. With all this darkness round me I feel less alone. [*Pause.*] In a way. [*Pause.*] I love to get up and move about in it, then back here to . . . [*hesitates*] . . . me. [*Pause.*] Krapp.

[*Pause.*]

The grain, now what I wonder do I mean by that, I mean . . . [*hesitates*] . . . I suppose I mean those things worth having when all the dust has—when all *my* dust has settled. I close my eyes and try and imagine them.

[*Pause.* KRAPP *closes his eyes briefly.*]

Extraordinary silence this evening, I strain my ears and do not hear a sound. Old Miss McGlome always sings at this hour. But not tonight. Songs of her girlhood, she says. Hard to think of her as a girl. Wonderful woman though. Connaught, I fancy. [*Pause.*] Shall I sing when I am her age, if I ever am? No. [*Pause.*] Did I sing as a boy? No. [*Pause.*] Did I ever sing? No.

[*Pause.*]

Just been listening to an old year, passages at random. I did not check in the book, but it must be at least ten or twelve years ago. At that time I was still living on and off with Bianca in Kedar Street. Well out of that, Jesus yes! Hopeless business. [*Pause.*] Not much about her, apart from a tribute to her eyes. Very warm. I suddenly saw them again. [*Pause.*] Incomparable! [*Pause.*] Ah well . . . [*Pause.*] These old P.M.s[1] are gruesome, but I often find them— [KRAPP *switches off, broods, switches on*] —a help before

---

1. Postmortems.

embarking on a new . . . [*hesitates*] . . . retrospect. Hard to believe I was ever that young whelp. The voice! Jesus! And the aspirations! [*Brief laugh in which* KRAPP *joins.*] And the resolutions! [*Brief laugh in which* KRAPP *joins.*] To drink less, in particular. [*Brief laugh of* KRAPP *alone.*] Statistics. Seventeen hundred hours, out of the preceding eight thousand odd, consumed on licensed premises alone. More than 20%, say 40% of his waking life. [*Pause.*] Plans for a less . . . [*hesitates*] . . . engrossing sexual life. Last illness of his father. Flagging pursuit of happiness. Unattainable laxation. Sneers at what he calls his youth and thanks to God that it's over. [*Pause.*] False ring there. [*Pause.*] Shadows of the opus . . . magnum. Closing with a— [*brief laugh*] —yelp to Providence. [*Prolonged laugh in which* KRAPP *joins.*] What remains of all that misery? A girl in a shabby green coat, on a railway-station platform? No?

[*Pause.*]

When I look—

[KRAPP *switches off, broods, looks at his watch, gets up, goes backstage into darkness. Ten seconds. Pop of cork. Ten seconds. Second cork. Ten seconds. Third cork. Ten seconds. Brief burst of quavering song.*]

KRAPP [*sings*]. Now the day is over,
Night is drawing nigh-igh,
Shadows—[2]

[*Fit of coughing. He comes back into light, sits down, wipes his mouth, switches on, resumes his listening posture.*]

TAPE. —back on the year that is gone, with what I hope is perhaps a glint of the old eye to come, there is of course the house on the canal where mother lay a-dying, in the late autumn, after her long viduity [KRAPP *gives a start*], and the— [KRAPP *switches off, winds back tape a little, bends his ear closer to machine, switches on*] —a-dying, in the late autumn, after her long viduity, and the—

[KRAPP *switches off, raises his head, stares blankly before him. His lips move in the syllables of "viduity." No sound. He gets up, goes backstage into darkness, comes back with an enormous dictionary, lays it on table, sits down and looks up the word.*]

KRAPP [*reading from dictionary*]. State—or condition of being—or remaining—a widow—or widower. [*Looks up. Puzzled.*] Being—or remaining? . . . [*Pause. He peers again at dictionary. Reading.*] "Deep weeds of viduity" . . . Also of an animal, especially a bird

---

2. "Now the Day Is Over," a hymn; the first verse continues: "Shadows of the evening / Steal across the sky."

. . . the vidua or weaver-bird . . . Black plumage of male . . . [*He looks up. With relish.*] The vidua-bird!

> [*Pause. He closes dictionary, switches on, resumes listening posture.*]

TAPE.   —bench by the weir from where I could see her window. There I sat, in the biting wind, wishing she were gone. [*Pause.*] Hardly a soul, just a few regulars, nursemaids, infants, old men, dogs. I got to know them quite well—on by appearance of course I mean! One dark young beauty I recollect particularly, all white and starch, incomparable bosom, with a big black hooded perambulator, most funereal thing. Whenever I looked in her direction she had her eyes on me. And yet when I was bold enough to speak to her—not having been introduced—she threatened to call a policeman. As if I had designs on her virtue! [*Laugh. Pause.*] The face she had! The eyes! Like . . . [*hesitates*] . . . chrysolite! [*Pause.*] Ah well . . . [*Pause.*] I was there when— [KRAPP *switches off, broods, switches on again*] —the blind went down, one of those dirty brown roller affairs, throwing a ball for a little white dog, as chance would have it. I happened to look up and there it was. All over and done with, at last. I sat on for a few moments with the ball in my hand and the dog yelping and pawing at me. [*Pause.*] Moments. Her moments, my moments. [*Pause.*] The dog's moments. [*Pause.*] In the end I held it out to him and he took it in his mouth, gently, gently. A small, old, black, hard, solid rubber ball. [*Pause.*] I shall feel it, in my hand, until my dying day. [*Pause.*] I might have kept it. [*Pause.*] But I gave it to the dog.

> [*Pause.*]

Ah well . . .

> [*Pause.*]

Spiritually a year of profound gloom and indigence until that memorable night in March, at the end of the jetty, in the howling wind, never to be forgotten, when suddenly I saw the whole thing. The vision, at last. This I fancy is what I have chiefly to record this evening, against the day when my work will be done and perhaps no place left in my memory, warm or cold, for the miracle that . . . [*hesitates*] . . . for the fire that set it alight. What I suddenly saw then was this, that the belief I had been going on all my life, namely— [KRAPP *switches off impatiently, winds tape forward, switches on again*] —great granite rocks the foam flying up in the light of the lighthouse and the wind-gauge spinning like a propellor, clear to me at last that the dark I have always struggled to keep under is in reality my most— [KRAPP *curses, switches off, winds tape forward, switches on again*] —unshatterable association until my dissolution of storm and night with the light of the understanding and the fire— [KRAPP *curses louder, switches off, winds tape forward, switches on again*] —my face in her breasts and my hand on her. We lay there without moving. But under us all moved, and moved us, gently, up and down, and from side to side.

[*Pause.*]

Past midnight. Never knew such silence. The earth might be uninhabited.

[*Pause.*]

Here I end—

[KRAPP *switches off, winds tape back, switches on again.*]

—upper lake, with the punt, bathed off the bank, then pushed out into the stream and drifted. She lay stretched out on the floorboards with her hands under her head and her eyes closed. Sun blazing down, bit of a breeze, water nice and lively. I noticed a scratch on her thigh and asked her how she came by it. Picking gooseberries, she said. I said again I thought it was hopeless and no good going on, and she agreed, without opening her eyes. [*Pause.*] I asked her to look at me and after a few moments— [*Pause.*] —after a few moments she did, but the eyes just slits, because of the glare. I bent over her to get them in the shadow and they opened. [*Pause. Low.*] Let me in. [*Pause.*] We drifted in among the flags and stuck. The way they went down, sighing, before the stem! [*Pause.*] I lay down across her with my face in her breasts and my hand on her. We lay there without moving. But under us all moved, and moved us, gently, up and down, and from side to side.

[*Pause.*]

Past midnight. Never knew—

[KRAPP *switches off, broods. Finally he fumbles in his pockets, encounters the banana, takes it out, peers at it, puts it back, fumbles, brings out the envelope, fumbles, puts back envelope, looks at his watch, gets up and goes backstage into darkness. Ten seconds. Sound of bottle against glass, then brief siphon. Ten seconds. Bottle against glass alone. Ten seconds. He comes back a little unsteadily into light, goes to front of table, takes out keys, raises them to his eyes, chooses key, unlocks first drawer, peers into it, feels about inside, takes out reel, peers at it, locks drawer, puts keys back in his pocket, goes and sits down, takes reel off machine, lays it on dictionary, loads virgin reel on machine, takes envelope from his pocket, consults back of it, lays it on table, switches on, clears his throat and begins to record.*]

KRAPP.   Just been listening to that stupid bastard I took myself for thirty years ago, hard to believe I was ever as bad as that. Thank

God that's all done with anyway. [*Pause.*] The eyes she had! [*Broods, realizes he is recording silence, switches off, broods. Finally.*] Everything there, everything, all the— [*Realizes this is not being recorded, switches on.*] Everything there, everything on this old muckball, all the light and dark and famine and feasting of . . . [*hesitates*] . . . the ages! [*In a shout.*] Yes! [*Pause.*] Let that go! Jesus! Take his mind off his homework! Jesus! [*Pause. Weary.*] Ah well, maybe he was right. [*Pause.*] Maybe he was right. [*Broods. Realizes. Switches off. Consults envelope.*] Pah! [*Crumples it and throws it away. Broods. Switches on.*] Nothing to say, not a squeak. What's a year now? The sour cud and the iron stool. [*Pause.*] Revelled in the word spool. [*With relish.*] Spooool! Happiest moment of the past half million. [*Pause.*] Seventeen copies sold, of which eleven at trade price to free circulating libraries beyond the seas. Getting known. [*Pause.*] One pound six and something, eight I have little doubt. [*Pause.*] Crawled out once or twice, before the summer was cold. Sat shivering in the park, drowned in dreams and burning to be gone. Not a soul. [*Pause.*] Last fancies. [*Vehemently.*] Keep 'em under! [*Pause.*] Scalded the eyes out of me reading *Effie*[3] again, a page a day, with tears again. Effie . . . [*Pause.*] Could have been happy with her, up there on the Baltic, and the pines, and the dunes. [*Pause.*] Could I? [*Pause.*] And she? [*Pause.*] Pah! [*Pause.*] Fanny came in a couple of times. Bony old ghost of a whore. Couldn't do much, but I suppose better than a kick in the crutch. The last time wasn't so bad. How do you manage it, she said, at your age? I told her I'd been saving up for her all my life. [*Pause.*] Went to Vespers once, like when I was in short trousers. [*Pause. Sings.*]

> Now the day is over,
> Night is drawing nigh-igh,
> Shadows— [*coughing, then almost
>   inaudible*] —of the evening
> Steal across the sky.

[*Gasping.*] Went to sleep and fell off the pew. [*Pause.*] Sometimes wondered in the night if a last effort mightn't— [*Pause.*] Ah finish your booze now and get to your bed. Go on with this drivel in the morning. Or leave it at that. [*Pause.*] Leave it at that. [*Pause.*] Lie propped up in the dark—and wander. Be again in the dingle on a Christmas Eve, gathering holly, the red-berried. [*Pause.*] Be again on Croghan[4] on a Sunday morning, in the haze, with the bitch, stop and listen to the bells. [*Pause.*] And so on. [*Pause.*] Be again, be again. [*Pause.*] All that old misery. [*Pause.*] Once wasn't enough for you. [*Pause.*] Lie down across her.

[*Long pause. He suddenly bends over machine, switches off, wrenches off tape, throws it away, puts on the other, winds it*

3. *Effi Briest* (1895), by German novelist Theodor Fontane (1819–98).
4. Mountain south of Dublin.

forward to the passage he wants, switches on, listens staring front.]

TAPE. —gooseberries, she said. I said again I thought it was hope-less and no good going on, and she agreed, without opening her eyes. [*Pause.*] I asked her to look at me and after a few mo-ments— [*pause*] —after a few moments she did, but the eyes just slits, because of the glare. I bent over her to get them in the shadow and they opened. [*Pause. Low.*] Let me in. [*Pause.*] We drifted in among the flags and stuck. The way they went down, sighing, before the stem! [*Pause.*] I lay down across her with my face in her breasts and my hand on her. We lay there without moving. But under us all moved, and moved us, gently, up and down, and from side to side.

[*Pause.* KRAPP's *lips move. No sound.*]

Past midnight. Never knew such silence. The earth might be un-inhabited.

[*Pause.*]

Here I end this reel. Box— [*pause*] —three, spool— [*pause*] — five. [*Pause.*] Perhaps my best years are gone. When there was a chance of happiness. But I wouldn't want them back. Not with the fire in me now. No, I wouldn't want them back.

[KRAPP *motionless staring before him. The tape runs on in silence.*]

BRIAN FRIEL

Translations[†]

Persons in the Play

MANUS

SARAH

JIMMY JACK

MAIRE

DOALTY

BRIDGET

HUGH

OWEN

CAPTAIN LANCEY

LIEUTENANT HOLLAND

The action takes place in a hedge-school in the townland of Baile Beag/Ballybeg, an Irish-speaking community in County Donegal.

ACT 1   *An afternoon in late August 1833.*

ACT 2   *A few days later.*

ACT 3   *The evening of the following day.*
One-interval—between the two scenes in Act 2.

Act 1

The hedge-school[1] is held in a disused barn or hay-shed or byre. Along the back wall are the remains of five or six stalls—wooden posts and chains—where cows were once milked and bedded. A double door left, large enough to allow a cart to enter. A window right. A wooden stairway without a banister leads to the upstairs living-quarters (off) of the schoolmaster and his son. Around the room are broken and for-

---

† Copyright © 1981 by Brian Friel. Reprinted by permission of Faber & Faber, Inc., an affiliate of Farrar, Straus, and Giroux, LLC.

1. A widespread but irregular educational system in rural areas where formal education was unavailable or illegal; in 1832, legislation introduced a national system that gradually replaced the hedge schools.

gotten implements: a cart-wheel, some lobster-pots, farming tools, a
battle of hay, a churn, etc. There are also the stools and bench-seats
which the pupils use and a table and chair for the master. At the door
a pail of water and a soiled towel. The room is comfortless and dusty
and functional—there is no trace of a woman's hand.

When the play opens, MANUS *is teaching* SARAH *to speak. He kneels*
beside her. She is sitting on a low stool, her head down, very tense,
clutching a slate on her knees. He is coaxing her gently and firmly
and—as with everything he does—with a kind of zeal.

MANUS *is in his late twenties/early thirties; the master's older son.*
He is pale-faced, lightly built, intense, and works as an unpaid assis-
tant—a monitor—to his father. His clothes are shabby; and when he
moves we see that he is lame.

SARAH's *speech is so bad that all her life she has been considered lo-*
cally to be dumb and she has accepted this: when she wishes to com-
municate, she grunts and makes unintelligible nasal sounds. She has
a waiflike appearance and could be any age from seventeen to thirty-
five.

JIMMY JACK CASSIE—*known as the Infant Prodigy—sits by himself,*
contentedly reading Homer in Greek and smiling to himself. He is a
bachelor in his sixties, lives alone, and comes to these evening classes
partly for the company and partly for the intellectual stimulation. He
is fluent in Latin and Greek but is in no way pedantic—to him it is
perfectly normal to speak these tongues. He never washes. His
clothes—heavy top coat, hat, mittens, which he wears now—are filthy
and he lives in them summer and winter, day and night. He now
reads in a quiet voice and smiles in profound satisfaction. For JIMMY
the world of the gods and the ancient myths is as real and as immedi-
ate as everyday life in the townland of Baile Beag.

MANUS *holds* SARAH's *hands in his and he articulates slowly and dis-*
tinctly into her face.

MANUS.   We're doing very well. And we're going to try it once
more—just once more. Now—relax and breathe in . . . deep . . .
and out . . . in . . . and out . . .

[SARAH *shakes her head vigorously and stubbornly.*]

MANUS.   Come on, Sarah. This is our secret.

[*Again vigorous and stubborn shaking of* SARAH's *head.*]

MANUS.   Nobody's listening. Nobody hears you.
JIMMY.   'Ton d'emeibet epeita thea glaukopis Athene . . .'[2]
MANUS.   Get your tongue and your lips working. 'My name—'
Come on. One more try. 'My name is—' Good girl.
SARAH.   My . . .
MANUS.   Great. 'My name—'
SARAH.   My . . . my . . .

2. But the gray-eyed goddess Athene then replied to him (Homer, *Odyssey* 13.420).

MANUS.   Raise your head. Shout it out. Nobody's listening.
JIMMY.   '. . . *alla hekelos estai en Atreidao domois . . .*'[3]
MANUS.   Jimmy, please! Once more—just once more—'My name—'
Good girl. Come on now. Head up. Mouth open.
SARAH.   My . . .
MANUS.   Good.
SARAH.   My . . .
MANUS.   Great.
SARAH.   My name . . .
MANUS.   Yes?
SARAH.   My name is . . .
MANUS.   Yes?

[SARAH *pauses. Then in a rush.*]

SARAH.   My name is Sarah.
MANUS.   Marvellous! Bloody marvellous!

[MANUS *hugs* SARAH. *She smiles in shy, embarrassed pleasure.*]

Did you hear that, Jimmy?—'My name is Sarah'—clear as a bell.
[*To* SARAH] The Infant Prodigy doesn't know what we're at.

[SARAH *laughs at this.* MANUS *hugs her again and stands up.*]

Now we're really started! Nothing'll stop us now! Nothing in the
wide world!

[JIMMY, *chuckling at his text, comes over to them.*]

JIMMY.   Listen to this, Manus.
MANUS.   Soon you'll be telling me all the secrets that have been in
that head of yours all these years. Certainly, James—what is it?
[*To* SARAH.] Maybe you'd set out the stools? [MANUS *runs up the
stairs.*]
JIMMY.   Wait till you hear this, Manus.
MANUS.   Go ahead. I'll be straight down.
JIMMY.   '*Hos ara min phamene rabdo epemassat Athene—*' 'After
Athene had said this, she touched Ulysses with her wand. She
withered the fair skin of his supple limbs and destroyed the
flaxen hair from off his head and about his limbs she put the skin
of an old man . . .'! The divil! The divil!

[MANUS *has emerged again with a bowl of milk and a piece of
bread.*]

JIMMY.   And wait till you hear! She's not finished with him yet!

[As MANUS *descends the stairs he toasts* SARAH *with his bowl.*]

JIMMY.   '*Knuzosen de oi osse—*' 'She dimmed his two eyes that were
so beautiful and clothed him in a vile ragged cloak begrimed with
filthy smoke . . .'! D'you see! Smoke! Smoke! D'you see! Sure look

3.   . . . but he sits at ease in the halls of the Sons of Athens . . . (Homer, *Odyssey* 13.423–4).

at what the same turf-smoke has done to myself! [*He rapidly removes his hat to display his bald head.*] Would you call that flaxen hair?

MANUS.   Of course I would.

JIMMY.   'And about him she cast the great skin of a filthy hind, stripped of the hair, and into his hand she thrust a staff and a wallet'! Ha-ha-ha! Athene did that to Ulysses! Made him into a tramp! Isn't she the tight one?

MANUS.   You couldn't watch her, Jimmy.

JIMMY.   You know what they call her?

MANUS.   '*Glaukopis Athene.*'

JIMMY.   That's it! The flashing-eyed Athene! By God, Manus, sir, if you had a woman like that about the house, it's not stripping a turf-bank you'd be thinking about—eh?

MANUS.   She was a goddess, Jimmy.

JIMMY.   Better still. Sure isn't our own Grania a class of a goddess and—

MANUS.   Who?

JIMMY.   Grania—Grania—Diarmuid's Grania.[4]

MANUS.   Ah.

JIMMY.   And sure she can't get her fill of men.

MANUS.   Jimmy, you're impossible.

JIMMY.   I was just thinking to myself last night: if you had the choosing between Athene and Artemis and Helen of Troy—all three of them Zeus's girls—imagine three powerful-looking daughters like that all in the one parish of Athens!—now, if you had the picking between them, which would you take?

MANUS [*to* SARAH].   Which should I take, Sarah?

JIMMY.   No harm to Helen; and no harm to Artemis; and indeed no harm to our own Grania, Manus. But I think I've no choice but to go bull-straight for Athene. By God, sir, them flashing eyes would fair keep a man jigged up constant!

> [*Suddenly and momentarily, as if in spasm,* JIMMY *stands to attention and salutes, his face raised in pained ecstasy.* MANUS *laughs. So does* SARAH. JIMMY *goes back to his seat, and his reading.*]

MANUS.   You're a dangerous bloody man, Jimmy Jack.

JIMMY.   'Flashing-eyed'! Hah! Sure Homer knows it all, boy. Homer knows it all.

> [MANUS *goes to the window and looks out.*]

MANUS.   Where the hell has he got to?

> [SARAH *goes to* MANUS *and touches his elbow. She mimes rocking a baby.*]

4. Lovers in Celtic rather than classical mythology.

MANUS.   Yes, I know he's at the christening; but it doesn't take them all day to put a name on a baby, does it?

[SARAH *mimes pouring drinks and tossing them back quickly.*]

MANUS.   You may be sure. Which pub?

[SARAH *indicates.*]

MANUS.   Gracie's?

[*No. Further away.*]

MANUS.   Con Connie Tim's?

[*No. To the right of there.*]

MANUS.   Anna na mBreag's?

[*Yes. That's it.*]

MANUS.   Great. She'll fill him up. I suppose I may take the class then.

[MANUS *begins to distribute some books, slates and chalk, texts, etc., beside the seats.* SARAH *goes over to the straw and produces a bunch of flowers she has hidden there. During this:*]

JIMMY.   '*Autar o ek limenos prosebe*—' 'But Ulysses went forth from the harbour and through the woodland to the place where Athene had shown him he could find the good swineherd who—'*o oi biotoio malista kedeto*'—what's that, Manus?

MANUS.   'Who cared most for his substance.'

JIMMY.   That's it! 'The good swineherd who cared most for his substance above all the slaves that Ulysses possessed . . .'

[SARAH *presents the flowers to* MANUS.]

MANUS.   Those are lovely, Sarah.

[*But* SARAH *has fled in embarrassment to her seat and has her head buried in a book.* MANUS *goes to her.*]

MANUS.   Flow-ers.

[*Pause.* SARAH *does not look up.*]

MANUS.   Say the word: flow-ers. Come on—flow-ers.

SARAH.   Flowers.

MANUS.   You see?—you're off!

[MANUS *leans down and kisses the top of* SARAH's *head.*]

MANUS.   And they're beautiful flowers. Thank you.

[MAIRE *enters, a strong-minded, strong-bodied woman in her twenties with a head of curly hair. She is carrying a small can of milk.*]

MAIRE.   Is this all's here? Is there no school this evening?

MANUS.   If my father's not back, I'll take it. [MANUS *stands awk-wardly, having been caught kissing* SARAH *and with the flowers almost formally at his chest.*]

MAIRE.   Well now, isn't that a pretty sight. There's your milk. How's Sarah?

[SARAH *grunts a reply.*]

MANUS.   I saw you out at the hay.

[MAIRE *ignores this and goes to* JIMMY.]

MAIRE.   And how's Jimmy Jack Cassie?

JIMMY.   Sit down beside me, Maire.

MAIRE.   Would I be safe?

JIMMY.   No safer man in Donegal.

[MAIRE *flops on a stool beside* JIMMY.]

MAIRE.   Ooooh. The best harvest in living memory, they say; but I don't want to see another like it. [*Showing* JIMMY *her hands.*] Look at the blisters.

JIMMY.   *Esne fatigata?*[5]

MAIRE.   *Sum fatigatissima.*

JIMMY.   *Bene! Optime!*

MAIRE.   That's the height of my Latin. Fit me better if I had even that much English.

JIMMY.   English? I thought you had some English?

MAIRE.   Three words. Wait—there was a spake I used to have off by heart. What's this it was? [*Her accent is strange because she is speaking a foreign language and because she does not understand what she is saying.*] 'In Norfolk we besport ourselves around the maypoll.' What about that!

MANUS.   Maypole.

[*Again* MAIRE *ignores* MANUS.]

MAIRE.   God have mercy on my Aunt Mary—she taught me that when I was about four, whatever it means. Do you know what it means, Jimmy?

JIMMY.   Sure you know I have only Irish like yourself.

MAIRE.   And Latin. And Greek.

JIMMY.   I'm telling you a lie: I know one English word.

MAIRE.   What?

JIMMY.   Bo-som.

MAIRE.   What's a bo-som?

JIMMY.   You know— [*he illustrates with his hands*] —bo-som—bo-som—you know—Diana, the huntress, she has two powerful bosom.

MAIRE.   You may be sure that's the one English word you would know. [*Rises.*] Is there a drop of water about?

5. Are you tired?/I am very tired/Good! Excellent!

[MANUS *gives* MAIRE *his bowl of milk.*]

MANUS.   I'm sorry I couldn't get up last night.

MAIRE.   Doesn't matter.

MANUS.   Biddy Hanna sent for me to write a letter to her sister in Nova Scotia. All the gossip of the parish. 'I brought the cow to the bull three times last week but no good. There's nothing for it now but Big Ned Frank.'

MAIRE [*drinking*].   That's better.

MANUS.   And she got so engrossed in that she forgot who she was dictating to: 'The aul drunken schoolmaster and that lame son of his are still footering about in the hedge-school, wasting people's good time and money.'

[MAIRE *has to laugh at this.*]

MAIRE.   She did not!

MANUS.   And me taking it all down. 'Thank God one of them new national schools is being built above at Poll na gCaorach.' It was after midnight by the time I got back.

MAIRE.   Great to be a busy man.

[MAIRE *moves away.* MANUS *follows.*]

MANUS.   I could hear music on my way past but I thought it was too late to call.

MAIRE [*to* SARAH].   Wasn't your father in great voice last night?

[SARAH *nods and smiles.*]

MAIRE.   It must have been near three o'clock by the time you got home?

[SARAH *holds up four fingers.*]

MAIRE.   Was it four? No wonder we're in pieces.

MANUS.   I can give you a hand at the hay tomorrow.

MAIRE.   That's the name of a hornpipe, isn't it?—'The Scholar In The Hayfield'—or is it a reel?

MANUS.   If the day's good.

MAIRE.   Suit yourself. The English soldiers below in the tents, them sapper fellas,[6] they're coming up to give us a hand. I don't know a word they're saying, nor they me; but sure that doesn't matter, does it?

MANUS.   What the hell are you so crabbed about?!

[DOALTY *and* BRIDGET *enter noisily. Both are in their twenties.* DOALTY *is brandishing a surveyor's pole. He is an open-minded, open-hearted, generous and slightly thick young man.* BRIDGET *is a plump, fresh young girl, ready to laugh, vain, and with a countrywoman's instinctive cunning.* DOALTY *enters doing his imitation of the master.*]

6. Military engineers.

DOALTY.   Vesperal salutations to you all.
BRIDGET.   He's coming down past Carraig na Ri and he's as full as a pig!
DOALTY.   *Ignari, stuli, rustici*—pot-boys and peasant whelps— semi-literates and illegitimates.
BRIDGET.   He's been on the batter since this morning; he sent the wee ones home at eleven o'clock.
DOALTY.   Three questions. Question A—Am I drunk? Question B—Am I sober? [*Into* MAIRE's *face.*] —*Responde—responde!*
BRIDGET.   Question C, Master—When were you last sober?
MAIRE.   What's the weapon, Doalty?
BRIDGET.   I warned him. He'll be arrested one of these days.
DOALTY.   Up in the bog with Bridget and her aul fella, and the Red Coats were just across at the foot of Croc na Mona, dragging them aul chains and peeping through that big machine they lug about everywhere with them—you know the name of it, Manus?
MAIRE.   Theodolite.[7]
BRIDGET.   How do you know?
MAIRE.   They leave it in our byre at night sometimes if it's raining.
JIMMY.   Theodolite—what's the etymology of that word, Manus?
MANUS.   No idea.
BRIDGET.   Get on with the story.
JIMMY.   *Theo-theos*—something to do with a god. Maybe *thea*—a goddess! What shape's the yoke?
DOALTY.   'Shape!' Will you shut up, you aul eejit you! Anyway, every time they'd stick one of these poles into the ground and move across the bog, I'd creep up and shift it twenty or thirty paces to the side.
BRIDGET.   God!
DOALTY.   Then they'd come back and stare at it and look at their calculations and stare at it again and scratch their heads. And cripes, d'you know what they ended up doing?
BRIDGET.   Wait till you hear!
DOALTY.   They took the bloody machine apart! [*And immediately he speaks in gibberish—an imitation of two very agitated and confused sappers in rapid conversation.*]
BRIDGET.   That's the image of them!
MAIRE.   You must be proud of yourself, Doalty.
DOALTY.   What d'you mean?
MAIRE.   That was a very clever piece of work.
MANUS.   It was a gesture.
MAIRE.   What sort of gesture?
MANUS.   Just to indicate . . . a presence.
MAIRE.   Hah!
BRIDGET.   I'm telling you—you'll be arrested.

7. "A portable surveying instrument, originally for measuring horizontal angles, and con- sisting essentially of a planisphere or horizontal graduated circular plate, with an alidad or index bearing sights." *OED.*

[*When* DOALTY *is embarrassed—or pleased—he reacts physically. He now grabs* BRIDGET *around the waist.*]

DOALTY.   What d'you make of that for an implement, Bridget? Wouldn't that make a great aul shaft for your churn?

BRIDGET.   Let go of me, you dirty brute! I've a headline to do before Big Hughie comes.

MANUS.   I don't think we'll wait for him. Let's get started.

[*Slowly, reluctantly they begin to move to their seats and specific tasks.* DOALTY *goes to the bucket of water at the door and washes his hands.* BRIDGET *sets up a hand-mirror and combs her hair.*]

BRIDGET.   Nellie Ruadh's baby was to be christened this morning. Did any of yous hear what she called it? Did you, Sarah?

[SARAH *grunts: No.*]

BRIDGET.   Did you, Maire?

MAIRE.   No.

BRIDGET.   Our Seamus says she was threatening she was going to call it after its father.

DOALTY.   Who's the father?

BRIDGET.   That's the point, you donkey you!

DOALTY.   Ah.

BRIDGET.   So there's a lot of uneasy bucks about Baile Beag this day.

DOALTY.   She told me last Sunday she was going to call it Jimmy.

BRIDGET.   You're a liar, Doalty.

DOALTY.   Would I tell you a lie? Hi, Jimmy, Nellie Ruadh's aul fella's looking for you.

JIMMY.   For me?

MAIRE.   Come on, Doalty.

DOALTY.   Someone told him . . .

MAIRE.   Doalty!

DOALTY.   He heard you know the first book of the Satires of Horace off by heart . . .

JIMMY.   That's true.

DOALTY.   . . . and he wants you to recite it for him.

JIMMY.   I'll do that for him certainly, certainly.

DOALTY.   He's busting to hear it.

[JIMMY *fumbles in his pockets.*]

JIMMY.   I came across this last night—this'll interest you—in Book Two of Virgil's *Georgics.*

DOALTY.   Be God, that's my territory alright.

BRIDGET.   You clown you. [*To* SARAH.] Hold this for me, would you? [*Her mirror.*]

JIMMY.   Listen to this, Manus. '*Nigra fere et presso pinguis sub vomere terra . . .*'

DOALTY.   Steady on now—easy, boys, easy—don't rush me, boys—
[*He mimes great concentration.*]
JIMMY.   Manus?
MANUS.   'Land that is black and rich beneath the pressure of the
plough . . .'
DOALTY.   Give *me* a chance!
JIMMY.   'And with *cui putre*—with crumbly soil—is in the main
best for corn.' There you are!
DOALTY.   There you are.
JIMMY.   'From no other land will you see more wagons wending
homeward behind slow bullocks.' Virgil! There!
DOALTY.   'Slow bullocks'!
JIMMY.   Isn't that what I'm always telling you? Black soil for corn.
That's what you should have in that upper field of yours—corn,
not spuds.
DOALTY.   Would you listen to that fella! Too lazy be Jasus to wash
himself and he's lecturing me on agriculture! Would you go and
take a running race at yourself, Jimmy Jack Cassie! [*Grabs*
SARAH.] Come away out of this with me, Sarah, and we'll plant
some corn together.
MANUS.   All right—all right. Let's settle down and get some work
done. I know Sean Beag isn't coming—he's at the salmon. What
about the Donnelly twins? [*To* DOALTY.] Are the Donnelly twins
not coming any more?

   [DOALTY *shrugs and turns away.*]

Did you ask them?
DOALTY.   Haven't seen them. Not about these days.

   [DOALTY *begins whistling through his teeth. Suddenly the atmosphere is silent and alert.*]

MANUS.   Aren't they at home?
DOALTY.   No.
MANUS.   Where are they then?
DOALTY.   How would I know?
BRIDGET.   Our Seamus says two of the soldiers' horses were found
last night at the foot of the cliffs at Machaire Buidhe and . . .
[*She stops suddenly and begins writing with chalk on her slate.*]
D'you hear the whistles of this aul slate? Sure nobody could
write on an aul slippery thing like that.
MANUS.   What headline did my father set you?
BRIDGET.   'It's easier to stamp out learning than to recall it.'
JIMMY.   Book Three, the *Agricola* of Tacitus.
BRIDGET.   God but you're a dose.
MANUS.   Can you do it?
BRIDGET.   There. Is it bad? Will he ate me?
MANUS.   It's very good. Keep your elbow in closer to your side.
Dolty?
DOALTY.   I'm at the seven-times table. I'm perfect, skipper.

[MANUS *moves to* SARAH.]

MANUS.   Do you understand those sums?

[SARAH *nods: Yes.* MANUS *leans down to her ear.*]

MANUS.   My name is Sarah.

[MANUS *goes to* MAIRE. *While he is talking to her the others swop books, talk quietly, etc.*]

MANUS.   Can I help you? What are you at?
MAIRE.   Map of America. [*Pause.*] The passage money came last Friday.
MANUS.   You never told me that.
MAIRE.   Because I haven't seen you since, have I?
MANUS.   You don't want to go. You said that yourself.
MAIRE.   There's ten below me to be raised and no man in the house. What do you suggest?
MANUS.   Do you want to go?
MAIRE.   Did you apply for that job in the new national school?
MANUS.   No.
MAIRE.   You said you would.
MANUS.   I said I might.
MAIRE.   When it opens, this is finished: nobody's going to pay to go to a hedge-school.
MANUS.   I know that and I . . .

[*He breaks off because he sees* SARAH, *obviously listening at his shoulder. She moves away again.*]

I was thinking that maybe I could . . .
MAIRE.   It's £56 a year you're throwing away.
MANUS.   I can't apply for it.
MAIRE.   You *promised* me you would.
MANUS.   My father has applied for it.
MAIRE.   He has not!
MANUS.   Day before yesterday.
MAIRE.   For God's sake, sure you know he'd never—
MANUS.   I couldn't—I can't go in against him.

[MAIRE *looks at him for a second. Then:*]

MAIRE.   Suit yourself. [*To* BRIDGET.] I saw your Seamus heading off to the Port fair early this morning.
BRIDGET.   And wait till you hear this—I forgot to tell you this. He said that as soon as he crossed over the gap at Cnoc na Mona— just beyond where the soldiers are making the maps—the sweet smell was everywhere.
DOALTY.   You never told me that.
BRIDGET.   It went out of my head.
DOALTY.   He saw the crops in Port?
BRIDGET.   Some.

MANUS.   How did the tops look?

BRIDGET.   Fine—I think.

DOALTY.   In flower?

BRIDGET.   I don't know. I think so. He didn't say.

MANUS.   Just the sweet smell—that's all?

BRIDGET.   They say that's the way it snakes in, don't they? First the smell; and then one morning the stalks are all black and limp.

DOALTY.   Are you stupid? It's the rotting stalks makes the sweet smell for God's sake. That's what the smell is—rotting stalks.

MAIRE.   Sweet smell! Sweet smell! Every year at this time some-body comes back with stories of the sweet smell. Sweet God, did the potatoes ever fail in Baile Beag? Well, did they ever—ever? Never! There was never blight here. Never. Never. But we're al-ways sniffing about for it, aren't we?—looking for disaster. The rents are going to go up again—the harvest's going to be lost—the herring have gone away for ever—there's going to be evic-tions. Honest to God, some of you people aren't happy unless you're miserable and you'll not be right content until you're dead!

DOALTY.   Bloody right, Maire. And sure St Colmcille prophesied there'd never be blight here. He said:

> The spuds will bloom in Baile Beag
> Till rabbits grow an extra lug.[8]

And sure that'll never be. So we're all right. Seven threes are twenty-one; seven fours are twenty-eight; seven fives are forty-nine—Hi, Jimmy, do you fancy my chances as boss of the new national school?

JIMMY.   What's that?—what's that?

DOALTY.   Agh, g'way back home to Greece, son.

MAIRE.   You ought to apply, Doalty.

DOALTY.   D'you think so? Cripes, maybe I will. Hah!

BRIDGET.   Did you know that you start at the age of six and you have to stick at it until you're twelve at least—no matter how smart you are or how much you know.

DOALTY.   Who told you that yarn?

BRIDGET.   And every child from every house has to go all day, every day, summer or winter. That's the law.

DOALTY.   I'll tell you something—nobody's going to go near them—they're not going to take on—law or no law.

BRIDGET.   And everything's free in them. You pay for nothing ex-cept the books you use; that's what our Seamus says.

DOALTY.   'Our Seamus'. Sure your Seamus wouldn't pay anyway. She's making this all up.

BRIDGET.   Isn't that right, Manus?

MANUS.   I think so.

BRIDGET.   And from the very first day you go, you'll not hear one

---

8. St. Colmcille (also St. Columba) (521–97), founder of churches in Ireland and in Scot-land; a "lug" is an ear.

word of Irish spoken. You'll be taught to speak English and every subject will be taught through English and everyone'll end up as cute as the Buncrana people.

[SARAH *suddenly grunts and mimes a warning that the master is coming. The atmosphere changes. Sudden business. Heads down.*]

DOALTY.   He's here, boys. Cripes, he'll make yella meal out of me for those bloody tables.

BRIDGET.   Have you any extra chalk, Manus?

MAIRE.   And the atlas for me.

[DOALTY *goes to* MAIRE *who is sitting on a stool at the back.*]

DOALTY.   Swop you seats.

MAIRE.   Why?

DOALTY.   There's an empty one beside the Infant Prodigy.

MAIRE.   I'm fine here.

DOALTY.   Please, Maire. I want to jouk⁹ in the back here.

[MAIRE *rises.*]

God love you. [*Aloud.*] Anyone got a bloody table-book? Cripes, I'm wrecked.

[SARAH *gives him one.*]

God, I'm dying about you.

[*In his haste to get to the back seat,* DOALTY *bumps into* BRIDGET *who is kneeling on the floor and writing laboriously on a slate resting on top of a bench-seat.*]

BRIDGET.   Watch where you're going, Doalty!

[DOALTY *gooses* BRIDGET. *She squeals. Now the quiet hum of work:* JIMMY *reading Homer in a low voice;* BRIDGET *copying her headline;* MAIRE *studying the atlas;* DOALTY, *his eyes shut tight, mouthing his tables;* SARAH *doing sums. After a few seconds:—*]

BRIDGET.   Is this 'g' right, Manus? How do you put a tail on it?

DOALTY.   Will you shut up! I can't concentrate!

[*A few more seconds of work. Then* DOALTY *opens his eyes and looks around.*]

False alarm, boys. The bugger's not coming at all. Sure the bugger's hardly fit to walk.

[*And immediately* HUGH *enters. A large man, with residual dignity, shabbily dressed, carrying a stick. He has, as always, a large quantity of drink taken, but he is by no means drunk. He is in his early sixties.*]

9. Hide.

HUGH.   *Adsum,*[1] Doalty, *adsum.* Perhaps not in *sobrietate perfecta*[2] but adequately *sobrius* to overhear your quip. Vesperal salutations to you all.

[*Various responses.*]

JIMMY.   *Ave*, Hugh.
HUGH.   James.

[*He moves his hat and coat and hands them and his stick to* MANUS, *as if to a footman.*]

Apologies for my late arrival: we were celebrating the baptism of Nellie Ruadh's baby.
BRIDGET [*innocently*].   What name did she put on it, Master?
HUGH.   Was it Eamon? Yes, it was Eamon.
BRIDGET.   Eamon Donal from Tor! Cripes!
HUGH.   And after the *caerimonia nominations*—Maire?
MAIRE.   The ritual of naming.
HUGH.   Indeed—we then had a few libations to mark the occasion. Altogether very pleasant. The derivation of the word 'baptize'?— where are my Greek scholars? Doalty?
DOALTY.   Would it be—ah—ah—
HUGH.   Too slow. James?
JIMMY.   *'Baptizein'*—to dip or immerse.
HUGH.   Indeed—our friend Pliny Minor speaks of the *'baptisterium'*—the cold bath.
DOALTY.   Master.
HUGH.   Doalty?
DOALTY.   I suppose you could talk then about baptizing a sheep at sheep-dipping, could you?

[*Laughter. Comments.*]

HUGH.   Indeed—the precedent is there—the day you were appropriately named Doalty—seven nines?
DOALTY.   What's that, Master?
HUGH.   Seven times nine?
DOALTY.   Seven nines—seven nines—seven times nine—seven times nine are—cripes, it's on the tip of my tongue, Master—I knew it for sure this morning—funny that's the only one that foxes me—
BRIDGET [*prompt*].   Sixty-three.
DOALTY.   What's wrong with me: sure seven nines are fifty-three, Master.
HUGH.   Sophocles from Colonus would agree with Doalty Dan Doalty from Tulach Alainn: 'To know nothing is the sweetest life.' Where's Sean Beag?
MANUS.   He's at the salmon.

1. I am present.
2. With complete sobriety.

HUGH.   And Nora Dan?

MAIRE.   She says she's not coming back any more.

HUGH.   Ah. Nora Dan can now write her name—Nora Dan's education is complete. And the Donnelly twins?

[*Brief pause. Then:*—]

BRIDGET.   They're probably at the turf. [*She goes to* HUGH.] There's the one-and-eight I owe you for last quarter's arithmetic and there's my one-and-six for this quarter's writing.

HUGH.   *Gratias tibi ago.*[3] [*He sits at his table.*] Before we commence our *studia* I have three items of information to impart to you— [*to* MANUS] a bowl of tea, strong tea, black—

[MANUS *leaves.*]

Item A: on my perambulations today—Bridget? Too slow. Maire?

MAIRE.   Perambulare—to walk about.

HUGH.   Indeed—I encountered Captain Lancey of the Royal Engineers who is engaged in the ordnance survey of this area. He tells me that in the past few days two of his horses have strayed and some of his equipment seems to be mislaid. I expressed my regret and suggested he address you himself on these matters. He then explained that he does not speak Irish. Latin? I asked. None. Greek? Not a syllable. He speaks—on his own admission—only English; and to his credit he seemed suitably verecund—James?

JIMMY.   *Verecundus*—humble.

HUGH.   Indeed—he voiced some surprise that we did not speak his language. I explained that a few of us did, on occasion—outside the parish of course—and then usually for the purposes of commerce, a use to which his tongue seemed particularly suited— [*shouts*] and a slice of soda bread—and I went on to propose that our own culture and the classical tongues made a happier conjugation—Doalty?

DOALTY.   *Conjugo*—I join together.

[DOALTY *is so pleased with himself that he prods and winks at* BRIDGET.]

HUGH.   Indeed—English, I suggested, couldn't really express us. And again to his credit he acquiesced to my logic. Acquiesced—Maire?

[MAIRE *turns away impatiently.* HUGH *is unaware of the gesture.*]

Too slow. Bridget?

BRIDGET.   *Acquiesco.*[4]

3. I thank you.
4. *Acquiesco, acquiescere:* to rest, to find comfort in.

HUGH.   *Procede.*
BRIDGET.   *Acquiesco, acquiescere, acquievi, acquietum.*
HUGH.   Indeed—and Item B . . .
MAIRE.   Master.
HUGH.   Yes?

[MAIRE *gets to her feet uneasily but determinedly. Pause.*]

Well, girl?
MAIRE.   We should all be learning to speak English. That's what
my mother says. That's what I say. That's what Dan O'Connell[5]
said last month in Ennis. He said the sooner we all learn to speak
English the better.

[*Suddenly several speak together.*]

JIMMY.   What's she saying? What? What?
DOALTY.   It's Irish he uses when he's travelling around scrounging
votes.
BRIDGET.   And sleeping with married women. Sure no woman's
safe from that fella.
JIMMY.   Who-who-who? Who's this? Who's this
HUGH.   *Silentium!* [*Pause.*] Who is she talking about?
MAIRE.   I'm talking about Daniel O'Connell.
HUGH.   Does she mean that little Kerry politician?
MAIRE.   I'm talking about the Liberator, Master, as you well know.
And what he said was this: 'The old language is a barrier to mod-
ern progress.' He said that last month. And he's right. I don't
want Greek. I don't want Latin. I want English.

[MANUS *reappears on the platform above.*]

I want to be able to speak English because I'm going to America
as soon as the harvest's all saved.

[MAIRE *remains standing.* HUGH *puts his hand into his pocket
and produces a flask of whiskey. He removes the cap, pours a
drink into it, tosses it back, replaces the cap, puts the flask
back into his pocket. Then:—*]

HUGH.   We have been diverted—*diverto*—*divertee*—Where were
we?
DOALTY.   Three items of information, Master. You're at Item B.
HUGH.   Indeed—Item B—Item B—yes—On my way to the christening this morning I chanced to meet Mr George Alexander,
Justice of the Peace. We discussed the new national school. Mr.
Alexander invited me to take charge of it when it opens. I
thanked him and explained that I could do that only if I were
free to run it as I have run this hedge-school for the past thirty-

5. "The Liberator" (1775–1847) and organizer of Catholic, Gaelic Ireland in mass meetings that helped achieve Catholic Emancipation; his reformist compromises, such as encouraging English, have long been subject to debate.

five years—filling what our friend Euripides calls the *'aplestos pithos'*—James?

JIMMY.   'The cask that cannot be filled'.

HUGH.   Indeed—and Mr Alexander retorted courteously and emphatically that he hopes that is how it will be run.

[MAIRE *now sits.*]

Indeed. I have had a strenuous day and I am weary of you all. [*He rises.*] Manus will take care of you.

[HUGH *goes towards the steps.* OWEN *enters.* OWEN *is the younger son, a handsome, attractive young man in his twenties. He is dressed smartly—a city man. His manner is easy and charming: everything he does is invested with consideration and enthusiasm. He now stands framed in the doorway, a traveling bag across his shoulder.*]

OWEN.   Could anybody tell me is this where Hugh Mor O'Donnell holds his hedge-school?

DOALTY.   It's Owen—Owen Hugh! Look, boys—it's Owen Hugh!

[OWEN *enters. As he crosses the room he touches and has a word for each person.*]

OWEN.   Doalty! [*Playful punch.*] How are you, boy? *Jacobe, quid agis?*[6] Are you well?

JIMMY.   Fine. Fine.

OWEN.   And Bridget! Give us a kiss. Aaaaaah!

BRIDGET.   You're welcome, Owen.

OWEN.   It's not—Yes, it *is* Maire Chatach! God! A young woman!

MAIRE.   How are you, Owen?

[OWEN *is now in front of* HUGH. *He puts his two hands on his* FATHER's *shoulders.*]

OWEN.   And how's the old man himself?

HUGH.   Fair—fair.

OWEN.   Fair? For God's sake you never looked better! Come here to me. [*He embraces* HUGH *warmly and genuinely.*] Great to see you, Father. Great to be back.

[HUGH's *eyes are moist—partly joy, partly the drink.*]

HUGH.   I—I'm—I'm—pay no attention to—

OWEN.   Come on—come on—come on—[*He gives* HUGH *his handkerchief.*] Do you know what you and I are going to do tonight? We are going to go up to Anna na mBreag's . . .

DOALTY.   Not there, Owen.

OWEN.   Why not?

DOALTY.   Her poteen's worse than ever.

BRIDGET.   They say she puts frogs in it!

6. James, how are you?

OWEN.   All the better. [*To* HUGH.] And you and I are going to get
footless drunk. That's arranged.

> [OWEN *sees* MANUS *coming down the steps with tea and soda
> bread. They meet at the bottom.*]

And Manus!

MANUS.   You're welcome, Owen.

OWEN.   I know I am. And it's great to be here. [*He turns round,
arms outstretched.*] I can't believe it. I come back after six years
and everything's just as it was! Nothing's changed! Not a thing!
[*Sniffs.*] Even that smell—that's the same smell this place always
had. What is it anyway? Is it the straw?

DOALTY.   Jimmy Jack's feet.

> [*General laughter. It opens little pockets of conversation
> round the room.*]

OWEN.   And Doalty Dan Doalty hasn't changed either!

DOALTY.   Bloody right, Owen.

OWEN.   Jimmy, are you well?

JIMMY.   Dodging about.

OWEN.   Any word of the big day?

> [*This is greeted with 'ohs' and 'ahs'.*]

Time enough, Jimmy. Homer's easier to live with, isn't he?

MAIRE.   We heard stories that you own ten big shops in Dublin—is
it true?

OWEN.   Only nine.

BRIDGET.   And you've twelve horses and six servants.

OWEN.   Yes—that's true. God Almighty, would you listen to them—
taking a hand at me!

MANUS.   When did you arrive?

OWEN.   We left Dublin yesterday morning, spent last night in
Omagh and got here half an hour ago.

MANUS.   You're hungry then.

HUGH.   Indeed—get him food—get him a drink.

OWEN.   Not now, thanks; later. Listen—am I interrupting you all?

HUGH.   By no means. We're finished for the day.

OWEN.   Wonderful. I'll tell you why. Two friends of mine are waiting outside the door. They'd like to meet you and I'd like you to
meet them. May I bring them in?

HUGH.   Certainly. You'll all eat and have . . .

OWEN.   Not just yet, Father. You've seen the sappers working in
this area for the past fortnight, haven't you? Well, the older man
is Captain Lancey . . .

HUGH.   I've met Captain Lancey.

OWEN.   Great. He's the cartographer in charge of this whole area.
Cartographer—James? [OWEN *begins to play this game—his father's game—partly to involve his classroom audience, partly to*

show he has not forgotten it, and indeed partly because he enjoys it.]

JIMMY.   A maker of maps.

OWEN.   Indeed—and the younger man that I traveled with from Dublin, his name is Lieutenant Yolland and he is attached to the toponymic department—Father?—*responde—responde!*

HUGH.   He gives names to places.

OWEN.   Indeed—although he is in fact an orthographer—Doalty?—too slow—Manus?

MANUS.   The correct spelling of those names.

OWEN.   Indeed—indeed!

[OWEN *laughs and claps his hands. Some of the others join in.*]

Beautiful! Beautiful! Honest to God, it's such a delight to be back here with you all again—'civilized' people. Anyhow—may I bring them in?

HUGH.   Your friends are our friends.

OWEN.   I'll be straight back.

[*There is general talk as* OWEN *goes towards the door. He stops beside* SARAH.]

OWEN.   That's a new face. Who are you?

[*A very brief hesitation. Then?—*]

SARAH.   My name is Sarah.

OWEN.   Sarah who?

SARAH.   Sarah Johnny Sally.

OWEN.   Of course! From Bun na hAbhann! I'm Owen—Owen Hugh Mor. From Baile Beag. Good to see you.

[*During this* OWEN–SARAH *exchange.*]

HUGH.   Come on now. Let's tidy this place up. [*He rubs the top of his table with his sleeve.*] Move, Doalty—lift those books off the floor.

DOALTY.   Right, Master; certainly, Master; I'm doing my best, Master.

[OWEN *stops at the door.*]

OWEN.   One small thing, Father.

HUGH.   *Silentium!*

OWEN.   I'm on their pay-roll.

[SARAH, *very elated at her success, is beside* MANUS.]

SARAH.   I said it, Manus!

[MANUS *ignores* SARAH. *He is much more interested in* OWEN *now.*]

MANUS.   You haven't enlisted, have you?!

[SARAH *moves away.*]

OWEN.   Me a soldier? I'm employed as a part-time, underpaid,
  civilian interpreter. My job is to translate the quaint, archaic
  tongue you people persist in speaking into the King's good English. [*He goes out.*]
HUGH.   Move—move—move! Put some order on things! Come on,
  Sarah—hide that bucket. Whose are these slates? Somebody
  takes these dishes away. *Festinate! Festinate!*[7]

  [MANUS *goes to* MAIRE *who is busy tidying.*]

MANUS.   You didn't tell me you were definitely leaving.
MAIRE.   Not now.
HUGH.   Good girl, Bridget. That's the style.
MANUS.   You might at least have told me.
HUGH.   Are these your books, James?
JIMMY.   Thank you.
MANUS.   Fine! Fine! Go ahead! Go ahead!
MAIRE.   You talk to me about getting married—with neither a roof
  over your head nor a sod of ground under your foot. I suggest you
  go for the new school; but no—'My father's in for that.' Well now
  he's got it and now this is finished and now you've nothing.
MANUS.   I can always . . .
MAIRE.   What? Teach classics to the cows? Agh—

  [MAIRE *moves away from* MANUS. OWEN *enters with* LANCEY
  and YOLLAND. CAPTAIN LANCEY *is middle-aged; a small, crisp
  officer, expert in his field as cartographer but uneasy with people—especially civilians, especially these foreign civilians. His
  skill is with deeds, not words.* LIEUTENANT YOLLAND *is in his
  late twenties/early thirties. He is tall and thin and gangling,
  blond hair, a shy, awkward manner. A soldier by accident.*]

OWEN.   Here we are. Captain Lancey—my father.
LANCEY.   Good evening.

  [HUGH *becomes expansive, almost courtly, with his visitors.*]

HUGH.   You and I have already met, sir.
LANCEY.   Yes.
OWEN.   And Lieutenant Yolland—both Royal Engineers—my fa-
  ther.
HUGH.   You're very welcome, gentlemen.
YOLLAND.   How do you do.
HUGH.   *Gaudeo vos hic adesse.*[8]
OWEN.   And I'll make no other introductions except that these are
  some of the people of Baile Beag and—what?—well you're
  among the best people in Ireland now. [*He pauses to allow*

7. Hurry!
8. Welcome.

LANCEY *to speak.* LANCEY *does not.*] Would you like to say a few words, Captain?

HUGH.   What about a drop, sir?

LANCEY.   A what?

HUGH.   Perhaps a modest refreshment? A little sampling of our *aqua vitae?*

LANCEY.   No, no.

HUGH.   Later perhaps when—

LANCEY.   I'll say what I have to say, if I may, and as briefly as possible. Do they speak *any* English, Roland?

OWEN.   Don't worry. I'll translate.

LANCEY.   I see. [*He clears his throat. He speaks as if he were addressing children—a shade too loudly and enunciating excessively.*] You may have seen me—seen me—working in this section—section?—working. We are here—here—in this place—you understand?—to make a map—a map—a map and—

JIMMY.   *Nonne Latine loquitur?*[9]

[HUGH *holds up a restraining hand.*]

HUGH.   James.

LANCEY [*to* JIMMY].   I do not speak Gaelic, sir. [*He looks at* OWEN.]

OWEN.   Carry on.

LANCEY.   A map is a representation on paper—a picture—you understand picture?—a paper picture—showing, representing this country—yes?—showing your country in miniature—a scaled drawing on paper of—of—of—

[*Suddenly* DOALTY *sniggers. Then* BRIDGET. *Then* SARAH. OWEN *leaps in quickly.*]

OWEN.   It might be better if you *assume* they understand you—

LANCEY.   Yes?

OWEN.   And I'll translate as you go along.

LANCEY.   I see. Yes. Very well. Perhaps you're right. Well. What we are doing is this.

[*He looks at* OWEN. OWEN *nods reassuringly.*]

His Majesty's government has ordered the first ever comprehensive survey of this entire country—a general triangulation which will embrace detailed hydrographic and topographic information and which will be executed to a scale of six inches to the English mile.

HUGH [*pouring a drink*].   Excellent—excellent.

[LANCEY *looks at* OWEN.]

OWEN.   A new map is being made of the whole country.

[LANCEY *looks to* OWEN: *Is that all?* OWEN *smiles reassuringly and indicates to proceed.*]

9. Does he not speak Latin?

LANCEY.   This enormous task has been embarked on so that the military authorities will be equipped with up-to-date and accurate information on every corner of this part of the Empire.

OWEN.   The job is being done by soldiers because they are skilled in this work.

LANCEY.   And also so that the entire basis of land valuation can be reassessed for purposes of more equitable taxation.

OWEN.   This new map will take the place of the estate agent's map so that from now on you will know exactly what is yours in law.

LANCEY.   In conclusion I wish to quote two brief extracts from the white paper which is our governing charter: [*Reads*] 'All former surveys of Ireland originated in forfeiture and violent transfer of property; the present survey has for its object the relief which can be afforded to the proprietors and occupiers of land from unequal taxation.'

OWEN.   The captain hopes that the public will cooperate with the sappers and that the new map will mean that taxes are reduced.

HUGH.   A worthy enterprise—*opus honestrum!* And Extract B?

LANCEY.   'Ireland is privileged. No such survey is being undertaken in England. So this survey cannot but be received as proof of the disposition of this government to advance the interests of Ireland.' My sentiments, too.

OWEN.   This survey demonstrates the government's interest in Ireland and the captain thanks you for listening so attentively to him.

HUGH.   Our pleasure, Captain.

LANCEY.   Lieutenant Yolland?

YOLLAND.   I—I—I've nothing to say—really—

OWEN.   The captain is the man who actually makes the new map. George's task is to see that the place-names on this map are . . . correct. [*To* YOLLAND.] Just a few words—they'd like to hear you. [*To class.*] Don't you want to hear George, too?

MAIRE.   Has he anything to say?

YOLLAND [*to* MAIRE].   Sorry—sorry?

OWEN.   She says she's dying to hear you.

YOLLAND [*to* MAIRE].   Very kind of you—thank you . . . [*To class.*] I can only say that I feel—I feel very foolish to—to—to be working here and not to speak your language. But I intend to rectify that—with Roland's help—indeed I do.

OWEN.   He wants me to teach him Irish!

HUGH.   You are doubly welcome, sir.

YOLLAND.   I think your countryside is—is—is—is very beautiful. I've fallen in love with it already. I hope we're not too—too crude an intrusion on your lives. And I know that I'm going to be happy, very happy, here.

OWEN.   He is already a committed Hibernophile—

JIMMY.   He loves—

OWEN.   All right, Jimmy—we know—he loves Baile Beag; and he loves you all.

HUGH.   Please . . . May I . . .? [HUGH *is now drunk. He holds on to the edge of the table.*]

OWEN.   Go ahead, Father. [*Hands up for quiet.*] Please—please.

HUGH.   And we, gentlemen, we in turn are happy to offer you our friendship, our hospitality, and every assistance that you may require. Gentlemen—welcome!

> [*A few desultory claps. The formalities are over. General conversation. The soldiers meet the locals.* MANUS *and* OWEN *meet down stage.*]

OWEN.   Lancey's a bloody ramrod but George's all right. How are you anyway?

MANUS.   What sort of translation was that, Owen?

OWEN.   Did I make a mess of it?

MANUS.   You weren't saying what Lancey was saying!

OWEN.   'Uncertainty in meaning is incipient poetry'—who said that?

MANUS.   There was nothing uncertain about what Lancey said: it's a bloody military operation, Owen! And what's Yolland's function? What's 'incorrect' about the place-names we have here?

OWEN.   Nothing at all. They're just going to be standardized.

MANUS.   You mean changed into English?

OWEN.   Where there's ambiguity, they'll be Anglicized.

MANUS.   And they call you Roland! They both call you Roland!

OWEN.   Shhhhh. Isn't it ridiculous? They seemed to get it wrong from the very beginning—or else they can't pronounce Owen. I was afraid some of you bastards would laugh.

MANUS.   Aren't you going to tell them?

OWEN.   Yes—yes—soon—soon.

MANUS.   But they . . .

OWEN.   Easy, man, easy. Owen—Roland—what the hell. It's only a name. It's the same me, isn't it? Well, isn't it?

MANUS.   Indeed it is. It's the same Owen.

OWEN.   And the same Manus. And in a way we complement each other. [*He punches* MANUS *lightly, playfully and turns to join the others. As he goes.*] All right—who has met whom? Isn't this a job for the go-between?

> [MANUS *watches* OWEN *move confidently across the floor, taking* MAIRE *by the hand and introducing her to* YOLLAND. HUGH *is trying to negotiate the steps.* JIMMY *is lost in a text.* DOALTY *and* BRIDGET *are reliving their giggling.* SARAH *is staring at* MANUS.]

Act 2

The sappers have already mapped most of the area. YOLLAND's *official task, which* OWEN *is now doing, is to take each of the Gaelic names— every hill, stream, rock, even every patch of ground which possessed its own distinctive Irish name—and Anglicize it, either by changing it into its approximate English sound or by translating it into English words. For example, a Gaelic name like Cnoc Ban could become Knockban or—directly translated—Fair Hill. These new standardized names were entered into the Name-Book, and when the new maps appeared they contained all these new Anglicized names.* OWEN's *official function as translator is to pronounce each name in Irish and then provide the English translation.*

The hot weather continues. It is late afternoon some days later.

Stage right: an improvised clothes-line strung between the shafts of the cart and a nail in the wall; on it are some shirts and socks.

A large map—one of the new blank maps—is spread out on the floor. OWEN *is on his hands and knees, consulting it. He is totally engrossed in his task which he pursues with great energy and efficiency.*

YOLLAND's *hesitancy has vanished—he is at home here now. He is sitting on the floor, his long legs stretched out before him, his back resting against a creel, his eyes closed. His mind is elsewhere. One of the reference books—a church registry—lies open on his lap.*

Around them are various reference books, the Name-Book, a bottle of poteen, some cups, etc.

OWEN *completes an entry in the Name-Book and returns to the map on the floor.*

OWEN.   Now. Where have we got to? Yes—the point where that stream enters the sea—that tiny little beach there. George!

YOLLAND.   Yes. I'm listening. What do you call it? Say the Irish name again?

OWEN.   Bun na hAbhann.

YOLLAND.   Again.

OWEN.   Bun na hAbhann.

YOLLAND.   Bun na hAbhann.

OWEN.   That's terrible, George.

YOLLAND.   I know. I'm sorry. Say it again.

OWEN.   Bun na hAbbann.

YOLLAND.   Bun na hAbbann.

OWEN.   That's better. Bun is the Irish word for bottom. And Abha means river. So it's literally the mouth of the river.

YOLLAND.   Let's leave it alone. There's no English equivalent for a sound like that.

OWEN.   What is it called in the church registry?

[*Only now does* YOLLAND *open his eyes.*]

YOLLAND.   Let's see . . . Banowen.

OWEN.   That's wrong. [*Consults text.*] The list of freeholders calls it Owenmore—that's completely wrong: Owenmore's the big river at the west end of the parish. [*Another text.*] And in the grand jury lists it's called—God!—Binhone!—wherever they got that. I suppose we could Anglicize it to Bunowen; but somehow that's neither fish nor flesh.

[YOLLAND *closes his eyes again.*]

YOLLAND.   I give up.

OWEN [*at map*].   Back to first principles. What are we trying to do?

YOLLAND.   Good question.

OWEN.   We are trying to denominate and at the same time describe that tiny area of soggy, rocky, sandy ground where that little stream enters the sea, an area known locally as Bun na hAbhann . . . Burnfoot! What about Burnfoot?

YOLLAND [*indifferently*].   Good, Roland, Burnfoot's good.

OWEN.   George, my name isn't . . .

YOLLAND.   B-u-r-n-f-o-o-t?

OWEN.   Are you happy with that?

YOLLAND.   Yes.

OWEN.   Burnfoot it is then. [*He makes the entry into the Name-Book.*] Bun na hAbhann—B-u-r-n-

YOLLAND.   You're becoming very skilled at this.

OWEN.   We're not moving fast enough.

YOLLAND [*opens eyes again*].   Lancey lectured me again last night.

OWEN.   When does he finish here?

YOLLAND.   The sappers are pulling out at the end of the week. The trouble is, the maps they've completed can't be printed without these names. So London screams at Lancey and Lancey screams at me. But I wasn't intimidated.

[MANUS *emerges from upstairs and descends.*]

'I'm sorry, sir,' I said, 'But certain tasks demand their own tempo. You cannot rename a whole country overnight.' Your Irish air has made me bold. [*To* MANUS.] Do you want us to leave?

MANUS.   Time enough. Class won't begin for another half-hour.

YOLLAND.   Sorry—sorry?

OWEN.   Can't you speak English?

[MANUS *gathers the things off the clothes-line.* OWEN *returns to the map.*]

OWEN.   We now come across that beach . . .

YOLLAND.   Tra—that's the Irish for beach. [*To* MANUS.] I'm picking up the odd word, Manus.

MANUS.   So.

OWEN.   . . . on past Burnfoot; and there's nothing around here that has any name that I know of until we come down here to the south end, just about here . . . and there should be a ridge of rocks there . . . Have the sappers marked it? They have. Look, George.

YOLLAND. Where are we?

OWEN. There.

YOLLAND. I'm lost.

OWEN. Here. And the name of that ridge is Druim Dubh. Put English on that, Lieutenant.

YOLLAND. Say it again.

OWEN. Druim Dubh.

YOLLAND. Dubh means black.

OWEN. Yes.

YOLLAND. And Druim means . . . what? a fort?

OWEN. We met it yesterday in Druim Luachra.

YOLLAND. A ridge! The Black Ridge! [*To* MANUS.] You see, Manus?

OWEN. We'll have you fluent at the Irish before the summer's over.

YOLLAND. Oh, I wish I were.

> [*To* MANUS *as he crosses to go back upstairs.*]

We got a crate of oranges from Dublin today. I'll send some up to you.

MANUS. Thanks. [*To* OWEN.] Better hide that bottle. Father's just up and he'd be better without it.

OWEN. Can't you speak English before your man?

MANUS. Why?

OWEN. Out of courtesy.

MANUS. Doesn't he want to learn Irish? [*To* YOLLAND.] Don't you want to learn Irish?

YOLLAND. Sorry—sorry? I—I—

MANUS. I understand the Lancey's perfectly but people like you puzzle me.

OWEN. Manus, for God's sake!

MANUS [*still to* YOLLAND]. How's the work going?

YOLLAND. The work?—the work? Oh, it's—it's staggering along—I think— [*to* OWEN] —isn't it? But we'd be lost without Roland.

MANUS [*leaving*]. I'm sure. But there are always the Rolands, aren't there? [*He goes upstairs and exits.*]

YOLLAND. What was that he said?—something about Lancey, was it?

OWEN. He said we should hide that bottle before Father gets his hands on it.

YOLLAND. Ah.

OWEN. He's always trying to protect him.

YOLLAND. Was he lame from birth?

OWEN. An accident when he was a baby: Father fell across his cradle. That's why Manus feels so responsible for him.

YOLLAND. Why doesn't he marry?

OWEN. Can't afford to, I suppose.

YOLLAND. Hasn't he a salary?

OWEN.   What salary? All he gets is the odd shilling Father throws him—and that's seldom enough. I got out in time, didn't I?

[YOLLAND *is pouring a drink.*]

Easy with that stuff—it'll hit you suddenly.

YOLLAND.   I like it.

OWEN.   Let's get back to the job. Druim Dubh—what's it called in the jury lists? [*Consults texts.*]

YOLLAND.   Some people here resent us.

OWEN.   Dramduff—wrong as usual.

YOLLAND.   I was passing a little girl yesterday and she spat at me.

OWEN.   And it's Drimdoo here. What's it called in the registry?

YOLLAND.   Do you know the Donnelly twins?

OWEN.   Who?

YOLLAND.   The Donnelly twins.

OWEN.   Yes. Best fishermen about here. What about them?

YOLLAND.   Lancey's looking for them.

OWEN.   What for?

YOLLAND.   He wants them for questioning.

OWEN.   Probably stolen somebody's nets. Dramduffy! Nobody ever called it Dramduffy. Take your pick of those three.

YOLLAND.   My head's addled. Let's take a rest. Do you want a drink?

OWEN.   Thanks. Now, every Dubh we've come across we've changed to Duff. So if we're to be consistent, I suppose Druim Dubh has to become Dromduff.

[YOLLAND *is now looking out the window.*]

You can see the end of the ridge from where you're standing. But D-r-u-m- or D-r-o-m-? [*Name-Book.*] Do you remember—which did we agree on for Druim Luachra?

YOLLAND.   That house immediately above where we're camped—

OWEN.   Mm?

YOLLAND.   The house where Maire lives.

OWEN.   Maire? Oh, Maire Chatach.

YOLLAND.   What does that mean?

OWEN.   Curly-haired; the whole family are called the Catachs. What about it?

YOLLAND.   I hear music coming from that house almost every night.

OWEN.   Why don't you drop in?

YOLLAND.   Could I?

OWEN.   Why not? We used D-r-o-m then. So we've got to call it D-r-o-m-d-u-f-f—all right?

YOLLAND.   Go back up to where the new school is being built and just say the names again for me, would you?

OWEN.   That's a good idea. Poolkerry, Ballybeg—

YOLLAND.   No, no; as they still are—in your own language.

OWEN.   Poll na gCaorach,

[YOLLAND *repeats the names silently after him.*]

Baile Beag, Ceann Balor, Lis Maol, Machaire Buidhe, Baile na
gGall, Carraig na Ri, Mullach Dearg—
YOLLAND.   Do you think I could live here?
OWEN.   What are you talking about?
YOLLAND.   Settle down here—live here.
OWEN.   Come on, George.
YOLLAND.   I mean it.
OWEN.   Live on what? Potatoes? Buttermilk?
YOLLAND.   It's really heavenly.
OWEN.   For God's sake! The first hot summer in fifty years and you
  think it's Eden. Don't be such a bloody romantic. You wouldn't
  survive a mild winter here.
YOLLAND.   Do you think not? Maybe you're right.

[DOALTY *enters in a rush.*]

DOALTY.   Hi, boys, is Manus about?
OWEN.   He's upstairs. Give him a shout.
DOALTY.   Manus! The cattle's going mad in that heat—Cripes, running wild all over the place. [*To* YOLLAND.] How are you doing,
  skipper?

[MANUS *appears.*]

YOLLAND.   Thank you for—I—I'm very grateful to you for—
DOALTY.   Wasting your time. I don't know a word you're saying. Hi,
  Manus, there's two bucks down the road there asking for you.
MANUS [*descending*].   Who are they?
DOALTY.   Never clapped eyes on them. They want to talk to you.
MANUS.   What about?
DOALTY.   They wouldn't say. Come on. The bloody beasts'll end up
  in Loch an lubhair if they're not capped. Good luck, boys!

[DOALTY *rushes off.* MANUS *follows him.*]

OWEN.   Good luck! What were you thanking Doalty for?
YOLLAND.   I was washing outside my tent this morning and he was
  passing with a scythe across his shoulder and he came up to me
  and pointed to the long grass and then cut a pathway round
  my tent and from the tent down to the road—so that my feet
  won't get wet with the dew. Wasn't that kind of him? And I have
  no words to thank him . . . I suppose you're right: I suppose I
  couldn't live here . . . Just before Doalty came up to me this
  morning, I was thinking that at that moment I might have been
  in Bombay instead of Ballybeg. You see, my father was at his wits
  end with me and finally he got me a job with the East India Company—some kind of clerkship. This was ten, eleven months ago.
  So I set off for London. Unfortunately I—I—I missed the boat.
  Literally. And since I couldn't face Father and hadn't enough

money to hang about until the next sailing, I joined the army. And they stuck me into the Engineers and posted me to Dublin. And Dublin sent me here. And while I was washing this morning and looking across the Tra Bhan, I was thinking how very, very lucky I am to be here and not in Bombay.

OWEN.   Do you believe in fate?

YOLLAND.   Lancey's so like my father. I was watching him last night. He met every group of sappers as they reported in. He checked the field kitchens. He examined the horses. He inspected every single report—even examining the texture of the paper and commenting on the neatness of the handwriting. The perfect colonial servant: not only must the job be done—it must be done with excellence. Father has that drive, too; that dedication; that indefatigable energy. He builds roads—hopping from one end of the Empire to the other. Can't sit still for five minutes. He says himself the longest time he ever sat still was the night before Waterloo when they were waiting for Wellington to make up his mind to attack.[1]

OWEN.   What age is he?

YOLLAND.   Born in 1789—the very day the Bastille[2] fell. I've often thought maybe that gave his whole life its character. Do you think it could? He inherited a new world the day he was born— The Year One. Ancient time was at an end. The world had cast off its old skin. There were no longer any frontiers to man's potential. Possibilities were endless and exciting. He still believes that. The Apocalypse is just about to happen . . . I'm afraid I'm a great disappointment to him. I've neither his energy, nor his coherence, nor his belief. Do I believe in fate? The day I arrived in Ballybeg—no, Baile Beag—the moment you brought me in here, I had a curious sensation. It's difficult to describe. It was a momentary sense of discovery; no—not quite a sense of discovery— a sense of recognition, of confirmation of something I half knew instinctively; as if I had stepped . . .

OWEN.   Back into ancient time?

YOLLAND.   No, no. It wasn't an awareness of *direction* being changed but of experience being of a totally different order. I had moved into a consciousness that wasn't striving nor agitated, but at its ease and with its own conviction and assurance. And when I heard Jimmy Jack and your father swapping stories about Apollo and Cuchulainn and Paris and Ferdia[3]—as if they lived down the road—it was then that I thought—I knew—perhaps I could live here . . . [*Now embarrassed.*] Where's the pot-een?

OWEN.   Poteen.[4]

YOLLAND.   Poteen—poteen—poteen. Even if I did speak Irish I'd

1. The duke of Wellington defeated Napoleon at Waterloo, in Belgium, on June 18, 1815.
2. The Paris jail destroyed on July 14, the onset of the French Revolution.
3. Figures of classical and Celtic mythology.
4. Distilled liquor.

always be an outsider here, wouldn't I? I may learn the password but the language of the tribe will always elude me, won't it? The private core will always be . . . hermetic, won't it?

OWEN.   You can learn to decode us.

[HUGH *emerges from upstairs and descends. He is dressed for the road. Today he is physically and mentally jaunty and alert—almost self-consciously jaunty and alert. Indeed, as the scene progresses, one has the sense that he is deliberately parodying himself. The moment* HUGH *gets to the bottom of the steps* YOLLAND *leaps respectfully to his feet.*]

HUGH.   [*as he descends*].

> *Quantumvis cursum longum fessumque moratur*
> *Sol, sacro tandem carmine vesper adest.*

I dabble in verse, Lieutenant, after the style of Ovid. [*To* OWEN.] A drop of that to fortify me.

YOLLAND.   You'll have to translate it for me.

HUGH.   Let's see—

No matter how long the sun may linger on his long and weary journey
At length evening comes with its sacred song.

YOLLAND.   Very nice, sir.

HUGH.   English succeeds in making it sound . . . plebeian.

OWEN.   Where are you off to, Father?

HUGH.   An *expeditio* with three purposes. Purpose A: to acquire a testimonial from our parish priest— [*to* YOLLAND.] a worthy man but barely literate; and since he'll ask me to write it myself, how in all modesty can I do myself justice? [*To* OWEN.] Where did this [*drink*] come from?

OWEN.   Anna na mBreag's.

HUGH [*to* YOLLAND].   In that case address yourself to it with circumspection. [*And* HUGH *instantly tosses the drink back in one gulp and grimaces.*] Aaaaaaagh! [*Holds out his glass for a refill.*] Anna na mBreag means Anna of the Lies. And Purpose B: to talk to the builders of the new school about the kind of living accommodation I will require there. I have lived too long like a journeyman tailor.

YOLLAND.   Some years ago we lived fairly close to a poet—well, about three miles away.

HUGH.   His name?

YOLLAND.   Wordsworth—William Wordsworth.[5]

HUGH.   Did he speak of me to you?

YOLLAND.   Actually I never talked to him. I just saw him out walking—in the distance.

HUGH.   Wordsworth? . . . No. I'm afraid we're not familiar with

5. The English Romantic poet (1770–1850).

your literature, Lieutenant. We feel closer to the warm Mediter-
ranean. We tend to overlook your island.

YOLLAND.   I'm learning to speak Irish, sir.

HUGH.   Good.

YOLLAND.   Roland's teaching me.

HUGH.   Splendid.

YOLLAND.   I mean—I feel so cut off from the people here. And I
was trying to explain a few minutes ago how remarkable a community this is. To meet people like yourself and Jimmy Jack who
actually converse in Greek and Latin. And your place names—
what was the one we came across this morning?—Termon, from
Terminus, the god of boundaries. It—it—it's really astonishing.

HUGH.   We like to think we endure around truths immemorially
posited.

YOLLAND.   And your Gaelic literature—you're a poet yourself—

HUGH.   Only in Latin, I'm afraid.

YOLLAND.   I understand it's enormously rich and ornate.

HUGH.   Indeed, Lieutenant. A rich language. A rich literature.
You'll find, sir, that certain cultures expend on their vocabularies
and syntax acquisitive energies and ostentations entirely lacking
in their material lives. I suppose you could call us a spiritual people.

OWEN [not unkindly; more out of embarrassment before YOLLAND].
Will you stop that nonsense, Father.

HUGH.   Nonsense? What nonsense?

OWEN.   Do you know where the priest lives?

HUGH.   At Lis na Muc, over near . . .

OWEN.   No, he doesn't. Lis na Muc, the Fort of the Pigs, has become Swinefort. [Now turning the pages of the Name-Book—a
page per name.] And to get to Swinefort you pass through Green-
castle and Fair Head and Strandhill and Gort and Whiteplains.
And the new school isn't at Poll na gCaorach—it's at Sheepsrock.
Will you be able to find your way?

[HUGH pours himself another drink. Then:—]

HUGH.   Yes, it is a rich language, Lieutenant, full of the mytholo-
gies of fantasy and hope and self-deception—a syntax opulent
with tomorrows. It is our response to mud cabins and a diet of
potatoes; our only method of replying to . . . inevitabilities. [To
OWEN.] Can you give me the loan of half-a-crown? I'll repay you
out of the subscriptions I'm collecting for the publication of my
new book. [To YOLLAND.] It is entitled: 'The Pentaglot Preceptor
or Elementary Institute of the English, Greek, Hebrew, Latin and
Irish Languages; Particularly Calculated for the Instruction of
such Ladies and Gentlemen as may Wish to Learn without the
Help of a Master'.

YOLLAND [laughs].   That's a wonderful title!

HUGH.   Between ourselves—the best part of the enterprise. Nor do
I, in fact, speak Hebrew. And that last phrase—'without the Help

of a Master'—that was written before the new national school
was thrust upon me—do you think I ought to drop it now? After
all you don't dispose of the cow just because it has produced a
magnificent calf, do you?

YOLLAND.   You certainly do not.

HUGH.   The phrase goes. And I'm interrupting work of moment.
[*He goes to the door and stops there.*] To return briefly to that
other matter, Lieutenant. I understand your sense of exclusion,
of being cut off from a life here; and I trust you will find access
to us with my son's help. But remember that words are signals,
counters. They are not immortal. And it can happen—to use an
image you'll understand—it can happen that a civilization can be
imprisoned in a linguistic contour which no longer matches the
landscape of . . . fact. Gentlemen. [*He leaves.*]

OWEN.   'An *expeditio* with three purposes': the children laugh at
him: he always promises three points and he never gets beyond A
and B.

YOLLAND.   He's an astute man.

OWEN.   He's bloody pompous.

YOLLAND.   But so astute.

OWEN.   And he drinks too much. Is it astute not to be able to ad-
just for survival? Enduring around truths immemorially posited—
hah!

YOLLAND.   He knows what's happening.

OWEN.   What is happening?

YOLLAND.   I'm not sure. But I'm concerned about my part in it. It's
an eviction of sorts.

OWEN.   We're making a six-inch map of the country. Is there something sinister in that?

YOLLAND.   Not in—

OWEN.   And we're taking place-names that are riddled with confusion and—

YOLLAND.   Who's confused? Are the people confused?

OWEN.   —and we're standardizing those names as accurately and
as sensitively as we can.

YOLLAND.   Something is being eroded.

OWEN.   Back to the romance again. All right! Fine! Fine! Look
where we've got to. [*He drops on his hands and knees and stabs a
finger at the map.*] We've come to this crossroads. Come here and
look at it, man! Look at it! And we call that crossroads Tobair
Vree. And why do we call it Tobair Vree? I'll tell you why. Tobair
means a well. But what does Vree mean? It's a corruption of
Brian— [*Gaelic pronunciation*] Brian—an erosion of Tobair
Bhriain. Because a hundred-and-fifty years ago there used to be a
well there, not at the crossroads, mind you—that would be too
simple—but in a field close to the crossroads. And an old man
called Brian, whose face was disfigured by an enormous growth,
got it into his head that the water in that well was blessed; and
every day for seven months he went there and bathed his face in

it. But the growth didn't go away; and one morning Brian was found drowned in that well. And ever since that crossroads is known as Tobair Vree—even though that well has long since dried up. I know the story because my grandfather told it to me. But ask Doalty—or Maire—or Bridget—even my father—even Manus—why it's called Tobair Vree; and do you think they'll know? I know they don't know. So the question I put to you, Lieutenant, is this: what do we do with a name like that? Do we scrap Tobair Vree altogether and call it—what?—The Cross? Crossroads? Or do we keep piety with a man long dead, long forgotten, his name 'eroded' beyond recognition, whose trivial little story nobody in the parish remembers?

YOLLAND.   Except you.

OWEN.   I've left here.

YOLLAND.   You remember it.

OWEN.   I'm asking you: what do we write in the Name-Book?

YOLLAND.   Tobair Vree.

OWEN.   Even though the well is a hundred yards from the actual crossroads—and there's no well anyway—and what the hell does Vree mean?

YOLLAND.   Tobair Vree.

OWEN.   That's what you want?

YOLLAND.   Yes.

OWEN.   You're certain?

YOLLAND.   Yes.

OWEN.   Fine. Fine. That's what you'll get.

YOLLAND.   That's what you want, too, Roland.

[*Pause.*]

OWEN [*explodes*].   George! For God's sake! *My name is not Roland!*

YOLLAND.   What?

OWEN [*softly*].   My name is Owen.

[*Pause.*]

YOLLAND.   Not Roland?

OWEN.   Owen.

YOLLAND.   You mean to say—?

OWEN.   Owen.

YOLLAND.   But I've been—

OWEN.   O-w-e-n.

YOLLAND.   Where did Roland come from?

OWEN.   I don't know.

YOLLAND.   It was never Roland?

OWEN.   Never.

YOLLAND.   O my God!

[*Pause. They stare at one another. Then the absurdity of the situation strikes them suddenly. They explode with laughter.* OWEN *pours drinks. As they roll about, their lines overlap.*]

YOLLAND.   Why didn't you tell me?
OWEN.   Do I look like a Roland?
YOLLAND.   Spell Owen again.
OWEN.   I was getting fond of Roland.
YOLLAND.   O my God!
OWEN.   O-w-e-n.
YOLLAND.   What'll we write—
OWEN.   —in the Name-Book?!
YOLLAND.   R-o-w-e-n!
OWEN.   Or what about Ol-
YOLLAND.   Ol- what?
OWEN.   Oland!

[*And again they explode.* MANUS *enters. He is very elated.*]

MANUS.   What's the celebration?
OWEN.   A christening!
YOLLAND.   A baptism!
OWEN.   A hundred christenings!
YOLLAND.   A thousand baptisms! Welcome to Eden!
OWEN.   Eden's right! We name a thing and—bang!—it leaps into existence!
YOLLAND.   Each name a perfect equation with its roots.
OWEN.   A perfect congruence with its reality. [*To* MANUS.] Take a drink.
YOLLAND.   Poteen—beautiful.
OWEN.   Lying Anna's poteen.
YOLLAND.   Anna na mBreag's poteen.
OWEN.   Excellent, George.
YOLLAND.   I'll decode you yet.
OWEN [*offers drink*].   Manus?
MANUS.   Not if that's what it does to you.
OWEN.   You're right. Steady—steady—sober up—sober up.
YOLLAND.   Sober as a judge, Owen.

[MANUS *moves beside* OWEN.]

MANUS.   I've got good news! Where's Father?
OWEN.   He's gone out. What's the good news?
MANUS.   I've been offered a job.
OWEN.   Where? [*Now aware of* YOLLAND.] Come on, man—speak in English.
MANUS.   For the benefit of the colonist?
OWEN.   He's a decent man.
MANUS.   Aren't they all at some level?
OWEN.   Please.

[MANUS *shrugs.*]

He's been offered a job.
YOLLAND.   Where?
OWEN.   Well—tell us!

MANUS.   I've just had a meeting with two men from Inis Meadhon. They want me to go there and start a hedge-school. They're giving me a free house, free turf, and free milk; a rood of standing corn; twelve drills of potatoes; and— [*He stops.*]

OWEN.   And what?

MANUS.   A salary of £42 a year!

OWEN.   Manus, that's wonderful!

MANUS.   You're talking to a man of substance.

OWEN.   I'm delighted.

YOLLAND.   Where's Inis Meadhon?

OWEN.   An island south of here. And they came looking for you?

MANUS.   Well, I mean to say . . .

> [OWEN *punches* MANUS.]

OWEN.   Aaaaagh! This calls for a real celebration.

YOLLAND.   Congratulations.

MANUS.   Thank you.

OWEN.   Where are you, Anna?

YOLLAND.   When do you start?

MANUS.   Next Monday.

OWEN.   We'll stay with you when we're there. [*To* YOLLAND.] How long will it be before we reach Inis Meadhon?

YOLLAND.   How far south is it?

MANUS.   About fifty miles.

YOLLAND.   Could we make it by December?

OWEN.   We'll have Christmas together. [*Sings.*] 'Christmas Day on Inis Meadhon . . .'

YOLLAND [*toast*].   I hope you're very content there, Manus.

MANUS.   Thank you.

> [YOLLAND *holds out his hand.* MANUS *takes it. They shake warmly.*]

OWEN [*toast*].   Manus.

MANUS [*toast*].   To Inis Meadhon. [*He drinks quickly and turns to leave.*]

OWEN.   Hold on—hold on—refills coming up.

MANUS.   I've got to go.

OWEN.   Come on, man; this is an occasion. Where are you rushing to?

MANUS.   I've got to tell Maire.

> [MAIRE *enters with her can of milk.*]

MAIRE.   You've got to tell Maire what?

OWEN.   He's got a job!

MAIRE.   Manus?

OWEN.   He's been invited to start a hedge-school in Inis Meadhon.

MAIRE.   Where?

MANUS.   Inis Meadhon—the island! They're giving me £42 a year and . . .

OWEN.   A house, fuel, milk, potatoes, corn, pupils, what-not!

MANUS.   I start on Monday.

OWEN.   You'll take a drink. Isn't it great?

MANUS.   I want to talk to you for—

MAIRE.   There's your milk. I need the can back.

[MANUS *takes the can and runs up the steps.*]

MANUS [*as he goes*].   How will you like living on an island?

OWEN.   You know George, don't you?

MAIRE.   We wave to each other across the fields.

YOLLAND.   Sorry-sorry?

OWEN.   She says you wave to each other across the fields.

YOLLAND.   Yes, we do; oh, yes; indeed we do.

MAIRE.   What's he saying?

OWEN.   He says you wave to each other across the fields.

MAIRE.   That's right. So we do.

YOLLAND.   What's she saying?

OWEN.   Nothing—nothing—nothing. [*To* MAIRE.] What's the news?

[MAIRE *moves away, touching the text books with her toe.*]

MAIRE.   Not a thing. You're busy, the two of you.

OWEN.   We think we are.

MAIRE.   I hear the Fiddler O'Shea's about. There's some talk of a dance tomorrow night.

OWEN.   Where will it be?

MAIRE.   Maybe over the road. Maybe at Tobair Vree.

YOLLAND.   Tobair Vree!

MAIRE.   Yes.

YOLLAND.   Tobair Vree! Tobair Vree!

MAIRE.   Does he know what I'm saying?

OWEN.   Not a word.

MAIRE.   Tell him then.

OWEN.   Tell him what?

MAIRE.   About the dance.

OWEN.   Maire says there may be a dance tomorrow night.

YOLLAND [*to* OWEN].   Yes? May I come? [*To* MAIRE.] Would anybody object if I came?

MAIRE [*to* OWEN].   What's he saying?

OWEN [*to* YOLLAND].   Who would object?

MAIRE [*to* OWEN].   Did you tell him?

YOLLAND [*to* MAIRE].   Sorry-sorry?

OWEN [*to* MAIRE].   He says may he come?

MAIRE [*to* YOLLAND].   That's up to you.

YOLLAND [*to* OWEN].   What does she say?

OWEN [*to* YOLLAND].   She says—

YOLLAND [*to* MAIRE].   What-what?

MAIRE [*to* OWEN].   Well?

YOLLAND [*to* OWEN].   Sorry-sorry?

OWEN [*to* YOLLAND].   Will you go?

YOLLAND [*to* MAIRE].   Yes, yes, if I may.
MAIRE [*to* OWEN].   What does he say?
YOLLAND [*to* OWEN].   What is she saying?
OWEN.   Oh for God's sake! [*To* MANUS, *who is descending with the empty can.*] You take on this job, Manus.
MANUS.   I'll walk you up to the house. Is your mother at home? I want to talk to her.
MAIRE.   What's the rush? [*To* OWEN.] Didn't you offer me a drink?
OWEN.   Will you risk Anna na mBreag?
MAIRE.   Why not.

> [YOLLAND *is suddenly intoxicated. He leaps up on a stool, raises his glass and shouts.*]

YOLLAND.   Anna na mBreag! Baile Beag! Inis Meadhon! Bombay! Tobair Vree! Eden! And poteen—correct, Owen?
OWEN.   Perfect.
YOLLAND.   And bloody marvellous stuff it is, too. I love it! Bloody, bloody, bloody marvellous!

> [*Simultaneously with his final 'bloody marvellous' bring up very loud the introductory music of the reel. Then immediately go to black. Retain the music throughout the very brief interval.*]

SCENE II

The following night.
    This scene may be played in the schoolroom, but it would be preferable to lose—by lighting—as much of the schoolroom as possible, and to play the scene down front in a vaguely 'outside' area.
    The music rises to a crescendo. Then in the distance we hear MAIRE *and* YOLLAND *approach—laughing and running. They run on, hand-in-hand. They have just left the dance. Fade the music to distant background. Then after a time it is lost and replaced by guitar music.* MAIRE *and* YOLLAND *are now down front, still holding hands and excited by their sudden and impetuous escape from the dance.*

MAIRE.   O my God, that leap across the ditch nearly killed me.
YOLLAND.   I could scarcely keep up with you.
MAIRE.   Wait till I get my breath back.
YOLLAND.   We must have looked as if we were being chased.

> [*They now realize they are alone and holding hands—the beginnings of embarrassment. The hands disengage. They begin to drift apart. Pause.*]

MAIRE.   Manus'll wonder where I've got to.
YOLLAND.   I wonder did anyone notice us leave.

> [*Pause. Slightly further apart.*]

MAIRE.   The grass must be wet. My feet are soaking.
YOLLAND.   Your feet must be wet. The grass is soaking.

> [*Another pause. Another few paces apart. They are now a long distance from one another.*]

YOLLAND [*indicating himself*].   George.

> [MAIRE *nods: Yes-yes. Then:—*]

MAIRE.   Lieutenant George.
YOLLAND.   Don't call me that. I never think of myself as Lieutenant.
MAIRE.   What-what?
YOLLAND.   Sorry-sorry. [*He points to himself again.*] George.

> [MAIRE *nods: Yes-yes. Then points to herself.*]

MAIRE.   Maire.
YOLLAND.   Yes, I know you're Maire. Of course I know you're Maire. I mean I've been watching you night and day for the past—
MAIRE [*eagerly*].   What-what?
YOLLAND [*points*].   Maire. [*Points.*] George. [*Points both.*] Maire and George.

> [MAIRE *nods: Yes-yes-yes.*]

I—I—I—
MAIRE.   Say anything at all. I love the sound of your speech.
YOLLAND [*eagerly*].   Sorry-sorry? [*In acute frustration he looks around, hoping for some inspiration that will provide him with communicative means. Now he has a thought: he tries raising his voice and articulating in a staccato style and with equal and absurd emphasis on each word.*] Every-morning-I-see-you-feeding-brown-hens-and-giving-meal-to-black-calf—[*the futility of it.*] —O my God.

> [MAIRE *smiles. She moves towards him. She will try to communicate in Latin.*]

MAIRE.   *Tu es centurio in—in—in exercitu Britannico—*[6]
YOLLAND.   Yes-yes? Go on—go on—say anything at all—I love the sound of your speech.
MAIRE.   *—et es in castris quae—quae—quae sunt in agro—*[7] [*the futility of it.*] —O my God.

> [YOLLAND *smiles. He moves towards her. Now for her English words.*]

George—water.
YOLLAND.   'Water'? Water! Oh yes—water—water—very good—water—good—good.

6. You are a soldier in the British Army.
7. And you are in the camp in the field.

MAIRE.   Fire.

YOLLAND.   Fire—indeed—wonderful—fire, fire, fire—splendid—splendid!

MAIRE.   Ah . . . ah . . .

YOLLAND.   Yes? Go on.

MAIRE.   Earth.

YOLLAND.   'Earth'?

MAIRE.   Earth. Earth.

> [YOLLAND *still does not understand.* MAIRE *stoops down and picks up a handful of clay. Holding it out.*]

Earth.

YOLLAND.   Earth! Of course—earth! Earth. Earth. Good Lord, Maire, your English is perfect!

MAIRE [*eagerly*].   What-what?

YOLLAND.   Perfect English. English perfect.

MAIRE.   George—

YOLLAND.   That's beautiful—oh, that's really beautiful.

MAIRE.   George—

YOLLAND.   Say it again—say it again—

MAIRE.   Shhh. [*She holds her hand up for silence—she is trying to remember her one line of English. Now she remembers it and she delivers the line as if English were her language—easily, fluidly, conversationally.*] George, 'In Norfolk we besport ourselves around the maypoll.'

YOLLAND.   Good God, do you? That's where my mother comes from—Norfolk. Norwich actually. Not exactly Norwich town but a small village called Little Walsingham close beside it. But in our own village of Winfarthing we have a maypole too and every year on the first of May— [*He stops abruptly, only now realizing. He stares at her. She in turn misunderstands his excitement.*]

MAIRE [*to herself*].   Mother of God, my Aunt Mary wouldn't have taught me something dirty, would she?

> [*Pause.* YOLLAND *extends his hand to* MAIRE. *She turns away from him and moves slowly across the stage.*]

YOLLAND.   Maire.

> [*She still moves away.*]

Maire Chatach.

> [*She still moves away.*]

Bun na hAbhann? [*He says the name softly, almost privately, very tentatively, as if he were searching for a sound she might respond to. He tries again.*] Druim Dubh?

> [MAIRE *stops. She is listening.* YOLLAND *is encouraged.*]

Poll na gCaorach. Lis Maol.

[MAIRE *turns towards him.*]

Lis na nGall.

MAIRE. Lis na nGradh.

[*They are now facing each other and begin moving—almost imperceptibly—towards one another.*]

MAIRE. Carraig an Phoill.
YOLLAND. Carraig na Ri. Loch na nEan.
MAIRE. Loch an lubhair. Machaire Buidhe.
YOLLAND. Machaire Mor. Cnoc na Mona.
MAIRE. Cnoc na nGabhar.
YOLLAND. Mullach.
MAIRE. Port.
YOLLAND. Tor.
MAIRE. Lag.

[*She holds out her hands to* YOLLAND. *He takes them. Each now speaks almost to himself/herself.*]

YOLLAND. I wish to God you could understand me.
MAIRE. Soft hands; a gentleman's hands.
YOLLAND. Because if you could understand me I could tell you how I spend my days either thinking of you or gazing up at your house in the hope that you'll appear even for a second.
MAIRE. Every evening you walk by yourself along the Tra Bhan and every morning you wash yourself in front of your tent.
YOLLAND. I would tell you how beautiful you are, curly-headed Maire. I would so like to tell you how beautiful you are.
MAIRE. Your arms are long and thin and the skin on your shoulders is very white.
YOLLAND. I would tell you . . .
MAIRE. Don't stop—I know what you're saying.
YOLLAND. I would tell you how I want to be here—to live here—always—with you—always, always.
MAIRE. 'Always'? What is that word—'always'?
YOLLAND. Yes-yes; always.
MAIRE. You're trembling.
YOLLAND. Yes, I'm trembling because of you.
MAIRE. I'm trembling, too.

[*She holds his face in her hand.*]

YOLLAND. I've made up my mind . . .
MAIRE. Shhhh.
YOLLAND. I'm not going to leave here . . .
MAIRE. Shhh—listen to me. I want you, too, soldier.
YOLLAND. Don't stop—I know what you're saying.
MAIRE. I want to live with you—anywhere—anywhere at all—always—always.
YOLLAND. 'Always'? What is that word—'always'?

MAIRE.   Take me away with you, George.

> [*Pause. Suddenly they kiss.* SARAH *enters. She sees them. She stands shocked, staring at them. Her mouth works. Then almost to herself.*]

SARAH.   Manus . . . Manus!

> [SARAH *runs off. Music to crescendo.*]

Act 3

The following evening. It is raining.

SARAH *and* OWEN *alone in the schoolroom.* SARAH, *more waiflike than ever, is sitting very still on a stool, an open book across her knee. She is pretending to read but her eyes keep going up to the room upstairs.* OWEN *is working on the floor as before, surrounded by his reference books, map, Name-Book, etc. But he has neither concentration nor interest; and like* SARAH *he glances up at the upstairs room.*

After a few seconds MANUS *emerges and descends, carrying a large paper bag which already contains his clothes. His movements are determined and urgent. He moves around the classroom, picking up books, examining each title carefully, and choosing about six of them which he puts into his bag. As he selects these books:—*

OWEN.   You know that old limekiln beyond Con Connie Tim's pub, the place we call The Murren?—do you know why it's called The Murren?

> [MANUS *does not answer.*]

I've only just discovered: it's a corruption of Saint Muranus. It seems Saint Muranus had a monastery somewhere about there at the beginning of the seventh century. And over the years the name became shortened to the Murren. Very unattractive name, isn't it? I think we should go back to the original—Saint Muranus. What do you think? The original's Saint Muranus. Don't you think we should go back to that?

> [*No response.* OWEN *begins writing the name into the Name-Book.* MANUS *is now rooting about among the forgotten implements for a piece of rope. He finds a piece. He begins to tie the mouth of the flimsy, overloaded bag—and it bursts, the contents spilling out on the floor.*]

MANUS.   Bloody, bloody, bloody hell!

> [*His voice breaks in exasperation: he is about to cry.* OWEN *leaps to his feet.*]

OWEN.   Hold on. I've a bag upstairs.

> [*He runs upstairs.* SARAH *waits until* OWEN *is off. Then:—*]

SARAH.   Manus . . . Manus, I . . .

> [MANUS *hears* SARAH *but makes no acknowledgement. He gathers up his belongings.* OWEN *reappears with the bag he had on his arrival.*]

OWEN.   Take this one—I'm finished with it anyway. And it's supposed to keep out the rain.

> [MANUS *transfers his few belongings.* OWEN *drifts back to his task. The packing is now complete.*]

MANUS.   You'll be here for a while? For a week or two anyhow?
OWEN.   Yes.
MANUS.   You're not leaving with the army?
OWEN.   I haven't made up my mind. Why?
MANUS.   Those Inis Meadhon men will be back to see why I haven't turned up. Tell them—tell them I'll write to them as soon as I can. Tell them I still want the job but that it might be three or four months before I'm free to go.
OWEN.   You're being damned stupid, Manus.
MANUS.   Will you do that for me?
OWEN.   Clear out now and Lancey'll think you're involved somehow.
MANUS.   Will you do that for me?
OWEN.   Wait a couple of days even. You know George—he's a bloody romantic—maybe he's gone out to one of the islands and he'll suddenly reappear tomorrow morning. Or maybe the search party'll find him this evening lying drunk somewhere in the sandhills. You've seen him drinking that poteen—doesn't know how to handle it. Had he drink on him last night at the dance?
MANUS.   I had a stone in my hand when I went out looking for him—I was going to fell him. The lame scholar turned violent.
OWEN.   Did anybody see you?
MANUS [*again close to tears*].   But when I saw him standing there at the side of the road—smiling—and her face buried in his shoulder—I couldn't even go close to them. I just shouted something stupid—something like, 'You're a bastard, Yolland.' If I'd even said it in English . . . 'cos he kept saying 'Sorry-sorry?' The wrong gesture in the wrong language.
OWEN.   And you didn't see him again?
MANUS.   'Sorry?'
OWEN.   Before you leave tell Lancey that—just to clear yourself.
MANUS.   What have I to say to Lancey? You'll give that message to the islandmen?
OWEN.   I'm warning you: run away now and you're bound to be—
MANUS [*to* SARAH].   Will you give that message to the Inis Meadhon men?
SARAH.   I will.

> [MANUS *picks up an old sack and throws it across his shoulders.*]

OWEN.   Have you any idea where you're going?

MANUS.   Mayo, maybe. I remember Mother saying she had cousins somewhere away out in the Erris Peninsula. [*He picks up his bag.*] Tell Father I took only the Virgil and the Caesar and the Aeschylus because they're mine anyway—I bought them with the money I got for that pet lamb I reared—do you remember that pet lamb? And tell him that Nora Dan never returned the dictionary and that she still owes him two-and-six for last quarter's reading—he always forgets those things.

OWEN.   Yes.

MANUS.   And his good shirt's ironed and hanging up in the press and his clean socks are in the butter-box under the bed.

OWEN.   All right.

MANUS.   And tell him I'll write.

OWEN.   If Maire asks where you've gone . . .?

MANUS.   He'll need only half the amount of milk now, won't he? Even less than half—he usually takes his tea black. [*Pause.*] And when he comes in at night—you'll hear him; he makes a lot of noise—I usually come down and give him a hand up. Those stairs are dangerous without a banister. Maybe before you leave you'd get Big Ned Frank to put up some sort of a handrail. [*Pause.*] And if you can bake, he's very fond of soda bread.

OWEN.   I can give you money. I'm wealthy. Do you know what they pay me? Two shillings a day for this—this—this—

[MANUS *rejects the offer by holding out his hand.*]

Goodbye, Manus.

[MANUS *and* OWEN *shake hands. Then* MANUS *picks up his bag briskly and goes towards the door. He stops a few paces beyond* SARAH, *turns, comes back to her. He addresses her as he did in Act One but now without warmth or concern for her.*]

MANUS.   What is your name? [*Pause.*] Come on. What is your name?

SARAH.   My name is Sarah.

MANUS.   Just Sarah? Sarah what? [*Pause.*] Well?

SARAH.   Sarah Johnny Sally.

MANUS.   And where do you live? Come on.

SARAH.   I live in Bun na hAbhann. [*She is now crying quietly.*]

MANUS.   Very good, Sarah Johnny Sally. There's nothing to stop you now—nothing in the wide world. [*Pause. He looks down at her.*] It's all right—it's all right—you did no harm—you did no harm at all. [*He stoops over her and kisses the top of her head—as if in absolution. Then briskly to the door and off.*]

OWEN.   Good luck, Manus!

SARAH [*quietly*].   I'm sorry . . . I'm sorry . . . I'm so sorry, Manus . . .

[OWEN *tries to work but cannot concentrate. He begins folding up the map. As he does:—*]

OWEN.   Is there a class this evening?

> [SARAH *nods: yes.*]

I suppose Father knows. Where is he anyhow?

> [SARAH *points.*]

Where?

> [SARAH *mimes rocking a baby.*]

I don't understand—where?

> [SARAH *repeats the mime and wipes away tears.* OWEN *is still puzzled.*]

It doesn't matter. He'll probably turn up.

> [BRIDGET *and* DOALTY *enter, sacks over their heads against the rain. They are self-consciously noisier, more ebullient, more garrulous than ever—brimming over with excitement and gossip and brio.*]

DOALTY.   You're missing the crack, boys! Cripes, you're missing the crack! Fifty more soldiers arrived an hour ago!

BRIDGET.   And they're spread out in a big line from Sean Neal's over to Lag and they're moving straight across the fields towards Cnoc na nGabhar!

DOALTY.   Prodding every inch of the ground in front of them with their bayonets and scattering animals and hens in all directions!

BRIDGET.   And tumbling everything before them—fences, ditches, haystacks, turf-stacks!

DOALTY.   They came to Barney Petey's field of corn—straight through it be God as if it was heather!

BRIDGET.   Not a blade of it left standing!

DOALTY.   And Barney Petey just out of his bed and running after them in his drawers: 'You hoors you! Get out of my corn, you hoors you!'

BRIDGET.   First time he ever ran in his life.

DOALTY.   Too lazy, the wee get, to cut it when the weather was good.

> [SARAH *begins putting out the seats.*]

BRIDGET.   Tell them about Big Hughie.

DOALTY.   Cripes, if you'd seen your aul fella, Owen.

BRIDGET.   They were all inside in Anna na mBreag's pub—all the crowd from the wake—

DOALTY.   And they hear the commotion and they all come out to the street—

BRIDGET.   Your father in front; the Infant Prodigy footless behind him!

DOALTY.   And your aul fella, he sees the army stretched across the countryside—

BRIDGET.   O my God!

DOALTY.   And Cripes he starts roaring at them!

BRIDGET.   'Visigoths! Huns! Vandals!'

DOALTY.   *'Ignari! Stulti! Rustici!'*[8]

BRIDGET.   And wee Jimmy Jack jumping up and down and shouting, 'Thermopylae! Thermopylae!'[9]

DOALTY.   You never saw crack like it in your life, boys. Come away on out with me, Sarah, and you'll see it all.

BRIDGET.   Big Hughie's fit to take no class. Is Manus about?

OWEN.   Manus is gone.

BRIDGET.   Gone where?

OWEN.   He's left—gone away.

DOALTY.   Where to?

OWEN.   He doesn't know. Mayo, maybe.

DOALTY.   What's on in Mayo?

OWEN [*to* BRIDGET].   Did you see George and Maire Chatach leave the dance last night?

BRIDGET.   We did. Didn't we, Doalty?

OWEN.   Did you see Manus following them out?

BRIDGET.   I didn't see him going out but I saw him coming in by himself later.

OWEN.   Did George and Maire come back to the dance?

BRIDGET.   No.

OWEN.   Did you see them again?

BRIDGET.   He left her home. We passed them going up the back road—didn't we, Doalty?

OWEN.   And Manus stayed till the end of the dance?

DOALTY.   We know nothing. What are you asking us for?

OWEN.   Because Lancey'll question me when he hears Manus's gone. [*Back to* BRIDGET.] That's the way George went home? By the back road? That's where you saw him?

BRIDGET.   Leave me alone, Owen. I know nothing about Yolland. If you want to know about Yolland, ask the Donnelly twins.

[*Silence.* DOALTY *moves over to the window.*]

[*To* SARAH.] He's a powerful fiddler, O'Shea, isn't he? He told our Seamus he'll come back for a night at Hallowe'en.

[OWEN *goes to* DOALTY *who looks resolutely out the window.*]

OWEN.   What's this about the Donnellys? [*Pause.*] Were they about last night?

DOALTY.   Didn't see them if they were. [*Begins whistling through his teeth.*]

OWEN.   George is a friend of mine.

DOALTY.   So.

8. Ignoramuses! Fools! Peasants!
9. Gap between mountain and sea defended by Greeks for three days in 480 B.C. against a far larger Persian force.

OWEN. I want to know what's happened to him.

DOALTY. Couldn't tell you.

OWEN. What have the Donnelly twins to do with it? [*Pause.*] Doalty!

DOALTY. I know nothing, Owen—nothing at all—I swear to God. All I know is this: on my way to the dance I saw their boat beached at Port. It wasn't there on my way home, after I left Bridget. And that's all I know. As God's my judge. The half-dozen times I met him I didn't know a word he said to me; but he seemed a right enough sort . . . [*With sudden excessive interest in the scene outside.*] Cripes, they're crawling all over the place! Cripes, there's millions of them! Cripes, they're levelling the whole land!

> [OWEN *moves away.* MAIRE *enters. She is bareheaded and wet from the rain; her hair in disarray. She attempts to appear normal but she is in acute distress, on the verge of being distraught. She is carrying the milk-can.*]

MAIRE. Honest to God, I must be going off my head. I'm halfway here and I think to myself, 'Isn't this can very light?' and I look into it and isn't it empty.

OWEN. It doesn't matter.

MAIRE. How will you manage for tonight?

OWEN. We have enough.

MAIRE. Are you sure?

OWEN. Plenty, thanks.

MAIRE. It'll take me no time at all to go back up for some.

OWEN. Honestly, Maire.

MAIRE. Sure it's better you have it than that black calf that's . . . that . . . [*She looks around.*] Have you heard anything?

OWEN. Nothing.

MAIRE. What does Lancey say?

OWEN. I haven't seen him since this morning.

MAIRE. What does he *think*?

OWEN. We really didn't talk. He was here for only a few seconds.

MAIRE. He left me home, Owen. And the last thing he said to me—he tried to speak in Irish—he said, 'I'll see you yesterday'— he meant to say 'I'll see you tomorrow.' And I laughed that much he pretended to get cross and he said 'Maypoll! Maypoll!' because I said that word wrong. And off he went, laughing—laughing, Owen! Do you think he's all right? What do *you* think?

OWEN. I'm sure he'll turn up. Maire.

MAIRE. He comes from a tiny wee place called Winfarthing. [*She suddenly drops on her hands and knees on the floor—where* OWEN *had his map a few minutes ago—and with her finger traces out an outline map.*] Come here till you see. Look. There's Winfarthing. And there's two other wee villages right beside it; one of them's called Barton Bendish—it's there; and the other's called Saxingham Nethergate—it's about there. And there's Little Walsing-ham—that's his mother's townland. Aren't they odd names? Sure they make no sense to me at all. And Winfarthing's near a big town called Norwich. And Norwich is in a county called Norfolk. And Norfolk is in the east of England. He drew a map for me on the wet strand and wrote the names on it. I have it all in my head now: Winfarthing—Barton Bendish—Saxingham Nethergate—Little Walsingham—Norwich—Norfolk. Strange sounds, aren't they? But nice sounds; like Jimmy Jack reciting his Homer. [*She gets to her feet and looks around; she is almost serene now. To* SARAH.] You were looking lovely last night, Sarah. Is that the dress you got from Boston? Green suits you. [*To* OWEN.] Some-thing very bad's happened to him, Owen. I know. He wouldn't go away without telling me. Where is he, Owen? You're his friend—where is he? [*Again she looks around the room; then sits on a stool.*] I didn't get a chance to do my geography last night. The master'll be angry with me. [*She rises again.*] I think I'll go home now. The wee ones have to be washed and put to bed and that black calf has to be fed . . . My hands are that rough; they're still blistered from the hay. I'm ashamed of them. I hope to God there's no hay to be saved in Brooklyn. [*She stops at the door.*] Did you hear? Nellie Ruadh's baby died in the middle of the night. I must go up to the wake. It didn't last long, did it?

[MAIRE *leaves. Silence. Then.*]

OWEN.   I don't think there'll be any class. Maybe you should : . .

[OWEN *begins picking up his texts.* DOALTY *goes to him.*]

DOALTY.   Is he long gone?—Manus.
OWEN.   Half an hour.
DOALTY.   Stupid bloody fool.
OWEN.   I told him that.
DOALTY.   Do they know he's gone?
OWEN.   Who?
DOALTY.   The army.
OWEN.   Not yet.
DOALTY.   They'll be after him like bloody beagles. Bloody, bloody fool, limping along the coast. They'll overtake him before night for Christ's sake.

[DOALTY *returns to the window.* LANCEY *enters—now the com-manding officer.*]

OWEN.   Any news? Any word?

[LANCEY *moves into the centre of the room, looking around as he does.*]

LANCEY.   I understood there was a class. Where are the others?
OWEN.   There was to be a class but my father—

LANCEY.   This will suffice. I will address them and it will be their responsibility to pass on what I have to say to every family in this section.

> [LANCEY *indicates to* OWEN *to translate.* OWEN *hesitates, trying to assess the change in* LANCEY's *manner and attitude.*]

I'm in a hurry, O'Donnell.

OWEN.   The captain has an announcement to make.

LANCEY.   Lieutenant Yolland is missing. We are searching for him. If we don't find him, or if we receive no information as to where he is to be found, I will pursue the following course of action. [*He indicates to* OWEN *to translate.*]

OWEN.   They are searching for George. If they don't find him—

LANCEY.   Commencing twenty-four hours from now we will shoot all livestock in Ballybeg.

> [OWEN *stares at* LANCEY.]

At once.

OWEN.   Beginning this time tomorrow they'll kill every animal in Baile Beag—unless they're told where George is.

LANCEY.   If that doesn't bear results, commencing forty-eight hours from now we will embark on a series of evictions and levelling of every abode in the following selected areas—

OWEN.   You're not—!

LANCEY.   Do your job. Translate.

OWEN.   If they still haven't found him in two days time they'll begin evicting and levelling every house starting with these townlands.

> [LANCEY *reads from his list.*]

LANCEY.   Swinefort.
OWEN.   Lis na Muc.
LANCEY.   Burnfoot.
OWEN.   Bun na hAbhann.
LANCEY.   Dromduff.
OWEN.   Druim Dubh.
LANCEY.   Whiteplains.
OWEN.   Machaire Ban.
LANCEY.   Kings Head.
OWEN.   Cnoc na Ri.
LANCEY.   If by then the lieutenant hasn't been found, we will proceed until a complete clearance is made of this entire section.
OWEN.   If Yolland hasn't been got by then, they will ravish the whole parish.
LANCEY.   I trust they know exactly what they've got to do. [*Pointing to* BRIDGET.] I know you. I know where you live. [*Pointing to* SARAH.] Who are you? Name!

[SARAH's *mouth opens and shuts, opens and shuts. Her face becomes contorted.*]

What's your name?

[*Again* SARAH *tries frantically.*]

OWEN.   Go on, Sarah. You can tell him.

[*But* SARAH *cannot. And she knows she cannot. She closes her mouth. Her head goes down.*]

OWEN.   Her name is Sarah Johnny Sally.
LANCEY.   Where does she live?
OWEN.   Bun na hAbhann.
LANCEY.   Where?
OWEN.   Burnfoot.
LANCEY.   I want to talk to your brother—is he here?
OWEN.   Not at the moment.
LANCEY.   Where is he?
OWEN.   He's at a wake.
LANCEY.   What wake?

[DOALTY, *who has been looking out the window all through* LANCEY's *announcements, now speaks—calmly, almost casually.*]

DOALTY.   Tell him his whole camp's on fire.
LANCEY.   What's your name? [*To* OWEN.] Who's that lout?
OWEN.   Doalty Dan Doalty.
LANCEY.   Where does he live?
OWEN.   Tulach Alainn.
LANCEY.   What do we call it?
OWEN.   Fair Hill. He says your whole camp is on fire.

[LANCEY *rushes to the window and looks out. Then he wheels on* DOALTY.]

LANCEY.   I'll remember you, Mr Doalty. [*To* OWEN.] You carry a big responsibility in all this. [*He goes off.*]
BRIDGET.   Mother of God, does he mean it, Owen?
OWEN.   Yes, he does.
BRIDGET.   We'll have to hide the beasts somewhere—our Seamus'll know where. Maybe at the back of Lis na nGradh—or in the caves at the far end of the Tra Bhan. Come on, Doalty! Come on! Don't be standing about there!

[DOALTY *does not move.* BRIDGET *runs to the door and stops suddenly. She sniffs the air. Panic.*]

The sweet smell! Smell it! It's the sweet smell! Jesus, it's the potato blight!
DOALTY.   It's the army tents burning, Bridget.

BRIDGET.   Is it? Are you sure? Is that what it is? God, I thought we were destroyed altogether. Come on! Come on!

[*She runs off.* OWEN *goes to* SARAH *who is preparing to leave.*]

OWEN.   How are you? Are you all right?

[SARAH *nods: Yes.*]

OWEN.   Don't worry. It will come back to you again.

[SARAH *shakes her head.*]

OWEN.   It will. You're upset now. He frightened you. That's all's wrong.

[*Again* SARAH *shakes her head, slowly, emphatically, and smiles at* OWEN. *Then she leaves.* OWEN *busies himself gathering his belongings.* DOALTY *leaves the window and goes to him.*]

DOALTY.   He'll do it, too.
OWEN.   Unless Yolland's found.
DOALTY.   Hah!
OWEN.   Then he'll certainly do it.
DOALTY.   When my grandfather was a boy they did the same thing. [*Simply, altogether without irony.*] And after all the trouble you went to, mapping the place and thinking up new names for it.

[OWEN *busies himself. Pause.* DOALTY *almost dreamily.*]

I've damned little to defend but he'll not put me out without a fight. And there'll be others who think the same as me.
OWEN.   That's a matter for you.
DOALTY.   If we'd all stick together. If we knew how to defend ourselves.
OWEN.   Against a trained army.
DOALTY.   The Donnelly twins know how.
OWEN.   If they could be found.
DOALTY.   If they could be found. [*He goes to the door.*] Give me a shout after you've finished with Lancey. I might know something then. [*He leaves.*]

[OWEN *picks up the Name-Book. He looks at it momentarily, then puts it on top of the pile he is carrying. It falls to the floor. He stoops to pick it up—hesitates—leaves it. He goes upstairs. As* OWEN *ascends,* HUGH *and* JIMMY JACK *enter. Both wet and drunk.* JIMMY *is very unsteady. He is trotting behind* HUGH, *trying to break in on* HUGH'S *declamation.* HUGH *is equally drunk but more experienced in drunkenness: there is a portion of his mind which retains its clarity.*]

HUGH.   There I was, appropriately dispositioned to proffer my condolences to the bereaved mother . . .
JIMMY.   Hugh—

HUGH.   . . . and about to enter the *domus lugubris*—Maire
Chatach?

JIMMY.   The wake house.

HUGH.   Indeed—when I experience a plucking at my elbow: Mister
George Alexander, Justice of the Peace. 'My tidings are infelici-
tous,' said he—Bridget? Too slow. Doalty?

JIMMY.   *Infelix*—unhappy.

HUGH.   Unhappy indeed. 'Master Bartley Timlin has been appointed to the new national school.' 'Timlin? Who is Timlin?' 'A
schoolmaster from Cork. And he will be a major asset to the
community: he is also a very skilled bacon-curer!'

JIMMY.   Hugh—

HUGH.   Ha-ha-ha-ha-ha! The Cork bacon-curer! *Barbarus hic ego
sum quia non intelligor ulli*—James?

JIMMY.   Ovid.

HUGH.   *Procede.*

JIMMY.   'I am a barbarian in this place because I am not understood by anyone.'

HUGH.   Indeed—[*Shouts.*] Manus! Tea! I will compose a satire on
Master Bartley Timlin, schoolmaster and bacon-curer. But it will
be too easy, won't it? [*Shouts.*] Strong tea! Black!

[*The only way* JIMMY *can get* HUGH's *attention is by standing
in front of him and holding his arms.*]

JIMMY.   Will you listen to me, Hugh!

HUGH.   James. [*Shouts.*] And a slice of soda bread.

JIMMY.   I'm going to get married.

HUGH.   Well!

JIMMY.   At Christmas.

HUGH.   Splendid.

JIMMY.   To Athene.

HUGH.   Who?

JIMMY.   Pallas Athene.

HUGH.   *Glaukopis Athene?*

JIMMY.   Flashing-eyed, Hugh, flashing-eyed! [*He attempts the gesture he has made before: standing to attention, the momentary
spasm, the salute, the face raised in pained ecstasy—but the body
does not respond efficiently this time. The gesture is grotesque.*]

HUGH.   The lady has assented?

JIMMY.   She asked *me*—I assented.

HUGH.   Ah. When was this?

JIMMY.   Last night.

HUGH.   What does her mother say?

JIMMY.   Metis from Hellespont? Decent people—good stock.

HUGH.   And her father?

JIMMY.   I'm meeting Zeus tomorrow. Hugh, will you be my best
man?

HUGH.   Honoured, James; profoundly honoured.

JIMMY.   You know what I'm looking for, Hugh, don't you? I mean to say—you know—I—I—I joke like the rest of them—you know?— [*Again he attempts the pathetic routine but abandons it instantly.*] You know yourself, Hugh—don't you?—you know all that. But what I'm really looking for, Hugh—what I really want—companionship, Hugh—at my time of life, companionship, company, someone to talk to. Away up in Beann na Gaoithe—you've no idea how lonely it is. Companionship—correct, Hugh? Correct?

HUGH.   Correct.
JIMMY.   And I always liked her, Hugh. Correct?
HUGH.   Correct, James.
JIMMY.   Someone to talk to.
HUGH.   Indeed.
JIMMY.   That's all, Hugh. The whole story. You know it all now, Hugh. You know it all.

[*As* JIMMY *says those last lines he is crying, shaking his head, trying to keep his balance, and holding a finger up to his lips in absurd gestures of secrecy and intimacy. Now he staggers away, tries to sit on a stool, misses it, slides to the floor, his feet in front of him, his back against the broken cart. Almost at once he is asleep.* HUGH *watches all of this. Then he produces his flask and is about to pour a drink when he sees the Name-Book on the floor. He picks it up and leafs through it, pronouncing the strange names as he does. Just as he begins,* OWEN *emerges and descends with two bowls of tea.*]

HUGH.   Ballybeg. Burnfoot. King's Head. Whiteplains. Fair Hill. Dunboy. Green Bank.

[OWEN *snatches the book from* HUGH.]

OWEN.   I'll take that. [*In apology.*] It's only a catalogue of names.
HUGH.   I know what it is.
OWEN.   A mistake—my mistake—nothing to do with us. I hope that's strong enough [*tea*]. [*He throws the book on the table and crosses over to* JIMMY.] Jimmy. Wake up, Jimmy. Wake up, man.
JIMMY.   What—what-what?
OWEN.   Here. Drink this. Then go on away home. There may be trouble. Do you hear me, Jimmy? There may be trouble.
HUGH [*indicating Name-Book*].   We must learn those new names.
OWEN [*searching around*].   Did you see a sack lying about?
HUGH.   We must learn where we live. We must learn to make them our own. We must make them our new home.

[OWEN *finds a sack and throws it across his shoulders.*]

OWEN.   I know where I live.
HUGH.   James thinks he knows, too. I look at James and three thoughts occur to me: A—that it is not the literal past, the 'facts' of history, that shape us, but images of the past embodied in language. James has ceased to make that discrimination.

OWEN.   Don't lecture me, Father.

HUGH.   B—we must never cease renewing those images; because once we do, we fossilize. Is there no soda bread?

OWEN.   And C, Father—one single, unalterable 'fact': if Yolland is not found, we are all going to be evicted. Lancey has issued the order.

HUGH.   Ah. *Edictum imperatoris.*[1]

OWEN.   You should change out of those wet clothes. I've got to go. I've got to see Doalty Dan Doalty.

HUGH.   What about?

OWEN.   I'll be back soon.

[*As* OWEN *exits.*]

HUGH.   Take care, Owen. To remember everything is a form of madness. [*He looks around the room, carefully, as if he were about to leave it forever. Then he looks at* JIMMY, *sleep again.*] The road to Sligo. A spring morning. 1798.[2] Going into battle. Do you remember, James? Two young gallants with pikes across their shoulders and the *Aeneid* in their pockets. Everything seemed to find definition that spring—a congruence, a miraculous matching of hope and past and present and possibility. Striding across the fresh, green land. The rhythms of perception heightened. The whole enterprise of consciousness accelerated. We were gods that morning, James; and I had recently married *my* goddess, Caitlin Dubh Nic Reactainn, may she rest in peace. And to leave her and my infant son in his cradle—that was heroic, too. By God, sir, we were magnificent. We marched as far as—where was it?—Glenties! All of twenty-three miles in one day. And it was there, in Phelan's pub, that we got homesick for Athens, just like Ulysses. The *desiderium nostrorum*—the need for our own. Our *pietas,*[3] James, was for older, quieter things. And that was the longest twenty-three miles back I ever made. [*Toasts* JIMMY.] My friend, confusion is not an ignoble condition.

[MAIRE *enters.*]

MAIRE.   I'm back again. I set out for somewhere but I couldn't remember where. So I came back here.

HUGH.   Yes, I will teach you English, Maire Chatach.

MAIRE.   Will you, Master? I must learn it. I need to learn it.

HUGH.   Indeed you may well be my only pupil. [*He goes towards the steps and begins to ascend.*]

MAIRE.   When can we start?

HUGH.   Not today. Tomorrow, perhaps. After the funeral. We'll begin tomorrow. [*Ascending.*] But don't expect too much. I will pro-

---

1. The decree of the commander.
2. A year of rebellious outbreaks leading to the landing of French supporters in August and quick British suppression of insurrection.
3. Piety.

vide you with the available words and the available grammar. But will that help you to interpret between privacies? I have no idea. But it's all we have. I have no idea at all. [*He is now at the top.*]

MAIRE.   Master, what does the English word 'always' mean?

HUGH.   *Semper—per omnia saecula.*[4] The Greeks called it *'aei'*. It's not a word I'd start with. It's a silly word, girl.

[*He sits.* JIMMY *is awake. He gets to his feet.* MAIRE *sees the Name-Book, picks it up, and sits with it on her knee.*]

MAIRE.   When he comes back, this is where he'll come to. He told me this is where he was happiest.

[JIMMY *sits beside* MAIRE.]

JIMMY.   Do you know the Greek word *endogamein?* It means to marry within the tribe. And the word *exogamein* means to marry outside the tribe. And you don't cross those borders casually— both sides get very angry. Now, the problem is this: Is Athene sufficiently mortal or am I sufficiently godlike for the marriage to be acceptable to her people and to my people? You think about that.

HUGH.   *Urbs antiqua fuit*—there was an ancient city which, 'tis said, Juno loved above all the lands. And it was the goddess's aim and cherished hope that here should be the capital of all nations—should the fates perchance allow that. Yet in truth she discovered that a race was springing from Trojan blood to overthrow some day these Tyrian towers—a people *late regem belloque superbum*—kings of broad realms and proud in war who would come forth for Lybia's downfall—such was—such was the course—such was the course ordained—ordained by fate . . . What the hell's wrong with me? Sure I know it backwards. I'll begin again. *Urbs antiqua fuit*—there was an ancient city which, 'tis said, Juno loved above all the lands.

[*Begin to bring down the lights.*]

And it was the goddess's aim and cherished hope that here should be the capital of nations—should the fates perchance allow that. Yet in truth she discovered that a race was springing from Trojan blood to overthrow some day these Tyrian towers—a people kings of broad realms and proud in war who would come forth for Lybia's downfall . . .

Black

---

4. Always—for all time.

CONOR McPHERSON

The Weir†

Characters

JACK, *fifties*.
BRENDAN, *thirties*.
JIM, *forties*.
FINBAR, *late forties*.
VALERIE, *thirties*.

The play is set in a rural part of Ireland, Northwest Leitrim or Sligo, Present day. Stage Setting: a small rural bar.

A counter; left with three bar taps. The spirits are not mounted, simply left on the shelf. There are three stools at the counter.

There is a fireplace, right. Near this is a low table with some small stools and a bigger, more comfortable chair, nearest the fire. There is another small table, front, with a stool or two.

On the wall, back, are some old black and white photographs, A ruined Abbey. People posing near a newly erected ESB weir.[1] A town in a cove with mountains around it.

An old television is mounted up in a corner, right. There is a small radio on a shelf behind the bar.

A door, right, is the main entrance to the bar. A door, back, leads to the toilets and a yard.

This bar is part of a house and the house is part of a farm.

The door, right, opens. JACK comes in. He wears a suit which looks a bit big for him, and a white shirt open at the collar. Over this is a dirty anorak:[2] He takes the anorak off and hangs it up. He wipes his boots aggressively on a mat.

---

† From *The Weir and Other Plays* by Conor McPherson. Copyright © 1999 by Conor McPherson. Published by Theatre Communications Group. Used by permission of Nick Hern Books Ltd.
1. Electricity Supply Board and a small dam that could be used to generate hydroelectric power.
2. Windbreaker.

He goes behind the counter. He selects a glass and pours himself a pint of stout. He puts it on the bar and turns to the till, which he opens with practised, if uncertain, ease. He puts the money in and takes the change.

As he does this, the door at back opens. BRENDAN *comes in. He wears a sweater, heavy cord pants and a pair of slip-on shoes. He carries a bucket with peat briquettes. He goes to the fire, barely acknowledging* JACK, *just his voice.*

BRENDAN.   Jack.
JACK.   Brendan.
BRENDAN. *[tending the fire.]*   That's some wind.
JACK *[topping up his pint].*   It is.
BRENDAN.   Must have been against you, was it?

   [JACK *comes out from behind the counter and stands looking at the fire.*]

JACK.   It was. It was against me till I came around the Knock. It was a bit of shelter then.

   [BRENDAN *also stands looking at the fire.*]

BRENDAN.   Yeah it's a funny one. It's coming from the north.
JACK.   Mm. Ah, it's mild enough though.
BRENDAN.   Ah yeah. It's balmy enough. *[Pause.]* It's balmy enough.

   [BRENDAN *goes in behind the counter.*]

JACK.   Were you in Carrick today?
BRENDAN.   I wasn't, no. I had the sisters over doing their rounds. Checking up on me.
JACK.   Checking their investments.
BRENDAN.   Oh yeah. Course, they don't have a fucking clue what they're looking for, d'you know? They're just vaguely . . . you know.
JACK.   Keeping the pressure on you.
BRENDAN.   This is it. *[Pause.]* At me to sell the top field.
JACK.   You don't use it much.
BRENDAN.   No. No I don't. Too much trouble. Driving a herd up. But I know they're looking at it, all they see is new cars for their hubbies, you know?
JACK.   Mm. You're not just trying to spite them? Get them vexed? Hah?
BRENDAN.   Not at all. I'm, just. It's a grand spot up there. Ah, I don't know. Just . . . *[Short pause.]*
JACK.   They over the whole day?
BRENDAN.   They got here about two. They'd gone for lunch in the Arms. Got their story straight. Ah they were gone and all about half four.
JACK.   They've no attachment to the place, no?

BRENDAN.   No they don't. They look around, and it's . . . 'Ah yeah . . .' you know? [*They laugh a little.*]

BRENDAN.   It's gas.

JACK.   Mm.

BRENDAN.   Were you in Carrick yourself?

JACK.   I was. I flew in about eleven, threw on a fast bet. Jimmy was there, we went for a quick one in the Pot.

BRENDAN.   How's Jimmy? And the ma?

JACK.   Ah. Jimmy. Be in tonight. He put me on to a nice one. We got her at eleven to four.

BRENDAN.   You're learning to listen, hah?

JACK.   Ah. Fuck that sure. I know, but I've been having the worst run of shit, you wouldn't believe. I was that desperate, I'd listen to anybody.

BRENDAN.   Go on out of that.

JACK.   Ah no. No no. Fair dues. I'll say it. He got us a right one. And it's good, you know. Break a streak like that.

BRENDAN.   You're a user.

JACK [*laughs*].   There's worse.

BRENDAN.   Yeah. There might be.

JACK.   But, ah, he was telling me. Did you know about Maura Nealon's house?

BRENDAN.   No.

JACK.   Well. Jim says he met Finbar Mack down in the Spar. Finally, either sold or's renting the, the thing, after how many years it's sat there?

BRENDAN.   Jays, four or five in anyway.

JACK.   Jim says five this month. And Finbar's going bananas with the great fella that he is. Patting himself on the back, goodo, and talking about the new resident. Who, he says, is a fine girl. Single. Down from Dublin and all this. And Finbar's nearly leaving the wife just to have a chance with this one. Only messing, like. But he's going to bring her in here tonight. This is the nearest place to old Maura's. Bring her in for a drink, introduce her to the natives.

BRENDAN.   The dirty bastard. I don't want him using in here for that sort of carry on. A married man like him.

JACK.   Ah he's only old shit. He wouldn't have the nerve. Sure, how far'd he get anyway? The fucking head on him. He's only having a little thrill. Bringing her around. And I'll tell you what it is as well. He's coming in here with her. And he's the one. He's the one that's 'with' her, in whatever fucking . . . sense we're talking about. He's bringing her in. And there's you and me, and the Jimmy fella, the muggins's, the single fellas. And he's the married fella. And he's going 'Look at this! There's obviously something the fuck wrong with yous. Yous are single and you couldn't get a woman near this place. And look at me. I'm hitched. I'm over and done with, and I'm having to beat them off.'

BRENDAN.   Yeah. That's the way cunts always go about their business. It's intrusive, it's bad manners, it's . . .

JACK.   Ah, it's a juvenile carry on. You know?

BRENDAN.   Mm.

JACK.   Let her come in herself.

BRENDAN.   Yeah. That'd be better. That'd make more sense, for fuck's sake.

JACK.   Leave her be . . . [*Short pause.*] Don't know if I'll stay actually.

BRENDAN.   Mm.

[*Pause.* JACK *drains his pint and brings his glass to the bar.*]

JACK.   Go on.

[BRENDAN *takes the glass and pours a fresh pint.*]

JACK.   Don't want to leave Jimmy in the lurch. You know? Trying to hold his own in the Finbar Mack world of big business.

[*They laugh a little.*]

BRENDAN.   Fucking . . . Jimmy talking all that crack with Finbar.

JACK.   But that's the thing though. The Jimmy fella's got more going on up here [*Head.*] than popular opinion would give him credit for.

BRENDAN.   Sure, don't we know too well, for God's sake?

JACK.   I know.

BRENDAN.   We know only too well.

[JACK *counts change out on the bar.*]

JACK.   Would you give us ten Silk Cut please, Brendan?

BRENDAN.   Red?

JACK.   Please.

[BRENDAN *hands over the cigarettes and finishes pulling the pint.*]

JACK.   Good man.

[BRENDAN *counts the money off the bar.* JACK *pauses before drinking.*]

JACK.   Are we right?

BRENDAN.   Close enough. Cheers.

JACK.   Good luck.

[JACK *takes a long drink. Pause.*]

JACK.   I know I do be at you. I'll keep at you though.

BRENDAN.   About what?

JACK.   Don't be messing. Come on.

BRENDAN.   Ah.

JACK.   A young fella like you. And this place a right going concern.

BRENDAN.   Ah. The odd time. You know, the odd time I'd think about it.

JACK.   You should though.

BRENDAN. Well then, so should you.

JACK. Would you go on? An auld fella like me!

BRENDAN. Would you listen to him?

JACK. Ah, sure what would I want with giving up my freedom?

BRENDAN. Well then me as well!

[*Pause.*]

JACK. Tch. Maybe. Maybe there's something to be said for the old independence.

BRENDAN. Ah there is.

[*Pause.*]

JACK. A lot to be said for it.

BRENDAN. Mm. [*Pause.*] Mm.

JACK. Cheers!

BRENDAN. Good luck.

[JACK *takes a long drink. The main door opens and* JIMMY *enters. He takes off an anorak to reveal a festive looking cardigan.* JACK *pretends not to notice him.*]

JACK [*winks*]. Oh yes, Brendan, the luck is changing. I got me and the Jimmy fella onto a nice one today. That fella would want to listen to me a little more often, I tell you.

JIM. I'm going to have to start charging you for tips, am I?

JACK. Ah James! What'll you have?

JIM. Teach you some manners. Teach him some manners Brendan, ha? Small one please Jack.

BRENDAN. Small one.

JACK. Sure it'd take more than money to put manners on me, ha? Brendan.

BRENDAN. It'd take a bomb under you.

JACK. Now you said it. Bomb is right. That wind still up, Jim?

JIM. Oh it is, yeah. Warm enough though.

JACK. We were just saying.

BRENDAN. For a Northerly.

JIM. Oh that's from the west now.

BRENDAN. Is it?

JIM. Oh yeah that's a Westerly.

JACK. Must've shifted.

JIM. Mm.

[*Pause.* JIM *comes to the bar.*]

JIM. Thanking you.

JACK. Good luck.

JIM. Good luck.

BRENDAN. Good luck.

[JACK *counts change out on the bar.*]

JACK. Are we right?

[BRENDAN *counts and pushes a coin back towards* JACK.]

BRENDAN [*taking rest*].   Now we are. Sure it's hard enough to come by without giving it away.

JACK.   This is it. Oh. [*To* JIM.] Are you doing anything tomorrow?

JIM.   What time?

JACK.   I have to get out to Conor Boland. His tractor is packed up. And I have Father Donal's jalopy in since Tuesday. Said I'd change the oil. Haven't done it yet. Would you come in and do it so I can go over to Boland's?

JIM.   It'd have to be early. I'm dropping the mother out to Sligo.

JACK.   Well, whatever. Is that all right?

JIM.   Ah, it should be yeah. Pint?

JACK.   Not for the moment. You go on.

JIM.   Pint please Brendan.

BRENDAN.   How's the mammy today?

JIM.   Ah you know?

JACK.   Tch. I have to get down and see her. I keep saying it.

JIM.   Well whenever, whenever you want.

BRENDAN.   Do you think you'll do anything?

JIM.   About?

BRENDAN.   About up there on your own and all that?

JIM.   Ah. Sure where would I go? And I was talking to Finbar Mack. Be lucky to get twenty thousand for the place. Sure where would you be going with that? [*Short pause.*] You know!

JACK.   With the acre?

JIM.   Ah yeah, the whole . . . the whole thing.

JACK.   Ah you're grand with the few little jobs around here.

JIM.   Ah.

JACK.   You'll be cosy enough.

[*Pause.*]

BRENDAN.   Jack was telling me about Finbar. And the new eh . . .

JIM.   Mmm, yeah, I was telling him earlier.

JACK.   I was telling him.

JIM.   I've seen her since.

BRENDAN.   Oh yeah?

JIM.   Yeah, they were in Finbar's car going up the Head.

[JACK *and* BRENDAN *exchange a look.*]

BRENDAN.   Fucking hell.

JACK.   Like a courting couple or something.

JIM.   He's showing her the area.

JACK.   Jesus. 'The area.' He's a terrible fucking thick.

JIM.   Ah, he has them all jabbering down in Carrick.

JACK.   Yeah. I wish he wasn't bringing her in here. You know?

BRENDAN.   Sure he hasn't been in here since Freddie Mack drowned.

JACK.   What the fuck, is he doing? You know?

JIM. Ah. She's new. This is the only place near to her.

JACK. She can . . . [*Nodding.*] find her own way surely, Jim, come on.

BRENDAN. Well it's, you know. If it's courtesy, which is one thing and a business . . . act or whatever, you know, you have to say, well . . . you know, okay. But if it's all messy, I'm trapped in here behind this fucking thing. And you wish he'd stop acting the mess. I have to respect whatever, they're . . .

JACK. Well this is it, we're here.

JIM. It's probably not really anything.

[*Short pause.*]

JACK. What age would she be, about, Jim?

JIM. Em, I only saw her for a sec. I'd say, [*Beat.*] like they were in the car and all, I'd say about thirties. Very nice looking.

[*Pause.*]

JACK. Dublin woman.

JIM. Dublin.

[*Short pause.*]

BRENDAN. She's no one in the area, no?

JIM. No she's . . . coming down, you know?

JACK. Mm. [*Pause.*] Yeah.

JIM. Good luck. [*Drinks.*]

JACK. Cheers. [*Drinks.*]

BRENDAN. Good luck, boys.

JACK. Another week or two now, You'll be seeing the first of the Germans.

BRENDAN. Mm. Stretch in the evening, yeah.

JACK. You wouldn't ever think of clearing one of the fields for a few caravans.[3]

BRENDAN. Ah.

JACK. The top field.

BRENDAN. Ah there wouldn't be a lot of shelter up there. There'd be a wind up there that'd cut you.

JIM. D'you know what you could do? The herd'd be grand up there, and you could, you know, down here.

BRENDAN. Ah. [*Short pause.*] They do be around anyway. You know yourself.

JIM. Ah, they do.

JACK. You're not chasing the extra revenue.

BRENDAN. Or the work!

JIM. They do be around right enough.

BRENDAN. I'll leave the campsites to Finbar, ha? He'll sort them out.

JACK. Ah, Finbar's in need of the few shekels.

---

3. Vacation trailers.

[*They laugh.*]

BRENDAN.   Ah, he's in dire need of the few bob, the poor fella, that's right, that's right.

JACK.   Mm.

[*Pause.*]

BRENDAN.   Yeah. If you had all the . . . families out there. On their holliers. And all the kids and all. You'd feel the evenings turning. When they'd be leaving. And whatever about how quiet it is now. It'd be fucking shocking quiet then. [*Short pause.*] You know?

[*Pause.*]

JACK.   Mm.

JIM.   D'you want a small one, Jack?

JACK.   Go on.

JIM.   Two small ones please Brendan.

BRENDAN.   The small fellas.

[BRENDAN *works.*]

JACK.   Are you having one yourself?

BRENDAN.   I'm debating whether to have one.

JACK.   Ah have one, and don't be acting the mess.

BRENDAN.   Go on then.

[*He pours himself a glass of whiskey.*]

JACK.   Good man. [*Short pause.*] A few shekels, ha? [*They smile.*] Mm.

[JACK *takes out his cigarettes.*]

JACK.   Jim?

JIM.   Oh cheers Jack.

[JIM *takes one.*]

JACK.   Brendan?

BRENDAN.   Fags and all, ha?

JACK.   Go on, they're good for you.

BRENDAN.   [*Taking one.*] Go on.

[*They light up from a match which* JACK *strikes. They puff contentedly for a moment.*]

JIM [*lifting glass*].   Keep the chill out.

JACK.   This is it. Cheers.

BRENDAN.   Cheers men.

JIM.   Good luck.

[*They drink.*]

JACK.   Now.

JIM.   D'yous hear a car?

[*Pause.*]

BRENDAN.   No.
JIM.   That's Finbar's car.

[*Pause.*]

JIM.   He's parked.
JACK.   I didn't see the lights.
JIM.   He came around the Knock.

[*From off, they hear* FINBAR's *voice.*]

FINBAR [*off*].   Ah yeah, sure half the townland used to nearly live in here.
JACK.   There we are now.

[*The door opens and* FINBAR *brings* VALERIE *in.*]

FINBAR.   That's it now.

[FINBAR *wears a light cream coloured suit and an open collar.* VALERIE *wears jeans and a sweater.*]

FINBAR.   Men. This is Valerie. She's just moved into Maura Nealon's old house.
JACK.   Hello, how are you?

[JACK *shakes her hand.*]

VALERIE.   Hello.
FINBAR.   This is Jack Mullen. He has a little garage up around the Knock.
VALERIE.   How are you?

[JACK *nods politely.*]

JACK.   Now.
FINBAR.   This is Jim Curran. Does a bit of work with Jack.

[VALERIE *and* JIM *shake hands.*]

VALERIE.   Pleased to meet you.
JIM.   Pleased to meet you.
FINBAR.   And this is Brendan. Brendan Byrne.
VALERIE.   Hello.

[*They shake hands.*]

BRENDAN.   How are you?
FINBAR.   This is his bar. And all the land I showed you. All back down the hill. That's all his farm.
VALERIE.   Oh right. It's all lovely here.
BRENDAN.   Oh yeah. It's a grand spot all along . . . for going for a walk or that, all down the cliffs.
FINBAR.   Oh it's lovely all down here. What'll you have?
BRENDAN.   Oh, I'll get this, Finbar. No. What, what do you want?

FINBAR. Oh now, ha ha. Eh, I'll have a pint, then, what? Says you,
     if it's going, ha?
BRENDAN. Pint. Valerie?
VALERIE. Em. Could I have . . . Do you have . . . em, a glass of
     white wine?

          [*Pause.*]

BRENDAN [*going*]. Yeah. I'm just going to run in the house.
VALERIE. Oh no. Don't. Don't put yourself to any trouble.
BRENDAN. No. No it's no trouble. I have a bottle.

          [*He goes.*]

FINBAR. He probably has a bottle of the old vino, from feckin . . .
     Christmas, what?
JACK. It's not too often the . . . the . . . wine does be flowing in
     here.
VALERIE. I'm all embarrassed now.
FINBAR. Don't be silly. Sit up there now, and don't mind us. Don't
     mind these country fellas.
JACK. Jays. You're not long out of it yourself, says the man, ha?
FINBAR [*winks*]. They're only jealous Valerie because I went to the
     town to seek my fortune. And they all stayed out here on the bog
     picking their holes.
JACK. Janey, now ha? You didn't have very hard to seek. Just a
     quick look in big Finbar's will, I think is more like it.
FINBAR. Big Finbar's will! That's shrewd investment, boy. That's
     an eye for the gap.
JACK. Yeah, he probably fleeced you on Maura Nealon's house,
     did he?
VALERIE. I have to say I don't think so.
FINBAR. Good girl.
VALERIE. But it's very reasonable all around here, isn't it?
FINBAR. Oh it is, yeah. You know . . .

          [*Short pause.*]

JACK. Is there much doing up in it?
FINBAR. Ah, hardly any.
VALERIE. There's one or two floorboards. A bit of paint.
JACK [*indicating* JIM]. Well, there's your man. If you're looking for
     a good pair of hands.
VALERIE. Is that right?
JIM. I'll have a look for you, if you like. I know that house.
FINBAR. Don't be charging her through the nose now.
JIM. Ah ha, now.

          [BRENDAN *returns with a bottle of wine.*]

FINBAR. You'd want to be giving her a neighbourly . . . rate, now, is
     the thing, ha?
JIM. Oh yeah.

JACK.   Would you listen to him? 'Neighbourly rates'. Wasn't by giving neighbourly rates you bought half the fucking town.

FINBAR.   Half the town! [*To* VALERIE, *winking.*] I bought the whole town. Eye for the gap, you see.

JACK.   Eye for your gap is right.

FINBAR [*To* BRENDAN].   How long has that been in there? Lying in some drawer . . .

BRENDAN [*corkscrewing the bottle*].   Ah, it was a . . . present or some . . . [*Looks at label.*] 1990. Now. Vintage, ha? [*They laugh.*] I hope it's all right now.

VALERIE.   It's grand. I won't know the difference.

[*They watch* BRENDAN *open the bottle. He pours a tumbler full and holds it up to the light and sniffs it.*]

BRENDAN.   I think it's all right.

FINBAR.   Ah, would you give the woman the feckin thing. The tongue's hanging out of her.

[*Again they watch as* VALERIE *takes the glass.*]

VALERIE.   Thanks Brendan.

[*She drinks.*]

VALERIE.   That's gorgeous. I'm not joking now. That's lovely.

FINBAR.   Good.

BRENDAN.   I'm putting it in the fridge for you Valerie.

[*He does.*]

FINBAR.   Good man.

[*Pause.* FINBAR *nods at* VALERIE, *a reassuring 'hello'.*]

[*To* JACK *and* JIM.] How d'yous do today, boys?

JACK.   Are you codding me? With this fella? Eleven to four we got her at, came down to six to four.

FINBAR.   Sheer Delight was it?

JACK.   Yeah. Kenny down in the shop, the knacker. Adjusting everything how this fella's betting.

JIM [*indicating* JACK].   This fella hardly listens to me.

JACK.   Ah now.

FINBAR.   He's too proud, Jimmy. Too proud to admit when he needs a tip off you.

JACK [*emphatically*].   I . . . have . . . my policy on this. And I have my principle. I am the first one to say it about this fella. See, usually, Valerie, usually, not all the time, Jim's not too far off the mark.

FINBAR.   'Too far off the mark' [*To* VALERIE.] He's bang on the nail!

[BRENDAN *places a pint on the bar.*]

FINBAR.   Thanks Brendan.

[*He puts his hand in his pocket,* BRENDAN *waves him away.*]

JACK. Not every time.

FINBAR. Thanks, thanks a million. [*To* VALERIE.] He is.

JACK. Bang on the nail is one thing, from judgement . . . and . . .
But, and Jimmy knows I don't mean anything by this, and I know
because we've spoken about this before. He has a scientific approach. He studies the form. And, no offence, he has a bit of
time to be doing that. He studies it Valerie, and fair play to him,
right? Do you bet on horses?

VALERIE. No.

FINBAR. Good girl.

JACK. Well he, how much, Jim, would you make in a month? On
the horses.

JIM. Ah it evens out Jack. Like I'm not eh . . . I don't . . .

JACK. How much was it you got that time? When Cheltenham
was on that time.

JIM. Two hundred and twenty.

JACK. Two hundred and twenty pounds, Valerie, in like three days,
now. Right?

JIM. Yeah but . . .

JACK. Yeah, I know, that'd be a bigger win. But he was planning
for Cheltenham for weeks, Valerie, and . . . tinkering with his figures and his . . . you know. He'd be in here with the paper up on
the counter there. Brendan? Before Cheltenham?

BRENDAN. Oh yeah.

JACK. Right? Now, but I'm more: 'Ah, sure, I'll have an old bet,
like.' Do you know that way? And that's what I do, and to tell you
the truth I don't be too bothered. It's a bit of fun and that's what
it should be. And so . . . I'm not going to listen to 'Do this and do
that, and you'll be right.' Just to get a few bob. There's no fun in
that. And the principle of it, you know?

FINBAR. Ah, the principle of the thing is to win a few quid and
don't be giving out.

JACK. Who's giving out? I'm not giving out. All I'm just saying is
that the way I go at it, the principle's not the science. It's the
luck, it's the something that's not the facts and figures of it.

FINBAR. Jaysus. And do you and Kenny get down on your knees
and lash a few quick Hail Marys out before he stamps your
docket or something?

JACK. Ah it's not like that. I'm not talking about that. For fuck's
sake.

FINBAR. Anyway, what the hell are you talking about? You took
Jimmy's tip today, and you won, so what the hell are you talking
about? [*To others.*] Ha?

JACK. Ah yeah but . . . now listen because . . .

[*The others are laughing and going 'ah' as though* FINBAR *has
caught* JACK *out.*]

I'll tell yous. If you won't listen. Right? I don't have a system. And I do. I do lose a few bob every now and then. Right? So I take a little tip from Jim. And then that'll finance having a few old bets for the next few weeks. [*They laugh.*] And I've been known to have one or two wins myself, as well yous know and don't forget. I have one or two.

BRENDAN.   You do not. Go on out of that you chancer.

JACK.   I do.

FINBAR.   I'd say the last win you had was fucking Red Rum or someone.

JACK [*aside to* VALERIE].   We do be only messing like this.

FINBAR.   What would anyone like? Jim?

JIM.   Eh, small one, then, thanks Finbar.

FINBAR.   Jack? Small one? Pint?

JACK.   I'll have a small one, go on.

FINBAR.   Good man. Valerie?

VALERIE.   Oh no, I'm okay for the moment, thanks.

FINBAR.   Are you sure? Top that up?

VALERIE.   No I'm fine, honestly.

FINBAR.   You're sure now?

VALERIE.   No really, I'm fine.

FINBAR [*hands up*].   Fair enough. We won't force you. Give us . . . eh three small ones, Brendan. Good man. Here, are you having one?

[BRENDAN *is pouring three glasses of whiskey.*]

BRENDAN.   I'm debating whether to have one.

JACK.   Ah he'll have one, go on Brendan. Who knows when the hell you'll see another drink off the Finbar fella, hah? Come on! Quick! He's all annoyed you're having one.

FINBAR [*to* VALERIE].   Would you listen to him?

JACK.   That fella'd peel a banana in his pocket.

JIM.   Is that what that is?

[*They laugh.*]

FINBAR.   First time I've been in here in ages, bringing nice company in and everything, getting this. Oh you'd have to watch the Jimmy fella. There's more going on there than he lets on. 'Is that what that is?'

[BRENDAN *places the drinks on the bar.*]

And look at this! Me buying the drinks and everything! Ah it's not right. What do you think Valerie?

VALERIE.   Oh, it's terrible.

FINBAR.   Oh, it's desperate.

[*He hands* BRENDAN *a twenty pound note.*]

There you go, Brendan. I wouldn't say you see too many twenties in here. With the boys, wouldn't be too often, I'd say. Cheers boys.

JACK.   Cheers.

JIM.   Good luck.

BRENDAN.   Good luck now.

VALERIE.   Cheers.

JACK.   How did you put up with this fella showing you around?

VALERIE.   Ah, he was a bit quieter today.

JACK.   Well you're seeing the real him now. And I bet you prefer the other one. We've never seen it. The quiet Finbar. This one comes out at night. You see.

VALERIE.   Oh, well I was getting the history of the place and everything today.

JACK.   He was probably making it up on the spot. Was he?

FINBAR.   Yeah. I was, that's right Jack. That's why all them photographs are fake, I had them done years ago just to fool Valerie tonight.

VALERIE [*going to the photographs*].   That's all around here, is it?

FINBAR [*going to the photographs*].   Yeah. That's the weir. When was that taken, Brendan?

BRENDAN.   Eh. That's 1951.

FINBAR.   1951. That's your father there.

BRENDAN.   Yeah. I think your father's in it too.

FINBAR.   Oh he is! Valerie look at this. That's Big Finbar. And that's Brendan's father, Paddy Byrne. This is when the ESB opened the weir.

VALERIE [*to* FINBAR].   You look like your father. [*To* BRENDAN.] You don't.

FINBAR.   He's like his mother. He's like the Mangans. Now . . . Who would you say that is there? In the shorts.

VALERIE.   Is it you?

FINBAR.   Would you go on! The big fucking head on that yoke! Excuse the language. That's Jack.

VALERIE.   Oh my God! How old were you there, Jack?

JACK.   Em. Oh I was about seven.

VALERIE.   I wouldn't have said that was you.

FINBAR.   You must be joking, you'd spot that big mutton head anywhere. The photographer nearly had to ask him to go home, there wasn't going to be room in the picture. Isn't that right, Jack?

JACK.   That's right and your dad nearly climbing into the camera there.

FINBAR.   He was a pillar of the community, Valerie. No one had anything against him. Except headers like your man there. [*Indicating* JACK.]

JACK.   That's right Finbar. And I'm just going in here to do something up against the pillar of the community now.

[JACK *goes out the door at back.*]

FINBAR.   Jays, he's a desperate fella, that one.

VALERIE.   Where was this taken?

BRENDAN. That's the view of Carrick from our top field up there.

VALERIE. It's an amazing view.

FINBAR. Oh I'd say that's probably one of the best views all around here, wouldn't it be?

BRENDAN. Oh yeah I'd say so.

JIM. Oh yeah it would be, yeah.

FINBAR. You get all the Germans trekking up here in the summer, Valerie. Up from the campsite.

VALERIE. Right.

FINBAR. They do all come up—this'd be the scenic part of all around here you know. Em. There's what's . . .? There was stories all, the fairies be up there in that field. Isn't there a fort up there?

BRENDAN. There's a kind of a one.

VALERIE. A fairy fort?

FINBAR. The Germans do love all this.

BRENDAN. Well there's a . . . ring of trees, you know.

FINBAR. What's the story about the fairy road that . . . Who used to tell it?

BRENDAN. Ah, Jack'd tell you all them stories.

FINBAR. There's all this around here, Valerie, the area's steeped in old folklore, and that, you know.

BRENDAN. Jack'd know . . . the what the, you'd know a few, Jim.

JIM. Ah Jack'd tell you better than me.

FINBAR [*pointing to another photograph*]. That's the Abbey now.

VALERIE. Oh yeah.

FINBAR. You can see more of it there now. What was there, Brendan? When was that?

BRENDAN. Oh, back in oh fifteen something there was a synod of bishops all came and met there, for . . . like . . . eh.

JIM. This townland used to be quite important back a few hundred years ago, Valerie. This was like the capital of the, the country, it would have been.

VALERIE. Right.

[JACK *comes back in.*]

FINBAR. Oh it's a very interesting place all, eh, Jack we were just saying about the, what was the story with the fairy road?

JACK. The fairy road? I go into the toilet for two minutes, I come out and you're talking about fairies. [*They laugh.*]

FINBAR. Ah, I was telling Valerie about the fort and everything. What was the story with the fairy road? Where was it?

[*Short pause.*]

JACK. Are you really interested? All the babies.

FINBAR. Ah it's a bit of fun, tell her, where was it?

JACK [*to* FINBAR]. You're going to regret me saying this now, 'cause you know whose house it was?

FINBAR. Where?

JACK. It was Maura Nealon's house.

324 CONOR McPHERSON

FINBAR [*self-chastising, remembering*]. Oh . . . Jesus.

[*They laugh.*]

JACK. You see? That's as much cop as you have now.

FINBAR. I fucking forgot it was Maura.

JACK. These are only old stories, Valerie.

VALERIE. No. I'd like to hear it.

JACK. It's only an old cod like.

FINBAR. You're not going to be scaring the woman.

JACK. Ah it's not scary.

VALERIE. I'm interested in it.

FINBAR. You hear all old shit around here, it doesn't mean anything.

BRENDAN. This is a good little story.

JACK. It's only short. It's just. Maura . . . Nealon used come in here in the evening, sit over there at the fire. How old was she, Jim? When she died?

JIM. Oh Jays, she would have been nearly ninety.

JACK. But she was a grand, you know, spritely kind of a woman 'til the end. And she had all her . . . She was on the ball, like, you know? And she swore that this happened. When she was only a girl. She lived in that house all her life. And she had older brothers and sisters. She was the youngest. And her mother eh . . .

JIM. Bridie.

JACK. Bridie. She was a well known woman in the area. A widow woman. She was a bit of a character. Bit of a practical joker and that you know? And Maura would say that when she was young she was, Bridie was, always doing things on the older kids, hiding their . . . clothes and this, you know. And she'd tell them old fibs about what a certain, prospective boyfriend or girlfriend had said about them out on the road and this about coming courting or that. And she was always shouting from upstairs or this 'There's someone at the door.' She was always saying there's someone at the back door or there's someone coming up the path. You know. This. And there'd never be anyone there. And people got used to her. That she liked her joke.

And Maura used to say that one Saturday evening back in about 1910 or 1911, the older ones were getting ready to go out for a dance or whatever was happening. And the mother, Bridie, came down the stairs and said 'Did no one get the door?'

And they were all 'Oh here we go,' you know? And Bridie came down and *opened* the door, and there was nobody there. And she didn't say anything. And she wasn't making a big thing out of it, you know? And Maura said, she was only young, but she knew there was something wrong. She wasn't cracking the jokes. And later on when the others were all out, it was just her and her mother sitting at the fire, And her mother was very quiet. Normally she'd send Maura up to bed, early enough like. But Maura

said she remembered this night because Bridie didn't send her
up. She wanted someone with her, you see. And in these days,
Valerie, as you know, there was no electricity out here. And
there's no dark like a Winter night in the country. And there was
a wind like this one tonight howling and whistling in off the sea.
You hear it under the door and it's like someone singing. Singing
in under the door at you. It was this type of night now.

Am I setting the scene for you?

[*They laugh.*]

Finbar's looking a bit edgy. You want to finish that small one I
think.

FINBAR.   Don't mind my small one. You're making very heavy
weather of this yarn Jack.

JACK.   Ah now, you have to enjoy it. You have to relish the details
of something like this, ha?

[*They laugh.*]

So there they were, sitting there and Bridie was staring into the
fire, a bit quiet. And smiling now and again at Maura, but Maura
said she could see a bit of wet in her eyes. And then there was a
soft knocking at the door. Someone. At the front door. And Bridie
never moved. And Maura said 'Will I get the door, mammy?' And
Bridie said 'No, sure, it's only someone playing a joke on us, don't
mind them.' So they sat there, and there was no more knocking
for a while. And em, in those days, there was no kitchen, where
the extension is, Valerie, that was the back door and only a little
latch on it, you know? And that's where the next knocking was.
Very soft, Maura said, and very low down the door. Not like
where you'd expect a grown man or a woman would be knocking,
up here, you know? And again Bridie was saying, ah, it's only
someone having a joke, they'll go away. And then it was at the
window. Maura couldn't see anything out in the night. And her
mother wouldn't let her go over. And then it stopped. But when it
was late and the fire went down, Bridie wouldn't get up to get
more turf for the fire. Because it was out in the shed. So they just
sat there until the others came back, well after midnight.

VALERIE.   What was it?

JACK.   Well Maura said her mother never told the others, and one
day when it was only the two of them there, a priest came and
blessed the doors and the windows. And then there was no more
knocking. And it was only years later that Maura heard from one
of the older people in the area that the house had been built on
what they call a fairy road. Like it wasn't a road, but it was a . . .

JIM.   It was like a row of things.

JACK.   Yeah, like a . . . From the fort up in Brendan's top field
there, then the old well, and the abbey further down, and into
the cove where the little pebbly beach is, there. And the . . . leg-

end would be that the fairies would come down that way to bathe, you see. And Maura Nealon's house was built on what you'd call . . . that . . . 'road'.

VALERIE. And they wanted to come through?

JACK. Well, that'd be the idea. But Maura never heard the knocking again except on one time in the fifties when the weir was going up. There was a bit of knocking then she said. And a fierce load of dead birds all in the hedge and this, but that was it. That's the story.

FINBAR. You're not bothered by that, are you, Valerie? 'Cause it's only old cod, you know? You hear these, all around, up and down the country.

VALERIE. I think there's probably *something* in them. No I do.

JACK. Ah there might be alright. But . . . it doesn't hurt. A bit of an old story like. But I'll tell what, it'd give a thirst, like. You know? What'll yous have?

[*They laugh.*]

Valerie, top that up.

VALERIE. Em . . .

JACK. Go on.

FINBAR. Ah she will. Brendan.

[BRENDAN *puts a clean tumbler on the bar.*]

VALERIE. This glass is fine.

FINBAR. Oh, country ways! Good girl.

[*They laugh.* BRENDAN *pours wine*]

JACK. Finbar. Pint?

FINBAR. Ah. Pint. Why not says you, ha?

JACK. Jim?

JIM. Ah.

JACK. Three pints please, Brendan.

BRENDAN. Three pints.

[*Pause.* BRENDAN *works.*]

FINBAR. Yep. Oh yeah.

JACK. Are you debating whether to have one yourself?

BRENDAN. I'm debating.

FINBAR. Who's winning?

BRENDAN. Ah, it's a draw. I'm going to have a glass.

FINBAR. Good man, have two, ha?

[*They laugh.* JACK *produces his cigarettes.*]

JACK. Valerie?

VALERIE. Eh, I will, thanks.

FINBAR [*pleasantly surprised*]. Oh! Good girl.

JACK. Finbar?

FINBAR.   No I won't, thanks Jack. Haven't had one of them fellas now, eighteen years this November.

JACK.   Eighteen years, ha?

[JACK *offers the pack to* BRENDAN *and* JIM *who both take one*.]

FINBAR.   Eighteen years. Not since I made the move. [*To* VALERIE.] Down to Carrick.

JACK [*lighting the cigarettes*].   Jays, you don't look any better for it, ha?

[*They laugh*.]

FINBAR.   Oh yeah? We'll see who'd look better after a round or two of the fisty footwork ha? And you with the lungs hanging out your back.

JACK.   Jaysus. An auldfella like me. Ten or more years between us and you wanting to give me a few digs. Business . . . killer instinct, is it?

FINBAR.   That's an eye for the gap. [*Winks at* VALERIE.] Exploit the weakness.

JACK.   'The weakness'? Sure, don't you have a grand little spooky story, about how brave you are.

FINBAR.   Ah no . . .

JACK.   Come on.

FINBAR.   Ah that was only the . . . Walsh young one having us all on. It was only a cod, sure.

JIM.   She's in America now. Niamh Walsh.

BRENDAN.   It was Niamh that time, yeah?

FINBAR.   Ah she was a header. Looking for attention.

VALERIE.   What happened?

JACK.   This was the brave fella.

FINBAR.   Ah, stop. It was nothing.

JACK.   This was a family lived up beside Big Finbar's place. The Walshes.

FINBAR.   Ah, they were only blow-ins, he was a guard.

VALERIE.   Blow-ins like me?

FINBAR.   Ah no. You know what I mean.

JACK.   Jays, you'll be losing business with them kind of remarks, ha? Valerie will agree with me there now.

[*They laugh*.]

FINBAR.   Ah she knows what I mean. Valerie's very welcome. She knows that, don't you?

JACK.   Ah leave her alone, you're embarrassing everybody now. Jaysus. [*They laugh*.] Tell her the story.

FINBAR.   Ah Janey. Sure you have her in a haunted house already! She won't be able to sleep.

VALERIE.   No I'd like to hear it.

FINBAR.   It's not even a real one.

JACK.   Ah, she wants to hear one, don't be moaning and tell her, come on.

FINBAR.   Tch. Just a crowd of headbangers[4] is all it was. There was a house out near where we were on the other side of the Knock there. It would have been the nearest place to us, Valerie, about a quarter mile down the road. And the old lad Finnerty lived on his own down there, and his family got him into a nursing home out by them down in Westport. And the people who moved in were the Walshes, your man was a sergeant in the guards, stationed in Carrick. And, like, he was fifty-odd and still only a sergeant, so, like he was no Sherlock Holmes. You know?

[*They laugh.*]

He wasn't 'Walsh of the yard' or anything like that. And they moved in. He had three daughters who were teenagers, and he had a youngfella who was married back near Longford there. So the . . . daughters were with him and the missus. And I knew them a little bit because that was the year Big Finbar died, God rest him, and they arrived about the time of the funeral so . . . you know, I met them, then. And I was living on my own because me and Big Finbar were the only two in it at the time. So I was the bachelor boy, and a gaggle of young ones after moving in next door, yo ho! You know?

[*They laugh.*]

And around that time I would have been wondering what to do, Valerie, do you know? Whether to sell it on or farm it or, you know. I was twenty-two, twenty-three, you know?

And it was, it would have been about eleven or twelve o'clock this night and there was a knock at the door and it was Mrs. Walsh. And she was all upset and asking me if I could come in, she didn't know what to do. The husband was at work out on a call, and she didn't know anyone in the area, and there was a bit of trouble. So, 'What kind of trouble?' I says. And she says she was after getting a phone call from the young one, Niamh and she was after doing the Luigi board, or what do you call it?

VALERIE.   Ouija board.

FINBAR.   Ouija board.

JACK.   'Luigi board!' She was down there in the chipper in Carrick, was she, Finbar?

FINBAR.   Ah fuck off. I meant the Ouija board. You know what I meant. She was after being down in . . .

JACK.   'The Luigi board.'

FINBAR.   She was after, come on now, she was after being down in a friend of hers house or this. And they were after doing the . . . Ouija board. And she phoned her mother to come and collect

---

4. Devotees of heavy-metal rock music.

her. They *said* they were after getting a spirit or this, you know, and she was scared, saying it was after her. And I just obviously thought, this was a load of bollocks, you know. If you'll . . . excuse the language Valerie, but here was the mother saying she'd gone and picked her up. I mean, like sorry, but I think it was all a bit mad. But on the way back they'd seen something, like the mother had seen it as well. Like a dog on the road, running with the car and running after it. Like there's dogs all around here, Valerie, you know? The farmers have them. There was a big dog up there, Jack, that Willie McDermott had that time.

JACK.   Oh, Jaysus, yeah, it was like a, if you saw it from the distance, you'd think it was a little horse. It was huge.

JIM.   Saxon.

FINBAR.   That was it. Saxon.

JIM.   It was an Irish Wolfhound. He got it off a fella in the North.

FINBAR.   Yeah, it was huge; you'd be used to seeing dogs all around the place. All kinds, but they'd be tame, like. Their bark'd be worse than their bite. So I wasn't too . . . taken with this story. But she wanted me to come down because when they'd got back to the house, the young one, Niamh, was going hysterical saying there was something on the stairs. Like no one else could see it. But she could, she said there was a woman, looking at her. And Mrs. Walsh didn't know what to do. They couldn't contact the hubbie, and would I come down? I mean, what made her think there was anything I could do, I don't know. But she was panicking, you know . . . So I got in the car and we went down. And Jesus, now, I've never seen the like of it. The young one was in . . . bits. They had a blanket around her and she was as white, now as . . . [*Points to* JACK's *shirt.*] as white as that. Well, whiter because that's probably filthy.

JACK.   Ha ha.

FINBAR.   But I'm not messing. And she wouldn't come out of the living room. Because she said there was a woman on the stairs. And I said, what's the woman doing? And she said, 'She's just looking at me.' She was terrified. Now I didn't know whether she was after taking drugs or drink or what she was after doing. So I says to phone for Dr. Joe in Carrick. This is Joe Dillon, Valerie, you'd see him in the town, he still has his surgery there beside the Spar. Very nice fella. And I got through to him, and he was on his way, and the Niamh one was shouting at me to close the living room door. Because I was out in the hall where the phone was, and she could see the woman looking at her over the banister. Like, she was that bad, now. So Mrs. Walsh phoned Fr. Donal, got him out of bed. And fair dues, like, he came down. And he sort of blessed the place a little bit. Like, he'd be more Vatican Two. There wouldn't be much of all the demons or that kind of carry-on with him.

JACK.   Jaysus, sure, he'd collapse. He's like that. [JACK *holds up his little finger.*] Him and a demon . . .

[*They laugh.*]

FINBAR. But Dr. Joe gave her a sedative and off she went then, you know. And we all had a little drink, and poor Mrs. Walsh was understandably, very, you know, shaken and everything. But Fr. Donal told her not to mind the Ouija, and it was only an old cod. And it was Niamh's imagination and this. And then, the phone rang, right? And it was the youngfella, the brother who was married in Longford. And he was all, that his baby was crying and he had it out of the cot and he was standing at the window and he saw a dead neighbour, of theirs out in the garden. A grown man. Ringing his mammy.

VALERIE. Out in the garden?

FINBAR. Standing out in the garden. Looking at the house, some old dear who'd died, a few weeks before. I mean, now either, they were all headers in that family or I'm, you know? And . . . when I went home then, that night, I was sitting at the fire having a last fag before the sack, and, Jack would know the house, the stairs come down into the, the main room. And I had my back to it, to the stairs, and it's stupid now, but at the time . . . I couldn't turn around. I couldn't get up to go to bed. Because I thought there was something on the stairs. [*Low laugh.*] And I just sat there, looking at an empty fireplace. And I sat there until it got bright. I was like a boy, you know? I wouldn't in case something saw me. You know that way. I wouldn't even light another fag. Like I was dying for one, and I wouldn't . . . mad. But when it was bright then, I was grand, you know? Obviously there was nothing there and everything, but that was the last fag I ever had. [*Short pause.*] They moved away then, though, after that, the Walshes. [*Pause.*] Yep.

VALERIE. And was that when you moved . . . down to Carrick?

FINBAR. Yeah. [*Nods slowly.*] Maybe that . . . had something to do with it. I don't know.

VALERIE. Mmm.

JACK. Moving down into the lights, yeah?

FINBAR. Mmm. Might be. Might be alright. Didn't want the loneliness maybe, you know? [*Pause.*] Yous all think I'm a lulah now. [*They laugh.*] Ha? I'm the header, says you, ha? I'm going to powder my nose I think. [*He goes out back.*]

JACK [*calling after him.*] Sure we knew you were a headbanger. Knew that all along.

[*They laugh. Pause.*]

Yeah.

VALERIE. I'd imagine, though, it can get very quiet.

JACK. Oh it can yeah. Ah you get used to it. Brendan.

BRENDAN. Ah yeah you don't think about it.

JACK. Me and Brendan are the fellas on our own. Jim has the mammy to look after, but we're, you know, you can come in here in the evenings. During the day you'd be working. You know, there's company around. Bit of a community all spread around the place, like.

JIM.   You can put the radio on.

[*Pause.*]

JACK.   Have you got any plans or that, for . . . here?

VALERIE.   Not really, I'm just going to try and have some . . .

JACK.   Peace and quiet.

VALERIE.   Mm.

JACK.   Jaysus, you're in the right place, so, ha?

[*They laugh.*]

You're going to have a peace and quiet . . . over . . . load. Oh yeah.

BRENDAN.   Sure, you can always stick the head in here. Or Jack, or me or whatever, be able to sort you out for anything.

VALERIE.   Thanks. I should be okay.

JACK.   You're only ten minutes up the road. And Jaysus, by the looks of things you'll have a job keeping Finbar away. Ha?

VALERIE.   Ah he's a dote.

JACK.   Jays, I never heard him called that before, ha? Lots of other things, never that though.

[FINBAR *comes back.*]

FINBAR.   What have you fecking heard? What are you talking about this time, Mullen, ha? About how twenty Germans were poisoned by the drink in here, last Summer. [*Winks at* BRENDAN.] Ha?

JACK.   No, I'd say the Arms is the place where that kind of carry on happens. You'd get a pint in there now, I believe, that'd put you on your back for a fortnight.

FINBAR.   Don't mind them, Valerie, they're only jealous.

VALERIE.   That's probably what it is, alright.

FINBAR.   You see now? At least there's one person on my side.

JACK.   Yeah. You. She's only sticking up for you to make sure she gets a lift after you scaring the living daylights out of her with your insistence on spooky stories.

FINBAR.   Go on. It's only headers like me get a fright like that, ha? Fecking lulahs.

[*They laugh.* JIM *counts some money.*]

JIM.   Does eh . . . is anybody?

JACK.   Ah no, Jim, I'm grand, you look after yourself.

JIM.   Are you sure? Valerie?

VALERIE.   No I'll get you one.

FINBAR.   Ah, no Valerie, you're . . .

JACK [*simultaneously.*]   No, you're alright.

FINBAR.   You're the guest. You're the guest.

JIM. Will you have a small one, Finbar?

FINBAR. Eh no, Jim. Thanks very much. I'm fine for the moment, finish this pint.

BRENDAN. Small one, Jim?

JIM. Thanks Brendan. I'll eh, I'll just lash a bit of turf on that, will I?

FINBAR. Good man, Jim.

[BRENDAN *gives* JIM *his drink.* JIM *leaves money on the bar and goes to the fire, leaving his drink on the mantel.*]

JACK. Keep the chill out, ha?

FINBAR. This is it.

[FINBAR *looks at his watch.*]

VALERIE. Do you want to?

FINBAR. Ah no, no, no. I'm just watching the time. We've a wedding tomorrow.

VALERIE. Would you be . . . directly . . . working in the hotel?

JACK. Saves him paying someone's wages.

FINBAR. Sure that's how I have it, boy. [*He winks at* VALERIE.]

JACK. We know.

FINBAR. No. There's certain things I'd do myself on a big day. One of the first things I ever learned in the business. The importance of good stock.

VALERIE. Soup stock?

FINBAR. For the soup. For the gravy, for the sauces, ah, you use it all over the place. And it's just a little thing I do. A little ritual. In the morning, I help do the stock. What do we have from yesterday, and so on. A little mad thing I do, but there you are.

VALERIE. I think that's lovely.

FINBAR. Ah, it's a little thing I do. Little superstition. These'll tell you. I'm famous for it.

JACK. It's a gimmick.

BRENDAN. Who's getting married, Finbar?

FINBAR. Do you know Nuala Donnelly? 'Nu' they call her. She used to work for me in the Arms. Declan Donnelly's girl. Gas young one.

BRENDAN. Oh yeah.

FINBAR. You used to be pals with Declan, Jim.

JIM. Poor Declan. Be ten years dead in July. God rest him. Lovely fella.

FINBAR. She's a gas young one, the daughter. 'Nu' they call her. 'Call me "Nu",' she says, the first day she was working for me. Not afraid to speak up for herself or anything. Used to tell us who was having affairs and all this. She was chambermaid, you see. She knew the couples who were being all illicit because she'd go in to do the room in the morning and the bed would be already made. The woman in the affair would have done it out of guilt, you see. Cover it all up, for herself as much as for anyone else. She's a mad young one.

VALERIE.   Would you get many people using the hotel like that?

FINBAR.   Not at all. I wouldn't say so. But Nuala just you know, she's a gabber and a talker.

JIM [*at fire*].   Who's she getting married to Finbar?

FINBAR.   Oh Jesus some fella from out the country. He must be in his forties. Shame, a young one getting hitched to an old fella like that. He must have plenty of money. [*To* VALERIE.] Be like getting married to that. [*Indicating* JACK.] He's a nice stash hidden away in that little garage, I'll tell you. Hoping to trap some little thing with it. Isn't that right, Jack?

JACK.   That's my plan.

FINBAR.   But you'd want to be careful of the old lads living on their own. They've a big pot of stew constantly on the heat, and they just keep throwing a few old bits of scraps in it every couple of days. And they survive off that, don't you Jack? That'd do you.

JACK.   It's a feast every day.

FINBAR.   Aw. Dreadful fellas. And then they manage to get a girl and the dust'd be like that on everything. And your man'd be after living in two rooms all his life, and the poor young one would have to get in and clean it all out. Thirty years of old newspapers and cheap thrillers, all lying there in the damp since their mammies died and that was the last bit of cleaning went on in the place. That right Jack?

JACK.   That's us to a tee.

BRENDAN.   Jaysus, speak for yourself, ha?

FINBAR.   Oh, they'd be desperate men. Changing the sheets in the bed every Christmas. And there'd be soot all over everything, and bits of rasher, and egg and pudding on the floor.

VALERIE.   The poor girl.

FINBAR.   The poor girl is right. So the least I can do is make sure her reception, in the Arms, is a little memory for her to have in the future, in the cold nights. Cheers.

[*They have all enjoyed this.*]

JACK.   You've a terrible warped mind, do you know that?

FINBAR [*winks at* VALERIE.].   Sure I'm only telling it like it is, ha?

JIM.   Nuala getting married. You don't feel the time.

FINBAR.   No.

JIM.   Mm. I remember, oh, it must have been twenty or more years ago, doing a job with him. Declan. Talking about what we were saying earlier. The priest over in Glen was looking for a couple of lads to do a bit of work. And he was down in Carrick in the Arms. He'd, come over, from Glen. You know? Which was an odd thing anyway. Like what was he doing coming over all the way just to get a couple of young fellas? But Declan Donnelly got put onto him. There was a few quid and he knocked up to me and we were to go over to the church in Glen the following day. And I remember I was dying with the 'flu and I had a terrible high temperature. The mother was telling me to stay in the leaba. Burn it off. But like it was a couple of quid on the Q.T. so I told Declan, yeah, I'd do it tomorrow. No problem. And then the next day it was lashing rain. I'll never forget it. He called for me in his dad's car. The smell of sheep in it like you wouldn't believe. God, it would kill you. He used to put them in the car, chauffeur them around, you know?

[*Smiles.*]

And we drove over to Glen. And the priest took us into the Sacristy, and the job, of all things was to dig a grave in the yard. That day was the removal of the remains and they needed the grave for the morning.

And fair dues, like, Declan said it to him. Was there no one else around the place could have done it? And the priest got a bit cagey and he was saying something about the local boys being busy with a game of Gaa, or something. And the rain was pelting down and he gave us leggings and wellies and the whole bit they had there and a couple of shovels. And then he put up his umbrella all annoyed, like, and he brought us out, over to a grave under a tree. It was a family one and there were two down in it already, the mother and the father, and this was going to be for the boy. Well, he was a man, like, a middle-aged fella. But there was two in it so we wouldn't have to go down for miles, like. So he went off to do his business and get ready, and me and Declan got stuck in. And with the rain and all, I was dying with the flu. My arms were sore and then my legs got sore. And then my neck got sore. And I was boiling. But we got down two, two and a half foot and we took a break. We got in Declan's car and he pulled out a bottle of poitín.[5] I couldn't eat, but I had a good belt of the bottle, like. Knocked me into some sort of shape.

And we just sat there for a while, listening to the radio, and the rain coming down, and then we got out and got stuck in again. Having a swig every half hour or so, keeping it going. And we saw the hearse arrive then. And the mad thing was there was only about two or three other fellas there for the service. Of course the removal is only a short thing mostly, but to have no one there, and for a man who's not an old man, it was funny, you know? And then that was over and the priest came out to us. We were nearly finished. And he just cleared us for the funeral in the morning, and then he went off. So me and Declan were the only two there then.

5 Poteen, distilled liquor.

[*Short pause.*]

And your man was laid out in the church. And Declan went off to get a tarp to stretch . . . over . . . the grave, and I put a big lump of a door over it. And I was just waiting on Declan and having the last drop, under the tree, dying to get in out of the rain, and thinking maybe we'd stick the head in somewhere for a quick pint on the way back. You know? And then, I saw this, fella, come out of the church. And he walked straight over to me. He was in a suit so I reckoned he was . . . paying his respects or whatever. And over he comes, through the gravestones. And he was looking around him a bit, like he didn't know the place. And he stood beside me, under the tree, looking at the grave. I didn't know what to say, you know? And he goes, 'Is this for so and so?' I forget the name. And I go, 'That's right, yeah.' And he says, 'That's the wrong grave.' And I'm like, 'No. This is where the priest said, like.' And he looked at me breathing hard, through his nose. Like he was holding his temper. And he goes, 'Come on, I'll show you.' And he walks off. And, I was all like 'fuck this' you know? And I was cursing Declan, waiting for him to come back. And your man turns around, you know 'Come on, it's over here.' I just, he was a lulah, you know? And I was nearly climbing into the grave myself, with the tiredness. And I was sick. So I followed him just to get it over with. And he stopped at a grave. Like a new enough one. A white one with a picture of a little girl on it.

And he says, 'It's this one, here.' And I just went, 'Okay, right you are mister, I'll have it done, no problem. See you now.' And he . . . sort of touched the gravestone and he went off, back into the church. I was breathing a few sighs of relief, I'll tell you. And Declan came back with the tarp and I said,' Did you see your man?' And he didn't know what I was talking about. So I told him and all this, and we just kind of had a bit of a laugh at it. And we just got out of there. Stopped into the Green Man on the way back for a few pints and that night, my fever broke. But I was knackered. The mother wouldn't let me go to the burial. Declan did it on his own I think. But I was laid up for a couple of days. And one day the mother brought me in the paper and on the obituaries, there was a picture of your man whose grave we'd dug. And you know what I'm going to say. It was the spit of your man I'd met in the graveyard. So I thought first it was a brother or a relative or someone, I'd met. And I forgot about it a bit and didn't think about it for ages until one night Declan told me he'd found out why the priest from Glen was looking for a couple of Carrick fellas, for the job.

The fella who'd died had had a bit of a reputation for 'em, being a pervert. And Jesus, when I heard that you know? If it was him. And he wanted to go down in the grave with the . . . little girl. Even after they were gone. It didn't bear . . . thinking about. It came back when you said about Declan's girl. Yeah.

[*Pause.*]

FINBAR.   Jaysus, Jim. That's a terrible story to be telling.

JIM.   Well, you know. I was very sick and we'd had the few little drinks. From Dick Lenihan's batch, you know?

JACK.   Oh Jesus. Firewater. Sure that'd put a hole in the glass, let alone give you hallucinations.

[*A little laugh. Pause.*]

VALERIE.   Do you think it was a, an hallucination Jim?

JIM.   God I don't know. I was flying like, but it was some coincidence him showing me where he wanted to be buried. And me knowing nothing about him like.

VALERIE.   Mm. [*Nods.*]

FINBAR.   Are you alright, Valerie? [*Little laugh.*] You look a bit peaky there.

VALERIE.   No, I'm fine. Just, actually is the Ladies out this way?

BRENDAN.   Ah. [*Short pause.*] Jays, I'll tell you what, Valerie, this is very embarrassing but the Ladies is busted. And with the . . . [JACK *laughs.*] I'm getting it fixed for the Germans like, but I haven't done it yet.

FINBAR.   Ah, you're a terrible man, Brendan.

BRENDAN.   No, I'll bring you in the house, come on.

VALERIE.   Are you sure?

BRENDAN.   Aw yeah, yeah, no problem.

JACK.   Don't worry Valerie, if you're not back in ten minutes we'll come and get you, ha?

BRENDAN.   Jaysus. Give it a rest. Come on, Valerie, I'll put the lights on for you. Out this way.

FINBAR.   Bye now.

VALERIE.   Bye.

[BRENDAN *and* VALERIE *leave by door, back.*]

[*Pause.*]

JACK.   Yep. [*Short pause.*]

FINBAR [*to* JIM].   Jaysus. That's some fucking story. To be telling a girl, like. Perverts out in the country. For fuck's sake.

[*Short pause.*]

JACK.   Like your story had nothing in it, ha?

FINBAR.   Ah that was only old headers in it.

JACK.   But you brought the whole thing up. With the fairies. The fairies! She's in that house.

FINBAR.   I forgot it was that house. I forgot it was Maura Nealon. It was an honest mistake.

JACK.   Honest mistake.

FINBAR.   What.

JACK.   Don't be giving it that old cod now.

FINBAR.   What do you mean?

JACK.   With bringing her around and all.

FINBAR.   What about it?

JACK.   Bringing her up the head and all. [*Short pause.*]

FINBAR.   Yeah?

JACK.   So don't be giving it the old cod now.

FINBAR.   What cod, Jack? [*Pause.*] I'm asking you. [*Short pause.*] What?

JIM.   Ah boys, we have a small one. Come on now.

FINBAR.   Hang on a minute, Jim. What?

JACK.   Well you get me to tell a story about the house she's in.

FINBAR.   I didn't *know* that though. I told you that.

JACK.   Whatever. And then you tell the story about the Walsh girl.

FINBAR.   Sure it was you told me to say that.

JACK.   What?

FINBAR.   Talking about the fags and giving up the fags and all that. When you offered them that time.

JACK.   Would you cop on? 'Ghosts' and 'giving up the fags'.

FINBAR.   Okay. I'm sorry. What? I regret the stories, then. I don't think we should have any more of them. But that's what I'm saying, like.

JIM.   I didn't think. I just said it. With Declan Donnelly and that. It just, you know . . .

FINBAR.   Ah no no no no. Jim. We're not blaming anybody. I regret it now. And just let's not have any more of them, and that's all.

JACK.   Oh, you regret it now?

FINBAR.   Yeah.

JACK.   It's not part of the tour.

FINBAR.   Ah now, come on.

JACK.   Bit of local colour.

FINBAR.   No. Jack.

JACK.   Just don't berate Jim for telling a story after you telling one yourself.

FINBAR.   I apologise, if that's what I did. Sorry Jim. Now, I'll say that. But stop with this . . . tour guide thing. That's not fair. The woman's moved out here on her own. For some reason. There's something obviously going on . . . in her life. I'm just trying to make it easier for her. Give her a welcome, for fuck's sake. So don't . . . be implying anything else. I don't like it. [*Pause.*] I've apologised to Jim. And I'm saying no more stories. [*Short pause.*] Sure I'm married! I mean really. Yous are the single boys. [*Short pause. Warm.*] Sure I can't remember the last time I saw a suit on you.

[*Pause.*]

JACK.   Oh now it's me?

JIM.   Ah now boys, come on. That's enough. That's enough of that.

JACK.   You think I have intentions, is it?

FINBAR.   I didn't know. You're entitled.

JACK.   I do often wear a suit. Don't come in here for the first time in God knows, thinking we're fucking hicks. 'Cause you're from round here.

[*Pause.*]

FINBAR. Nobody's saying that. You've got the wrong idea, Jack. And it's not worth falling out over. Now, I'll buy you a drink. And that'll be the fucking end of it now. Alright?

JACK. You will not buy me a fucking drink. [*Short pause.*] I'll buy *you* one, and *that'll* be the end of it.

[*He extends his hands. They shake.*]

JIM. That's more like it, men. That's more like it, ha?

[JACK *goes behind the bar.*]

JACK. What'll yous have?

FINBAR [*offering hand to* JIM]. Sorry Jim.

JIM. Ah no no no. Stop. [*Shaking hands.*] It's forgotten.

JACK. Finbar.

FINBAR. Ah. I think I'll just have a glass, Jack, I think.

JACK. Ah, you'll have a small one with that.

FINBAR. Jays, you'll fucking kill me now, ha? I think he's trying to kill me Jim, is he?

JIM. Oh now.

JACK. Jim?

JIM. Small one, Jack, thanks.

JACK. You'll have a little pint with that, I think.

JIM. Go on, ha?

FINBAR. Ah good man. [*Pause.*] Jays. That was a hot one there for a minute, ha?

JACK. We'll say no more about it. We might tell a few jokes when she comes back. [*They laugh.*]

FINBAR. Jays. This is it. How's the mammy, Jim?

JIM. Ah, do you know what it is? She's just old. And everything's going on her.

FINBAR. Ah Jaysus, ha? I'll have to get up and see her.

JACK. I was saying that earlier. It would be the time, you think, Jim.

JIM. Ah.

FINBAR. She does be alright on her own, with you coming out for an old jar or that?

JIM. Oh don't mind her. She's well able to tell you what's what. The only thing would be the eyes, but she's the one, I'm always mixing up the tablets.   She knows exactly what she's supposed to be taking when. So. But we have the telly in that room. And she'll listen to that and drop off.

FINBAR. Well that's alright, isn't it?

JIM. Oh she's still . . . I'm taking her over tomorrow to see her sister in the, in the order.

JACK. That's a closed order, Jim, yeah?

JIM.   Yeah, you know. They don't talk and all that. But the sister is six years older than the mammy, now, you know, so?

FINBAR.   Gas. She'll be alright for the drive?

JIM.   Oh, she'll be knackered, she'll be out like a light when we get back.

FINBAR.   Ah.

JIM.   Ah, yeah.

[BRENDAN *and* VALERIE *come back.*]

BRENDAN.   So this was all the original. Before the house.

VALERIE.   Right.

FINBAR.   There you are, we thought we were going to have to send out a search party.

VALERIE.   I was having a good nosy around.

FINBAR.   Wasn't too much of a state, no?

VALERIE.   Tidier than I normally am.

JACK.   That's he had the sisters over today. That's all that is.

FINBAR.   I saw them having their lunch in my place today.

BRENDAN.   Don't be talking.

FINBAR [*gingerly*].   Oh . . . back off there. Sensitive area. Eh, Valerie, darling, I don't want you to be stranded here with me now if I'm keeping you.

BRENDAN.   Sure we can look after her.

FINBAR.   Ah no, I'm grand for a while yet.

VALERIE.   I, em. Hearing about. All these . . . you know, stories. It's . . .

FINBAR.   Ah that's the end of them, now. We've had enough of them old stories, they're only an old cod. We've just been joking about it there when you were out. We'll all be witless, ha? We won't be able to sleep in our beds!

VALERIE.   No, see, something happened to me. That just hearing you talk about it tonight. It's important to me. That I'm not . . . bananas.

I mean, I'm a fairly straight. . . . down the line . . . person. Working. I had a good job at D.C.U.[6] I had gone back to work after having my daughter, Niamh. My husband is a teacher at D.C.U. We had Niamh in 1988. And I went back to work when she was five, when she started school. And we'd leave her with Daniel's parents, my husband's parents. His mother always picked her up from school. And I'd collect her after work. And last year she, she was dying to learn how to swim. And the school had a thing. They'd take the class down to the C.R.C.[7] in Clontarf on Wednesdays. She was learning very well. No problem. Loved the water. She couldn't wait for Wednesdays and swimming. Daniel used to take her to the pool on Saturdays and everything.

6. Dublin City University.
7. Central Remedial Clinic, facility for treatment of physical disabilities.

But for such a bright, outgoing, happy girl she was a big em . . . She had a problem sleeping at night. She was afraid of the dark. She never wanted you to leave the room.

One of us would have to lie there with her until she went off, and even when she did, she'd often have to come in and sleep with us.

And I'd say to her, 'What's wrong, when you go to bed?' But in the daytime, you know, she wouldn't care. Night time was a million years away. And she wouldn't think about it. But at night there were people at the window, there were people in the attic, there was someone coming up the stairs. There were children knocking, in the wall. And there was always a man standing across the road who she'd see. Like there was loads of things. The poor thing. I wanted to bring her to a doctor, but Daniel said she'd grow out of it. And we should be careful, just, about books we got her, and what she saw on the telly and all of this.

But I mean, she used to be even be scared that when she got up in the morning that Mammy and Daddy would have gone away and she'd be in the house on her own. That was one she told Daniel's mother. And all the furniture and carpets and everything would be gone. I mean, you know? So I told her after that, you know, we'd never, you know, it was ridiculous. And that if she was scared or worried at all during the day to ring me, and I'd come and get her, and there was nothing to worry about. And she knew our number, she was very good at learning numbers off and everything. She knew ours and her nana's and mine at work. She knew them all.

But then, in March, last year, the school had a, a sponsored swim, and the kids were going to swim a length of the pool. And I promised I was going to go and watch her. But I got . . . I was late, out of work, and I was only going to be in time to meet her afterwards, but em, when I got there . . . There was an ambulance and I thought, like, the pool is in the Central Remedial Clinic, so I thought like it was just somebody being dropped there. I didn't really pay any attention.

But when I got in, I saw that there was no one in the pool and one of the teachers was there with a group of kids. And she was crying and some of the children were crying. And this woman, another one of the mums came over and said there'd been an accident. And Niamh had hit her head in the pool and she'd been in the water and they had been trying to resuscitate her. But she said she was going to be alright. And I didn't believe it was happening. I thought it must have been someone else. And I went into, I was brought into, a room and Niamh was on a table. It was a table for table-tennis, and an ambulance man was giving her the . . . kiss of life.

She was in her bathing suit. And the ambulance man said he didn't think that what he was doing was working. And he didn't know if she was alive. And he wrapped her in a towel and carried her out to the ambulance. And I got in the back with him. And they radioed on ahead, they were going to put her on a machine in Beaumont and try to revive her there. But the ambulance man knew, I think. She wasn't breathing, and he just knew and he said if I wanted to just say goodbye to her in the ambulance in case I didn't get a chance in the hospital.

And I gave her a little hug. She was freezing cold. And I told her Mammy loved her very much. She just looked asleep but her lips were gone blue and she was dead.

And it had happened so fast. Just a few minutes. And I don't think I have to tell you. How hard it was. Between me and Daniel, as well. It didn't seem real. At the funeral I just thought I could go and lift her out of the coffin and that would be the end of all this.

I think Daniel was. I don't know if he actually, blamed me, there was nothing I could do. But he became very busy in his work. Just. Keeping himself . . . em. But I was, you know, I was more, just I didn't really know what I was doing. Just walking around or sitting in the house, with Daniel's mother, fussing around the place.

Just, months of this. Not really talking about it, like.

[*Pause.*]

But, and then one morning. I was in bed, Daniel had gone to work. I usually lay there for a few hours, trying to stay asleep, really, I suppose. And the phone rang. And I just left it. I wasn't going to get it. And it rang for a long time. Em, eventually it stopped, and I was dropping off again. But then it started ringing again, for a long time. So I thought it must have been Daniel trying to get me. Someone who knew I was there.

So I went down and answered it. And. The line was very faint. It was like a crossed line. There were voices, but I couldn't hear what they were saying. And then I heard Niamh. She said, 'Mammy?' And I . . . just said, you know? 'Yes?' And she said . . . she wanted me to come and collect her.

I mean, I wasn't sure whether this was a dream or her leaving us had been a dream. I just said 'Where are you?'

And she said she thought she was at Nana's. In the bedroom. But Nana wasn't there. And she was scared. There were children knocking in the walls and the man was standing across the road, and he was looking up and he was going to cross the road. And could I come and get her?

And I said I would, of course I would. And I dropped the phone and I ran out to the car in just a tee-shirt I slept in. And I drove to Daniel's mother's house. And I could hardly see, I was crying so much. I mean, I knew she wasn't going to be there. I knew she was gone. But to think wherever she was . . . that . . . And there was nothing I could do about it. Daniel's mother had to get a doctor and I . . . slept for a day or two. But it was . . .

Daniel felt that I . . . needed to face up to Niamh being gone.
But I just thought he should face up to what happened to me. He
was insisting I got some 'treatment' and then . . . everything
would be okay. But you know, what can help that, if she's out
there? She still . . . she still needs me. [*Pause.*]

JACK.   You don't think it could have been a dream you were having,
no? [*Short pause.*]

VALERIE.   I heard her. [*Short pause.*]

FINBAR.   Sure, you were after getting a terrible shock, Valerie.
These things can happen. Your brain is . . . trying to deal with it,
you know? [*Pause.*] Is your husband going to . . . come down?

VALERIE.   I don't think so.

FINBAR.   Ah, it'd be a terrible shame if you don't . . . if you didn't
see him because of something as, as, you know . . . that you don't
even know what it was. [*Short pause.*]

BRENDAN.   She said she knew what it was.

FINBAR.   But, sure you can't just accept that, that you, you know
. . . I mean . . . surely you, you have to look at the broader thing
of it here.

JIM.   It might have been a wrong number.

BRENDAN.   What?

JIM.   It could have been a wrong number or something wrong with
the phone, you know? And you'd think you heard it. Something
on the line.

BRENDAN.   But you wouldn't hear someone's voice on the fucking
thing, Jim.

JIM.   Just it might have been something else.

JACK.   Here, go easy, Brendan, Jim's only trying to talk about the
fucking thing.

FINBAR.   Ah lads.

JACK.   Just take it easy.

VALERIE.   Stop. I don't want . . . it's something that happened. And
it's nice just to be here and . . . hear what you were saying. I
know I'm not crazy.

FINBAR.   Valerie, love, nobody's going to think that. But . . . just . . .
no one knows about these things, sure, they're not real even. You
hear all sorts of old cod, all round. But there's usually some kind
of . . . explanation for it. Sure, Jim said himself he was delirious
with the 'flu that time. Jim.

JIM.   I had a right temperature.

FINBAR.   Maura . . . eh . . . Nealon, sure she was in here every
night of the week. Brendan. About how much would she drink?
Be honest now.

BRENDAN.   How much did she drink?

JACK.   Have a bit of respect, Finbar.

FINBAR.   I'm trying to make a point, Jack. The woman was a
drinker.

JACK.   We're all drinkers.

FINBAR.   But, come on. She was an alcoholic, Valerie. She used to have a bottle of whiskey put away before you knew where you were. Sure, who wouldn't be hearing knocking on the door after that?

JACK. Ah you're not being fair on her now. The woman's dead, she can't defend herself.

FINBAR. I'm not casting anything on her. If she came in that door now, if she was alive, I'd be buying her drink, and more power to her, I'd hope she'd enjoy it. I'd be the first to buy her a drink. But I run a bar myself down in the Arms. I know all about what a right few drinks'll do to you. She liked her drop is what I'm saying.

BRENDAN. What about you? And the Walshes?

FINBAR. Look. How many times do I have to say it? They were all a bunch of fucking headers!

[Pause.]

I got the wind put up me that night. Fair enough. But that's what these stories do. But I resent that now. What I went through that night. But I was only young. And that's over with. Fucking head-bangers.

[Pause.]

And after all that, I'm ignoring the bigger thing, I'm very sorry about your daughter, Valerie, I'm very sorry indeed.

JACK. Oh we all are. Of course we are. It's terrible.

[Long pause.]

FINBAR. I'm going to have to go, I'm afraid. I don't want to, but . . .

VALERIE. Okay.

BRENDAN. Ah here, I'll leave her down.

FINBAR. But you might want to come on now, no?

VALERIE. Em.

BRENDAN. Ah, have another drink and relax for a little while.

VALERIE. Yeah, I think I'm going to hang on for another little while.

FINBAR. Are you going to go easy on the old stories?

JACK. Ah stop being an old woman. She'll be grand.

FINBAR. Alright?

JACK. She'll be grand.

JIM. Could I get a lift, Finbar?

FINBAR. Of course you can, Jim.

JACK. You're okay for Father Donal's car in the morning?

JIM [counting money]. No problem. I'll be there about quarter to nine.

JACK. Grand, just, I've got to get out to Conor Boland.

JIM. Yeah. It's fine. Brendan, em . . .

BRENDAN. Naggin?

JIM. Please.

344

CONOR MCPHERSON

[BRENDAN *puts a small bottle of whiskey in a plastic bag and gives it to* JIM.]

FINBAR. Yep.

JIM. Well. Valerie.

VALERIE. It was very nice to meet you.

JIM [*taking her hand*]. I'm very sorry about what's happened to you. And I'm sure your girl is quite safe and comfortable wherever she is, and I'm going to say a little prayer for her, but I'm sure she doesn't need it. She's a saint. She's a little innocent. And that fella I saw in the churchyard that time was only the rotten poitín and the fever I had. Finbar's right. You enjoy your peace and quiet here now. And we'll see you again. You're very nice. Goodnight now.

VALERIE. Goodnight. Thanks Jim.

JIM. That's alright.

FINBAR. Valerie. [*He takes her hand.*]

VALERIE. Thanks for everything.

FINBAR. My pleasure, darling. And I'll call up to you now in the next day or two . . .

VALERIE. Fine.

FINBAR. And we'll make sure you're all right and you're settling in with us. You're very welcome.

[*He kisses her awkwardly on the cheek.*]

VALERIE. Thanks for everything, Finbar.

FINBAR. That's quite alright. Men.

JACK. Finbar.

FINBAR. I'll see you soon, I hope, Jack.

[*They shake hands.*]

FINBAR. Alright?

JACK. See you soon.

FINBAR. Brendan.

BRENDAN. Take it easy now, Finbar. Look after yourself.

FINBAR. I won't leave it so long next time.

BRENDAN. Okay.

JIM. Goodnight.

BRENDAN. Goodnight Jim.

VALERIE. See you soon.

JACK. See you in the morning.

JIM. Quarter to nine.

FINBAR. See yous now.

[JIM *and* FINBAR *leave.*]

JACK. There you are now.

BRENDAN. Mm.

JACK. I'm sorry for snapping that time.

BRENDAN. Ah no. Sure. I was . . .

VALERIE. I think it was my fault.
JACK. Would you go on? Of course it wasn't your fault. You know, it's all very well, us sitting around, fecking about with these old stories. But then, for something personal like that. That's happened to you. People are, going to deal with it in different ways. Jim, was . . . you know . . .
BRENDAN. Yeah . . .
JACK. He didn't mean anything.
BRENDAN. He didn't really mean there was anything wrong with your phone, I don't think.

[*They laugh a little. Pause.*]

JACK. It's em . . . a terrible thing that happened. Do you ever get over something like that, I wonder? I don't mean the . . . phone . . . call, you know.
VALERIE. I know. [*Pause.*] I don't know. [*Pause.*]
JACK. We're very sorry.
BRENDAN. Come on we sit at the fire. It's getting cold. We'll have a last one.
JACK. Good idea.
BRENDAN. Give us your glass, Valerie. Jack, you'll have a small one, for the road.
VALERIE. Can I get this?
JACK. Ah no no no.
BRENDAN. It's on the house now. Bar's officially closed. Go on.

[JACK *and* VALERIE *move to the fire.*]

JACK. You get yourself in there now. We'll be grand in a minute.
BRENDAN. I'm going to give you a little brandy, Valerie. This wine is freezing in the fridge.
JACK. Good man.
VALERIE. Oh lovely. Thanks.
JACK. Good girl. That's it now. [*To* BRENDAN.] Jim'll be in a bad way, all the same when the mammy goes, what do you think Brendan?
BRENDAN. Oh definitely. She's been very sick, Valerie, for years now. Fading fast, like, for years! She still spoils that boy rotten, ha? Though.
JACK. Oh definitely. Oh yeah.

[BRENDAN *brings the drinks over.*]

VALERIE. That's an awful lot.
BRENDAN. Ah it's not really.
JACK. There's no law says you have to drink it all, ha? Your man does put it back in the bottle.
BRENDAN. Would you ever fuck off?
JACK. I think we should drink this to you, sweetheart.
BRENDAN. Yes. To Valerie.
JACK. Hope it's all . . . [*Raises glass.*] In the end . . .

BRENDAN. Cheers.
VALERIE. Cheers.

[*They drink.*]

VALERIE. You've no children, Jack, no?
JACK. No, darling, never married. But I do be telling this fella to be on the lookout. A young fella like him to end up like me.
VALERIE. Do you wish you had married?
JACK. Sure who'd have me? A cantankerous old fucker like me.
BRENDAN. Too right.
JACK. Yeah . . . it's a thing, you know? I do say it to Brendan. I'm down in the garage. And the fucking tin roof on the thing. On my own on that country road. You see it was bypassed by the main road into Carrick. And there's no . . . like in the summer the heat has the place like an oven, with the roof, or if it's not that, it's the rain pelting down on it like bricks, the noise of it. You've heard it Brendan. You can't even hear the radio anymore. And there'll you'd be, the only car'd be stopping in be someone that knows the area real well. Ah you'd definitely feel it, like. But you know. I get down here for a pint and that. There's a lot to be said for the company. And the . . . you know, the . . . someone there. Oh yeah.
VALERIE. Did you never consider it? When you were young.
JACK. Oh sure, yeah, of course I did, sure what the hell else does a youngfella be thinking about? You know? And Brendan knows. I had a girl, a lovely girl back then. We were courting for three years, and em, 1963 to '66. But she wanted to go up to Dublin, you know. She would have felt that that's what we should have done. And I don't know why it was a thing with me that I . . . an irrational fear, I suppose, that kept me here. And I couldn't understand why she wanted to be running off up to Dublin, you know? And she did in the end, anyway, like. And she was working up there waiting for me to come. But it was with me that it was like a mad thing, that I thought it was a thousand fucking miles away. Hated going up. I went up a few times like.

But . . . I was going up for . . . you know . . . she had a room. A freezing, damp place. I was a terrible fella. It became that that was the only thing I was going for. I couldn't stand being away. I don't know why. Ah I'd be all excited about going up for . . . the physical . . . the freedom of it. But after a day and a night, and I'd had my fill, we'd be walking in the park and I'd be all catty and bored, and moochy. [*Pause.*] Breaking the poor girl's heart. Ah, you get older and you look back on why you did things, you see that a lot of the time, there wasn't a reason. You do a lot of things out of pure cussedness. I stopped answering her letters. And I'd fucking dread one coming to the house. And her in it wondering how I was and was there something wrong with the post or this. [*Pause.*] I can't explain what carry on I was up to. I had just . . . left her out. Being the big fella, me dad handing over the business to me. Me swanning around. A man of substance. And then I had the gall to feel resentful when she wrote and said she was getting married to a fella.

[*Pause.*]

And I was all that it was her fault for going in the first place. Tss.

There was a delegation of people from all around here going up to the wedding on a bus. And I was just one of the crowd. Just one of the guests. In my suit, and the shoes nearly polished off me. And a hangover like you wouldn't believe. I'd been up 'til five or more, swilling this stuff, looking at the fire. And we were all on the bus at nine. And all the chat all around was why she hadn't come home to get married. And me sick as a dog. The smell of Brylcreem off all us culchies[8]—sitting in the church in Phibsboro. All her lovely-looking nurse friends and their guard boyfriends. She was marrying a guard.[9] Huge fella. Shoulders like a big gorilla. And they were going down the aisle after, and I caught her eye. And I gave her the cheesiest little grin you've ever seen. A little grin that was saying, 'Enjoy your big gorilla, 'cause the future's all ahead of me.'

And she just looked at me like I was only another guest at the wedding. And that was that. And the future *was* all ahead of me. Years and years of it. I could feel it coming. All those things you've got to face on your own. All by yourself. And you bear it 'cause you're showing everybody you're a great fella altogether. But I left the church like a little boy. And I walked away. I couldn't go to the reception. I just kept walking. There was a light rain. And then I was in town. It was a dark day. Like there was a roof on the city. And I found myself in a little labyrinth of streets. With nothing doing. And I ducked into a pub. Little dark place. Just one or two others there. A businesslike barman. Like yourself Brendan, ha?

Businesslike, dutiful. And I put a pint or two away. And a small one or two. And I sat there, just looking down at the dirty wooden bar. And the barman asked me if I was alright? Simple little question. And I said I was. And he said he'd make me a sandwich. And I said okay. And I nearly started crying—because you know, here was someone just . . . And I watched him. He took two big slices off a fresh loaf and buttered them carefully, spreading it all around. I'll never forget it. And then he sliced some cheese and cooked ham and an onion out of a jar, and put it all on a plate and sliced it down the middle. And, just someone doing this for me. And putting it down in front of me. 'Get that down you, now,' he said. And then he folded up his newspaper and put on his jacket, and went off on his break. And there was another barman then. And I took this sandwich up and I could hardly swallow it, because of the lump in my throat. But I ate it

8. Country persons, not urban.
9. *Garda Síochána*, "Guardians of the Peace," or civil police.

all down because someone I didn't know had done this for me. Such a small thing. But a huge thing. In my condition.

It fortified me, like no meal I ever had in my life. And I went to the reception. And I was properly ashamed of myself. There was a humility I've tried to find since. But goodness wears off. And it just gets easier to be a contrary bollocks.

Down in the garage. Spinning small jobs out all day. Taking hours to fix a puncture. Stops you thinking about what might of been and what you should have done. It's like looking away. Like I did at that reception. You should only catch someone's eye for the right reason.

But I do be at this fella, don't I? [*Pause.*]

Yep. [*Pause.*] I may be on my way now. [*Pause.*]

BRENDAN.   Will you be alright in that wind?

JACK.   Jaysus I should be used to that road by now, says you, ha?

BRENDAN.   I'll get you the torch.

JACK.   Am I a moaner?

BRENDAN [*going*].   There's well fucking worse, I'll tell you.

[*Exits*]

JACK.   Well. That wasn't a ghostly story. Anyway, At least, ha?

VALERIE.   No.

JACK.   We've had enough of them. [*Pause.*] We'll all be ghosts soon enough, says you ha?

VALERIE.   Mmm.

JACK.   We'll all be sitting here. Sipping whiskey all night with Maura Nealon. [*Pause.*] Yeah. [*Short pause.*] This has been a strange little evening, for me.

VALERIE [*a little laugh*].   For me as well.

JACK.   Fuck, We could do worse. It was lovely to meet you.

VALERIE.   You too.

JACK.   Didn't mean to go on there.

VALERIE.   No, please . . .

JACK.   Something about your company. Inspiring, ha? And this of course. [*Glass.*]

[*They smile.*]

I wonder if being out here in the country is the best place for to . . . you know . . .

VALERIE.   Why?

JACK.   Ah. Girl like you. Hiding yourself away, Listening to old headers like us talking about the fairies. Having all your worst fears confirmed for you. Tuh. Ghosts and angels and all this? Fuck them. I won't have it. Because I won't see someone like you being upset by it. You've enough to deal with for fuck's sake. I am very, sorry, love, about what happened.

VALERIE.   Thanks.

JACK [*standing up*].   Makes you feel very powerless. I'll say that much.

[BRENDAN *comes in turning the torch on and off.*]

BRENDAN.   The batteries are a bit weak. Come on I'll drop you.

JACK.   Are you sure?

BRENDAN.   Sure, I'm giving Valerie a lift.

VALERIE.   Come with us.

JACK.   Okay, then. Grand.

[BRENDAN *is clearing their glasses, going in behind the bar, tidying up.*]

VALERIE.   Do you want a hand, Brendan?

BRENDAN.   Oh no! Stay where you are, I'll be finished in a sec.

[JACK *takes his anorak, joking.*]

JACK.   Is this yours, Valerie?

VALERIE.   Yeah right.

[JACK *takes her jacket and holds it for her.*]

JACK.   Come on.

VALERIE.   Oh now. Very nice.

JACK.   These are the touches, ha, Brendan?

BRENDAN.   That's them.

JACK.   Now.

VALERIE.   Thanks.

JACK.   Mmm. Have a last fag I think. [*Taking cigarette packet.*] Anyone else?

VALERIE.   No, I won't thanks.

BRENDAN.   No thanks, Jack.

JACK.   Up early in the morning. Over to Conor Boland. He's over the other side of Carrick there. Has about fifteen fucking kids. Mmm.

[*Pause.*]

VALERIE.   Will you be in here again soon?

JACK.   Ah I'm always in and out. Got to keep the place afloat at least, you know?

BRENDAN [*working*].   Don't mind him now, Valerie. Him and the Jimmy fella'll be fierce scarce around here the next few weeks.

VALERIE.   Why?

BRENDAN [*stops work and lights a cigarette*].   All the Germans'll be coming and they love it in here.

VALERIE [*to* JACK].   You don't like that?

[JACK *makes a face.*]

BRENDAN.   He thinks they're too noisy.

JACK.   See, you don't know what they do be saying or anything.

BRENDAN.   Him and Jimmy be sitting there at the bar with big sour pusses on them. Giving out like a couple of old grannies.

JACK.   Ah we're not that bad.

BRENDAN. You're like a pair of bloody auld ones, you should see them.

VALERIE. Where do you go instead?

JACK. Ah, place down in Carrick, the Pot.

BRENDAN [derision]. 'The Pot'. There does be just as many of them down there, don't be codding yourself.

JACK. Ah no, it doesn't seem as bad down there, now.

VALERIE. That's because this is your place.

JACK. Now. You've hit it on the head. You see, Brendan, Valerie's defending us. It's out of respect for this place.

BRENDAN. It is in my fucking barney, respect! The two of yous leaving me standing behind that bar with my arms folded picking my hole and not knowing what the hell is going on. And them playing all old sixties songs on their guitars. And they don't even know the words.

And nothing for me to do except pull a few pints and watch the shadow from the Knock moving along the floor, with the sun going down. I'm like some fucking mentaller, I do be watching it! Watching it creeping up on the Germans. And they don't even notice it.

I must be cracking up if that's my entertainment of an evening.

JACK. Ah don't be moaning. I'll tell you what. If Valerie's willing to come in and brave the Germans, then I'm sure me and Jim'll come in and keep yous company, how's that now?

BRENDAN. Oh you'll *grace* us with your ugly mushes, will you?

JACK. Don't push it, boy. Ah sure, Jaysus, what am I talking about? Sure you'll have Finbar in here sniffing around Valerie every night anyway.

VALERIE. Ah now stop.

[*They laugh a little.*]

JACK. He'll be like a fly on a big pile of shite, so he will. Jesus. That came out all wrong, didn't it?

BRENDAN. It certainly did, you big messer.

JACK. Couldn't have come out worse, sorry about that.

VALERIE. Would you relax?

[BRENDAN *is putting his jacket on.*]

JACK. Sorry. Will you anyway?

VALERIE. What? Come in . . . with the . . . Germans?

JACK. Yeah.

VALERIE. Doesn't bother me.

JACK. Ah, I think that's the right attitude. You should stay with the company and the bright lights.

BRENDAN. Do you see my keys?

[*He is looking around.* VALERIE *and* JACK *look around a little.*]

VALERIE. Sure I might even pick up some German.

JACK.   Ah, I don't know. They're eh . . . Are they from Germany, Brendan?

BRENDAN.   What?

JACK.   The Germans. [*To* VALERIE.] We call them the Germans.

[VALERIE *picks keys off the mantelpiece.*]

VALERIE.   Is this them?

BRENDAN.   Yeah, thanks. Are we right?

[*They are moving towards the door.*]

JACK.   Where are they from? Is it Denmark, or Norway? [*To* VAL-ERIE.] It's somewhere like that.

[JACK *goes out, followed by* VALERIE.]

BRENDAN.   Ah, I don't know where the fuck they're from.

[BRENDAN *turns off the light and leaves.*]

MARINA CARR

By the Bog of Cats[†]

Characters

HESTER SWANE, *forty*
CARTHAGE KILBRIDE, *thirty*
JOSIE KILBRIDE, *seven, Hester and Carthage's daughter*
MRS KILBRIDE, *sixties, Carthage's mother*
MONICA MURRAY, *sixties, a neighbour*
THE CATWOMAN, *sixties, lives on the bog*
XAVIER CASSIDY, *sixties, a big farmer*
CAROLINE CASSIDY, *twenty, his daughter*
THE GHOST FANCIER
THE GHOST OF JOSEPH SWANE, *eighteen*
YOUNG DUNNE, *a waiter*
FATHER WILLOW, *eighty*
TWO OTHER WAITERS

Time and place

The present.

ACT ONE *takes place in the yard of Hester Swane's house and by the caravan*[1] *on the Bog of Cats.*

ACT TWO *takes place in Xavier Cassidy's house.*

ACT THREE *opens in Hester's yard and then reverts to the caravan on the Bog of Cats.*

Accent

Midland. I've given a slight flavour in the text, but the real midland accent is a lot flatter and rougher and more guttural than the written word allows.

† Reproduced by permission of The Agency (London) Ltd. Copyright © Marina Carr 1998. First published by The Gallery Press, Ireland, in 1998. All rights reserved and enquiries to The Agency (London) Ltd.
1. Vacation trailer.

Act 1

SCENE ONE

Dawn. On the Bog of Cats. A bleak white landscape of ice and snow. Music, a lone violin. HESTER SWANE *trails the corpse of a black swan after her, leaving a trail of blood in the snow. The* GHOST FANCIER *stands there watching her.*

HESTER.   Who are you? Haven't seen you around here before.

GF.   I'm a ghost fancier.

HESTER.   A ghost fancier. Never heard tell of the like.

GF.   You never seen ghosts?

HESTER.   Not exactly, felt what I thought were things from some other world betimes, but nothin' I could grab onto and say, that is a ghost.

GF.   Well, where there's ghosts there's ghost fanciers.

HESTER.   That so? So what do you do, Mr Ghost Fancier? Eye up ghosts? Have love affairs with them?

GF.   Dependin' on the ghost. I've trailed you a while. What're you doin' draggin' the corpse of a swan behind ya like it was your shadow?

HESTER.   This is auld Black Wing. I've known her the longest time. We used play together when I was a young wan. Wance I had to lave the Bog of Cats and when I returned years later this swan here came swoopin' over the bog to welcome me home, came right up to me and kissed me hand. Found her frozen in a bog hole last night, had to rip her from the ice, left half her underbelly.

GF.   No one ever tell ya it's dangerous to interfere with swans, especially black wans?

HESTER.   Only an auld superstition to keep people afraid. I only want to bury her. I can't be struck down for that, can I?

GF.   You live in that caravan over there?

HESTER.   Used to; live up the lane now. In a house, though I've never felt at home in it. But you, Mr Ghost Fancier, what ghost are you ghoulin' for around here?

GF.   I'm ghoulin' for a woman be the name of Hester Swane.

HESTER.   I'm Hester Swane.

GF.   You couldn't be, you're alive.

HESTER.   I certainly am and aim to stay that way.

GF [*Looks around, confused*].   Is it sunrise or sunset?

HESTER.   Why do ya want to know?

GF.   Just tell me.

HESTER.   It's that hour when it could be aither dawn or dusk, the light bein' so similar. But it's dawn, see there's the sun comin' up.

GF.   Then I'm too previous. I mistook this hour for dusk. A thousand apologies.

[*Goes to exit,* HESTER *stops him.*]

HESTER.   What do ya mean you're too previous? Who are ya? Really?

GF.   I'm sorry for intrudin' upon you like this. It's not usually my style.

[*Lifts his hat, walks off.*]

HESTER [*Shouts after him*].   Come back!—I can't die—I have a daughter.

[MONICA *enters.*]

MONICA.   What's wrong of ya, Hester? What are ya shoutin' at?

HESTER.   Don't ya see him?

MONICA.   Who?

HESTER.   Him!

MONICA.   I don't see anywan.

HESTER.   Over there. [*Points.*]

MONICA.   There's no wan, but ya know this auld bog, always shiftin' and changin' and coddin' the eye. What's that you've there? Oh, Black Wing, what happened to her?

HESTER.   Auld age, I'll wager, found her frozed last night.

MONICA [*Touches the swan's wing*].   Well, she'd good innin's, way past the life span of swans. Ya look half frozed yourself, walkin' all night again, were ya? Ya'll cetch your death in this weather. Five below the forecast said and worser promised.

HESTER.   Swear the age of ice have returned. Wouldn't ya almost wish if it had, do away with us all like the dinosaurs.

MONICA.   I would not indeed—are you lavin' or what, Hester?

HESTER.   Don't keep axin' me that.

MONICA.   Ya know you're welcome in my little shack.

HESTER.   I'm goin' nowhere. This here is my house and my garden and my stretch of the bog and no wan's runnin' me out of here.

MONICA.   I came up to see if ya wanted me to take Josie down for her breakfast.

HESTER.   She's still asleep.

MONICA.   The child, Hester, ya have to pull yourself together for her, you're goin' to have to stop this broodin', put your life back together again.

HESTER.   Wasn't me as pulled it asunder.

MONICA.   And you're goin' to have to lave this house, isn't yours anymore. Down in Daly's doin' me shoppin' and Caroline Cassidy there talkin' about how she was goin' to mow this place to the ground and build a new house from scratch.

HESTER.   Caroline Cassidy. I'll sourt her out. It's not her is the problem anyway, she's just wan of the smaller details.

MONICA.   Well, you've left it late for dealin' with her for she has her heart set on everythin' that's yours.

HESTER.   If he thinks he can go on treatin' me the way he's been treatin' me, he's another thing comin'. I'm not to be flung aside at his biddin'. He'd be nothin' today if it wasn't for me.

MONICA.   Sure the whole parish knows that.

HESTER.   Well, if they do, why're yees all just standin' back and gawkin'. Think yees all Hester Swane with her tinker blood is gettin' no more than she deserves. Think yees all she's too many notions, built her life up from a caravan on the side of the bog. Think yees all she's taken a step above herself in gettin' Carthage Kilbride into her bed. Think yees all yees knew it'd never last. Well, yees are thinkin' wrong. Carthage Kilbride is mine for always or until I say he is no longer mine. I'm the one who chooses and discards, not him, and certainly not any of yees. And I'm not runnin' with me tail between me legs just because certain people wants me out of their way.

MONICA.   You're angry now and not thinkin' straight.

HESTER.   If he'd only come back, we'd be alright, if I could just have him for a few days on me own with no wan stickin' their nose in.

MONICA.   Hester, he's gone from ya and he's not comin' back.

HESTER.   Ah you think ya know everythin' about me and Carthage. Well, ya don't. There's things about me and Carthage no wan knows except the two of us. And I'm not talkin' about love. Love is for fools and children. Our bond is harder, like two rocks we are, grindin' off of wan another and maybe all the closer for that.

MONICA.   That's all in your own head, the man cares nothin' for ya, else why would he go on the way he does.

HESTER.   My life doesn't hang together without him.

MONICA.   You're talkin' riddles now.

HESTER.   Carthage knows what I'm talkin' about—I suppose I may bury auld Black Wing before Josie wakes and sees her.

[*Begins walking off.*]

MONICA.   I'll come up to see ya in a while, bring yees up some lunch, help ya pack.

HESTER.   There'll be no packin' done around here.

[*And exit both in opposite directions.*]

SCENE 2

The sound of a child's voice comes from the house. She enters after a while, JOSIE KILBRIDE, *seven, barefoot, pyjamas, kicking the snow, singing.*

JOSIE.   By the Bog of Cats I dreamed a dream of wooing.
         I heard your clear voice to me a-calling

That I must go though it be my undoing.
By the Bog of Cats I'll stay no more a-rueing—
Mam—Mam—[*Continues playing in the snow, singing*]

To the Bog of Cats I one day will return,
In mortal form or in ghostly form,
And I will find you there and there with you sojourn,
Forever by the Bog of Cats, my darling one.

[MRS KILBRIDE *has entered, togged up against the biting cold, a shawl over her face.*]

MRS K. Well, good mornin', ya little wagon of a girl child.

JOSIE. Mornin' yourself, y'auld wagon of a Granny witch.

MRS K. I tould ya not to call me Granny.

JOSIE. Grandmother—Did ya see me Mam, did ya?

MRS K. Aye, seen her whooshin' by on her broom half an hour back.

JOSIE. Did yees crash?

MRS K. Get in, ya pup, and put on some clothes before Jack Frost ates your toes for breakfast. Get in till I dress ya.

JOSIE. I know how to dress meself.

MRS K. Then dress yourself and stop braggin' about it. Get in. Get in.

[*And exit the pair to the house.*]

SCENE 3

Enter HESTER *by the caravan. She digs a grave for the swan. Enter the* CATWOMAN, *a woman in her late fifties, stained a streaky brown from the bog, a coat of cat fur that reaches to the ground, studded with cat's eyes and cat paws. She is blind and carries a stick.*

CATWOMAN. What're ya doin' there?

HESTER. None of your business now, Catwoman.

CATWOMAN. You're buryin' auld Black Wing, aren't ya?

HESTER. How d'ya know?

CATWOMAN. I know everythin' that happens on this bog. I'm the Keeper of the Bog of Cats in case ya forgotten? I own this bog.

HESTER. Ya own nothin', Catwoman, except your little house of turf and your hundred odd mousetraps and anythin' ya can rob and I'm missin' a garden chair so ya better bring it back.

CATWOMAN. I only took it because ya won't be needin' it anymore.

HESTER. Won't I? If ya don't bring it back I'll have to go down meself and maybe knock your little turf house down.

CATWOMAN. You just dare.

HESTER. I'll bring down diesel, burn ya out.

CATWOMAN. Alright! Alright! I'll bring back your garden chair, fierce uncomfortable anyway, not wan of the cats'd sleep on it. Here, give her to me a minute, auld Black Wing.

[HESTER *does.*]

She came to my door last night and tapped on it as she often did, only last night she wouldn't come in. I bent down and she puts her wing on me cheek and I knew this was farewell. Then I heard her tired auld wingbeat, shaky and off kilter and then the thud of her fallin' out of the sky onto the ice. She must've died on the wing or soon after. [*Kisses the black swan*] Goodbye, auld thing, and safe journey. Here, put her in the ground.

[HESTER *does and begins shovelling in clay.* CATWOMAN *stands there leaning on her stick, produces a mouse from her pocket.*]

CATWOMAN. A saucer of milk there, Hester Swane.

HESTER. I've no milk here today. You may go up to the house for your saucer of milk and, I told ya, I don't want ya pawin' mice around me, dirty auld yokes, full of diseases.

CATWOMAN. And you aren't, you clean as the snow, Hester Swane?

HESTER. Did I say I was?

CATWOMAN. I knew your mother, I helped her bring ya into the world, knew ya when ya were chained like a rabied pup to this auld caravan, so don't you look down on me for handlin' a mouse or two.

HESTER. If ya could just see yourself and the mouse fur growin' out of your teeth. Disgustin'.

CATWOMAN. I need mice the way you need whiskey.

HESTER. Ah, go on and lave me alone, Catwoman, I'm in no mood for ya today.

CATWOMAN. Bet ya aren't. I had a dream about ya last night.

HESTER. Spare me your visions and dreams, enough of me own to deal with.

CATWOMAN. Dreamt ya were a black train motorin' through the Bog of Cats and, oh, the scorch off of this train and it blastin' by and all the bog was dark in your wake, ya even quinched the jack-a'-lantern and I had to run from the burn. Hester Swane, you'll bring this place down by evenin'.

HESTER. I know.

CATWOMAN. Do ya now? Then why don't ya lave? If ya lave this place you'll be alright. That's what I came by to tell ya.

HESTER. Ah, how can I lave the Bog of Cats, everythin' I'm connected to is here. I'd rather die.

CATWOMAN. Then die ya will.

HESTER. There's sympathy for ya! That's just what I need to hear.

CATWOMAN. Ya want sugar plum platitudes, go talk to Monica Murray or anyone else around here. You're my match in witchery, Hester, same as your mother was, it may even be ya surpass us both and the way ya go on as if God only gave ya a little frog of a

brain instead of the gift of seein' things as they are, not as they
should be, but exactly as they are. Ya know what I think?

HESTER.   What?

CATWOMAN.   I been thinkin' a while now that there's some fierce
wrong ya done that's caught up with ya.

HESTER.   What fierce wrong?

CATWOMAN.   Don't you by talk me, I'm the Catwoman. I know
things. Now I can't say I know the exact wrong ya done but I'd
put a bet on it's somethin' serious judgin' by the way ya go on.

HESTER.   And what way do I go on?

CATWOMAN.   What was it ya done, Hester?

HESTER.   I done nothin'—Or if I did I never meant to.

CATWOMAN.   There's a fine answer, a half a lie and a half a truth.

HESTER.   Everywan has done wrong at wan time or another.

CATWOMAN.   Aye, but not everywan knows the price of wrong. You
do and it's the best thing about ya and there's not much in ya I'd
praise. No, most manage to stay a step or two ahead of the pigsty
truth of themselves, not you though.

HESTER.   Ah, would ya give over. Ya lap up people's fears, you've
too much time on your own, concoctin' stories about others. Go
way and kill a few mice for your dinner, only lave me alone—Or
tell me about me mother, for what I remember doesn't add up.

CATWOMAN.   What ya want to know about big Josie Swane?

HESTER.   Everythin'.

CATWOMAN.   Well, what ya remember?

HESTER.   Only small things—Like her pausin'.

CATWOMAN.   She was a great wan for the pausin'.

HESTER.   'G'wan to bed, you,' she'd say, 'I'll just be here pausin'.'
And I'd watch her from the window. [*Indicates window of caravan.*] Times she'd smoke a cigar which she had her own particular way of doin'. She'd hould it stretched away from her and,
instead of takin' the cigar to her mouth, she'd bring her mouth to
the cigar. And her all the time pausin'. What was she waitin' for,
Catwoman? And did she ever find it?

CATWOMAN.   Ya'd often hear her voice comin' over the bog at night.
She was the greatest song stitcher ever to have passed through
this place and we've had plenty pass through but none like Josie
Swane. But somewhere along the way she stopped weavin' them
songs and became small and bitter and mean. By the time she
ran off and left ya I couldn't abide her.

HESTER.   There's a longin' in me for her that won't quell this while
gone.

CATWOMAN.   I wouldn't long for Josie Swane if I was you. Sure the
night ya were born she took ya over to the black swan's lair, auld
Black Wing ya've just buried there, and laid ya in the nest alongside her. And when I axed her why she'd do a thing like that with
snow and ice everywhere, ya know what she says, Swane means
swan. That may be so, says I, but the child'll die of pneumonia.
That child, says Josie Swane, will live as long as this black swan,

not a day more, not a day less. And each night for three nights
she left ya in the black swan's lair and each night I snuck ya out
of the lair and took ya home with me and brung ya back to the
lair before she'd come lookin' for ya in the mornin'. That's when
I started to turn again' her.

HESTER.   You're makin' it up to get rid of me like everywan else
round here. Xavier Cassidy put ya up to this.

CATWOMAN.   Xavier Cassidy put me up to nothin'. I'm only tellin'
ya so ya know what sourt of a woman your mother was. Ya were
lucky she left ya. Just forget about her and lave this place now or
ya never will.

HESTER.   Doesn't seem to make much difference whether I stay or
lave with a curse like that on me head.

CATWOMAN.   There's ways round curses. Curses only have the
power ya allow them. I'm tellin' ya, Hester, ya have to go. When
have I ever been proved wrong? Tould ya ya'd have just the wan
daughter, tould ya the day and hour she'd be born, didn't I now?

HESTER.   Ya did alright.

CATWOMAN.   Tould ya Carthage Kilbride was no good for ya, never
grew his backbone, would ya listen? Tould Monica Murray to
stop her only son drivin' to the city that night. Would she listen?
Where's her son? In his grave, that's where he is. Begged her till
she ran me off with a kittle of bilin' water. Mayhap she wanted
him dead. I'll say nothin'. Gave auld Xavier Cassidy herbs to cure
his wife. What did he do? Pegged them down the tilet and took
Olive Cassidy to see some swanky medicine man in a private hospital. They cured her alright, cured her so well she came back
cured as a side of ham in an oak coffin with golden handles.
Maybe he wanted her dead too. There's many gets into brown
studies over buryin' their loved wans. That a fact, Hester Swane.
I'll be off now and don't say the Catwoman never tould ya. Lave
this place now or ya never will.

HESTER.   I'm stoppin' here.

CATWOMAN.   Sure I know that too. Seen it writ in a bog hole.

HESTER.   Is there anythin' them blind eyes doesn't see writ in a bog
hole?

CATWOMAN.   Sneer away. Ya know what the Catwoman says is true,
but sneer away and we'll see will that sneer be on your puss at
dusk. Remember the Catwoman then for I don't think I'll have
the stomach for this place tonight.

[*And exit the* CATWOMAN *and exit* HESTER.]

SCENE 4

JOSIE *and* MRS KILBRIDE *enter and sit at the garden table as the* CAT-
WOMAN *and* HESTER *exit.* JOSIE *is dressed: wellingtons, trousers,
jumper on inside out. They're playing Snap.* MRS KILBRIDE *plays
ruthlessly, loves to win.* JOSIE *looks on in dismay.*

MRS K.   Snap—snap! Snap! [*Stacking the cards.*] How many games is that I'm after winnin' ya?

JOSIE.   Five.

MRS K.   And how many did you win?

JOSIE.   Ya know right well I won ne'er a game.

MRS K.   And do ya know why ya won ne'er a game, Josie? Because you're thick, that's the why.

JOSIE.   I always win when I play me Mam.

MRS K.   That's only because your Mam is thicker than you. Thick and stubborn and dangerous wrong-headed and backwards to top it all. Are ya goin' to start cryin' now, ya little pussy babby, don't you dare cry, ya need to toughen up, child, what age are ya now?—I says what age are ya?

JOSIE.   Seven.

MRS K.   Seven auld years. When I was seven I was cookin' dinners for a houseful of men, I was thinnin' turnips twelve hour a day, I was birthin' calves, sowin' corn, stookin' hay, ladin' a bull be his nose, and you can't even win a game of Snap. Sit up straight or ya'll grow up a hunchback. Would ya like that, would ya, to grow up a hunchback? Ya'd be like an auld camel and everyone'd say, as ya loped by, there goes Josie Kilbride the hunchback, would ya like that, would ya? Answer me.

JOSIE.   Ya know right well I wouldn't, Granny.

MRS K.   What did I tell ya about callin' me Grandmother.

JOSIE [*Defiantly*].   Granny.

MRS K [*Leans over the table viciously*].   Grandmother! Say it!

JOSIE [*Giving in*].   Grandmother.

MRS K.   And you're lucky I even let ya call me that. Ya want another game?

JOSIE.   Only if ya don't cheat.

MRS K.   When did I cheat?

JOSIE.   I seen ya, loads of times.

MRS K.   A bad loser's all you are, Josie, and there's nothin' meaner than a bad loser. I never cheat. Never. D'ya hear me, do ya? Look me in the eye when I'm talkin' to ya, ya little bastard. D'ya want another game?

JOSIE.   No thanks, Grandmother.

MRS K.   And why don't ya? Because ya know I'll win, isn't that it? Ya little coward ya, I'll break your spirit yet and then glue ya back the way I want ya. I bet ya can't even spell your name.

JOSIE.   And I bet ya I can.

MRS K.   G'wan then, spell it.

JOSIE [*Spells*].   J-o-s-i-e K-i-l-b-r-i-d-e.

MRS K.   Wrong! Wrong! Wrong!

JOSIE.   Well, that's the way Teacher taught me.

MRS K.   Are you back-answerin' me?

JOSIE.   No, Grandmother.

MRS K.   Ya got some of it right. Ya got the 'Josie' part right, but ya got the 'Kilbride' part wrong, because you're not a Kilbride. You're a Swane. Can ya spell Swane? Of course ya can't. You're Hester Swane's little bastard. You're not a Kilbride and never will be.

JOSIE.   I'm tellin' Daddy what ya said.

MRS K.   Tell him! Ya won't be tellin' him anythin' I haven't told him meself. He's an eegit, your Daddy. I warned him about that wan, Hester Swane, that she'd get her claws in, and she did, the tinker. That's what yees are, tinkers. And your poor Daddy, all he's had to put up with. Well, at least that's all changin' now. Why don't yees head off in that auld caravan, back to wherever yees came from, and give your poor Daddy back to me where he rightfully belongs. And you've your jumper on backwards.

JOSIE.   It's not backwards, it's inside out.

MRS K.   Don't you cheek me—and tell me this, Josie Swane, how much has your Mam in the bank?

JOSIE.   I don't know.

MRS K.   I'll tell ya how much, a great big goose egg. Useless, that's what she is, livin' off of handouts from my son that she flitters away on whiskey and cigars, the Jezebel[2] witch. [*Smugly*] Guess how much I've saved, Josie, g'wan, guess, guess.

JOSIE.   I wish if me Mam'd came soon.

MRS K.   Ah g'wan, child, guess.

JOSIE.   Ten pound.

MRS K [*Hysterical*].   Ten pound! A' ya mad, child? A' ya mad! Ten pound! [*Whispers avariciously*] Three thousand pound. All mine. I saved it. I didn't frig it away on crame buns and blouses. No. I saved it. A thousand for me funeral, a thousand for the Little Sisters of the Poor and a thousand for your Daddy. I'm lavin' you nothin' because your mother would get hould of it. And d'ya think would I get any thanks for savin' all that money? Oh no, none, none in the world. Would it ever occur to anywan to say, well done, Mrs Kilbride, well done, Elsie, not wance did your Daddy ever say, well done, Mother, no, too busy fornicatin' with Hester Swane, too busy bringin' little bastards like yourself into the world.

JOSIE.   Can I go and play now?

MRS K.   Here, I brung ya sweets, g'wan ate them, ate them all, there's a great child, ya need some sugar, some sweetie pie sweetness in your life. C'mere and give your auld Grandmother a kiss. [*JOSIE does*] Sure it's not your fault ya were born a little girl bastard. D'ya want another game of Snap? I'll let ya win.

JOSIE.   No.

MRS K.   Don't you worry, child, we'll get ya off of her yet. Me and your Daddy has plans. We'll batter ya into the semblance of legitimacy yet, soon as we get ya off—

2. Heretic Queen of Israel.

[*Enter* CARTHAGE.]

CARTHAGE.   I don't know how many times I tould ya to lave the
child alone. You've her poisoned with your bile and rage.
MRS K.   I'm sayin' nothin' that isn't true. Can't I play a game of
Snap with me own granddaughter?
CARTHAGE.   Ya know I don't want ya around here at the minute.
G'wan home, Mother, g'wan.
MRS K.   And do what? Talk to the range? Growl at God?
CARTHAGE.   Do whatever ya like, only lave Josie alone, pick on
somewan your own size. [*Turning* JOSIE's *jumper the right way
around*] You'll have to learn to dress yourself.
MRS K.   Ah now, Carthage, don't be annoyed with me. I only came
up to say goodbye to her, found her in her pyjamas out here
playin' in the snow. Why isn't her mother mindin' her?
CARTHAGE.   Don't start in on that again.
MRS K.   I never left you on your own.
CARTHAGE.   Ya should have.
MRS K.   And ya never called in to see the new dress I got for today
and ya promised ya would. [CARTHAGE *glares at her*] Alright, I'm
goin', I'm goin'. Just don't think now ya've got Caroline Cassidy
ya can do away with me, the same as you're doin' away with Hester Swane. I'm your mother and I won't be goin' away. Ever.

[*And exit* MRS KILBRIDE.]

CARTHAGE.   Where's your Mam?
JOSIE.   Isn't she always on the bog? Can I go to your weddin'?
CARTHAGE.   What does your mother say?
JOSIE.   She says there'll be no weddin' and to stop annoyin' her.
CARTHAGE.   Does she now?
JOSIE.   Will you ax her for me?
CARTHAGE.   We'll see, Josie, we'll see.
JOSIE.   I'll wear me Communion dress. Remember me Commu-
nion, Daddy?
CARTHAGE.   I do.
JOSIE.   Wasn't it just a brilliant day?
CARTHAGE.   It was, sweetheart, it was. Come on we go check the
calves.

[*And exit the pair.*]

SCENE 5

Enter CAROLINE CASSIDY *in her wedding dress and veil. Twenty,
fragile-looking and nervous. She goes to the window of Hester's house
and knocks.*

CAROLINE.   Hester—are ya there?

[HESTER *comes up behind her.*]

HESTER.   Haven't you the gall comin' here, Caroline Cassidy.

CAROLINE [*Jumps with fright*].   Oh! [*Recovers*] Can come here whenever I want, this is my house now, sure ya signed it over and all.

HESTER.   Bits of paper, writin', means nothin', can as aisy be unsigned.

CAROLINE.   You're meant to be gone this weeks, it's just not fair.

HESTER.   Lots of things isn't fair, Daddy's little ice-pop.

CAROLINE.   We're goin' ahead with the weddin', me and Carthage,
ya think ya'll disrupt everythin', Hester Swane. I'm not afraid of
ya.

HESTER.   Ya should be. I'm afraid of meself—What is it ya want
from me, Caroline? What have I ever done on you that ya feel
the need to take everythin' from me?

CAROLINE.   I'm takin' nothin' ya haven't lost already and lost this
long while gone.

HESTER.   You're takin' me husband, you're takin' me house, ya even
want me daughter. Over my dead body.

CAROLINE.   He was never your husband, he only took pity on ya,
took ya out of that auld caravan on the bog, gave ya a home, built
ya up from nothin'.

HESTER.   Them the sweet nothin's he's been tellin' ya? Let's get
wan thing straight, it was me built Carthage Kilbride up from
nothin', him a labourer's son you wouldn't give the time of day to
and you trottin' by in your first bra, on your half-bred mare, your
nose nudgin' the sun. It was me who tould him he could do better. It was my money that bought his first fine acres. It was in my
bed he slowly turned from a slavish pup to a man and no frigid
little Daddy's girl is goin' to take him from me. Now get off of my
property before I cut that dress to ribbons.

CAROLINE.   I'll have to get Daddy. He'll run ya off with a shotgun if
he has to.

HESTER.   Not everyone is as afraid of your Daddy as you are, Caroline.

CAROLINE.   Look, I'll give ya more money if ya'll only go. Here's me
bank book, there's nearly nineteen thousand pounds in it, me inheritance from me mother. Daddy gave it to me this mornin'. Ya
can have it, only please go. It's me weddin' day. It's meant to be
happy. It's meant to be the best day of me life.

[*She stands there, close to tears.* HESTER *goes over to her,
touches her veil.*]

HESTER.   What ya want me to do, Caroline? Admire your dress?
Wish ya well? Hah? I used babysit you. Remember that?

CAROLINE.   That was a long time ago.

HESTER.   Not that long at all. After your mother died, several
nights ya came down and slept with me. Ya were glad of the auld

caravan then, when your Daddy'd be off at the races or the mart or the pub, remember that, do ya? A pasty little thing, and I'd be awake half the night listenin' to your girly gibberish and grievances. Listen to me now, Caroline, there's two Hester Swanes, one that is decent and very fond of ya despite your callow treatment of me. And the other Hester, well, she could slide a knife down your face, carve ya up and not bat an eyelid.

[*Grabs her hair suddenly and viciously—*]

CAROLINE.   Ow! Lave go!
HESTER.   Listen to me now, Caroline. Carthage Kilbride is mine and only mine. He's been mine since he was sixteen. You think ya can take him from me? Wrong. All wrong. [*Lets go of her*] Now get out of me sight.
CAROLINE.   Ya'll be sorry for this, Hester Swane.
HESTER.   We all will.

[*And exit* CAROLINE, *running.*]

SCENE 6

HESTER *lights a cigar, sits at her garden table. Enter* JOSIE *with an old shawl around her head and a pair of high heels. She is pretending to be her Granny.*

JOSIE.   Well good mornin', Tinker Swane.
HESTER [*Mock surprise*].   Oh, good mornin', Mrs Kilbride, what a lovely surprise, and how are ya today?
JOSIE.   I've been savin' all night.
HESTER.   Have ya now, Mrs Kilbride.
JOSIE.   Tell me, ya Jezebel witch, how much have ya in the bank today?
HESTER.   Oh, I've three great big goose eggs, Mrs Kilbride. How much have ya in the bank yourself?
JOSIE.   Seventeen million pound. Seventeen million pound. I saved it. I didn't frig it away on love stories and silk stockin's. I cut back on sugar and I cut back on flour. I drank biled socks instead of tay and in wan night I saved seventeen million pound.
HESTER.   Ya drank biled socks, Mrs Kilbride?
JOSIE.   I did and I had turf stew for me dinner and for dessert I had snail tart and a big mug of wee-wee.
HESTER.   Sounds delicious, Mrs Kilbride.
JOSIE.   Ya wouldn't get better in Buckin'am Palace.
HESTER.   Josie, don't ever say any of that in front of your Granny, sure ya won't?
JOSIE.   I'm not a total eegit, Mam.
HESTER.   Did ya have your breakfast?
JOSIE.   I had a sugar sammige.

HESTER.   Ya better not have.

JOSIE.   Granny made me disgustin' porridge.

HESTER.   Did she? Did ya wash your teeth?

JOSIE.   Why do I always have to wash me teeth? Every day. It's so
    borin'. What do I need teeth for anyway?

HESTER.   Ya need them for snarlin' at people when smilin' doesn't
    work anymore. G'wan in and wash them now.

   [*Enter* CARTHAGE *in his wedding suit.* HESTER *looks at him,
   looks away.*]

JOSIE.   Did ya count the cattle, Daddy?

CARTHAGE.   I did.

JOSIE.   Were they all there?

CARTHAGE.   They were, Josie.

JOSIE.   Daddy says I can go to his weddin'.

CARTHAGE.   I said maybe, Josie.

HESTER.   G'wan round the back and play, Josie.

JOSIE.   Can I go, Mam, can I? Say yeah, g'wan, say yeah.

HESTER.   We'll see, g'wan, Josie, g'wan, good girl.

   [*And exit* JOSIE. *They both watch her. Silence.*]

CARTHAGE.   I'd like to know what ya think you're playin' at.

HESTER.   Take a better man than you to cancel me out, Carthage
    Kilbride.

CARTHAGE.   Ya haven't even started packin'.

HESTER.   Them your weddin' clothes?

CARTHAGE.   They're not me farm clothes, are they?

HESTER.   Ya've a cheek comin' here in them.

CARTHAGE.   Well, you missus, are meant to be gone.

HESTER.   And ya've a nerve tellin' Josie she can go to your weddin'.

CARTHAGE.   She's mine as well as yours.

HESTER.   Have ya slept with her yet?

CARTHAGE.   That's none of your business.

HESTER.   Every bit of me business. Ya think ya can wipe out four-
    teen years just like that. Well she's welcome to ya and any satis-
    faction she can squeeze out of ya.

CARTHAGE.   Never heard ya complainin' when I was in your bed.

HESTER.   Ya done the job, I suppose, in a kindergarten sourt of
    way.

CARTHAGE.   Kindergarten, that what ya call it?

HESTER.   You were nothin' before I put me stamp on ya and ya'll be
    nothin' again I'm finished with ya.

CARTHAGE.   Are you threatenin' me, Hetty? Because, if ya are, ya
    better know who you're dealin' with, not the sixteen year auld
    fool snaggin' hares along the Bog of Cats who fell into your
    clutches.

HESTER.   It was you wooed me, Carthage Kilbride, not the other
    way round as ya'd like everywan to think. In the beginnin' I
    wanted nothin' to do with ya, should've trusted me first instinct,

but ya kept comin' back. You cut your teeth on me, Carthage Kilbride, gnawed and sucked till all that's left is an auld bone ya
think to fling on the dunghill, now you've no more use for me. If
you think I'm goin' to let you walk over me like that, ya don't
know me at all.

CARTHAGE.   That at least is true. I've watched ya now for the best
part of fourteen years and I can't say for sure I know the first
thing about ya. Who are ya and what sourt of stuff are ya made
of?

HESTER.   The same as you and I can't abide to lose ya. Don't lave
me. Don't—is it I've gotten old and you just hittin' thirty?

CARTHAGE.   Ya know right well it isn't that.

HESTER.   And I haven't had a drink since the night ya left.

CARTHAGE.   I know.

HESTER.   I only ever drank anyway to forget about—

CARTHAGE.   I don't want to talk about that. Lave it.

HESTER.   And still ya took the money and bought the land, the Kilbrides who never owned anythin' till I came along, tinker and all.
Tell me what to do, Carthage, and I'll do it, anythin' for you to
come back.

CARTHAGE.   Just stop, will ya—

HESTER.   Anythin', Carthage, anythin', and I'll do it if it's in me
power.

CARTHAGE.   It's not in your power—Look, I'm up to me neck in another life that can't include ya anymore.

HESTER.   You're sellin' me and Josie down the river for a few lumpy
auld acres and notions of respectability and I never thought ya
would. You're better than all of them. Why must ya always look
for the good opinion from them that'll never give it. Ya'll only ever
be Xavier Cassidy's work horse. He won't treat ya right. He
wouldn't know how.

CARTHAGE.   He's treatin' me fine, signin' his farm over to me this
evenin'.

HESTER.   Ya know what they're sayin' about ya? That you're a
jumped-up land-hungry mongrel but that Xavier Cassidy is greed-
ier and craftier and he'll spancel ya back to the scrubber ya are.[3]

CARTHAGE.   And ya know what they're sayin' about you? That it's
time ya moved onto another haltin' site.

HESTER.   I was born on the Bog of Cats and on the Bog of Cats I'll
end me days. I've as much right to this place as any of yees,
more, for it holds me to it in ways it has never held yees. And as
for me tinker blood, I'm proud of it. It gives me an edge over all
of yees around her, allows me see yees for the inbred, underbred,
bog-brained shower yees are. I'm warnin' ya now, Carthage, you
go through with this sham weddin' and you'll never see Josie
again.

CARTHAGE.   If I have to mow ya down or have ya declared an unfit

3. Tie you back to the menial you are.

mother to see Josie I will, so for your own sake don't cause any trouble in that department. Look, Hetty, I want Josie to do well in the world, she'll get her share of everythin' I own and will own. I want her to have a chance in life, a chance you never had and so can never understand—

HESTER.   Don't tell me what I can and can't understand!

CARTHAGE.   Well understand this. Ya'll not separate me and Josie or I'll have her taken off of ya. I only have to mention your drinkin' or your night roamin' or the way ya sleep in that dirty auld caravan and lave Josie alone in the house.

HESTER.   I always take Josie to the caravan when I sleep there.

CARTHAGE.   Ya didn't take her last night.

HESTER.   I wasn't in the caravan last night. I was walkin' the bog, but I checked on her three, four times.

CARTHAGE.   Just don't cross me with Josie because I don't want to have to take her off of ya, I know she's attached to ya, and I'm not a monster. Just don't cross me over her or I'll come down on ya like a bull from heaven.

HESTER.   So I'm meant to lie back and let Caroline Cassidy have her way in the rearin' of me child. I'm meant to lave her around Xavier Cassidy—sure he's capable of anythin'. If it's the last thing I do I'll find a way to keep her from ya.

CARTHAGE.   I want you out of here before dusk! And I've put it to ya now about Josie. Think it over when ya've calmed down. And here. [*Producing envelope*] There's your blood money. It's all there down to the last penny.

HESTER.   No! I don't want it!

CARTHAGE.   [*Throws it in the snow*] Neither do I. I never should've took it in the first place. I owe ya nothin' now, Hester Swane. Nothin'. Ya've no hold over me now.

[*Goes to exit.*]

HESTER.   Carthage—ya can't just walk away like this.

CARTHAGE.   I can and I am—Ya know what amazes me, Hetty?

HESTER.   What?

CARTHAGE.   That I stayed with ya so long—I want peace, just peace—Remember, before dusk.

[*And exit* CARTHAGE. HESTER *looks after him, a low heartbroken wail.* JOSIE *comes running on.*]

JOSIE.   What's wrong of ya, Mam?

HESTER.   Ah go 'way, would ya, and lave me alone.

JOSIE.   Can I go down to Daly's and buy sweets?

HESTER.   No, ya can't. Go on off and play, you're far too demandin'.

JOSIE.   Yeah well, just because you're in a bad humour it's not my fault. I'm fed up playin' on me own.

HESTER.   You'll get a clatter if you're not careful. I played on me own when I was your age, I never bothered me mother, you're spoilt rotten, that's what ya are. [*In a gentler tone*] G'wan and play with your dolls, give them a bath, cut their hair.

JOSIE.   Ya said I wasn't to cut their hair.

HESTER.   Well now I'm sayin' ya can, alright.

JOSIE.   But it won't grow back.

HESTER.   So! There's worse things in this world than your dolls' hair not growin' back, believe me, Josie Swane.

JOSIE.   Me name is Josie Kilbride.

HESTER.   That's what I said.

JOSIE.   Ya didn't, ya said Josie Swane. I'm not a Swane. I'm a Kilbride.

HESTER.   I suppose you're ashamed of me too.

[*Enter* XAVIER CASSIDY *and* CAROLINE, *both in their wedding clothes.*]

JOSIE.   Caroline, your dress, is that your weddin' dress? It's beautiful.

CAROLINE.   Hello Josie.

[JOSIE *runs over to* CAROLINE *to touch her dress.* HESTER *storms after her, picks her up roughly, carries her to corner of the house. Puts her down.*]

HESTER.   Now stay around the back.

[*And exit* JOSIE.]

XAVIER.   Was hopin' I wouldn't find ya still here, Swane.

HESTER.   So ya came back with your Daddy, ya know nothin', Caroline, nothin'.

[*Sits at her garden table, produces a naggin of whiskey from her pocket, drinks.*]

XAVIER.   Thought ya'd given up the drink.

HESTER.   I had. Me first in months, but why should I try and explain meself to you?

XAVIER.   Might interest Carthage to know you lashin' into a naggin of whiskey at this hour.

HESTER.   Carthage. If it wasn't for you, me and Carthage'd be fine. Should've eradicated ya, Cassidy, when I could've. God's punishin' me now because I didn't take steps that were right and proper concernin' you. Aye. God's punishin' me but I won't take his blows lyin' down.

CAROLINE.   What are ya talking about, Hester?

HESTER.   What am I talkin' about? I'm talkin' about you, ya little fool, and I'm talkin' about James.

CAROLINE.   Me brother James?

XAVIER.   You keep a civil tongue, Swane, over things ya know nothin' about.

HESTER.   Oh, but I do know things, and that's why ya want me out of here. It's only your land and money and people's fear of ya that has ya walkin' free. G'wan home and do whatever it is ya do with your daughter, but keep your sleazy eyes off of me and Josie. This is my property and I've a right to sit in me own yard without bein' ogled by the likes of you.

XAVIER.   There's things softer on the eye than you, Swane, if it's oglin' I was after. This is no longer your property and well ya know it, ya signed it over six months ago, for a fine hefty sum, have the papers here.

HESTER.   I wasn't thinkin' right then, was bein' coerced and bullied from all sides, but I have regained me pride and it tells me I'm stayin'. Ya'll get your money back.

[*Picks up envelope* CARTHAGE *has thrown in the snow.*]

Here's some of it.

XAVIER.   I'm not takin' it. A deal's a deal.

HESTER.   Take it! Take it! [*Stuffs it into his breast pocket*] And it might interest ya to know, Caroline, that Carthage was just here in his weddin' clothes and he didn't look like no radiant groom and he axed me to take him back, but I said—

XAVIER.   I'd say he did alright—

HESTER.   He did! He did! Or as much as, but I said I couldn't be played with anymore, that I was made for things he has lost the power to offer. And I was. I was made for somethin' different than these butchery lives yees all lead here on the Bog of Cats. Me mother taught me that.

XAVIER.   Your mother. Your mother taught ya nothin', Swane, except maybe how to use a knife. Let me tell ya a thing or two about your mother, big Josie Swane. I used see her outside her auld caravan on the bog and the fields covered over in stars and her half covered in an excuse for a dress and her croonin' towards Orion in a language I never heard before or since. We'd peace when she left.

HESTER.   And what were ya doin' watchin' her? Catwoman tould me ya were in a constant swoon over me mother, sniffin' round the caravan, lavin' little presents and Christmas dinners and money and drink, sure I remember the gatch of ya meself and ya scrapin' at the door.

XAVIER.   Very presumptuous of ya, Swane, to think I'd have any interest in your mother beyond Christian compassion.

HESTER.   Christian compassion! That what it's called these days!

XAVIER.   Aye, Christian compassion, a thing that was never bet into you. Ya say ya remember lots of things, then maybe ya remember that that food and money I used lave was left so ya wouldn't starve. Times I'd walk by that caravan and there'd be ne'er a sign of this mother of yours. She'd go off for days with anywan who'd buy her a drink. She'd be off in the bars of Pullagh and Mucklagh gettin' into fights. Wance she bit the nose off a

woman who dared to look at her man, bit the nose clean off her
face. And you, you'd be chained to the door of the caravan with
maybe a dirty nappy on ya if ya were lucky. Often times—

HESTER.   Lies! All lies!

XAVIER.   Often times I brung ya home and gave ya over to me
mother to put some clothes on ya and feed ya. More times than I
can remember it'd be from our house your mother would collect
ya, the brazen walk of her, and not a thank you or a flicker of
guilt in her eye and her reekin' of drink. Times she wouldn't even
bother to collect ya and meself or me mother would have to bring
ya down to her and she'd hardly notice that we'd come and gone
or that you'd returned.

HESTER.   Ya expect me to believe anythin' that comes from your
siled lips, Xavier Cassidy.

XAVIER.   And wan other thing, Swane, for you to cast aspersions
on me just because I'm an auld widower, that's cheap and low.
Not everywan sees the world through your troubled eyes. There's
such a thing as a father lovin' his daughter as a father should, no
more, no less, somethin' you have never known, and I will—

HESTER.   I had a father too! Ya'd swear I was dropped from the sky
the way ya go on. Jack Swane of Bergit's Island, I never knew
him—but I had a father. I'm as settled as any of yees—

XAVIER.   Well, he wasn't much of a father, never claimin' ya when
your mother ran off.

HESTER.   He claimed me in the end—

XAVIER.   Look, Swane, I don't care about your family or where ya
came from. I care only about me own and all I've left is Caroline
and if I have to plough through you to have the best for her, then
that's what I'll do. I don't want to unless I have to. So do it the
aisy way for all of us. Lave this place today.

[*Takes envelope from breast pocket, puts it into her hand.*]

This is yours. Come on, Caroline.

CAROLINE.   Ya heard what Daddy says. Ya don't know his temper,
Hester.

HESTER.   And you don't know mine.

[*And exit* XAVIER *followed by* CAROLINE. HESTER *sits at her garden table, has a drink, looks up at the cold winter sky.*]

[*A whisper*] Dear God on high, what have ya in store for me at
all?

[*Enter* JOSIE *in her Communion dress, veil, buckled shoes,
handbag, the works.*]

[*Looks at her a minute*] What are ya doin' in your Communion
dress?

JOSIE.   For Daddy's weddin'. I'm grown out of all me other dresses.

HESTER.   I don't think ya are.

JOSIE.   I am. I can go, can't I, Mam?

HESTER.　Ya have her eyes.

JOSIE.　Whose eyes—whose eyes, Mam?

HESTER.　Josie Swane's, me mother.

JOSIE.　Granny said me real name is Josie Swane.

HESTER.　Don't mind your Granny.

JOSIE.　Did ya like her, Josie Swane?

HESTER.　—More than anythin' in this cold white world.

JOSIE.　More than me and Daddy?

HESTER.　I'm talkin' about when I was your age. Ya weren't born then, Josie—Ya know the last time I saw me mother I was wearin' me Communion dress too, down by the caravan, a beautiful summer's night and the bog like a furnace. I wouldn't go to bed though she kept tellin' me to. I don't know why I wouldn't, I always done what she tould me. I think now—maybe I knew. And she says, I'm goin' walkin' the bog, you're to stay here, Hetty. And I says, No, I'd go along with her, and made to folly her. And she says, No, Hetty, you wait here, I'll be back in a while. And again I made to folly her and again she stopped me. And I watched her walk away from me across the Bog of Cats. And across the Bog of Cats I'll watch her return.

　　　[*Lights down. End of Act 1.*]

Act 2

Interior of Xavier Cassidy's house. A long table covered in a white tablecloth, laid for the wedding feast. Music off, a band setting up. The CATWOMAN *sits at centre table lapping wine from a saucer. A* WAITER, *a lanky, gawky young fellow hovers with a bottle of wine waiting to refill the saucer.*

WAITER.　You're sure now ya wouldn't like a glass, Catwoman?

CATWOMAN.　No, no, I love the saucer, young man. What's your name? Do I know ya?

WAITER.　I'm a Dunne.

CATWOMAN.　Wan of the long Dunnes or wan of the scutty fat legged Dunnes?

WAITER.　Wan of the long Dunnes. Ya want a refill, Catwoman?

CATWOMAN.　I will. Are ya still in school? Your voice sounds as if it's just breakin'.

WAITER.　I am.

CATWOMAN.　And what're ya goin' to be when ya grow up, young Long Dunne?

WAITER.　I want to be an astronaut but me father wants me to work on the bog like him and like me grandfather. The Dunnes has always worked on the bog.

CATWOMAN.　Oh go for the astronaut, young man.

WAITER.　I will so, Catwoman. Have ya enough wine?

CATWOMAN.　Plenty for now.

[*Exit young* DUNNE *crossed by the ghost of* JOSEPH SWANE, *entering; blood-stained shirt and trousers, a throat wound. He walks across the stage.* CATWOMAN *cocks her ear, starts sniffing.*]

JOSEPH. Hello. Hello.

CATWOMAN. Ah Christ, not another ghost.

JOSEPH. Who's there?

CATWOMAN. Go 'way and lave me alone. I'm on me day off.

JOSEPH. Who are ya? I can't see ya.

CATWOMAN. I can't see you aither. I'm the Catwoman but I tould ya I'm not talkin' to ghosts today, yees have me heart scalded, hardly got a wink's sleep last night.

JOSEPH. Please, I haven't spoken to anywan since the night I died.

CATWOMAN. Haven't ya? Who are ya anyway?

JOSEPH. I'm Joseph Swane of Bergit's Island. Is this Bergit's Island?

CATWOMAN. This is the Bog of Cats.

JOSEPH. The Bog of Cats. Me mother had a song about this place.

CATWOMAN. Josie Swane was your mother?

JOSEPH. Ya know her?

CATWOMAN. Oh aye, I knew her. Then Hester must be your sister?

JOSEPH. Hester, ya know Hester too?

CATWOMAN. She lives only down the lane. I never knew Hester had a brother.

JOSEPH. I doubt she'd be tellin' people about me.

CATWOMAN. I don't mean to be short with ya, Joseph Swane, but Saturday is me day off. I haven't a minute to meself with yees, so tell me what is it ya want and then be on your way.

JOSEPH. I want to be alive again. I want to stop walkin'. I want to rest, ate a steak, meet a girl, I want to fish for wild salmon and sow pike on Bergit's Lake again.

CATWOMAN. You'll never do them things again, Joseph Swane.

JOSEPH. Don't say that to me, Catwoman, I'm just turned eighteen.

CATWOMAN. Eighteen. That's young to die alright. But it could be worse. I've a two-year-old ghost who comes to visit, all she wants to do is play Peep. Still eighteen's young enough. How come ya went so young? An accident, was it? Or by your own hand?

WAITER [*Going by*]. Ya talkin' to me, Catwoman?

CATWOMAN. No, Long Dunne, just a ghost, a poor lost ghost.

WAITER. Oh. [*And exit*]

JOSEPH. Are ya still there, Catwoman?

CATWOMAN. I am but there's nothin' I can do for ya, you're not comin' back?

JOSEPH. Is there no way?

CATWOMAN. None, none in this world anyway, and the sooner ya realize that the better for ya. Now be on your way, settle in to your new world, knock the best out of it ya can.

JOSEPH.   It's fierce hard to knock the best out of nothin', fierce hard to enjoy darkness the whole time, can't I just stay here with ya, talk to ya a while?

CATWOMAN.   Ya could I suppose, only I'm at a weddin' and they might think I'm not the full shillin' if I have to be talkin' to you all day. Look, I'll take ya down to Hester Swane's house, ya can talk to her.

JOSEPH.   Can she hear ghosts?

CATWOMAN [*Getting up*].   Oh aye, though she lets on she can't.

JOSEPH.   Alright so, I suppose I may as well since I'm here.

CATWOMAN.   C'mon, folly me voice till I lead ya there.

JOSEPH [*Following her*].   Keep talkin' so I don't take a wrong turnin'.

CATWOMAN.   I will and hurry up now, I don't want to miss the weddin'. Ya still there?

JOSEPH.   I am.

> [*And they're off by now. Enter* CAROLINE *and* CARTHAGE *as they exit.*]

CAROLINE.   This is the tablecloth me mother had for her weddin' and it's the same silver too. I'd really like for her to have been here today—Aye, I would.

CARTHAGE.   A soft-boned lady, your mother. I used see her in town shoppin' with you be the hand, ya wanted to bow when she walked by, she had class. And you have too, Caroline, like no wan else around here.

CAROLINE.   I can't stop thinkin' about Hester.

CARTHAGE [*Kisses her*].   Hester'll be fine, tough as an auld boot. Ya shouldn't concern yourself with her on your weddin' day. I've provided well for her, she isn't goin' to ever have to work a day in her life, Josie's the wan I worry about. The little sweetheart all done up in her Communion dress. Hetty should've got her a proper dress.

CAROLINE.   But Hester didn't want her here, Carthage.

CARTHAGE.   Ya know what I wish?

CAROLINE.   What?

CARTHAGE.   That she'd just give Josie to me and be done with it.

CAROLINE.   You're still very tangled up with Hester, aren't ya?

CARTHAGE.   I'm not wan bit tangled with her, if she'd just do what she's supposed to do which is fierce simple, clear out of the Bog of Cats for wance and for all.

CAROLINE.   And I suppose ya'll talk about me as callously wan day too.

CARTHAGE.   Of course I won't, why would I?

CAROLINE.   It's all fierce messy, Carthage. I'd hoped ya'd have sourted it out by today. It laves me in a fierce awkward position. You're far more attached to her than ya'd led me to believe.

CARTHAGE.   Attached to her? I'm not attached to her, I stopped lovin' her years ago!

CAROLINE. I'm not jealous as to whether ya love her or don't love
her, I think maybe I'd prefer if ya still did.
CARTHAGE. Then what's botherin' ya?
CAROLINE. You and Hester has a whole history together, stretchin'
back years that connects yees and that seems more important
and real than anythin' we have. And I wonder have we done the
wrong thing.
CARTHAGE. Ya should've said all this before ya took your vows at
the altar.
CAROLINE. I've been tryin' to say it to ya for weeks.
CARTHAGE. So what do we do now?
CAROLINE. Get through today, I suppose, pretend it's the best day
of our lives. I don't know about you but I've had better days than
today, far better.
CARTHAGE. Caroline, what's wrong of ya?
CAROLINE. Nothin', only I feel like I'm walkin' on somewan's
grave.

> [*Enter* MRS KILBRIDE *in what looks extremely like a wedding
> dress, white, a white hat, with a bit of a veil trailing off it,
> white shoes, tights, bag, etc.*]

MRS K [*Flushed, excited, neurotic*]. Oh the love birds! The love
birds! There yees are, off hidin'. Carthage, I want a photo of yees.
Would you take it, Caroline?
CARTHAGE. She means she wants wan of herself.
MRS K. Shush now, Carthage, and stand up straight.

> [*They pose like a bride and groom,* CARTHAGE *glaring at* MRS
> K.]

That's it. Wan more, smile, Carthage, smile, I hate a glowery de-
meanour in a photograph. That's great, Caroline, did ya get me
shoes in?
CAROLINE. I don't think I—
MRS K. Doesn't matter, doesn't matter, thank ya, what a glorious
day, what a glorious white winter's day, nothin' must spoil today
for me, nothin'.

> [*Begins photographing her shoes, first one, then the other.*]

CARTHAGE. What in the name of God are ya at now?
MRS K. I just want to get a photo of me shoes while they're new
and clean. I've never had such a beautiful pair of shoes, look at
the diamonds sparklin' on them. I saved like a Shylock for them,
seen them in O'Brien's six months ago and I knew instantly them
were to be me weddin' shoes. And I put by every week for them.
Guess how much they were, Carthage, g'wan guess, Caroline,
guess, guess.
CAROLINE. I don't know, Mrs Kilbride.
MRS K. Elsie! Elsie! Call me Elsie, ah g'wan guess.
CAROLINE. Fifty pound.

MRS K [*Angrily*].   Fifty pound! Are ya mad! Are ya out of your tiny mind!

CARTHAGE.   Tell us how much they were, Mother, before we die of the suspense.

MRS K [*Smug, can hardly believe it herself*].   A hundred and fifty pound. The Quane herself wouldn't pay more.

> [MONICA *and* XAVIER *have entered*, MONICA *has* JOSIE *by the hand.*]

MONICA.   —And Father Willow seems to have lost the run of himself entirely.

XAVIER.   They should put him down, he's eighty if he's a day.

MONICA.   The state of him with his hat on all durin' the Mass and the vestments inside out and his pyjamas peepin' out from under his trousers.

XAVIER.   Did you hear he's started keepin' a gun in the tabernacle?

MONICA.   I did, aye.

XAVIER.   For all them robbers, is it?

MONICA.   No, apparently it's for any of us that's late for Mass. Ya know what I was thinkin' and I lookin' at Caroline up there on the altar, I was thinkin' about my young fella Brian and I decided not to think about him today at all.

XAVIER.   God rest him.

MONICA.   If only I'd heeded the Catwoman he'd be here today. Didn't you think about your own young fella too?

XAVIER.   Never, I never think about him. Never. Children! If they were calves we'd have them fattened and sould in three weeks. I never think of James. Never.

MONICA.   Or Olive aither?

XAVIER.   Ah, Olive had no fight in her, wailed like a ewe in a storm after the young lad and then lay down with her face to the wall. Ya know what she died of, Monica? Spite. Spite again' me. Well, she's the wan who's dead. I've the last laugh on her.

MONICA.   Strange what these weddin's drag up.

XAVIER.   Aye, they cost a fortune.

> [*Takes two glasses of champagne from a passing* WAITER.]

Here, Monica, and cheers. [*To* JOSIE] Child, a pound for your handbag.

MRS K.   What d'ya say, Josie?

XAVIER.   Lave her. Two things in this world get ya nowhere, sayin' sorry and sayin' thanks—that right, Josie?

JOSIE.   That's right, Mr Cassidy.

MRS K [*Taking* JOSIE *a little aside*].   Here give me that pound till I mind it for ya.

JOSIE.   First give me back me Communion money.

MRS K.   What Communion money?

CARTHAGE.   So it was you took her Communion money.

[*The* CATWOMAN *and* FATHER WILLOW *have entered, linking arms, both with their sticks.* FATHER WILLOW *has his snuff on hand, pyjamas showing from under his shirt and trousers, hat on, adores the* CATWOMAN.]

FR WILLOW.   I'm tellin' ya now, Catwoman, ya'll have to cut back on the mice, they'll be the death of ya.

CATWOMAN.   And you'll have to cut back on the snuff.

FR WILLOW.   Try snails instead, far better for ya, the French ate them with garlic and tons of butter and Burgundy wine. I tried them wance meself and I in Avalon. Delicious.

CATWOMAN.   We should go on a holiday, you and me, Father Willow.

FR WILLOW.   Ah, ya say that every winter and come the summer I can't budge ya.

CATWOMAN.   I'll go away with ya next summer and that's promise.

FR WILLOW.   Well, where do ya want to go and I'll book the tickets in the mornin'?

CATWOMAN.   Anywhere at all away from this auld bog, somewhere with a big hot sun.

FR WILLOW.   Burgundy's your man then.

MONICA.   God help Burgundy is all I say.

CATWOMAN.   Anywhere it's not rainin' because it's goin' to rain here all next summer, seen it writ in the sky.

MRS K.   Writ in the sky, me eye, sure she's blind as a bat. Xavier, what did ya have to invite the Catwoman for? Brings down the tone of the whole weddin'.

MONICA.   Hasn't she as much right to walk God's earth as you, partake of its pleasures too.

MRS K.   No, she hasn't! Not till she washes herself. The turf-smoke stink of her. Look at her moochin' up to Father Willow and her never inside the door of the church and me at seven Mass every mornin' watchin' that auld fool dribblin' into the chalice. And would he call to see me? Never. Spends all his time with the Catwoman in her dirty little hovel. I'd write to the Archbishop if I thought he was capable of anythin'. Why did ya have to invite her?

XAVIER.   Ya know as well as me it's bad luck not to invite the Catwoman.

[FATHER WILLOW *shoots* MRS K *in the back of the head with an imaginary pistol as he walks by or as she walks by.*]

MRS K.   I'd love to hose her down, fling her in onto the milkin' parlour floor, turn the water on full blast and hose her down to her kidneys.

CARTHAGE [*With his arm around* CAROLINE].   Well, Catwoman, what do ya predict for us?

CATWOMAN.   I predict nothin'.

CARTHAGE.   Ah g'wan now, ya must have a blessin' or a vision or somethin'.

CAROLINE.   Lave it, Carthage. You're welcome, Catwoman and Father Willow.

FR WILLOW.   Thank you, Hester, thank you.

CARTHAGE.   You mean, Caroline, Father Willow, this is Caroline.

FR WILLOW.   Whatever.

CARTHAGE.   Come on now, Catwoman, and give Caroline and me wan of your blessin's.

CATWOMAN.   Seein' as ya insist. Separate tombstones. I'm sorry but I tould ya not to ax me.

JOSIE.   Granny, will ya take a photo of just me and Daddy for to put in me scrapbook?

MRS K.   Don't be so rude, you, to Caroline. [*Hisses*] And I tould ya to call me Grandmother!

JOSIE [*Whispers boldly from the safety of her father's side*].   Granny, Granny, Granny.

CAROLINE.   She's alright. Here, I'll take the photo of you and Carthage for your scrapbook. [*Does*]

MRS K.   She's ruined, that's what she is, turnin' up in her Communion dress, makin' a holy show of us all.

CARTHAGE.   It's you that's the holy show in that stupid dress.

MRS K.   What! I am not! There's gratitude for ya. Ya make an effort to look your best. [*Close to tears*] I cut back on everythin' to buy this dress. How was I supposed to know the bride'd be wearin' white as well.

CARTHAGE.   Don't start whingin' now in front of everywan, sit down will ya, ya look fine, ya look great—Alright, I'm sorry. Ya look stunnin'!

MRS K [*Beginning to smile*].   I don't, do I?

CARTHAGE.   Christ! Yes!

FR WILLOW [*Leading the* CATWOMAN *to the table, whispers to her*].   If ya were a bar of chocolate I'd ate ya.

CATWOMAN.   If I was a bar of chocolate I'd ate meself.

> [*They've all made their way to the table by now and are seated,* XAVIER *tinkles his glass for silence.*]

XAVIER.   Thank you. Now before we dig in I'd like to welcome yees all here on wan of the happiest days of me life. Yees have all long known that Caroline has been my greatest joy and reason for livin'. Her mother, if she was here today, would've been proud too at how she has grown into a lovely and graceful woman. I can take no credit for that, though I've taken the greatest pride these long years in watchin' her change from a motherless child to a gawky girl, to this apparition I see before me eyes today. We auld fathers would like to keep our daughters be our sides forever and enjoy their care and gentleness but it seems the world does have a different plan entirely. We must rear them up for another man's benefit. Well if this is so, I can't think of a better man than Carthage Kilbride to take over the care of me only child. [*Raises his glass*] I wish yees well and happiness and infants rompin' on the hearth.

ALL. Hear! Hear!

XAVIER. Father Willow, would ya do us the—

MRS K [*Standing up*]. I'd like to say a few words too—

XAVIER. Go ahead, Mrs Kilbride.

MRS K. As the proud mother of the groom—

CARTHAGE. Mother, would ya whisht up—

MRS K [*Posh public speaking voice*]. As the proud mother of the groom, I feel the need to answer Xavier's fine speech with a few words of me own. Never was a mother more blessed than me in havin' Carthage for a son. As a child he was uncommon good, never cried, never disobeyed, never raised his voice wance to me, never went about with a grumpy puss on him. Indeed he went to the greatest pains always to see that me spirits was good, that me heart was uplifted. When his father died he used come into the bed to sleep beside me for fear I would be lonely. Often I woke from a deep slumber and his two arms would be around me, a small leg thrown over me in sleep—

CATWOMAN. The craythur—

MRS K. He was also always aware of my abidin' love for Our Lord, unlike some here [*Glares at the* CATWOMAN] and on wan occasion, me birthday it was, I looked out the back window and there he was up on the slope behind our house and what was he doin'? He was buildin' Calvary for me. He'd hammered three wooden crosses and was erectin' them on the slope Calvary-style. Wan for him, wan for me and wan for Our Lord. And we draped ourselves around them like the two thieves in the holy book, remember, Carthage?

CARTHAGE. I do not, would ya ever sit down.

MRS K. Of course ya do, the three crosses ya made up on the slope and remember the wind was howlin' and the pair of us yellin' 'Calvary! Calvary!' to wan another. Of course ya remember. I'm only tellin' yees this story as wan of the countless examples of Carthage's kind nature and I only want to say that Caroline is very welcome into the Kilbride household. And that if Carthage will be as good a son to Caroline as he's been a husband to me then she'll have no complaints. [*Raises her glass*] Cheers.

ALL. Hear! Hear!

XAVIER. And now, Father Willow, ya'll say grace for us?

FR WILLOW. It'd be an honour, Jack, thank you—

MRS K. Who's Jack?

FR WILLOW. (*Getting up*) In the name of the Father and of the Son and of the Holy Ghost, it may or may not surprise yees all if I tould yees I was almost a groom meself wance. Her name was Elizabeth Kennedy, no that was me mother's name, her name was—it'll come to me, anyway it wasn't to be, in the end we fell out over a duck egg on a walkin' holiday by the Shannon, what was her name at all? Helen? No.

MRS K.   Would ya say the grace, Father Willow, and be—

FR WILLOW.   The grace, yes, how does it go again?

MRS K.   Bless us, oh Lord, and these thy gifts which of—

FR WILLOW.   Rowena. That was it. Rowena Phelan. I should never have ate that duck egg—no—[*Stands there lost in thought*]

[*Enter* HESTER *in her wedding dress, veil, shoes, the works.*]

MRS K.   Ya piebald knacker ya.

XAVIER.   What's your business here, Swane, besides puttin' a curse on me daughter's weddin'?

MRS K.   The brazen nerve of her turnin' up in that garb.

HESTER.   The kettle callin' the pot white. Remember this dress, Carthage? He bought it for me—

CAROLINE.   Daddy, would ya do somethin'.

HESTER.   Oh must be near nine year ago. We'd got to the stage where we should've parted and I said it to ya and ya convinced me otherwise and axed me to marry ya. Came home wan evenin' with this dress in a box and somehow it got put away. Ya only ever wanted me there until ya were strong enough to lave me.

CARTHAGE.   Get outa here right now!

HESTER.   Ya thought ya could come swaggerin' to me this mornin' in your weddin' clothes, well, here I am, in mine. This is my weddin' day be rights and not wan of yees can deny it. And yees all just sit there glarin' as if I'm the guilty wan. [*Takes* CARTHAGE's *glass of wine, drinks from it*]

MRS K.   Run her off, Xavier! Run her off or I will. [*Gets up*]

CARTHAGE [*Pulls her back*].   Would you keep out of this!

MRS K.   And let her walk all over us?

MONICA.   Hester, go home, g'wan.

MRS K [*Getting up again*].   I've had the measure of you this long time, the lazy shiftless blood in ya, that savage tinker eye ya turn on people to frighten them—

CARTHAGE.   Would ya shut up! Ya haven't shut up all day! We're not havin' a brawl here.

MRS K.   There's a nice way to talk to your mother on your weddin' day, I'm not afraid of ya, Hester Swane, you're just a sad lost little woman—

HESTER.   I still stole your son from ya, didn't I, Elsie? Your sissy boy that I tried to make a man of.

MRS K.   Ya took advantage of him, ya had to take advantage of a young boy for your perverted pleasures for no grown man would stomach ya.

HESTER.   And weren't they great, Carthage, all them nights in the caravan I 'took advantage' of ya and you bangin' on the window and us stuffin' pillows in our mouths so ya wouldn't hear us laughin'—

MRS K.   You're absolutely disgustin', that's what ya are!

HESTER.   Have you ever been <u>discarded,</u> Elsie Kilbride?—the way I've been dis- —

MRS K.   No, I've never been discarded, Hester Swane! Ya know why? Because I've never overstepped meself. I've always lived be the rules.

HESTER.   Ah rules! What rules are they? Teach them to me and I'll live by them. Yees don't know what it's like, to be flung on the ashpit and you still alive—

XAVIER.   No wan's flingin' ya anywhere! We done everythin' proper by you—

HESTER.   Proper! Yees have taken everythin' from me. I've done nothin' again' any of yees. I'm just bein' who I am, Carthage, I'm axin' ya the wance more, come away with me now, with me and—

MRS K.   Come away with her, she says—

HESTER.   Yes! Come away with me and Josie and stop all this—

XAVIER.   Come away with ya! Are ya mad! He's married to Caroline now—

CARTHAGE.   Go home, Hester, and pack your things.

MONICA.   C'mon, Hester, I'll take ya home.

HESTER.   I have no home anymore for he's decided to take it from me.

MONICA.   Then come and live with me, I've no wan—

HESTER.   No, I want to stay in me own house. Just let me stay in the house, Carthage. I won't bother anywan if yees'd just lave me alone. I was born on the Bog of Cats, same as all of yees, though ya'd never think it the way yees shun me. I know every barrow and rivulet and bog hole of its nine square mile. I know where the best bog rosemary grows and the sweetest wild bog rue. I could lead yees around the Bog of Cats in me sleep.

CARTHAGE.   There's a house bought and furnished for ya in town as ya agreed to—

HESTER.   I've never lived in a town. I won't know anywan there—

MONICA.   Ah, let her stay in the house, the Bog of Cats is all she knows—

MRS K.   And since when do we need you stickin' your snout in, Monica Murray?

MONICA.   <u>Since you and your son have forgotten all dacency, Elsie Kilbride. Ya've always been too hard on her. Ya never gave her a chance</u>—

MRS K.   A waste of time givin' chances to a tinker. All tinkers understands is the open road and where the next bottle of whiskey is comin' from.

MONICA.   Well, you should know and your own grandfather wan!

MRS K.   My grandfather was a wanderin' tinsmith—

MONICA.   And what's that but a tinker with notions!

FR WILLOW.   What year is this wine?

MONICA.   Go home, Hester. Don't plead your case with this shower. They'd sicken ya!

HESTER.   Carthage, ya could aisy afford another house for yourself and Caroline if ya wanted—

CARTHAGE.   No! We're stickin' by what we agreed on—

HESTER.   The truth is you want to eradicate me, make out I never existed—

CARTHAGE.   If I wanted to eradicate ya, I could've, long ago. And I could've taken Josie off of ya. Facts are, I been more than generous with ya.

HESTER.   You're plentiful with the guilt money alright, showerin' buckets of it on me. [*Flings envelope he had given her in Act One at him*] There's your auld blood money back. Ya think you're gettin' away that aisy! Money won't take that guilt away, Carthage, we'll go to our grave with it!

CARTHAGE.   I've not an ounce of guilt where you're concerned and whatever leftover feelin' I had for ya as the mother of me child is gone after this display of hatred towards me. Just go away, I can't bear the sight of ya!

HESTER.   I can't lave the Bog of Cats—

MRS K.   We'll burn ya out if we have to—

HESTER.   Ya see—

MRS K.   Won't we, Xavier—

XAVIER.   Ya can lave me out of any low-boy tactics. You're lavin' this place today, Swane, aren't ya?

HESTER.   I can't lave—Ya see me mother said she'd come back here—

MRS K.   Your mother! That tramp hasn't been seen round here in over thirty—

HESTER.   Don't call her that! Father Willow, tell them what they're doin' is wrong. They'll listen to you.

FR WILLOW.   They've never listened to me, sure they even lie in the Confession box. Ya know what I do? I wear ear-plugs.

HESTER [*Close to tears*].   I can't lave till me mother comes. I'd hoped she'd have come before now and it wouldn't come to this. Don't make me lave this place or somethin' terrible'll happen. Don't.

XAVIER.   We've had enough of your ravin', Swane, so take yourself elsewhere and let us try to recoup these marred celebrations.

JOSIE.   I'll go with ya, Mam, and ya look gorgeous in that dress.

CARTHAGE.   Stay where ya are, Josie.

JOSIE.   No, I want to go with me Mam.

CARTHAGE [*Stopping her*].   Ya don't know what ya want. And reconsiderin', I think it'd be better all round if Josie stays with me till ya've moved. I'll bring her back to ya then.

HESTER.   I've swallyed all me pride over you. You're lavin' me no choice but a vicious war against ya.

[*Takes a bottle of wine from the table.*]

Josie, I'll be back to collect ya later. And you just try keepin' her from me!

[*And exit* HESTER. *End of Act Two.*]

Act 3

Dusk. HESTER, *in her wedding dress, charred and muddied. Behind her, the house and sheds ablaze.* JOSEPH SWANE *stands in the flames watching her.*

HESTER. Well, Carthage, ya think them were only idle threats I made? Ya think I can be flung in a bog hole like a bag of newborn pups? Let's see how ya like this—Ya hear that sound? Them's your cattle howlin'. Ya smell that smell? That's your forty calves roastin'. I tied them all in and flung diesel on them. And the house, I burnt the bed and the whole place went up in flames. I'd burn down the world if I'd enough diesel—Will somewan not come and save me from meself before I go and do worse.

[JOSEPH *starts to sing.*]

JOSEPH. By the Bog of Cats I finally learned false from true,
Learned too late that it was you and only you
Left me sore, a heart brimfull of rue
By the Bog of Cats in the—
HESTER. Who's there? Who dares sing that song? That's my song that me mother made up for me. Who's there?
JOSEPH. I think ya know me, Hester.
HESTER. It's not Joseph Swane, is it?
JOSEPH. It is alright.
HESTER. I thought I done away with you. Where are ya? I can't see ya. Keep off! Keep away! I'm warnin' ya.
JOSEPH. I'm not here to harm ya.
HESTER. Ya should be. If you'd done to me what I done to you I'd want your guts on a platter. Well come on! I'm ready for ya! Where are ya!
JOSEPH. I don't know, somewhere near ya. I can't see you aither.
HESTER. Well, what do ya want, Joseph Swane, if you're not here to harm me? Is it an apology you're after? Well, I've none for ya. I'd slit your throat again if ya stood here in front of me in flesh and bone.
JOSEPH. Would ya? What're ya so angry about? I've been listenin' to ya screamin' your head off for the last while.
HESTER. You've a nerve singin' that song. That song is mine! She made it for me and only me. Can't yees lave me with anythin'!
JOSEPH. I didn't know it was yours. She used sing it to me all the time.
HESTER. You're lyin'! Faithless! All of yees! Faithless! If she showed up now I'd spit in her face, I'd box the jaws off of her, I'd go after her with a knife, I'd make her squeal like a cornered badger. Where is she? She said she'd return. I've waited so long. I've waited so long—Have you come across her where you are?
JOSEPH. Death's a big country, Hester. She could be anywhere in it.

HESTER.   No, she's alive. I can smell her. She's comin' towards me.
   I know it. Why doesn't she come and be done with it! If ya see
   her tell her I won't be hard on her, will ya?
JOSEPH.   Aye, if I see her.
HESTER.   Tell her there's just a couple of things I need to ax her,
   will ya?
JOSEPH.   I will.
HESTER.   I just want to know why, that's all.
JOSEPH.   Why what?
HESTER.   Was it somethin' I done on her? I was seven, same as me
   daughter Josie, seven, and there isn't anythin' in this wide world
   Josie could do that'd make me walk away from her.
JOSEPH.   Ya have a daughter?
HESTER.   Aye, they're tryin' to take her from me. Just let them try!
JOSEPH.   Who's tryin'?
HESTER.   If it wasn't for you, me and Carthage'd still be together!
JOSEPH.   So it's my fault ya killed me, that what you're sayin'?
HESTER.   He took your money after we killed ya—
JOSEPH.   To my memory Carthage did nothin' only look on. I think
   he was as shocked as I was when ya came at me with the fishin'
   knife—
HESTER.   He took your money! He helped me throw ya overboard!
   And now he wants to put it all on me.
JOSEPH.   Ya came at me from behind, didn't ya? Wan minute I'm
   rowin' and the next I'm a ghost.
HESTER.   If ya hadn't been such an arrogant git I may have left
   ya alone but ya just wouldn't shut up talkin' about her as if she
   wasn't my mother at all. The big smug neck of ya! It was axin' to
   be cut. And she even called ya after her. And calls me Hester.
   What sourt of a name is Hester? Hester's after no wan. And she
   saves her own name for you—Didn't she ever tell ya about me?
JOSEPH.   She never mentioned ya.
HESTER.   She must've. It's a long time ago. Think, will ya. Didn't
   she ever say anythin' about me?
JOSEPH.   Only what she tould me father. She never spoke to me
   about ya.
HESTER.   Listen to ya! You're still goin' on as if she was yours and
   you only an auld ghost! You're still talkin' as if I never existed.
JOSEPH.   I don't know what you're on about, Hester, but if it's any
   consolation to ya, she left me too and our father. Josie Swane
   hung around for no wan.
HESTER.   What age were ya when she left ya?
JOSEPH.   Goin' on ten.
HESTER.   Goin' on ten—that's three year more ya had of her than
   me—and me all that time waitin' for her and her all the time
   molly cuddlin' you—What was she like, Joseph? Every day I forget more and more till I'm startin' to think I made her up out of
   the air. If it wasn't for this auld caravan I'd swear I only dreamt
   her. What was she like?

JOSEPH.   Well, she was big for starters.

HESTER.   Aye, a big rancorous hulk.

JOSEPH.   And she was fierce silent—gentle I suppose in her way.

HESTER.   Gentle! She'd a vicious whiskey temper on her and a whiplash tongue and fists that'd land on ya like lightnin'.

JOSEPH.   She never laid a hand on me—though I remember her fightin' with me father alright. He wasn't able for her at all. He'd be skulkin' round the house and her blowin' off about somethin' or other and her twice the size of him. I remember her goin' after him with a brush wan time. 'What're ya at?' says he and he backin' away from her. 'I'm spring cleanin',' says she and she sweepin' him out the door—It wasn't his fault, Hester, she told him you were dead, that ya died at birth, it wasn't his fault. Ya would've liked the old man, but she told him ya died, that ya were born with your heart all wrong.

HESTER.   Nothin' wrong of me heart till she set about banjaxin' it. The lyin' tongue of her. And he just believed her.

JOSEPH.   Didn't he send me lookin' for ya in the end, see was there any trace of ya, told me to split the money with ya if I found ya. Hester, I was goin' to split the money with ya. I had it there in the boat. I was goin' to split it with ya when we reached the shore, ya didn't have to cut me throat for it.

HESTER.   Ya think I slit your throat for a few auld pound me father left me?

JOSEPH.   Then why?

HESTER.   She stole my life from me.

JOSEPH.   So you stole mine.

HESTER.   Well somewan had to pay.

JOSEPH.   If ya knew what it was like here ya'd never have done what ya done.

HESTER.   Oh I think I know, Joseph, and I this years an apprentice ghost.

JOSEPH.   I'll be off, Hester, I didn't come for a row, I just wanted to say hello.

HESTER.   Where are ya goin'?

JOSEPH.   Just stravagin[4] the shadows.

HESTER.   Look out for me over there.

JOSEPH.   It's not wan bit romantic bein' dead, let me tell ya.

HESTER.   I never thought it was.

> [*And exit* JOSEPH. HESTER *sits on the steps of the caravan, drinks some wine from the bottle she took from the wedding, lights a cigar.* MONICA *shouts offstage.*]

MONICA.   Hester! Hester! Your house! It's on fire! Hester! [*Runs on*] Come quick, I'll get the others!

HESTER.   Don't bother.

MONICA.   But your house—Ya set it yourself?

4. Wandering with.

HESTER.   I did.

MONICA.   Christ almighty woman, are ya gone mad!

HESTER.   Ya want a drink?

MONICA.   A drink, she says! I better go and get Carthage, the live-stock, the calves—

HESTER.   Would ya calm down, Monica, only an auld house, it should never have been built in the first place. Let the bog have it back. In a year or so, it'll be covered in gorse and furze, a tree'll grow out through the roof, maybe a big bog oak. I never liked that house anyway.

MONICA.   That's what the tinkers do, isn't it, burn everythin' after them?

HESTER.   Aye.

MONICA.   They'll skin ya alive, Hester, I'm tellin ya, they'll kill ya.

HESTER.   And you with them.

MONICA.   I stood up for ya as best I could, I've to live round here, Hester. I had to pay me respects to the Cassidys. Sure Xavier and meself used walk to school together.

HESTER.   Wan of these days you'll die of niceness, Monica Murray.

MONICA.   A quality you've never had any time for.

HESTER.   I'm just wan big lump of maneness and bad thoughts. Sit down, have a drink with me, I'll get ya a glass. [*Goes into the caravan, gets one.*] Sit down before ya fall.

MONICA [*Sitting on steps, tipsily*].   We'll go off in this yoke, you and me.

HESTER.   Will we?

MONICA.   Flee off from this place, flee off to Eden.

HESTER.   Eden—I left Eden, Monica, at the age of seven. It was on account of a look be this caravan at dusk. A look from a pair of nonchalant eyes, the colour of which I'm still not sure of.

MONICA.   And who was it gave ya this look, your mother, was it? Josie Swane?

HESTER.   Oh aye, Monica, she was the wan alright who looked at me so askance and strangely—Who'd believe a look could destroy ya? I never would've 'cept it happened to me.

MONICA.   She was a harsh auld yoke, Hester, came and went like the moon. Ya'd wake wan mornin' and look out over the bog and ya'd see a fire and know she had returned. And I'd bring her down a sup of milk or a few eggs and she'd be here sittin' on the step just like you are, with her big head of black hair and eyes glamin' like a cat and long arms and a powerful neck all knotted that she'd stretch like a swan in a yawn and me with ne'er a neck at all. But I was never comfortable with her, riddled by her, though, and I wasn't the only wan. There was lots spent evenin's tryin' to figure Josie Swane, somethin' cold and dead about her except when she sang and then I declare ya'd fall in love with her.

HESTER.   Would ya now?

MONICA.   There was a time round here when no celebration was

complete without Josie Swane. She'd be invited everywhere to
sing, funerals, weddin's, christenin's, birthdays of the bigger
farmers, the harvest. And she'd make up songs for each occasion.
And it wasn't so much they wanted her there, more they were
afraid not to have her.

HESTER.   I used go with her on some of them singin' sprees before
she ran off. And she'd make up the song as we walked to wherever we were goin'. Sometimes she'd sing somethin' completely
different than the song she'd been makin' on the road. Them
were her 'Blast from God' songs as opposed to her 'Workaday'
songs, or so she called them. And they never axed us to stay,
these people, to sit down and ate with them, just lapped up her
songs, gave her a bag of food and a half a crown and walked us
off the premises, for fear we'd steal somethin', I suppose. I don't
think it bothered her, it did me—and still rankles after all these
years. But not Josie Swane, she'd be off to the shop to buy cigars
and beer and sweets for me.

MONICA.   Is there another sup of wine there?

HESTER [Pours for her].   I'm all the time wonderin' whatever happened to her.

MONICA.   You're still waitin' on her, aren't ya?

HESTER.   This thirty-three years and it's still like she only walked
away yesterday.

MONICA.   She's not comin' back, Hester. I know what it's like to
wait for somewan who's never walkin' through the door again.
But this waitin' is only a fancy of yours. Now I don't make out to
know anythin' about the workin's of this world but I know this
much, it don't yield aisy to mortal wishes. And maybe that's the
way it has to be. You up on forty, Hester, and still dreamin' of sto-
rybook endin's, still whingin' for your Mam.

HESTER.   I made a promise, Monica, a promise to meself a long
while back, all them years I was in the Industrial school I swore
to meself that wan day I'm comin' back to the Bog of Cats to wait
for her there and I'm never lavin' again.

MONICA.   Well, I don't know how ya'll swing to stay now, your
house in ashes, ya after appearin' in that dress. They're sayin' it's
a black art thing ya picked up somewhere.

HESTER.   A black art thing. [Laughs] If I knew any black art things,
by Christ, I'd use them now. The only way I'm lavin' this place is
in a box and if it comes to that I'm not lavin' alone. I'll take yees
all with me. And, yes, there's things about me yees never understood and makes yees afraid and yees are right for other things
goes through my veins besides blood that I've fought so hard to
keep wraps on.

MONICA.   And what things are they?

HESTER.   I don't understand them meself.

MONICA.   Stop this wild talk then, I don't like it.

HESTER.   Carthage still at the weddin'?

MONICA.   And where else would he be?

HESTER.   And what sourt of mood is he in?

MONICA.   I wasn't mindin'. Don't waste your time over a man like him, faithless as an acorn on a high wind—wine all gone?

HESTER.   Aye.

MONICA.   I'll go up to the feast and bring us back a bottle unless you've any objections.

HESTER.   I'll drink the enemy's wine. Not the wine's fault it fell into the paws of cut-throats and gargiyles.

MONICA.   Be back in a while, so.

HESTER.   And check see Josie's alright, will ya?

MONICA.   She's dancin' her little heart out.

[*Exit* MONICA. HESTER *looks around, up at the winter sky of stars, shivers.*]

HESTER.   Well, it's dusk now and long after and where are ya, Mr Ghost Fancier. I'm here waitin' for ya, though I've been tould to flee. Maybe you're not comin' after all, maybe I only imagined ya.

[*Enter* JOSIE *running, excited.*]

JOSIE.   Mam!—Mam! I'm goin' on the honeymoon with Daddy and Caroline.

HESTER.   You're goin' no such where.

JOSIE.   Ah, Mam, they're goin' drivin' to the sea. I never seen the sea.

HESTER.   It's just wan big bog hole, Josie, and blue, that's all, nothin' remarkable about it.

JOSIE.   Well, Daddy says I'm goin'.

HESTER.   Don't mind your Daddy.

JOSIE.   No, I want to go with them. It's only for five days, Mam.

HESTER.   There's a couple of things you should know about your precious Daddy, ya should know how he has treated me!

JOSIE.   I'm not listenin' to ya givin' out about him. [*Covers her ears with her hands*]

HESTER.   That's right, stand up for him and see how far it'll get ya. He swore to me that after you'd been born he'd marry me and now he plans to take ya off of me. I suppose ya'd like that too.

JOSIE [*Still with ears covered*].   I said I'm not listenin'!

HESTER [*Pulls* JOSIE's *hands from her ears*].   You'll listen to me, Josie Swane, and you listen well. Another that had your name walked away from me. Your perfect Daddy walked away from me. And you'll walk from me too. All me life people have walked away without a word of explanation. Well, I want to tell ya somethin', Josie, if you lave me ya'll die.

JOSIE.   I will not.

HESTER.   Ya will! Ya will! It's a sourt of curse was put on ya be the Catwoman and the black swan. Remember the black swan?

JOSIE.   Aye. [*Frightened*]

HESTER. So ya have to stay with me, d'ya see, and if your Daddy or anywan else axes ya who ya'd prefer to live with, ya have to say me.

JOSIE. Mam, I would've said you anyway.

HESTER. Would ya?—Oh, I'm sorry, Josie, I'm sorry, sweetheart. It's not true what I said about a curse bein' put on ya, it's not true at all. If I'm let go tonight I swear I'll make it up to ya for them awful things I'm after sayin'.

JOSIE. It's alright, Mam, I know ya didn't mean it—Can I go back to the weddin'? The dancin's not over yet.

HESTER. Dance with me. [*Begins waltzing with* JOSIE, *music*] Come on, we'll have our own weddin'.

[*Picks her up, they swirl and twirl to the music.*]

Ya beautiful, beautiful child, I could ate ya.

JOSIE. I could ate ya too—Can I go back to the weddin' for a while?

HESTER. Ya can do anythin' ya want 'cept lave me. [*Puts her down*] G'wan then, for half an hour.

JOSIE. I brung ya a big lump of weddin' cake in me handbag. Here. Why wasn't it your weddin', Mam?

HESTER. It sourt of was. G'wan and enjoy yourself.

[*And exit* JOSIE *running.* HESTER *looks after her eating the wedding cake.* XAVIER CASSIDY *comes up behind her from the shadows, demonic, red-faced, drink taken, carries a gun.*]

XAVIER. Ya enjoyin' that, are ya, Swane, me daughter's weddin' cake?

HESTER. Oh it's yourself, Xavier, with your auld gun. I was wonderin' when I'd see ya in your true colours. Must've been an awful strain on ya behavin' so well all day.

XAVIER. Ya burnt the bloody house to the ground.

HESTER. Did ya really think I was goin' to have your daughter livin' there?

XAVIER. Ya won't best me, Swane, ya know that. I ran your mother out of here and I'll run you too like a frightened hare.

HESTER. It's got nothin' to do with ya, Cassidy, it's between me and Carthage.

XAVIER. Got everythin' to do with me and ya after makin' a mockery of me and me daughter in front of the whole parish.

HESTER. No more than yees deserve for wheedlin' and cajolin' Carthage away from me with your promises of land and money.

XAVIER. He was aisy wheeled.

HESTER. He was always a feckless fool.

XAVIER. Aye, in all respects bar wan. He loves the land and like me he'd rather die than part with it wance he gets his greedy hands on it. With him Cassidy's farm'll be safe, the name'll be gone, but never the farm. And who's to say but maybe your little bastard and her offspring won't be farmin' my land in years to come.

HESTER.   Josie'll have nothin' to do with anythin' that's yours. I'll see to that. And if ya'd looked after your own son better ya wouldn't be covetin' Josie nor any that belongs to me.

XAVIER.   Don't you talk about my young fella.

HESTER.   Wasn't it me that found him, strychnined to the eyeballs, howlin' 'long the bog and his dog in his arms?

XAVIER.   How was I supposed to know he'd go and dig the dog up?

HESTER.   You're not a farmer for nothin', somethin' about that young lad bothered ya, he wasn't tough enough for ya probably, so ya strychnined his dog, knowin' full well the child'd be goin' lookin' for him. And ya know what strychnine does, a tayspoon-full is all it takes, and ya'd the dog showered in it. Burnt his hands clean away. Ya knew what ya were at, Cassidy, and ya know I know. I can tell the darkness in you, ya know how? Because it mirrors me own. And that's why ya want me out of here. And maybe you're right. I can't tell anymore.

XAVIER.   Fabrications! Fabrications of a mind unhinged! My son died in a tragic accident of no wan's makin'. That's what the in-quest said. My conscience is clear.

HESTER.   Is it now? Well, I don't believe in tragic accidents and es-pecially not where you're concerned.

XAVIER.   If ya could just hear the mad talk of yourself, Swane, and the cut of ya. You're mad as your mother and she was a lunatic.

HESTER.   Nothin' lunatic about her 'cept she couldn't breathe the same air as yees all here by the Bog of Cats.

XAVIER.   We often breathed the same air, me and Josie Swane, she was a loose wan, loose and lazy and aisy, a five shillin' hoor, like you.

HESTER.   If you're tryin' to destroy some high idea I have of her you're wastin' your time. I've spent long hours of all the long years thinkin' about her. There isn't a situation I haven't imag-ined her in. I've lived through every mood there is to live con-cernin' her. Sure there was a time I hated her and wished the worst for her, but I've taught meself to rise above all that is cruel and unworthy in me thinkin' about her. So don't you think your five shillin' hoor stories will ever change me opinion of her. I have memories your cheap talk can never alter.

XAVIER.   And what memories are they, Swane? I'd like to know if they exist at all.

HESTER.   Oh they exist alright and ya'd like to rob them from me along with everythin' else. But ya won't because I'm stronger than ya and ya'll take nothin' from me I don't choose to give ya.

XAVIER [*Puts gun to her throat*].   Won't I now? Think ya'll outwit me with your tinker ways and—

HESTER.   Let go of me!

XAVIER [*A tighter grip*].   Now let's see the leftovers of Carthage Kil-bride. [*Uses gun to look down her dress*]

HESTER.   I'm warnin' ya, let go!

[*A struggle, a few blows, he wins this bout.*]

XAVIER.   Now are ya stronger than me? I could do what I wanted with ya right here and now and no wan would believe ya. Now what I'd really like to know is when are ya plannin' on lavin'?

HESTER.   What're ya goin' to do, Cassidy? Blow me head off?

XAVIER.   I married me daughter today, now I don't care for the whiny little rip that much, but she's all I've got, and I don't want Carthage changin' his mind after a while. So when are ya lavin', Swane? When?

HESTER.   Ya think I'm afraid of you and your auld gun.

[*Puts her mouth over the barrel.*]

G'wan shoot! Blow me away! Save me the bother meself.

[*Goes for the trigger.*]

Ya want me to do it for ya?

[*Another struggle, this time* XAVIER *trying to get away from her.*]

XAVIER.   You're a dangerous witch, Swane.

HESTER [*Laughs at him*].   You're sweatin'. Always knew ya were yella to the bone. Don't worry, I'll be lavin' this place tonight, though not the way you or anywan else expects. Ya call me a witch, Cassidy? This is nothin', you just wait and see the real—

[*Enter* CARTHAGE *running, enraged, shakes her violently.*]

CARTHAGE.   The cattle! The calves! Ya burnt them all, they're roarin' in the flames! The house in ashes! A' ya gone mad altogether! The calves! A' ya gone mad!

HESTER [*Shakes him off*].   No, I only meant what I said. I warned ya, Carthage, ya drove me to it.

XAVIER.   A hundred year ago we'd strap ya to a stake and roast ya till your guts exploded.

CARTHAGE.   That's it! I'm takin' Josie off of ya! I don't care if I've to drag ya through the courts. I'll have ya put away! I'll tell all about your brother! I don't care!

HESTER.   Tell them! And tell them your own part in it too while you're at it! Don't you threaten me with Josie! This pervert has just been gropin' me with his gun and you want Josie round him—

XAVIER.   The filthy lies of her—

HESTER.   Bringin' a child on a honeymoon, what are ya at, Carthage? Well, I won't let ya use Josie to fill in the silences between yourself and Caroline Cassidy—

XAVIER.   She's beyond reasonin' with, if she was mine I'd cut that tinker tongue from her mouth, I'd brand her lips, I'd—

CARTHAGE [*Exploding at* XAVIER].   Would you just go back to the weddin' and lave us alone, stop interferin'. If ya'd only let me handle it all the way I wanted to, but, no, ya had to push and bring the weddin' forward to avoid your taxes, just lave us alone, will ya!

XAVIER.   I will and gladly. You're a fiasco, Kilbride, like all the Kilbrides before ya, ya can't control a mere woman, ya'll control nothin', I'm havin' serious doubts about signin' over me farm—

CARTHAGE.   Keep your bloody farm, Cassidy. I have me own. I'm not your scrubber boy. There's other things besides land.

XAVIER.   There's nothin' besides land, boy, nothin', and a real farmer would never think otherwise.

CARTHAGE.   Just go back to the weddin', I'll follow ya in a while and we can try hammerin' out our differences.

XAVIER.   Can we?

[*Exit* XAVIER.]

HESTER.   All's not well in Paradise.

CARTHAGE.   All'd be fine if I could do away with you.

HESTER.   If ya just let me stay I'll cause no more trouble. I'll move into the caravan with Josie. In time ya may be glad to have me around. I've been your greatest friend around here, Carthage, doesn't that count for nothin' now?

CARTHAGE.   I'm not havin' me daughter livin' in a caravan!

HESTER.   There was a time you loved this caravan.

CARTHAGE.   Will ya just stop tryin' to drag up them years! It won't work!

HESTER.   Ya promised me things! Ya built that house for me. Ya wanted me to see how normal people lived. And I went along with ya again' me better judgement. All I ever wanted was to be by the Bog of Cats. A modest want when compared with the wants of others. Just let me stay here in the caravan.

CARTHAGE.   And have the whole neighbourhood makin' a laughin' stock of me?

HESTER.   That's not why ya won't let me stay. You're ashamed of your part in me brother's death, aren't ya?

CARTHAGE.   I had no part in it!

HESTER.   You're afraid I'll tell everywan what ya done. I won't. I wouldn't ever, Carthage.

CARTHAGE.   I done nothin' except watch!

HESTER.   Ya helped me tie a stone around his waist!

CARTHAGE.   He was dead by then!

HESTER.   He wasn't! His pulse was still goin'!

CARTHAGE.   You're only sayin' that now to torture me! Why did ya do it, Hetty? We were doin' fine till then.

HESTER.   Somethin' evil moved in on me blood—and the fishin' knife was there in the bottom of the boat—and Bergit's Lake was wide—and I looked across the lake to me father's house and it went through me like a spear that she had a whole other life there—How could she have and I a part of her?

CARTHAGE.   Ya never said any of this before—I always thought ya
killed your brother for the money.
HESTER.   I met his ghost tonight, ya know—
CARTHAGE.   His ghost?
HESTER.   Aye, a gentle ghost and so lost, and he spoke so softly to
me, I didn't deserve such softness—
CARTHAGE.   Ah, would you stop this talk!
HESTER.   You rose in the world on his ashes! And that's what
haunts ya and that's why ya want to forget I ever existed. Well, I
won't let ya. You'll remember me, Carthage, when the dust settles, when ya grow tired scourin' acres and bank balances. Ya'll
remember me when ya walk them big empty childless rooms in
Cassidy's house. Ya think now ya won't, but ya will.
CARTHAGE.   Ya always had a high opinion of yourself. Aye, I'll remember ya from time to time. I'll remember ya sittin' at the
kitchen table drinkin' till all hours and I'll remember the sound
of the back door closin' as ya escaped for another night roamin'
the bog.
HESTER.   The drinkin' came after, long after you put it into your
mind to lave me. If I had somewan to talk to I mightn't have
drunk so hard, somewan to roam the bog with me, somewan to
take away a tiny piece of this guilt I carry with me, but ya never
would.
CARTHAGE.   Seems I done nothin' right. Did I not?
HESTER.   You want to glane lessons for your new bride. No,
Carthage, ya done nothin' right, your bull-headed pride and
economy and painful advancement never moved me. What I
wanted was somewan to look me in the eye and know I was understood and not judged. You thought I had no right to ax for
that. Maybe I hadn't, but the way ya used judge me—didn't it
ever occur to ya, that however harshly ya judged me, I judged
meself harsher. Couldn't ya ever see that.
CARTHAGE.   I'm takin' Josie, Hester. I'm takin' her off of ya. It's
plain as day to everywan 'cept yourself ya can't look after her. If
you're wise ya'll lave it at that and not take us muckin' through
the courts. I'll let ya see her from time to time.
HESTER.   Take her then, take her, ya've taken everythin' else. In me
stupidity I thought ya'd lave me Josie. I should've known ya always meant to take her too.

[*Enter* CAROLINE *with a bottle of wine.*]

CAROLINE [*To* CARTHAGE].   Oh, this is where ya are.
CARTHAGE.   She's after burnin' all the livestock, the house, the
sheds in ruins. I'm away up there now to see what can be sal-
vaged. G'wan back home, I'll be there in a while.

[*And exit* CARTHAGE.]

CAROLINE.   Monica said ya wanted wine, I opened it for ya.

HESTER.   Take more than wine to free me from this place. Take some kind of dark sprung miracle. [*Takes the wine.*]

CARTHAGE [*Coming back*].   Caroline, come on, come on, I don't want ya around her.

HESTER.   G'wan back to your weddin' like Carthage says.

[CAROLINE *goes to exit, stops.*]

CAROLINE.   I just wanted to say—

HESTER.   What? Ya just wanted to say what?

CAROLINE.   Nothin'—Only I'll be very good to Josie whenever she stays with us.

HESTER.   Will ya now?

CAROLINE.   I won't let her out of me sight—I'll go everywhere with her—protect her from things—That's all.

[*Goes to exit.*]

HESTER.   Didn't ya enjoy your big weddin' day, Caroline?

CAROLINE.   No, I didn't—Everywan too loud and frantic—and when ya turned up in that weddin' dress, knew it should've been you—and Daddy drinkin' too much and shoutin', and Carthage gone away in himself, just watchin' it all like it had nothin' to do with him, and everywan laughin' behind me back and pityin' me—When me mother was alive, I used go into the sick room to talk to her and she used take me into the bed beside her and she'd describe for me me weddin' day. Of how she'd be there with a big hat on her and so proud. And the weddin' was goin' to be in this big ballroom with a fountain of mermaids in the middle, instead of Daddy's idea of havin' the do at home like his own weddin'—None of it was how it was meant to be, none of it.

HESTER.   Nothin' ever is, Caroline. Nothin'. I've been a long time wishin' over me mother too. For too long now I've imagined her comin' towards me across the Bog of Cats and she would find me here standin' strong. She would see me life was complete, that I had Carthage and Josie and me own house. I so much wanted her to see that I had flourished without her and maybe then I could forgive her—Caroline, he's takin' Josie from me.

CAROLINE.   He's not, he wouldn't do that, Hester.

HESTER.   He's just been here tellin' me.

CAROLINE.   I won't let him, I'll talk to him, I'll stand up for ya on that account.

HESTER.   Ya never stood up for nothin' yet, I doubt ya'll stand up for me. Anyway, they won't listen to ya. You're only a little china bit of a girl. I could break ya aisy as a tay cup or a wine glass. But I won't. Ya know why? Because I knew ya when ya were Josie's age, a scrawky little thing that hung on the scraps of my affection. Anyway, no need to break ya, you were broke a long while back.

CAROLINE.   I wanted to be a kindergarten teacher or a air hostess or a beautician.

[*Stands there, lost-looking.*]

HESTER. G'wan back to your weddin' and lave me be.

CAROLINE. I promise ya I'll do everythin' I can about Josie.

HESTER [*Softly*]. G'wan. G'wan.

> [*Exit* CAROLINE. HESTER *stands there alone, takes a drink, goes into the caravan, comes out with a knife. She tests it for sharpness, teases it across her throat, shivers.*]

Come on, ya done it aisy enough to another, now it's your own turn.

> [*Bares her throat, ready to do it. Enter* JOSIE *running, stops, sees* HESTER *with the knife poised.*]

JOSIE. Mam—What's that ya've got there?

HESTER [*Stops*]. Just an auld fishin' knife, Josie, I've had this years.

JOSIE. And what are ya doin' with it?

HESTER. Nothin', Josie, nothin'.

JOSIE. I came to say goodbye, we'll be goin' soon. [*Kisses* HESTER.]

HESTER. Goodbye, sweetheart—Josie, ya won't see me again now.

JOSIE. I will so. I'm only goin' on a honeymoon.

HESTER. No, Josie, ya won't see me again because I'm goin' away too.

JOSIE. Where?

HESTER. Somewhere ya can never return from.

JOSIE. And where's that?

HESTER. Never mind. I only wanted to tell ya goodbye, that's all.

JOSIE. Well, can I go with ya?

HESTER. No, ya can't.

JOSIE. Ah, Mam, I want to be where you'll be.

HESTER. Well, ya can't, because wance ya go there ya can never come back.

JOSIE. I wouldn't want to if you're not here, Mam.

HESTER. You're just bein' contrary now. Don't ya want to be with your Daddy and grow up big and lovely and full of advantages they tell me I have not the power to give ya.

JOSIE. Mam, I'd be watchin' for ya all the time 'long the Bog of Cats. I'd be hopin' and waitin' and prayin' for ya to return.

HESTER. Don't be sayin' those things to me now.

JOSIE. Just take me with ya, Mam.

> [*Puts her arms around* HESTER.]

HESTER. No, ya don't understand. Go away, get away from me, g'wan now, run away from me quickly now.

JOSIE [*Struggling to stay in contact with* HESTER]. No, Mam, stop! I'm goin' with ya!

HESTER. Would ya let go!

JOSIE [*Frantic*]. No, Mam. Please!

HESTER.   Alright, alright! Shhh! [*Picks her up.*] It's alright, I'll take ya with me, I won't have ya as I was, waitin' a lifetime for some-wan to return, because they don't, Josie, they don't. It's alright. Close your eyes.

[JOSIE *closes her eyes.*]

Are they closed tight?

JOSIE.   Yeah.

[HESTER *cuts* JOSIE's *throat in one savage movement.*]

JOSIE [*Softly*].   Mam—Mam—

[*And* JOSIE *dies in her arms.*]

HESTER [*Whispers*].   It's because ya wanted to come, Josie.

[*Begins to wail. Enter the* CATWOMAN.]

CATWOMAN.   Hester, what is it? What is it?

HESTER.   Oh, Catwoman, I knew somethin' terrible'd happen, I never thought it'd be this.

[*Continues wailing.*]

CATWOMAN.   What have ya done, Hester? Have ya harmed your-self?

HESTER.   No, not meself and yes meself.

CATWOMAN [*Comes over, feels around* HESTER, *feels* JOSIE].   Not Josie, Hester? Not Josie? Lord on high, Hester, not the child. I thought yourself, maybe, or Carthage, but never the child.

[*Runs to the edge of the stage shouting.*]

Help, somewan, help! Hester Swane's after butcherin' the child! Help!

[HESTER *walks around demented with* JOSIE. *Enter* CARTHAGE *running.*]

CARTHAGE.   What is it, Catwoman? Hester? What's wrong with Josie? There's blood all over her.

HESTER.   Lave off, you. Lave off. I warned ya and I tould ya, would ya listen, what've I done, what've I done?

[*The others drift on in ones and twos.*]

CARTHAGE.   Give her to me!

MONICA.   Sweet Jesus, Hester—

CARTHAGE.   Give her to me! Will somewan go and get somewan. You've killed her, ya've killed her.

HESTER.   Yees all thought I was just goin' to walk away and lave her at yeer mercy. I almost did. But she's mine and I wouldn't have her waste her life dreamin' about me and yees thwartin' her with black stories against me.

CARTHAGE.   You're a savage!

[*Enter the* GHOST FANCIER. HESTER *sees him, the others don't. He picks up the fishing knife.*]

HESTER.   You're late, ya came too late.

CARTHAGE.   What's she sayin'? What? Give her to me, come on now.

[*Takes* JOSIE *off* HESTER.]

HESTER.   Ya won't forget me now, Carthage, and when all of this is over or half remembered and ya think ya've almost forgotten me again, take a walk along the Bog of Cats and wait for a purlin' wind through your hair or a soft breath be your ear or a rustle behind ya. That'll be me and Josie ghostin' ya.

[*She walks towards the* GHOST FANCIER.]

Take me away, take me away from here.

GF.   Alright, my lovely.

[*They go into a death dance with the fishing knife, which ends plunged into* HESTER's *heart. She falls to the ground.*]

HESTER [*Whispers as she dies*].   Mam—Mam—

[MONICA *goes over to her after a while.*]

MONICA.   Hester—She's gone—Hester—She's cut her heart out—it's lyin' there on top of her chest like some dark feathered bird.

[*Music. Lights. End.*]

Songs of Josie Swane[5]

By the Bog of Cats

By the Bog of Cats I finally learned false from true,
Learned too late that it was you and only you
Left me sore, a heart brimfull of rue
By the Bog of Cats in the darkling dew.

By the Bog of Cats I dreamed a dream of wooing.
I heard your clear voice to me a-calling
That I must go though it be my undoing.
By the Bog of Cats I'll stay no more a-rueing.

To the Bog of Cats I one day will return,
In mortal form or in ghostly form,
And I will find you there and there with you sojourn,
Forever by the Bog of Cats, my darling one.

The Black Swan

I know where a black swan sleeps
On the bank of grey water,
Hidden in a nest of leaves
So none can disturb her.

I have lain outside her lair,
My hand upon her wing,
And I have whispered to her
And of my sorrows sung.

I wish I was a black swan
And could fly away from here,
But I am Josie Swane,
Without wings, without care.

5. To be recorded and used during the play. [*Author's note*].

BACKGROUNDS
AND CRITICISM

The Irish Dramatic Revival

LADY GREGORY

Our Irish Theatre†

* * *

On one of those days at Duras in 1898,[1] Mr. Edward Martyn, my neighbour, came to see the Count, bringing with him Mr. Yeats, whom I did not then know very well, though I cared for his work very much and had already, through his directions, been gathering folk-lore. They had lunch with us, but it was a wet day, and we could not go out. After a while I thought the Count wanted to talk to Mr. Martyn alone; so I took Mr. Yeats to the office where the steward used to come to talk,—less about business I think than of the Land War or the state of the country, or the last year's deaths and marriages from Kinvara to the headland of Augh-anish. We sat there through that wet afternoon, and though I had never been at all interested in theatres, our talk turned on plays. Mr. Martyn had written two, *The Heather Field* and *Maeve*. They had been offered to London managers, and now he thought of trying to have them produced in Germany where there seemed to be more room for new drama than in England. I said it was a pity we had no Irish theatre where such plays could be given. Mr. Yeats said that had always been a dream of his, but he had of late thought it an impossible one, for it could not at first pay its way, and there was no money to be found for such a thing in Ireland.

We went on talking about it, and things seemed to grow possible as we talked, and before the end of the afternoon we had made our plan. We said we would collect money, or rather ask to have a certain sum of money guaranteed. We would then take a Dublin theatre and give a performance of Mr. Martyn's *Heather Field* and one of Mr. Yeats's own plays, *The Countess Cathleen*. I offered the first guarantee of £25.

† From *Our Irish Theatre: A Chapter of Autobiography* (New York: Oxford University Press; Bucks: Colin Smythe Ltd., 1972).
1. In fact 1897.

A few days after that I was back at Coole,[2] and Mr. Yeats came
over from Mr. Martyn's home, Tillyra, and we wrote a formal letter
to send out. We neither of us write a very clear hand, but a friend
had just given me a Remington typewriter and I was learning to use
it, and I wrote out the letter with its help. That typewriter has done
a great deal of work since that day, making it easy for the printers to
read my plays and translations, and Mr. Yeats's plays and essays,
and sometimes his poems. I have used it also for many, many hundreds of letters that have had to be written about theatre business
in each of these last fifteen years. It has gone with me very often up
and down to Dublin and back again, and it went with me even to
America last year that I might write my letters home. And while I
am writing the leaves are falling, and since I have written those last
words on its keys, she who had given it to me has gone. She gave
me also the great gift of her friendship through more than half my
lifetime, Enid, Lady Layard, Ambassadress at Constantinople and
Madrid, helper of the miserable and the wounded in the Turkish-
Russian war; helper of the sick in the hospital she founded at
Venice, friend and hostess and guest of queens in England and
Germany and Rome. She was her husband's good helpmate while
he lived—is not the Cyprus treaty set down in that clear handwriting I shall never see coming in here again? And widowed, she kept
his name in honour, living after him for fifteen years, and herself
leaving a noble memory in all places where she had stayed, and in
Venice where her home was and where she died.

Our statement—it seems now a little pompous—began:

"We propose to have performed in Dublin in the spring of every
year certain Celtic and Irish plays, which whatever be their degree
of excellence will be written with a high ambition, and so to build
up a Celtic and Irish school of dramatic literature. We hope to find
in Ireland an uncorrupted and imaginative audience trained to listen by its passion for oratory, and believe that our desire to bring
upon the stage the deeper thoughts and emotions of Ireland will
ensure for us a tolerant welcome, and that freedom to experiment
which is not found in theatres of England, and without which no
new movement in art or literature can succeed. We will show that
Ireland is not the home of buffoonery and of easy sentiment, as it
has been represented, but the home of an ancient idealism. We are
confident of the support of all Irish people, who are weary of mis-
representation, in carrying out a work that is outside all the political questions that divide us."

I think the word "Celtic" was put in for the sake of Fiona
Macleod, whose plays however we never acted, though we used to

2. Coole Park, county Galway, her home and the subject of several Yeats poems [*Editor*].

amuse ourselves by thinking of the call for "author" that might follow one, and the possible appearance of William Sharp in place of the beautiful woman he had given her out to be, for even then we had little doubt they were one and the same person. I myself never quite understood the meaning of the "Celtic Movement," which we were said to belong to. When I was asked about it, I used to say it was a movement meant to persuade the Scotch to begin buying our books, while we continued not to buy theirs.

We asked for a guarantee fund of £300 to make the experiment, which we hoped to carry on during three years. The first person I wrote to was the old poet, Aubrey de Vere. He answered very kindly, saying, "Whatever develops the genius of Ireland, must in the most effectual way benefit her; and in Ireland's genius I have long been a strong believer. Circumstances of very various sorts have hitherto tended much to retard the development of that genius; but it cannot fail to make itself recognised before very long, and Ireland will have cause for gratitude to all those who have hastened the coming of that day."

I am glad we had this letter, carrying as it were the blessing of the generation passing away to that which was taking its place. He was the first poet I had ever met and spoken with; he had come in my girlhood to a neighbour's house. He was so gentle, so fragile, he seemed to have been wafted in by that "wind from the plains of Athenry" of which he wrote in one of his most charming little poems. He was of the Lake School, and talked of Wordsworth, and I think it was a sort of courtesy or deference to him that I determined to finish reading *The Excursion*, which though a reader of poetry it had failed me, as we say, to get through. At last one morning I climbed up to a wide wood, Grobawn, on one of the hillsides of Slieve Echtge, determined not to come down again until I had honestly read every line. I think I saw the sun set behind the far-off Connemara hills before I came home, exhausted but triumphant! I have a charming picture of Aubrey de Vere in my mind as I last saw him, at a garden party in London. He was walking about, having on his arm, in the old-world style, the beautiful Lady Somers, lovely to the last as in Thackeray's day, and as I had heard of her from many of that time, and as she had been painted by [George Frederick] Watts.

Some gave us their promise with enthusiasm but some from good will only, without much faith that an Irish Theatre would ever come to success. One friend, a writer of historical romance, wrote: "October 15th. I enclose a cheque for £1, but confess it is more as a proof of regard for *you* than a belief in the drama, for I cannot with the best wish in the world to do so, feel hopeful on that subject. My experience has been that any attempt at treating Irish history is a fatal handicap, not to say absolute *bar*, to anything in the shape of popularity, and I cannot see how any drama can flourish which is not to some degree supported by the public, as it is even more dependent on it than literature is. There *are* popular Irish dramatists, of course, and *very* popular ones, but then unhappily they did not treat of Irish subjects, and *The School for Scandal* and *She Stoops to Conquer*³ would hardly come under your category. You will think me very discouraging, but I cannot help it, and I am also afraid that putting plays experimentally on the boards is a very costly entertainment. Where will they be acted in the first instance? And has any stage manager undertaken to produce them? Forgive my tiresomeness; it does not come from want of sympathy, only from a little want of hope, the result of experience."

"October 19th: I seize the opportunity of writing again as I am afraid you will have thought I wrote such a unsympathetic letter. It is not, believe me, that I would not give anything to see Irish literature and Irish drama taking a good place, as it ought to do, and several of the authors you name I admire extremely. It is only from the practical and *paying* point of view that I feel it to be rather rash. Plays cost more, I take it, to produce than novels, and one would feel rather rash if one brought out a novel at one's own risk."

I think the only actual refusals I had were from three members of the Upper House. I may give their words as types of the discouragement which we have often met with from friends: "I need not, I am sure, tell you how I gladly would take part in anything for the honour of Old Ireland and especially anything of the kind in which you feel an interest; but I must tell you frankly that I do not much believe in the movement about which you have written to me. I have no sympathy, you will be horrified to hear, with the 'London Independent Theatre', and I am sure that if Ibsen and Co. could know what is in my mind, they would regard me as a 'Philistine' of the coarsest class! Alas! so far from wishing to see the Irish characters of Charles Lever⁴ supplanted by more refined types, they have always been the delight of my heart, and there is no author in whose healthy, rollicking company, even nowadays, I spend a spare hour with more thorough enjoyment. I am very sory that I cannot agree with you in these matters, and I am irreclaimable; but all the same I remain with many pleasant remembrances and good wishes for you and yours, Yours very truly———"

Another, the late Lord Ashbourne, wrote: "I know too little of the matter or the practicability of the idea to be able to give my name to your list, but I shall watch the experiment with interest and be

---

3. By Irish-born playwrights, respectively, Richard Brinsley Sheridan (1751–1816) and Oliver Goldsmith (1730–74) [*Editor*].
4. Irish novelist (1806–72) whose characters were by many Irish considered gross caricatures [*Editor*].

glad to attend. The idea is novel and curious and how far it is capable of realisation I am not at all in a position to judge. Some of the
names you mention are well known in literature but not as dramatists or playwriters, and therefore the public will be one to be
worked up by enthusiasm and love of country. The existing class of
actors will not, of course, be available, and the existing playgoers
are satisfied with their present attractions. Whether 'houses' can be
got to attend the new plays, founded on new ideas and played by
new actors, no one can foretell."

One, who curiously has since then become an almost too zealous
supporter of our theatre, says: "I fear I am not too sanguine about
the success in a pecuniary way of a 'Celtic Theatre' nor am I familiar with the works, dramatic or otherwise, of Mr. Yeats or of Mr.
Martyn. Therefore, at the risk of branding myself in your estima-
tion as a hopeless Saxon and Philistine, I regret I cannot see my
way to giving my name to the enterprise or joining in the guarantee." On the other hand, Professor [John Pentland] Mahaffy says,
rather unexpectedly, writing from Trinity College: "I am ready to
risk £5 for your scheme and hope they may yet play their drama in
Irish. It will be as intelligible to the nation as Italian, which we so
often hear upon our stage."

And many joined who had seemed too far apart to join in any
scheme. Mr. William Hartpole Lecky sent a promise of £5 instead
of the £1 I had asked. Lord Dufferin, Viceroy of India and Canada,
Ambassador at Paris, Constantinople, St. Petersburg, and Rome,
not only promised but sent his guarantee in advance. I returned it
later, for the sums guaranteed were never called for, Mr. Martyn
very generously making up all loss. Miss Jane Barlow, Miss Emily
Lawless, the Lord Chancellor of Ireland ("Peter the Packer" as he
was called by Nationalists), John O'Leary, Mr. T. M. Healy, Lord
and Lady Ardilaun, the Duchess of St. Albans, Doctor Douglas
Hyde, the Rt. Hon. Horace Plunkett, Mr. John Dillon, M.P., all
joined. Mr. John Redmond supported us, and afterwards wrote me
a letter of commendation with leave to use it. Mr. William O'Brien
was another supporter. I did not know him personally but I remember one day long ago going to tea at the Speaker's house, after I had
heard him in a debate, and saying I thought him the most stirring
speaker of all the Irish party, and I was amused when my gentle and
dignified hostess, Mrs. Peel, said, "I quite agree with you. When I
hear William O'Brien make a speech, I feel that if I were an Irishwoman, I should like to go and break windows."

Then Mr. Yeats and Mr. Martyn went to Dublin to make preparations, but the way was unexpectedly blocked by the impossibility of
getting a theatre. The only Dublin theatres, the Gaiety, the Royal,
and the Queen's, were engaged far ahead, and in any case we could

not have given them their price. Then we thought of taking a hall or a concert room, but there again we met with disappointment. We found there was an old Act in existence, passed just before the Union, putting a fine of £300 upon any one who should give a performance for money in any unlicensed building. As the three large theatres were the only buildings licensed, a claim for a special license would have to be argued by lawyers, charging lawyer's fees, before the Privy Council. We found that even amateurs who acted for charities were forced to take one of the licensed theatres, so leaving but little profit for the charity. There were suggestions made of forming a society like the Stage Society in London, to give performances to its members only, but this would not have been a fit beginning for the National Theatre of our dreams. I wrote in a letter at that time: "I am all for having the Act repealed or a Bill brought in, empowering the Municipality to license halls when desirable." And although this was looked on as a counsel of perfection, it was actually done within the year. I wrote to Mr. [W. E. H.] Lecky for advice and help, and he told me there was a Bill actually going through the House of Commons, the Local Government (Ireland) Bill, in which he thought it possible a clause might be inserted that would meet our case. Mr John Redmond and Mr. Dillon promised their help; so did Mr. T. M. Healy, who wrote to Mr. Yeats: "I am acquainted with the state of the law in Dublin which I should gladly assist to alter as proposed. Whether the Government are equally well disposed may be doubted, as the subject is a little outside their Bill, and no adequate time exists for discussing it and many other important questions. They will come up about midnight or later and will be yawned out of hearing by our masters."

A Clause was drawn up by a Nationalist member, Mr. Clancy, but in July, 1898, Mr. Lecky writes from the House of Commons: "I have not been forgetting the Celtic Theatre and I think the enclosed Clause, with the Government have brought forward, will practically meet its requirements. The Attorney-General objected to Mr. Clancy's Clause as too wide and as interfering with existing patent rights, but promised a Clause authorising amateur acting. I wrote to him, however, stating the Celtic case, and urging that writers should be able, like those who got up the Ibsen plays in London, to get regular actors to play for them, and I think this Clause will allow it . . . . After Clause 59 insert the following Clause: (1) Notwithstanding anything in the Act of Parliament of Ireland of the twenty-sixth year of King George the Third, Chapter fifty-seven, intituled an Act for regulating the stage in the city and county of Dublin, the Lord Lieutenant may on the application of the council for the county of Dublin or the county borough of Dublin grant an occasional license for the performance of any stage play or other

dramatic entertainment in any theatre, room or building where the
profits arising therefrom are to be applied for charitable purpose or
in aid of funds of any society instituted for the purpose of science,
literature, or the fine arts exclusively. (2) The license may contain
such conditions and regulations as appear fit to the Lord Lieutenant, and may be revoked by him."

This Clause was passed but we are independent now of it,—the
Abbey Theatre holds its own Patent. But the many amateur societies which play so often here and there in Dublin may well call for
a blessing sometimes on the names of those by whom their charter
was won.

We announced our first performance for May 8, 1899, nearly a
year after that talk on the Galway coast, at the Ancient Concert
Rooms. Mr. Yeats's *Countess Cathleen* and Mr. Martyn's *Heather
Field* were the plays chosen, as we had planned at the first. Mr.
George Moore gave excellent help in finding actors, and the plays
were rehearsed in London. But then something unexpected happened. A writer who had a political quarrel with Mr. Yeats sent out a
pamphlet in which he attacked *The Countess Cathleen*, on the
ground of religious unorthodoxy.[5] The plot of the play, taken from
an old legend, is this: during a famine in Ireland some starving
country people, having been tempted by demons dressed as mer-
chants to sell their souls for money that their bodies may be saved
from perishing, the Countess Cathleen sells her own soul to redeem
theirs, and dies. The accusation made was that it was a libel on the
people of Ireland to say that they could under any circumstances
consent to sell their souls and that it was a libel on the demons that
they counted the soul of a countess of more worth than those of the
poor. At Cathleen's death, the play tells us, "God looks on the intention, not the deed," and so she is forgiven at the last and taken into
Heaven; and this it was said is against the teaching of the Church.

Mr. Martyn is an orthodox Catholic, and to quiet his mind, the
play was submitted to two good Churchmen. Neither found heresy
enough in it to call for its withdrawal. One of them, the Rev. Dr.
Barry, the author of *The New Antigone*, wrote:

> "BRIDGE HOUSE, WALLINGFORD,
> March 26, 1899

DEAR MR. YEATS,

"I read your *Countess Cathleen* as soon as possible after seeing
you. It is beautiful and touching. I hope you will not be kept back
from giving it by foolish talk. Obviously, from the literal point of
view theologians, Catholic or other, would object that no one is free

5. Frank Hugh O'Donnell (1848–1916) and his pamphlet *Souls for Gold! Pseudo-Celtic
   Drama in Dublin* (1899) [*Editor*].

to sell his soul in order to buy bread even for the starving. But St. Paul says, 'I wish to be anathema for my brethren'; which is another way of expressing what you have put into a story. I would give the play first and explanations afterwards.

"Sometimes perhaps you will come and spend a night here and I shall be charmed. But don't take a superfluous journey now. It is an awkward place to get at. I could only tell you, as I am doing, that if people will not read or look at a play of this kind in the spirit which dictated it, no change you might make would satisfy them. You have given us what is really an Auto,[6] in the manner of Calderon, with the old Irish folk-lore as a perceptive; and to measure it by the iron rule of experts and schoolmen would be most unfair to it. Some one else will say that you have learned from the Jesuits to make the end justify the means—and much that man will know of you or the Jesuits. With many kind wishes for your success, and fraternal greetings in the name of Ireland,

Ever yours,
"WILLIAM BARRY."

So our preparations went on. Mr. Yeats wrote a little time before the first performance: "Everybody tells me we are going to have good audiences. My play, too, in acting goes wonderfully well. The actors are all pretty sound. The first Demon is a little over-violent and restless but he will improve. Lionel Johnson has done a prologue which I enclose."

That prologue, written by so Catholic and orthodox a poet, was spoken before the plays at the Ancient Concert Rooms on May 8, 1899:

> The May fire once on every dreaming hill
> All the fair land with burning bloom would fill;
> All the fair land, at visionary night,
> Gave loving glory to the Lord of Light.
>
> Have we no leaping flames of Beltaine[7] praise
> To kindle in the joyous ancient ways;
> No fire of song, of vision, of white dream,
> Fit for the Master of the Heavenly Gleam;
> For him who first made Ireland move in chime
> Musical from the misty dawn of time?
>
> Ah, yes; for sacrifice this night we bring
> The passion of a lost soul's triumphing;
> All rich with faery airs that, wandering long,

6. A play [Editor].
7. Gaelic for the festival of May 1 and the beginning of summer [Editor].

Uncaught, here gather into Irish song;
Sweet as the old remembering winds that wail,
From hill to hill of gracious Inisfail;
Sad as the unforgetting winds that pass
Over her children in her holy grass
At home, and sleeping well upon her breast,
Where snowy Deirdre and her sorrows rest.

Come, then, and keep with us an Irish feast,
Wherein the Lord of Light and Song is priest;
Now, at this opening of the gentle May,
Watch warring passions at their storm and play;
Wrought with the flaming ecstasy of art,
Sprung from the dreaming of an Irish heart.

But alas! His call to "watch warring passions at their storm and play," was no vain one. The pamphlet, *Souls for Gold*, had been sent about, and sentences spoken by the demons in the play and given detached from it were quoted as Mr. Yeats's own unholy beliefs. A Cardinal who confessed he had read none of the play outside these sentences condemned it. Young men from the Catholic University were roused to come and make a protest against this "insult to their faith." There was hooting and booing in the gallery. In the end the gallery was lined with police, for an attack on the actors was feared. They, being English and ignorant of Ireland, found it hard to understand the excitement, but they went through their parts very well. There was enthusiasm for both plays, and after the first night London critics were sent over, Mr. Max Beerbohm among them, and gave a good report. Yet it was a stormy beginning for our enterprise, and a rough reception for a poetic play. The only moment, I think, at which I saw Mr. Yeats really angry was at the last performance. I was sitting next him, and the play had reached the point where the stage direction says, "The Second Merchant goes out through the door and returns with the hen strangled. He flings it on the floor." The merchant came in indeed, but without the strangled hen. Mr. Yeats got up, filled with suspicions that it also might have been objected to on some unknown ground, and went round to the back of the stage. But he was given a simple explanation. The chief Demon said he had been given charge of the hen, and had hung it out of a window every night, "And this morning," he said, "when I pulled up the string, there was nothing on it at all."

But that battle was not a very real one. We have put on *Countess Cathleen* a good many times of late with no one speaking against it at all. And some of those young men who hissed it then are our good supporters now.

* * *

JOHN EGLINTON

What Should Be the Subjects of National Drama?†

Supposing a writer of dramatic genius were to appear in Ireland, where would he look for the subject of a national drama? This question might serve as a test of what nationality really amounts to in Ireland—a somewhat trying one, perhaps, yet it is scarcely unfair to put the question to those who speak of our national literature with hardly less satisfaction in the present than confidence in the future. Would he look for it in the Irish legends, or in the life of the peasantry and folk-lore, or in Irish history and patriotism, or in life at large as reflected in his own consciousness? There are several reasons for thinking that the growing hopes of something in store for national life in this country are likely to come to something. In the great countries of Europe, although literature is apparently as prosperous as ever and is maintained with a circumstance which would seem to ensure it eternal honour, yet the springs from which the modern literary movements have been fed are probably dried up—the springs of simplicity, hope, belief, and an absolute original-ity like that of Wordsworth. If also, as seems likely, the approaching ages on the Continent are to be filled with great social and political questions and events which can hardly have immediate expression in literature, it is quite conceivable that literature, as it did once before, would migrate to a quiet country like Ireland, where there is no great tradition to be upset or much social sediment to be stirred up, and where the spectacle of such changes might afford a purely intellectual impulse. More important, of course, and certain than any such chances from without, is the positive feeling of encour-agement which is now taking the place of the hatreds and despon-dencies of the past. We may think that the peasantry are outside the reach of culture, that the gentry exhaust their function in con-tributing able officers to the British army, and that, frankly, there is nothing going on in the political or ecclesiastical or social life of Ireland on which to rest any but the most sober hopes for the fu-ture, still no one can say that political feebleness or stagnation might not be actually favourable to some original manifestation in the world of ideas. What [Ernest] Renan says, in speaking of the Jews, that "a nation whose mission it is to revolve in its bosom spir-itual truths is often weak politically," may be used with regard to

† From *Literary Ideals in Ireland*, a collection of essays by Eglinton, W. B. Yeats, and oth-ers, published in 1899.

Ireland as an argument that at least nothing stands in its way in this direction.

The ancient legends of Ireland undoubtedly contain situations and characters as well suited for drama as most of those used in the Greek tragedies which have come down to us. It is, nevertheless, a question whether the mere fact of Ireland having been the scene of these stories is enough to give an Irish writer much advantage over anyone else who is attracted by them, or whether anything but belles lettres, as distinguished from a national literature, is likely to spring from a determined pre-occupation with them. Belles lettres seek a subject outside experience, while a national literature, or any literature of a genuine kind, is simply the outcome and expression of a strong interest in life itself. The truth is, these subjects, much as we may admire them and regret that we have nothing equivalent to them in the modern world, obstinately refuse to be taken up out of their old environment and be transplanted into the world of modern sympathies. The proper mode of treating them is a secret lost with the subjects themselves. It is clear that if Celtic traditions are to be an active influence in future Irish literature they must seem to us worthy of the same compliment as that paid by Europe to the Greeks; we must go to them rather than expect them to come to us, studying them as closely as possible, and allowing them to influence us as they may. The significance of that interest in folklore and antiquities, which is so strong in this country, can hardly be different from that of the writings of [Johann Gottfried] Herder and others in German literature, and may lie in this, that some hint is caught in such studies of the forgotten mythopoetic secret.

As to Irish history and the subjects which it offers—a well-known Scotch Professor once said that Ireland was not a nation because it had never had a Burns nor a Bannockburn.[1] It is, however, as reasonable to think that these glorious memories of Scottish nationality will form a drag on its further evolution as that the want of a peasant poet, or of a recollection of having at least once given the Saxons a drubbing, will be fatal to an attempt to raise people above themselves in this country by giving expression to latent ideals. Ireland must exchange the patriotism which looks back for the patriotism which looks forward. The Jews had this kind of patriotism, and it came to something, and the Celtic peoples have been remarkable for it. The Saxon believes in the present, and, indeed, it belongs to him. The Romance nations, from whose hold the world has been

---

1. Scottish poet Robert Burns (1759–96); the battle, described in Burns's "Lord of the Isles," in which in 1314 the Scots under Robert Bruce defeated the English under Edward II [*Editor*].

slipping, can hardly be expected just yet to give up the consolations of history.

In short, we need to realise in Ireland that a national drama or literature must spring from a native interest in life and its problems and a strong capacity for life among the people. If these do not, or cannot exist, there cannot exist a national drama or literature. In London and Paris they seem to believe in theories and "movements," and to regard individuality as a noble but "impossible" savage; and we are in some danger of being absorbed into their error. Some of our disadvantages are our safeguards. In all ages poets and thinkers have owed far less to their countries than their countries have owed to them.

W. B. YEATS

An Irish National Theatre†

[The performance of Mr. Synge's *Shadow of the Glen* started a quarrel with the extreme National party, and the following paragraphs are from letters written in the play's defence. The organ of the party was at the time *The United Irishman*, but the first serious attack began in *The Independent*. *The United Irishman*, however, took up the quarrel, and from that on has attacked almost every play produced at our theatre, and the suspicion it managed to arouse among the political clubs against Mr. Synge especially led a few years later to the organised attempt to drive *The Playboy of the Western World* from the stage.—1908.]

When we were all fighting about the selection of books for the New Irish Library some ten years ago, we had to discuss the question, What is National Poetry? In those days a patriotic young man would have thought but poorly of himself if he did not believe that *The Spirit of the Nation*[1] was great lyric poetry, and a much finer kind of poetry than Shelley's *Ode to the West Wind*, or Keat's *Ode on a Grecian Urn*. When two or three of us denied this, we were told that we had effeminate tastes or that we were putting Ireland in a bad light before her enemies. If one said that *The Spirit of the Nation* was but salutary rhetoric, England might overhear us and take up the cry. We said it, and who will say that Irish literature has not a greater name in the world to-day than it had ten years ago?

To-day there is another question that we must make up our minds about, and an even more pressing one, What is a National

---

† From *Explorations* by W. B. Yeats (New York: Macmillan/Collier Books, 1973).
1. Anthology of patriotic verse compiled by Sir Charles Gavan Duffy (1816–1903) [*Editor*].

Theatre? A man may write a book of lyrics if he have but a friend or two that will care for them, but he cannot write a good play if there are not audiences to listen to it. If we think that a national play must be as near as possible a page out of *The Spirit of the Nation* put into dramatic form, and mean to go on thinking it to the end, then we may be sure that this generation will not see the rise in Ireland of a theatre that will reflect the life of Ireland as the Scandinavian theatre reflects the Scandinavian life. The brazen head has an unexpected way of falling to pieces. We have a company of admirable and disinterested players, and the next few months will, in all likelihood, decide whether a great work for this country is to be accomplished. The poetry of Young Ireland,[2] when it was an attempt to change or strengthen opinion, was rhetoric; but it became poetry when patriotism was transformed into a personal emotion by the events of life, as in that lamentation written by Doheny 'on his keeping' among the hills. Literature is always personal, always one man's vision of the world, one man's experience, and it can only be popular when men are ready to welcome the visions of others. A community that is opinion-ridden, even when those opinions are in themselves noble, is likely to put its creative minds into some sort of a prison. If creative minds preoccupy themselves with incidents from the political history of Ireland, so much the better, but we must not enforce them to select those incidents. If, in the sincere working-out of their plot, they alight on a moral that is obviously and directly serviceable to the National cause, so much the better, but we must not force that moral upon them. I am a Nationalist, and certain of my intimate friends have made Irish politics the business of their lives, and this made certain thoughts habitual with me, and an accident made these thoughts take fire in such a way that I could give them dramatic expression. I had a very vivid dream one night, and I made *Cathleen ni Houlihan* out of this dream. But if some external necessity had forced me to write nothing but drama with an obviously patriotic intention, instead of letting my work shape itself under the casual impulses of dreams and daily thoughts, I would have lost, in a short time, the power to write movingly upon any theme. I could have aroused opinions; but I could not have touched the heart, for I would have been busy at the oakum-picking that is not the less mere journalism for being in dramatic form. Above all, we must not say that certain incidents which have been a part of literature in all other lands are forbidden to us. It may be our duty, as it has been the duty of many dramatic move-

2. Mid-nineteenth-century nationalistic movement led by writers and editors of the journal *The Nation*, especially Charles Gavan Duffy, Thomas Davis (1814–45), and, named below, Michael Doheny (1805–63), who wrote a rebel's autobiography, *The Felon's Track* (1849) [*Editor*].

ments, to bring new kinds of subjects into the theatre, but it cannot
be our duty to make the bounds of drama narrower. For instance,
we are told that the English theatre is immoral, because it is preoccupied with the husband, the wife, and the lover. It is, perhaps, too
exclusively preoccupied with that subject, and it is certain it has
not shed any new light upon it for a considerable time, but a subject that inspired Homer and about half the great literature of the
world will, one doubts not, be a necessity to our National Theatre
also. Literature is, to my mind, the great teaching power of the
world, the ultimate creator of all values, and it is this, not only in
the sacred books whose power everybody acknowledges, but by
every movement of imagination in song or story or drama that
height of intensity and sincerity has made literature at all. Literature must take the responsibility of its power, and keep all its freedom: it must be like the spirit and like the wind that blows where it
listeth; it must claim its right to pierce through every crevice of human nature, and to describe the relation of the soul and the heart
to the facts of life and of law, and to describe that relation as it is,
not as we would have it be; and in so far as it fails to do this it fails
to give us that foundation of understanding and charity for whose
lack our moral sense can be but cruelty. It must be as incapable of
telling a lie as Nature, and it must sometimes say before all the
virtues, 'The greatest of these is charity.' Sometimes the patriot will
have to falter and the wife to desert her home, and neither be followed by divine vengeance or man's judgment. At other moments it
must be content to judge without remorse, compelled by nothing
but its own capricious spirit that has yet its message from the foundation of the world. Aristophanes held up the people of Athens to
ridicule, and even prouder of that spirit than of themselves, they invited the foreign ambassadors to the spectacle.

I would sooner our theatre failed through the indifference or
hostility of our audiences than gained an immense popularity by
any loss of freedom. I ask nothing that my masters have not asked
for, but I ask all that they were given. I ask no help that would limit
our freedom from either official or patriotic hands, though I am
glad of the help of any who love the arts so dearly that they would
not bring them into even honourable captivity. A good Nationalist
is, I suppose, one who is ready to give up a great deal that he may
preserve to his country whatever part of her possessions he is best
fitted to guard, and that theatre where the capricious spirit that
bloweth as it listeth has for a moment found a dwelling-place, has
good right to call itself a National Theatre.

FRANK J. FAY

An Irish National Theatre†

In a well-meaning, but cocky, contemporary of ours, there appeared a couple of weeks ago an article headed 'An Irish National Theatre,' the writer of which suggests that we in Ireland should emulate the example of the Tyrolese, who, it appears, annually represent in dramatic form, 'the exploits of their heroes in the struggle against the Napoleonic invasion of 1809.' While the suggestion is quite feasible, and might be productive of no small amount of good, an Irish National Theatre could never be treated from such a basis.

My notion of an Irish National Theatre is that it ought to be the nursery of an Irish dramatic literature which, while making a world-wide appeal, would see life through Irish eyes. For myself, I must say that I cannot conceive it possible to achieve this except through the medium of the Irish language. English as spoken by educated Irishmen differs from that spoken by Englishmen chiefly by reason of the difference in quality of voice between the two countries; in difference in inflexion or intonation and accentuation; in the use of expressions which show the subtle Gaelic mind vainly struggling for expression through an unsympathetic medium. I have read and seen many plays purporting to be Irish written in English, but save that they told an Irish story, the only real distinction was in the employment of a dialect more or less accurate, generally less. It is the old saying over again: No language, no nation, and consequently no drama. English is not our language; it is foreign to our nature, and weighs us down. If we must speak a foreign tongue, French is nearer to us; indeed the Irish voice is very like the French. But if happily, and the splendid success of the Gaelic movement would seem to point to it, the Irish nature is determined to assert its individuality, our old tongue will be found an ideal one for dramatic utterance, and I am convinced that plays given in it would not only be an invaluable boon to students, but would win us converts, and become a powerful weapon with which to fight the spread of Saxonism in this country. Certainly plays in English dealing with Irish heroic, legendary, or historical subjects cannot be written in dialect; instinctively, they will be written in as pure English as an Irishman can command, and so the national note will not be struck. Now that the Gaelic movement is so large, the time is

† From *Towards a National Theatre: The Dramatic Criticism of Frank J. Fay*, edited by Robert Hogan (Dublin: Dolmen Press, 1970).

ripe, if not for an Irish National Theatre, at least for the nucleus of
one in the shape of the frequent performance of plays in the Irish
language.

We have now several very capable Anglo-Irish dramatists, but the
Irish Literary Theatre is their proper place, unless they will take the
trouble, as many people of much less eminence have done, of
learning to express themselves in Irish.

There have also been published recently several plays in Irish,
and it is with these that an Irish National Theatre should begin its
work. And here it may be well to remind those who write plays in
Irish to aim at simplicity both as regards plot and scenery. We must
creep before we walk. There will be no Coquelins, or Mounet
Sullys, or Irvings on our Irish boards for many years to come.

The modern drama owes its origin largely to the old mystery
plays, which used to be acted by amateur actors, and these becoming enamoured of the pursuit or of their own real or fancied ability,
gradually turned a pastime into a profession. In the same way, the
first actors of an Irish National Theatre must be amateurs and
there is plenty of talent to be had by those who choose to seek for
it. Acting is a matter of temperament; constant practice before an
audience and unremitting rehearsal will do the rest. Annual performances are all but useless. It would be well if in our Irish National Theatre we could have for our first actors well-educated
native Irish speakers, and if possible, they should speak Connaught
Irish. In this way an Irish National Theatre would be able to set a
standard diction before its audiences. I fear, however, we shall not
be so lucky as to get people of this sort, firstly because they have
other things to do and could not devote the time and attention and
study which go to making actors, and secondly, because side by side
with the histrionic temperament and delight in dramatic display
which is very common in Ireland, there exists a scathing contempt
for the 'play-actor'; he is not considered respectable, and we have
been long suffering from an acute attack of respectability. Our actors would have to be got from the advanced pupils of the Gaelic
classes, now happily spread over the land, who show ability as re-
citers in Irish. I, myself, had the pleasure of hearing a number of
boys recite in Irish at the recent Leinster Feis,[1] most of whom
would have been able to give a very creditable account of themselves in a play, and nearly all of whom were gifted with splendid
voices. The Irish language is a fine voice producer. They had, to be
sure, been trained after the methods of the conventional reciter, so
far as gesture was concerned, but that could easily be remedied.

The article in our contemporary to which I allude has been fol-

1. Gaelic word for festival.

lowed by a letter from a gentleman who strongly advocates the formation of a National Theatre, either through the medium of subscription, by which means a wonderfully successful People's Theatre has been working for some years in Berlin, or by floating a company. The last suggestion makes one boil with rage. We don't want any of the financial gang, who would run the Universe, Limited, if they could, in connection with an Irish National Theatre. Those who have lately been abusing the English stage should abuse the syndicates who are running it, and who are the real authors of the vulgarity now rampant there. Only the other day, at a meeting of the Lyceum Theatre, Limited, or whatever they call it, one of these money-grubbers, who are making earth hideous, suggested turning that theatre into a variety show. Let us keep cursed commercialism at arm's length. It pollutes everything it touches. The writer of this letter gives the names of several people whom he would constitute patrons. You see there's no getting over the Irish nature, or perhaps, one should say, the Anglo-Irish nature—we must have patrons. It is, of course, characteristic of the paper to which this correspondent writes that Mr. Yeats's name should be omitted from the list of proposed patrons, although he is better entitled to be mentioned than Mr. George Moore. But, stay, perhaps the pious editor's hidebound prejudice moved him to expunge Mr. Yeats's name, which may, after all, have been in the original letter.

Personally, I see the way clear before me to a National Theatre. I do not think we need financial bounders or aristocratic patrons. The people who support the Gaelic movement will support a Gaelic Theatre. We would have a very, very small beginning, but many great things have started from less promising surroundings than an Irish National Theatre such as I conceive would have to encounter.

I will next week give a very short description of what Norway has done in this direction. The only superiority she had to Ireland was that she stuck to her own language.

COLM TÓIBÍN

[The Collaborations of Yeats and Lady Gregory]†

* * *

Cathleen ni Houlihan was Yeats's third play. At Coole in the summer of 1901, Yeats told Lady Gregory of a dream "almost as distinct as a vision, of a cottage where there was well-being and firelight

† From "Lady Gregory's Toothbrush." Reprinted with permission from the *New York Review of Books*, copyright © 2001, NYREV, Inc.

and talk of a marriage, and into the midst of that cottage there came an old woman in a long cloak" who was "Ireland herself, that Cathleen ni Houlihan for whom so many songs have been sung, and about whom so many stories have been told and for whose sake so many have gone to their death." This woman would lead the young man of the house away from domestic happiness to join the French who had landed to fight the British at Killala in County Mayo in 1798.

It is now absolutely clear that this play *Cathleen ni Houlihan* was actually written by Lady Gregory rather than Yeats. The idea belonged to Yeats and Yeats wrote the chant of the old woman at the end. But he could not write naturalistic peasant dialogue, and the play depends on the naturalistic setting, the talk of money and marriage, the sense of ease in family life in a small holding. In the manuscript held in the Berg Collection in the New York Public Library, Lady Gregory has written in pencil on the first section of ten pages "All this mine alone" and "This with WBY" at the beginning of the second section. James Pethica has described how Lady Gregory managed in the play to temper Yeats's tendency "to symbolize rather than to represent life" and grounded the development of the play within a realistic framework.[1]

In her journal for 1922, Lady Gregory said that she wrote "all but all" of *Cathleen ni Houlihan*. Lennox Robinson stated that "the verses in it are the poet's, but all the homely dialogue is Lady Gregory's. Indeed Yeats has told me more than once that the authorship of the play should be ascribed to her." Willie Fay also reported that Lady Gregory had written all of the play "except the part of Cathleen."

It is clear that Lady Gregory contributed "directly and abundantly," in James Pethica's phrase, to Yeats's work for the theater, especially to *On Baile's Strand*, *The Pot of Broth*, *The King's Threshold*, and *Deirdre*. In his dedication of *Where There Is Nothing* to Lady Gregory in 1902, Yeats wrote:

> I never did anything that went so easily and quickly; for when I hesitated, you had the right thought ready, and it was always you who gave the right turn to the phrase and gave it the ring of daily life. We finished several plays, of which this is the longest, in so few weeks, that if I were to say how few, I do not think anybody would believe me.

In public Yeats gave Lady Gregory some credit for this collaboration, but he never acknowledged the extent of her work on *Cathleen ni Houlihan*. In a diary entry in 1925 Lady Gregory

1. *Lady Gregory's Diaries* (Oxford: Oxford UP, 1996).

complained that not giving her name with the play was "rather hard on me." Elizabeth Coxhead, in her literary portrait of Lady Gregory, wrote that "when her family . . . urged her to stake her claim, she always refused with a smile, saying that she could not take from [Yeats] any part of what had proved, after all, his one real popular success."[2]

The play was performed with George Russell's play *Deirdre* in Dublin in April 1902 with Maud Gonne playing Cathleen. Lady Gregory, according to Roy Foster,[3] attended one rehearsal and "slipped away to Venice well before the first night." Yeats, in an interview with the *United Irishman,* said that his subject was "Ireland and its struggle for independence." "Apparently," Roy Foster wrote, "neither of them anticipated the response to their joint production." The hall was packed every night, and the effect of the play was powerful. It was short and stark, with no subplots or stylized dialogue until Cathleen herself appeared, and its message was clear: that young men would have to give up everything for Ireland. The audience and the ordinary people on the stage were as one, and both were visited by this haunting force, a woman both old and young, Platonic Ireland, who would pull them toward heroism and away from everyday materialism. The critic Stephen Gwynn attended the performance and wrote:

> I went home asking myself if such plays should be produced unless one was prepared for people to go out to shoot and be shot. . . . Yeats was not alone responsible; no doubt but Lady Gregory helped him to get the peasant speech so perfect; but above all Miss Gonne's impersonation had stirred the audience as I have never seen another audience stirred . . .

George Bernard Shaw later said that it was a play "which might lead a man to do something foolish." By 1904, Yeats was ready to deny that "it was a political play of a propaganda kind," but he was not convincing. Many years later, he would wonder, "Did that play of mine send out / Certain men the English shot."[4]

Two other one-act plays to which Lady Gregory gave her name as sole author, *Gaol Gate* and *The Rising of the Moon,* both produced and published over the next few years, made no bones about her support for rebellion. Lennox Robinson wrote that *Cathleen ni Houlihan* and *The Rising of the Moon* "made more rebels in Ireland than a thousand political speeches or a hundred reasoned books."

How she managed her two separate worlds in these years is a

2. *Lady Gregory: A Literary Portrait* (London: Secker and Warburg, 1966).
3. *W. B. Yeats: A Life,* vol. 1 (Oxford: Oxford UP, 1997).
4. "The Man and the Echo" [*Editor*].

mystery, but she managed superbly. In these same years, she could write Yeats a description of a dance at Coole:

> Our dance last night went off splendidly, lasted till three o'clock this morning, I wished you could have been there it was such a pretty bright sight, the drawing room cleared and lighted by close of fifty wax candles, the supper served on the twenty silver dishes, all the table silver and flowers and tempting dishes. . . . We were about thirty, chiefly cousins of Robert's and also two or three officers and a sister of Lord Westmeath's, Lady Emily Nugent. It was the merriest dance I ever saw (my experience has not been great, Buckingham Palace and Indian Viceregal and Embassy Balls chiefly).

In *Cathleen ni Houlihan, The Rising of the Moon*, and *Gaol Gate*, indeed in the story of Cuchulain himself, the lone male hero was ready to sacrifice himself. He was an idealistic, inspirational figure, free from the mire of the struggle for land which preoccupied most Irish peasants in these years. In *Cathleen ni Houlihan*, the family's desire for more land is something the son will have no truck with now that the old woman has come to the house and the French have landed at Killala. There was no grubby land-hunger in the rhetoric of these heroes.

Thus it was easier for Lady Gregory to apply the same zeal to collecting her folklore as to collecting her rents. She was, however, on at least one occasion, frightened enough by what she herself had created to write to Frank Fay in 1907: "I particularly didn't wish to have *Gaol Gate* [produced in Galway] in the present state of agrarian excitement, it [might] be looked on as a direct incitement to crime."

Her plays could incite crime; and when crime came close to her, it kept her awake. In May 1912 she wrote to Yeats about her tenants:

> Dear Willie, I am in great trouble this week—my brother wrote last week that he had had a meeting with the tenants but that they could not come to terms at present. Then Monday was rent day and he wired "Tenants demand 6/—in the pound reduction—no rents paid." This was a shock and gave me a sleepless night and in the morning I had a letter from him saying the tenants are trying to blackmail us—and that he is making preparations to seize their cattle end of this week or beginning of next, which will he thinks bring them to reason, especially as the bulk of them are really anxious to pay.

She wrote to her son that their agent "was sure that the seizures would bring them to their senses . . . . He had arranged to start from Gort at 7 o'clock Friday morning, with eight Gort men, four Coole men and twenty police; to begin with the stock of the small tenants, and to sweep that of the larger ones as well."

The cattle raid in Coole did not take place, however, since a settlement was negotiated. Robert, who was away, owned the estate and the rents were his income. "I hope you think I have done right," she wrote to him, "I have done what I think best for your happiness." This is the key to understanding Lady Gregory's role as landlord at Coole. The cold, ruthless tone in her letters to Yeats and Robert about the tenants was not because she was a landlord's daughter who could not shake off this tone. She held Coole for Robert. It was his heritage and his inheritance. However much she may have changed in other matters, she remained steadfast in this.

Lady Gregory's mixture of high ideals and natural haughtiness gave her an inflexibility and sturdy determination which were invaluable when dealing with those who opposed her. Her gifts for governing men, her passion and precision, as Yeats put it, came into their own in the early years of the twentieth century when she became involved with the Abbey Theatre.

Her first battle was with Miss Horniman, the tea heiress from Manchester who bankrolled the theater in its early days and made great demands on the management and fellow directors while also making a pitch for the affections of W. B. Yeats. In many letters to Yeats, Lady Gregory deplored Miss Horniman's "vulgar arrogance and bullying" and suggested that she "should be locked up." She also called her "cracked," "a blood sucker," "a crocodile," "the Saxon shilling," "wicked," "a mad woman," "insane," and "a raving lunatic." If this was not enough to dislodge her, Lady Gregory pulled rank. "I have never treated her as an equal," she wrote to Yeats, "without regretting it." And later: "I think it is a mistake treating tradespeople as if they had one's own table of values."

This hauteur and invective were accompanied, however, over several years by Lady Gregory's slow and deliberate and tireless preparations to have Miss Horniman removed. While Miss Horniman ranted and raved, Lady Gregory never lost her nerve. By early 1911, she had succeeded.

This readiness to do battle, this tough attitude toward opposition, made all the difference when the artistic integrity of the Abbey Theatre was under attack. The importance of Yeats's and Lady Gregory's collaboration at the Abbey was not so much that words of theirs sent out certain men the English shot, as that during the time when they ran the theater a number of enduring masterpieces were produced, notably the plays of Synge and O'Casey, and also

George Bernard Shaw's *The Shewing-up of Blanco Posnet*. Both
Yeats and Lady Gregory maintained their relationship to a peasant
culture they had dreamed into being, and at the same time made
no effort to repudiate their own Anglo-Irish heritage. This gave
them an enormous advantage in both Ireland and London: they
were members of a ruling class who lost none of their edge or high
manners or old friends while espousing a new politics and a new art
in Ireland. They were independent and they did what they liked,
subject to no peer group or class pressure. It was the mixture of
ambiguity and arrogance in their position which made them ready
for the exemplary battles they were now to fight for artistic freedom
in Ireland, the right to stage the plays of Synge, Shaw, and O'Casey.
They, and no one else, had the strength of will and the class confidence and the belief in their cause to do battle with the rabble, the
Catholic Church, the Lord Lieutenant, and, when the time came,
the new Irish state.

The young Catholic revolutionaries who had been so inspired by
the simple message of *Cathleen ni Houlihan* were not ready for the
mocking ironies and wild paganism of John Millington Synge's *The
Playboy of the Western World*, which the Abbey Theatre first produced in 1907. Yeats and Lady Gregory were ready to stand up to
them, insisting on their own nationalist credentials, but reverting
also to Ascendancy hauteur. After a week of riots in the theater
against the presentation of Irish peasants as less than holy, there
was, on Yeats's suggestion, a public debate held in the Abbey on
February 4. Yeats took the stage, announcing that he spoke as the
author of *Cathleen ni Houlihan*. Referring to a priest in Liverpool
who had withdrawn a play because of the public's objection, he said
of the Abbey directors, who were all Protestants: "We have not such
pliant bones and did not learn in the houses that bred us a suppliant knee." The audience would have understood this very clearly as
a statement of arrogant Ascendancy values over suppliant Roman
ones. When Yeats's father in the same debate referred to Ireland as
an island of saints and scholars and then, sneeringly, referred to
"plaster saints" ("his beautiful mischievous head thrown back," as
Yeats described him many years later in "Beautiful Lofty Things"),
the audience would also have understood his remark as an insult to
Catholicism.

Lady Gregory's nephew led a group of Trinity students to the theater to defend the play and offer what was perhaps most missing in
the debate—a rendering of "God Save the King." And as the disturbances continued in the theater, the Abbey directors, as property
owners, knew what to do: they called the police, who arrested rioters. The calling of the police did not win them many friends in

nationalist Ireland. In 1909, two years after *The Playboy*, Lady
Gregory placed the conflict between the Abbey directors and the
Catholic nationalist mob in terms both stark and superior: "It is the
old battle," she wrote to Yeats, "between those who use a toothbrush and those who don't."

On W. B. Yeats

W. B. YEATS

An Introduction for My Plays†

I

The theatre for which these plays were written was the creation of seven people: four players, Sara Allgood, her sister Maire O'Neill, girls in a blind factory who joined a patriotic society; William Fay, Frank Fay, an electric light fitter and an accountant's clerk who got up plays at a coffee-house; three writers, Lady Gregory, John Synge, and I. If we all told the story we would all tell it differently. Somewhere among my printed diaries is a note describing how on the same night my two sisters and their servant dreamt the same dream in three different grotesque forms. Once I was in meditation with three students of the supernormal faculties; our instructor had given us the same theme, what, I have forgotten; one saw a ripe fruit, one an unripe, one a lit torch, one an unlit. Science has never thought about the subject and so has no explanation of those parallel streams that make up a great part of history. When I follow back my stream to its source I find two dominant desires: I wanted to get rid of irrelevant movement—the stage must become still that words might keep all their vividness—and I wanted vivid words. When I saw a London play, I saw actors crossing the stage not because the play compelled them, but because a producer said they must do so to keep the attention of the audience; and I heard words that had no vividness except what they borrowed from the situation. It seems that I was confirmed in this idea or I found it when I first saw Sarah Bernhardt play in *Phèdre*,[1] and that it was I who converted the players, but I am old, I must have many false memories; perhaps I was Synge's convert. It was certainly a day of triumph

† Reprinted with the permission of Scribner, an imprint of Simon & Schuster Adult Publishing Group, from *Essays and Introductions* by W. B. Yeats. Copyright © 1961 by Mrs. W. B. Yeats. All rights reserved.
1. By the French playwright Jean Racine (1639–99) [*Editor*].

when the first act of *The Well of the Saints* held its audience, though the two chief persons sat side by side under a stone cross from start to finish. This rejection of all needless movement first drew the attention of critics. The players still try to preserve it, though audiences accustomed to the cinema expect constant change; perhaps it was most necessary in that first period when the comedies of Lady Gregory, the tragi-comedies of Synge, my own blank-verse plays, made up our repertory, all needing whether in verse or prose an ear attentive to every rhythm.

I hated the existing conventions of the theatre, not because conventions are wrong but because soliloquies and players who must always face the audience and stand far apart when they speak—'dressing the stage' it was called—had been mixed up with too many bad plays to be endurable. Frank Fay agreed, yet he knew the history of all the conventions and sometimes loved them. I would put into his hands a spear instead of a sword because I knew that he would flourish a sword in imitation of an actor in an eighteenth-century engraving. He knew everything, even that Racine at rehearsal made his leading lady speak on musical notes and that Ireland had preserved longer than England the rhythmical utterance of the Shakespearean stage. He was openly, dogmatically, of that school of Talma[2] which permits an actor, as Gordon Craig[3] has said, to throw up an arm calling down the thunderbolts of Heaven, instead of seeming to pick up pins from the floor. Were he living now and both of us young, I would ask his help to elaborate new conventions in writing and representation; for Synge, Lady Gregory, and I were all instinctively of the school of Talma. Do not those tragic sentences, 'shivering into seventy winters,' 'a starved ass braying in the yard,' require convention as much as a blank-verse line? And there are scenes in *The Well of the Saints* which seem to me over-rich in words because the realistic action does not permit that stilling and slowing which turns the imagination in upon itself.

II

I wanted all my poetry to be spoken on a stage or sung and, because I did not understand my own instincts, gave half a dozen wrong or secondary reasons; but a month ago I understood my reasons. I have spent my life in clearing out of poetry every phrase written for the eye, and bringing all back to syntax that is for ear alone. Let the eye take delight in the form of the singer and in the panorama of

2. Francis Joseph Talma (1763-1826), French actor [*Editor*].
3. Edward Gordon Craig (1872–1966), stage designer and theorist of modern drama [*Editor*].

the stage and be content with that. Charles Ricketts[4] once designed for me a black jester costume for the singer, and both he and Craig helped with the panorama, but my audience was for comedy—for Synge, for Lady Gregory, for O'Casey—not for me. I was content, for I knew that comedy was the modern art.

As I altered my syntax I altered my intellect. Browning said that he could not write a successful play because interested not in character in action but in action in character. I had begun to get rid of everything that is not, whether in lyric or dramatic poetry, in some sense character in action; a pause in the midst of action perhaps, but action always its end and theme. 'Write for the ear,' I thought, so that you may be instantly understood as when actor or folk singer stands before an audience. I delight in active men, taking the same delight in soldier and craftsman; I would have poetry turn its back upon all that modish curiosity, psychology—the poetic theme has always been present. I recall an Indian tale: certain men said to the greatest of the sages, 'Who are your Masters?' And he replied, 'The wind and the harlot, the virgin and the child, the lion and the eagle.'

NICHOLAS GRENE

Strangers in the House†

'All art,' Synge was to say, 'is a collaboration' and there were many more collaborators besides Yeats and Gregory in the theatrical event of the first production of *Kathleen ni Houlihan*. Adrian Frazier has shown just how far the play fulfilled the aesthetic and political demands set out by Frank Fay, the need for a drama to 'send men away filled with the desire for deeds'. Antoinette Quinn argues convincingly for the ideological significance of Maud Gonne's performance, and for the production by Inghinidhe na hEireann within the context of their political objectives. The theatrical realisation of *Kathleen ni Houlihan* was not in the hands of Yeats and Gregory. It was not first produced by the Irish Literary Theatre over which they had primary control, neither of them were involved with rehearsals and Gregory did not even attend the performances. The theatrical event represented by *Kathleen ni Houlihan* as performed in St Teresa's Hall, Clarendon Street, in April 1902 by a nationalist company of amateur actors with the expectations of an audience at-

---

4. Charles Ricketts (1866–1931), designer and editor [*Editor*].
† From *The Politics of Irish Drama*. Reprinted with the permission of Cambridge University Press.

tracted by such a company, cannot be considered wholly the creation of either Yeats or Gregory or both.

What is at issue [in *Kathleen ni Houlihan*] is the political meaning which the play generated and the potential for such meaning which the text offered. Again and again the testimony was to the extraordinary kinetic impact of the play. This was without doubt the play which Fay had demanded, sending 'men away filled with the desire for deeds'. Stephen Gwynn's reaction is often taken as representative when he recalled wondering 'whether such plays should be produced unless one was prepared for people to go out and shoot or be shot'.[1] Lennox Robinson was convinced that *Kathleen ni Houlihan*, along with Gregory's popular *The Rising of the Moon*, 'made more rebels in Ireland than a thousand political speeches or a hundred reasoned books'.[2] The play's power could work surprisingly even with those of very unnationalist convictions. Gregory recorded the reaction of Shaw watching a London performance in 1909: 'When I see that play I feel it might lead a man to do something foolish.' She was, she said, 'as much surprised as if I had seen one of the Nelson lions scratch himself.'[3] What was there in *Kathleen ni Houlihan* to move even the normally immovable G.B.S.?

The effectiveness of the play in part derives from the very concrete ordinariness of the peasant setting as established by Gregory in the first scene. This makes for the kind of literalism in the allegory attested to by Patrick Pearse. In his 1916 essay 'The Spiritual Nation' he wrote of how in his childhood he believed in the actual existence of a woman called Erin, 'and had Mr Yeats' "Kathleen ni Houlihan" been then written and had I seen it, I should have taken it not as an allegory, but as a representation of a thing that might happen any day in my house'.[4] The liaison between the realised typicality of the Gillanes' cottage as 'home' and the strange Old Woman that visits it facilitates this sort of child-like literal reaction. What is more, the representativeness of the Gillanes as a peasant family gives to the play its popular and populist quality. In the Yeatsian imagination it is normally the exceptional heroic figures who are susceptible to the dream of a transcendent, immortal destiny— Cuchulain being the archetype of such a hero. Although Mary

1. Stephen Gwynn, *Irish Literature and Drama in the English Language: a Short History* (London: Nelson, 1936), p. 158, cited by Maria Tymoczko in 'Amateur Political Theatricals, *Tableaux Vivants*, and *Cathleen ni Houlihan*', *Yeats Annual*, 10 (1993), 33–64.
2. Lennox Robinson, *Curtain Up* (London: Michael Joseph, 1942), p. 17, also quoted by Tymoczko, 'Amateur Political Theatricals', 59.
3. Lady Gregory, *Seventy Years* (Gerrards Cross: Colin Smythe, 1973), p. 444. [Nelson lions: statuary in Trafalgar Square, London (*Editor*).]
4. Pádraic H. Pearse, *Political Writings and Speeches* (Dublin: Talbot Press, 1952), pp. 300–1.

Bruin the changeling bride may not seem to fit such a pattern, even she (with her husband Shawn) can articulate a vision of love quite antithetical to the values of ordinary hearth and home. But the call of Kathleen ni Houlihan, like the call of Christ, can come to anyone and everyone. Though Michael must forsake the common good of marriage, family, house and comfort in the self-sacrificial act which marks him out from those who cleave to such things, his action in doing so is paradigmatic, indeed exemplary, rather than the tragic doom of the special hero. His role therefore is openly available to any audience member, if gender-skewed towards males. The challenge is to all, and the reward is the infinitely desirable transformation of old woman into young girl.

That transformation, miraculous, instantaneous, brought about by the willingness of the young man to lay down his life, is infinitely desirable for a nationalist community as it figures a revolution capable of restoring the country from its oppressed state of colonisation to renewed sovereignty. But the trope of strangers in the house as embodied in *Kathleen ni Houlihan* brings out the peculiar nature of that imagined dream of liberation. In so far as the original myth of the king's marriage to the sovereignty goddess Eire can be construed as a ritual both of kingship and of fertility, the blood sacrifice restores the land to health and establishes the legitimacy of the true king whom she marries. But in the context of a colonised Ireland, the nature and identity of that true king is highly problematic. In the Norman period, the bardic poet might celebrate the prowess of his individual chieftain, treating the invader/occupiers as no different from other rival chieftains to be outmatched in valour. But from the seventeenth century on, with Gaelic culture and the clan system definitely broken, the *aisling*[5] poets increasingly had to look outside the country for liberation and for the true sovereign. Hence the repeated focus on the various Stuart kings and pretenders under their several aliases; hence the constantly renewed hope of succour from France or Italy or Spain: 'Oh! the French are on the sea, / Says the *Shan Van Vocht*'; 'There's wine . . . from the royal Pope / Upon the ocean green; / And Spanish ale shall give you hope / My Dark Rosaleen!'[6]

This produces the special complexity of *Kathleen ni Houlihan*'s image of strangers in the house. It is strangers in the house which have put the Old Woman wandering in the first place, the colonial invaders who have taken away her land. She acts as stranger in the house of the Gillanes, disturbing and troubling them with the imagination of a pristine Ireland of the past which might be realised again in the future. The play's climax comes with the news that the

---

5. Irish Gaelic "vision" poets embodying Ireland in female form [*Editor*].
6. Thomas Kinsella (ed.), *New Oxford Book of Irish Verse* (Oxford: Oxford University Press, 1986), pp. 256, 273.

French have landed in Killala Bay, that the 1798 Rebellion is about to start. These strangers to Ireland need to invade in order to make possible the liberation/restoration of Kathleen ni Houlihan as sovereign Ireland. But who gets to marry her? There is a telling political ellipsis in the way the original structure of the myth is re-embodied in Yeats-Gregory's play. Michael must forego the sexual consummation of marriage to die instead for Kathleen. The stranger French are necessary catalysts for the expulsion of the stranger English. What then: The power of *Kathleen ni Houlihan* derives not only from the potency with which it imagines revolution as a miraculous transformation, but the skill with which it leaves unanswered the question of what is to follow the revolution.

ANTOINETTE QUINN

Cathleen ni Houlihan Writes Back†

Cathleen ni Houlihan, set in a cottage kitchen in Killala at the time of the French landing in 1798, stages two conflicting narratives of Irish peasant womanhood. Mrs. Gillane and, potentially, Delia, her son's pretty, well-dowered bride-to-be, represent a realist, maternal order, the values of hearth and home; the Poor Old Woman, Cathleen, also dressed as a peasant,[1] represents a contrary order of being—symbolic, nomadic, virginal, sacrificial rather than procreative, not subject to the imperatives of generational replacement, metamorphosing magically from age to youth. Two forms of continuity are opposed: continuity in the corporeal dimension expressed through reproduction and inheritance; continuity at an ideological level in which an old symbol (Sean Bhean Bhocht/Cathleen) is revitalized through her success in obtaining adherents in the dramatic present (1798) and in the present tense of the play's production, just over a century later. *Cathleen ni Houlihan* concludes with a diptych of Irish peasant womanhood. The notorious transformation scene—in which the old crone who has lured away the bridegroom turns into a beautiful young girl with the walk of a queen—occurs offstage;[2] onstage, two bereft women, mother and

---

† Reprinted by permission of the University of Massachusetts Press from *Gender and Sexuality in Modern Ireland*, Anthony Bradley and Maryann Gialanella Valiulis, eds., copyright © 1997 by the American Conference for Irish Studies.
1. "I have a beautiful untidy grey wig, a torn grey [flannil] flannel dress *exactly* like the old women wear in the west, bare feet and a big hoooded cloak." *The Gonne-Yeats Letters 1893–1938*, ed. with introductions by Anna MacBride White and A. Norman Jeffares (London: Hutchinson, 1992), 151.
2. The *Daily Express* review makes it clear that the rejuvenated Cathleen was not seen by the audience.

jilted bride, comfort one another.[3] Inghinidhe members played both
sets of contrasting female roles: the charismatic Cathleen who subverts the values of cradle, hearth, and smallholding, and the realist
peasant women who lose out to the symbolic woman-nation. Nationalists, far from being perturbed by this dramatization of the
split between the materialist and familist priorities of peasant con-
servatism and the abandonment of *kinder* and *kuchen*[4] advocated
by physical-force nationalism, were elated by the triumph of the
woman-nation. *Cathleen ni Houlihan*, which subordinated the interests of women to a sacrificial paradigm of male patriotism and
invoked a literary tradition of political allegory, was enshrined as
the exemplary nationalist play. It was appropriate that a scheduled
performance at the Abbey Theatre during Easter Week had to be
canceled because the Rising, which the play adumbrated, had actually occurred.

It is now well attested that Lady Gregory scripted the roles of the
realist peasants in *Cathleen ni Houlihan*, the Gillane family and
Delia,[5] but to what extent was the role of Cathleen, which was au-
thored by Yeats, authorized by Maud Gonne? All the part of Cathleen
really needed, Lady Gregory famously quipped, was "a hag and a
voice."[6] Would the play have proved as successful if the part had originally been played by any old hag? Or was it Maud Gonne's creation
of the title role that was largely responsible for the play's mystique?

Cathleen ni Houlihan, now probably the best-known female symbol of Ireland, was by no means as familiar as Dark Rosaleen in
1902. She derived from a much less popular poem by Mangan,
"Kathleen-ny-Houlihan," a translation of William Heffernan The
Blind's eighteenth-century poem "Caitilin ni Uallachain." Her accessibility in the play as a personification of Ireland was largely due
to her conflation with the Shan Van Vocht from the popular 1798
ballad. She appears as The Poor Old Woman, not as Cathleen, in
the list of "Persons in the Play," and the authors toyed with the idea
of using "The Poor Old Woman" as the title. Lady Gregory feared
that audiences might confuse Cathleen ni Houlihan with the
Countess Cathleen from Yeats's earlier play.[7]

The first-night audience had difficulty negotiating the transition
from the play's realist representation of peasantry to the figurative
role of Cathleen. Yeats reported that they were slow to turn from

3. Delia and Bridget's final embrace was suggested by the Inghinidhe and the Fays during
   rehearsals. *The Gonne-Yeats Letters*, 150.
4. By extension, "home and hearth" [*Editor*].
5. See James Pethica, " 'Our Kathleen': Yeats's Collaboration with Lady Gregory in the writing of *Cathleen ni Houlihan*," *Yeats Annual*, no. 6 (1988).
6. Lady Gregory, *Selected Writings*, ed. Lucy McDiarmid and Maureen Waters (Har-
   mondsworth: Penguin, 1995), 436.
7. Pethica, " 'Our Kathleen,' " 14.

"delighted laughter" to an appreciation of the "tragic meaning" of Cathleen's part. By the third performance they had been educated, and crowds were being turned away from the packed theater.[8] Yeats's report betrays the risk that he and Lady Gregory were taking in staging Ireland as a female symbol in a realist setting. Without Maud Gonne's collaboration they might not have pulled it off. Edward Martyn comments that "her sheer talent saved the disaster which otherwise must have come to destroy the high poetic significance of the play by reason of the low comedy-man air adopted by another actor." That other actor was Willie Fay and Yeats, in his reply to Martyn, pointed out that the reason for the laughter that greeted him was that Dublin audiences associated him with comedy and were "ready to laugh before even he speaks."[9] Fortunately, Fay's associations with comedy, which almost ruined the play, were more than compensated for by Maud Gonne's considerable notoriety in Dublin as an exceptionally ardent and beautiful nationalist. It was her credentials on both counts that authenticated the role of Cathleen, making the final transformation credible.

In 1902 Maud Gonne was at the apogee of her career as an Irish nationalist. A public speaker who was much in demand, she had undertaken lecture tours in France and the United States as well as speaking at many Irish venues. She was a prolific journalist, a prominent pro-Boer campaigner, one of the organizers of the 1798 centenary celebrations, and she was generally prominent in anti-British demonstrations in Dublin. In the role of Cathleen, Maire Nic Shiubhlaigh recalls, she appeared to the young people in the theater as "the very personification of the figure she portrayed on the stage."[1] The *All-Ireland Review* noted the connection between Maud's theatrical role and her more customary role of nationalist orator, making her performance continuous with her politics: "The well-known nationalist orator did not address the other actors as is usual in drama, but spoke directly to the audience, as if she was addressing them in Beresford Place . . . she can scarcely be said to act the part, she lived it." How much of the play's success in translating a female symbol of the nation from balladry and iconography onto the stage was due to Maud Gonne's charisma and her political "street cred."?

As George L. Mosse observes, theater which creates "sexed bodies as public spectacles" helps "to instill through representational practices an erotic investment in the national romance."[2] Maud Gonne

8. Robert Hogan and James Kilroy, *Laying the Foundations, 1902–1904* (Dublin: Dolmen Press, 1976), 15.
9. Ibid., 17–18.
1. Maire Nic Shiubhlaigh, *The Splendid Years* (Dublin: Duffy, 1955), 19.
2. George L. Mosse, "Nationalism and Sexuality," in *Nationalisms and Sexualities*, ed. Andrew Parker (London: Routledge, 1992), 12.

ANTOINETTE QUINN

brought to the part of the *femme fatale* an erotic charge all the more potent for being covert, her disguised beauty colluding with the dialogue, titillating by its promise of a final unveiling. Her late arrival for the premiere, sweeping through the auditorium in her costume when the audience was already seated, consciously or unconsciously anticipated the play's conclusion, preempting Yeats's script.[3]

Moreover, Maud Gonne, who like Yeats was a member of the mystical order of the Golden Dawn, invested the role of Cathleen with occult power. Yeats was not alone in attributing a "weird power" to her characterization of Cathleen; Maire Nic Shiubhlaigh described her appearance as "ghostly"; Joseph Holloway applied the adjectives "mysterious," "weird," "uncanny," "strange" to her playing and remarked that she "realised" the role "with creepy realism."[4] Through her personal alliance of nationalism and the occult Maud rendered the woman-nation *unheimlich*,[5] antithetical both to material values and to the home.

The upstaging of real women by the nationalist female icon, which contemporary feminists decry, was not only thematized in the script of *Cathleen ni Houlihan* but was inseparable from its first production. Lady Gregory's co-authorship was ignored on the playbill and neither her co-authorship nor the Inghinidhe's sponsorship was acknowledged in Yeats's postperformance speeches. That the nationalist cause was privileged over the claims of sisterhood is evidenced by the fact that the play went ahead despite the death of Anna Johnston (Ethna Carbery), a vice president of the Inghinidhe[6] and the first of its members to die.[7] A year later, the Inghinidhe broke away from the newly formed Irish National Theatre Society because they disapproved of the Society's denationalized attitude to female representation as manifested in its staging of *In the Shadow of the Glen*.[8]

---

3. "Her beauty was *startling* . . .," Nic Shiubhlaigh, *The Splendid Years*, 19. For Mary Colum too "her beauty was startling in its greatness, its dignity, its strangeness . . ." *Life and the Dream* (Dublin: Dolmen Press, 1966), 124. Her late arrival is from *The Splendid Years*, 17.
4. Yeats quoted in Hogan and Kilroy, *Laying the Foundations*, 15; Nic Shiubhlaigh, *The Splendid Years*, 17; Holloway in Levenson, *Maud Gonne*, 195.
5. Supernatural [*Editor*].
6. Inghinidhe na hEireann (Daughters of Ireland), political and cultural nationalist organization [*Editor*].
7. Anna Johnston died on 2 April 1902, the date of the premiere. Jenny Wyse-Power wrote to Alice Milligan: "it pained me more than I can tell to think they went on with the plays the night of the day she passed away—out of respect for her memory they should have been postponed that evening. . . ." She continued, "Mr Russel and Mr Yates [sic] each made speeches . . . and never once referred to the Society that had financed the whole affair." Letters to Alice Milligan, ms. 5048, The National Library of Ireland.
8. In her letter of resignation from the recently formed National Theatre Society to which she had been elected vice president following her success as Cathleen ni Houlihan, Gonne reveals that she had joined because she thought it shared the same theatrical aims as the Inghinidhe. *The Gonne-Yeats Letters*, 178.

R. F. FOSTER

[At the Hawk's Well]†

* * * The effect [of the lyric drama of the Noh] relied on a blend of formalism and intimacy, using strategies which wBy [W. B. Yeats] had already established at the centre of his ideal drama: symbolic scenery, masks, dance. Much in his article 'The Tragic Theatre', written for Edward Gordon Craig's journal the *Mask* in October 1910, was perfectly in line with the conventions of Noh. Just as strikingly, the subject matter concerned aristocratic values, archetypal personalities, duty, and the otherworld, and the dramatic presentation involved choruses, pauses, and repetitions. Put like this, proto-Noh elements are discernible in many of Yeats's earlier plays, notably *Deirdre* and the 1911 production of *The Hour-Glass*— though often coexisting, not uncomfortably, with the formulations of classical tragedy. wBy consciously followed the main lines of the classical Noh play in *At the Hawk's Well*, but only in so far as it fitted the format he had already grasped.

What happened at Stone Cottage[1] in January 1916 was that the imagery, concision, and ellipsis which Pound found in Fennolosa's translations, and wrote about in his essay ' "Noh", or Accomplishment', showed wBy how his core poetic values, so painfully evolved, could be expressed in drama. This was done by finding a theatrical form which had at its centre the presentation of occult themes, and for which an elite audience was a requirement rather than a disadvantage. A long letter to jBy[2] in March shows vividly both how much Pound's modernist associations had influenced him in this—and how little.

> You asked for examples of 'imitation' in poetry. I suggest that the corresponding things are drama & the pictorial element & that in poetry those who lack them are rhetoricians. I feel in Wyndham Lewis's Cubist pictures an element corresponding to rhetoric arising from his confusion of the abstract with the rhythmical. Rhythm implies a living body a breast to rise & fall or limbs that dance while the Abstract [is] incompatible with life. The cubist is abstract. At the same time you must not leave out rhythm & this rhythm is not imitation. Impression-

---

† From *W. B. Yeats: A Life II: The Arch-Poet, 1915–1939*. Reprinted by permission of Oxford University Press.
1. Country retreat in Sussex, England, where Yeats spent time with the American poet Ezra Pound (1885–1972) during World War I [*Editor*].
2. His father, John Butler Yeats [*Editor*].

ism by leaving it out brought all this rhetoric of the abstract
upon us. I have just been turning over a book of Japanese
paintings. Everywhere there is delight in form, repeated yet
varied, in curious patterns of lines but these lines are all an or-
dering of natural objects though they are certainly not imitation. In every case the artist one feels has had to *consciously* &
deliberately arrange his subject. It was the impressionists
beleif [sic] that this arrangement should be only unconscious
& instinctive that brought this violent reaction. They are right
in beleiving [sic] that they should be conscious but wrong in
substituting abstract scientific thought for conscious feeling. If
I delight in rhythm I love Nature though she is not rhythmical.
I express my love in rhythm. The more I express it the less
can I forget her.

I think Keats perhaps greater than Shelley and beyond
words greater than Swinbourne because he makes pictures one
cannot forget & sees them as full of rhythm as a Chinease [sic]
painting. Swinbourne's poetry all but some early poems is as
abstract as a Cubist picture. Carlyle is abstract—ideas, never
things or only their common worn out images taken up from
some preacher, & today he is as dead as MacPhersons Ossian.
In sincere and theatrical he knew nothing, he saw nothing. His
moral zeal cast before his mind perpetually 'God' 'Eternity'
'Work' & these ideas corresponding to no exact pictures have
their analogy in all art which is without imitation. I doubt if I
have made myself plane. I seperate the rhythmical & the abstract. They are brothers but one is Abel & one is Cain. In poetry they are not confused for we know that poetry is rhythm
but in music hall verses we find an abstract cadence, which is
vulgar because it is a part from imitation. The cadence is a
mechanism, it never suggests a voice shaken with joy or sorrow
as poetrical rhythm does. It is but the noise of a machine &
not the coming & the going of the breath.

It is Midnight & I must stop.[3]

In fact, though *At the Hawk's Well* relies for its scenario on the Noh
play *Yoro* (not published by Pound), it is built around familiar
themes which invoke Celtic mythology as well as William Morris's
Well at the World's End. Cuchulain as a young man comes in search
of immortality to a miraculous well whose waters appear and disappear (like the lake at Coole). The well's guardian, a miraculous figure who takes the guise of a hawk, mesmerizes him by a marvellous

3. WBY to JBY, 14 Mar. [1916], Boston College and *L*, 608–9. (Wyndham Lewis
(1882–1957), Canadian-born writer and painter; John Keats (1795–1821), English Romantic Poet; Percy Bysshe Shelley (1792–1922), English Romantic Poet; Algernon
Charles Swinburne (1837–1909), English Victorian Poet; Thomas Carlyle (1795–1881),
Scottish-born essayist and historian [*Editor*].)

dance; during this, the waters run and dry up again, unnoticed by the hero until it is too late. The first draft ended with a reflection (later excised) which exactly repeated the conclusion to [Yeats's] *Reveries*: 'Accursed is the life of man—between passion and empti- ness what he longs for never comes. All his days are in preparation for what never comes.'[4] Thus the drama would take its place in the series of Cuchulain plays which WBY returned to throughout his life. It establishes the pattern of the Promethean hero doomed to disappointment, and the Yeatsian moral—as expressed in the play's conclusion—that 'wisdom must live a bitter life'. The bleakness re- flects the lonely conditions of his life when he began to write it. Stylistically, WBY was determined on austerity: written in a kind of free verse, the play was cut down, draft after draft, to remove de- scriptive passages and focus on 'a single metaphor, as deliberate as the echoing rhythm of line in Chinese and Japanese painting'.[5] But the two apparently Eastern innovations in the play's presentation were derived from nearer home. One was the use of marvellous masks worn by the players, designed by Edmund Dulac; the other was the dance performed by Michio Ito.

By 1916 the 34-year-old Dulac was one of the most eminent il- lustrative artists of the day, his status recently confirmed by work for the bestselling 'Gift Books' produced for the war effort. A reti- cent, dapper, Anglophile Frenchman, who had moved to London in 1904 and subsequently taken out British citizenship, his unassum- ing manner belied the sensuous, erotically charged style of his art, which owed as much to [Aubrey] Beardsley as to [Arthur] Rackham (whose mantle he assumed); he was much influenced by Persian miniatures, Léon Bakst, and Japanese prints. Though celebrated for his fairy-tale illustrations, the projects which most suited his style were perhaps *The Arabian Nights* (1907) and *The Rubáiyát of Omar Khayyám* (1909). Dulac's world had intersected with WBY's for several years: he had worked for the theatre, illustrated Verlaine's *Fêtes Galantes* (1910), and frequented the Ricketts– Shannon salon from 1912, when he moved to the artists' studios built by Edmund Paris in Ladbroke Road, Holland Park. Through his wife Elsa Bignardi he became interested in seances and spiritu- alism. His Leicester Gallery exhibition of November 1914 had in- cluded a caricature of WBY, physically supporting the Abbey Theatre: by then they were well acquainted, and Dulac was a natu-

---

4. Ellmann, *IY*, 216. The text is full of echoes, not only from WBY himself: for instance, he may have remembered the phrase 'a mouthful of air' from Seumas O'Sullivan's 'Nelson Street' in the Cuala 'Broadside', no. 1, Fourth Year (June 1911).
5. *Certain Noble Plays of Japan*. Influences in the play are fully dealt with in F. A. C. Wil- son, *Yeat's Iconography* (London, 1960), Chapter 1.

ral choice to design *At the Hawk's Well*.[6] He had already done costumes and sets for Maud Allan's unperformed ballet *Khamma* (with
music by Debussy), and for Thomas Beecham's 1915 production of
the Bach cantata *Phoebus and Pan*.

Dulac was notoriously expensive as an illustrator but in 1916 was
ready to collaborate on a new venture, tempted by the stimulation
of working with WBY, and hoping to revive his own flagging energies. In a recent accident he had nearly lost the sight of one eye,
wartime commissions were not lucrative, and his wife was suffering
severe nervous trouble. His influence on the production was immense, and through it he developed a close friendship with WBY.
The multi-talented Dulac created costumes, properties (including a
black backcloth with a symbolic gold hawk), and the famous masks,
and was also a passionate advocate of modern and exotic music: a
visitor once found him sitting cross-legged on his studio floor, with
a cotton-wool plug up one nostril to let a steady stream of air from
the other into a Polynesian nose-flute which he had just constructed; he was also able to provide Puccini with chinoiserie musical themes for *Turandot*, and to introduce Constant Lambert to
Diaghilev. (Another route to the WBY circle may have been through
Pound's friend the avant-garde composer Walter Morse Rummel,
who was close to Dulac as well.) Much influenced by [Erik] Satie,
Dulac felt that *At the Hawk's Well* needed music based on simple
chords, with a flute melody underlying vocal intonations. This was
in line with current thought; Pound was preaching that music and
poetry were essentially connected, and this should be made dramatically effective.[7] WBY had already approached the violinist Maud
Mann (brought by Horton[8] to his Monday evenings). An aggressive
devotee of Indian musical instruments, she had improvised a word-
less song to her own accompaniment. Dulac found this repellent.
First he forced her to perform behind a backcloth, then engineered
a public row, and finally saw to it that her services were dispensed
with after the first performance. Then he was free to alter the score
and increase the musicians to three—one playing a series of bam-
boo flutes in different scales (inevitably constructed by Dulac), another a harp, while the composer himself performed on drum and
gong.[9]

The effect was archaic and remote, just as WBY wanted; he had
recently decided there were definite tunes behind the rhythms of

6. Dulac to Hone, 16 Apr. 1940, NLI MS 5919, puts their first meeting 'in 1912 or 1913',
adding that they often met at Pound's or with Ricketts and Shannon, but their close association began with *At the Hawk's Well*.
7. See his 'Vers Libre and Arnold Dolmetsch', *The Egoist*, July 1917, 90.
8. William Thomas Horton (1864–1919), English artist [Editor].
9. These arrangements are preserved in the correspondence, sketches, and musical scores
in the Dulac collection at the Harry Ransom Humanities Research Center [HRHRC].

his own verse (alerted to them, ironically, by the ill-fated Maud Mann). Dulac's musical contribution fascinated him, but the painter's influence did not stop there. In November 1915 Dulac had begun an oil painting of a Japanese dancer, Michio Ito, in the costume of a medieval Japanese *daimyo*[1] jointly designed by Ricketts and Dulac. Thus he also brought to WBY the ideally authentic Noh interpreter of the Guardian's dance.

Or so it must have seemed. In fact, the dramatically handsome Ito was a habitué of the Café Royal and a disciple of Nijinsky and the *Ballet Russe*; he had come to England after several years in Germany studying Dalcroze's 'eurhythmics'. He was also patronized by Lady Cunard, who launched his performances on London drawing rooms, where WBY first saw him dance. Much as the language in [Yeats's] *Diarmuid and Grania* had achieved 'authentic' Irishness by transmigrating through French and English, the Japanese Ito was reborn as a Noh performer under the instruction of a Frenchman, an Irishman—and an American, since Pound was arranging for Ito to perform five dance-poems in Noh mode by October 1915. There were inevitable gaps of comprehension (when WBY read his poems aloud Ito thought he was speaking Gaelic), but the Japanese dancer took to it all the more readily as there were echoes of Mallarmé, Maeterlinck, and the aestheticism of the 1890s. He was the logical interpreter for WBY's new passion; in early March 1916 he went to the zoo in Regent's Park with Dulac and WBY to spend an absorbing Sunday studying the movements of birds of prey. (The birds remained sleepily uncooperative, despite encouraging prods from an umbrella.) But this approach owed more to Isadora Duncan than to the traditions of Noh. True to his real passions, Ito would subsequently gravitate to New York, where he partnered Martha Graham, before returning to Japan to run a dance studio and a few 'discreetly lit bars'.[2]

* * *

* * * Formal, watchful, and withdrawn, from early 1915 he entered Pound's London circle, attending his Thursday dining club at Belotti's restaurant in Soho; he first met WBY in January 1915.[3] In literary terms, they rubbed shoulders in issues of the *Egoist* as well as in Pound's *Catholic Anthology*, where the landmark 'Love Song of

1. Leaders of samurai warriors [*Editor*].
2. See Anthony Thwaite, 'A Talk with Ito', *Truth*, 3 Aug. 1956.
3. Stella Bowen, in *Drawn from Life* (London, 1941), mentions Eliot and WBY attending the Soho evenings in 1914/15. Eliot wrote on 30 Sept. 1914 that he hoped to meet WBY with the Pounds; but on 4 Apr. 1915 he told Mrs Jack Gardner 'the last time I was [in London] I had the pleasure of meeting Yeats', implying that this encounter (in Jan.) had been the first. See Valerie Eliot (ed.), *The Letters of T. S. Eliot. Volume 1: 1898–1922* (London, 1988), 58, 95. In 1920 WBY allegedly told Quinn he disliked Eliot's work: Quinn to Pound, 6 Mar. 1920 [copy], NYPL.

J. Alfred Prufrock' had appeared the previous November after its first outing in *Poetry*, again at the inevitable insistence of Pound. For Eliot—as avid for intellectual enterprise as Pound but in a more feline way—*At the Hawk's Well* confirmed 'Yeats rather as a more eminent contemporary than as an elder from whom we could learn'.[4] The influence would recur in his own drama, and perhaps in 'Ash Wednesday'.[5]

'No press, no photographs in the papers, no crowd,' WBY had told Quinn. 'I shall be happier than Sophocles.'[6] There was a photographer involved, but it was the experimental and artistic Alvin Langdon Coburn; at Lady Islington's a press man who offered 'a whole page somewhere or other' was disdainfully dismissed. As for the audience, the reaction of the shrewd social butterfly and literary man-about-town Eddie Marsh (who got into the select preview at Lady Cunard's) was probably fairly typical:

> I had to go away in the middle, which was wretched, as I was getting quite worked up and impressed. I find I can manage quite well without *any* scenery at all, but they had been a little too careful not to disturb the room, and I couldn't help being disconcerted. Just when I had persuaded myself that I had before me a wild mountain track of semi-historic Ireland, to notice the characters skirting round a Louis XV table covered with French novels. The actors wore masks made by Dulac, awfully good, and I found it quite easy to accept the convention. But I had an odd sensation before the play began. Henry Ainley had a mask very like his own face and I didn't know it wasn't his own self till he came up to me roaring with laughter and not a muscle of his mouth moving, it was quite uncanny. The play began with atmospheric keening and a man in black solemnly pacing to the front—he got there, made an impressive bow to the audience, then started, and said, 'Oh, we've forgotten to light the lanterns!'—lighted them, retired, paced solemnly forward again and began his speech.[7]

For WBY, however, the success was not necessarily to be confined to aristocratic drawing rooms. The Noh enterprise had restored his old faith in an experimental Irish travelling theatre. He wrote excitedly to Gregory from rehearsals, suggesting that they adapt a room

4. James Longenbach, *Stone Cottage: Pound, Yeats & Modernism* (Oxford, 1988), 211.
5. See Wilson, *Yeats's Iconography*, 69–72.
6. *L*, 610.
7. Letter to Cathleen Nesbitt, quoted in D. Fielding, *Emerald and Nancy: Lady Cunard and Her Daughter* (London, 1968), 70–1. Sturge Moore reported on the same performance to his wife (n.d., Sturge Moore Papers, University of London, MS 978/35/401 A): he was impressed but disliked Maud Mann's singing. 'After the play there was a sort of council of war & Lady Cunard shone. It was very interesting—she has good sense, great ability, not much taste, but courage and energy.'

in the Dublin Mechanics' Institute for plays of this kind, with masks and no scenery. 'We would not invite the press and would have some form of society. The aim would be to get those who cared for poetry and nobody else.' Their old Abbey collaborator Frank Fay might even come back to teach there; they could undertake tours; perhaps they could play in Irish, working with the Gaelic League.[8] The 'accomplishment' which Pound had associated with the Noh form had infused a decisive new energy into WBY's drama, but it also brought him back to familiar ideas, though they had long proved unfeasible on the Abbey stage. There, crises continued to erupt. Ervine's insistence on rehearsing two plays a day would lead to a mutiny and dismissal notices in May. In June things reached such a pass that the directors seriously thought of bringing in Pound as manager: there could have been no more eloquent signal of desperation.[9]

As it happened, Dublin was denied this spectacle, and Pound himself, as usual, moved on after his raid into Japanese exoticism. A year later he was telling Quinn, 'China is fundamental, Japan is not. Japan is a special interest, like Provence or 12–13 century Italy (apart from Dante). I dont mean to say there aren't interesting things in Fenollosa's Jap stuff . . . But China is solid.'[1] Equally characteristically, WBY's interest would be sustained: the mask Dulac made for Henry Ainley ended up hanging on his wall, a permanent inspiration as well as a reminder.

He had composed, in January 1916, 'Lines Written in Dejection', reflecting the feeling that his creative life had reached a crossroads:

> When have I last looked on
> The round green eyes and the long wavering bodies
> Of the dark leopards of the moon?
> All the wild witches those most noble ladies,
> For all their broom-sticks and their tears,
> Their angry tears, are gone.
> The holy centaurs of the hills are banished;
> And I have nothing but harsh sun;
> Heroic mother moon has vanished,
> And now that I have come to fifty years
> I must endure the timid sun.

Almost immediately moonstruck inspiration had flooded in, with *At the Hawk's Well*: he felt he had hit upon a new form which re-

8. 5 Mar. 1916, Berg.
9. Pound to Quinn, 19 July 1916, NYPL. Also *FJ*, 30 May 1916, for troubles at the Abbey: theatre-goers who turned up for a performance in Limerick the day before had been greeted by the players with hand-outs denouncing Ervine. Though Bailey, for one, thought him wasteful, extravagant, and headstrong (letter to WBY, 9 June 1916, Berg), Pound would certainly have trumped his record.
1. 10 Jan. 1917, NYPL.

sponded to the harsh new age, and he ended his 'Note' on the first performance with a rallying call reminiscent of the manifestos he had issued in *Samhain* when shaping the Irish National Dramatic Society.

> We must recognise the change as the painters did when, find-ing no longer palaces and churches to decorate, they made framed pictures to hang upon a wall. Whatever we lose in mass and in power we should recover in elegance and in sub-tlety. Our lyrical and our narrative poetry alike have used their freedom and have approached nearer, as Pater said all the arts would if they were able, to 'the condition of music'; and if our modern poetical drama has failed, it is mainly because, always dominated by the example of Shakespeare, it would restore an irrevocable past.

TERENCE BROWN

[*Purgatory*]†

* * * The inexorable as a given of existence is the grim theme of *Purgatory*, the short play which Yeats wrote in the spring and early summer of 1938. It had its première, with stage design by his daughter Anne, at the Abbey on 10 August during a festival of plays and lectures at the theatre (there were revivals of *Cathleen ni Houlihan* and of *On Baile's Strand*, while F. R. Higgins gave a lec-ture on 'Yeats and Poetic Drama in Ireland'). Austin Clarke at-tended the first night of *Purgatory* and gave a jaundiced report in a letter to a friend (the newspaper reviews in Dublin were kinder):

> Yeats's play was pathetic. It had the usual interesting idea— this time the eternal recurrence in terms of the bridal night, or as the old man coarsely puts it, the sexual act. The scene is the ruin of a great house looking a bit like the Coliseum. In the foreground the tramp scion of a great family which gave states-men and generals to the empire. With him his get. Coconut horse hoofs indicated haunted house. Father and mother ap-pear in tableaux vivants at the windows. The tramp had mur-dered his roistering progenitor and now stabs his son who was grovelling on the ground for some pennies. The author hob-bled on the stage and made a speech about his infirmities. The dearer seats were full but the back pit half empty.[1]

† From *The Life of W. B. Yeats: A Critical Biography*. Reprinted with permission of Black-well Publishing Ltd.
1. Mary Thompson, *Austin Clarke: A Literary Life—Chronology*. Diss. UC Dublin (1997), 659.

Clarke's scathing summary catches some of the play's savage horror and lets us glimpse Yeats on a final occasion in public in his native city. Yet it is wide of the mark in failing to grasp the tragic import of an excoriating vision of irrevocable action as ineluctable destiny.

Purgatory in less than 250 lines of tautly dramatic verse, mostly the old tramp's monologue, manages to induce a sense of time and eternity in intimate proximity (though its brevity on stage makes this a difficult play to carry off theatrically). Of the play Yeats stated on the first night: 'I have put there my own conviction about this world and the next.' In both dimensions there can be no escape from the consequences a crime of miscegenation has wrought. The Old Man's mother had married a jockey to satisfy her lust. She died in childbirth giving birth to him, her only child. He murdered his own father but not before that base-born product of a base bed had in his cups burnt down the family seat which had become his by marriage. Now with the son whom he 'got/Upon a tinker's daughter in a ditch' the Old Man revisits the wreck of the great house to see the ghost of his parents beget him and to kill his own offspring with the blade he used on his father. He hopes the pollution of a dynasty can be arrested by this second murder and his mother's ghost released from its purgatorial, repetitive re-enactment of her crime. At curtain-fall the Old Man realizes there can be no such escape and the play ends with his anguish and guilt: 'Appease/The misery of the living and the remorse of the dead.' Only silence answers this haunted cry.

Elitist ideals and eugenic panic certainly find expression in this packed dramatic text. The notion of a polluted genealogy is made the more horrific in a stage image of a blasted tree before a ruin which replaces the rich fertility that had once marked an aristocratic tradition. And the Old Man's murder of his son can be read indeed as a very practical act of eugenic cleansing (*Purgatory* was first published with [Yeats's] *On the Boiler*). The fact that the Old Man declared the destruction of what is manifestly an Anglo-Irish, eighteenth-century house 'a capital offence' also gave a distinct social and political significance to the work.

The social references in the text, as W. J. McCormack has tellingly argued,[2] are not restricted to the eighteenth-century origin of the house but bear more precisely on recent nineteenth-century Irish social history when Protestant Ireland was beginning to take cognizance of its essential insecurity in the country. Accordingly the Old Man's caste prejudice, revolted as he is by his mother's infringement of a class taboo and the sectarian debasement that that

2. W. J. McCormack, *Ascendancy and Tradition in Anglo-Irish History from 1789–1939*. Oxford: Clarendon Press (1985), 382–84.

implies in the play, makes him more than the celebrant of an idealized Irish eighteenth century. He becomes the voice of urgent,
more contemporary Protestant anxieties, expressing in local terms
the crisis for social privilege implicit in democratic mass society in
the twentieth century. Yet he is also the fruit of a flawed pedigree,
and his action in bringing his son to witness the appearance of his
progenitor making love to his mother, which in the play he can almost be said to stage himself, is inescapably the action of a cor-
rupted being. For in his own person and actions he is the
embodiment of a familial doom, played out in the strange 'white
light' of eternity which falls on the stricken tree in the final movements of the drama.

The awful sense of necessity that this irony releases on stage
(which makes all the Old Man's actions and utterances partake of
an ineluctable pollution), renders elitism and eugenics the ideological machinery of a tragic vision, implicating them with the evil in
whose coils the participants in the drama will be trapped for ever.
History in this severe study in a dynasty's fall from grace, in a context which reflects a universal crisis for distinction of any kind in a
heterogeneous, levelling modernity, can only be experienced as
tragedy, entered under the signature of a terminal irony. In *Purgatory*, therefore, the eugenic 'enthusiasm' is subsumed as a dubious
attraction to a nasty theory in a profoundly disturbing apprehension
of the determinism implicit in consciousness experienced as unappeasable consequence.

It must be said however that the work, even as such a heavily
ironized tragedy, is as sinister a performance as some of the poems
composed in the poet's last year. For *Purgatory*, far from giving us a
hero for whom 'joy' is the achievement of suffering as the audience
experiences a cathartic release in a religious expansion of awareness at his death, leaves us only in a state of stunned horror at its
shocking conclusion. In effect the play throws down the gauntlet of
its own cruel, despairing cynicism that not even a tragic redemption can be imagined in the modern world. The play, I am arguing,
is an example of the eschatological nihilism of reaction *in extremis*,
in which in the 1930s Fascism often found a not-unsympathetic
climate for its own lethally nihilistic vision of social destiny.* * *

On Lady Gregory

LADY GREGORY

Spreading the News†

The idea of this play first came to me as a tragedy. I kept seeing as in a picture people sitting by the roadside, and a girl passing to the market, gay and fearless. And then I saw her passing by the same place at evening, her head hanging, the heads of others turned from her, because of some sudden story that had risen out of a chance word, and had snatched away her good name.

But comedy and not tragedy was wanted at our theatre to put beside the high poetic work, [Yeats's] *The King's Threshold, The Shadowy Waters, On Baile's Strand,* [and Synge's] *The Well of the Saints;* and I let laughter have its way with the little play. I was delayed in beginning it for a while, because I could only think of Bartley Fallon as dull-witted or silly or ignorant, and the handcuffs seemed too harsh a punishment. But one day by the sea at Duras a melancholy man who was telling me of the crosses he had gone through at home said—"But I'm thinking if I went to America, its long ago today I'd be dead. And it's a great expense for a poor man to be buried in America." Bartley was born at that moment, and, far from harshness, I felt I was providing him with a happy old age in giving him the lasting glory of that great and crowning day of misfortune.

It has been acted very often by other companies as well as our own, and the Boers[1] have done me the honour of translating and pirating it.

---

† This and the next two "notes" are from *The Comedies of Lady Gregory, Being the First Volume of The Collected Plays,* ed. Ann Saddlemyer (New York: Oxford University Press; Bucks: Colin Smythe Ltd., 1970).
1. Dutch settlers of South Africa at odds with Britain, especially in the Boer War (1899–1902), in which Britain reasserted its colonial control [*Editor*].

A Note on *Spreading the News*

Some time ago at a debate in Dublin a speaker complained that the Irish peasantry were slandered in *Spreading the News,* because nowhere in Ireland would so improbable a story grow out of so little; and in the same speech he said our Theatre was not worthy of support, because we "had given our first performance at the Castle."[1] Another speaker pointed to this fiction as a very Spreading of the News. Since that day it has been said of us that we never play but in Irish, that our Theatre is "something done for the Roman Catholics," that it has been "got up by the Irish Parliamentary Party with Mr. Healy at the head of them," that we have a special fee of fifty pounds a performance for anybody from Trinity College who wishes to hire the Theatre, that our "attitude to the Irish peasant arises out of class prejudice which keeps us from seeing anything that is good in him," that we encourage agrarian outrage by the performance of "Cathleen Ni Houlihan," that through fear of offending the English we will not play anything founded upon events that happened since their arrival under Strongbow, that we are neglecting Dublin for England, that we are "a Fenian lot," and that we give ourselves airs. Some at least of these accusations must be founded on evidence as airy as that given in the case of the murder of Jack Smith.

The Rising of the Moon

When I was a child and came with my elders to Galway for their salmon fishing in the river that rushes past the gaol, I used to look with awe at the window where men were hung, and the dark, closed gate. I used to wonder if ever a prisoner might by some means climb the high, buttressed wall and slip away in the darkness by the canal to the quays and find friends to hide him under a load of kelp in a fishing boat, as happens to my ballad-singing man. The play was considered offensive to some extreme Nationalists before it was acted, because it showed the police in too favourable a light, and a Unionist paper attacked it after it was acted because the policeman was represented "as a coward and a traitor"; but after the Belfast police strike that same paper praised its "insight into Irish character." After all these ups and downs it passes unchallenged on both sides of the Irish Sea.

---

1. Dublin Castle, at the time seat of British administration of Ireland. The references that follow include: Timothy Healy (1855–1931) MP, advocate of several and occasionally conflicting causes; Richard FitzGilbert, "Strongbow," leader of Normans from Wales to Ireland in 1170; and "Fenians," both the Irish Republican Brotherhood founded in 1858 and the nationalist tradition in Ireland [*Editor*].

JUDITH HILL

[*Spreading the News*]†

The impending realisation of the Abbey Theatre dominated hearts and minds in the summer. The patent application[1] was challenged by the three established Dublin theatres, which meant a court hearing in early August. Yeats wired, asking Augusta to be the patentee because she was a 'resident of good standing' in Ireland. Annie Horniman would take the financial risk.

Synge and [George] Russell visited Coole in July, and Yeats wrote a memo about the theatre in which he claimed the non-politically partisan theatre as a significant intellectual influence in the country. Historians of the Abbey inevitably emphasise Yeats's vision and, of course, without his trenchant views, his overbearing and irresistible judgement, and his poetic ideals there would have been no Abbey. Much of what he represented was distilled into the '*Samhain* principles' enunciated for the controversial 1903 season: art must override propaganda, speech must have the vitality of poetry, acting and scenery should be simplified.

Although Augusta, consistently idealistic about Yeats, followed this agenda with loyalty and passion, she approached the theatre, as we have seen, from a different angle, valuing it as a conduit for retransmitting the voice of the people who had traditionally either been ignored or patronised. Much of this would be articulated in 1911 and 1912, in lectures for her American audience,[2] She depicted folk culture as a river whose overwhelming current had swept the theatre into its wake. With this she even, subtly, marginalised Yeats's 'beautiful verse plays'. These, she wrote, were sparked by folklore, but sustained by his free interpretation of it and so were not part of the mainstream. Synge, who had 'collaborated with the people,' deriving his 'fable, emotion, style' from them to give them back works that would change their perception of themselves, she characterised as completely caught in the current. She did not, of course, explicitly refer to her plays, but she obviously saw them as an important part of this mainstream.

She observed that the excitement of the discovery that a theatre could spring from folk culture made it 'a living thing'. A responsive

---

† From *Lady Gregory: An Irish Life*. Copyright © 2005 by Judith Hill. Reproduced by permission of Sutton Publishing.
1. Request for a theater license [*Editor*].
2. "The Theatre and the Return of the People," dated November 1911, National Library of Ireland, printed in *Our Irish Theatre* (London: G. P. Putnam, 1913), 140–43.

audience was also vital, both in Dublin and the provinces.[3] In
Dublin her broadly democratic bent was translated into a demand
for sixpenny seats in the theatre (not achieved until after the departure of Annie Horniman), and a favouring of the pit over the stalls.
In February 1914, when the company had left Dublin for their
third tour of America, Augusta, left in charge of a second company,
did a few experiments 'to go in the direction of a "People's Theatre".'[4] She enlarged the pit to entice people away from music hall,
and trained a number of people new to acting.

But this was all to come. In the late summer of 1904 Augusta's
contribution to the debate about the direction in which the theatre
should be going was to write a one-act comedy, *Spreading the News*,
the first play that was immediately satisfying both to her (she never
revised it significantly) and to Yeats. Her idea was to present the
losing of a good reputation. Given the fear she had experienced
over 20 years previously about the loss of her own good name, it is
not surprising that her first thoughts were of a young girl and
tragedy. But Yeats and the Fays insisted on a comedy.[5] So she imagined a fair in a small country town plagued by a newly appointed
magistrate on the lookout for illegal alcohol and agrarian crimes.
Into this she put Bartley, who is observed pursuing a man with a
hay fork. At each retelling of this incident his crimes multiplied until he was charged with murder. At first she could only think of
Bartley as dull-witted but, after meeting a lugubrious old man on
Kinvara beach, she had a character who could enjoy his misfortunes and would meekly comply with the unjust accusation of murder that she planned.[6]

With this comedy set in a convincing evocation of everyday life
Augusta had found a theatrical voice which would carry her far.
She had a comic technique based on characters that could be let
loose on the plot. She had an inherently theatrical idea that relied
on her formulating the necessary stories. And it was funny: 'delight'
and 'joy' were the first words that Yeats used to describe it. She had
also successfully removed herself, creating a fictional self-sufficient
community that would in *Hyacinth Halvey* become Cloon. Further,
the play had a nationalist slant without politics as she allowed the
audience to savour the different vocabulary, syntax and assump-

3. She wrote several times about her desire to see her history plays touring to schoolchildren to ground them in the myths of their forebears, and her letters reveal that she was
   diligent in preparing programmes and itineraries for tours in Ireland. Augusta Gregory to
   John Quinn, 24 July 1906, Berg Collection, New York Public Library; *Book Monthly* article April 1904.
4. *Seventy Years* (London: Macmillan, 1976) 473.
5. Augusta Gregory to Yeats, 18 January 1904, Berg.
6. See Notes in Ann Saddlemyer, ed., *Augusta Gregory: The Collected Plays*, Vol. I (Gerrard's Cross: Colin Smyth, 1970), 253–55.

tions of the magistrate and the villagers so that they could become aware of the clash of cultures, while the comedy precluded any heavy-handed moralising. However, to modern ears she still falls into the trap of lumping the country people together and laughing at communal characteristics rather than individual foibles. Also, producing comedy out of the inclination towards innocent exaggeration pandered to the old stereotypes and, laughing at the foolish rather than with the wise, Augusta was closer to the comic world of Samuel Lover's[7] buffooning Paddy Whack and Handy Andy than she thought she was.

'But I'm thinking if I went to America its long ago the day I'd be dead! . . . And it's a great expense for a poor man to be buried in America.' So said Bartley within the first few minutes of the play, repeating (except 'the day' had replaced 'to-day') the words of the man at Kinvara. The rest of the dialogue ran along the current of everyday speech, reproducing the cadences, rhythms, phraseology and vocabulary of Hiberno-English. Augusta's 'Kiltartan' has been received sceptically, especially in the years after her death; in 1974 Micheál Ó hAodha claimed that her knowledge of the dialect was only superficial. But if her dialogue is translated into natural Irish and then re-translated into English the result comes very close to her Hiberno-English, only differing when the literal translation would not be readily understandable in English.[8]

Yeats thought it was a 'little masterpiece'. 'She seems to me,' he wrote to John Quinn (Augusta was typing), 'to have suddenly found herself in drama, and I foresee that the *Pot of Broth* will fade before its popularity.'[9] One who would appreciate the commercial value of her popularity, as well as the nature of her comedy, was Annie Horniman: 'Lady Gregory's work must be well treated—she is the best "draw" of the lot of you. I am so proud of her because she makes the people laugh in a witty manner, and I felt murderous when her work was treated as wickedly as at Edinburgh,' she would write to Yeats in November 1906.[1]

Finding George Bernard Shaw's long promised *John Bull's Other Island* too strange, dangerous and impractical to stage, Yeats and Augusta decided that *Spreading the News*, maybe not the better play, was certainly right for the Abbey and for the opening night when it would be performed with *Cathleen ni Houlihan*, *In the Shadow of the Glen* and the premiere of Yeats's *On Baile's Strand*.

---

7. Irish novelist (1797–1868) whose novels for English audiences were thought to patronize the Irish [*Editor*].
8. Private communication from Dr Maura Cronin. The phrases are also very similar to those spoken in parts of Ireland today.
9. 28 September 1904, in John Kelly and Ronald Schuchard, eds., *The Collected Letters of W. B. Yeats*, Vol. III (Oxford: Oxford UP, 1994), 652.
1. 26 November 1906, in Saddlemyer, 162.

The theatre was ready for rehearsals by the end of October. By now John Quinn[2] had joined an increasingly overwrought group in Dublin. Augusta was busy entertaining. She was also directing rehearsals of *Spreading the News*, her first experience of working with the actors. Before meeting them she made paper figures of her characters so that she could work out groupings and movements, and arrange their entrances and exits.[3] Sara Allgood, as Bartley's mother, was particularly responsive to her direction, and the *United Irishman*, which would find the play an 'improbable farce', would praise Allgood for living 'through every minute of her part'.[4] Augusta had found an actress who would be adept at interpreting her comedies and contribute greatly to their success.

The theatre was finally ready for 27 December. Although the Abbey was significantly less grand than the Gaiety, carpet greeted the audience as they entered, polished brass, scarlet leather and electric light defined the auditorium, and there were separate entrances for the wealthy and the not so wealthy. But there was a simplicity and artiness that was not to be found elsewhere. The stage dominated, allowing actors to perform with subdued voices and natural actions, contributing to a feeling of intimacy between actors and audience. 'Standing on the Abbey stage, the feeling, absent in so many other theatres, of being one with the audience was always present,' Máire Nic Shiubhlaigh claimed.[5]

The decorative restraint in Holloway's building expressed the new theatre's earnest emphasis on the spoken word. Where there was decoration it was to be Irish made and, preferably, Irish in theme. In the foyer the stained glass windows designed by Sarah Purser depicted uncontroversial trees (to satisfy Annie Horniman) while the walls were hung with oil paintings of the Fays, Máire Nic Shiubhlaigh and Annie Horniman by John Butler Yeats. It gave a strong impression of sincerity and spontaneity, exactly the tone Yeats and Augusta wished to set for the reception of the plays.

Neither Augusta, who was suffering from a severe bout of influenza (her first day in bed for nine years according to the housemaid), nor Annie Horniman were present for the first night.[6] But Augusta and Yeats were in close contact. With long days to contemplate the recent weeks, Augusta was overwhelmed by what they all owed to Yeats: 'But for your genius, which of us would have had the faith to do anything at all? I couldn't & you have kept in such a

2. American lawyer (1870–1924), collector of arts, and proponent of the Irish Literary Renaissance [*Editor*].
3. *Seventy Years*, 412.
4. 31 December 1904 in Robert Hogan and James Kilroy, *The Modern Irish Drama*, Vol. II (Atlantic Highlands, NJ: Humanities Press, 1976) 130.
5. Maire Nic Shiubhlaigh, *The Splendid Years* (Dublin: J. Duffy, 1955) 57.
6. 24 December 1904, Berg Collection.

straight line—& you have conquered.'⁷ Was Augusta staying away on purpose to give Yeats the opportunity to get the full credit? As he moved loquaciously between the many invited journalists the Abbey was indeed inaugurated as Yeats's theatre.

Before the opening Yeats's letters to Augusta were full of doubt and last-minute changes to costumes and scenery, and a nervous over-sensitiveness to the possible impact of the plays. He, too, was guiltily aware of what he owed Augusta, advocating that she take a long rest: 'You take care of everybody but yourself.'⁸ At 10.50 pm on the first night he sent her a telegram: 'Your play immense success. all [sic] plays successfully packed house.'⁹ A few days later he went through the event in detail in a letter, and his conclusion was generous: 'Our success could not have been greater.'¹

ANN SADDLEMYER

Image-Maker for Ireland: Augusta, Lady Gregory†

. . . but we are "image-makers," and must carry out our dreams.
(Letter to Sir Hugh Lane)

Ups and downs, ups and downs; and we know nothing till all is over. . . . I would like my name set in clean letters in the book of the people.
(Sarsfield in *The White Cockade*)

Throughout Lady Gregory's work and constant in her collaborations with Yeats is a delight in what she called "our incorrigible genius for myth-making," and despite the courage with which she struggled to keep the Abbey Theatre going for so many years, it is perhaps as myth-maker and mythologizer that she can best be recognized in "the book of the people." For even in her dream of an Irish theatre, Lady Gregory's main ambition was to restore once again to Ireland her native dignity:

I had had from the beginning a vision of historical plays being sent by us through all the countries of Ireland. For to have a real success and to come into the life of the country, one must touch a real and eternal emotion, and history comes only next to religion in our country. And although the realism of our

7. [24 December 1904], Berg.
8. 17 December 1904, in Kelly and Schuchard, 687.
9. *Ibid.*, 690.
1. 17 December 1904, in Kelly and Schuchard, 687.
† From *The World of W. B. Yeats*, Rev. ed., ed. Robin Skelton and Ann Saddlemyer. Reprinted by permission of the University of Washington Press.

young writers is taking the place of fantasy and romance in the cities, I still hope to see a little season given up every year to plays on history and in sequence at the Abbey, and I think schools and colleges may ask to have them sent and played in their halls, as a part of the day's lesson.

Her first play, *Colman and Guaire*, was written not with stage production in mind, but as a play in rhyme which "might perhaps be learned and acted by Kiltartan school-children." Consistently she saw the theatre as part of the same movement which had earlier given impetus to the Gaelic League:

It was a movement for keeping the Irish language a spoken one, with, as a chief end, the preserving of our own nationality. That does not sound like the beginning of a revolution, yet it was one. It was the discovery, the disclosure of the folk-learning, the folk-poetry, the folk-tradition. Our Theatre was caught into that current, and it is that current, as I believe, that has brought it on its triumphant way. It is chiefly known now as a folk-theatre. It has not only the great mass of primitive material and legend to draw on, but it has been made a living thing by the excitement of that discovery.

Twenty years after she wrote these passages in *Our Irish Theatre* she was still writing plays that children as well as adults could enjoy. Unlike Yeats's, her dream of an Irish theatre was fulfilled, with her own work playing a far more important part than she had ever dreamed possible. In 1934 Yeats wrote that her plays were "constantly acted, not only in Dublin but by little companies in village halls. Their names are as familiar as old proverbs."[1] A visitor to Ireland will still find her work popular, both in English and in Irish, at the Abbey and in the provinces. Always she wrote for Ireland: writing of her people as she had observed them during her childhood and widowhood in Galway; of Irish history and folklore as she had collected it for her books; for the children and countryfolk of her nation.

Patriotism for Lady Gregory was a simpler ideal, founded on a much smaller scale than the literary nationalism of her colleagues. Descendant of the Persses of Roxborough who arrived in Ireland with Cromwell, and of the O'Gradys of literary and legal fame, until her marriage with Sir William Gregory of Coole she had seen little of Ireland beyond her own county, Galway. But the west of Ireland she did know well; as a young girl she had eagerly observed the great working-estate, and as a young widow she capably managed the Coole property for her son Robert, later for her grandson Richard.

1. *The Irish National Theatre* (Roma: Reale Accademia D'Italia, 1935), 6.

Yeats had memories of tales told by Mary Battle in the kitchen at Sligo; Lady Gregory heard tales of the faery—even more stirring, of the rebellion of '98—from her old nurse Mary Sheridan. Later she herself participated in the foundation of village libraries, visited the cottages on the estate, acted as secretary to the families of American immigrants. Her marriage for some years interrupted her firm relationship with the peasantry but did not dissolve it, and after her husband died she once more picked up the threads of her friendship with those who still hold her memory dear in Ireland. "She has been like a serving-maid among us," said an old peasant to Yeats.

Patriotic she had always been, ever since the first Fenian pamphlet she bought as a child in the small village of Loughrea:

> For a romantic love of country had awakened in me, perhaps through the wide beauty of my home . . . or it may be through the half revealed sympathy of my old nurse for the rebels whose cheering she remembered when the French landed at Killala in '98; or perhaps but through the natural breaking of a younger child of the house from the conservatism of her elders.[2]

However, it was not until she found herself turning against England that she became intensely nationalistic. In 1898 her edition of her husband's grandfather's papers was published, and when questioned concerning the Home Rule sentiments that crept into her comments, she replied: "I defy anyone to study Irish History without getting a dislike and distrust of England." (At the unexpected success of Martyn's re-written play, *The Bending of the Bough*, she assured the bewildered authors, "We are not working for Home Rule; we are preparing for it.") It was not, in fact, until after she had become involved with the Irish Literary Theatre that she met John O'Leary and the other political rebels who had influenced Yeats. Through her husband, one-time Member of Parliament and Governor of Ceylon, she had made many friends among English Unionists, but at all times she managed to reconcile, if at times uneasily, the friendships formed during Sir William's work for England and those she herself made in her work for Ireland. In this sense alone, she was invaluable to Yeats; he was willing to accept "the baptism of the gutter" for the sake of his national dream, but she preferred "the baptism of clean water."[3] Involvement in the idea of a national theatre, however, increased her nationalism still more, and where Yeats subordinated his ideals of art to no nation, she avowed her determination to work principally for "the dignity of

2. Introduction to *The Kiltartan Poetry Book* (London: Putnam's Sons, 1919), 3–4.
3. *Our Irish Theatre* (London: Putnam's Sons, 1913), 71.

Ireland." As her interest in art increased, so too did her love for her country. The one inspiration fed on the other.

As she herself sought for the dignity her nationalism demanded for her country, so she also demanded it of others. The patriotic verses in *The Spirit of the Nation* appealed to her because of "a certain dignity, an intensity born of continuity of purpose; they are roughly hammered links in a chain of unequal workmanship, but stretching back through the centuries to the Munster poets of the days of Elizabeth." In her own work she strove for this same dignity and "continuity of purpose." (Many years later Yeats was to place her—along with Queen Victoria—in Phase Twenty-four of *A Vision* in which the true mask is self-reliance and organization.) She, like Yeats, was moved by the death of Parnell, not realizing until later, however, that by tearing from the corner of a newspaper Katharine Tynan's lament she had

> unwittingly taken note of almost the moment of a new impulse in literature, in poetry. For with that death, the loss of that dominant personality, and in the quarrel that followed, came the disbanding of an army, the unloosing of forces, the setting free of the imagination of Ireland.

Always her nationalism retained this strong desire to win once more the dignity of Ireland, and like Yeats, she believed it possible through the arts. One day while collecting folk tales on Aran, she happened to glance through a volume of *Don Quixote*, and the thought of England's false half-vision of Ireland crossed her mind:

> They see in us one part boastful quarrelsome adventurer, one part vulgar rollicking buffoon . . . . But we begin to think after all that truth is best, that we have worn the mask thrust upon us too long, and that we are more likely to win at least respect when we appear in our own form . . . . Poetry and pathos may be granted to us, but when we claim dignity, those who see only the sham fights of Westminister shake their heads. But here, in real Ireland, dignity can live side by side with the strongest political feeling.[4]

The words re-echo through the Irish Literary Theatre's manifesto of 1897: "We will show that Ireland is not the home of buffoonery and easy sentiment . . . but of ancient idealism."

* * *

---

4. "Ireland, Real and Ideal," *Nineteenth Century* 1898, 769–782.

On J. M. Synge

J. M. SYNGE

Preface to *The Playboy of the Western World*†

In writing *The Playboy of the Western World,* as in my other plays, I
have used one or two words only that I have not heard among the
country people of Ireland, or spoken in my own nursery before I
could read the newspapers. A certain number of the phrases I employ I have heard also from herds and fishermen along the coast
from Kerry to Mayo, or from beggar-women and ballad-singers
nearer Dublin; and I am glad to acknowledge how much I owe to
the folk-imagination of these fine people. Anyone who has lived in
real intimacy with the Irish peasantry will know that the wildest
sayings and ideas in this play are tame indeed, compared with the
fancies one may hear in any little hillside cabin in Geesala, or Car-
raroe, or Dingle Bay. All art is a collaboration; and there is little
doubt that in the happy ages of literature, striking and beautiful
phrases were as ready to the story-teller's or the playwright's hand,
as the rich cloaks and dresses of his time. It is probable that when
the Elizabethan dramatist took his ink-horn and sat down to his
work he used many phrases that he had just heard, as he sat at dinner, from his mother or his children. In Ireland, those of us who
know the people have the same privilege. When I was writing "The
Shadow of the Glen," some years ago, I got more aid than any
learning could have given me from a chink in the floor of the old
Wicklow house where I was staying, that let me hear what was being said by the servant girls in the kitchen. This matter, I think, is
of importance, for in countries where the imagination of the people, and the language they use, is rich and living, it is possible for a
writer to be rich and copious in his words, and at the same time to
give the reality, which is the root of all poetry, in a comprehensive
and natural form. In the modern literature of towns, however, rich-
ness is found only in sonnets, or prose poems, or in one or two

† From *The Complete Plays of John M. Synge* (New York: Random House, 1935). Vintage
Books edition.

elaborate books that are far away from the profound and common interests of life. One has, on one side, Mallarmé and Huysmans producing this literature; and on the other, Ibsen and Zola[1] dealing with the reality of life in joyless and pallid words. On the stage one must have reality, and one must have joy; and that is why the intellectual modern drama has failed, and people have grown sick of the false joy of the musical comedy, that has been given them in place of the rich joy found only in what is superb and wild in reality. In a good play every speech should be as fully flavoured as a nut or apple, and such speeches cannot be written by anyone who works among people who have shut their lips on poetry. In Ireland, for a few years more, we have a popular imagination that is fiery and magnificent, and tender; so that those of us who wish to write start with a chance that is not given to writers in places where the springtime of the local life has been forgotten, and the harvest is a memory only, and the straw has been turned into bricks.

W. B. YEATS

Preface to the First Edition of
The Well of the Saints†

Six years ago I was staying in a students' hotel in the Latin Quarter [of Paris], and somebody, whose name I cannot recollect, introduced me to an Irishman, who, even poorer than myself, had taken a room at the top of the house. It was J. M. Synge, and I, who thought I knew the name of every Irishman who was working at literature, had never heard of him. He was a graduate of Trinity College, Dublin, too, and Trinity College does not, as a rule, produce artistic minds. He told me that he had been living in France and Germany, reading French and German literature, and that he wished to become a writer. He had, however, nothing to show but one or two poems and impressionistic essays, full of that kind of morbidity that has its root in too much brooding over methods of expression, and ways of looking upon life, which come, not out of life, but out of literature, images reflected from mirror to mirror. He had wandered among people whose life is as picturesque as the Middle Ages, playing his fiddle to Italian sailors, and listening to

---

1. Stéphane Mallarmé (1842–98), French poet; Joris-Karl Huysman (1848–1907) French novelist; Henrik Ibsen (1828–1906), Norwegian playwright; Émile Zola (1840–1902), French novelist [*Editor*].

† Reprinted with the permission of Scribner, an imprint of Simon & Schuster Adult Publishing Group, from *Essays and Introductions* by W. B. Yeats. Copyright © 1961 by Mrs. W. B. Yeats. All rights reserved.

stories in Bavarian woods, but life had cast no light into his writings. He had learned Irish years ago, but had begun to forget it, for the only language that interested him was that conventional language of modern poetry which has begun to make us all weary. I was very weary of it, for I had finished *The Secret Rose*,[1] and felt how it had separated my imagination from life, sending my Red Hanrahan, who should have trodden the same roads with myself, into some undiscoverable country.[2] I said: 'Give up Paris. You will never create anything by reading Racine, and Arthur Symons will always be a better critic of French literature. Go to the Aran Islands. Live there as if you were one of the people themselves; express a life that has never found expression.' I had just come from Aran, and my imagination was full of those grey islands where men must reap with knives because of the stones.

He went to Aran and became a part of its life, living upon salt fish and eggs, talking Irish for the most part, but listening also to the beautiful English which has grown up in Irish-speaking districts, and takes its vocabulary from the time of Malory and of the translators of the Bible, but its idiom and its vivid metaphor from Irish. When Mr. Synge began to write in his language, Lady Gregory had already used it finely in her translations of Dr. Hyde's[3] lyrics and plays, or of old Irish literature, but she had listened with different ears. He made his own selection of word and phrase, choosing what would express his own personality. Above all, he made word and phrase dance to a very strange rhythm, which will always, till his plays have created their own tradition, be difficult to actors who have not learned it from his lips. It is essential, for it perfectly fits the drifting emotion, the dreaminess, the vague yet measureless desire, for which he would create a dramatic form. It blurs definition, clear edges, everything that comes from the will, it turns imagination from all that is of the present, like a gold background in a religious picture, and it strengthens in every emotion whatever comes to it from far off, from brooding memory and dangerous hope. When he brought *The Shadow of the Glen*, his first play, to the Irish National Theatre Society, the players were puzzled by the rhythm, but gradually they became certain that his Woman of the Glen, as melancholy as a curlew, driven to distraction by her own sensitiveness, her own fineness, could not speak with any other tongue, that all his people would change their life if the rhythm changed. Perhaps no Irish countryman had ever that exact rhythm in his voice, but certainly if Mr. Synge had been born a

1. Collection of stories published in 1897 [*Editor.*]
2. Since writing this I have, with Lady Gregory's help, put *Red Hanrahan* into the common speech.
3. Dr. Douglas Hyde (1860–1947), writer, translator, founder of the Gaelic league [*Editor*].

countryman, he would have spoken like that. It makes the people of his imagination a little disembodied; it gives them a kind of innocence even in their anger and their cursing. It is part of its maker's attitude towards the world, for while it makes the clash of wills among his persons indirect and dreamy, it helps him to see the subject-matter of his art with wise, clear-seeing, unreflecting eyes; to preserve the integrity of art in an age of reasons and purposes. Whether he write of old beggars by the roadside, lamenting over the misery and ugliness of life, or of an old Aran woman mourning her drowned sons, or of a young wife married to an old husband, he has no wish to change anything, to reform anything; all these people pass by as before an open window, murmuring strange, exciting words.

* * *

JOSEPH HOLLOWAY

[Journal 1907]†

Saturday, Matinee and Evening, January 12. The Eloquent Dempsy[1] wooed back to the Abbey large audiences at both performances, and Henderson beamed on all patrons as they entered the vestibule. He is like a barometer—bad house, he is gloomy and down in the mouth; good house, and a summer day is not more bright and cheerful . . . . The matinee was very well attended, and everyone seemed profoundly impressed with the weird, strange sorrow created by Synge's gem of sadness *Riders to the Sea* . . . . Few things finer than Sara Allgood's portrait of the old mother have been seen on the stage. It was a masterpiece of acting, quite flawless in every detail. To see her return with the bit of bread the girls had sent her with after "Bartley," and totteringly reach the chair by the fire with a look of dread on her face that was thrilling, was to witness as fine a moment of realistic acting as could be desired. . . . *Riders to the Sea* was superbly acted in the evening, and I overheard the author say to D. J. O'Donoghue who sat behind me that he had never seen it better played. When an author thinks the child of his brain realised on the stage, the audience very well may be satisfied.

By the way, a trifle light as air spoiled this almost perfect per-

---

† From *Joseph Holloway's Abbey Theatre: A Selection from His Unpublished Journal, "Impressions of a Dublin Playgoer,"* edited by Robert Hogan and Michael J. O'Neill. Copyright © 1967 by Southern Illinois University Press. Reprinted by permission of Southern Illinois University Press.
1. By William Boyle (1853–1922), one of the major popular successes while W. A. Henderson was manager of the Abbey Theatre [*Editor*].

formance for me, and it was nothing more or less than a label bearing the legend, "National Theatre Co." pasted on the side of the shaft of the stretcher on which the body of "Bartley" was borne into the cottage.

Thursday, January 24 . . . . Yeats, before he left for England, told F. J. Fay he did not like his teaching of poetic speaking, and Frank had given up doing so in disgust since. There is great dissatisfaction in the camp.

Saturday, January 26. The Abbey was thronged in the evening to witness the first performance of Synge's three-act comedy *The Playboy of the Western World*, which ended in fiasco owing to the coarseness of the dialogue. The audience bore with it for two and a half acts and even laughed with the dramatist at times, but an unusually brutally coarse remark[2] put into the mouth of "Christopher Mahon," the playboy of the title, set the house off into hooting and hissing amid counter applause, and the din was kept up till the curtain closed in.

On coming out, Lady Gregory asked me, "What was the cause of the disturbance?"

And my monosyllabic answer was, "Blackguardism!"

To which she queried, "On which side?"

"The stage!" came from me pat, and then I passed on, and the incident was closed . . . .

"This is not Irish life!" said one of the voices from the pit, and despite the fact that Synge in a note on the programme says, "I have used one or two words only that I have not heard among the country people of Ireland, or spoken in my own nursery before I could read the newspapers," I maintain that his play of *The Playboy* is not a truthful or just picture of the Irish peasants, but simply the outpouring of a morbid, unhealthy mind ever seeking on the dunghill of life for the nastiness that lies concealed there . . . . Synge is the evil genius of the Abbey and Yeats his able lieutenant. Both dabble in the unhealthy. Lady Gregory, though she backs them up when they transgress good taste and cast decency to the winds, keeps clean in her plays, and William Boyle is ever and always wholesome . . . .

W. G. Fay as "Christopher Mahon," the hero, was inimitable in a

---

2. "Widow Quin" wants "Christy" to leave "Pegeen" and go with her—"Come on, I tell you, and I'll find you finer sweethearts at each waning moon." And he answers, "It's Pegeen I'm seeking only, and what'd I care if you brought me a drift of chosen females, standing in their shifts itself, maybe, from this place to the eastern world?" It was made more crudely brutal on the first night by W. G. Fay. "Mayo girls" was substituted for "chosen females."

very disagreeable role. Miss Maire O'Neill as "Margaret Flaherty," the publican's daughter who sets her cap at "Mahon" and gives the cold shoulder to "Shawn Keogh" (F. J. Fay), a sheepish admirer of her (played after the fashion of "Hyacinth Halvey" by Fay) was excellent, and Sara Allgood as "Widow Quin" who had designs on "Mahon" was also good. Two more undesirable specimens of Irish womankind could not be found in this isle I be thinking. A. Power, repulsively got-up, played "Old Mahon" with some effect. Arthur Sinclair as the drunken bar-keeper, and J. M. Kerrigan as "Jimmy Farrell," a small farmer, interpreted the characters . . . carefully. I only pitied the actors and actresses for having to give utterance to such gross sentiments and only wonder they did not refuse to speak some of the lines.

Sunday, January 27. Met W. G. Fay and Mrs. Fay together with Frank on Pembroke Road while out for a walk, and we chatted about last night's fiasco, and the feeling of the actors during and leading up to the scene. The players had expected the piece's downfall sooner, and W. G. Fay expressed it that "Had I not cut out a lot of the matter, the audience would not have stood an act of it." I praised the acting and said it was a fine audience to play to. It frankly did not like the play and frankly expressed itself on the matter, having patiently listened to it until the fatal phrase came and proved the last straw. Frank excused Synge on the score that he has had no joy in his life, and until he has had some you may expect drab plays from him . . . . The influence of the Elizabethan dramatists was on Synge, and he loved vigorous speech. Frank partly defended him on this score. He told me Lawrence came round after the comedy and was in a terrible state about the piece. Both brothers wondered what would be the result of last night's scene, and I said, "Bad houses next week, but a return when the right stuff would be forthcoming again."

Monday, January 28 . . . . Henderson and I went down to the Abbey . . . and on our way spoke of Synge's nasty mind—to store those crude, coarse sayings from childhood and now present them in a play. The influence of Gorki must be upon him. Henderson also told me that the new English manager had arrived, and he was thinking of retiring before being dismissed. The new man was to get £5 a week; he was only getting 30 /-.

By this time we arrived at the Abbey. Two stalwart police at the vestibule suggested trouble, and we found plenty and to spare when we went in. The performance was just concluding amid a terrific uproar (the piece had not been listened to, we were told). The curtains were drawn aside, and W. G. Fay stood forward amid the din.

After some minutes, in a lull, he said, "You who have hissed to-night will go away saying you have heard the play, but you haven't."

"We heard it on Saturday!" came from the back of the pit, and the hissing and hooting were renewed.

The scene which followed was indescribable. Those in the pit howled for the author, and he with Lady Gregory and others held animated conversation in the stalls. Denis O'Sullivan made himself very conspicuous railing against the noise producers, and Signor Esposito gesticulated abundantly. Small knots of people argued the situation out anything but calmly, and after about a quarter of an hour's clamour, the audience dispersed hoarse. "Heblon,"[3] in a half-tight state, blackguarded the Irish people and upheld the dramatist, and George Roberts said, "The play is the finest ever written if you had only the wit to see it!" I wished him joy of the dungheap of a mind he must possess to arrive at that conclusion, and Lawrence and I departed.

Tuesday, January 29 . . . . Arrived at the Abbey when *Riders to the Sea* was half through. D. J. O'Donoghue was going in at the same time. We waited in the side passage near the radiator until it was over. A number of youths were dimly seen in the stalls. The piece was well received. We joined W. J. Lawrence in the back row of the stalls during the interval. I noticed that the youths in the stalls were mostly under the influence of drink (and learned that the management had allowed them in for nothing to back up the play that the crowded pit had come there to howl down). This precious gang of noisy boys hailed from Trinity, and soon after *The Playboy* commenced one of their number (Mr. Moorhead) made himself objectionable and was forcibly removed by Synge and others, after a free fight amongst the instruments of the orchestra.

W. B. Yeats came before the curtain after *Riders to the Sea,* and made a speech "inviting a free discussion on the play on Monday night next in the theatre." Shortly after the commencement of the police-protected play, a remark from the pit set the college boys to their feet, and for a moment they looked like going for those in the pit, but didn't. The uproar was deafening, and it was here Moorhead got put out. One of the theatre's bullies removed by the people who wanted him in struck me as a funny sight. This set the noise in motion, and W. B. Yeats again came on the scene and with raised hand secured silence. He referred to the removal of one drunken man and hoped all that were sober would listen to the

3. Joseph O'Connor, police office clerk and feature writer of "Studies in Blue" as Heblon of *The Evening Herald.* From 1933–47 he was a brilliant criminal lawyer and circuit judge of Cork.

play. The noise continued, and shortly after a body of police led on by W. B. marched out of the side door from the scene dock and ranged along the walls of the pit. Hugh Lane now made himself very conspicuous by pointing out some men in the pit and demanding their arrest as disturbers of the peace. Yeats also was busy just now as a spy aiding the police in picking out persons disapproving of the glorification of murder on the stage. . . . A gent addressed the audience from the stalls, and the students with Hugh Lane in their midst behaved themselves like the drunken cads they were. At the end chaos seemed to have entered the Abbey, and the college youths clambered onto the seats and began the English national anthem, while those in the body of the hall sang something else of home growth. I felt very sad while the scene continued. The college boys had ultimately to be forcibly ejected by the police, and they marched off in a body singing, police-protected, to the college. One of them was arrested for beating the police and fined £5. Two of those who were ejected from the pit were fined 40 / - each, W. B. Yeats prosecuting.

Despite all, *The Playboy* was not heard!

Wednesday, January 30. I sauntered down about 7:45 to Abbey Street, and saw an immense crowd awaiting the pit-door to be opened, and police everywhere. Met Sinclair in the crowd and had a chat about the turn things had taken. He was hopeful that the success of scandal would be the makings of the theatre, and said Miss Horniman had telegraphed over her delight at the turn things had taken. . . .

A loud-voiced, glorified music-hall patron took up his seat in front of me after *Riders to the Sea* had been perfectly played and enthusiastically received, and commenced shouting in grating, piercing tones, "Shut up!" making more noise than all the house put together. He was a distinctly vulgar type and began to call the play "rotten" during Act III. The house listened to the piece in patches to-night. Every time Synge would appear, he was hissed. Over fifty police were in the theatre, and uproar was frequent; nevertheless, a few were ejected from the pit. W. B. Yeats was eager to get people charged. . . .

The theatre was full to-night to witness a row, and was very disappointed that they did not get value for their money. Several I spoke to thought the play a poor one—the first act having some slight merit, but the others none whatever, and as to the plot it was too absurd for words. All the very nasty bits have vanished. Mr. Short is of opinion that the excitement will do the theatre good. I have my doubts. Outside the theatre in Abbey Street, the place was thronged with people and police, but I did not wait developments.

Did I ever think I would see the Abbey protected from an Irish audience by the police!

Thursday, January 31. The police-protected drama by the dramatist of the dungheap . . . got a fair hearing tonight, and was voted by those around me very poor, dull, dramatic stuff indeed. After the first act all interest of any kind ceases, and were it not for the claque imported into the stalls very little applause would be forthcoming. A Free Theatre is a droll cry where police line the walls and block the passages . . . ready to pounce on anyone who dares say "boo" to the filth and libels of the Irish peasant girl on the stage. "Free" indeed! The theatre is forever damned in the eyes of all right-thinking Irishmen. One sack, one sample. Yeats, Synge, and Gregory are all degenerates of the worst type; the former pair indulge in sensuality in their later work, and the latter condones with them. . . .

Over two hundred police guarded the Abbey to-night, with the only result of two arrests for leaving the theatre before the programme was ended. The prestige of the theatre has fled, and Henderson's work of creating an audience frustrated.

Friday, February 1. William Boyle has publicly withdrawn his plays from the Abbey. As an Irish Theatre, the Abbey's knell is rung. This was the biggest blow to the National Theatre Society received since it became a police-protected society.

Saturday, February 2 . . . . After dinner I went to the matinee at the Abbey, and found the police in large numbers around the building. The first act had concluded as I went in. Everything was quiet and matinee-like inside, except the number of police lining the walls and blocking up the passages. The audience was not very large and mostly ladies. W. B. Yeats came and had a few words with me about the arrest last night, and I told him what I thought of it and others, and also of the drunken Trinity students of Tuesday night.

He replied. "There were plenty of drunken men in the pit, and I prefer drunken men who applaud on in the right than drunken men who hiss in the wrong." A beautiful sentiment quite worthy of his pal Synge, I thought.

When I pressed him further about the freedom of every man to judge for himself, and yet if a man hissed or left the theatre before the play was over he was likely to be taken, he fled. He would not work in the art-for-art's-sake theory into an answer to that question, and so his flowers of speech did not blossom on the subject. "Humbug," thy name is Yeats.

* * *

W. B. YEATS

The Controversy over
The Playboy of the Western World†

We have claimed for our writers the freedom to find in their own land every expression of good and evil necessary to their art, for Irish life contains, like all vigorous life, the seeds of all good and evil, and a writer must be free here as elsewhere to watch where weed or flower ripens. No one who knows the work of our theatre as a whole can say we have neglected the flower; but the moment a writer is forbidden to take pleasure in the weed, his art loses energy and abundance. In the great days of English dramatic art the greatest English writer of comedy was free to create *The Alchemist* and *Volpone*,[1] but a demand born of Puritan conviction and shopkeeping timidity and insincerity, for what many second-rate intellects thought to be noble and elevating events and characters, had already at the outset of the eighteenth century ended the English drama as a complete and serious art. Sheridan and Goldsmith, when they restored comedy after an epoch of sentimentalities, had to apologise for their satiric genius by scenes of conventional love-making and sentimental domesticity that have set them outside the company of all—whether their genius be great or little—whose work is pure and whole. The quarrel of our theatre to-day is the quarrel of the theatre in many lands; for the old Puritanism, the old dislike of power and reality have not changed, even when they are called by some Gaelic name.

[On the second performance of *The Playboy of the Western World*, about forty men who sat in the middle of the pit succeeded in making the play entirely inaudible. Some of them brought tin trumpets and the noise began immediately on the rise of the curtain. For days articles in the Press called for the withdrawal of the play, but we played for the seven nights we had announced; and before the week's end opinion had turned in our favour. There were, however, nightly disturbances and a good deal of rioting in the surrounding streets. On the last night of the play there were, I believe, five hundred police keeping order in the theatre and in its neigh-

---

† From *Explorations* by W. B. Yeats (New York: Macmillan/Collier Books, 1973).

1. Plays by Ben Jonson (1572–1637); Richard Brinsley Sheridan (1751–1816) and Oliver Goldsmith (1730–74), named below, English Restoration playwrights of Irish birth [*Editor*].

bourhood. Some days later our enemies, though beaten so far as
the play was concerned, crowded into the cheaper seats for a debate on the freedom of the stage. They were very excited, and kept
up the discussion until near twelve. The last paragraphs of my
opening statement ran as follows.]

From Mr. Yeats's opening Speech in the Debate on February 4, 1907, at the Abbey Theatre.

The struggle of the last week has been long a necessity; various
paragraphs in newspapers describing Irish attacks on theatres had
made many worthy young men come to think that the silencing of a
stage at their own pleasure, even if hundreds desired that it should
not be silenced, might win them a little fame, and, perhaps, serve
their country. Some of these attacks have been made on plays which
are in themselves indefensible, vulgar and old-fashioned farces and
comedies. But the attack, being an annihilation of civil rights, was
never anything but an increase of Irish disorder. The last I heard of
was in Liverpool, and there a stage was rushed, and a priest, who
had set a play upon it, withdrew his play and apologised to the audience. We have not such pliant bones, and did not learn in the
houses that bred us a so suppliant knee. But behind the excitement
of example there is a more fundamental movement of opinion.
Some seven or eight years ago the National movement was democ-
ratised and passed from the hands of a few leaders into those of
large numbers of young men organised in clubs and societies. These
young men made the mistake of the newly enfranchised everywhere: they fought for causes worthy in themselves with the unworthy instruments of tyranny and violence. Comic songs of a certain
kind were to be driven from the stage; everyone was to wear Irish
cloth; everyone was to learn Irish; everyone was to hold certain
opinions; and these ends were sought by personal attacks, by viru-
lent caricature and violent derision. It needs eloquence to persuade
and knowledge to expound; but the coarser means come ready to
every man's hand, as ready as a stone or a stick, and where these
coarse means are all, there is nothing but mob, and the commonest
idea most prospers and is most sought for.

Gentlemen of the little clubs and societies, do not mistake the
meaning of our victory; it means something for us, but more for you.
When the curtain of *The Playboy* fell on Saturday night in the midst
of what *The Sunday Independent*—no friendly witness—described
as 'thunders of applause', I am confident that I saw the rise in this
country of a new thought, a new opinion, that we had long needed.
It was not all approval of Mr. Synge's play that sent the receipts of
the Abbey Theatre this last week to twice the height they had ever

touched before. The generation of young men and girls who are now leaving schools or colleges are weary of the tyranny of clubs and leagues. They wish again for individual sincerity, the eternal quest of truth, all that has been given up for so long that all might crouch upon the one roost and quack or cry in the one flock. We are beginning once again to ask what a man is, and to be content to wait a little before we go on to that further question: What is a good Irishman? There are some who have not yet their degrees that will say to friend or neighbour, 'You have voted with the English, and that is bad'; or 'You have sent away your Irish servants, or thrown away your Irish clothes, or blacked your face for your singing. I despise what you have done, I keep you still my friend; but if you are terrorised out of doing any of these things, evil things though I know them to be, I will not have you for my friend any more.' Manhood is all, and the roof of manhood is courage and courtesy.

PAIGE REYNOLDS

The First *Playboy*†

* * * Critics [have] long debated not only Synge's aesthetic objectives, but also whether or not he had political intents for this play. It seems to me that in its initial run, *The Playboy of the Western World* worked powerfully—if ultimately, unsuccessfully—to manipulate its first audiences into a critical self-awareness about their authority in both cultural and national politics.

Immediately after this first performance, Gregory wired a telegraph to Scotland, where Yeats was lecturing. It explained simply: 'Audience broke up in disorder at the word shift.[1] The welter of eyewitness accounts and critical analyses of this first production generally reflect Gregory's concise explanation of why the upheaval occurred: Synge's affront to Irish womanhood—his reference to women's underwear—had so outraged the audience that they felt impelled to protest. There was, of course, much on stage to offend and confuse, and critics have linked the controversy to factors ranging from rising unionist anxiety about Home Rule[2] to a growing awareness of venereal disease.[3] For the most part, however, these

---

† From *Playboys of the Western World: Production Histories* (A. Frazier, ed.). Reprinted by permission of Carysfort Press.
1. Augusta Gregory, *Our Irish Theatre: A Chapter of Autobiography* (1913; New York: Capricorn, 1965), 112.
2. Lionel Pilkington, *Theatre and State in Twentieth-Century Ireland: Cultivating the People* (London: Routledge, 2001), 59.
3. Susan Cannon Harris, *Gender and Modern Irish Drama* (Bloomington: Indiana UP, 2002), 69–122.

appraisals reaffirm the stance of Dubliners who talked about the production in 1907. The Abbey, which professed to be a national theatre, had offered its public an offensive and unflattering picture of Irish peasant life, rather than an affirmative depiction of national folk culture. Consequently, the week-long run of *Playboy* was accompanied not only by vociferous remonstrations, but also by a lively debate about its representations of Irish life and its artistic merit and, hence, about its suitability for performance by the self-proclaimed 'National Theatre Society, Ltd.'—the company run by Gregory, Synge, and Yeats that staged the play.

The ruckus at Saturday's premiere was merely a prelude to further chaos: the theatre was dark on Sunday, but Monday's newspapers offered detailed, if sometimes inaccurate, reports of the play's content and the protests. The second performance on Monday night attracted a small audience of around eighty, seated mostly in the inexpensive pit seats. As soon as the curtain rose on *Playboy*, the audience began stomping its feet, hurling Irish-language invective, and singing refrains from nationalist songs like 'A Nation Once Again'. This same rowdy behaviour characterized Tuesday night. A full house of playgoers, many of whom were not quite sober, ignored Yeats's appeal for a fair hearing for the play and his promises for a fruitful debate the following Monday on 'The Freedom of the Theatre.' After this performance, a brawl erupted in Westmoreland Street. By Wednesday night, crowds gathered in the streets outside the theatre, as hundreds stormed the doors. Strangely, on this evening *The Freeman's Journal* reported that *Riders to the Sea* 'never had a more sympathetic audience'.[4] But when Christy entered the stage, once more the shouts, the skirmishes, and the competing choruses of 'God Save the King' and 'God Save Ireland' began. Audience members trooped through Abbey Street and O'Connell Street after the play, followed closely by the police. By Thursday night, the disturbances decreased and unlike the previous two evenings, no arrests were made. The protests had played themselves out, and the Friday and Saturday performances proceeded smoothly.

The audiences for these first productions sometimes have been represented as unenlightened philistines who failed to recognize Synge's genius and attacked his masterpiece for political reasons, much to the surprised dismay of the Abbey directors and performers. But Synge and his cohorts should not be seen sympathetically as the bewildered victims of a nationalist audience's attack. From its inception, the Abbey Theatre placed a great deal of thought and energy into creating a coherent theory of the Irish national audi-

4. *The Freeman's Journal* 31 Jan. 1907: 7–8.

ence. Its frequently shifting perceptions of and intentions for these audiences pour out of the promotional, the editorial, and—I would argue—the creative work of its members. This was a theatre that attended to its audiences, even if it refused to welcome what it understood about them. The Abbey associates were aware that Dublin audiences had engaged directly with the stage for centuries: the eighteenth century was rife with theatre riots, like those at Smock Alley, and throughout the nineteenth and early twentieth centuries, audiences had engaged in call-and-response with popular plays, howled at performers, stormed the stage, and shouted down controversial productions, like the 1903 Dublin premiere of Ibsen's *A Doll's House*.[5]

Motivated by a mixture of optimism and hubris, the early Abbey tried to hammer these boisterous audiences into well-behaved spectators who would adhere to bourgeois norms. The architecture of the Abbey directed and focused the spectator's vision toward its proscenium stage, as did its practice of darkening the theatre. In the Abbey's occasional publications and from its stage, Yeats regularly lectured audience members, demanding they arrive promptly, sit quietly, and not ruffle their programmes during performances. Nonetheless, Irish audiences had forced the Abbey, early in its career, to acknowledge that they were not a passive body in full sway of the dramatic spectacle on hand. From its inception, the institution had a troubled history with controversial plays and rowdy theatre-goers. Yeats's *The Countess Cathleen* (1899), for instance, had been hissed during its first performance owing to its depiction of a woman who sold her soul; and Synge's *In the Shadow of the Glen* (1902) had elicited jeers and had even driven Maud Gonne from the theatre for what she perceived as the play's slurs on Irish women. The Abbey grudgingly came to recognize that its audiences were sometimes antipathetic, raucously antipathetic, to their work.

It seems the Abbey's management anticipated a similarly spirited response to *Playboy*. Prior to the opening, rehearsals were held in secret, an unusual practice for the theatre. Mary Maguire Colum recalled that during these two weeks of rehearsal, 'reports spread through Dublin that there were improprieties in the play and that the womanhood of Ireland was being slandered, and these rumors were received with hilarity by some, with solemnity by others'.[6]

5. For a brief account of this 1903 premiere, see Joseph Holloway, *Impressions of a Dublin Playgoer*, 22 August 1903, reproduced in *Laying the Foundations 1902–1904*, eds. Robert Hogan and James Kilroy, vol. 2, *Modern Irish Drama: A Documentary History*, ed. Robert Hogan (Dublin: Dolmen Press, 1976), 65. Helen M. Burke provides a rich study of eighteenth-century Irish audiences and their behaviour at sites such as Smock Alley in her *Riotous Performances: The Struggle for Hegemony in the Irish Theatre, 1712–1784* (Notre Dame: University of Notre Dame Press, 2003).
6. Mary Maguire Colum, *Life and the Dream: Memories of a Literary Life in Europe and America* (London: Macmillan & Co., 1947), 137.

Meanwhile, the theatre management and performers expressed anxieties about how the public might respond to *Playboy*'s rough language. Gregory compensated for these concerns by encouraging Yeats to remove his play *The Pot of Broth* from the evening's bill and by replacing it with Synge's popular one-act *Riders to the Sea*. Additionally, both Yeats and Gregory made arrangements to go abroad for the premiere, though only Yeats succeeded in missing the first performance.

In studies of historical popular culture in America, England, and Ireland, scholars often attribute the vociferous engagement of audiences with the stage to their conflation of reality and representation.[7] The first production of *Playboy*, it appears, actually encouraged the audience to confuse the real world and the fictive world. Padraic Colum credited this mistake to the play's visual realism, and in particular to the graphic image of Old Mahon's reappearance; according to Colum, this figure with a 'horribly bloodied bandage about his head . . . took the whole thing out of the atmosphere of comedy'.[8] *The Irish Times* praised both the play's ' "remorseless truth" in characterization' and its uncannily accurate duplication of peasant speech, even as it acknowledged that Dubliners 'will not publicly approve of the indiscriminate use of the Holy Name on every possible occasion'.[9] Meanwhile, the Abbey actress Maire nic Shiubhlaigh ascribed the audience's upset to Synge's direction, claiming roles were 'played seriously, almost sombrely, as though each character had been studied and its nastiness made apparent'.[1] The realism of the production encouraged its audiences to ignore the fourth wall, and believe they could somehow alter the course of events on stage.

Accounts of the riots underscore the notion that the audience mistook representation for reality and, consequently, conflated the stage and the stalls. On Wednesday night, for instance, when the third act began and Philly declared, 'There will be right sport before night will fall', one press account asserted, 'This was so very apropos to the exciting situation that all parties in the theatre joined in an outburst of hearty laughter'.[2] The sport, obviously,

7. Elaine Hadley, *Melodramatic Tactics: Theatricalized Dissent in the English Marketplace, 1800–1885* (Stanford: Stanford UP, 1995); Lawrence W. Levine, *Highbrow/Lowbrow: The Emergence of Cultural Hierarchy in America* (Cambridge: Harvard UP, 1988); Stephen Watt, *Joyce, O'Casey, and the Irish Popular Theatre* (Syracuse: Syracuse UP, 1991).
8. Padraic Colum, *The Road Round Ireland* (New York: Macmillan, 1926), 368.
9. "Public Amusements: Abbey Theatre," *The Irish Times*, 28 Jan. 1907: 7.
1. Maire nic Shiubhlaigh, *The Splendid Years* (Dublin: J. Duffy, 1955), 81. In Nic Shiubhlaigh's assessment, Dublin audiences correctly attributed this 'nasty' characterization to Synge's efforts to retaliate for the poor reception of *The Shadow of the Glen* and *The Well of the Saints*.
2. *The Freeman's Journal*, 31 Jan. 1907: 7.

refers both to the 'sport' that the fictive Mayo community engages in on stage and to the boisterous 'sport' found in the Abbey, which was filled with individuals from the Dublin community primed to support this artful comedy or to protest a play rumoured to slight the Irish. This description also reveals the sheer fun of the protest for its audiences—the playful repartee that night was received with laughter from 'all parties'.

BEN LEVITAS

[The Playboy of the Western World]†

* * * Synge's capacity to unsettle drew power from his capacity to combine direct language, poetic register, and dramatic symbol. His language is embedded in action, and audience objection found each reinforcing the other. During the *Playboy* riots, one interviewer insisted the provocation was not that the playwright called a spade a spade: "the complaint is, Mr. Synge, that you call it a bloody shovel."[1] That distinction calls to mind the hinge upon which *The Playboy of the Western World* changes direction, namely, the appearance of Christy's father, Old Mahon, in act 2 and his exchange with Widow Quin:

> MAHON. I want to destroy him for breaking the head on me with the clout of a loy. [*He takes off a big hat, and shows his head in a mass of bandages and plaster, with some pride.*] It was he did that, and amn't I a great wonder to think I've traced him ten days with that rent in my crown?
>
> WIDOW QUIN [*taking his head in both hands and examining it with extreme delight.*]. That was a great blow. And who hit you? Robber maybe?
>
> MAHON. It was my own son hit me, and he the divil a robber or anything else but a dirty, stuttering lout.[2]

As Mahon explains, no spade or shovel did the damage. It was a loy. From the opening of the play, Synge's insistence on the cultural specificity of the weapon fixes the action in the particular. Naming the tool of rural Irish labor makes the violence socially and economically determined. It is no weapon of choice, but the instru-

---

† From "Censorship and Self-Censure in the Plays of J. M. Synge," *Princeton University Library Chronicle* 68. Reprinted by permission of the author.
1. *Dublin Evening Mail*, 28 Jan. 1907.
2. J. M. Synge, *The Playboy of the Western World*, in *Collected Works*, vol. 4, *Plays: Book II*, ed. Ann Saddlemyer (London: Oxford University Press, 1968), 121. Further references to this edition of the play will be cited by page number in the text.

ment of circumstance. And with the introduction of its target, Mahon's head, the loy gains new weight. As several witnesses to the first production on January 26, 1907, would vouch, this point marks the place at which the mood of the audience shifted from indulgence to discomfort, before evolving into downright hostility.[3] From this moment, we are made acutely aware of a "dirty deed" forcing its way into the "gallous story" told thus far. As the brutal evidence of violence, the exaggeratedly bloody bandage offers an overtly physical counterpoint to Christy's lyrical elaborations. A corresponding phrase, "dirty, stuttering lout," confirms the impact by insisting on a return to the real world that reins in Christy's speech to a haltering dumbness.

It was no coincidence that this juncture of language and image of violence was the precise point that Arthur Griffith thought most important to censor as "the foulest language we have ever listened to from a public platform."[4] Griffith actually misheard the word "stuttering" as something altogether more obscene, and the projection of sexual disgust upon the misheard is only further testament to the provoking, sickening insistence of the formative past. When the father appears, the allegorical possibilities are narrowed, and a generalized violence is forced into specific form, with identifiable victims and known localities. To anticipate a sexual connotation is an acknowledgment of the degree to which the physical facts of sex, procreation, and family are bound in with the social violence that marks boundaries of difference defining gender, class, and nation.

Similar processes are in operation in the crucial scene where the action became unbearable to the first Abbey audience, that gap between the second strike of the loy and the father's second survival. This, the lynching episode, quickly rendered the play as unplayable. It is marked by two critical junctures. The first is a famous sexual image, followed by an odd juxtaposed action:

> CHRISTY. It's Pegeen I'm seeking only, and what'd I care if you brought me a drift of chosen females, standing in their shifts itself maybe, from this place to the Eastern World.
>
> SARA [*runs in, pulling off one of her petticoats*]. They're going to hang him. [*Holding out petticoat and shawl.*] Fit these upon him and let him run off to the east. (167)

The potency of Christy's declaration has been much analyzed as a deftly ironic evocation conjuring the sexually wanton image to

3. The change was marked by Padraic Colum, *The Road Round Ireland* (New York: Macmillan, 1926) 211–12 and Maire Nic Shiubhlaigh, *The Splendid Years* (Dublin: J. Duffy, 1955) 81–82. See also Nicholas Grene, *Synge: A Critical Study of the Plays* (London: Macmillan, 1975).

4. *Sinn Féin*, 2 Feb. 1907.

emphasize chastity, prompting an outrage at licentiousness at the moment when it is denied. The corresponding image of Christy cross-dressing, using Sara's surrendered undergarment, is no less notable, however. This transgression obviously tests the conservative allocation of gender roles, already challenged by the feistiness of Pegeen and the Widow Quin. The fantasy of the harem is paired with over-romantic delusion, though neither can match the contingent gender roles of real live men or women.

But there is another possible dimension to the image, thrown up by Peter Hart's analysis of the social roots of youth culture in the Irish Volunteers. The wearing of women's clothes by local male youths (along with the wearing of clothes inside out, with faces masked, blackened, or rouged, and legs bound with hay or straw) was a feature of festival days in Irish folk culture. Particularly on Skelling Night (Shrove Tuesday), gangs of Straw Boys would ridicule the transgressive to impose a carnival coercion. Bachelors, old maids, adulterers, difficult drunks, and lusty widows were all targets.[5] Such groups often established the social ties underlying the revolutionary bands that formed the Irish Republican Army. Christy's suggestive drag can be interpreted as a further layering of inversions and coercions that resonates with the attempt at social censoring of *The Playboy*. Christy's supposed purity of intent is echoed by his dress, but the attempt to "shift" his gender and escape retribution only returns him to the uniform of the young male intent on policing communal conformity.

The image thus invites consideration of Christy's revolutionary potential. Straw Boys were ambiguous forces, coercive in their targets, subversive in their rowdiness. Just as Synge had drawn upon social trespass in *The Tinker's Wedding* to break a theatrical taboo, the echo of the Boys' presence in *The Playboy* appropriates a folk unruliness to the theatrical idiom. This dynamic is further elaborated in the closing image of the sequence, in which Pegeen lifts the "lighted sod" to Christy's leg.

PEGEEN [*coming over*]. God help him so. [*Burns his leg.*]

CHRISTY [*kicking and screaming*]. Oh, glory be to God! (171)

The spare contrast between the brutality of the action and the twin providential injunctions constitutes an extreme polarity. At one end, the contact is metaphorically and literally grounded. The scorching turf, like the loy and the petticoat/shift, is both domestically specific and politically resonant: the lighted sod had been a common symbol of the Land War. It carries, therefore, connota-

---

5. Peter Hart, *The I.R.A. and Its Enemies: Violence and Community in Cork 1916–1923* (Oxford: Clarendon Press, 1998), 178–79.

tions of resistance as well as of home and hearth. At the same time, deploying the blasphemy of religious language at a moment of unholy torture brings into tight proximity the detachment of the divine and the immediacy of physical harm. This juxtaposition is doubled up with Pegeen's sudden renunciation of intimacy ("a strange man is a marvel" [169]). With that estrangement comes a jarring replacement of pleasure with pain, forcing the moment of rejection to recognize in its violence a sublimation of repressed sexual attraction.

Synge's calculated provocation in *The Playboy* did more than expose his audiences' sexual repression and force them to sublimate their own desires as defensive outrage. The language of Synge's theatricality is always assertive in its testing interplay between the ideal and the real, and always alert to the ambiguous powers of concerted action. As in *The Well of the Saints*, the commentary operates in a meta-dramatic dimension as well as a thematic one. Provoking the riot, Synge's incitement brings his audience into the play, completing the explosive action by engaging his public in a common manifestation of staged ideas.

In one sense this intended complicity is prototypically avant-gardist. In a draft letter to Stephen MacKenna in January 1904, Synge suggested that "I think the Law-Maker and Law-Breaker are both needful in society—as the lively and volcanic forces are needed to make earth's crust inhabitable—and I think the Law-Maker is tending to reduce Ireland or parts of Ireland to a dismal morbid hypocracy [*sic*] that is not a blessed unripeness."[6] By this logic Synge finds himself happily thrown into the company of the socially transgressive tinkers, tramps, and outlaws he imagines providing Ireland's energy for change. On the other hand, Synge's physical symbols are always carefully selected for their evocation of social struggles. Such denotations detonate within any easy, romanticized associations. Bringing the audience in as protagonists draws attention to the relationship between the stage and the auditorium and notice to the demarcations of power explicit in the physical space of the Abbey Theatre. In this sense *The Playboy* is Synge's most overt dramatic attempt to acknowledge his social and cultural position in what Ronan McDonald has described as an "art of guilt."[7]

To recognize Synge in the playboy Christy is to identify Synge

6. *The Collected Letters of J. M. Synge*, ed. Anne Saddlemyer (New York: Oxford University Press, 1983), I: 76. See also Gale Schricker Swiontkowski, "The Devil and Auld Mahoun: Exposing the Trickster Archetype in Synge's Christy Mahon by Way of Rushdie's Muhammad/Mahound," in *Assessing the Achievement of J. M. Synge*, ed. Alexander G. Gonzales (Westport, Conn.: Greenwood Press, 1996), 163.
7. Ronan McDonald, *Tragedy in Irish Literature: Synge, O'Casey, Beckett* (London: Palgrave, 2002), 54.

with a character whose expectant anticipation of a "romping life-time" shouts a return to the line of shift-clad females he had once declined as empty fantasy. If the author is to be redeemed from his tendency to objectify, it begs an interruption to the process of alienation the play describes. This is not a one-way street: scrutiny of Synge's self-aware social class position is demanded, but at the price that the spectators scrutinize their own implication in other systems of control. The possibility that the dialectic between the real and the idealized Ireland may in this context be further enlarged as a dynamic between play and spectators enjoins all participants in an expanding drama of censorship. * * *

On Bernard Shaw

BERNARD SHAW

Preface for Politicians†

John Bull's Other Island was written in 1904 at the request of Mr William Butler Yeats, as a patriotic contribution to the repertory of the Irish Literary Theatre. Like most people who have asked me to write plays, Mr Yeats got rather more than he bargained for. The play was at that time beyond the resources of the new Abbey Theatre, which the Irish enterprise owed to the public spirit of Miss A. E. F. Horniman (an Englishwoman, of course), who, twelve years ago, played an important part in the history of the modern English stage as well as in my own personal destiny by providing the necessary capital for that memorable season at the Avenue Theatre which forced my Arms and The Man and Mr Yeats's Land of Heart's Desire on the recalcitrant London playgoer, and gave a third Irish playwright, Dr John Todhunter, an opportunity which the commercial theatres could not have afforded him.[1]

There was another reason for changing the destination of John Bull's Other Island. It was uncongenial to the whole spirit of the neo-Gaelic movement, which is bent on creating a new Ireland after its own ideal, whereas my play is a very uncompromising presentment of the real old Ireland. The next thing that happened was the production of the play in London at the Court Theatre by Messrs. Vedrenne and Barker, and its immediate and enormous popularity with delighted and flattered English audiences. This constituted it a successful commercial play, and made it unnecessary to resort to the special machinery or tax the special resources of the Irish Literary Theatre for its production.

1. Todhunter (1839–1916), poet as well as "Ibsenite" playwright, whose "Comedy of Sighs," generally ridiculed, was paired with Yeats's play in 1894 [*Editor*].

How Tom Broadbent Took It

Now I have a good deal more to say about the relations between the
Irish and the English than will be found in my play. Writing the
play for an Irish audience, I thought it would be good for them to
be shewn very clearly that the loudest laugh they could raise at the
expense of the absurdest Englishman was not really a laugh on
their side; that he would succeed where they would fail; that he
could inspire strong affection and loyalty in an Irishman who knew
the world and was moved only to dislike, mistrust, impatience and
even exasperation by his own countrymen; that his power of taking
himself seriously, and his insensibility to anything funny in danger
and destruction, was the first condition of economy and concentration of force, sustained purpose, and rational conduct. But the
need for this lesson in Ireland is the measure of its demoralizing
superfluousness in England. English audiences very naturally swallowed it eagerly and smacked their lips over it, laughing all the
more heartily because they felt that they were taking a caricature of
themselves with the most tolerant and large-minded goodhumor.
They were perfectly willing to allow me to represent Tom Broadbent as infatuated in politics, hypnotized by his newspaper leader-
writers and parliamentary orators into an utter paralysis of his
common sense, without moral delicacy or social tact, provided I
made him cheerful, robust, goodnatured, free from envy, and above
all, a successful muddler-through in business and love. Not only
did no English critic allow that the success in business of Messrs
English Broadbent and Irish Doyle might possibly have been due to
some extent to Doyle, but one writer actually dwelt with much feeling on the pathos of Doyle's failure as an engineer (a circumstance
not mentioned nor suggested in my play) in contrast with Broadbent's solid success. No doubt, when the play is performed in Ireland, the Dublin critics will regard it as self-evident that without
Doyle Broadbent would have become bankrupt in six months. I
should say, myself, that the combination was probably much more
effective than either of the partners would have been alone. I am
persuaded further—without pretending to know more about it than
anyone else—that Broadbent's special contribution was simply the
strength, self-satisfaction, social confidence and cheerful bump-
tiousness that money, comfort, and good feeling bring to all healthy
people; and that Doyle's special contribution was the freedom from
illusion, the power of facing facts, the nervous industry, the sharp-
ened wits, the sensitive pride of the imaginative man who has
fought his way up through social persecution and poverty. I do not
say that the confidence of the Englishman in Broadbent is not for
the moment justified. The virtues of the English soil are not less

real because they consist of coal and iron, not of metaphysical sources of character. The virtues of Broadbent are not less real because they are the virtues of the money that coal and iron have produced. But as the mineral virtues are being discovered and developed in other soils, their derivative virtues are appearing so rapidly in other nations that Broadbent's relative advantage is vanishing. In truth I am afraid (the misgiving is natural to a by-this-time slightly elderly playwright) that Broadbent is out of date. The successful Englishman of today, when he is not a transplanted Scotchman or Irishman, often turns out on investigation to be, if not an American, an Italian, or a Jew, at least to be depending on the brains, the nervous energy, and the freedom from romantic illusions (often called cynicism) of such foreigners for the management of his sources of income. At all events I am persuaded that a modern nation that is satisfied with Broadbent is in a dream. Much as I like him, I object to be governed by him, or entangled in his political destiny. I therefore propose to give him a piece of my mind here, as an Irishman, full of an instinctive pity for those of my fellow-creatures who are only English.

What Is an Irishman?

When I say that I am an Irishman I mean that I was born in Ireland, and that my native language is the English of Swift and not the unspeakable jargon of the mid-XIX century London newspapers. My extraction is the extraction of most Englishmen: that is, I have no trace in me of the commercially imported North Spanish strain which passes for aboriginal Irish: I am a genuine typical Irishman of the Danish, Norman, Cromwellian, and (of course) Scotch invasions. I am violently and arrogantly Protestant by family tradition; but let no English Government therefore count on my allegiance: I am English enough to be inveterate Republican and Home Ruler. It is true that one of my grandfathers was an Orangeman[2]; but then his sister was an abbess; and his uncle, I am proud to say, was hanged as a rebel. When I look round me on the hybrid cosmopolitans, slum poisoned or square pampered, who call themselves Englishmen today, and see them bullied by the Irish Protestant garrison as no Bengalee now lets himself be bullied by an Englishman; when I see the Irishman everywhere standing clear-headed, sane, hardily callous to the boyish sentimentalities, susceptibilities, and credulities that make the Englishman the dupe of every charlatan and the idolater of every numskull, I perceive that

---

2. Protestant, loyalist sympathizer; hence, like Shaw's other contrasts here, opposed to a Catholic abbess or Republican rebel [*Editor*].

Ireland is the only spot on earth which still produces the ideal Englishman of history. Blackguard, bully, drunkard, liar, foulmouth,
flatterer, beggar, backbiter, venal functionary, corrupt judge, envi-
ous friend, vindictive opponent, unparalleled political traitor: all
these your Irishman may easily be, just as he may be a gentleman (a
species extinct in England, and nobody a penny the worse); but he
is never quite the hysterical nonsense-crammed, fact-proof, truth-
terrified, unballasted sport of all the bogey panics and all the silly
enthusiams that now calls itself "God's Englishman." England cannot do without its Irish and its Scots today, because it cannot do
without at least a little sanity.

The Protestant Garrison

The more Protestant an Irishman is—the more English he is, if it
flatters you to have it put that way, the more intolerable he finds it
to be ruled by English instead of Irish folly. A "loyal" Irishman is an
abhorrent phenomenon, because it is an unnatural one. No doubt
English rule is vigorously exploited in the interests of the property,
power, and promotion of the Irish classes as against the Irish
masses. Our delicacy is part of a keen sense of reality which makes
us a very practical, and even, on occasion, a very coarse people.
The Irish soldier takes the King's shilling and drinks the King's
health; and the Irish squire takes the title deeds of the English settlement and rises uncovered to the strains of the English national
anthem. But do not mistake this cupboard loyalty for anything
deeper. It gains a broad base from the normal attachment of every
reasonable man to the established government as long as it is bear-
able; for we all, after a certain age, prefer peace to revolution and
order to chaos, other things being equal. Such considerations produce loyal Irishmen as they produce loyal Poles and Fins, loyal
Hindus, loyal Filipinos, and faithful slaves. But there is nothing
more in it than that. If there is an entire lack of gall in the feeling
of the Irish gentry towards the English, it is because the Englishman is always gaping admiringly at the Irishman as at some clever
child prodigy. He overrates him with a generosity born of a traditional conviction of his own superiority in the deeper aspects of human character. As the Irish gentleman, tracing his pedigree to the
conquest or one of the invasions, is equally convinced that if this
superiority really exists, he is the genuine true blue heir to it, and
as he is easily able to hold his own in all the superficial social ac-
complishments, he finds English society agreeable, and English
houses very comfortable, Irish establishments being generally
straitened by an attempt to keep a park and a stable on an income

which would not justify an Englishman in venturing upon a wholly detached villa.

Our Temperaments Contrasted

But however pleasant the relations between the Protestant garrison and the English gentry may be, they are always essentially of the nature of an *entente cordiale* between foreigners. Personally I like Englishmen much better than Irishmen (no doubt because they make more of me) just as many Englishmen like Frenchmen better than Englishmen, and never go on board a Peninsular and Oriental steamer when one of the ships of the Messageries Maritimes is available. But I never think of an Englishman as my countryman. I should as soon think of applying that term to a German. And the Englishman has the same feeling. When a Frenchman fails to make the distinction, we both feel a certain disparagement involved in the misapprehension. Macaulay, seeing that the Irish had in Swift an author worth stealing, tried to annex him by contending that he must be classed as an Englishman because he was not an aboriginal Celt. He might as well have refused the name of Briton to Addison because he did not stain himself blue and attach scythes to the poles of his sedan chair.[3] In spite of all such trifling with facts, the actual distinction between the idolatrous Englishman and the fact-facing Irishman, of the same extraction though they be, remains to explode those two hollowest of fictions, the Irish and English "races." There is no Irish race any more than there is an English race or a Yankee race. There *is* an Irish climate, which will stamp an immigrant more deeply and durably in two years, apparently, than the English climate will in two hundred. It is reinforced by an artificial economic climate which does some of the work attributed to the natural geographic one; but the geographic climate is eternal and irresistible, making a mankind and a womankind that Kent, Middlesex, and East Anglia cannot produce and do not want to imitate.

How can I sketch the broad lines of the contrast as they strike me? Roughly I should say that the Englishman is wholly at the mercy of his imagination, having no sense of reality to check it. The Irishman, with a far subtler and more fastidious imagination, has one eye always on things as they are. If you compare [Thomas] Moore's visionary "Minstrel Boy" with Mr Rudyard Kipling's quasi-

3. Thomas Babington Macaulay (1800–59), MP, writer, colonial administrator of India; Jonathan Swift (1667–1745), Dubliner by birth, career, and burial; Joseph Addison (1672–1719), English essayist who twice served as aide to the lord lieutenant of Ireland [*Editor*].

realistic "Soldiers Three," you may yawn over Moore or gush over him, but you will not suspect him of having had any illusions about the contemporary British private; whilst as to Mr Kipling, you will see that he has not, and unless he settles in Ireland for a few years will always remain constitutionally and congenitally incapable of having, the faintest inkling of the reality which he idolizes as Tommy Atkins. Perhaps you have never thought of illustrating the contrast between English and Irish by Moore and Mr Kipling, or even by Parnell and Gladstone. Sir Boyle Roche and Shakespeare may seem more to your point. Let me find you a more dramatic instance. Think of the famous meeting between the Duke of Wellington, that intensely Irish Irishman, and Nelson, that intensely English Englishman.[4] Wellington's contemptuous disgust at Nelson's theatricality as a professed hero, patriot, and rhapsody, a theatricality which in an Irishman would have been an insufferably vulgar affectation, was quite natural and inevitable. Wellington's formula for that kind of thing was a well-known Irish one: "Sir: dont be a damned fool." It is the formula of all Irishmen for all Englishmen to this day. It is the formula of Larry Doyle for Tom Broadbent in my play, in spite of Doyle's affection for Tom. Nelson's genius, instead of producing intellectual keenness and scrupulousness, produced mere delirium. He was drunk with glory, exalted by his fervent faith in the sound British patriotism of the Almighty, nerved by the vulgarest anti-foreign prejudice, and apparently unchastened by any reflections on the fact that he had never had to fight a technically capable and properly equipped enemy except on land, where he had never been successful. Compare Wellington, who had to fight Napoleon's armies, Napoleon's marshals, and finally Napoleon himself, without one moment of illusions as to the human material he had to command, without one gush of the "Kiss me, Hardy" emotion which enabled Nelson to idolize his crews and his staff, without forgetting even in his dreams that the normal British officer of that time was an incapable amateur (as he still is) and the normal British soldier a never-do-well (he is now a depressed and respectable young man). No wonder Wellington became an accomplished comedian in the art of anti-climax, scandalizing the unfortunate Croker,[5] responding to the demand for glorious sentiments by the most disenchanting

4. Again, Irish figures of British careers contrasted with English: Parliamentarians Charles Stewart Parnell (1846–91) and William Ewart Gladstone (1809–98); rhetoricians Sir Boyle Roche (1743–1807), said to have perpetrated the inflated, senseless "Irish Bull"; military commanders the duke of Wellington (1769–1852) and Viscount Nelson (1758–1805) [*Editor*].

5. John Wilson Croker (1780–1857), a comical literary figure who published his own papers, including letters from Wellington; "Kiss me, Hardy," above, are said to have been Nelson's last words [*Editor*].

touches of realism, and, generally, pricking the English windbag at its most explosive crises of distention. Nelson, intensely nervous and theatrical, made an enormous fuss about victories so cheap that he would have deserved shooting if he had lost them, and, not content with lavishing splendid fighting on helpless adversaries like the heroic De Brueys or Villeneuve (who had not even the illusion of heroism when he went like a lamb to the slaughter), got himself killed by his passion for exposing himself to death in that sublime defiance of it which was perhaps the supreme tribute of the exquisite coward to the King of Terrors (for, believe me, you cannot be a hero without being a coward: supersense cuts both ways), the result being a tremendous effect on the gallery. Wellington, most capable of captains, was neither a hero nor a patriot: perhaps not even a coward; and had it not been for the Nelsonic anecdotes invented for him—"Up guards, and at em" and so forth—and the fact that the antagonist with whom he finally closed was such a master of theatrical effect that Wellington could not fight him without getting into his limelight, nor overthrow him (most unfortunately for us all) without drawing the eyes of the whole world to the catastrophe, the Iron Duke would have been almost forgotten by this time. Now that contrast is English against Irish all over, and is the more delicious because the real Irishman in it is the Englishman of tradition, whilst the real Englishman is the traditional theatrical foreigner.

The value of the illustration lies in the fact that Nelson and Wellington were both in the highest degree efficient, and both in the highest degree incompatible with one another on any other footing than one of independence. The government of Nelson by Wellington or of Wellington by Nelson is felt at once to be a dishonorable outrage to the governed and a finally impossible task for the governor.

I daresay some Englishman will now try to steal Wellington as Macaulay tried to steal Swift. And he may plead with some truth that though it seems impossible that any other country than England could produce a hero so utterly devoid of common sense, intellectual delicacy, and international chivalry as Nelson, it may be contended that Wellington was rather an eighteenth century aristocratic type, than a specifically Irish type. George IV and Byron, contrasted with Gladstone, seem Irish in respect of a certain humorous blackguardism, and a power of appreciating art and sentiment without being duped by them into mistaking romantic figments for realities. But faithlessness and the need for carrying off the worthlessness and impotence that accompany it, produce in all nations a gay, sceptical, amusing, blaspheming, witty fashion which suits the flexibility of the Irish mind very well; and the contrast between this fashion and the energetic infatuations that have

enabled intellectually ridiculous men, without wit or humor, to go
on crusades and make successful revolutions, must not be confused with the contrast between the English and Irish idiosyn-
crasies. The Irishman makes a distinction which the Englishman is
too lazy intellectually (the intellectual laziness and slovenliness of
the English is almost beyond belief) to make. The Englishman, impressed with the dissoluteness of the faithless wits of the Restoration and the Regency, and with the victories of the willful zealots of
the patriotic, religious, and revolutionary wars, jumps to the conclusion that willfulness is the main thing. In this he is right. But he
overdoes his jump so far as to conclude also that stupidity and
wrong-headedness are better guarantees of efficiency and trustwor-
thiness than intellectual vivacity, which he mistrusts as a common
symptom of worthlessness, vice, and instability. Now in this he is
most dangerously wrong. Whether the Irishman grasps the truth as
firmly as the Englishman may be open to question; but he is certainly comparatively free from the error. That affectionate and admiring love of sentimental stupidity for its own sake, both in men
and women, which shines so steadily through the novels of Thackeray, would hardly be possible in the works of an Irish novelist.
Even Dickens, though too vital a genius and too severely educated
in the school of shabby-genteel poverty to have any doubt of the national danger of fatheadedness in high places, evidently assumes
rather too hastily the superiority of Mr Meagles to Sir John Chester
and Harold Skimpole.[6] On the other hand, it takes an Irishman
years of residence in England to learn to respect and like a block-
head. An Englishman will not respect nor like anyone else. Every
English statesman has to maintain his popularity by pretending to
be ruder, more ignorant, more sentimental, more superstitious,
more stupid than any man who has lived behind the scenes of public life for ten minutes can possibly be. Nobody dares to publish
really intimate memoirs of him or really private letters of his until
his whole generation has passed away, and his party can no longer
be compromised by the discovery that the platitudinizing twaddler
and hypocritical opportunist was really a man of some perception
as well as of strong constitution, peg-away industry, personal ambition, and party keenness.

* * *

6. Characters from Dickens's novels, respectively, *Little Dorrit, Barnaby Rudge,* and *Bleak House* [Editor].

NORMA JENCKES

The Rejection of Shaw's Irish Play:
John Bull's Other Island†

* * *

Yeats conceived and created the Abbey Theatre as a vehicle for a certain type of dramaturgy. Ten years earlier Shaw had been able to see the value of much that Yeats attempted. He concluded in a letter to Florence Farr written in 1894 at the time of the production of *The Land of Heart's Desire*, that Yeats was a gifted playwright and that his play was exquisite.[1] Yeats was never able to be so generous. Although he can admit the talent and energy of Shaw's *Arms and the Man*, his judgment is never unmixed. He cannot resist noting what is for him the play's "inorganic, logical straightness."[2] Ten years only intensified Yeats's hatred of the logical and unromantic presentation of the world that Shaw represented. When Shaw turned his sights to Ireland, he created *John Bull's Other Island*, with its attack on the mood of dreaminess, Celticism, and escapism. In 1904 too much of the repertory of the Irish Literary Theatre included those plays that treated Celticism and the Irish past as staples. Yeats might later, as described in "The Circus Animals' Desertion," leave behind his gay and heroic images of Ireland, but in 1904 these were still central to his poetic inspiration. Also, he believed that any political improvement in Ireland would only come through a revitalization of the figures of Ireland's heroic past.

Once the Abbey had rejected Shaw's play as diplomatically as possible, and when it was finally produced in London, Yeats expressed his dislike for it in a letter to Lady Gregory he wrote after seeing that performance: "I have seen Shaw's play; it acts very much better than one could have foreseen, but is immensely long. It begins at 2:30 and ends at 6. I don't really like it. It is fundamentally ugly and shapeless, but certainly keeps everybody amused."[3]

William Fay, the director of the amateur acting group that joined with Yeats in reviving Irish drama, registers an equally amazing shift of opinion. When he first read it he found it "a wonderful piece of work." When he saw it in London, his only objections were to the difficulty of casting it:

---

† From *Eire-Ireland* 10 (Spring 1975). Reprinted by permission of the Irish American Cultural Institute.
1. *Florence Farr, Bernard Shaw, W. B. Yeats: Letters*, ed. Clifford Box (London, 1946), p ix.
2. W. B. Yeats, *Autobiographies* (New York: Doubleday, 1958), 283.
3. *Letters*, ed. Allan Wade (London: Rupert Hart-Davis, 1954), 442.

Our company could not do it adequately in their present circumstances. Their experience was far too limited. To my thinking the play depends on having a Broadbent who can carry the weight of it, for without him it is *Hamlet* without the Prince. Besides, he must both look and sound English, and we had nobody who could take the part of the Cockney valet, Hodson. In Frank I had a splendid Keegan, but I had no Larry. The rest of the cast I might have managed, though my people were really too young for the parts. Rather reluctantly I had to advise against attempting the play.[4]

But by 1930 Fay had turned against it violently. In the 1912 revival of the play under the direction of Granville-Barker, and with the famous William Poel as Keegan, Fay's wife had "the genteel but not very exciting part of Nora, while I burbled along about 'me sufferings' as old Haffigan." Remembering this, he pronounces a sweeping condemnation of the play and convicts Shaw of garrulity and of ignorance of his subject:

. . . *John Bull's Other Island* ranks among Shaw's failures. It is interesting as the first play of his later manner, where action is nothing and talk everything, but its talk was out of date before it was written down. Mr. Shaw left Ireland in 1876, and it was only by hearsay that he knew of the Land League, the Plan of Campaign, and what Parnell meant to Ireland. By the time he had grasped the significance of all these things, Ireland had put them away and was busy organizing the Gaelic League which produced Sinn Fein, followed by two revolutions and the formation of the Free State. There is half a century between the Ireland of *John Bull's Other Island* and the Ireland of Sean O'Casey, and yet to O'Casey's name one might add with profound reverence, the name of J. M. Synge.[5]

More recent critics, who should know better, have likewise belittled the play. Writing in 1971, Michael J. Sidnell conjectures that "the initial rejection of his *John Bull's Other Island* by the Abbey-to-be may even be a matter of rejoicing." He relegates Shaw to the position of a kind of middle-man in Anglo-Irish literary life: "Like Swift, Shaw was to be most useful and dear to Ireland when addressing England or at least seeing Ireland in its relation to England." Sidnell concludes his comments with the note that "Dublin in 1904 according to the best testimony for that year, Joyce's farraginous chronicle, stood more in need of unifying vision than analytical criticism: more in need of creative image than the intellectual structure erected by Shaw as a gallery in which to hand the

4. *The Abbey Theatre* (London: Rich and Coward, 1935), 206–07.
5. *The Abbey Theatre*, 251.

caricatures of the time."[6] Like Fay, Sidnell performs a feat of literary second-guessing, and he encourages the notion that Shaw could not write a truly Irish play because he was remote from the cultural events of his native land.

This notion, though a persistent one, will not withstand an objective perusal of the events of Shaw's career. Shaw's experience of Irishness and its effect upon his career was quite different from that of Yeats's. At an early age, in 1875, Shaw had felt that he must leave Dublin if he was to make a career as a writer. He perceived that "My business in life could not be transacted in Dublin out of an experience confined to Ireland. I had to go to London just as my father had to go to the Corn Exchange. London was the literary centre for the English language, and for such culture as the realm of the English language (in which I proposed to be king) could afford. There was no Gaelic League in those days, nor any sense that Ireland had in herself the seed of culture."[7] Shaw's concern for Ireland continued throughout his life, but it was the concern of an Irishman residing in England. His English experience greatly affected his view of Ireland. When Shaw turned to analyze the woes of that "most distressful country," he did so with an intimacy that birth can bestow and an objectivity that distance made possible.

Shaw's politics also colored his view of his native land. His Fabian studies, which had taught him that class oppression was common to all nations, made him immune to the "fanatical" Irish nationalism that saw England as the source of all Irish woes and emancipation from England as the solution to all Irish problems. Shaw insisted that there was nothing peculiar or special about the misery of the Irish people. It was the result of British imperialism and feudal land relations, and Ireland shared her miseries with other British colonies. He saw nothing magical or charming in the superstition and backwardness of the Irish peasant, but only an ignorance that must be removed. He agreed with the nationalists that Ireland must sever her connection with England to realize her nationhood. But, once accomplished, this first advance must be followed by the removal of all classes and class oppression and the achievement of socialism. Shaw explains his movement from nationalism to internationalism thus: "I was drawn into the Socialist revival of the early eighties, among Englishmen intensely serious and burning with indignation at every real and very fundamental evil that affected all the world; so that the reaction against them bound the finer spirits of all the nations together instead of making

6. "Hic and Ille: Shaw and Yeats," *Theatre and Nationalism in 20th Century Ireland*, ed. Robert O'Driscoll (Toronto: University of Toronto Press, 1971), 157, 161, 168.
7. "Preface to *Immaturity*," Ayot St. Lawrence Edition of *Collected Works*, I, xxxvii–xxxviii.

them cherish hatred of one another as a national virtue."[8] Shaw's internationalism did not preclude nationalism; it transcended it.

Throughout the 1880's and 1890's Shaw continued to comment on the Irish scene from his Fabian perspective. Repeatedly in articles with such titles as "The Making of the Irish Nation" (1886), "A Balfour Ballad" (1888), "The Tories and Ireland" (1888), "A Crib for Home Rulers" (1888), "The Parnell Forger" (1889), "Shall Parnell Go?" (1890), he used a Marxist analysis to sort out the complexities of the Irish political scene and insisted that "there is no federating nationalities without first realizing them."[9] Shaw remained an Irishman in the thirty years between his departure from Ireland and his re-creation of Ireland in *John Bull's Other Island*, but an Irishman with a difference: a socialist and an internationalist.

Artistically Shaw's interest in Irish subjects finds its highest expression in the play the Abbey Theatre rejected. The fate of Ireland and the Irish, of those who leave Ireland and those who remain, dominates this play, which is a kind of dramatic collision of dreams of Ireland's future. Doyle, Broadbent, and Keegan present their separate hopes and plans for the future of Ireland. Their dreams are juxtaposed against a scathingly realistic picture of Irish rural poverty and exploitation. Shaw had not forgotten Ireland. Perhaps it would be more accurate to say that he remembered things that Yeats had never known. With his reverence for the "Big Houses" and the aristocracy, Yeats could never agree with the insight that illuminated Shaw's work: that class oppression weighed as heavily as national oppression on the Irish poor.

The rejection of Shaw's "uncongenial play," although probably inevitable considering the aims of the new theatre and the biases of its directors, has been seen as a mistake by commentators close to the events. Lennox Robinson considered the rejection to be an error in the Abbey management equalled only by the rejection of *The Silver Tassie* by O'Casey.[1] George Moore, who had parted from active involvement in the theatre by 1902, wrote a great deal about Yeats's attempts to keep out the works of playwrights other than those he had discovered. Although Moore does not mention *John Bull's Other Island*, he would say by 1908 that "The Celtic Renaissance does not exist, it is a myth."[2] O'Casey also saw the rejection of Shaw's play as a loss to the Abbey Theatre and a surrender to Yeats's narrowness.[3]

8. "Preface to *Immaturity*," xxxvi.
9. Collected in *The Matter with Ireland*, eds. David Greene and Dan H. Laurence (London: Rupert Hart-Davis, 1962).
1. *Ireland's Abbey Theatre* (London: Sedgwick and Jackson, 1951), 152.
2. *Hail and Farewell* (London: Heinemann, 1947).
3. Letter to O'Casey, June 19, 1928; quoted by Eileen O'Casey in *Sean* (New York: Coward-McCann, 1972), 84–85.

The question of Yeats's personal antipathy to Shaw and the influence of this attitude on his rejection of Shaw's play is a difficult and delicate one. In an oft-quoted passage from his *Autobiographies*, Yeats remembers his nightmare vision of Shaw: "Presently I had a nightmare that I was haunted by sewing machines, that clicked and shone, but the incredible thing was that the machine smiled, smiled perpetually." The image of Shaw which this conjures up is not attractive. But that was not Yeats's whole opinion. He goes on to record his admiration of and debt to Shaw: "Yet I delighted in Shaw, the formidable man. He could hit my enemies and the enemies of all I loved, as I could never hit, as no living author that was dear to me could ever hit."[4] Yeats appreciated Shaw's powers and wanted him as an ally. But when Shaw denounced the twilight dreaming of the neo-Celtic revival, he struck too close to Yeats, and seemed to give aid and support to the enemy.

The differences over his Irish play did not stifle Shaw's relationships with the directors of the Abbey Theatre. Lady Gregory's journals witness her continuing and close relationship with the Shaws. She was a frequent guest at their home and considered Shaw to be her most gentle friend. Shaw's later play, *The Shewing-Up of Blanco Posnet*, was presented at the Abbey in 1909 and occasioned one of the famous battles with censors. In a letter to James Joyce, years later, Yeats notes that Shaw and he are founding an Irish Academy in which they hope to include Joyce. And Shaw's defense of the maligned Roger Casement must have vindicated him in Yeats's eyes.[5]

Bernard Shaw was undeterred by the rejection of his play. Even while awaiting Yeats's decision he was busy planning the London opening with Granville-Barker. Lennox Robinson and O'Casey may have been right in their judgment that the play reflected more on the Abbey management than on Shaw. But, from the vantage point of 70 years, perhaps it would be more accurate to say that the rejection of the play actually reflected on neither.

Shaw had a very special feeling for the play which he had written about his native land. In a letter to Siegfried Trebitsch he ranks it as one of his "big three."[6] At the time of the play's composition he writes to Ada Rehan with enthusiasm: "This is the first time I have tried my hand on Ireland; and of course, being an Irishman, I get a quality into the play that is quite unlike anything in any other plays. It is not particularly complimentary to either the Irish or the English; but it is fascinating."[7] In these lines Shaw

4. *Autobiographies*, 134.
5. *Letters*, 442.
6. MS. Berg Collection, New York Public Library.
7. Letters to Ada Rehan, *Collected Letters, 1898–1910*, ed. Dan H. Laurence (London: Max Reinhardt, 1972), p. 458.

refers to the main problem with the play as seen by those who were trying to establish an Irish National Theatre. This same problem was in turn to split the Abbey and cause innumerable internal struggles on the questions of art versus politics. It was the question of nationalism. Shaw's play was not partisan enough to suit the needs of the hour. Like some by Yeats, Shaw's play claims to be political but is not nationalist, and so it was an anomaly in the Ireland of 1904. In a historical sense, its rejection marks the spirit of the time more than the theatrical aims of any particular group. Events in Ireland, which were to culminate in the Easter Rising of 1916, a bloody civil war, and the declaration of the Irish Free State, demanded that a partisan position at least pro-Irish, but also anti-British, be reflected in every aspect of Irish cultural life. The Abbey plays were usually pro-Irish. When they were not, they occasioned riots. But Shaw's play did not satisfy either half of this demand, and so it would not do. Nationalism is a simple creed with simple slogans—"A nation once again" and "Ireland her own"—but Shaw's politics, as dramatized in *John Bull's Other Island*, were more complex.

MARTIN MEISEL

Irish Romance†

John Bull's Other Island is a discussion of the realities of Irish life and character in terms of their theatrical conventions. It belongs to that group of plays, including *Arms and the Man* and *Mrs. Warren's Profession*, which makes direct attacks upon the fundamental romantic elements of a particular dramatic genre, elements which Shaw considered pernicious and illusory. But *John Bull's Other Island* follows the tendency of Shaw's later dramaturgy, and accordingly conventions are invoked chiefly to provide points of reference and to illustrate a discussion. For its wholeness, connection, and rational interest, the play depends upon a dialectically pursued argument on the nature of Irish Reality; for its background materials, and points of departure, it draws upon the conventions of Irish Romance. The discussion of Irish Reality and the disintegration of Irish Romance thus proceed simultaneously.

Shaw's dramatic attack upon the Irish Romance might have been tolerably sketched in advance from his review in 1896 of a re-

† From *Shaw and the Nineteenth Century Theatre*. © 1963 Princeton University Press, 1968 revised ed., 1991 renewed Princeton University Press. Reprinted by permission of Princeton University Press.

vival of Dion Boucicault's germinal play, *The Colleen Bawn* (1860). Under the acid title "Dear Harp of My Country," Shaw told his readers:

> "When I imply . . . that the Irishmen in The Colleen Bawn are not real Irishmen, I do not mean for a moment to challenge the authenticity of [actor] Mr Richard Purdon, who succeeds Dion Boucicault as Myles. Nor do I even accuse him of demonstrating the undeniable fact that the worst stage Irishmen are often real Irishmen. What I mean is that Dion Boucicault, when he invented Myles, was not holding the mirror up to nature, but blarneying the British public precisely as the Irish car-driver, when he is 'cute' enough, blarneys the English tourist. To an Irishman who has any sort of social conscience, the conception of Ireland as a romantic picture, in which the background is formed by the Lakes of Killarney by moonlight, and a round tower or so, whilst every male figure is 'a broth of a bhoy,' and every female one a colleen in a crimson Connemara cloak, is . . . exasperating . . . The occupation of the Irish peasant is mainly agricultural; and I advise the reader to make it a fixed rule never to allow himself to believe in the alleged Arcadian virtues of the half-starved drudges who are sacrificed to the degrading, brutalizing, and, as far as I can ascertain, entirely unnecessary pursuit of unscientific farming. The virtues of the Irish peasant are the intense melancholy, the surliness of manner, the incapacity for happiness and self-respect that are the tokens of his natural unfitness for a life of wretchedness. His vices are the arts by which he accommodates himself to his slavery—the flattery on his lips which hides the curse in his heart; his pleasant readiness to settle disputes by 'leaving it all to your honor,' in order to make something out of your generosity in addition to exacting the utmost of his legal due from you; his instinctive perception that by pleasing you he can make you serve him; his mendacity and mendicity; his love of a stolen advantage; the superstitious fear of his priest and his Church which does not prevent him from trying to cheat both in the temporal transactions between them . . . Of all the tricks which the Irish nation have played on the slow-witted Saxon, the most outrageous is the palming off on him of the imaginary Irishman of romance."[1]

The details of this outline of the Irish stage romance are nearly all put to account in *John Bull's Other Island*. The contrasts are made explicit, as shall be shown below, between the Stage Irishman and the real peasant, with his real virtues and vices; between the "colleen" as she is imagined by the Englishman and the "colleen" as

1. *Our Theatre in the Nineties* (London: Constable, 1954), 28–29.

she is; between Ireland as romantic picture, with moonlight and a genuine round tower in the background, and Ireland as reality. Yet Shaw was not concerned to enlighten the "slow-witted Saxon" alone, for the Englishman was not the only one who had succumbed to the illusion. Shaw wrote *John Bull's Other Island* in 1904 "at the request of Mr William Butler Yeats, as a patriotic contribution to the repertory of the Irish Literary Theatre."[2] His first experience of the atmosphere and appeal of *The Colleen Bawn* had taken place, not in London, but in Dublin.

"The worst of it is," complains Shaw of the imaginary Irishman of romance, "that when a spurious type gets into literature, it strikes the imagination of boys and girls. They form themselves by playing up to it; and thus the unsubstantial fancies of the novelists and music-hall song-writers of one generation are apt to become the unpleasant and mischievous realities of the next."[3] The stage Irishman, who had been a welcome favorite in Dublin long before *The Colleen Bawn*, became an institution after. Irish Romance, which could claim exoticism as an excuse for its appeal in England, was evidently not compromised by the proximity of the reality in Ireland; and, indeed, the romance was even paraded as the genuine reality. When [Edmund] Falconer's *Eileen Oge* (1871) opened in Dublin, it was announced in advertisements as "A Drama illustrative of Irish Character and the Romance of Life in the Land of the Shamrock."[4] The Stage Irishman was so sure to be popular that when Joseph Jefferson brought the Gaiety audience his Rip Van Winkle, by all testimony one of the great character creations of the century, "One of the managers (I think it was Mr. Michael Gunn) seemed to have a presentiment of my failure; for, after witnessing the rehearsal, he asked my agent if he thought I could be prevailed upon to make *Rip Van Winkle* an Irishman. I thought at first that this suggestion was meant as a joke; but upon asking Mr. Gunn if he were serious he assured me that he was, adding that he was quite certain that the audience would understand and appreciate the character more fully if I would give the performance a Hibernian coloring instead of a Dutch one. I told him that if I did this, in order to make an harmonious entertainment it would be necessary to alter the entire play—lay the scene in Ireland, and change the names of all the characters; that poor *Rip* would have to be called *Misther O'Winkle*; and to me these alterations would be very absurd. The manager argued that such violent changes were not nec-

2. In "Preface for Politicians" (see page 47.
3. *Our Theatre in the Nineties*, 29–30.
4. *Dublin Evening Mail*, 29 April 1872.

essary, and he only suggested that I should act the part with just a 'shlight taste of the brogue.' "[5] Michael Gunn no doubt perceived in Rip's whimsical, drunken, good-hearted humours the elements of the Stage Irishman, and a better chance of success. Dublin, Jefferson reports, was one of the very few places in the world where Rip in a Dutch accent flatly failed.

Complementing the Gaiety's partiality to a stage-Irish hero, the Theatre Royal refused to accept a stage-Irish villain if he were not offset, as in Buckstone's *Green Bushes* (1845), by an abundance of Irish virtue. A vigorous disturbance occurred, for example, over Mulhowther, a low-comedy Irish villain in T. W. Robertson's *M.P.* (1870). When the play was presented in Dublin for the first time by "Richard Younge's celebrated London Comedy Company," Younge found it necessary "to come before the curtain and beg of the audience to allow the piece to proceed without interruption, stating that it was an author's right to pourtray any character he pleased, and that Mr. Canninge was merely fulfilling to the best of his ability the part assigned him."[6] Later in the week, it was reported that "the Irish character of 'Mulhowther' . . . has been entirely changed."[7] A low comedy auxiliary villain was a regular feature of Irish Romance, but he was generally made an Ulsterman or Scot.

The term "Stage Irishman," as Shaw used it, meant something other than the Irishman put on the stage. It implied a stereotype, a developed body of conventions forming a vigorous dramatic mask, instantly recognizable and easily distinguished from the limited number of other dramatic masks. Tim Haffigan, Shaw's Stage Irishman, flaunts the type insignia, both visual and verbal. He presents a bullet head, a red nose, *"a show of reckless geniality and high spirits, helped out by a rollicking stage brogue."* His first words are "Tim Haffigan, sir, at your service. The top o the mornin to you, Misther Broadbent." He rattles off, in a single breath, all the other tell-tale phrases: "More power to your elbow! an may your shadda never be less! for youre the broth of a boy intirely." He seems warmhearted, impulsive, and whimsically witty, with a weakness for drink. He acts the stereotype, and Broadbent accepts him as "a thorough Irishman, with all the faults and all the qualities of your race: rash and improvident but brave and good-natured; not likely to succeed in business on your own account perhaps, but eloquent, humorous, a lover of freedom, and a true follower of that great Englishman Gladstone."

5. *The Autobiography of Joseph Jefferson* (New York: Century, 1890), 378.
6. *Dublin Evening Mail*, 29 Aug. 1871.
7. *Dublin Evening Mail*, 1 Sept. 1871.

Broadbent is incredulous when his partner tells him that Haffigan was born in Glasgow, and was never in Ireland in his life.

> BROADBENT. But he spoke—he behaved just like an Irishman.
> DOYLE. Like an Irishman!! Man alive, dont you know that all this top-o-the-morning and broth-of-a-boy and more-power-to-your-elbow business is got up in England to fool you, like the Albert Hall concerts of Irish music? No Irishman ever talks like that in Ireland, or ever did, or ever will. But when a thoroughly worthless Irishman comes to England . . . he soons learns the antics that take you in. He picks them up at the theatre or the music hall. Haffigan learnt the rudiments from his father, who came from my part of Ireland.

Irish character parts were not unusual on the stage before the nineteenth century, from Shakespeare's slave of passion, Captain Macmorris, to Sheridan's whimsical gentleman, Sir Lucius O'Trigger; but only in the nineteenth century did the Stage Irishman develop the importance and consistent individuality to become more than a specialty by which certain actors (like "Irish" [John] Johnstone) were best known. John Brougham and Tyrone Power and, in the golden age of Irish drama, Dion Boucicault and Edmund Falconer wrote plays for themselves that raised the Stage Irishman to "leading business." Only in the nineteenth century did a distinct genre develop with a Stage Irish lead and a setting that was Ireland itself.

* * *

Shaw is not content just to present a counterfeit Stage Irishman in *John Bull's Other Island*; he also presents a gallery of true Irish types, set in deliberate contrast with the romantic stereotypes. Shaw's true Irish peasant is no attractive, ebullient Conn the Shaughraun, all play and no work; he is Matthew Haffigan, Tim Haffigan's genuine Irish uncle, ugly, morose, and brutalized, with "*a surliness that is meant to be aggressive, and is in effect pathetic.*" When Broadbent expresses surprise at the possibility of an industrious Irishman, Doyle replies, "Industrious! That man's industry used to make me sick, even as a boy. I tell you, an Irish peasant's industry is not human: it's worse than the industry of a coral insect. An Englishman has some sense about working: he never does more than he can help . . . but an Irishman will work as if he'd die the moment he stopped." After making a farm out of "a patch of stones on the hillside," and losing it when the landlord put a rent upon it to fit its new value, Haffigan has finally become a small peasant proprietor in his own right, tenacious, greedy, inefficient, and worked out. "The real tragedy of Haffigan," cries Larry Doyle "is the tragedy of his wasted youth, his stunted mind, his drudging

over his clods and pigs until he has become a clod and a pig himself—until the soul within him has smouldered into nothing but a
dull temper that hurts himself and all around him. I say let him die,
and let us have no more of his like."

If Matthew Haffigan embodies most of the "virtues" of the real
Irish peasant as Shaw had sketched them in his review of *The
Colleen Bawn*, most of the "vices" are embodied in Patsy Farrell,
the worthless and seemingly witless young man whom Haffigan is
anxious to exploit and keep down. Patsy is described as having *"an
instinctively acquired air of helplessness and silliness, indicating, not
his real character, but a cunning developed by his constant dread of a
hostile dominance . . . Englishmen think him half-witted, which is
exactly what he intends them to think."* Barney Doran, a third member of Shaw's gallery, presents Shaw's view of the high spirits and
abundant humor which, in the Shaughraun, shows in Conn's enjoyment of the grief at his own wake. Barney Doran leads the mirth
over the catastrophe which ensued when Broadbent took Haffigan's
pig for a drive. Doran is described as stout bodied, middle-aged,
*"with an enormous capacity for derisive, obscene, blasphemous, or
merely cruel and senseless fun, and a violent and impetuous intolerance of other temperaments and other opinions, all this representing
energy and capacity wasted and demoralized by want of sufficient
training and social pressure to force it into beneficent activity and
build a character with it."*

Shaw has literally analyzed the Stage Irishman by splitting him
into his various aspects: peasants, ingratiating incompetent, and
humorist. In addition to this analysis, Shaw brings other elements
of the conventional Irish Romance into his discussion: the colleen
and the "Irish heiress"; the Irish priest; and the romantic appeal of
the Irish scene for Englishmen.

* * *

DECLAN KIBERD

John Bull's Other Islander—Bernard Shaw†

* * *

Like [Oscar] Wilde, Shaw was another Irishman who used England as a laboratory in which he could redefine what it meant to

† Reprinted by permission of the publisher from *Inventing Ireland: The Literature of the
Modern Nation* by Declan Kiberd, Cambridge, Mass.: Harvard University Press. Copy-
right © 1995 by Declan Kiberd. Published by Jonthan Cape. Reprinted by permission of
The Random House Group Ltd. and by Harvard University Press.

be Irish. In *John Bull's Other Island,* the defrocked priest Peter Keegan finds wonders in Oxford that he had never seen at home, but
on his return to Ireland he discovers that the wonders had been
there all the time. "I did not know what my own house was like", he
concludes, "because I had never been outside it".[1] In similar fashion, the mock-villain Broadbent only discovers what it means to be
an Englishman when he pays a visit to Ireland. "Ireland", declared
Shaw, "is the only spot on earth which still produces the ideal Englishman of history".[2] *John Bull's Other Island* is Shaw's attempt to
show how the peoples of the two islands spend most of their time
acting an approved part before their neighbours' eyes: and these assigned parts are seen as impositions by the other side rather than
opportunities for true self-expression. In the play, stereotypes are
exploded, for it is the Englishman Tom Broadbent who is a romantic duffer, while the Irishman Larry Doyle is a cynical realist. The
underlying reasoning is sound, for the Irish have become fact-
facers through harsh poverty, while the English have enjoyed a
scale of wealth so great that it allows them to indulge their victims
with expansively sentimental gestures.

On the one hand, Broadbent cynically plots the ruin of the village of Roscullen and packs a gun before his visit to the place; on
the other, he fills his head with sentimental claptrap about the
charms of rural Ireland. As his caustic Irish partner observes, he
keeps these separate ideas in watertight compartments, each "warranted impervious to anything it doesn't suit you to understand".[3]
The very ambivalence of Broadbent's gestures evokes the common
English oscillation between coercion and conciliation, between
contempt for and envy of all that the imperialist denies in himself.
A similar ambiguity will mark the gestures of the Englishman
Haines in the opening chapter of Joyce's *Ulysses;* he, also, will take
refuge from bad dreams behind an imported gun, yet he also will
have come over to Ireland to savour the wit and wordplay of the
Celtic revival at first hand. So, too, in the opening act of Shaw's
play, Broadbent is charmed by the antics of Tim Haffigan, a stage
Irishman who wishes him the top-o-the-mornin', until Doyle ex-
poses him as a fraud and an impostor, born not in Ireland but in
the streets of Glasgow. Doyle insists that the stage Irishman is a
creation of the British folk mind: "all Haffigan has to do is to sit
there and drink your whiskey while you humbug yourself", he
warns Broadbent, but to no avail, for his English partner attributes

1. G. B. Shaw, *John Bull's Other Island,* in *The Field Day Anthology of Irish Writing,* Vol. 2 (Derry: Field Day, 1991), 438.
2. *The Matter with Ireland,* ed. David H. Greene and Dan H. Laurence (London: Rupert Hart-Davis, 1962), 33.
3. Shaw, *John Bull's Other Island,* 432.

this anger to "the melancholy of the Celtic race".[4] Doyle remarks that sweeping generalizations about the Celtic race constitute the most insidiously aggressive of all the tactics used by Englishmen— because they imply that the English are invariably the surveyors and the Irish the surveyed (with the depressing inference that the Irish can neither analyze nor represent themselves). Such talk does more harm than ten coercion acts.

Froude's[5] theory that Celts would thrive only under the benign guidance of Saxons, is voiced confidently by Broadbent, despite his pretensions to liberalism: "I saw at once that you are a thorough Irishman, with all the faults and all the qualities of your race: rash and improvident but brave and good natured: not likely to succeed in business on your own account perhaps, but eloquent, humorous, a lover of freedom . . ."[6] The fact that the reverse might actually be true—that the Englishman needs the Irish to help him determine his own identity, just as Broadbent relied heavily on Doyle for their joint business success—would not have struck many in Shaw's London audience. Yet the play is at pains to stress that all nationalisms rely for their construction on outsiders and others.

If the very notion of a centrally administered, united Ireland is an English invention, then many of the features of English nationalism are patented by German Jews, according to the anti-semitic Broadbent: "If my name was Breitstein, and I had a hooked nose and a house in Park Lane, I should carry a Union Jack handkerchief".[7] He goes on to refer to a nationalist English song as one written "by a German jew, like most English patriotic sentiment". The Germans thereby help to create the fiction, the "imagined community", that is England; and the English help to invent the idea of Ireland and, in return, are assisted by those Irish in sharpening the definition of themselves. This, indeed, is one of the services to his London audience offered by Shaw in the play.

As an empirical, fact-facing Irishman, Larry Doyle felt uneasy in his own country: his youthful desire was to learn how to do something and then to get out of Ireland in order to have the chance to do it. The plot itself seems to suggest that an Irishman will succeed far better in England than in Ireland, where the only successful men are all English. In Ireland, Broadbent plays the role of a lover of the Celts, the English liberal in search of round towers and fresh-faced colleens. So, by his outrageous antics in the role of English duffer, he manages to see only the Ireland he has come to see, a land of buffoons, derisive laughter and whimsy, where a pig

4. Ibid., 429.
5. James Anthony Froude (1818–94), English historian [*Editor*].
6. Shaw, *John Bull's Other Island*, 427.
7. Ibid., 426.

can be taken for a ride in his car and an Englishman (i.e., himself) voted the fittest man to represent Roscullen in parliament. He adopts the protective coloration of the stage-English buffoon to the enormous entertainment of the natives, who reciprocate by adopting the protective coloration of the stage-Irish peasant, taking tea at the wrong time of the day and laughing hysterically at every event which ensues. Larry Doyle foresees that, for his antics, Broadbent will not be mocked out of town but will be rewarded with Larry's sweetheart and Larry's seat in Westminster: "He'll never know they're laughing at him—and while they're laughing, he'll win the seat".[8]

The driver who ferried Broadbent into Roscullen told him that the finest hotel in Ireland was there, but there is no hotel, just seventeen pubs. Aunt Jude excuses the driver: "Sure he'd say whatever was the least trouble to himself and the pleasantest to you".[9] This is the psychology which underlies the acting of both sides, Irish and English. For the Irish, the callow labourer Patsy Farrell exudes an air of helpless silliness which, says a Shavian stage direction, "is not his real character, but a cunning developed by his constant dread of a hostile dominance, which he habitually tries to disarm by pretending to be a much greater fool than he really is. Englishmen think him half-witted, which is exactly what he wants them to think".[1] This, however, is precisely the strategy adopted by the conquering Englishman, who, according to Larry Doyle, "does what the caterpillar does. He instinctively makes himself look like a fool, and eats up all the real fools at his ease while his enemies let him alone and laugh at him for being a fool like the rest. Oh, nature is cunning, cunning".[2]

In other words, at root the English and Irish are rather similar peoples, who have nonetheless decided to perform versions of Englishness and Irishness to one another, in the attempt to wrest a material advantage from the unsuspecting audience of each performance. Each group projects onto the other many attributes which it has denied in itself, but at bottom both peoples are alike. This socialist perception is embodied in Hodson, the servant of Broadbent, who does indeed find in Ireland the flexibility of mind to disown his master and to point to the common cause of the dispossessed Irish labourer and the exploited English proletariat. He is, moreover, as impatient of Irish whining as of English repression, pointing to the fact that the bulk of the English work-force was exploited at even closer hand than the Irish peasantry by the imperial

8. Ibid., 459.
9. Ibid., 440.
1. Ibid., 436.
2. Ibid., 433.

system. In all of this, he speaks for the Shaw who wrote: "The people of England have done the people of Ireland no wrong whatever . . . in factory, mine and sweatshop they had reason to envy the Irish peasant who at the worst starved on an open hillside . . . the most distressful country . . . has borne no more than her fair share of the growing pains of human society . . ."[3]

Shaw's play, like Wilde's career, is a radical critique of the Anglo-Irish antithesis so beloved of the Victorians and of many Irish revivalists. By the simple expedient of presenting a romantic Englishman and an empirical Irishman *John Bull's Other Island* mocks the ancient stereotype. Of course, that is not the end of the story, for, by his performance of absurd sentimentality, Broadbent effectively takes over the entire village on the terms most favourable to himself, while Larry Doyle loses his cynical self-composure in the face of the ruin of his people. Larry's sophisticated intellect paralyses him into inactivity, for he has grown too subtle and too cynical, foolish in his very cleverness, whereas Broadbent's blinkered vision is what allows him to be so efficient, so finally clever in his very foolishness. In the end, the Anglo-Irish antithesis has been questioned only to be reasserted in a slightly modified form.[4]

3. Shaw, *Matter*, 16.
4. On this, see Alfred J. Turco, Jr., *Shaw's Moral Vision: The Self and Salvation* (Ithaca: Cornell UP, 1976), 178ff.

On Sean O'Casey

JOSEPH HOLLOWAY

[Journal 1923–24]†

* * *

Monday, September 10. . . . I went on to the Abbey and was just in time to see the curtains rise on *Cathleen ni Houlihan* . . . Sara All-good was impressive in the title role. Sean O'Casey was behind me, and I joined him after Yeats's play and had a chat with him between whiles. He told me he had been raided several times lately. Last week he was awakened out of his sleep with hands pulling the sheet off him, and a light full in his eyes, and three revolvers pointed out. He was hauled out of bed and roughly handled, as they queried his name, etc. He knew of a young fellow, a member of the I.R.A., who was on the run, being taken in the middle of the night by the C.I.D. men and brought out towards Finglas and bru-tally beaten with the butt end of their revolvers, and then told to run for his life while they fired revolver shots after him, taking bits off his ears, etc., and catching up on him again renewed their beat-ing. Next day O'Casey saw the chap and could hardly recognise him, so battered and bruised was he. Such brutality demoralises a country. Flogging demoralises, but does not correct. . . .

* * *

Monday, March 3. "It is powerful and gripping and all that, but too damned gruesome; it gets you, but it is not pleasant," is the way Dan Maher summed up *Juno and the Paycock,* O'Casey's new play at the Abbey. . . . The last act is intensely tragic and heart-rendingly real to those who passed through the terrible period of 1922. . . . The tremendous tragedy of Act III swept all before it, and made the do-ings on the stage real and thrilling in their intensity. The acting all

† From *Joseph Holloway's Abbey Theatre: A Selection From His Unpublished Journal "Im-pressions of a Dublin Playgoer,"* ed. Robert Hogan and Michael J. O'Neill. Copyright © 1967 by Southern Illinois University Press. Reprinted by permission of Southern Illinois University Press.

round was of the highest quality, not one in the long cast being misplaced or for a moment out of the picture. [Barry] Fitzgerald and
[F. J.] McCormick as "Captain Jack Boyle" and his bar-room pal "Joxer
Daly," an old Forester, make a splendid pair of workers who never
work. Sara Allgood as "Juno Boyle," with all the worries of trying to
keep everything together was excellent, and in Act III she had great
moments of heart-rending sorrow. Arthur Shields as the haunted,
maimed boy "Johnny," got the right note of dread into his study from
the very first, and Eileen Crowe as "Mary" presented every side of the
character cleverly and realistically, and her singing of the duet, "Home
to our Mountains," with her mother at the hooley was deliciously
droll. Maureen Delaney, as the talkative "Mrs. Maisie Madigan"
was most amusing, and Christine Hayden, as the sorrowing mother
"Mrs. Tancred" sorrowed for her son most touchingly. . . .

In Act III some in the pit were inclined at first to laugh at the
tragedy that had entered into the "Boyle" family, but they soon lost
their mirth and were gripped by the awful actuality of the incidents
enacted so realistically and unassumingly before them. As I left the
theatre, cries of "Author, Author!" were filling the air, and I suppose
O'Casey had to bow his acknowledgment. He sat with a friend in
the second row of the stalls with his cap on all the while, I noticed.
He is a strange, odd fish, but a genius in his way.

* * *

Tuesday, March 18. . . . I had a chat with Sean O'Casey in the
vestibule. He told me that when he started to write plays he
thought he was a second Shaw sent to express his views through his
characters, and was conceited enough to think that his opinions
were the only ones that mattered. It was Lady Gregory who advised
him to cut out all expression of self, and develop his peculiar apt-
ness for character drawing. At first he didn't take kindly to her advice, but afterwards on consideration felt she was right.

He was so poor when he took to writing first that he hadn't the
money to supply himself with paper to write his stuff on, and a pal
supplied him with paper filched from his employer's store. His first
two plays were written in his cramped handwriting, and yet the
Abbey directors read his script and expressed sorrow at having to
reject both plays, and gave him sound critical advice which he resented at first, but on second thought accepted, and was determined to profit by and did. He was determined to succeed. . . .

He has a small typewriter now. He intends to stick to playwriting;
he thinks Robinson has too many irons in the fire to do himself justice. O'Casey reads [Lennox] Robinson's *Observer* article each
week, but doesn't think very much of it. He should concentrate
more; only those do who reach the very top. This is the age of the
specialist.

Friday, March 21. . . . I had a chat with lame Maguire.[1] . . . Speaking of Sean O'Casey, he remembered him as being one of the first to join the Piper's Band and wear the kilt, and an ungainly figure he cut in it. He was more like a country lad than a Dubliner. He always walked with a near-sighted bend of the head. He was always strong and energetic, and when he played hurling he looked a guy in short knickers, and once in a match in the park—so it is said—he killed a sparrow, thinking he was swiping at the ball. He agreed with nobody and believed in nothing. He was strangely distant and silent always. He wrote for *The Irish Worker* and was secretary to the Citizen Army. The book he wrote about the Citizen Army wasn't thought much of by those connected with it.[2] He was a shunter on the Northern Railway in those days. He was always sore-eyed and took an active part in the Gaelic movement. He was very energetic in all he undertook. Now he has struck oil as a playwright, he is determined to work hard to reach the top in that branch of literature. His friend out of Webb's joined us in the latter part of our conversation about O'Casey. It was he told the sparrow incident.

Friday, March 28. A bitterly sharp evening with an icy cutting wind about. I had a long chat with O'Casey in the vestibule of the Abbey. He thinks the Government is proving a set of woeful incompetents—egotistical and intolerant of criticism. They are going from bad to worse. They'll be nobody's friend shortly. He spoke of the hypocrisy over the shooting of the soldier at Cork. "The honour of Ireland is at stake over it, people say who don't know what honour is!"

He witnessed terrible deeds during recent years; a friend of his was riddled with bullets and mutilated in a horrible way by the Green and Tans, a young Tipperary lad. Nothing could be more brutal than the treatment he got. It is hard to think Irish people capable of such savagery. Savages would be decent in comparison to them. After the inquest his remains were brought to his digs, and O'Casey helped to carry in the coffin to his friend's upstairs. Another lad he knew was taken out and tied up by his hands—his feet dangling some distance from the ground, while they poured salts through a tin dish down his throat. The poor fellow was cut down alive, but he is a human wreck ever since—always shaking, though as brave as ever.

* * *

Thursday, August 14. . . . I witnessed a strange incident last night in seeing W. B. Yeats and Mrs. Yeats being crowded out of the Abbey,

---

1. Maguire was the proprietor of a book barrow on the quays.
2. *The Story of the Irish Citizen Army* (1919), by "P. O'Cathasaigh," faulted the organization for stressing nationalism more than labor reform [*Editor*].

and having to seek the pictures to allay their disappointment. O'Casey's play, *The Shadow of a Gunman*, had been staged for three nights with the usual result—that crowds had to be turned away each performance. This and his other play, *Juno and the Paycock*, have wonderful drawing power. The same people want to see them over and over again. . . . And the author stood chatting to me in the vestibule the other night as the audience came thronging in, proud of the fact, but in no way swell-headed, his cloth cap cocked over his left eye, as his right looked short-sightedly at the audience's eager rush. Certainly he has written the two most popular plays ever seen at the Abbey, and they both are backgrounded by the terrible times we have just passed through, but his characters are so true to life and humourous that all swallow the bitter pill of fact that underlies both pieces. The acting in both reaches the highest watermark of Abbey acting. It looks as if the Abbey is coming into its own at long last, and it's about time. In December next it will reach its twentieth year of existence. [Padraic] Colum was present in the front row of the stalls last night, and he became so excited during the events in the second act that he kept unconsciously jumping up and down in his seat, and even at times went over to the stage front and placed his elbows on the stage ledge as he gazed intently at what was talking place thereon.

* * *

LADY GREGORY

[Journal 1923–24]†

* * *

12 APRIL 1923 At the Abbey I found an armed guard; there has been one ever since the theatres were threatened if they kept open.[1] And in the green room I found one of them giving finishing touches to the costume of Tony Quinn, who is a Black and Tan in the play, and showing him how to hold his revolver. *The Shadow of a Gunman* was an immense success, beautifully acted, all the political points taken up with delight by a big audience. Sean O'Casey the author only saw it from the side wings the first night but had to appear to make his bow. I brought him into the stalls the other two nights and have had some talk with him. Last night there was an

---

† From *Lady Gregory's Journals: Volume 1*, Coole Edition (New York: Oxford University Press; Bucks: Colin Smythe Ltd, 1978).
1. That is, during the Irish Civil War threatened by Republicans if they opened, thus suggesting a state of normalcy, and by Free Staters if they did not open [*Editor*].

immense audience the largest I think since the first night of
[Shaw's] *Blanco Posnet*. Many, to my grief, had to be turned away
from the door. Two seats had been kept for Yeats and me, but I put
Casey in one of them and sat in the orchestra for the first act, and
put Yeats in the orchestra for the second. I had brought Casey
round to the door before the play to share my joy in seeing the
crowd surging in (Dermod O'Brien caught in the queue) and he introduced me to two officers, one a Colonel. (Yeats has wanted me
to go with them to a *ball* given by the army, "good names being
wanted"!)

Casey told me he is a labourer, and as we talked of masons said
he had "carried the hod". He said "I was among books as a child,
but I was sixteen before I learned to read or write. My father loved
books, he had a big library, I remember the look of the books high
up on shelves." I asked why his father had not taught him and he
said "He died when I was three years old, through those same
books. There was a little ladder in the room to get to the shelves,
and one day when he was standing on it, it broke and he fell and
was killed." I said "I often go up the ladder in our library at home"
and he begged me to be careful. He is learning what he can about
Art, has bought books on Whistler and Raphael, and takes *The Studio*. All this was as we watched the crowd. I forget how I came to
mention the Bible, and he asked "Do you like it"? I said "Yes, I read
it constantly, even for the beauty of the language". He said he ad-
mires that beauty, he was brought up as a Protestant but has lost
belief in religious forms. Then, in talking of our war here, we came
to Plato's *Republic*, his dream-city, whether on earth or in heaven
not far away from the city of God. And then we went in to the play.
He says he sent us a play four years ago *Frost and Flowers* and it
was returned, but marked "Not far from being a good play". He has
sent others, and says how grateful he was to me because when we
had to refuse the Labour one "The Crimson in the Tri-Colour" I
had said "I believe there is something in you" and "your strong
point is characterisation". And I had wanted to pull that play together and put it on to give him experience, but Yeats was down on
it. Perrin says he has offered him a pass sometimes when he happened to come in, but he refused and said "No one ought to come
into the Abbey Theatre without paying for it". He said "All the
thought in Ireland for years past has come through the Abbey. You
have no idea what an education it has been to the country". That,
and the fine audience on this our last week, put me in great spirits.

* * *

8 MARCH 1924 In the evening to the Abbey with W.B.Y. *Juno and
the Paycock* a long queue at the door, the theatre crowded, many
turned away, so it will be run on next week. A wonderful and terri-

ble play of futility, of irony, humour, tragedy. When I went round to the green room I saw O'Casey and had a little talk with him. He is very happy. I asked him to come to tea after the next day matinée as I had brought up a barmbrack for the players, but he said "No I can't come, I'll be at work till the afternoon, and I'm working with cement, and that takes such a long time to get off". "But after that?" "Then I have to cook my dinner. I have but one room and I cook for myself since my mother died." He is of course happy at the great success of the play and I said "You must feel now that we were right in not putting on that first one you sent in *The Crimson in the Tricolour*. I was inclined to put it on because some of it was so good and I thought you might learn by seeing it on the stage, though some was very poor, but Mr. Yeats was firm". He said "You were right not to put it on. I can't read it myself now. But I will tell you that was a bitter disappointment for I not only thought at the time it was the best thing I had written, but I thought that no one in the world had ever written anything so fine". Then he said "You had it typed for me, and I don't know how you could have read it as I sent it in with the bad writing and the poor paper. But at that time it was hard for me to afford even the paper it was written on". And he said "I owe a great deal to you and Mr. Yeats and Mr. Robinson, but to you above all. You gave me encouragement. And it was you who said to me upstairs in the office—I could show you the very spot where you stood—'Mr. O'Casey, your gift is characterisation'. And so I threw over my theories and worked at characters, and this is the result."

Yeats hadn't seen the play before, and thought it very fine, re-minding him of Tolstoi. He said when he talked of that imperfect first play "Casey was bad in writing of the vices of the rich which he knows nothing about, but he thoroughly understands the vices of the poor". But that full house, the packed pit and gallery, the fine play, the call of the mother for the putting away of hatred—"give us Thine own eternal love!" made me say to Yeats "This is one of the evenings at the Abbey that makes me glad to have been born".

* * *

GABRIEL FALLON

[*Juno and the Paycock*]†

* * *

I didn't see much of Sean O'Casey during the rehearsals of *Juno and the Paycock*. The Abbey's work of weekly repertory went on and I was kept fairly busy. In the week preceding the dress rehearsal of *Juno* Lady Gregory came to town. If she attended rehearsals I didn't see her. My part of Bentham was almost wholly rehearsed at the 1 o'clock luncheon break; the old difficulty of getting the professionals and the 'part-timers' together saw to that. I have no doubt that the Old Lady, as we called her, spent some time in the company of her beloved actress, 'Sally' Allgood, but whatever views she may have expressed about the play I had no means of finding out. Not, indeed, that I was particularly interested. The play would go on and that was that.

The dress-rehearsal was planned for Sunday March 2nd at 11.30 a.m. That would give everyone ample time for Mass, or Church, or a long sleep. But there was a difficulty. For some time past an Abbey party had been planned to take place on the night of Saturday March 1st, after the final curtain. Now an Abbey party was a party that *was* a party; at least it was so in those far-off days and nothing was ever allowed to stand in the way of it, neither civil wars nor fights for freedom. Abbey parties had been held under armed guards of various political persuasions and as often as not the guards themselves added much to the revelry. Sometimes directors were present; sometimes not; but whatever the company one thing was certain and that, to use the popular phrase, was that a good time was had by all. But what was to be done on this occasion? Obviously, no one could be expected to dress-rehearse at such an unearthly hour as 11.30 a.m. after a party the night before. Indeed, it was as much as some of us could do to put in a sleepy attendance at the 6 a.m. Mass in the Pro-Cathedral down the street. Sean O'Casey or no Sean O'Casey this dress-rehearsal would have to be postponed, that was all about it. Someone approached the directors, and the directors agreed to postponement. The dress-rehearsal of *Juno and the Paycock* would be held at 5 p.m. on the Sunday.

I arrived at the theatre at 4.30 p.m. and found the author there before me looking rather glum and wondering if a rehearsal would

---

† From *The Life of Sean O'Casey*. Reprinted by permission of Taylor & Francis.

take place since so far as he could find out there was no one else in the theatre. I assured him that everything would be all right even though I privately thought otherwise. Sara Allgood, who had spent the night feasting us with song and story, had left the theatre in or around 3 a.m. a very tired woman. I tried to persuade Sean that dress-rehearsals were always like this but he was only half convinced. Although I did not know it at the time he was suffering much pain with his eyes and was attending the Royal Eye and Ear Hospital where he was a patient of the Senior Surgeon, the sensitive and perceptive Mr. Joe Cummins, who took a particular interest in the dramatist and in the theatre.

Gradually the players filed in and quietly went to their dressing-rooms. Lennox Robinson arrived shortly before 5 o'clock and was followed by Yeats and Lady Gregory. Under the direction of Seaghan Barlow the stage staff were putting finishing touches to the setting. Yeats, Lady Gregory and Robinson took seats in the stalls. The author sat a few seats away from them. The curtain rose about 5.36 p.m. So far as I could see and hear while waiting for my cue in the wings the rehearsal seemed to be proceeding smoothly. As soon as I had finished my part of Bentham at the end of the second act I went down into the stalls and sat two seats behind the author. Here for the first time I had an opportunity of seeing something of the play from an objective point of view. I was stunned by the tragic quality of the third act which the magnificent playing of Sara Allgood made almost unbearable. But it was the blistering irony of the final scene which convinced me that this man sitting two seats in front of me was a dramatist of genius, one destined to be spoken of far beyond the confines of the Abbey Theatre.

The third act had been dominated by Allgood's tragic quality even though Barry Fitzgerald and F. J. McCormick were uproariously funny as Captain Boyle and Joxer. This was always so with Allgood in the part of Juno. She had the quality of pinning down preceding laughter to freezing point. When Juno returns from the doctor with Mary the author's simple directions are: 'Mrs. Boyle enters: it is apparent from the serious look on her face that something has happened. She takes off her hat and coat without a word and puts them by. She then sits down near the fire, and there is a few moments pause.' That is all. Yet Sara Allgood's entrance in this scene will never be forgotten by those who saw it. Not a word was spoken: she did not even sigh: her movements were few and simply confined to the author's directions. She seemed to have shrunken from the Juno we saw in Acts 1 and 2 as if reduced by the catalytic effect of her inner consciousness.

We watched the act move on, the furniture removers come and

go, the ominous entry of the I.R.A. men, the dragging of Johnny to summary execution, the stilted scene between Jerry Devine and Mary Boyle, and then as with the ensnaring slow impetus of a ninth great wave Allgood's tragic genius rose to an unforgettable climax and drowned the stage in sorrow. Here surely was the very butt and sea-mark of tragedy! But suddenly the curtain rises again: are Fitzgerald and McCormick fooling, letting off steam after the strain of rehearsal? Nothing of the kind; for we in the stalls are suddenly made to freeze in our seats as a note beyond tragedy, a blistering flannel-mouthed irony sears its maudlin way across the stage and slowly drops an exhausted curtain on a world disintegrating in 'chassis'.

I sat there stunned. So, indeed, so far as I could see, did Robinson, Yeats and Lady Gregory. Then Yeats ventured an opinion. He said that the play, particularly in its final scene, reminded him of a Dostoievsky novel. Lady Gregory turned to him and said: 'You know, Willie, you never read a novel by Dostoievsky.' And she promised to amend this deficiency by sending him a copy of *The Idiot*. I turned to O'Casey and found I could only say to him: 'Magnificent, Sean, magnificent.' Then we all quietly went home.

* * *

* * * What shocked me about the author was that he was by no means as certain as I was about the validity of [the final] scene. Indeed, he left me with the impression that he was by no means as knowledgeable about his play as I was for he seemed to be quietly surprised when I drew attention to what I considered to be this excellence or that. I was to learn in time, of course, that an artist is seldom conscious of the effect of what he has created. I recalled O'Casey's insistence that he was writing a play about a young man called Johnny Boyle. Yet Johnny was only one character amongst other and greater characters. We were seeing much more of each other than formerly and on each occasion *Juno* and the craft of the playwright provided the main talking-point. The critics, public and private, with the exception of [W. V.] Lawrence had used as a whip the mixture of tragedy with comedy. There was some talk of Aristotle and I took my first glance into the *Poetics*. While I was not prepared to agree with O'Casey that 'Aristotle was all balls', I conceded that the Greeks were great in their own time and fashion but that there were great playwrights since that time who had thrown Aristotle's *Poetics* (or rather the misconception derived from them by Italian and French theorists) to the winds. Shakespeare had mixed tragedy and comedy and what had been good enough for Shakespeare ought to be good enough for a 'neo-Elizabethan'.

During one of our conversations he told me that when he submitted *Juno and the Paycock* to the Abbey it had an additional scene which the directors cut. He gave me the impression that he was rather aggrieved at this. I asked him what the scene was and he told me it was the shooting of Johnny Boyle which took place in darkness in a roadside setting. I tried to assure him that the directors were perfectly right and that the shooting of Johnny Boyle was in the imagination of the audience infinitely more terrible in those lines where the Second Irregular asks him: 'Have you your beads?' and Johnny replies, 'Me beads! Why do you ass me that, why do you ass me that?' At this point the audience knows only too well what is going to happen, and hardly needs Johnny's agonised 'Mother o' God, pray for me—be with me now in the agonies o' death . . .' to convince them that judicial murder is afoot. After this an actual shooting scene would be truly anti-climax. After some argument on my part he seemed satisfied. Again it was borne in on me that the artist is not always the best judge of his work.

It was obvious that one of the effects of these conversations was to blunt the remarks of the critics. I still maintained that what made this play something greater than great was its final scene and I repeatedly told him so. The fact was that I couldn't get this play and its author out of my mind. The play itself had stirred up all kinds of problems for me. I suppose in a sense it heralded the birth of a drama critic. I was conscious of the play's faults, the poverty of Bentham as a character, the mawkish artificiality of the scenes between Jerry Devine and Mary Boyle. Yet these faults, and I could find no others, were far outweighed by the play's greatness. One of the critics said that O'Casey knew nothing about the art of construction. On this point what struck me about *Juno* was that its characters came and went without let or hindrance. 'Construction' as it was seen in the work of Abbey dramatists had hitherto consisted of situations in which A, B and C are on stage and the dramatist invents some plausible or (as in most cases) implausible reason to get rid of B in order that A and C may discuss something not intended for B's hearing. If this was 'construction' they could keep it so far as I was concerned, for I reasoned that when one could see a man's framework sticking out there was something wrong with the man. There is nothing particularly attractive about a skeleton and no one wants to see the bones of a play.

I believed I saw the reason why Sean O'Casey was not fully conscious of the value of what he had achieved. This work of his was not art for Art's sake, a phrase very much in fashion in the literary Dublin of those days. It was something much more akin to what Paul Claudel had in mind when he wrote to Jacques Riviere in 1912: 'Do you believe for a moment that Shakespeare or Dostoievsky or Reubens or Titian or Wagner did their work for art's sake? No! They did it to free themselves of a great incubus of living matter, *opus non factum*. And certainly not to colour a cold artificial design by borrowings from reality.' *Juno and the Paycock*, I reflected, was an outstanding example of a play which simply had to be written, which, so to speak, erupted from its author, a fact which gave it that 'red-hot contemporaneity' which Lawrence praised. It pulsed with what Henry James had in mind when he demanded 'felt life' from the writer. No doubt Sean O'Casey sat down consciously to write a play about a tragic young man called Johnny Boyle, but underneath other forces were at work and the total result emerged in a blistering indictment of the stupidity of men and (as I thought then on that March evening in 1924 and think so still) in one of the great tragic masterpieces of our time.

This man Sean O'Casey was attracted towards me (I didn't know why) but from that dress-rehearsal of *Juno and the Paycock* I was forcibly attracted towards him. Like him I was a Dubliner who loved my native city. He had lived most of his years in grinding poverty and I had lived mine on the fringe of it. In *Juno and the Paycock* I had found an overwhelming sense of pity which I myself had sometimes felt but was unable to express. I had also, I believed, found a very great dramatist, one who was destined, I said to him, to write very many great plays. I looked back on my theatre-going experience but could recall nothing which equalled this. The highest peak point in the graph of Abbey Theatre dramaturgy was undoubtedly John Millington Synge's *The Playboy of the Western World. Juno and the Paycock*, I believed, was as high if not higher.

CHRISTOPHER MURRAY

[*Juno and the Paycock*]†

* * *

To prove himself to the Abbey audience which had scorned his *Kathleen* O'Casey began work on *Juno and the Paycock*. He had been pondering the material, for he told Holloway on 10 September [1923] about recent raids by rogue elements in the Free State army with scores to settle. 'Last week he was awakened out of his sleep with hands pulling the sheet off him, and a light full in his eyes, and three revolvers pointed out. He was hauled out of bed and roughly handled, as they queried his name, etc.' They were after a young man who had shot one of their own. O'Casey was to describe his fate in the autobiographies as the Free State forces exacted swift revenge:

† From *Sean O'Casey: Writer at Work—A Biography*. Reprinted by permission of McGill-Queen's University Press.

—Jesus! whimpered the half-dead lad, yous wouldn't shoot an
old comrade, Mick!
The Colonel's arm holding the gun shot forward suddenly, the
muzzle of the gun, tilted slightly upwards, splitting the lad's
lips and crashing through his shattering teeth.
—Be Jasus! We would, he said, and then he pulled the trigger.[1]

In his conversation with Holloway O'Casey described something
more in the style of a 'punishment beating' which left the young
man barely recognisable next day. What leaps out of this account is
the detail of the young IRA man 'being taken in the middle of the
night [. . .] and brought out towards Finglas'. Here was the germ
of *Juno and the Paycock*, which opens with Mary Boyle reading
from a newspaper about Robbie Tancred's end: 'On a little bye-
road, out beyant Finglas, he was found.' As O'Casey commented to
Holloway, 'Such brutality demoralises a country.'[2] It was out of that
sense of moral outrage that the action of *Juno* was conceived.
     The idea of the Boyle legacy and all its melodramatic possibili-
ties, although stemming from a real case O'Casey knew of in 1921,
was grafted on later. As Fallon recalled: 'He had been telling me for
some time about a play he had mapped out, a play which would
deal with the tragedy of a crippled I.R.A. man, one Johnny Boyle.
He mentioned this play many times and always it was the tragedy of
Johnny. I cannot recall that he once spoke about Juno or Joxer or
the Captain; always Johnny.[3] Indeed, as he wrote the play O'Casey
included an off-stage scene in act 3 depicting Johnny's assassination which was cut in rehearsal. It is unlikely that he was 'aggrieved' at this, as Fallon claimed, since he never included the
scene in the published text:

> [*They go out leading Johnny*]
> *During the last few sentences, the room has been growing
> darker, and darker, till it disappears, to give place to a lonely,
> narrow boreen on the hip of one of the Dublin mountains. It is
> pitch dark; the hedge is scarcely perceptible, except for its darker
> silhouette. A few stars are faintly showing in a clouded sky. An
> hour has gone by. A motor is heard coming rapidly along, stop-
> ping some distance away. After a pause, some figures emerge
> from the darkness on left, and slowly cross to the right.*

1. Sean O'Casey, *Autobiographies 2* (New York: Carroll and Graf, 1984), 91.
2. Robert Hogan, Michael J. O'Neill, and Joseph Holloway, *Joseph Holloway's Abbey Theatre: A Selection from His Unpublished Journal, Impressions of a Dublin Playgoer* (Carbondale: Southern Illinois University Press, 1967), pp. 220–21. Garry O'Connor
   assumes that this young man was killed, and identifies him as one Captain Hogan in
   Sean O'Casey: A Life, p. 148.
3. Gabriel Fallon, *Sean O'Casey: The Man I Knew* (London: Routledge & Kegan Paul,
   1965), p. 17.

VOICE OF JOHNNY. Are yous goin' to do in a comrade—look at me arm, I lost it for Ireland.

VOICE OF IRREGULAR. Commandant Tancred lost his life for Ireland.

VOICE OF JOHNNY. Sacred Heart of Jesus, have mercy on me! Mother o' God, pray for me—be with me now in the agonies o' death! . . . Hail, Mary, full o' grace . . . the Lord is . . . with Thee.

[*They pass out of sight* [sic]
A pause; then several shots are heard, followed by a cry; then silence again. Figures cross the stage from right to left; the motor is heard starting, and moving away, the sound growing fainter in the distance. The scene gradually brightens, till the room of the Boyles is again revealed. The most of the furniture is gone. Mary and Mrs Boyle, one on each side, are sitting in a darkened room, by the fire: it is an hour later.[4]

Juno was submitted to the Abbey on 28 December. It was thus written inside three months, which is extraordinary. Ronald Ayling attests that there were three versions, now in private hands: a manuscript entitled 'Juno and the Peacock', with notes and full drafts for acts 1 and 2; a typescript of act 2, using the phonetic 'Paycock' in the title and the subtitle 'Rough Copy'; a typescript draft of the three acts. Johnny's final scene made it into the latter, while other possibilities, such as Captain Boyle's having an eye for one 'Julia Jennins', to Juno's annoyance, were cut and names of characters changed (the Captain was first Billy Kelly, Joxer was Andy Murphy). The remarkable thing is how quickly and surely O'Casey reshaped his original idea into a many-layered tragicomedy. He told the scribbler Holloway that the comedy of life appealed to him most. When he read [Thomas] Hardy's *Tess of the d'Urbervilles* he stayed awake all night crying. 'It had a surprising effect on him though he is not a sentimental fellow.'[5] To a degree, he used the story of Tess in *Juno*, in part a tale of seduction and betrayal. (But he said nothing to Holloway of his sister Bella, whose real-life tragedy had for him been the equal of anything in Hardy's fiction.) He was temperamentally at odds with pure tragedy. Not for him the Yeatsian axiom, 'We begin to live when we have conceived life as tragedy.'[6] He had to have joy, colour, hope, laughter and song in his life and therefore in the lives of his imagined characters.

4. Ronald Ayling, "*Juno and the Paycock*: A Textual Study," *Modernist Studies: Literature & Culture 1920–1940*, 2.1 (1976): 24.
5. *Joseph Holloway's Abbey Theatre*, p. 220.
6. W.B. Yeats, *Autobiographies* (London: Macmillan, 1961), p. 189.

Juno is the best-constructed of all of O'Casey's plays. Some of the credit must go to Robinson, a master craftsman who tried to get him trained in the writing of the so-called 'well-made play'. Following Dolan's advice O'Casey read *The Whiteheaded Boy*, describing it as 'a glorious work' and expressing envy for 'every word' of it.[7] In turn, when Robinson wrote a short handbook on playmaking he invoked *Juno* as a model of a good opening:

> In five minutes or so, Seán O'Casey has "planted" four of the chief protagonists [*sic*] in his drama. Nothing they do or say is extraneous to the plot. We get his scene, a slum room (producer's business and wardrobe-mistress's and property-man's), we get that the scene is laid in Dublin by the accent of the players (players' business); we get Juno's character, worried over her thriftless husband but a good anxious mother; we get Mary, a little vain, a little selfish; we get Johnny, we suspect something from his nervousness, his reaction to the reading of the details of the assassination; we get vigorous young Jerry Devine; we have talk about the Paycock and his wastrel friend Joxer—though we have not yet seen them their shadows have already fallen quite distinctly across the play—and all this has been done in a few minutes of superb stage-craft. Most of the main ingredients which go to the making of the play are here [. . .]; in short, it is difficult to think of a better example of a theme being more perfectly and economically enunciated, there is not a superfluous word in the dialogue, everything is pregnant with meaning, even the sausages which Juno brings in for the Paycock's breakfast are going to play an important part later on.[8]

Robinson's admiration shows us that *Juno* was the sort of play the Abbey preferred. There are three plots, all neatly dovetailed, while at the same time the impression is created of life drifting and unfolding.

O'Casey's own interest, however, lay considerably less in structure than in characterization, language and theme. He delighted in the Captain and Joxer, irresponsible though they are, and took a savage delight also in exposing on the one hand the pretensions of the socially respectable Bentham and on the other the limitations of Jerry Devine, '*a type, becoming very common now* [*sic*] *in the Labour Movement, of a mind knowing enough to make the mass of his associates, who know less, a power, and too little to broaden that power for the benefit of all.*'[9] That 'now' indicates the force of

7. Sean O'Casey [SOC] to Robinson, 29 Dec. 1923, in David Krause, ed., *The Letters of Sean O'Casey*, Vol. 1 (New York: Macmillan, 1978), 108.
8. Lennox Robinson, *Towards an Appreciation of the Theatre* (Dublin: Metropolitan Publishing Co.), 1945, pp. 18–19.

O'Casey's dissatisfaction with the Labour movement. His article published in the *Irish Statesman* in December 1923 shows clearly his bitterness on this theme. There he deplored the ignorance of the 'present-day Trade Unionist' and his failure to learn that 'self-realisation is more important than class-consciousness'. To learn is the worker's greatest need, if the people of Ireland are going to be more than 'a race of fools during an election, and a race of madmen during a civil war.'[1] The social apathy and parasitic natures of Captain Boyle and Joxer are illuminated by the inadequacies of the likes of Jerry Devine to alter them. In the vacuum created by the civil war and the failure of the workers' revolution there are only Juno's common sense and rich humanity. Her 'What can God do agen the stupidity o' men!' is an exclamation rather than a question, a gesture against the male-dominated politics of the day.[2] O'Casey was now able to embody such ideas in three-dimensional characters. The result was Chekhovian naturalism, marking his advance past Synge's style of realism, for to him 'Chekhov seems to let his characters speak as they please and get them into his play's scheme.'[3]

O'Casey's use of language raises a similar issue: art or nature? On the one hand, it is argued, the urban Dubliner's speech is (or was) particularly lively and characteristically peppered with malapropisms and puns, available for O'Casey to record; on the other hand, his successful stage speech drew, and to a lesser degree continues to draw, attention back to the similar strengths of actual Dublin dialect (if the speech can be so described). Thus when Kevin C. Kearns in his oral history allows several older folk to comment on the liveliness of Dublin speech in days gone by, each witness ends up relating the actual speech to O'Casey's humorous exploitation of it in his plays, e.g. 'I've *absolutely no doubt* that Sean O'Casey didn't invent a single thing. All he did was keep his ears open. Because when I go to the Abbey or the Gaiety and I see an O'Casey play I hear all the Americans and the Irish bursting their sides laughing at the way they [the characters] mangle the English language. Well, I was listening to it *every* day! It's *totally* authentic.'[4] Flattering though such evidence is to the native wit of Dubliners it rather leaves out of account that O'Casey was a native Dubliner himself, not short of invention. Colbert Kearney has emphasised what he calls the 'the glamour of grammar', the interest of an oral

9. Stage direction, *Juno and the Paycock*, act 1, soc, *CP*, 1, 8.
1. "Literature and Life," *Irish Statesman* 22 Dec. 1923: 467–68.
2. SOC, *CP*, 1, 86.
3. *Joseph Holloway's Abbey Theatre*, p. 224. The diary entry is for 3 Jan. 1924, shortly after SOC had submitted *Juno* to the Abbey.
4. Kevin C. Kearns, *Dublin Tenement Life: An Oral History* (Dublin: Gill and Macmillan, 1994), p. 143.

culture in a literary one, as the Dublin working class formed a love of fine expression through public speeches, sermons and popular drama using some aristocratic speech. The characters who possess this dangerous glamour, such as Donal Davoren in the *Gunman*, or Charles Bentham in *Juno*, speak a language admired by the less well educated, a language which also deceives and deludes. The wit, the 'vandalisation' of language by the ordinary Dublin people, derives from a comic aping of one's betters, as when Captain Boyle refers to his 'attackey case' and his 'dockyments'.[5] In the *Plough*, all the working-class characters except the Covey fall captive to the rhetoric of the high-toned Figure in the Window. O'Casey's language is never as innocent as it looks on the page. It is shot through at all times with historical, cultural and political implications. In production, the language has to show (or expose) these registers and betrayals. It cannot be played straight. It engages ironically with its own origins.

In the first production of *Juno* at the Abbey this authenticity was provided by an unsurpassable cast, who were themselves Dubliners capable of responding to the layers of tone and meaning to be found in O'Casey's mainly comic style. Sara Allgood, back from an ill-fated sojourn in Australia and New Zealand (where her husband died), triumphed in the role of Juno. She was to play it as the undisputed owner for twenty years. Barry Fitzgerald, likewise, the original Captain Boyle, was definitive; F.J. McCormick lent Joxer closely observed detail, while his fiancée Eileen Crowe was perfect casting as Mary Boyle. All the other roles were equally well cast— Arthur Shields as Johnny, Maureen Delany as Mrs Madigan, Gabriel Fallon as Charles Bentham. Even the small part of Needle Nugent was given to a major Dublin actor, Michael J. Dolan (who had recently succeeded Robinson as manager and who also directed *Juno*). 'There was not a weak spot in the acting,' said the *Irish Times*. 'It probably attained the most level standard of good work that has been witnessed on the Abbey stage of late.'[6] On opening night, the actors were called back so often 'that in the end the exhausted stage-hands left the curtain up for good'.[7]

5. Colbert Kearney, 'Sean O'Casey and the Glamour of Grammar', in *Anglo-Irish and Irish Literature: Aspects of Language and Culture*, ed. Birgit Bramsbäck and Martin Croghan, vol. 2 (Uppsala: Uppsala University, 1988), pp. 63–70. See also Kearney, *The Glamour of Grammar* (Westport, CT: Greenwood, 2000), pp. 75–96.
6. *Irish Times*, 4 March 1924, cited by Robert Hogan and Richard Burnham, eds., in *Modern Irish Drama: The Years of O'Casey, 1921–1926* (Newark: U of Delware P, 1992), p. 192.
7. Elizabeth Coxhead, 'Sally and Molly: Sara Allgood and Maire O'Neill', in *Daughters of Erin: Five Women of the Irish Renascence* (London: Secker and Warburg, 1965), p. 211. Holloway also testified that 'the acting all round [in *Juno*] was of the highest quality, not one in the long cast being misplaced or for a moment out of the picture,' *Joseph Holloway's Abbey Theatre*, p. 226.

On Friday 7 March Lady Gregory came up by train from Galway
and went with Yeats to *Juno*, 'a wonderful and terrible play of futility, of irony, humour, tragedy'. The house was packed—the manager
had to find a chair for James Stephens—with long queues outside.
She met O'Casey in the green room. 'He is very happy. I asked him
to come to tea after the next day['s] matinée as I had brought up a
barmbrack for the players.' Maybe it was the thought of the barmbrack. O'Casey declined and elaborating his excuse said that he
would be 'working with cement, and that takes such a long time to
get off'. He was useless at making excuses. For Lady Gregory immediately said, 'But after that?' Well, then, 'I have to cook my dinner. I have but one room and I cook for myself since my mother
died.' All the more reason, one would have thought, to accept a free
dinner or even high tea. But he disliked dining out, having 'a delicate palate'[8] and also being naturally uncertain of the necessary social graces. In compensation he gushed outrageously. 'I owe a great
deal to you and Mr. Yeats and Mr. Robinson, but to you above all.
You gave me encouragement. And it was you who said to me upstairs in the office—I could show you the very spot where you
stood—"Mr. O'Casey [yet she always, like Yeats, called him 'Casey'],
your gift is characterisation". And so I threw over my theories and
worked at characters, and this is the result.'[9] Little did he suspect
that his every word would go straight into Lady Gregory's *Journals*
the next day. Between Holloway on the one side and Lady Gregory
on the other he was, in Dublin parlance, being nicely 'chronicled'.
Yet he must have been pleased to hear Lady Gregory's remark to
Yeats, 'This is one of the evenings at the Abbey that makes me glad
to have been born.' He was obviously meant to hear it. Although he
dodged the green-room party next afternoon he met Lady Gregory
again at the (Saturday) evening performance—another full house—
and had to agree to attend Yeats's Monday evening on 10 March.
Unlike Captain Boyle, he was unable to invent a job in Killester
which might excuse him.

* * *

8. SOC, *Letters*, 2, 1023. In this letter (26 Jan. 1954), SOC outlined the menu he had
when living at 422 NCR: boiled eggs, raw tomatoes, cooked prunes and figs or apple
rings with tea, bread and butter. He ate meat only once a week, preferably roast pork.
9. Daniel J. Murphy, ed., *Lady Gregory's Journals*, Vol. I (Gerrard's Cross: Colin Smythe,
1978), pp. 511–12.

SUSAN CANNON HARRIS

Sensationalizing Sacrifice†

Gabriel Fallon, writing about *Juno* in his memoirs, professes himself baffled at O'Casey's insistence that *Juno* was a play "about a
young man called Johnny Boyle."¹ It was Fallon's conviction that
the play was about the young man's parents, Juno and "Captain"
Jack Boyle.² The only vestige of this reported original intention is
the subplot involving Johnny, Juno's only son, who is abducted and
executed by his former republican comrades for having informed
on a neighbor named Tancred. The play's famous ending seems to
support Fallon's reading. In the penultimate scene, Juno learns
from a neighbor that the police have found Johnny's body. After de-
livering her lament, Juno and the other women leave the stage. Instead of bringing down the curtain, however, O'Casey then brings
on Juno's husband and his buddy Joxer, whose drunken, incoherent
conversation is the play's final scene.

The juxtaposition of these two scenes, while baffling to some of
O'Casey's contemporary reviewers, was immediately hailed by Fallon
and others as the first positive proof that the Abbey had a genius on
its hands. *Juno*'s ending is a blatant departure from the melodramatic conventions that, as Stephen Watt points out, O'Casey both
borrows and undermines in his Dublin trilogy. At the same time, the
ending indicates that O'Casey's subversion of the "dominant ideology" about Ireland and the Irish through his undermining of the
"very devices which, on the popular stage, conveyed it"³ has its limits. While this formal departure from melodrama does help O'Casey
make his point about the failure of masculinist sacrificial rhetoric, it
makes a dangerous argument about why that rhetoric fails.

As an example of O'Casey flouting melodramatic conventions,
Watt cites the disappearance of the sensationalist execution scene
that so often closed the nationalist melodrama: "O'Casey appropriates no extravagant tableaux from nineteenth-century historical
drama to heighten his characters' deaths; in fact, we never see Min-
nie after she leaves Davoren's apartment."⁴ Similarly, in *Juno*,

† From *Gender and Modern Irish Drama*. Reprinted by permission of Indiana University
Press.
1. See p. 502 in this volume [*Editor*].
2. Fallon originated the role of Charles Bentham, the English Schoolteacher who seduces
and then abandons Mary Boyle.
3. Stephen Watt, *Joyce, O'Casey, and the Irish Popular Theater* (Syracuse: Syracuse UP,
1991), 149.
4. Watt, 179.

Johnny Boyle is killed offstage between scenes. But the absence of this particular "sensation scene" does not mean that O'Casey has abandoned sensationalism as a strategy. In fact, what O'Casey is trying to do in *Juno* is to produce a treatment of Irish history that is *more* sensational than the sacrificial paradigm, and melodramatic conventions are valuable to him insofar as they help him do so. One of the arguments *Juno* makes is precisely that republican rhetoric denies the importance of sensation—the power of pain and the experience of the suffering body. While O'Casey does not stage Johnny Boyle's death, the presentation of his body on stage is an attempt to make political violence "sensational" to the audience—to "render suffering so palpable because so visible that the viewer will be convinced that an injustice is being done"[5].

Juno's opening scene demonstrates the problem O'Casey faced in his quest to make suffering sensational to his public. Mary, Juno's daughter and Johnny's sister, is reading a newspaper account of the death of Tancred, a republican who has been assassinated by the Free State. The newspaper account certainly seems sensationalist enough: "The full details are in it this mornin'; seven wounds he had—one enterin' the neck, with an exit wound beneath the left shoulder-blade; another in the left breast penethratin' the heart." As Mary's dispassionate reading indicates, Dubliners had already gotten "used to newspaper headlines" sensationalizing political violence as best they could;[6] after three years of war with England, violence and its effects were more familiar to the Irish reading public than they had been during the Volunteers' heyday. Graphic and detailed as this description is, however, it lacks affective power. Although both of them know the victim, Mary and Juno are not particularly moved by the report. Their discussion of it does, however, provoke a response from Johnny: "Oh, quit that readin' for God's sake! Are yous losin' all your feelin's?"

As "realistic" as this medical description of Tancred's body is, it fails to make Tancred's suffering as vivid or painful to its readers as it is to Johnny, who is lame in one hip and missing an arm as a result of his exposure to political violence. For the audience, Johnny functions primarily as a way of making that violence accessible by embodying its consequences. As Mary says, Johnny's wounds have left him "very sensitive"; many of Johnny's lines are cries of pain in one form or another, and he seems to respond somatically to intangible stimuli. He complains, for instance, that the noise from the upstairs apartment is "like thunderclaps in me brain," and when his

5. Ann Cvetkovich, *Mixed Feelings: Feminism, Mass Culture, and Victorian Sensationalism* (New Brunswick: Rutgers UP, 1992), 169.
6. Robert Hogan and Richard Burnham, *The Years of O'Casey, 1921–1926: A Documentary History* (Gerrard's Cross: Colin Smythe, 1992), 72.

devotional candle blows out, he experiences it like a gunshot: "I'm afther feelin' a pain in me breast, like the tearin' by of a bullet!"

While Mary and Juno, like O'Casey's audiences, are "losing their feelings" as a result of long exposure to this kind of violence (and this kind of reporting), Johnny's have become hyper-real, manifesting in physical symptoms extreme enough to become sensible to the audience. The most dramatic example of this process of sensationalization is during the party scene in Act II. Bentham, the British schoolteacher and theosophist who is courting Mary, offers this explanation of ghost stories:

> Scientists are beginning to think that what we call ghosts are sometimes seen by persons of a certain nature. They say that sensational actions, such as the killing of a person, demand great energy, and that that energy lingers in the place where the action occurred. People may live in the place and see nothing, when someone may come along whose personality has some peculiar connection with the energy of the place, and, in a flash, the person sees the whole affair.

What is speculation for Bentham soon becomes reality for Johnny, who moments later runs into the room with "his face pale, his lips twitching, his limbs trembling" after having a vision of the dying Tancred:

> I seen him. . . . I seen Robbie Tancred kneelin' down before the statue . . . an' the red light shinin' on him . . . an' when I went in . . . he turned an' looked at me . . . an' I seen the wouns bleedin' in his breast . . . . Oh, why did he look at me like that? . . . It wasn't my fault that he was done in.

What Johnny sees is an image that is obscured both in sacrificial rhetoric and in newspaper accounts: a living, suffering, bleeding body—no longer a hale and hearty Irish Volunteer but not yet an immortal martyr or a dissectable corpse. This vision provokes the physical sensations that the newspaper account could not when Johnny's agitation produces a sympathetic response in Mary: "Mother o' God, he made me heart lep!"

Tancred's ghost is treated by the other characters as a figment of Johnny's superstitious imagination, and its placement (directly after Bentham's speech) strongly suggests that they are right. Thus, the play offers a "realistic" explanation for this visitation that otherwise comes straight out of the sensationalist tradition. But the ghost's unreality does not mean that its effect on Johnny is less pronounced or that its appearance does not affect his audiences on stage or in the theater. Here, then, we see O'Casey drawing on the sensationalist techniques of melodrama in order to render his "realism" more affectively powerful than the newspaper account with which the play opens, using Johnny to translate this imaginary vision into experienced sensation for the audience. If his sudden scream makes Mary's "heart lep," it also jolts the audience in their seats; the same theatergoers who listened without surprise or fear to the description of Tancred's dead body are startled by Johnny's scream into sharing his terror.

* * *

On Samuel Beckett

Correspondence of Samuel Beckett
and Alan Schneider†

Ussy
4.1.60

Dear Alan[1]

Thanks for your two letters, second today. I hasten to reply. First your specific points:

1. *Spool* instead of *reel* if you wish.
2. *Post Mortems* by all means.
3. Instead of *weir* suggest *sluice* or *lock*.
4. Should prefer you to keep *stem*.
5. If *dell* is clearer than *dingle* by all means. Same thing.

Now the rest.

Know nothing whatever about "extra speaker to tape recorder" in Berlin and am not sure what this means. If it does what I fear it is plain murder and unpardonable. I dream sometimes of all German directors of plays with perhaps one exception united in one with his back to the wall and me shooting a bullet into his balls every five minutes till he loses his taste for improving authors. Krapp has nothing to talk to but his dying self and nothing to talk to him but his dead one. I think we discussed the technical problems raised by the machine. The text recorded should be spoken obviously in a much younger and stronger voice than Krapp's for his last tape (though as McWhinnie remarked voices don't always age abreast of the rest), but unmistakably his. The visible machine on the table should obviously be a dummy (too risky otherwise with all the violent manipulations), by which I mean of course a real machine visibly working and stopping when switched on and off but the tape silent. The machine heard has to be worked off stage which in-

---

1. These letters between the playwright and the director concern a production of *Krapp's Last Tape* at the Provincetown Playhouse in New York City that opened 14 Jan. 1960, with Edward Albee's *Zoo Story* [Editor].

volves very delicate cue work from the wings but there seems no other way of doing it. By the way for God's sake make sure in your script that there are no omissions or variations in the repeated passages. What helps for the cue is for Krapp to have a very special gesture for switching on and off which though it has to be abrupt may be prepared by a change of posture (straightening a little out of his crouch for example), the same each time. Hard to explain these things in writing. When writing the piece if I had been more familiar with tape recorders I might have had Krapp wind back and forward *without* switching off for the sake of the extraordinary sound that can be had apparently in this way (Blin did it), but it would certainly complicate things technically and better not try it. I told you about the beautiful and quite accidental effect in London of the luminous eye burning up as the machine runs on in silence and the light goes down. It is not visible from all parts of the house unless you can manage two eyes, one on each side, or the eye in front in the middle! This requires of course a slow fade out at the end which I think is good in any case, but not a fade on at the beginning. It is better the curtain should go up on a dark stage and then suddenly full blaze on Krapp seated at his table. He should be in a pool of light and of course near the front (just enough room between table and edge of stage for banana gag and walk backstage). All backstage as black as possible, he can disappear through black drapes for his drinks and dictionary. Nothing whatever on stage but table. We also I think discussed his itinerary from table backstage. The one I recommend and which we used in London is quite unnatural but correct dramatically, it is

and has the great advantage of lengthening the walk (to compensate immobility) and of allowing Krapp to be inspected in motion as he would not be if he took the normal route in a straight line from behind table backstage. I think this is important. With regard to costume it should be sufficiently clear from text (don't be afraid of exaggerating with boots). Black and white (both dirty), the whole piece being built up in one sense on this simple antithesis of which you will find echoes throughout the text (black ball, white nurse, black pram, Bianca, Kedar—anagram of "dark"—Street, black storm, light of understanding, etc.) Black dictionary if you can and ledger. Similarly black and white set. Table should be small (plain kitchen table) cluttered up with tapes and boxes until he sweeps them to the ground (maximum of violence). In the light everything as visible as possible, hence unnatural opening of drawers towards audience, i.e. when he extracts spool from left drawer he holds it up so that it can be seen before he puts it back, similarly with bananas as soon as taken from drawer, similarly with envelope and keys and whenever else possible, almost (only almost!) like a conjuror exhibiting his innocent material. Another good effect is for the transition from repose to motion to be made as abrupt as possible. He is motionless at table then suddenly (shock) in laborious motion, not fast because he can't go fast, but looking fast because of sudden start and effort entailed. Similarly when having eaten first banana he broods. What next? Suddenly back to table. Similarly when after second banana he "has an idea." Sudden turn and as fast as he can backstage. At the end, towards close of third repeat of boat passage, he can steal his arm round machine and sink his head on table. Then slowly up and staring front on "past midnight etc" to end. Throughout when listening to tape even if crouched down over machine he should have his face up and full front maximally visible, staring eyes etc. Lot to be done with eyes. They can close for example for boat passage. Pity Davis is tall[2] I saw Krapp small and wizened. What else? Can't think. Bit late in day anyhow. Hope you have the right old tune for "Now the day etc." Herewith in case not.[3]

Hope these hurried notes may be of some service. Let me know how it goes.

Affectionately to you all.

Sam [handwritten]

Saturday Jan. 16 [1960]†

Dear Sam,

Well, by now you have read the notices and I have slept 48 hours straight—so we can talk. It went well Thursday night, very well, and I think you would have been pleased.[4] The critics, of course,

---

2. Donald Davis (1928–98), Canadian actor.
3. The Irish chorale for "Now the Day Is Over."
† Reprinted with permission of the John J. Burns Library, Boston College.
4. Produced by Theatre 1960 (Richard Barr, H. B. Lutz, and Harry Joe Brown, Jr.), *Krapp's Last Tape* opened at the Provincetown Playhouse, New York, 14 January 1960. Donald Davis (Krapp). Performed in conjunction with Albee's *Zoo Story*, directed by Milton Katselas, who was Albee's original choice, then "let go"; Barr and Albee directed, although Katselas's name was on the program (*Entrances*, 275). Settings and lighting, William Ritman. Moved to Players Theatre 19 April, then Cricket Theatre, closed 21 May after 582 performances. Davis succeeded by Henderson Forsythe, then by Mark Rickman. Reviews: Walter Kerr, *NY Herald-Tribune*, 15 January 1960; Richard Watts, Jr., *NY Post*, 15 January; Brooks Atkinson, *NY Times*, 15 and 31 January; Frank Aston, *NY Telegram*, 15 January; *New Yorker*, 23 January; *Saturday Review*, 30 January; *Time*, 8 February. Each play received Obie Awards for "Distinguished Plays," Davis for "Distinguished Performance."

showed their usual lack of perception; but the response was generally favorable even if they didn't know what or why. Davis was superb, both on the tape and live. In spite of his height I think you would have liked him, and there are times when he looks a bit like Pat Magee[5] even . . . And one thing is certain: you could have heard half a pin drop except in all those places where they were laughing.

Your letter came a week ago in last stages of rehearsal, and followed as scrupulously as circumstances permitted. I was delighted by your comments regarding that extra speaker because I had had a big argument with Ed Albee[6] about it. He said it had worked well in the Berlin production and gave me the impression you had approved, which is why I asked. We used one standard RCS tape recorder, with an EYE which we added since it didn't have one of its own. Visible from all parts of the house and very effective . . . You may be surprised, however, that we actually have Davis manipulate the tape, finding the cueing from offstage (there is no offstage at the Provincetown—where O'Neill got started, by the way) practically impossible. Have settled the winding and re-winding problem very simply although explaining it is complicated, using a new kind of unbreakable tape, and Davis has never missed a cue! And we even get some of Blin's extraordinary sounds on the recorder when Krapp goes forward or backward. . . . Our lighting is also very good, I think, albeit simple. Krapp in a pool of light except when he literally disappears upstage center for his stuff there. The only liberty we have taken and I trust it is not enough to justify any type of firing squad is to have a plain black funnel of an overhead lamp with an actual light bulb in it, which helps to create the pool, light Krapp's face, make him stoop more, and in general give the feeling of a work table. We didn't start out with it, but soon found that in order to see his eyes we needed a light source closer and more directly overhead than was possible in this particular theatre . . . Don't be misled by the publicity photos which appear with some of the notices; they were taken weeks ago before rehearsals started and in no way resemble our present Krapp. He has no mustache, no scarf of that kind, etc. We'll send you some actual photos as soon as there are any. . . . Davis does wonderful things with his eyes, hands, entire body; subtle yet always meaningful.

I love the play, it moves me every time, and I can hardly stand the ending. Really beautiful and true, and I could kill a critic who says 'no enduring value'[7] when every moment will be equally true one hundred years from now . . . Judith Schmidt equally moved, sorry

5. Irish actor who originated the role of Krapp at the Royal Court Theatre in London, 1958 [*Editor*].
6. Edward Albee (b. 1928), American playwright [*Editor*].
7. Brooks Atkinson *New York Times*, 15 January 1960.

Barney away, he'll come. . . . . . In the meantime, business is good, management pleased, the other play strange but interesting. . . . You know, this is first time I have directed one of your plays without seeing a previous production; maybe this turned out well in the case.

Kept 'Stem', naturally. Also dingle. LOCK for weir.

The weeklies should be even better because more intelligent. And I saw [Critic] Jerry Tallmer tonight, who said he liked it very much.[8] Looking [ending missing]

[Alan]

JAMES KNOWLSON

[*Krapp's Last Tape*]†

On December 11, 1957, Beckett heard from Con Leventhal that his wife and Beckett's own former love, Ethna MacCarthy, was suffering from terminal cancer of the throat. He was utterly devastated. He wrote immediately to ask whether there was any specialist whom they could consult or any form of specialized treatment that they could obtain, either in Britain or America, adding: "I needn't tell you you may count on me financially up to the limit."[1] He was to repeat his offer on several subsequent occasions.

From December until Ethna's death eighteen months later, Beckett wrote her long, sometimes very beautiful letters, which can only be described as touching love letters written to someone for whom he had never lost his deep affection. Uncharacteristically, he deliberately padded his letters out with what he called "my silly news"[2] so as to interest and entertain her while she was ill at home or in hospital: "I suppose the best I have to do," he wrote to her, "is to open for you my little window on my little world."[3]

During the opening weeks of 1958, while he was in a mood of very deep depression,[4] he stayed alone at Ussy.[5] Memories of Ethna when she was young and full of life and wit were juxtaposed with thoughts of her now, sick and dying. These memories helped to inspire the short, now famous play that he wrote fairly quickly in February 1958.

8. *Village Voice*, 15 January.
† From *Damned to Fame: The Life of Samuel Beckett*. Copyright © 1996 by James Knowlson. Reprinted by permission of Aitken Alexander Associates Ltd. and Bloomsbury Publishing, PLC.
1. Samuel Beckett [SB] to A. J. Leventhal (AJL), 11 Dec. 1957 (Texas).
2. SB to Ethna MacCarthy, 14 Aug. 1958 (Texas).
3. SB to Ethna MacCarthy, 27 Sept. 1958 (Texas).
4. Interview with Avigdor Arikha, 23 Feb. 1994.
5. Normandy, France [*Editor*].

This play, which he eventually called *Krapp's Last Tape*, is unusual in Beckett's theatrical opus for its tender lyricism and for a
poignancy that verges on sentimentality. Rehearsing many years
later with the San Quentin Drama Workshop, Beckett commented:
"A woman's tone goes through the entire play, returning always, a
lyrical tone. . . . Krapp feels tenderness and frustration for the feminine beings."[6] And if the old man, Krapp, who listens to the tape
recordings he made in his younger days, is fascinated by his recollections of the various women he has known in his life, he is ob-
sessed by the eyes of one woman in particular. "The eyes she had!
. . . Everything there, everything on this old muckball, all the light
and dark and famine and feasting of . . . (*hesitates*) . . . the ages!"[7]
The eyes of one woman are the touchstone for all the others, even
for a woman whom Krapp encounters casually by the side of the
canal, commenting admiringly: "The face she had! The eyes! Like
. . . chrysolite!"[8]

When a biographical source has been suggested for the woman
who inspired the yearning for what has long since past, Beckett's
cousin Peggy Sinclair has been mentioned. Memories of visits to
and farewells from Peggy are certainly evoked in the play. Peggy often wore green, and Krapp asks rhetorically: "What remains of all
that misery? A girl in a shabby green coat, on a railway-station platform?"[9] Krapp reads again, "with tears again,"[1] Theodor Fontane's
novel *Effi Briest*, a book of which Beckett was very fond and over
which Peggy often used to cry. But the play, like Beckett's own life
up to that time, contains several different loves and there seems little doubt that the source for the girl with the haunting eyes is
Ethna MacCarthy. For, as *Dream of Fair to Middling Women* had
made clear a quarter of a century before; the "Alba," who on Beckett's own admission was closely modeled on Ethna,[2] had eyes like
dark, deep pools.

The scene with the girl in the punt to which the middle-aged,
then old man, Krapp, harks back in his recordings has also been
related to an incident with Peggy Sinclair.[3] An incident in *Dream
of Fair to Middling Women* off an Irish beach suggests such an
affinity. Beckett himself did not remember the scene this way, however, denying that the girl in the boat in *Krapp's Last Tape* had

6. James Knowlson, ed., *Samuel Beckett: Krapp's Last Tape*, Theatre Workbook 1 (London:
   Brutus Books Ltd., 1980), p. 130.
7. SB, *Krapp's Last Tape* in *Collected Shorter Plays* (London: Faber and Faber, 1984), p. 62.
8. Ibid., p. 60.
9. Ibid., p. 58.
1. Ibid., p. 62.
2. Interview with SB, 13 Sept. 1989.
3. Deirdre Bair, *Samuel Beckett: A Biography* (New York: Harcourt Brace Jovanovich,
   1978), p. 87.

anything at all to do with Peggy.[4] And the feelings expressed in this passage seem much closer to the tender yearning inspired by Ethna than to the emotion aroused by the more overtly physical Peggy. Small wonder that Beckett felt able to write to Ethna Mac-Carthy when the play was finished: "I've written in English a stage monologue for Pat Magee which I think you will like if no one else."[5]

If Ethna's terminal illness inspired Beckett by drawing him back in memory to the days of his youth in Ireland, other factors contributed to the composition of the play. George Devine wrote to Beckett in December 1957 saying that he wanted to present his translation of *Endgame* at the Royal Court Theatre in the Spring, not with the mime *Act Without Words* that had accompanied the earlier French production, but with N. F. Simpson's play *A Resounding Tinkle*. Beckett replied that he was not at all happy about this proposal and commented to Donald McWhinnie that he would rather they did not proceed until he could offer them "something else from my own muckheap more acceptable than the mime. This is not nosiness God knows and I have no doubt, having read Mr Tynan, that I would be in excellent company with Mr Simpson. I simply prefer right or wrong to be unrelieved."[6] Beckett was searching therefore at this time for an idea for a short play to accompany *Endgame* on the Royal Court program.

Also in December 1957, he heard Patrick Magee reading extracts from *Molloy* and *From an Abandoned Work* on the BBC Third Programme. In spite of the static through which he again strained to listen, first in Paris then, later in the month, in Ussy, when the readings were repeated, Beckett was impressed and moved by the cracked quality of Magee's distinctively Irish voice, which seemed to capture a sense of deep world-weariness, sadness, ruination, and regret. He had not yet met the actor, who had also been in *All That Fall*.[7] But he had heard enough through the interference to "thank my stars for Magee."[8] A few weeks later, he began to compose a dramatic monologue, which he first called the Magee Monologue, for a character who is described in the first draft as a "wearish old

4. Interview with SB, 17 Nov. 1989.

5. SB to Ethna MacCarthy, 2 June 1958 (Texas).

6. SB to Donald McWhinnie, 23 Dec. 1957 (McWhinnie). Beckett had written to George Devine on December 14, 1957, objecting to his proposal (Herbert).

7. Bair claims that Beckett had been over in London for the recording of *All That Fall* the previous year when he had met Patrick Magee (*Samuel Beckett*, p. 489). But according to Barbara Bray and Michael Bakewell, although he had intended to come, he had been either unable or unwilling to travel (interviews with Barbara Bray, July 1991, and with Michael Bakewell, 21 Mar. 1994). It is also clear from letters to Donald McWhinnie that Beckett had still not yet met Magee in April 1958 (SB to Donald McWhinnie, 27 April 1958 [McWhinnie]).

8. SB to Mary Hutchinson (MH), 21 Dec. 1957 (Texas).

man" with a "wheezy ruined old voice with some characteristic accent."[9]

It has often been said (by Beckett among others) that he had no knowledge at all of tape recorders when he wrote a play that uses such a machine, sophisticated technology at the time, as its central device. However true this may at first have been in matters of detail, his correspondence shows that he had seen a tape recorder in operation when he went along in January 1958 to the BBC studio on the avenue Hoche in Paris, where Cecilia Reeves played for him the tapes of Magee's readings that had been sent over from London.[1] Staring at the reels that held his own words as they revolved on the tape deck and seeing, in a casual way at least, how the tape recorder worked helped him to imagine a play in which different moments of time could be captured, juxtaposed, and relived later. Beckett started to write the play on February 20; during the final stages of composition in March, when he needed detailed operating instructions, he wrote to ask Donald McWhinnie if he would send him a tape recorder manual.

Krapp's Last Tape contains many personal elements. Beckett's walks in the hills with his father and his favorite Kerry Blue terrier lie behind the memory of the younger Krapp tramping on a hazy Crohan mountain with the bitch, stopping to listen to the peal of the church bells. "At night, when I can't sleep," Beckett had written earlier to Susan Manning, "I do the old walks again and stand beside him again one Xmas morning in the fields near Glencullen, listening to the chapel bells."[2] Beckett had also experienced a lack of success resembling Krapp's. "Seventeen copies sold . . . to free circulating libraries beyond the seas"[3] with the French *Murphy*, and had spent many an evening sitting alone at the "Wine-house" or village pub "before the fire with closed eyes, separating the grain from the husks."[4] Experiences of a very different order of importance to Beckett have lost their personal, purely local significance and have been more successfully integrated into the play's thematic structure. Even the most poignant memory of all, that of his mother's death some eight years before, has now been absorbed into a carefully structured pattern of images of black and white, sense and spirit, that Beckett later described in terms of Manichean dualism. Personal elements cannot simply be pinned down, then, to com-

9. The first draft is in a notebook entitled "Eté 56." The manuscript is dated 20.2.58. Ms.1227/7/7/1 (Reading).
1. "I heard the tapes with the keenest enjoyment and appreciation. Magee's performance is unforgettable. I hope it may be possible for me to acquire them, or have copies made, for my personal use" (SB to Donald McWhinnie, 28 Jan. 1958 [McWhinnie]).
2. SB to Susan Manning, 21 May 1955 (Texas).
3. SB, *Krapp's Last Tape* in *Collected Shorter Plays*, p. 62.
4. Ibid., p. 57.

fortable real-life equivalences. They convey more universal feelings of yearning or loss, nostalgia or regret, aspiration or failure.

Beckett always felt a great deal of affection for this play: "I feel as clucky and beady and one-legged and bare-footed about this little text as an old hen with her last chick," he wrote to Barney Rosset.[5] And, mocking himself, he wrote to Jacoba van Velde that the short play was "nicely sad and sentimental; it will be like the little heart of an artichoke served before the tripes with excrement of Hamm and Clov. People will say: good gracious, there is blood circulating in the man's veins after all, one would never have believed it; he must be getting old."[6]

* * *

JOHN P. HARRINGTON

The Irish Beckett†

When *Waiting for Godot* was in its first productions, the matter of its universal and humanist or local and Irish import was an issue. Expectation of local import was as axiomatic then as the humanistic image of Beckett is now. In Dublin the issue was of some particular interest because of the author's Irish portfolio and the general configuration of Irish drama in the 1950s around privileged regionalism, a.k.a. Peasant Quality. The case was not closed, as it has been since. *Godot* had affinities with modern Irish drama that were apparent to frequenters of the Abbey. But the play came from an author who in their memory had been branded in court a bawd and blasphemer from Paris, and the play left them, like others, with the enigma of Godot. A. J. Leventhal, who years later could be more decisive, presented the case without verdict in *The Dublin Magazine* on the occasion of The Pike Theatre's Dublin premiere of *Godot* in 1956. Familiar with the previous Paris and London productions, Leventhal took up the issue because "the real innovation in the Irish production lies in making the two tramps (Austin Byrne and Dermot Kelly faithfully efficient) speak with the accent of O'Casey's Joxer tempered by Myles na gCopaleen's 'Dubalin' man." Locally, at least, Leventhal wrote with the authority of personal familiarity: years later Denis Johnston, a notable omission from Beck-

5. SB to Barney Rosset (BR), 1 April 1958 (Syracuse). A few days later he also wrote to Rosset: "I feel—to a disturbing degree—the strangest of solicitudes for this little work" (SB to BR, 10 April 1958 [Syracuse]).
6. SB to Jacoba van Velde, 12 April 1958 (Bibliothèque Nationale).
† From *The Irish Beckett* (Syracuse: Syracuse UP, 1990). Printed by permission of Syracuse University Press.

ett's memory of Dublin's drama of the late 1920s, would always refer to Leventhal as Beckett's secretary as Beckett had been Joyce's.
Perhaps with support or on instructions from the author, Leventhal
responded to the "Dubalin" accents somewhat imperiously: "It
seemes [sic] evident that the author had in mind a universal rather
than a regional application of his vision of mankind in perpetual expectation, desperately endeavouring to fill the hiatus between birth
and death" (52). His sole printed rationale for that claim was that
the names of the four characters indicate different nationalities. (It
is interesting to note that Sigfried Unseld reports a luncheon with
T. W. Adorno, who proposed the same theory of names in *Endgame*,
and Beckett, who denied any such use of names in that play [93].)
Responding to local hearsay, Leventhal observed in his review of
the Dublin production of *Godot* that:

> Mr. Beckett's origin has caused the view to be widely ac-
> cepted that the whole conception of *Waiting for Godot* is Irish,
> a fact which the original French has been unable to conceal, it
> is claimed. The Pike Theatre production lends support to this
> view, and it may well be that *Waiting for Godot* will go down in
> the local records as a lineal descendant of the works of the
> high literary kings of the Irish dramatic renascence. It is un-
> derstood that there is a proposal to translate the play into Irish
> which would assist in bringing about a general acceptance
> here of this theory. Indeed later literary historians might align
> Mr. Beckett with George Moore, who, in his efforts to help in
> the revival of the Irish language, suggested that he might com-
> pose his work in French which could be translated into Eng-
> lish for the convenience of the Gaelic Leaguers who would
> then, in their turn, have little difficulty in turning the text into
> Irish. (52–53)

In 1956 Leventhal only offered by way of verdict the speculation
that "the point might be made that the effective use of local idiom
would also be a proof of the universal applicability of the play since
its intrinsic quality would lose nothing by the change" (52). That is
wholly ambiguous, of course, if the point was made: if local idiom
was a change, then it would prove little about the intrinsic quality
of the play. In any case, the assumption of the strictly universal
context of *Godot*, argued somewhat uneasily by Leventhal in 1956,
eventually became as axiomatic in Ireland as elsewhere.

That axiom, though, needs examination. Production lore is replete with incidental evidence of Beckett's working links with Irish
drama. A number of works were written for Irish actors; Beckett's
favorite actors included a string of Irish ones; and Roger Blin's
qualifications for the first Paris production of *Godot*, however universal its intention, seem to have included his previous appearance

in a French production of *The Playboy of the Western World* (Bair 404). Irish actors, if they thought Beckett not Irish, thought he was something other than universal. Jack MacGowran was performing O'Casey's *The Shadow of a Gunman* in London when he was recruited for the BBC taping of *All That Fall*. "I didn't know then who Beckett was," MacGowran said. "I'd never heard of him. I thought he was a Frenchman whose work had been translated into English" (Young 52). Beckett, though, knew what to make of an Irish character actor like MacGowran. Beckett adds to these suggestive links his multiple tributes to Irish dramatists, his willing information about his formative encounters with productions of plays at the Abbey and Gate Theatres, and even use of fundamental local images in works like *Not I*: " 'I knew that woman in Ireland,' Beckett said, 'I knew who she was—not 'she' specifically, one single woman, but there were so many of those old crones, stumbling down the lanes, in the ditches, beside the hedgerows. Ireland is full of them. And I heard 'her' saying what I wrote in *Not I*. I actually heard it' " (Bair 622). None of this is to suggest that Samuel Beckett was aspiring to be an Abbey playwright. His relation to Irish theater in the 1950s was, rather, as impatient and as antagonistic as his dudgeon on Irish censorship in the 1930s. That was clear enough when he withdrew mimes from the 1958 Dublin Theatre Festival as part of a dispute provoked by the Archbishop of Dublin's disapproval of O'Casey's *The Drums of Father Ned* and of a stage adaptation of *Ulysses*. O'Casey and others managed to shut down the festival because of perceived censorship. Beckett's mimes were not generally missed, but he extended his own ban to productions of any of his works in Ireland. That lasted until 1960: "it is now time I fell off my high Eire moke" (Murray 108). Relation by antagonism is relation nonetheless. Specialized criticism of Beckett, assuming the universal frame of reference, and never entertaining MacGowran's assumption that the author was really French, often quite clearly contradicts that assumption or at least opens the way for qualification. In his formidable study *The Intent of Undoing in Samuel Beckett's Dramatic Texts*, S. E. Gontarski takes as problem the principle that "Beckett is unable to slough his literary past, the culturally coded forms of literature, as easily as he would like. As much as Beckett might resist the notion, he finds himself already written into the text of Western literature. In much of his creative process, he struggles to undo himself" (xiv). This is instructive and useful. There are niches of cultural forms within Western literature, though, and Gontarski's persuasive theory of Beckett's plays, undoing, also has reference to literary pasts and cultural codes more specific than Western literature.

In "the French period" Beckett's dramatic productions are, in a decade, two plays in French, *En attendant Godot* and *Fin de partie*, which he translated into English; two plays in English, *Krapp's Last Tape* and *Happy Days*, which he translated into French; and a pivotal radio play, *All That Fall*, in English, set in Ireland, and only translated into French by another hand. Beckett's novels, roughly contemporary with the same "period," are consistently about place and more often than not about Ireland. Drama differs from the maieutics of Beckett's narrative fiction in easy effacement of specific locale: it is more conducive, in the phrase of the narrator of *Watt*, to very interesting exercises. But those plays most effaced of geographically identifiable setting also refer to Ireland's features, such as Connemara in *Godot* or Connaught in *Krapp*. Like Beckett's novels, these plays also draw on more personal, autobiographical material, always Irish, like the revelation on the pier in Dun Laoghaire in *Krapp*. But such connections as have been made about Beckett's plays and Irish drama are often glosses of the sort that at this time of heightened awareness of the mechanics of cultural relativity can be taken as patronizing. Katherine Worth in *The Irish Drama of Europe*, for example, adds to the national definitions of Beckett: "an Irishman who lives in France, writes with equal facility in French and English, regularly translates himself from one to the other and always keeps in his English an Irish lilt" (241). In 1983 Hugh Kenner wrote that Beckett "is not Irish as Irishness is defined today by the Free State" and that Beckett is instead "willing to be the last Anglo-Irishman" (270).

Argument for the "Irishness" of Beckett's plays might take two tacks. One would be examination of the Irish material in Beckett's plays, including such as the helpfully flagged vision of the Irish crone in *Not I* and also less obvious representations of action constructed in and refined out of local material. Another would be examination of the place of Beckett's plays in Irish drama, of, in Gontarski's terms, the plays' relations to culturally coded forms of literature distinctly Irish. There is interesting secondary evidence for this argument. When the Irish-language version of *Godot* promised by Leventhal finally materialized for two nights in 1971, the *Irish Times* reviewer of *Ag Fanacht Le Godot* offered the opinion, in Irish, that "Until I saw *Godot* in Irish I didn't properly understand how exactly Beckett takes hold of the Irish literary heritage" (Murray 107 n9)—the literary heritage, that is, rather than the general cultural heritage.

Contemporary with the admission of Beckett's works such as *More Pricks Than Kicks* into Irish studies was an Irish Theatre Company production of *Godot* in 1982 accompanied by revivals of Yeats's *On Baile's Strand* and Synge's *The Well of the Saints*. The artistic director of the company announced its thesis that "these plays show Irish drama as firmly rooted in the European tradition" (Murray 121). The subject of Katherine Worth's book was a strain in modern Irish drama derived from the Continent, usually in circumnavigation of England, as represented by Wilde, Synge, Yeats, and O'Casey, all leading to Beckett. This is a select list of Irish playwrights, and it has in mind a selection of their works, but it is a provocative selection. Synge, Yeats, and O'Casey are the names most prominent in Beckett's own memories of the Abbey Theatre in his student days. For a gallery catalogue, *Samuel Beckett: An Exhibition*, Beckett offered to James Knowlson the information that the Irish dramas most vivid in his memory were "several" of O'Casey's plays, Yeats's plays including but not limited to two Sophocles "versions," "most" productions of Synge in the late 1920s, and two plays by Lennox Robinson (22–23). Shaw appeared in Beckett's comments as a negative aside, and Beckett's well-known response to a request for a tribute to Shaw, also recorded in Knowlson's catalogue, brought forth again a preference for specific works by Yeats, Synge, and O'Casey: "What I would do is give the whole unupsettable applecart for a sup of the Hawk's Well, or the Saints', or a whiff of Juno, to go no further" (23). As he was selective in his praise for Yeats's poetry and the state of Irish writing in "Recent Irish Poetry" in 1934, so Beckett was selective on these later dates in reference to Irish drama. Those names—Yeats, Synge, and O'Casey—may at this date seem a fairly comprehensive compendium, but a reading of Joseph Holloway's theater diaries from the late 1920s gives a corrective sense of the great mass of productions that go unmentioned by Beckett. Certainly, those recollections owe something to the moment of the question, which as posed by Knowlson was forty years or so after the fact. But they also point to the degree to which Beckett's plays constitute an extension of one strain in Irish drama, a strain most antithetical to a local dramatic "realism," and a strain generally ignored by the Abbey in the years between first productions of that trinity of Irish playwrights and of Beckett. That gap in time, between the 1920s and the 1950s, helps account for the interesting local effect of Beckett's dramatic work as retroactive influence. Beckett's plays help extricate a strain in the national drama for a time obscured. That retroactive action is evident in the new proposals for ideal programs of Irish plays lately offered by many critics. John Rees Moore would join *The Cat and the Moon* with *Godot* (246); Worth would join *Godot* with *The Well of the Saints* or *At the Hawk's Well* with *Endgame* (260); Robin Skelton would join *The Shadow of the Glen, Juno and the Paycock*, and *Godot* (63). For better or worse, these groupings shift the canon of Irish drama, alter the sense of individual plays, and suggest that the exclusively universal "application," as Leventhal said of *Godot*, may be arbitrary.

Works Cited

Bair, Dierdre. *Samuel Beckett: A Biography*. New York: Harcourt Brace Jovanovich, 1978.
Gontarski, S. E. *The Intent of Undoing in Samuel Beckett's Dramatic Texts*. Bloomington: Indiana UP, 1985.
Kenner, Hugh. *A Colder Eye: The Modern Irish Writers*. New York: Knopf, 1983.
Knowlson, James. *Samuel Beckett: An Exhibition*. London: Turret Books, 1971.
Leventhal, A. J. "Dramatic Commentary." *The Dublin Magazine* ns 31.1 (1956): 52–54.
Moore, John Rees. *Masks of Love and Death: Yeats as Dramatist*. Ithaca: Cornell UP, 1971.
Murray, Christopher. "Beckett Productions in Ireland: A Survey." *Irish University Review* 14.1 (1984): 103–25.
Skelton, Robin. *The Writings of J. M. Synge*. Indianapolis: Bobbs-Merrill, 1971.
Unseld, Siegfried. "To the Utmost: To Samuel Beckett on His Eightieth Birthday." *As No Others Dare Fail: For Samuel Beckett on His Eightieth Birthday By His Friends and Admirers*. New York: Riverrun, 1986. 91–95.
Worth, Katherine. *The Irish Drama of Europe from Yeats to Beckett*. Atlantic Highlands: Humanities Press, 1978.
Young, Jordan R. *The Beckett Actor: Jack MacGowran, Beginning to End*. Beverly Hills: Moonstone Press, 1987.

ANTHONY ROCHE

Beckett and Yeats: Among the Dreaming Shades†

On 22 December 1989 Samuel Beckett died in Paris of respiratory problems at the age of 83 and was buried at the Montparnasse Cemetery. His death evoked a complicated reaction: having been such an absent presence for so long and having described in his writings more than once the sensation of never having been born, Beckett still seems strangely present even in death. With the completion of Beckett's life work, it has become more apparent just how much and to what extent he and W. B. Yeats came to occupy similar imaginative terrain. They did so from widely divergent earlier positions. Yeats was the promoter of a school of self-consciously 'Irish' poets, who wore their prescribed nationalist emblems on their sleeves and in the lines of their verse. The direction the young Beckett took was towards Europe, modernism, and an experimental prose and verse, as far away as he could get from the mystification of the Celtic Twilight.

The major Irish writer Beckett literally followed was Joyce, not Yeats: by going to Paris, making deliberate contact with the Joyce family, assisting with the transcription of *Work in Progress*, and achieving his first publication in 1929 by contributing a critical es-

† From *Contemporary Irish Drama: From Beckett to McGuiness*. Published 1995 St. Martin's Press. Reproduced with permission of Palgrave MacMillan.

say, 'Dante . . . Bruno . . . Vico . . . Joyce', to *Our Exagmination Round his Factification for Incamination of Work in Progress*. But if Beckett began his writing career under the shadow of Joyce, there are two related points to be made. The first is that there naturally came a time when he had to declare his independence as a writer of prose from Joyce. Beckett did so in the following terms: 'the difference [between us] is that Joyce was a superb manipulator of material—perhaps the greatest. He was making words do the absolute maximum of work. . . . The kind of work I do is one in which I'm not master of my material. The more Joyce knew the more he could. He's tending towards omniscience and omnipotence as an artist. I'm working with impotence, ignorance.'[1] This adumbration of a poetics of failure by Beckett is something to which I will return, as constituting a major link with the later writings of Yeats.

But if Beckett began under the shadow of Joyce, by the end of his life and career the 'deepening shade' had become that of Yeats. On what proved to be his last visit in 1989, critic Hugh Kenner heard Beckett say: 'Now shall I make my soul'. With a jolt, Kenner recognised the first line of the last movement of Yeats's long poem, 'The Tower'. Beckett, with 'but a halt or two of memory',[2] slowly spoke the remaining lines of Yeats's poem, all the while relishing the sounds:

> Now shall I make my soul,
> Compelling it to study
> In a learned school
> Till the wreck of body,
> Slow decay of blood,
> Testy delirium
> Or dull decrepitude,
> Or what worse evil come—
> The death of friends, or death
> Of every brilliant eye
> That made a catch in the breath—
> Seem but the clouds of the sky
> When the horizon fades;
> Or a bird's sleepy cry
> Among the deepening shades.[3]

The content of one of Beckett's last mouthfuls of air might have come as less of a surprise to Kenner had he recalled the television play of 1976 entitled '. . . *but the clouds* . . .'. There, one of the objects of attention is the face of a woman repeatedly muttering words which only become fully audible, at the end of the play, as

1. Israel Shenker, "Moody Man of Letters," *New York Times* 6 May 1956: sect. 2, 1, 3.
2. *Irish Times*, 21 Nov. 1989.
3. *Poems* (Dublin: Gill and Macmillan, 1993), 199–200.

the last four lines of 'The Tower'. And Ulick O'Connor recalls Beckett at a Paris production of Yeats's *The Countess Cathleen*, 'reciting lovingly' the last three lines.

> The years like great black oxen tread the world,
> And God the herdsman goads them on behind,
> And I am broken by their passing feet.[4]

What makes these occasions so striking is, for one, the rare acknowledgment by a writer like Beckett, marked by radical originality, of this loving debt to a major precursor; and the no less surprising choice of Yeats rather than Joyce for the role. In the shift from one to the other is involved not only Beckett's freeing himself from Joyce's direct influence so he could continue to write prose, a prose concerned as he says to explore the implications not of linguistic mastery but of impotence and ignorance, but his equally crucial decision in 1947 to take up writing drama, an area where he found much more common ground with Yeats than he did in the radical difference of their poetry.

[It is the drama of both Yeats and Beckett that is] the site of the two Irish writers' greatest interaction. For Beckett, the drama offered a more tangible medium in which to work after the increasing abstractions of his prose. The theatre forced him to deal with objects in space and to take on a medium which restored the primacy of speech. For Yeats, what it offered was less rigidity rather than more, a place of refuge and remaking, not so much from Irish history as from the battery of personal and Gaelic icons with which he had opposed it. Symbolically, the theatre proved less of a prison and a more malleable site for Yeats than the tower, making possible a withdrawal from public assertions about Irish identity into the deeps of the mind where the problematic nature of that self could be examined. And it is in the drama that Beckett most clearly emerges as the successor to Yeats, taking up and developing the challenge of those difficult works.

* * *

* * * [Beckett's sojourning in the environs of the Abbey Theatre during the 1930s] coincided with the last ten years of Yeats's life, a decade which saw him return to the Abbey Theatre as a practising conventional straightforward plot is rejected, to be replaced by the formal elements of stasis, circularity and repetition.

When used to dramatise the encounter between the living and the dead in Yeats's plays, these structuring principles are incorporated formally into what he calls the 'dreaming back', a ghostly scenario in every sense. When 'the man is now in what is called the

---

4. *Collected Plays* (London: Macmillan, 1952), 50.

Dreaming Back . . . the murderer may be seen committing his murder night after night . . . or it may be that the dream is happy . . . or half tragic and half happy as when the mother, as the folklore of all nations and spiritualistic annals recalls, comes to her orphan children'.[5] Here, one can sense Yeats developing the 'dreaming back's' potential for drama as he goes on to stress the isolation of the dreamer, even with the ghosts of other people present. He argues that the dream may be dreamed 'once or many times' (the latter is usually the case with the tormented characters in his plays) and that it is now undergone, not with the ignorance which may then have accompanied it, but with full knowledge and experience of the consequences which followed it: 'the man must dream the event to its consequence as far as his intensity permit; not that consequence only which occurred while he lived, and was known to him, but those that were unknown, or have occurred after his death.' Examples of the 'dreaming back' occur in a great many Yeats plays, giving these plays their plot *and* content: the ghosts in *The Dreaming of the Bones*, for instance, who relive their original love affair with the added burden of knowing what has happened to Ireland in the intervening centuries as a result of their deed. The Old Man's mother in *Purgatory* now realises the consequences of her primal act and is drawn back to relive it repeatedly. But the question asked here and elsewhere in Yeats is: is she drawn to the sexual act again solely by remorse or also by pleasure? The double import of the 'dreaming back' for drama emerges as a way of dramatising history and its consequences, of foreshortening chronological time the better to disclose cause and effect, of framing and representing some historically primal act as a means of submitting it to questioning and revision.

Beckett has made dramatic capital of the Yeatsian 'dreaming back'. Even more than its deftness in submitting historical process to examination is the value of the 'dreaming back' as a means of deconstructing personal history. With both Yeats and Beckett the historical fate of their Anglo-Irish caste is implicated within the psychic dilemmas of their individual protagonists. In their plays based upon the process, a single dreamer is alone while events from a past life are being replayed and relived. As Yeats puts it: 'Every event so dreamed is the expression of some knot, some concentration of feeling separating off a period of time, or portion of the being, from the being as a whole and the life as a whole, and the dream is as it were a smoothing out or an unwinding.' The equation here of different periods of time with different portions of the self and the technical term 'unwinding' provide the clues as to which Beckett play is most relevant in relation to the 'dreaming back': *Krapp's Last Tape* (1958).

Krapp, all alone in his den, celebrates his seventieth birthday with the ritual of replaying an earlier taped autobiographical reminiscence from thirty years before. The theatrical development is the way in which Beckett technologises the procedure by using an on-stage tape-recorder to represent the content of the 'dreaming back'. The gap between the way the title character is now and his earlier self can be measured and compared by the audience in the course of the presentation, aided by the reactions of the spectator Krapp: the earlier preference for big, impressive words such as 'viduity', which he no longer understands and has to look up in a dictionary; the all too evident failure to renounce an addiction to bananas, despite a thirty-year-old resolution to do so. Above all else the present Krapp and the past, the old man and the young man, no longer mystified as two separate dramatic characters but here projected as two temporal aspects of the same self, are most differentiated by their/his changed attitudes to women and work. The tape concentrates on the progress of his intellectual life and career; it says goodbye to a 'girl in a shabby green coat, on a railway-station platform'. What the listening Krapp fast-forwards through is the lengthy account of intellectual discovery; what he obsessively returns to and replays is the erotic monologue in the punt:

> I lay down across her with my face in her breasts and my hand on her. We lay there without moving. But under us all moved, and moved us, gently, up and down, and from side to side.

Its form demonstrates that the present Krapp and his tastes are not to be given preference over those of the 39-year-old on the tape. For that voice in turn disdains an earlier taped self. We are shown the self as made up of so many layers of the onion or, to provide a more exact and denatured comparison, so many unwindings and rewindings of the spool. The taped voice reanimating the reverie in the punt finally takes over and is played out to the end. In this case, the sexual pleasure is vocally uppermost, but the framing context is one of remorse.

* * *

535

CONOR McPHERSON

Chronicles of the Human Heart†

At one stage in his memoir, *Almost a Gentleman*, the great British playwright John Osborne lets slip his true feelings about his 1950s Royal Court contemporary Samuel Beckett. He writes with languid derision about the "apostolic awe" Beckett inspired in the Royal Court's founding director, George Devine. "Uncle Sam had the monstrous good fortune of actually looking like one of his own plays, a graven icon of his own texts. The bristled cadaver and mountain-peak stare were the ultimate purifier that deified all endeavour, pity or hope." He goes on to say that, were Beckett's face fatter and less heroic-looking, "the response to that toneless voice might not have been so immediate." He finishes by declaring with barely hidden distaste—and not a little glee—that George Devine was unable to secure an actor to star as Hamm in the English-language premiere of *Endgame* and he "was reduced to having to attempt it himself. . . . It was brave but unmoving. It seemed a pretty long chew on a very dry prune [but] I would never have dreamed of saying so."

Obviously, Osborne's view of Beckett is coloured by a natural and (from a fellow playwright's point of view) understandable professional wariness of another big noise on the theatre block at that time. Indeed, the apostolic awe Beckett still provokes in certain theatre practitioners and academics has perhaps not done him any great service in the eyes of his critics. Fandom of Beckett can easily tip into a kind of fetishism typified by theatres who never produce one Beckett play when they can mount whole festivals of his work (as is happening at the Barbican this month), or actors who perform so many of his plays that they become known, almost exclusively, as Beckett actors. But there is no denying his influence. No other modern playwright has inspired so many disparate types of artists and thinkers. He has influenced painters, sculptors, designers, film-makers, philosophers, choreographers, directors, actors, musicians, and, of course, writers, in a way that could only have bewildered John Osborne.

In my opinion, Beckett's plays are probably best seen in (ahem) isolation, as each one is a beautifully honed, determined, focused world unto itself. While seeing lots together will raise awareness of the similarity between the plays, it may not help us to see how dis-

† From *The Guardian*, March 1, 2006. Reprinted by permission of the author.

tinct his best work is, even within his own canon. I believe that his plays will continue to echo through time because he managed to articulate a feeling as opposed to an idea. And that feeling is the unique human predicament of being alive and conscious. Of course, it's a very complicated feeling (and it's a complicated idea), but he makes it look simple because his great genius, along with his incomparable literary power, was the precision and clarity he brought to bear in depicting the human condition itself. That he did it with great warmth, humour, and moments of deep sadness, which are some of the most moving one could experience in the theatre, also speaks of his craft as a monumental playwright.

Any perusal of his plays must begin with *Waiting for Godot* (1952). This play has taken on, and will continue to have, a resonance similar to some of Shakespeare's greatest plays. Even people who have never seen it will have some idea of what it is like. In a bare, bleak landscape, two seemingly homeless old men, Vladimir and Estragon, attempt to pass the time while they wait for someone called Godot. The play spans two days (or two evenings really), and during both they experience oppressive boredom, random violence, unfruitful spiritual contemplation, real friendship, uneasy co-dependence, profound longing, and, ultimately, a deep, crushing uncertainty. They have problems remembering the day before. They don't know whether to leave or keep waiting. There is no resolution in the traditional sense. But it's really a revolutionary play because it takes the human mind itself as its subject matter and brilliantly dramatises it by splitting it in two.

Vladimir and Estragon speak to each other in the anxious, cajoling way human beings speak to themselves in their private moments. Fears are expressed and dismissed only to be unhelpfully reiterated in slightly different ways. Their feelings of love and hatred for each other jostle and even combine in the same impossible, tiny moment.

Psychologists suggest that the difference between productive thinking and worrying is that productive thinking flows; it moves forward to some kind of conclusion or sense of resolve. Worrying is just the same few unsettling thoughts going round and round like an annoying tune. This is how Vladimir and Estragon communicate, and how they dramatise the subjective experience itself. Their quarrels and musings often conjoin to form a kind of inclusive flow, as though they share one mind, but it always ends in dissatisfaction. For example, near the beginning of act two, when they nervously talk about "all the dead voices":

VLADIMIR.   What do they say?
ESTRAGON.   They talk about their lives.

VLADIMIR.   To have lived is not enough for them.
ESTRAGON.   They have to talk about it.
VLADIMIR.   To be dead is not enough for them.
ESTRAGON.   It is not sufficient.

[*Silence*]

VLADIMIR.   They make a noise like feathers.
ESTRAGON.   Like leaves.
VLADIMIR.   Like ashes.
ESTRAGON.   Like leaves.

[*Long silence*]

VLADIMIR.   Say something!
ESTRAGON: I'm trying.

Without a third party to become a benchmark for their wandering speculations, they are doomed to encircle the same futile topics forever—and they don't like it. They are waiting for Godot, but they are also contemplating suicide. Like Hamlet, they are even power-less to end their lives as they suspect it may only deliver them into another, perhaps even more painful existence.

Waiting for Godot, like *Hamlet*, is a benchmark in world litera-ture because, in an entirely new way, it presents the anxious, mod-ern, divided self as it witnesses the wanton cruelty of existence, unable to understand it, yet condemned to live it. It is the logical and emotional conclusion to the Cartesian foundation of our con-temporary western world: "I think therefore I am." With the exis-tence of thought itself as our only constant, no higher being or deity can adjudicate for the modern rational mind.

Considering that Beckett began writing plays in the aftermath of the horrific genocide of the Second World War, a war in which he fought alongside the French resistance, it is a testament to his character that the plays, while skating on the thin ice of our mortality, can be so funny. *Godot* is full of verbal jokes and visual slapstick routines based upon—what else?—confusion and misun-derstanding. While he opens the wound of the post-religious mind, at the same time he pours a salve of blessed warmth made possible only through the communal act of public presentation and laugh-ter. The very experience of enjoying and understanding the play be-comes its optimistic message, as opposed to anything glibly uttered by a character on the stage.

With his next play, *Endgame* (1957), Beckett shifts his focus from his ruminations on human thinking and turns to an examina-tion of human morals. It is a masterful play, full of jokes and real profundity, constructed like a vice that holds its ideas and pursuits centre stage in a riveting and disquieting way.

Where *Godot* is set in an unforgiving, almost featureless exterior, *Endgame* is set in a kind of claustrophobic bunker. Hamm is blind and unable to walk. He is attended upon by Clov, who can just about get around, coming and going from the room to fulfil Hamm's childlike whims. He does so not only because Hamm holds the combination to the larder that feeds them, but also because there seems to be nowhere else to go. They can see out of two grimy little windows, which Clov hoists a ladder to reach, but there is nothing (or "zero") out there. The two other occupants of the room are Nagg and Nell, Hamm's parents, whom he has consigned to live in dustbins. It is a truly apocalyptic vision, almost a bulletin from the height of the cold war, with its constant threat of nuclear annihilation.

But again, I like to see this play as a moving picture of the human mind—only this time it's what happens in the mind when we think about other human beings. The characters are racked with notions of responsibility and our desire to be free of it. Hamm works his way through the play trying to tell a story, or "chronicle" as he calls it, about how he was asked to take in a child to save him from starvation. This story causes Hamm great discomfort as he painstakingly pieces it back together, using many diversionary footnotes to prolong its conclusion. We come to understand that he is reluctant to reveal the ending as it places him in a moral catch-22 situation. If he refuses to save the child, does he have personal responsibility for his death, even though he did not personally cause it? And if he does save the child, has he accepted a logical responsibility to save anyone who is in a similar situation? He cannot possibly save everybody in the world and he fears that his inability to do so will only cause him further psychic pain.

In response to this puzzling problem, he seems to have chosen to shut down his whole life. He implores Clov (who may be the child he once saved) to "screw downs the lids" of the bins where his parents dwell. Cruelty seems easier than mercy to Hamm—it causes him less personal anguish. But Beckett strews the play with great humour and intriguing clues to Hamm's inner distress, suggesting that the sharp sting of moral choice is the price of being alive.

An echo of the reluctant storyteller resurfaces in *Krapp's Last Tape* (1958). Once again we are presented with a divided self, but this time brilliantly and realistically achieved with the presence of a tape recorder. Tucked away in his little "den," Krapp listens back to old diary entries and comments on them with curses and angry fast-forwarding, as he prepares to add a new one. The tension in the play is generated by his search for and, we come to realise, fear of a meaningful moment. He seems to dismiss the recordings of his past selves with disgust, implying that his present self and tonight's recording of it will also be dismissed in the future. His life appears to be an exercise in literally marking time, recording his diminishing sexual adventures and his laughable inability to kick his dependence on alcohol—and bananas.

But Beckett surprises the audience by allowing Krapp to stumble upon his 30-year-old account of a moment of perfect, almost trance-like bliss, in a punt on a stream with a past lover: "We lay there without moving. But under us all moved, and moved us, gently, up and down, and from side to side. (*Pause*) Past midnight. Never knew such silence. The earth might be uninhabited."

Krapp then attempts to dismiss this account with a new recording but finds himself listening to it again, motionless and spellbound as the play ends. It is a spine-tingling few minutes in the theatre, as Beckett illustrates that even our own attempts to duck life's experiences and cast our memories aside are impossible, for to experience even a moment of happiness blesses us with a kind of cosmic faith that is beyond language, and thus beyond denial.

Perhaps the supreme irony at the heart of Beckett's plays, and precisely the point that John Osborne missed, is that while he is often carelessly described as a 20th-century European existentialist who created hymns to "nothingness," he was in fact an Irish pagan who sought to celebrate the infinite mystery and endurance of the human heart through public rituals. His plays are not easy to perform and none can have been easy to write. But I believe that each one is enormously personal (perhaps this is why he never gave interviews), and while he always mercilessly stripped the work to its barest bones, at the same time he allowed his real feelings to shine through. This is what imbues his plays with their great power. They are also lovingly and respectfully shaped for an audience: this is what has made them enduring. And as long as they are performed with one eye on our spiritual longing, and another on the banana skin, they will continue to endure for generations yet to be born.

On Brian Friel

FIELD DAY THEATRE COMPANY

[Program Notes for *Translations*]†

Extract from The Hedge Schools of Ireland *by P. J. Dowling:–*

'The Hedge Schools owed their origin to the suppression of all the ordinary legitimate means of education, first during the Cromwellian regime and then under the Penal Code introduced in the reign of William III and operating from that time till within less than twenty years from the opening of the nineteenth century . . .

'The Hedge Schools were clearly of peasant institution. They were maintained by the people who wanted their children educated; and they were taught by men who came from the people . . .

'The poorest and humblest of the schools gave instruction in reading, writing and arithmetic; Latin, Greek, Mathematics and other subjects were taught in a great number of schools; and in many cases the work was done entirely through the medium of the Irish language. Though the use of the vernacular was rapidly falling into decay during the eighteenth century, it was owing to the greater value of English on the fair and market rather than to any shifting of ground on the part of the schools . . .

'The Hedge Schools were the most vital force in popular education in Ireland during the eighteenth century. They emerged in the nineteenth century more vigorous still, outnumbering all other schools, and so profoundly national as to hasten the introduction of a State system of education in 1831 . . .'

---

† Reprinted by permission of the Field Day Theatre Company.

Extract from The Autobiography of William Carleton (*born in County Tyrone, 1794*):–

'The only place for giving instruction was a barn. The barn was a loft over a cowshed and stable . . . It was one of the largest barns in the parish.

'(At the age of fourteen) I had only got as far as Ovid's *Metamorphoses*, Justin, and the first chapter of John in the Greek Testament.'

Extract from the memoirs of the Reverend Mr Alexander Ross, Rector, Dungiven, County Derry. 1814:–

'Even in the wildest districts, it is not unusual to meet with good classical scholars; and there are several young mountaineers of the writer's acquaintance, whose knowledge and taste in the Latin poets, might put to the blush many who have all the advantages of established schools and regular instruction.'

Extract from A History of Ireland *by Edmund Curtis:–*

'In 1831 Chief Secretary Stanley introduced a system of National Education . . . The system became a great success as an educational one but it had fatal effects on the Irish language and the old Gaelic tradition. According to Thomas Davis, at this time the vast majority of the people living west of a line drawn from Derry to Cork spoke nothing but Irish daily and east of it a considerable minority. It seems certain that at least two millions used it as their fireside speech . . . But the institution of universal elementary schools where English was the sole medium of instruction, combined with the influence of O'Connell, many of the priests, and other leaders who looked on Irish as a barrier to progress, soon made rapid inroads on the native speech . . .'

Extract from Ordnance Survey of Ireland *by Thomas Colby, Colonel, Royal Engineers (1835.):–*

'To carry on a minute Survey of all Ireland no collection of ready instructed surveyors would have sufficed. It, therefore, became indispensable to train and organise a completely new department for the purpose. Officers and men from the corps of Royal Engineers formed the basis of this new organisation, and very large numbers of other persons possessing various qualifications, were gradually added to them to expedite the great work . . .'

*   *   *

The mode of spelling the names of places was peculiarly vague and unsettled, but on the maps about to be constructed it was desirable to establish a standard orthography, and for future reference, to identify the several localities with the names by which they had formerly been called . . .'

Extract from the Spring Rice Report (advocating a general survey of Ireland) to the British Government; 21 June 1824:–

'The general tranquillity of Europe, enables the state to devote the abilities and exertions of a most valuable corps of officers to an undertaking, which, though not unimportant in a military point of view, recommends itself more directly as a civil measure. Your committee trust that the survey will be carried on with energy, as well as with skill, and that it will, when completed, be creditable to the nation, and to the scientific acquirements of the present age. In that portion of the Empire to which it more particularly applies, it cannot but be received as a proof of the disposition of the legislature to adopt all measures calculated to advance the interests of Ireland.'

Extracts from the letters of John O'Donovan, a civilian employee with the Ordnance Survey, later Professor of Celtic Studies, Queen's College, Belfast:–

Buncrana
23 August 1835
'On Friday we travelled through the Parish of Clonmary and ascended the Hill of Beinnin. Clonmany is the most Irish Parish I have yet visited; the men only, who go to markets and fairs, speak a little English, the women and children speak Irish only. This arises from their distance from Villages and Towns and from their being completely environed by mountains, which form a gigantic barrier between them and the more civilized and less civil inhabitants of the lower country.'

Dun Fionnchada? Dun Fionnchon?
Dunfanaghy
9 September 1835
'I am sick to death's door of the names on the coast, because the name I get from one is denied by another of equal intelligence and authority to be correct. The only way to settle these names would be to summon a Jury and order them to say and present 'uppon ther Oathes" what these names are and ought to be. But there are several of them such trifling places that it seems to me that it matters not which of two or three appelations we give them. For example,

the name Timlin's Hole is not of thirty years standing and will give way to another name as soon as that dangerous hole shall have swallowed a fisherman of more illustrious name than Tim Lyn.'

Glenties
15 October 1835
'Yesterday being a fair-day at Dunglow we were obliged to leave it in consequence of the bustle and confusion. We directed our course southwards through the Parish of Templecroan, keeping Traigh Eunach (a name which I find exceedingly difficult to Anglicise) to the right . . . On the road we met crowds of the women of the mountains who were loaded with stockings going to the stocking fair of Dunglow and who bore deep graven on their visages the effects of poverty and smoke, of their having been kept alive by the potatoe only . . . I have seen several fields of oats on this coast, some prostrated and rotting, others with the grain completely blown off the stalk—and some so green in October as to preclude the possibility of ripening at all.'

Ballyshanny
1 November 1835
'I have met in this town a fine old man named Edward Quin, from whom I have received a good deal of information. He has been employed by Lieutenant Vickers to give the Irish names of places about Ballyshannon, and has saved me a good deal of trouble—I wish you could induce Mr Vickers to take him to his next district, and keep him employed writing in the Name Books, and taking down the names from the pronounciation of the country people.'

BRIAN FRIEL

Making a Reply to the Criticisms of *Translations* by J. H. Andrews (1983)†

* * *

Perhaps the simplest thing might be if I were to tell you, very briefly, something about the genesis of *Translations* and the notions I was flirting with before I came across *A Paper Landscape*[1] and how those notions were adjusted and how they evolved after reading that book.

† From Christopher Murray, ed., *Brian Friel: Essays, Diaries, Interviews 1964–1999*. Reprinted by permission of Faber & Faber, Inc., an affiliate of Farrar, Straus, and Giroux, LLC.
1. By J. H. Andrews (Oxford: Clarendon Press, 1975 [*Editor*].

At any given time every playwright has half a dozen ideas that drift in and out of his awareness. For about five years before I wrote *Translations* there were various nebulous notions that kept visiting me and leaving me: a play set in the nineteenth century, somewhere between the Act of Union and the Great Famine; a play about Daniel O'Connell and Catholic emancipation; a play about colonialism; and the one constant—a play about the death of the Irish language and the acquisition of English and the profound effects that that change-over would have on a people. These were the kinds of shadowy notions that visited me and left me. But even when they had left me, from some of those ideas I was still getting persistent and strong signals.

During that same period (I am talking about the period prior to attempting the play that became *Translations*) I made two accidental discoveries. One, I learned that a great-great-grandfather of mine, a man called McCabe from County Mayo, had been a hedge-schoolmaster, had left Mayo and had come up to Donegal where he settled; and it was whispered in the family that he was fond of a drop. That discovery sent me into reading about the hedge-schools in this country and particularly to [P. J.] Dowling's *The Hedge Schools of Ireland*. And the second casual discovery I made at that time—this was really shameful but I hadn't known it until that point—was that directly across the River Foyle from where I live in Muff is a place called Magilligan and it was at Magilligan that the first trigonometrical base for the ordnance survey was set up in 1828; and the man in charge of that survey was Colonel Colby. And that discovery sent me to Colby's book, *A Memoir of the City and the North-West Liberties of Londonderry*, a very rich and wonderful book. And about the same time, too, as I made these discoveries, I began reading the letters that John O'Donovan wrote when he was working for the Ordnance Survey. He was surveying in Donegal in 1835, 'taking place-names'—if I may quote approximately from the play—'that were riddled with confusion and standardizing those names as accurately and as sensitively as he could.' So that was the general background: fugitive notions of a play about language, and simultaneously an incipient interest in the ordnance survey itself and particularly in the orthographical pursuits and torments of John O'Donovan.

Then in 1976 I came across *A Paper Landscape*. And suddenly here was the confluence—the aggregate—of all those notions that had been visiting me over the previous years: the first half of the nineteenth century: an aspect of colonialism; the death of the Irish language and the acquisition of English. Here were all the elements I had been dallying with, all synthesized in one very comprehensive and precise text. Here was the perfect metaphor to accommodate and realize all those shadowy notions—map-making. Now, it seemed to me, all I had to do was dramatize *A Paper Landscape*. (It seemed an excess of good luck that even Daniel O'Connell appeared in the book: 'A newspaper report of 1828 drew the idyllic picture of how the people of Glenomara, Country Clare, had helped the engineers to build a trigonometrical station, climbing their mountain in a great crowd with flutes, pipes and violins, and young women bearing laurel leaves; although they insisted on naming the station "O'Connell's Tower".' Even the detail of the young women bearing laurel leaves had the reassuring echoes of Ibsen.)

I plunged straight off into a play about Colonel Colby, the prime mover in the ordnance survey of this island. Writers sometimes allow themselves to be seduced by extraneous and altogether trivial elements in their material; and what fascinated me about Colby was not that he masterminded the huge task of mapping this country for the best part of forty years but the fact that he had one hand. That Oedipal detail seemed crucial to me, mesmerized me. And for many deluded months I pursued Colby and tried to make him amenable to my fictional notion of him. The attempt failed. And Colby appears in *Translations* as a minor character called Captain Lancey.

When Colby escaped me, I turned my attention to John O'Donovan. And just as I allowed myself to be misled by Colby's missing hand, so now I indulged in an even more bizarre and dangerous speculation: I read into O'Donovan's exemplary career as a scholar and orthographer the actions and perfidy of a quisling. (The only excuse I can offer for this short-lived delusion is that the political situation in the North was particularly tense about that time.) Thankfully, that absurd and cruel reading of O'Donovan's character was short-lived. But it soured a full tasting of the man. And O'Donovan appears in the play as a character called Owen.

I now went back to the earlier notion of trying to do something with O'Connell. But he had no part in the map-making metaphor, to which I was now wedded. And in my disappointment poor O'Connell gets only a few lines in the play.

Finally and sensibly I abandoned the idea of trying to dramatize *A Paper Landscape* and embarked on a play about a drunken hedge-schoolmaster.

Now that I meet Professor Andrews for the first time I want to thank him for providing me with that metaphor and to apologize to him for the tiny bruises inflicted on history in the play. He has pointed out the [historical] error of the bayonet. I would like to admit to a couple of other sins. One is having Donegal renamed in 1833 when in fact the task was not undertaken until two years later. Another is calling one of the characters Yolland and placing him in Donegal in 1833 when in fact the actual Yolland did not join the survey department until 1838. But I am sure that Professor Andrews will agree that the imperatives of fiction are as exacting as the imperatives of cartography and historiography.

Writing an historical play may bestow certain advantages but it also imposes particular responsibilities. The apparent advantages are the established historical facts or at least the received historical ideas in which the work is rooted and which give it its apparent familiarity and accessibility. The concomitant responsibility is to acknowledge those facts or ideas but not to defer to them. Drama is first a fiction, with the authority of fiction. You don't go to *Macbeth* for history.

Thomas Heywood, a contemporary of Shakespeare, defined historical plays—or chronicle plays, as he called them—in these terms:

> Chronicle plays are written with this aim and carried with this method: to teach the subjects obedience to their king; to show the people the untimely ends of such as have moved tumults, commotions and insurrections; to present them with the flourishing estate of such as live in obedience, exhorting them to allegiance, dehorting them from all traitorous and felonious stratagems.

If we accept that definition of an historical play, *Translations* is a total failure. But viewed from a different age—and maybe a different island—perhaps some merit can be found in it.

CHRISTOPHER MORASH

[*Translations*: A Night at the Theatre]†

* * *

* * * When Friel finished writing *Translations* on 5 November 1979, he could have handed it to the Abbey, or looked for a venue in New York, where his previous play, *Faith Healer*, had opened. However, Friel wanted greater control over the staging of his plays, telling Ciaran Carty in the *Sunday Independent* he was 'very doubtful about the whole idea of a director interpreting a play in any kind of way that's distinctive to him'.[1] Similarly, [Stephen] Rea could have remained in London, where he had an established acting career at the National Theatre. However, he too was chaffing at the

† From *History of Irish Theatre, 1601–2000*. Copyright © Christopher Morash 2002. Reprinted with the permission of Cambridge University Press.
1. *Sunday Independent*, 5 Oct. 1980.

limitations imposed by success. 'Friel and I often talked of our no-tion of theatre in Ireland', Rea told an interviewer in October 1980. 'You know, an Irishman in English theatre is very conscious of be-longing to a sub-culture rather than a culture proper. I felt less ex-pressed in terms of England than I did over here, but not in the narrow national way.'[2]

A few years earlier, these aspirations might have come to noth-ing. There had been almost no Arts Council money for new theatre companies throughout the 1970s, but by early 1980 cultural policy was edging towards the idea of decentralisation. Consequently, when Friel and Rea decided to stage *Translations* themselves, the Northern Ireland Arts Council told them that they would be eligible for funding if they were members of an existing regional com-pany—whereupon they formed a company called Field Day, a play on their combined names: Friel / Rea. The Northern Ireland Arts Council gave them £40,000, while the Arts Council in the Repub-lic later added £10,000. Meanwhile, Derry City offered them use of the Victorian Guildhall, and voted out of their own funds an addi-tional £13,000 with which to build a lighting rig and construct a stage. By 6 June 1980, Friel, Rea, and Derry's Lord Mayor Marlene Jefferson were able to announce the date of the opening.

At that point, the play had already been cast in a way that would give the production its shape. The plot of *Translations* is both sim-ple and conventional, a cross-cultural romantic triangle that ends in tragedy. It is set in 1833 on the Irish-speaking Inishowen penin-sula of Donegal, in a hedge school run by a polyglot master, Hugh O'Donnell, and his son Manus. A British Army Ordnance Survey team arrive, accompanied by Manus's brother, Owen, to begin tri-angulation work for what will become the standard map of the whole island. An attraction quickly develops between one of the school's adult students, Maire, who had been betrothed to Manus, and an English officer, Lieutenant Yolland. Yolland then disappears, and the play ends with Yolland's superior officer, Captain Lancey, threatening to destroy the entire parish unless he is found, driving Manus into hiding.

Described in these terms, *Translations* sounds like a naturalistic play with a triangular love story plot. However, of the three charac-ters at the centre of this story, in the Field Day production only Manus was played by a well-known actor, Mick Lally, while the roles of Maire and Yolland were filled by two relatively unknown performers, Nuala Hayes and Shaun Scott. By contrast, Stephen Rea cast himself as Owen, and chose Ray McAnally as the school-master, Hugh. Owen and Hugh may be background characters in

2. *Irish Times*, 10 Oct. 1980.

the love story, but they are at the crux of the meeting between two cultures—Owen as the translator accompanying the Ordnance Survey, and Hugh as the play's linguistic philosopher. In a sense therefore, the casting of the first *Translations* recognised that it is a love story in which the foreground and background have been reversed.

While Rea played Owen with the kind of economy of gesture that would characterise his later film work, McAnally's performance was at the heart of the Derry *Translations*. His film career went back to *Shake Hands with the Devil* in 1959, and his stage work began with the Abbey's days in the Queen's,[3] when he played the lead in Walter Macken's *Twilight of a Warrior*. 'Watching this actor at work is sheer joy', wrote Gus Smith reviewing the play. McAnally was at his best playing characters who are self-consciously playing a part. The title role in Sam Thompson's *The Evangelist* gave him one such role in 1961; Commandant Frank Butler, who he played in the first production of Friel's *Living Quarters* in 1977 was another; and so, of course, is Hugh in *Translations*. While such roles are easily overplayed, McAnally's Hugh 'verged on slow motion', so that 'with a mere flicker of his eyes, or movement of his hand he conveyed a world of meaning'. Dressed, unlike any of the other characters, in a flowing knee-length greatcoat, he 'dominated the stage each time he appeared', in spite of the fact that his character—like Stephen Rea's Owen—has almost no influence on the development of the plot.[4]

Weighting the play towards Hugh creates a palpable sense of loss in the play's final moments. With Owen torn between two sets of responsibilities, Manus on the run, and the hedge school dispersed, Hugh stands alone on the stage at the curtain with Maire and the 'infant prodigy', Jimmy Jack, an aging, gently-mad scholar who dreams of wedding the Greek goddess, Pallas Athene. In later productions, Jimmy Jack would often be played as a wizened old man; in Derry, however, Roy Hanlon's Jimmy Jack was a heavy-set, bearded figure, whose strong physical resemblance to McAnally's Hugh (also bearded) made him into a kind of admonitory *doppelganger*. 'It is not the literal past, the "facts" of history, that shape us, but images of the past embodied in language', Hugh tells Owen in the play's closing scene. 'James has ceased to make that discrimination.' In the diminuendo slide to the curtain, Hugh and Jimmy Jack merge, their erudition turning them into helpless prisoners of 'a linguistic contour which no longer matches the landscape of fact'.

---

3. The Abbey Company performed in Dublin's Queen's Theatre from the burning of its old building in 1951 and the opening of a new one in 1966 [*Editor*].
4. *Irish Press*, 13 Jan. 1981; *Sunday Independent*, 12 Oct. 1980; *Belfast Telegraph*, 24 Sept. 1980.

Apart from his commanding stage presence, McAnally had another great advantage in playing Hugh: he was born in Moville, just up the banks of Lough Foyle from Derry on the Donegal side. When Friel and Rea cast him in *Translations*, McAnally had just finished directing a young Ballymena actor, Liam Neeson, in a Dublin production of John Steinbeck's *Of Mice and Men*, and Neeson followed the older actor to Derry to play Doalty. Selecting a predominantly Ulster cast was a conscious decision, with Brenda Scallon (from Enniskillen, County Fermanagh) playing Bridget, and Ann Hasson (from Derry) as the mute Sarah. In performance, there was no mistaking the cast's origins, as their native Ulster accents, nurtured by six weeks' rehearsal in Derry, were allowed to come through strongly—so much so that one Dublin-based critic thought they 'may have to be toned down when the play comes south'.[5] In particular, Liam Neeson gave such free rein to his Northern vowels that some Southern critics could not understand him. By contrast, Captain Lancey, 'the perfect colonial servant' who threatens to destroy the parish at the end of the play, was played by an English actor, David Heap.

Translations is, of course, a play about 'the meeting of two cultures, and specifically of two languages', as Friel told the *Derry People*.[6] On the stage, this was clearly underlined in the contrast between the clean lines and primary colours of the British army uniforms, and the rumpled layers and mottled earth tones worn by the Irish characters. However, *Translations* is also about a collision between the values of a local community and a centralised state. The need to change place names arises not so much from a will to dominate on the part of the Ordnance Survey cartographers, as from the need for uniformity throughout the entire island. By contrast, when a name is used locally, it need only correspond to the communal lore out of which it arises. 'Look at that crossroads, Tobair Vree', Owen tells Yolland. 'Why do we call it Tobair Vree? . . . Tobair means a well . . . Because a hundred and fifty years ago there used to be a well there . . . and an old man called Brian, whose face was disfigured by an enormous growth, got it into his head that the water in the well was blessed; and every day for seven months he went there and bathed his face in it. But the growth didn't go away; and one morning Brian was found drowned in that well.'

Staging *Translations* in Derry thus generated the kind of local, community passion usually associated with the amateur theatre

5. *Evening Herald*, 24 Sept. 1980.
6. *Derry People*, 27 Sept. 1980.

(and, indeed, amateur companies would quickly make the play a staple of the festival circuit). Considered in the context of some of the concerns about the nature of language in *Translations*, this can be seen as part of the production's meaning, rather than simply a strategy to generate press interest and fill seats. 'The play has a great deal of political resonance', Stephen Rea told the *Derry Journal*. 'If we put it on in a place like Dublin's Abbey Theatre, its energy would be contained within the theatre and its clientele. But its energy is bound to spread much more profoundly through a place like Derry.'[7] Performing *Translations* with a largely Ulster cast in a building only a few miles from its Donegal setting allowed the audience to feel the same kind of local pride that the play itself sets against any kind of centralising, standardising authority, be it imperial or national. Like the character of Hugh, the audience's experience of the Derry production drew heavily on what he calls 'the *desiderium nostorum*—the need for our own'.

This feeling was powerfully vindicated on 23 September 1980, when Derry became the cultural centre of Ireland for the night. Joining Cyril Cusack, Friel and local politicians on their way to the Guildhall for the première were two future Nobel Laureates, Seamus Heaney and John Hume, as well as the Abbey's Artistic Director, Joe Dowling, Colm O'Briain and Michael Longley from the two Arts Councils, Tom Murphy, Seamus Deane, and reporters from all of the major Irish and British newspapers, including Eamonn McCann, who had been behind the protest over *A State of Chassis* in 1970. Also in the audience was the Catholic Bishop of Derry, Most Rev. Dr Edward Daly, a founder of the '71 Players. 'I have always emphasized the importance of culture as an antidote to violence', Bishop Daly told a reporter. '*Translations* could not have come at a better time.'[8]

When this audience first took their seats, there was initially little to suggest that they were about to watch what Friel would later describe as 'a three-act naturalistic play'. Consolata Boyle's design was not a conventional naturalistic box set, in that it lacked side flats, and the stage was a seven-sided thrust with 1:16 rake, lacking the proscenium arch usually associated with naturalism. Along the back of the stage, she built a simple wall of unfinished, vertical wooden boards, angled along the top so as to create a false perspective. In this wall were two unframed doors, one stage right, and one opening to a small platform, just left of centre at the set's highest point (rising to about 12 feet (3.6 metres)) reached by six stairs. There was almost no stage furniture, apart from a table down left,

7. *Derry Journal*, 23 Sept. 1980.
8. *Derry Journal*, 26 Sept. 1980.

and a few very low scattered stools, so that the set's most prominent feature was the large, open playing space, projecting out towards the audience—ideal for an actor like McAnally.

'The play has to do with language', Friel wrote in his diary as he
was working on *Translations*, 'and only with language.'[9] Just as casting decisions pushed the two characters most intimately associated
with language—Owen and Hugh—to the fore, so too did the thrust
stage emphasise the play's linguistic focus (even if the Guildhall's
high ceilings were an acoustic nightmare). In order to emphasise
this point, the love scene between Yolland and Maire was the only
scene in the play to be played completely downstage, creating a moment in which the two characters are alone, surrounded by a void
of darkness. As they reach out to each other from their linguistically separate worlds, the play's most important theatrical device—
that characters speaking English are accepted by the audience as
speaking Irish—is at its most self-exposed. In a sense, this was the
point towards which the entire production moved. Everything afterwards was, in a sense, an extended coda, and was played as such—
so much so that some reviewers criticised Art O Briain's direction
for allowing too much of a falling off in the final act.

In his diary, however, Friel also wrote 'it is a political play—how
can that be avoided?' Towering above Consolata Boyle's set on that
opening night was the Guildhall's mighty pipe organ (which was
left unmasked) framed by neo-Gothic oak panels and coats of arms.
More than any other building in Derry, the Guildhall was a symbol
of unionist power. Indeed, in his play set in the aftermath of a Civil
Rights march seven years earlier, *The Freedom of the City*, Friel had
used the building in precisely this way, an irony not lost on anyone
who attended the opening night of *Translations*. '*Translations* deals
powerfully with a number of themes of particular interest to Republicans', wrote the Sinn Féin weekly, *An Phoblacht*: 'language
and identity, the meaning of education and its relation to political
reality, colonial conquest through cultural imperialism'.[1] At the
same time, it was possible for the unionist Lord Mayor of Derry to
lead a standing ovation on the opening night.

The Derry production of *Translations* was clearly designed to provoke debate, and in this it succeeded. While the show was still on
its Irish tour, and on the eve of the IRA Hunger Strikes, Seamus
Heaney set the agenda for much that would follow when he wrote
in *The Times Literary Supplement* in October 1980 that the play
forced us to examine 'the need we have to create enabling myths of

---

9. *Essays, Diaries, Interviews: 1964–1999*, ed. Christopher Murray (London: Faber and
   Faber, 1999) 75.
1. *An Phoblacht*, 11 Oct. 1980.

ourselves and the danger we run if we too credulously trust to the
sufficiency of these myths'. A few years later, in a public debate
held in January 1983, the historian J. H. Andrews, whose study of
the Ordnance Survey, *A Paper Landscape*, suggested the mapping
metaphor in *Translations*, took Friel gently to task for what the playwright admitted were 'tiny bruises inflicted on history in the play'.
The debate's moderator, Kevin Barry, developed this exchange into
a wider discussion on *Translations* as a 'collision between fiction
and history that re-interprets the past in such a way as to project an
imagined and persuasive future'.[2]

* * *

SEAMUS HEANEY

[Review of *Translations*]†

Brian Friel's *Translations*, which has just finished its very successful
run at the Dublin Theatre Festival, plays elaborate variations on an
old theme. Perhaps Joyce stated it most succinctly in the classic
passage towards the end of *A Portrait of the Artist* where the English
Jesuit confuses Stephen Dedalus by calling a tundish a funnel, and
Stephen goes on to meditate on the consequences of the language
shift in Ireland from Irish to English: "The language we are speaking is his before it is mine . . . my soul frets in the shadow of his
language". For a moment Joyce allows Stephen to indulge the myth
of dispossession, though he is careful to allow him another, steelier
moment when Stephen tells Davin that his people threw off their
own language willingly.

The play is set in Irish-speaking Donegal in the 1830s, at a time
when the dispossession or abandonment began to accelerate. A
corps of the Royal Engineers is at work on the Ordnance Survey of
Ireland, anglicizing and standardizing the place-names—"making
sense" of them. Captain Lancey and Lieutenant Yolland are being
assisted in their work by Owen, son of the local hedge-
schoolmaster, Hugh O'Donnell, while being resented by his other
son, Manus. Yolland falls for Manus's fiancée (or perhaps one
should translate this to his "intended"), tribal lines get tangled and
things fall apart.

Traditional characters (redcoat soldier, shawled girl, hedge-
schoolmaster—this last a drily realized portrait by Ray McAnally)

2. "*Translations* and a Paper Landscape," *Crane Bag* 7.2 (1983): 120, 123.
† *Times Literary Supplement* 24 Oct. 1980. Reprinted by permission of the *Times Literary Supplement*.

and traditional motifs (eviction, potato-blight, poteen) are woven together with a mixture of irony and elegy. Friel knows that there were
certain inadequacies within the original culture that unfitted it to
survive the impact of the English presence and domination, but the
play is not simply a historical entertainment. What the schoolmaster says to Lieutenant Yolland in Act 2 is symptomatic of Friel's vig-
ilant concern with the way we still use language in Ireland (and in
England?). "It can happen that a civilization can be imprisoned in a
linguistic contour that no longer matches the landscape of fact."

In the 1830s the landscape of fact included the new National
Schools where the instruction was free and in English, but Friel's
scene is a hedge-school—a kind of fit-up classical academy—where
the first language is Irish, although Latin and Greek are to be heard
almost as frequently. We do not hear Irish on the stage, of course—
and that "of course" tells us how successful the National School
system was—yet once the English soldiers arrive we understand
that it is the language of the Donegal characters, because Owen,
the son who has arrived back from Dublin with them, begins to act
as go-between and interpreter. This allows Friel to show, at times
comically and at times angrily, that there are still two kinds of
speech within what appears to be a common language shared by
the two islanders. It also allows him to show Owen assisting in the
annihilation of the place he came from as he translates the place-
names into English and literally changes the map.

Owen (played with brio and a proper bewilderment by Stephen
Rea) is a key figure in the dispossession / abandonment uncertainty.
His brother Manus sees him as a betrayer, his father, more cautiously, sees him as a kind of success, and he cannot quite manage
to see to himself. Significantly, he cannot settle for a name: he is Owen
to the natives but his soldier friends call him Roland and he does
not quite deny them their mistake. There is a lovely moment at the
end when the place-names he has anglicized are read out by Captain
Lancey in their new versions and Owen must translate them back
into Irish for the benefit of his neighbours. It is a list of places that
the army is now intent on devastating in retaliation for the presumed killing of Lieutenant Yolland. The betrayer is betrayed.

Brian Friel has by now [1980] produced a more significant body of
work than any other playwright in Ireland, and it is time that he was,
as it were, translated. I am sure this piece would come home like a
remembrance in, for example, Derek Walcott's theatre in Trinidad.
His recent plays—*Aristocrats* and *Faith healer* last year, and now
Translations—show him in the grip of a major theme. He has come
in from different angles but with a constant personal urgency upon
the need we have to create enabling myths of ourselves and the danger we run if we too credulously trust to the sufficiency of these

myths. In the opening moment of *Translations*, a girl who has been
mute is being taught by Manus to say: "My name is Sarah". Nothing
can stop her now, Manus assures her, she can say who she is so she
is safe. Towards the end of the play, however, when the English captain demands who she is, his command and strangeness scare her:
"My name . . . my name is . . ." is all she can manage. It is as if some
symbolic figure of Ireland from an eighteenth-century vision poem,
the one who once confidently called herself Cathleen Ni Houlihan,
has been struck dumb by the shock of modernity. Friel's work, not
just here but in his fourteen preceding plays, constitutes a powerful
therapy, a set of imaginative exercises that give her the chance to
know and say herself properly to herself again.

MARILYNN J. RICHTARIK

[*Translations*: On the Page and On the Stage]†

* * *

In *Translations* the playwright concerns himself consistently with
language and what it means. As mentioned earlier, the displacement of one language by another in the play, epitomized by the
changing of place-names, is a metaphor for the alienation experienced by Irish people under English rule. The two most remarkable
features of the play, noted by virtually all contemporary reviewers
from the most sophisticated London and Dublin critics to anonymous correspondents for small local papers, are: (1) the convention
whereby the audience is led to believe that it is hearing both Irish
and English spoken when in fact everyone is speaking English, and
(2) the love scene between Maire and Yolland in which they manage to convey their affection for each other without the benefit of a
common language.[1]

For many of the ideas informing his treatment of language in the
play Friel was indebted to George Steiner, whose book *After Babel*
he was reading while writing *Translations* and working on a version
of Chekhov's *Three Sisters*. Friel acknowledged Steiner in the pro-

† From *Acting Between the Lines: The Field Day Theatre Company and Irish Cultural Politics*. Used with permission: the Catholic University of America Press, Washington, D.C.
1. Friel says 'Of course a fundamental irony of this play is that it should have been written
in Irish.' (Friel, 'Talking to Ourselves', interview by Paddy Agnew, *Magill*, Dec. 1980,
59.) The approach also raises the question of whether the English and Irish would have
been able to communicate any better if they had spoken the same language (as they do
today). The idea that this was a deliberate effect is borne out by the fact that when Friel
gave permission to Chomhlachas Náisiúnta Drámaíochta to produce *Translations* in
Irish he did so only on the condition that the entire play be translated. '*Translations* Le
hAistriu—Go Gaeilge!', *Inniu*, 16 Jan. 1981 (trans. by Marc Caball).

gramme notes, and several of the play's most memorable lines are taken almost verbatim from this book. For example, Hugh's remark that 'it can happen that a civilization can be imprisoned in a linguistic contour which no longer matches the landscape of . . . fact' is an echo of Steiner's dictum that 'A civilization is imprisoned in a linguistic contour which no longer matches . . . the changing landscape of fact.'[2]

Steiner's fundamental point is that translation is only a special case of communication in general. All human speech involves a large component of interpretation:

> Any model of communication is at the same time a model of translation, of a vertical or horizontal transfer of significance. No two historical epochs, no two social classes, no two localities use words and syntax to signify exactly the same things, to send identical signals of valuation and inference. Neither do two human beings.[3]

Perhaps his most radical suggestion is that 'communication outward is only a secondary, socially stimulated phase in the acquisition of language. Speaking to oneself would be the primary function.'[4] He argues that the greatest power of language is its capacity for 'counter-factuality' (*Language is the main instrument of man's refusal to accept the world as it is*') and that 'Human speech conceals far more than it confides; it blurs much more than it defines; it distances more than it connects.'[5]

Steiner's model of communication is one of concentric circles spreading outwards from the most inner, private speech to a speech that includes larger and larger groups of people:

> We speak first to ourselves, then to those nearest us in kinship and locale. We turn only gradually to the outsider, and we do so with every safeguard of obliqueness, of reservation, of conventional flatness or outright misguidance. At its intimate centre, in the zone of familial or totemic immediacy, our language is most economic of explanation, most dense with intentionality and compacted implication. Streaming outward it thins, losing energy and pressure as it reaches an alien speaker.[6]

---

2. George Steiner, *After Babel* (Oxford: Oxford UP, 1975). Other examples of this 'translation' include: 'To remember everything is a condition of madness' (Steiner, 29); '[T]here will be in every complete speech-act a more or less prominent element of translation. All communication "interprets" between privacies' (Steiner, 198); 'Often, cultures seem to expend on their vocabulary and syntax acquisitive energies and ostentations entirely lacking in their material lives. Linguistic riches seem to act as a compensatory mechanism' (Steiner, 55). Compare Hugh's lines; 'certain cultures expend on their vocabularies and syntax acquisitive energies and ostentations entirely lacking in their material lives.'
3. Steiner, 45.
4. Ibid., 120.
5. Ibid., 217–18, 229.
6. Ibid., 231.

This substantial element of exclusiveness in language means that 'there is in every act of translation—and specially where it succeeds—a touch of treason'.[7]

In the debate between the 'universalists' (who believe differences between languages are surface phenomena) and the 'monadists', Steiner aligns himself more with the latter in maintaining that each language creates its own particular 'mapping' of conscious being, of 'reality'. Nevertheless, Steiner does not contend, as some extreme monadists have, that translation is therefore impossible. It would be logically inconsistent for him to argue this without arguing as well that communication of any kind is an impossibility. Instead he asserts that, though good translation is extremely rare and there is no such thing as perfect translation, there are 'examples which seem to approach the limits of empirical possibility'.[8] He seems to say, like Hugh at the end of *Translations*, 'It's all we have.'

Richard Kearney sees the contrast between two conceptions of language, 'one ontological, the other positivistic', as the central focus of Friel's play: 'The former treats language as a house of Being; the latter treats it as a mechanical apparatus for the representation of objects.'[9] He is impressed by Friel's refashioning of Steiner's sholarly work in popular terms, calling the play an outstanding example of how 'criticism may be retranslated back into imaginative practice'.[1] James Simmons agrees, 'the boldness and deftness that makes large audiences dwell on the subtle importance of changing the names of places is stunning'.[2] The diary Friel kept while he was writing *Translations* records his struggle to incorporate this linguistic theory without betraying the play itself. On 3 July 1979 he wonders, 'Are the characters only mouthpieces. . . . Is the play only an ideas play? And indeed are those ideas amenable to dramatic presentation?' On 6 July he isolates one of the problems he faces as 'the almost wholly *public* concern of the theme. . . . How long can a *society* live without its tongue?' and reminds himself of his belief that the play should 'concern itself only with the exploration of the dark and private places of individual souls'.[3]

Judging from the evident appeal of *Translations* to a large and very diverse group of people, we might conclude that Friel overcame these difficulties to write a play full of human interest. That play none the less deals with theoretical linguistic questions. How-

7. Ibid., 233.
8. Ibid., 407.
9. Kearney, *Transitions: Narratives in Modern Irish Culture* (Manchester, 1988), 155, 136.
1. Ibid., 138.
2. James Simmons, "Brian Friel, Catholic Playwright," *Honest Ulsterman* 79 (Autumn 1985): 65–66.
3. Friel, 'Extracts from a Sporadic Diary', in Tim Pat Coogan (ed.), *Ireland and the Arts* (a Special Issue of *Literary Review*) (London, 1983), 60.

ever, it is somewhat disingenuous to say, as Friel did once (and as numerous people have quoted him as saying since) that 'the play has to do with language and only language.'[4] When an Irish playwright talks about language, it has a political edge. As Friel remarked in another context, 'The problem with the Northern situation is how you can tip-toe through the minefields of language where language has become so politicized. You see, whenever you have a war, language is always the first casualty.'[5]

This general problem is intensified in Ireland by the close association through many years of Gaelic revival and Irish nationalism. The national self-consciousness that preceded and helped to shape the movement for political independence was largely fostered by the Gaelic League, founded in 1893. The classic statement of the League's position was made the year before by its founder, Douglas Hyde, in a speech before the National Literary Society in Dublin entitled 'The Necessity for de-Anglicizing Ireland'. The gist of his argument was that the 'failure of the Irish people in recent times has been largely brought about by the race diverging during this century from the right path, and ceasing to be Irish without becoming English'. He called special attention to

> the illogical position of men who drop their own language to speak English, of men who translate their euphonious Irish names into English monosyllables, of men who read English books, and know nothing about Gaelic literature, nevertheless protesting as a matter of sentiment that they hate the country which at every hand's turn they rush to imitate. . . .
>
> [W]e must strive to cultivate everything that is most racial, most smacking of the soil, most Gaelic, most Irish, because in spite of the little admixture of Saxon blood in the north-east corner, this island *is* and will *ever* remain Celtic at the core.[6]

Hyde went on to become the first President of Ireland, holding office from 1938–45. Many Republican activists, including Éamon de Valera and Ernest Blythe, received their first quasi-political experience in the Gaelic League. The membership of the League frequently overlapped with that of the Volunteers, Sinn Féin, and the Irish Republican Brotherhood.[7] As Ronan Fanning has pointed out, cultural nationalism became even more important after the creation of the Irish Free State: 'The collapse of an agreed political

4. Ibid., 58.
5. Friel, interview with Christopher Morash in 'Flamethrowers: Contemporary Northern Irish Playwrights', M. Phil. diss., Trinity College, Dublin, 1986, 41.
6. Quoted in A. C. Hepburn, *The Conflict of Nationality in Modern Ireland* (London, 1980), 60–1 and P. S. O'Hegarty, *A History of Ireland Under the Union 1801 to 1922* (London, 1952), 617–19.
7. Ronan Fanning, *Independent Ireland* (Dublin, 1983), 80.

ideal in a partitioned, non-republican Ireland scarred by civil war
made the government hold all the more fervently to an intact cultural ideal.[8] After the adoption of the 1937 Constitution the issue
of 'Gaelicization' became particularly sensitive because it was related to what might be regarded as the abandonment of the North.
As de Valera said in February 1939, 'I would not tomorrow, for the
sake of a united Ireland, give up the policy of trying to make this a
really Irish Ireland'. In the same speech he nominated language revival as the keystone of that policy: 'I believe that as long as the language remains you have a distinguishing characteristic of
nationality which will enable the nation to persist.'[9]

The combination, in *Translations*, of language and education
would naturally be especially suggestive to politically sensitive Irish
men and women because of the Republic's long-standing and ill-
fated policy of language revival centred on the schools.[1] At first
schoolchildren were taught through the medium of Irish for several
hours each day, whether or not their home language was Irish.
Gradually, in response to protests from parents and teachers who
were worried about the effect this policy was having on students
acquiring proficiency in other subjects, the line was modified. To-
day the emphasis is on including Irish language classes in the curriculum. Thus, although most citizens of the Republic have been
exposed to Irish in school, if the goal of the original Gaelic Revivalists was to restore Irish as the everyday language of the people they
must be said to have failed.

Nevertheless, Irish remains important for Irish writers on both
sides of the border, if not as a medium then as a symbol. The decline of the language stands in a great deal of Irish writing for the
loss or suppression of Gaelic culture as a whole. Tim Pat Coogan,
in editing a recent supplement on the arts in Ireland, found the
'references to the Irish tongue, if not to the writing in Irish, remarkable—for Irish is commonly held to be a dying tongue, spoken
daily as an original means of communication by possibly as few as
30,000 people'.[2]

* * *

8. Ibid., 81.
9. Ibid., 140.
1. For a chronological discussion of Irish language revival in the Republic of Ireland see
   Terence Brown, *Ireland: A Social and Cultural History 1922–79* (London, 1981).
2. Coogan, 11.

On Conor McPherson

CONOR McPHERSON

[*The Weir*]†

I wrote this play in Leicester where [my girlfriend] Rionach had a job as an academic. She'd rented a little house, and I sat there avoiding writing. The problem was that I'd worked the play out in my head and writing it down just seemed to damage the idea. I'd write two pages and get up and go for long fraught walks around the suburbs, stopping at the off-license for beer and returning to start preparing dinner for us. Dinner was an endeavor I could drag out for hours. I didn't have to write it.

Finally all these short bursts of writing emerged as a complete narrative, all handwritten. I went back to Dublin and paid my little sister, Margaret, a hundred quid to type it up. I couldn't look at it. I wasn't sure people would think it would work. Some characters telling each other ghost stories in a pub. Were the stories they told any good? Why should we care about the people who told them? I knew I liked them, but why should an audience agree with me? But as my sister typed she kept telling me how much she loved it. She's always been a critical person. She won't watch much television or go to many movies. And she'd never go to a play unless there was a very good reason. She sits reading a book while everyone watches something else. And if she liked *The Weir* it meant it was either very good or completely shite.

I passed the typed script on to Kevin Hely to see what he thought. He rang me the next day to say he hadn't been able to sleep. He'd been scared shitless and kept the light on all night.

I sent it to my agent to pass on to the Royal Court who'd commissioned it. The response was strong. They scheduled it pretty quickly, with Ian Rickson directing. Ian is a man from Lewisham, South London. The play is set in rural Leitrim in the Republic of Ireland. Only six hundred miles away, but worlds apart. We sat in a

† *Afterword—The Weir*, from *The Weir and Other Plays* by Conor McPherson. Copyright © 1999 by Conor McPherson. Published by Theatre Communications Group. Used by permission of Theatre Communications Group.

cramped little patisserie in Soho with Margaret's horrendously typed script in front of us. Ian made notes on it with a pencil. He had few quibbles. I think I agreed to change a few lines and that was it. We were on.

Under no illusions that he knew anything about Ireland, Ian flew over a few weeks later with set designer, Rae Smith. I met them at the airport and we hired a car. The plan was to drive up to Leitrim and do a tour of pubs in the countryside. Rae had her video camera with her. We were looking for ideas. I also wanted to show them the tiny hamlet where I thought the play takes place, Jamestown, with the weir on the Shannon. It had been about two years since I'd been there. And as I showed Ian and Rae around, I had some pangs of guilt and remorse. What gave me the right to situate a piece of fiction so firmly in a real place? I became slightly reluctant to talk about it anymore.

I remembered sitting with my grandad, Jack, in his little house outside Jamestown where he lived alone. Smoking, tipping ash into the fire, drinking bottled stout from a six-pack. And a world, half imagined, half rooted in reality, just about visible to me in the dark. A world of lost afternoons in suburban and rural bars. Of closing your eyes in the dim light, with a community who couldn't or wouldn't judge you.

There was all this stuff in me and it was all very real and I couldn't explain it. We got out of there, and went to bars and places more anonymous to me.

We drove around. Rae sketched things in a book. I showed them Yeats's grave near Ben Bulben. Ian chatted to people in deserted bars, telling them the story of the play. I sat back, a little embarrassed. We ended up in Bundoran where we booked into a hotel. We went to a pub run by two sisters, and Ian told them what we were doing. Some suitable places were suggested to us. This turned into a bit of a session. Ian was our designated driver, and Rae and I were getting steadily pissed.

One bar we went into was tiny. It was Saturday night. The clientele was sitting up at the counter. Middle-aged, chatting away. But as soon as we ordered drinks everything stiffened. Me clearly from Dublin and Ian and Rae (the only woman in the place) with their London accents. The locals threw us curious glances over their shoulders. When we finally left I could sense them relax.

The next morning was beautiful. We went for a walk on the beach after breakfast and then drove back down to Leitrim. This time we went looking for places even more out of the way than the day before. We ended up in the little town of Dromahair. On Sundays in Ireland there's a "holy hour" between two o'clock and four o'clock when you can't buy a drink in a pub. We made it into a cozy bar in Dromahair just before two.

Two men sat at the bar. One at one end and one at the other. They seemed out of each others' earshot but managed to have a conversation mainly consisting of grunts and sighs. The man nearest us was small and skinny. My father always said that people from Leitrim had a haunted look. This man had it. High, gaunt cheekbones and an almost suspicious squinting grin. The other man was round and wore a shiny suit that had to be twenty years old and worn every day. His face was red and he wore a cap.

The skinny fellow was drunk in that way that's carried on from last night. Half hungover, half not knowing what the hell's wrong with you. He fell into conversation with us. Where were we from and so on. Ian told him the story of the play while I drank Guinness, taking the edge off my own hangover. We in turn got his story of an American woman who'd moved to Dromahair. This was told with supportive grunts and indecipherable elaboration from the round man at the other end of the pub.

She had moved here the previous summer and our skinny friend, Fergus, had inveigled his way into her life by helping repair her house, which had been badly built. It turned out she was married back in America, and though everyone wondered what the hell she was doing, at the same time they just assumed she was a bit mad. This didn't stop Fergus from pursuing her, however. And at the bar he slapped his legs and rubbed his hands together telling us how he'd been the one to get into bed with her. Yes indeed, him and no one else. Good God, he'd been riding her morning, noon and night. Then one day, out of the blue, she decided to go and sort out her affairs at home in America. But she told Fergus that her plan was to definitely come back and settle in Dromahair. She asked him to mind her dogs while she was gone. But that was a year ago and Fergus was still minding her dogs. Every day he'd go up to her empty house and feed them, keeping his foot in the door as it were, waiting for her to return. Then he rubbed his hands together again in anticipation, and bought ten cans of Budweiser to take with him up to her house. He liked to get hammered while he fed the dogs.

After our fact-finding mission we returned to Dublin. Rae with her sketchbook and video footage, and me and Ian ready to cast the play. We auditioned people in Dublin and London. The original cast was Brendan Coyle as Brendan, Kieran Ahern as Jim, Julia Ford as Valerie, Jerry Horan as Finbar and Jim Norton as Jack.

The run was only supposed to be for three and a half weeks at the Royal Court in their small sixty-seat venue. We rehearsed in the Drill Hall, off the Tottenham Court Road.

Ian tries to cast ensemble plays with an eye as to how everyone is going to get on with one another. The atmosphere between the actors is important to the quality of their performance together, especially in a play where it's vital that they be seen to be listening to each other. A way that Ian bonds the cast is to bring extra people into the rehearsal room—experts whom the cast can question about what their characters might be experiencing. The first week of rehearsal was spent simply reading the play and talking about it, and then someone would come in and chat to us. We spoke with a bereavement counselor and two experts on the paranormal. The atmosphere was great. We were all learning together and a generosity of spirit seeped into the work.

I went home to Dublin after the first week of rehearsal confident that everything was alright. It was more than that. I found the whole process redemptive and I didn't want to leave. But with drama, for film or for stage, there often comes a point where the person with absolutely nothing more to give is the writer. And no one wants to feel like they're in the way.

I returned for the final week of rehearsal to find everyone in pretty good shape. The set in the Ambassador was extraordinary. The seating was arranged so that the audience was pretty much in the bar with the characters. It had a rare intimacy which must be a joy for any actor to work with.

The dress rehearsals went great, the only problem being me. Nitpicking about blocking and getting on Ian's nerves. And then we started previews. And every night, people in the audience fainted and had to be carried out of the theatre. It was awful. It usually happened when Julia, as Valerie, told her story about her daughter. Because these were previews and nothing had appeared in the papers about the play, no one knew the story. No one was prepared. And Julia's performance was devastating. When you've written something, you forget that each night the audience is hearing it for the first time.

Brain Cox came to the opening night and told me it was shit. It was the worst play he'd ever seen. I stood gaping at him, dumbfounded, not only because he seemed to hate it so much, but also that he'd be so insensitive as to say it to my face on opening night. But then he couldn't hold back his laugh. Rionach had got him to wind me up. People with nothing better to do. I feel sorry for them.

I was staying at Brian's house, and the morning the reviews came out Ian rang me and told me to buy the papers. I sleepily went around the corner to a local garage and took them back to bed with me. And I went back to sleep. I still feel like the raves we got are a weird dream because of this.

Well, so much for a three-week run. It's early 1999. There's sun streaming in the windows and *The Weir* is still running in the West End.

It's strange when people ask me about the success of the play. I don't feel very responsible. I owe so much to all the good actors I've learned from. Good actors are out there doing things by instinct, and so often blessed with excellent judgment. I'm constantly surprised by them. And often I receive praise which I know is rightfully theirs.

I've been lucky so far. I've had the opportunity to work with so many talented people. There's been a lot of laughs, maybe a bit too much messing, but not too many tantrums. So here's to lots more late nights and regrettable proclamations. See yous in the bar.

CHRISTOPHER A. GROBE

Secular Morality in the Plays of Conor McPherson†

* * *

Conor McPherson earned a master's degree in philosophy—specializing in ethics—at the prestigious University College Dublin. His thesis, "Logical Constraint and Practical Reasoning: On Attempted Refutations of Utilitarianism," is a defense of moral utilitarianism against its contemporary critics. Through a scholarly analysis of anti-utilitarian philosophy, McPherson seeks to undermine it by, among other tactics, showing its dependence on a utilitarian understanding of the role of consequences in determining the moral status of an action. Although the work is mainly a dissection of logic and moral procedures, the introduction gives a deeper sense of McPherson's own stance. He writes that "ethical statements must be construed in consequentialist terms if they are to mean *anything* at all. Furthermore, consequences are only relevant to us in terms of our preferences, how we are disposed to view them in terms of satisfaction."[1]

One can glean two principle ideas from this statement. First, McPherson does not believe in rules or maxims as objective sources of morality, but instead relies on the consequences to give actions their ethical weight. This dependence on preferences places McPherson firmly in the utilitarian tradition. Second, he defines these consequences in terms of the highly subjective "preferences" of the individual agent. This reference does not mean that McPher-

---

† From *Princeton University Library Chronicle* 67. Reprinted by permission of the author.
1. Conor McPherson, "Logical Constraint and Practical Reasoning: On Attempted Refutations of Utilitarianism," diss. University College Dublin, 1993, 1.

son's morality is entirely subjective or relativistic. As he argues later in his thesis, no human being can purport to separate himself or herself from the concerns of the surrounding society and still be considered a moral being. After all, "moral terms, we may hold, have no meaning in a purely individualistic context."[2] Nevertheless, morality can make sense to any given individual only in relation to his or her own feelings of satisfaction.

This interpretation makes McPherson's own stance a radically arational take on utilitarian philosophy, more in line with David Hume's sympathy-based proto-utilitarianism than with J. S. Mill's and Jeremy Bentham's hairsplitting calculi for the mathematical determination of "exact" moral ramifications for every action. In fact, McPherson passionately defends the antirational moral philosophy of Hume against the hyperrational anti-utilitarianism of Alisdair MacIntyre. In this defense, he specifically calls attention to one assertion in Hume's *A Treatise of Human Nature* (1739–1740): "these two particulars are to be consider'd as equivalent . . . *virtue* and the power of producing love or pride, *vice* and the power of producing humility or hatred."[3] This equation is particularly useful to McPherson's own Humean conception of ethics because it ties Hume's somewhat nebulous idea of "sympathy" to a measurable commodity: lovability. Identifying lovability as the central notion of a utilitarian philosophy guards against the possibility of selfish hedonism in a morality that defines itself merely through personal satisfaction. Individuals, to secure their own moral satisfaction, must bolster the satisfaction of those around them.

McPherson's plays assume this same kind of moral utilitarianism. That is not to say that the characters—not even Ray in *This Lime Tree Bower*, who is, incidentally, a professor of utilitarianism—philosophize or even speak explicitly about ethics. Gerald Wood puts it best when he notes that a McPherson play "turns on the dramatic moment when lives become a matter of morality." Amid the (im)morally loaded circumstances of a McPherson play, for a character to speak of his actions and his life is for him to speak about his morality. Wood also writes about "the absence of potent benign authority" in McPherson's plays, recognizing that the lack of religious or societal strictures (in the plays as in contemporary Ireland) leaves a moral vacuum. However, Wood claims that this moral vacuum is filled with rational reflection. He portrays all of McPherson's work as a struggle between the opposing forces of "mischief" and "responsibility," and sums up McPherson's moral

2. McPherson, "Logical Constraint," 22.
3. McPherson, "Logical Constraint," 116.

project by saying, "The lure of irresponsibility needs to be played off against the humanising need to reflect, to engage reason."[4]

* * *

Of all of McPherson's plays, *The Weir* (1997) deals most explicitly and thoroughly with the duality of love and loneliness. In the "Author's Note," McPherson once again invokes the image of his grandfather's loneliness:

> This play was probably inspired by my visits to Leitrim to see my grandad. He lived on his own. . . . I remember him telling me once that it was very important to have the radio on because it gave him the illusion of company. . . . I can still see him standing on the platform at the station. He always waved for much too long. Much longer than a person who was glad to have their privacy back.[5]

As this and McPherson's previous comment about his grandfather suggest, *The Weir* is a play about the moral implications of loneliness and the quiet despair of the lonely. Three of the play's characters are bachelors of different ages: Brendan, the thirty-something owner of the pub where it is set, and two of the pub's regulars, Jack (in his fifties) and Jim (in his forties). Brendan has no living relatives except his sisters, who swing by occasionally to check up not on Brendan but on the family property: "Checking their investments," as Jack says. Jim takes care of his dying mother, who seems to be his only relative. Jack is the most confirmed bachelor of the bunch and a complete loner. His weak defense of his situation is that "maybe there's something to be said for the old independence," but he admits to being lonely.

The characters' aura of isolation is accentuated by the setting, the dark rural countryside of Northwest Ireland, and by the injection of two provocative guests: Finbar, the forty-year-old businessman who left the rest behind to find love and money in the city, and Valerie, a female figure who becomes a powerful catalyst to the bachelors' feelings of loneliness. Vying for her attention and approval, Jack, Finbar, and Jim tell ghost stories from their lives; but, as Ben Brantley wrote in his review of the Broadway production, as the night wears on "a moment arrives . . . when you realize that you have strayed into territory that scrapes the soul. Suddenly the subject isn't just things that go bump in the night, but the loss and loneliness that eventually haunt every life."[6] After Valerie reveals

4. Gerald Wood, *Conor McPherson: Imagining Mischief* (Dublin: Liffey Press, 2003), 6, 118.
5. *The Weir and Other Plays* (New York: Theatre Communications), 3.
6. Ben Brantley, "Dark Yarns Casting Light," *New York Times*, 2 April 1999: E-1.

her own, more personal ghost story, that of her dead daughter's phone call from beyond the grave, the men sober up and leave, except Brendan and Jack.

Jack goes on to tell the fifth and final story of the play, which deals with a girl he had dated in his younger days and how he failed her "out of pure cussedness". Years later, when he attended her wedding to a man in the Dublin area, he realized "that was that. And the future was all ahead of me. Years and years of it. I could feel it coming. All those things you've got to face on your own. All by yourself." At this lowest point, he finds a loving gesture in a dark Dublin-area pub, where a barman takes special interest in him and, without demanding any information about Jack's troubles, makes him a free sandwich. The meal takes on the religious connotations of a holy communion when Jack says, "I ate it all down because someone I didn't know had done this for me. [. . .] It fortified me, like no meal I ever had in my life." These hints of secular spirituality provoke in him a moral interpretation of the loneliness he has experienced ever since. From that day, he says, "There was a humility I've tried to find since. But goodness wears off. And it just gets easier to be a contrary bollocks." He concludes his story by confessing, "there's not one morning I don't wake up with her name in the room." Even though he says, "That wasn't a ghostly story. Anyway. At least, ha?" it is clear that his life is more haunted by this memory of failed love than by a whole countryside's worth of fairies, ghosts, and goblins.

If Jack's experience and the secular communion he describes establish loneliness as a moral and spiritual matter, then McPherson suggests that each of the other ghost stories is—somewhat more guardedly—an attempt to address the same issues of loneliness. When asked what his own fascination with ghosts and the supernatural amounts to, McPherson replied,

> Well, it's the fascination with life in all its messiness, you know? . . . I think probably all the kind of things in your life that are unresolved or whatever have to be compacted in order to find some resolution, but in a way they have to exist in a sort of spiritual place. . . . In any ghost story, ghosts come back because there's some sort of unfinished business. And I think it's about that: the sort of existential unfinished business.[7]

As Jack's last monologue makes clear, this spiritualized resolution and "existential unfinished business" in the world of *The Weir* has all to do with the inability to find love and the consequent masking of one's desires that is evident in dozens of little exchanges:

7. Conor McPherson, interview with the author.

VALERIE. I'd imagine though, it can get very quiet.

JACK. Oh it can, yeah. Ah, you get used to it. Brendan.

BRENDAN. Ah yeah you don't think about it.

JACK. [. . .] You know, there's company all around. Bit of a community all spread around the place, like.

Not only do the men's ghost stories address the haunting quality of the loss of love, they also serve as a remedy (albeit a fleeting one) for their spiritual loneliness. The act of telling the story creates a "bit of a community" among all of the participants, and perhaps even among the audience members who are put into the room with Jack and the rest during the storytelling by identification with the onstage listeners. In his review of the play, Ben Brantley used vivid language to describe the ephemeral connection established through the act of storytelling: "Though a feeling of individual isolation in a baffling and often hostile world pervades *The Weir*, the stories woven by its characters become solid, if temporary, bridges among them."[8] We see the existential loneliness of these men staved off for a short time, but these moments only serve to deepen our sense of the profundity of that loneliness, which is ultimately a moral issue.

As McPherson's generation and younger generations of Irish men and women drift out to sea like McPherson's younger characters for lack of a reliable moral lifeline, perhaps the kind of secular morality developed beneath the deceptively debaucherous surface of McPherson's plays will gain some credibility. In any case, in a time when the Irish generally lend less and less credence to institutions of moral "authority," McPherson's brand of theater, with its reliance on audience interpretation and interpolation, provides a comfortingly independent alternative to institutionalized morality. The theater could be in contemporary Ireland what it was in ancient Greece: a place for the community to gather and work out their values and communal identity apropos of the people and events depicted onstage. Instead of actively promoting a specific moral dogma, theater can reveal the essential humanity that underpins every effective morality.

8. Brantley, E-1.

KEVIN KERRANE

The Structural Elegance
of Conor McPherson's *The Weir*†

Conor McPherson's play *The Weir* (1997) achieved critical and popular success at three world-renowned theaters in the late 1990s: the Royal Court in London, the Gate in Dublin, and the Walter Kerr in New York. In London, it won the Lawrence Olivier BBC Award as the "Best New Play" of 1997–98, and McPherson received the Critics' Circle Award as the most promising playwright. In New York, where *The Weir* ran for eight months on Broadway, the *New York Times* described the play as "beautiful and devious" and hailed the playwright, only twenty-seven at the time, as "a first-rate story-teller."[1] The original production, directed by Ian Rickson, went on to further triumphs in Toronto and Belfast, and *The Weir* has been staged, almost always to fine reviews, by troupes in Boston, Philadelphia, Pittsburgh, and Los Angeles. Of particular note were productions by the Steppenwolf Company in Chicago and the Round House Theatre in Washington.

McPherson himself claimed to be baffled by all the fanfare. "It was just people talking," he said, "so it shouldn't have worked—it should have been boring."[2] At one level, his point is correct: *The Weir* includes little physical action, and its major events occur in the past, being recalled by the characters. But the same observation would apply to great Greek tragedies. And like those tragedies, *The Weir* observes the unities of time and place—unfolding without intermission in real time, about one hundred minutes, within the frame of a simple set: a small pub in the West of Ireland that becomes a site of both conflict and bonding. This compression is only one of the basic principles of dramatic construction in *The Weir*. McPherson's script also balances six other structural principles of drama—climactic order, reversal, synthesis, cause and effect, internalized action, and circularity—and the deft handling of these elements helps to explain why the play has been acclaimed so widely and so quickly as a modern classic.

These elemental plot premises generate strong emotions while conveying a subtle and compassionate sense of human life. Each el-

† From *New Hibernia Review* 10.4 (2006). Reprinted by permission of the author and the *New Hibernia Review*, University of St. Thomas.
1. Ben Brantley, "Dark Yarns Casting Light," *New York Times*, 2 April 1999: E-1.
2. *The Stage*, 28 Feb. 2002: 11.

ement can be traced back to masterworks of Western drama, from
the Greeks to Shakespeare to the modern realists. But they are also
prominent in such major Irish plays as *The Playboy of the Western
World, Endgame, Translations,* and *Pentecost.* In this respect, the
"classic" design of *The Weir* also highlights distinctly Irish features of
drama, and, most especially, the integration of tragedy and comedy.

The Weir's structural elegance rests upon a unique rhythm of action, alternating between casual bar talk and a series of stories told
by four of the five characters. McPherson began his theatrical career by scripting monologues—first for university and fringe groups
in Dublin, and later for the Bush Theatre in London. He achieved
early recognition for dramas of dissipation, especially *Rum and
Vodka* (1994) and *St. Nicholas* (1997), in which a single character
delivers a long confessional narrative. Even as each tale becomes
more convoluted, the telling remains simple: instead of trying to act
out the episodes or to assume the voices of other characters,
McPherson's narrator tells a story. When McPherson was commissioned to write a play for the Royal Court Theatre in 1997, the
artistic director, Stephen Daldry, attached a condition: the new
drama could not be another monologue. Scott T. Cummings describes the resulting script as "McPherson's characteristically
cheeky response to the call for him to write characters who talk to
each other instead of the audience. He has them tell stories."[3]

In *The Weir* these stories emerge naturally out of realistic conversation, and are separated by breathing spaces for comments, arguments, or fresh rounds of drinks. As in the plays of Eugene O'Neill
or Edward Albee, drink fuels the evening's successive revelations,
and the particular choices—Guinness versus Harp, Irish whiskey,
white wine, or glasses of brandy—can serve to mark the characters'
individuality, and sometimes to establish commonality. Moreover,
the simple setting of a country pub evokes a familiar picture of traditional Ireland.

According to McPherson's stage notes, "The bar is part of a house
and the house is part of a farm."[4] The audience does not see these
exterior features. The play unfolds within realistic boundaries, beginning with a brief fade-in. Before any characters appear, the audience sees a bar with stools in front, and a peat-burning stove at
stage right flanked by smaller stools, a low table, and an easy chair;
near the end of the play, this hearthside will become a stage within
the stage. On the walls are several old black-and-white photos that
provoke discussion in the course of the evening. The cozy effect is

3. Scott T. Cummings, "Homo Fabulator: The Narrative Impulses in Conor McPherson's
   Plays," *Theatre Stuff,* ed. Eamonn Jordan (Dublin: Carysfort Press, 2000), 308.
4. See the text in this volume [*Editor*].

heightened as the audience is made aware, through sound effects and dialogue, that the night outside is full of strange winds.

McPherson establishes a note of easy familiarity with the entrance of the first character, Jack, who acts as if the pub were his. He goes behind the bar and, frustrated that the Guinness tap fails to work, opens a bottle. As he counts out his change, Jack is greeted by the real owner, Brendan—who expresses no surprise or suspicion at seeing a customer in front of the open cash register. The two talk casually about the weather, about Jack's success that day at betting the horses, about "the Germans"—their generic name for Continental tourists—and, at length, about the likely visit of Finbar, a successful businessman who has rented out a local property to a single woman from Dublin. Finbar plans to bring the woman to the pub that evening, and the two bachelors—Jack in his fifties, Brendan in his thirties—resent his attempt to show off by treating them as local color. "The dirty bastard," Brendan says. "I don't want him using in here for that sort of carry on. A married man like him." A secondary point of tension appears in Brendan's references to his two sisters, who want him to sell the farm's unused top field so that they can all split the proceeds. Brendan resists without being able to say exactly why.

The third character, Jim, is a bachelor handyman who lives with his ill mother. Jim seems both sly and slow-witted: though well known as a shrewd bettor, he remains slightly behind the pulse of conversation. In contrast, Finbar is overbearing. Soon after entering the pub with Valerie, the Dublin woman, Finbar refers to the other men as "country fellas," and jokes: "They're only jealous Valerie because I went the town to seek my fortune. And they all stayed out here on the bog picking their holes."

A subtle interplay of competition for Valerie's attention follows. The men try earnestly to put her at ease—Brendan has to go offstage, inside the house, to find white wine for her—even when they cannot help expressing small courtesies in vulgar language. Valerie is a good audience, engaged and amiable as Jack explains his betting strategy, which trusts more to luck than "the facts and figures of it." Genuinely curious about the history of the area, Valerie is told about the framed photos, which commemorate the 1951 dedication of the local weir, a small dam that first provided electricity to this rural outpost. The unspoken question in these exchanges clearly intrigues all the men: Why has this attractive, unattached woman moved here from Dublin?

The play's inciting moment comes when Jack exits to the men's room and Valerie studies a panoramic photo taken from Brendan's top field. Finbar offers a touch of local lore: "There was stories all, the fairies be up there in that field. Isn't there a fort up there?" Finbar is referring to a ring of trees once believed to be inhabited by beings who had their own "road" to the river—past an old well, an abbey, and down to a pebbly cove. Along that road was a house whose residents experienced a strange visitation.

When Jack returns, the others prevail on him to tell the story of the fairy road, but he first discloses that the house in question is the very one that Finbar has just rented out to Valerie. As Finbar sputters in embarrassment, Jack launches into the evening's first story, the recollection of a tale told by Maura Nealon, who had lived in the house as a child. At first Jack plays the story for laughs by heightening the spooky atmosphere:

> And in those days, Valerie, as you know, there was no electric-ity out here. And there's no dark like a winter night in the country. And there was a wind like this one tonight, howling and whistling in off the sea. You hear it under the door and it's like someone singing. Singing under the door at you. It was this type of night now. Am I setting the scene for you?

Thus, McPherson puts his play in motion by evoking a fairy legend. As Angela Bourke has noted, such legends have long been told "to amuse adults and frighten children, to entertain tourists, and to mark the distance we have come from the supposed credulity of our ancestors."[5] In this resonant cultural setting, the city woman who has come to rural Leitrim will encounter traces of a traditional Ireland—benign at first, but darkening steadily as the entertain-ment turns toward first-person testimony.

Jack's story is the first in a sequence of narratives. Each, as Ben Brantley observes, "deepens and expands the others. And the order in which they are arranged offers a master lesson in dramatic con-struction."[6] That lesson extends beyond the world of *The Weir* and takes us deep into the art of storytelling. In McPherson's concen-trated play, the structural principles are seamless, not schematic: each depends on, and reinforces, the others.

The most obvious structural principle in *The Weir* is climactic or-der. The play incorporates five stories in all, and the first four offer models of intensification, as each narrative becomes more personal and more unsettling than the one before. The pace of the telling also accelerates; the time frame of each tale comes ever closer to the present; and, as Scott T. Cummings notes, "the presence of the supernatural becomes progressively more real, tangible, and omi-nous."[7]

* * *

5. Angela Bourke, "The Virtual Reality of Irish Fairy Legend," *Eire-Ireland* 30 (1996): 8.
6. Brantley, E-26.
7. Cummings, 309.

EAMONN JORDAN

Pastoral Exhibits: Narrating Authenticities in Conor McPherson's *The Weir*†

* * *

When McPherson was commissioned by the Royal Court's Artistic Director, Stephen Daldry, the agreement between the writer and the theatre stipulated that the new play must not be another monologue. *The Weir* is what McPherson delivered.[1] From the apparent naturalistic tradition of Irish theatre, McPherson, inspired most of all by Friel's *Faith Healer* (1979), allowed in a rival sensibility, ensuring that story-telling spaces are liminal ones, between the conscious and unconscious, between reality and dream life. However, the links between story-telling, the ghost story, memory, and the past, and between identity and narrative formation, within the frame of the pastoral, are the facets of *The Weir* that most interest me. Black and white photos of 'a ruined abbey and the once new Weir', a 'town in a cove with mountains around it' are placed in the pub setting. By means of memory, something additional is allowed to enter the frame. Truths and trust link up in a way that ensures that communication is intimate and deliberate, particularly through the form of narrative. Here all the characters, apart from Brendan, tell a story. Brendan through his lack of narrative desire is perhaps the most grounded character. (By contrast, Artie in Billy Roche's *Belfry* (1991) rejoices in at least now having a story, despite the pain and trauma of a failed relationship).

In a play so inhibited and immobile in terms of space and movement, narrative offers consolation, through the framework of otherness and through the manipulation of absence. In [Tom] Murphy's *Bailegangaire*, Mommo constructs meaning through traditional story-telling. An audience can be drawn in by the spell of the story, can begin to generate imaginative worlds, and can construct a reality based on the details provided by the teller. In Frank McGuinness's *Someone Who'll Watch Over Me* (1992), the characters alter through the faculty of story-telling. They grow by embracing each other's stories and by psychologically absorbing the testimony and resistance at the core of another's narrative. The absence of a reluctance to tell is vital.

---

† From *Irish University Review* 34.2 (Autumn 2004). Reprinted by permission of *Irish University Review*.
1. Scott T. Cummings, "Homo Fabulator: The Narrative Imperative in Conor McPherson's Plays," *Theatre Stuff*, ed. Eamonn Jordan (Dublin: Carysfort Press, 2000), 308.

Personal stories emerge as the individual begins to assemble the sensations and memories of trauma or pleasure. Stories or experiences set to memory, shaped as narrative, are ways inside a private world. They give access to a level of spirit or internal realities that normal interactions do not make available. In Ireland, people tend to exchange stories more than they involve themselves in discussion or debate. Dialogue often takes the form of narrative. Sometimes people exchange/inhabit the same conversations/narratives again and again, even with the same people. In *The Weir* each character has some dominant memory or remembrance narrative that provides a sense of where he/she has come from and of the events and circumstances that have shaped each of them. Each character has his/her own internal narrative rhythm that is made external through narrative activity. So, the characters trace themselves through narratives and locate themselves too by marshalling the narratives of others. Throughout the play's action, individual characters are placed by and placed within narratives, as the narrator is simultaneously inside and outside the role. A personal story can become an individual's fixation, a way of constructing a sense of self. The story can also be a way of seducing the listener into a way of thinking and a means of postponing judgement and of seeking acceptance. If a narrative breaks down or if one can no longer make sense of the world through one's own narrative, then problems emerge. Personal narratives can also use differing distancing features. One can disguise the personal relevance of a story by filtering it through different temporal or spatial frames or one can displace oneself from the centre of such narratives. One can also, as the characters do in this play, strain individual concerns through imaginative narratives like ghost stories.

From the point of view of the spectator, does one listen for the flaws and contradictions in the story being told or will the entry point be simply acceptance? Or might one interrogate the clues that point to something else, for often beneath what is said or hurried over, something altogether different is happening? The relative coherence of the story does not necessarily presuppose a coherent subjectivity, because there is no 'aboriginal or 'true' self to which we can return for guidance.' Ciarán Benson uses Antonio Damasio's framework of 'proto-self, core self and autobiographical self'. The first two are 'largely under the automatic control of the brain in its body,' and the final category, 'while dependent on the constantly self-renewing foundations of the proto-self and the core self', is still 'significantly a matter of learning.'[2] Auto-narratives duly enable

---

2. Ciarán Benson, *The Cultural Psychology of Self* (London: Routledge, 2001), 45, 225, 239.

and inhibit. In them we are also operating within the specificity of play and its efficacy. Play adds to articulation by making it sensual and also by sensationalizing memory formation. There is also the reformulation of the performative self through narrative delivery. Narratives are driven partly by the requirements of a form that demand the delivery of a story with impact. The narrative imperative is to ensure that the teller is most alive because between the narrator and audience a form of community is negotiated. The concept of play is in a way not so much about ratifying an older sense of being, rather its looseness is its primary insistence, releasing both the predatoriality or the territoriality of identity. Identity is fabricated thus as much out of the narrative structure as it is out of the variable of performance. It is the agreed, shared ritual of narrative exchange that offers, in part, the consolation of the pastoral. Then there is also the national narrative; Ireland as a nation has primarily structured its narrative on defiance, misfortune, hard luck, missed opportunity, and disaster. Giving coherence to the story comes at the expense of the chaos. While it is difficult to let go of the past, it is something that cannot be changed, but one can challenge its meaning and the significance given to it. It has to be said that international audiences, in particular, enjoy such a traumatic burden when articulated emotively in theatres by characters from nations other than their own or by circumstances that are unusually isolated and/or past tense.

Jack's story centres on Maura Nealon. She was a bit of a trickster and enjoyed scaring people. His story is a response to the sounds and noises of the natural world as if these confirmed the presence of the supernatural. The wind is like 'someone singing', according to Jack. Bridie, Maura's mother, disbelieved initially her daughter's responses to the strange happenings and eerie sensations. Then, she too heard low down knocks on the door that shook her. The local priest is asked to come round to pray. It is revealed that the 'house had been built on a fairy road' along which the fairies would progress to 'bathe'. The noise returned to the house when the Weir was being built, according to Maura. Dead birds were the only other sign of unnatural disturbance. Valerie, on her first night in the neighbourhood, learns that her recently purchased house may be haunted, whatever that happens to mean.

Finbar's story is next and, rather than diminish the threat implicit in local folklore, his own is again about the supernatural. Niamh Walsh has an experience after consulting an Ouija board. Her parents pick her up from a friend's house. Once back home there was the presence of a ghostly woman on the staircase. A priest was called again. Later the same night, the family received a telephone call, announcing the death of a previous neighbour, an old woman, who used to baby-sit the girls when they were young. As he had been called upon to offer assistance to the Walsh family, Finbar ended that evening, by staying up all night, unable to face the staircase. While Jack's story does not involve him personally, Finbar manages to place himself indirectly within the narrative. The events affected him enough to force him to give up cigarettes and to move away from the locality soon afterwards.

Jim's story becomes more personal again. Despite being sick with the flu, he had responded to a request from (another) priest in a distant parish to open a grave. While Jim worked alone, a stranger arrived and tells him that he was digging the 'wrong grave'. The stranger pointed out an alternative resting place for the dead male, a place where a recently deceased young girl had been buried. Later in a newspaper Jack saw a photo of the deceased man who was the '. . . spit of your man' he had 'met in the graveyard'. This person was a 'Pervert', who had abused children. Finbar wants to put a halt to things: 'We've had enough of them old stories, they're only an old cod'. The males may have used the form of the supernatural narrative against Valerie, both consciously and unconsciously. She is, in a sense, an intruder upon the male preserve, just like the non-nationals. But from such a position of subtle weakness, Valerie brings something radical to the action. Unlike the narratives of the men, Valerie's story is of a different order. Married to Daniel and with a good job in Dublin City University, her world is turned upside down when her daughter, Niamh, is drowned in a swimming pool accident. As a young girl, Niamh had anxieties: 'Valerie: . . . But at night . . . there were people at the window, there were people in the attic, there was someone coming up the stairs. There were children knocking, in the wall. And there was always a man standing across the road whom she'd see'. In addition, Niamh feared abandonment.

Valerie calmed her by inviting her to phone her if she was ever at all worried. After the child's death, Valerie received a phone call. 'Valerie: I couldn't hear what they were saying. And then I heard Niamh'. Niamh wanted to be collected and brought home. 'Valerie: . . . I mean, I wasn't sure whether this was a dream or her leaving us had been a dream'. It is intimated that Valerie's hold on reality is suspect. Finbar is most unnerved by the revelation, but Brendan supports Valerie's convictions. Explanations are offered by all for the supernatural elements in the previous stories. The supernatural is thus naturalized. Jim was suffering from flu and had been drinking when he had his experience; Maura Nealon was a heavy drinker and therefore she is not to be trusted; the Walshes were 'fucking headbangers'; Finbar's own experience is excused by the fact that he got 'the wind put up' him that night.

As Finbar departs, he asks that they go easy on Valerie. Jack in-
tervenes telling Finbar to stop 'being an old woman' and declaring
that she will be grand. When Jim leaves, he remarks that the dead
child, Niamh, is 'a little innocent' and he promises to pray for her.
Valerie's narrative leads to the most intimate story, delivered by
Jack. Once in love, Jack's girlfriend went to work in Dublin. The relationship stalled. One day he was told that she was about to get
married. He turned up as a mere invited guest. Upset by the occasion, he left the church 'like a little boy', and went to a bar, where
the Barman made him a sandwich. Jack nearly started to cry, so
moved was he by the act of charity. His former girlfriend has become a ghost. 'Jack: . . . there's not one morning I don't wake up
with her name in the room'. Although he says 'at least' it wasn't 'a
ghostly story', it, in fact, is. He is haunted by his failure to be more
responsive and responsible by turning down an opportunity that
would have required compromise and acceptance. Instead he felt it
better to hold out, but for what?

Maturation may be about the acceptance of death at a deep level.
Of course, the tradition of singing a song and telling a story also
overlaps with something else—wake rituals. The play is in a way a
wake for Valerie's dead daughter and other lost things. The characters might be seen to be enacting a wake ritual through ghost stories. The play thus works on one level as a pastoral elegy. Further,
for Julia Kristeva, death is a site of abjection. People avoid corpses
and the talk of death in order to live. Conversely, people tell stories
in order to accommodate the ideas of death in a distancing fashion.
Sue Vice cites Kristeva's notion that 'the corpse, most sickening of
wastes, is a border that has encroached upon everything', it is
'death infecting life'.[3] Death is containable within the pastoral. But
the sense of order associated with the pastoral landscape and the
cohesion imposed by the play's form promise one thing and deliver
something else. It appears as if the pastoral offers containment, but
it does not. Jack states that they will 'all be ghosts soon enough',
adding that all of them will 'be sitting here. Sipping whiskey all
night with Maura Nealon'. In pastoral, loss, or a communal acknowledgement of it, to put it more accurately, is ultimately the key
ingredient. In the lived world, loss has less and less currency or
value.

* * *

3. *Introducing Bakhtin* (Manchester: Manchester UP, 1997), 175.

On Marina Carr

MARINA CARR

[Introduction to Plays]†

When I was a scut we built a theatre in our shed; we lay boards across the stacked turf, hung an old blue sheet for a curtain and tied a bicycle lamp to a rafter at the side of the shed so its light would fall at an angle on the stage. For costumes we wore brown nylons over our faces. There were always robbers in our plays. Even when you weren't playing a robber, you dressed like one, for any second you could be caught or hung or shot. Even the Good Guy dressed like a robber, so if the worst came to the worst he could arrest himself. Everyone was interchangeable. One minute you were the heroine on the swing and the next you were in the stocks pleading guilty to every crime invented. Our dramas were bloody and brutal. Everyone suffered: the least you could hope to get away with was a torturing. And still we all lived happily ever after. Good and bad got down from their ropes or off the rack or out of the barrel of boiling oil, apologized to the Goodie—who was usually more perverse than all the Baddies put together—and made long soliloquies about "never doing it again." Everyone was capable of redemption except Witches. We had no mercy for Witches, but since the Witch had all the power and all the magic, we could never finally throttle her with all the righteous savagery of our scuttish hearts. Just when we had her choked down to her last cheekful of air or had her chest bared for the stake, she'd cast one of her spells and escape on the handle of an old spade.

Scuts know instinctively that morality is a human invention, fallible and variable as the wind, and so our dramas were strange and free and cruel. But scuts also have a sense of justice—bar the Witch, I don't know what she was about—and hence our desire for the thing to end well. We loved the havoc, the badness, the blood spillage, but loved equally restoring some sort of botched order and

† From *Marina Carr: Plays One*. Reproduced by permission of The Agency (London) Ltd. © 1999 Marina Carr. Faber & Faber. All rights reserved and enquiries to The Agency (London) Ltd.

harmony. Ignorantly we had hit upon the first and last principles of dramatic art. And the Witch? Maybe she was Time. Time we didn't understand or fully inhabit, and yet we respected and feared her. And fell away humbly under her spells and charms and curses. If I'm after anything when I'm writing plays, it's the scuts' view of things as they are or were or should be, and perhaps once in a blue moon be given a sideways glance of it all as the first dramatist might see it and how it should be done.

OLWEN FOUÉRÉ

[Interview: On Playing in *By the Bog of Cats*]†

Your response to By the Bog of Cats . . . ? *What was it initially, and did it change over time?*

My initial response to the script was a very powerful one. I remember reading an early draft—not the penultimate draft, but the one before that—when Hester was called Angel—I remember reading it and finishing it in bed one morning, and when I got to the end I experienced a very powerful physical release. I remember being in floods of tears. I knew that the play had hit me in a very deep place, and it also seemed to articulate something that I had never fully articulated in anything I'd done before. Some deep grief to do with . . . yes, some deep grief. I think that deep feeling of grief was brought on by the seamless transition in the play from the intensely personal to the hugely mythic. And the power of this juxtaposition of the detailed and the local against the mythic is that it is not a single action. It's an accumulation of actions which you experience as you're reading or playing. This peaks during the sequence in the final moments of the play. When Josie doesn't want to be left alone, she begs her mother, pleading, 'Take me with you', and it is in order to comfort her that Hester kills her. It is the loving nature of that gesture from Hester, and something about that 'Take me with you' that I find extraordinarily touching, the idea that someone asks to travel with you into death.

My response to the character Angel/Hester was immediate. I immediately connected to her. I felt the greatest difficulty would be to give her a quiet place because the fire of her rage was so hot, and I knew my task would be to contain that rage in some way. Not to repress it but to contain it so that it could burn all the way through

† From "Journeys in Performance: On Playing in *The Mai* and *By the Bog of Cats*," from *The Theater of Marina Carr: "before rules was made."* Reprinted by permission of Carysfort Press.

two and a half hours, or whatever length the show would be and
not to let it burn out too fast. The characters in the play are unciv-
ilized, they have a savage quality. They cut across all the boundaries, and this makes them funny as well. Those were my initial
responses to the script and they didn't actually change. When I
read the next two drafts and when we started rehearsing, I felt very
much the same about the script and the character.

*Hester is at once a passionate person, and a mythic figure from
Greek tragedy. Does this yoking together relate to your work in the
part?*

Yes, it does of course. You're dealing with very primal energies, the
stuff of myth. I believe that all those Greek mythic figures are classical archetypes, and are representations of the primal energies
within us. They are an embodiment of those energies and that's
why they survive through time. They're in our DNA, in our physical, spiritual, and psychic DNA. As I said, Hester was there in front
of me and I just needed to step into this person who was like a furnace inside, but who was exultant within it as well.

*How did you work on the dialogues with the ghosts and with Cat-
woman?*

I worked on the dialogues with the ghost characters and with the
'real' characters in a similar way. When Hester speaks with the
Ghost Fancier, she quickly realizes that he is a form of ghost, but it
doesn't particularly alter her conversation with him, except insofar
as her curiosity is aroused and she begins to engage more fully. Her
last line as he leaves is 'Come back. I can't die. I have a daughter'—
recognizing that, in some way, his appearance is a warning that she
has one day left to complete her life. I love how the Ghost Fancier is
confused by mortal time and gets his dawn and his dusk mixed up!
    The Catwoman I regarded very much as a 'real' or local charac-
ter, who is the midwife or the local witch in the community. I don't
know whether those people exist in communities in rural Ireland
still. To a certain extent they must. As we know, midwives over the
last few centuries were also the healers and the witches. Hester
knows that Catwoman tells the truth. A lot of the other characters
don't. The truth in the deepest sense.
    The appearance of Joseph's ghost at the beginning of Act Three
and Hester's conversation with him is the dialogue that disturbs her
the most and that scene was the most difficult part of the play from
my point of view. I think it was problematic for all of us to find the
arc of that scene and I think it was rewritten quite a few times during the four week rehearsal period.

How was Monica Frawley's set [for the Abbey production of By the Bog of Cats . . .] to work in?

I found it a superb set. It was classical, stripped down. It was as empty as the bog. It created a mythic space for the play to exist in, and it demanded a nakedness from us on the stage. There was some talk about whether there should be a caravan on the set. In the San Jose production apparently, there was a caravan at several different moments, but I think that the nakedness of our set was right. Also, when I felt the need to mark Hester's more personal territory, as opposed to her larger landscape, I established it by choosing the stage right side, which I imagined to be the steps of the caravan. Monica reinforced this for me by putting stuff around that area, and when I went off stage right, that was the inside of the caravan. So, reading the image of the stage from stage left to stage right, as the audience does, Hester's territory begins stage left (the house) and ends on stage right (the caravan). The stage left area is dominant, since it's known to be where an audience looks first. So you could theorize that, at the beginning of the play, the audience and the people from the town share the same world (stage right), and Hester is the intruder on stage left. But Hester's territory moves to stage right, drawing the audience with her, so towards the end of the play Hester shares her world with the audience, and the people from the town all enter from the dominant stage left. Hester never really left that stage right side towards the end as the world of the town came in on her, driving her out. In all those final moments, for instance in that final exchange with Xavier Cassidy, it was very useful for me to be able to cling to that side of the stage, until the Ghost Fancier releases Hester in death. Yes, I think the set expressed and released the mythic dimension of the piece, and the mythic dimension of Hester's space.

How did you manage the dialect in By the Bog of Cats . . .?

I could see how important the dialect was. When I did *The Mai*, it was written in straight English, (with the exception of Grandma Fraochlán), not in dialect form, and the sound of The Mai, the sound of the characters in *The Mai* was not at all as crucial as it was in *By the Bog of Cats* . . . The dialect form is a departure that Marina undertook with *Portia Coughlan*, where all of her characters speak with this very particular sound, and it's essential that they speak with that sound. The music of the piece is crucial. I was very anxious to get that right in *By the Bog of Cats* . . . because I feel it is the key to a number of things that are lurking underneath the language. It is certainly one of the keys to the primal energy that drives Hester, and many of Marina's characters. So what I did was a lot of listening. I was rehearsing another play in Edinburgh before I started rehearsing *By the Bog of Cats* . . . in Dublin, and I flew over one weekend in order to spend some time with Marina and asked if I could record her saying some of the lines for me, so that I could listen back to the tape and start getting the sound into my head. She also gave me a few guidelines and mentioned certain people who could speak like that. So I think I pretty much had the music of it by the time I came in to day one of rehearsals. When we did the first readings I would simply stop and repeat the sentence if I felt that my sound wasn't right. So I managed the dialect by a lot of preparation beforehand, and by the time I got into rehearsal if I lost the sound it would throw me off my track completely. It was an essential part of the performance. Because the part of your body that this sound needs to come from is a very resonant gut place, the audience then receives the sound in that gut place; (Artaud often talked about this). By the end of *By the Bog of Cats* . . ., Hester lets out a cry of grief. It was an extension of the sounds I'd been using all evening, so it wasn't hard to go to that place. Marina has talked about the charge the characters must carry, and how playwriting is not about the beautiful sentence. Much of this charge, this unspoken information which the audience receives is through the dialect.

What were the most difficult moments in rehearsal?

The rehearsal period was short and intense. It was four weeks, which is very short for a few play. A lot of new plays get more time than that. It so happened that four weeks was all we had, so I don't remember the most difficult moments [laughing] because it was full on and I never stopped and I don't think I ever had a break—I was on stage for so much of the time. I knew that I could access the end scene, when I would have to murder my child, and so I didn't experience any difficulty about it but I was aware that I had to maintain a trust in myself—that I could tap into that place every time. And Patrick [Mason] was wonderful. I remember a couple of times drawing towards the close of the play when the whole thing would get to me and I would be a bit shaky afterwards, Patrick would come and put his arm around me and we'd have a bit of a laugh, and it was fine. Then there was a period when we started running the play where I realized I was in some sort of overdrive. I was going too fast and it all started to sound the same, at the same pitch. That comes from not properly containing the rage and the drive that I was talking about earlier on (where I knew that was going to be one of my tasks). So when we started running it I was thinking 'Oh my god, it's all up there. What am I going to do?' And Marina and I went out for a meal that night and she gave me a few pointers. She said, yes, you are overdriving it. Just take your time here and there, and she gave me a few pointers like that. Initially, it was hard to avoid overdriving because of the amount of emotional baggage that I was carrying in order to work through the piece, so it was a question of applying a conscious degree of craft to contain it, and to modulate it a little bit more. I suppose that was the most difficult aspect of the rehearsal period, but it was a joyous time because I knew I was being given an opportunity that was rare. I don't think they come around that often—those kinds of roles.

Why does Hester kill her child as well as herself?

In my view Hester kills her child as an act of love. Her child wants to come with her. Her child is otherwise going to enter a world that Hester feels is worse than death. But she certainly does not kill her child as an act of revenge, which is what some people seem to regard the classical Medea as doing. I don't think it's got anything to do with that. I think revenge is a very reductive way of putting it. It has nothing to do with revenge. It has to do with love.

* * *

MELISSA SIHRA

A Cautionary Tale:
Marina Carr's *By the Bog of Cats*†

* * *

The mother-figure in Irish theatre has traditionally been viewed as a personification of the nation. Carr presents the myth of Big Josie Swane as an alternative to the romanticised literary Mother Ireland figure. Big Josie is described by the Catwoman as being ". . . a harsh auld yoke, [who] came and went like the moon . . . except when she sang and then I declare ya'd fall in love with her". This is Yeats' *Cathleen Ní Houlihan* re-imagined. With the legend of Big Josie, Yeats' "Mother Ireland" now metamorphoses into a "rancorous hulk" with a "brazen walk . . . and her reekin' of drink" as opposed to the comely young girl who previously had the "walk of a queen". Illegitimate and unapologetic, like her daughter and granddaughter, Big Josie is an outlaw spending her nights "Off in the bars of Pullagh and Mucklagh gettin' into fights". The nation as female is now depicted as an overweight, erotic, foul-mouthed transgressive energy who, according to Xavier Cassidy was "loose and lazy and aisy, a five shillin' hoor", in contrast to Yeats' martyric wanderer.

† From *Theatre Stuff: Critical Essays on Contemporary Irish Theatre*. Reprinted by permission of Carysfort Press.

Yeats' literary configuration of the nation as female is thought by the *dramatis personae* of his 1902 play to have been: "a woman from beyond the world?" [who has led] "many that have been free to walk the hills and the bogs and the rushes [to be] sent to walk hard streets in far countries". Both Cathleen and Big Josie have the power to compel and to seduce those around them. Cathleen states that: "many a man has died for love of me". Hester comments on her mother's Medusian quality: "Who'd believe a look [from her] could destroy ya?" In Yeats' drama Cathleen's name is remembered by Peter in a song from his boyhood: "I think I heard that name once. Who was it, I wonder? It must have been someone I knew when I was a boy. No, no: I remember, I heard it in a song". Big Josie is also re-membered in a song entitled *The Black Swan*, and is described as "the greatest song stitcher ever to have passed through this place".

Like Cathleen, Big Josie is thought to have been in communion with some otherness. Xavier Cassidy, who was known to have been "in a constant swoon" over the larger than life figure, describes her 'Outside her ould caravan on the bog covered over in stars and her half covered over in an excuse of a dress and her croonin' towards Orion in a language I never heard before or since". This dead or forgotten language is hermetic to the people that now live on the bog. Big Josie embodies the unattainability of the past and its nar-ratives and the changes that can be imposed on a nation. Her war-blings to the moon are reminiscent of the unintelligible ramblings of Doalty imitating the "King's good English" or the "quaint, ar-chaic tongue" heard by Captain Lancey in Friel's *Translations*.

Through the figure of Big Josie, Carr dramatises the notion of otherness and how it is viewed socially and politically. The "settled" locals in *By the Bog of Cats* display suspicion engendered by fear of difference. Both Hester and her mother are accused of dabbling in some "black art thing" because they refuse to conform to the pre-requisites of social convention. Similar to the plight of Hester Prynne in Hawthorne's *The Scarlet Letter* the accusations of black magic are based on a distrust of the extra-ordinary. In his inability to understand Hester's mentality Xavier concludes: "You're a dan-gerous witch Swane! . . . . You're as mad as your mother and she was a lunatic". Carr emphasises that "There is no black magic in the play. There is nothing black magic about Hester. It is about how she is perceived."[1]

Repeatedly compelled to the dramatic possibility of the outsider, Carr's depiction of Hester, The Mai in *The Mai* and Portia in *Portia Coughlan*, as women who "will not bow down [and] will not accept things the way they are", completes what can be regarded as a tril-

1. Unpublished interview with Melissa Sihra, Dublin, 8 Feb. 1999.

ogy. Amphibiously Hester is both in and out of social convention.
The conceptualising of space and property in *By the Bog of Cats* is
unstable and indicative of the nature of identity. Hester crosses
spatial boundaries more radically than in Carr's previous work (The
Mai remains indoors, while Portia flirts with the threshold). Her
representation in contrasting spaces such as the indeterminate bog
"always shiftin' and changin' and coddin' the eye", a caravan and a
fixed house lead to the representation of the self with which they
are entwined. "Half-settled", she is neither one thing nor the other.[2]
Hester displays anomie, itinerancy and exile, all recurring motifs of
a century of Irish playwriting.

Viewed as a "savage" by the settled community, Hester's situation
is similar to that of Christy Mahon's in *The Playboy of the Western
World*. The sitting of the savage is inverted in both plays. The locals' desire that Hester should "Go to the next haltin' site" mirrors
Christy's enforced exile. Now "a lepping savage" the former playboy
is ritualistically scorched on the shins with a lighted sod while Hester is warned: "We'll burn ya out if we have to". Carr subverts the
notion of the outsider in *By the Bog of Cats*. Instead of detachedly
observing the excentric figure from within, the audience, through
its engagement with Hester also becomes marginalised from the so-
called "settled community" in the play. This results in the audience
ironically observing themselves (as members of the "settled-
community"), a collusion which gives both Hester and the audience "an edge over all of yees . . . [and] . . . allows me see yees for
the inbred, underbred, bog-brained shower yees are".

The suffering of the outsider is articulated by Jimmy Jack in
Translations: "I am a barbarian in this place because I am not understood by anyone". Hester's sense of displacement is furthered
by the deliberate ambiguity surrounding her paternity and the
mythical quality of her father-land: "I had a father too! . . . Jack
Swane from Bergit's Island . . . Ya'd swear I was dropped from the
sky the way ya go on. . . . I'm as settled as any of yees—". Olwen
Fouéré notes the dialectical tension of Hester's existence: "she sets
herself apart from the society she is in, yet she desires to be a part
of it".[3]

Through the figures of Big Josie and Hester, Carr represents the
female as outlaw or deviant. Roaming the bog by day and night
Hester is both *maenad* and *mater familias*. With her inherited association to the outdoors and nature comes the tendency to excessive
behaviour and anarchism. Simon Goldhill writes about fifth-
century Athenian drama and "the regular association of women

2. Public Reading, Trinity College, Dublin, 29 June 1999.
3. Unpublished interview with Melissa Sihra, 30 April 1999.

with the inside and the dangers associated with women when they
go outside [and how the] requirement to keep women on the inside
is so forcefully stated"[4]. Hester persistently interrogates the rhetoric
of authority and demonstrates how the written law possesses no
hold over her. Accused by Caroline of breaking a signed and sealed
contract, Hester states "Bits of paper, writin', means nothin', can as
aisy be unsigned". Mrs. Kilbride, Carthage's mother, is complicit
with existing codes of practice. She is perpetuator *and* cog of the
law in all its forms. Hester confronts Mrs. Kilbride: "Have you ever
been discarded Elsie Kilbride?" To which she replies: "No, I've
never been discarded, Hester Swanel Ya know why? Because I've
never overstepped myself. I've always lived by the rules". "Ah rules!
What rules are they?" questions Hester.

Carr's drama articulates the dynamics of ownership in relation to
personal and political identity. Domineering and manipulative, Mrs.
Kilbride is a key figure of the play in her will to overpower and control those around her. Allusions to imperialism are directed at Mrs.
Kilbride on two occasions in the play. At the wedding she observes of
her shoes that: "The Quane herself wouldn't pay more". Similarly in
scene six of the first act when Josie pretends to be Mrs. Kilbride, she
says to Hester: "I had turf stew for me dinner and for dessert I had
a snail tart . . . Ya wouldn't get better in Buckin'am Palace".

In scene four of act one Mrs. Kilbride seeks to possess and re-
write somebody else's identity. Just as the orthographer in Friel's
Translations works with the toponymic department in order to ensure the correct spelling of new names of places, Mrs. Kilbride as-
cribes a different name to Hester's child. Upon asking the child to
spell her name aloud, Mrs. Kilbride informs little Josie that she is:
"wrong! wrong! wrong! . . . Ya got some of it right. Ya got the "Josie"
part right, but ya got the "Kilbride" part wrong, because you're not
a Kilbride. You're a Swane . . . . You're Hester Swane's little bastard.
You're not a Kilbride and never will be". Mrs. Kilbride continues:
"Don't you worry, child, we'll get ya off her yet. Me and your Daddy
has plans. We'll batter ya into the semblance of legitimacy yet . . .
I'll break your spirit yet and then glue ya back the way I want ya".

The re-named child Josie Kilbride suffers a subsequent crisis of
her identity. When her mother addresses her as "Josie Swane" she
replies: "Me name is Josie Kilbride . . . . I'm not a Swane, I'm a Kilbride". As Hugh asserts in *Translations*: "Confusion is not an ignoble condition". Josie's confusion is born out of having a
Grandmother who spoke in a different tongue and whose own
name has been changed. The reality intrinsic to re-naming as

4. Simon Goldhill, *Reading Greek Tragedy* (Cambridge: Cambridge University Press,
   1992), 15.

dramatised by Friel, is articulated by Hester in act three when she states to the locals: "The truth is you want to eradicate me, make out I never existed".

Clothing and costume are directly relational to the performative nature of identity. Christy Mahon assumes a persona as the *Playboy* upon the acquirement of new clothes. He sees a different image of himself in the looking-glass and conditions his identity according to the reflection: "Didn't I know rightly, I was handsome". Hester's arrival at the marriage celebrations in a wedding dress is similarly a signifier of what she is not. In the scene between Mrs. Kilbride and her granddaughter, it is noted in the text that little Josie's jumper is "*on inside out*". This is an indication of the deranged state of the child's subjectivity. When Carthage arrives on the scene he tellingly informs his daughter that she must learn to dress herself.

Sense of place is integral to Irish theatre. The repetition of the name "Bog of Cats" throughout the play highlights the link between place, identity and memory. Samuel Beckett is unique in the canon of Irish playwrights in his consistent refusal to localise his drama. Carr's play can be linked with the Beckettian anti-landscape. The bog, a place and a non-place (hovering somewhere between the actual and the imaginary), transcends what Beckett viewed as the aesthetic reductivism of specific geographic allusion. Carr's *mise en scene* has the best of both worlds. While on the one hand it is recognisably Irish, it belongs as much in the domain of Greek tragedy, Gothic horror, Absurdism and Grotesque surrealism. The play possesses the mythic dimension of timelessness. There is a sparseness in the setting of *By the Bog of Cats* that is suggestive of the inescapable limbo of Beckett's "*A country road. A tree. Evening*". Carr offers: "*Dawn . . . . A bleak white landscape of ice and snow. Music, a lone violin*".

The genre of the Fantastic, which does not invent other worlds but inverts elements of the *known* world, allows for a distance that affords oblique access to the culture and society in question. By entering spaces outside the frame of the real, Carr replaces familiarity and comfort with estrangement and unease, thus offering the necessary objectivity for self-scrutiny. The rise in materialism and intolerance of otherness currently gripping contemporary Ireland is commented upon in *By the Bog of Cats*. "Why don't yees head off . . . back to wherever yees came from" declares Mrs. Kilbride to her granddaughter. An upwardly mobile mentality is portrayed in the characters Xavier, Carthage and Mrs. Kilbride. Hester accuses Carthage of being a "jumped-up land hungry mongrel [who is] selling me and Josie down the river for a few lumpy auld acres and notions of respectability".

* * *

BERNADETTE BOURKE

Grotesque and Carnivalesque Elements in
By the Bog of Cats†

* * *

Hester Swane, Carr's female protagonist in *By the Bog of Cats*, is
the forty-year-old 'tinker'[1] woman whose mother abandoned her on
the Bog of Cats at the tender age of seven. As the action of the play
begins she has once more been abandoned, this time by her lover of
fourteen years, Carthage Kilbride. The father of her seven-year-old
daughter Josie, Carthage is about to marry into a local landowning
family for, as Hester accuses, 'a few lumpy auld acres and notions
of respectability'. Hester is determined not to leave her home, despite Catwoman's prophetic dreams. In medieval folklore, death's
headless harbinger travels in a black horse-drawn coach which
stops at the abode of the victim. Carr presents the post-modern appropriation,[2] with a 'black train motorin' through the Bog of Cats',
scorching and blasting everything in its wake. Catwoman interprets
the dream and urges Hester to leave or she will 'bring this place
down by evening'. Hester Swane contradicts the departure motif
central to Synge. His plays usually end with the departure of the
hero/heroine whose alternative viewpoint is rejected by a closed society. Nora in *The Shadow of the Glen* chooses to escape from the
repression of her fruitless life and marriage, and to embrace the
wild outdoors with the tramp. The Douls face a similar fate when
they choose a dubious freedom at the end of *The Well of the Saints*,
and the most famous departure of all is probably that of Christy
Mahon. He vacates the space at the end of *The Playboy*, leaving behind him a static society, which had been temporarily invigorated
by the vital energy he brought with him. In Carr's play, Synge's departure motif is subverted, and ultimately expanded, as Hester refuses from the beginning to leave the bog, and avoids the necessity
by taking her own life.

At times, one detects in Carr's work grotesque allusions which

† From *The Theater of Marina Carr: "before rules was made."* Reprinted by permission of
Carysfort Press.
1. Before the word acquired the connotations associated with it today, a tinker was a travelling mender of pots and pans. Hester Swane is proud of her heritage and claims that
her tinker blood gives her 'the edge over all of yees around here'.
2. Hutcheon says postmodern parody, whether ironic quotation or appropriation, notes the
continuum, but also the difference induced by the history which separates the two representations. See Linda Hutcheon, *The Politics of Postmodernism* (London: Routledge,
1989), 93–94.

seem like deliberate appropriations from Synge. [In *Playboy*,] Sarah
Tansey, who 'yoked the ass cart and drove ten miles' to see 'the man
bit the yellow lady's nostril on the northern shore,' strikingly illustrates Synge's fascination with the grotesque. This story finds
echoes in *By the Bog of Cats* where Big Josie Swane is recalled as
a pugnacious individual, who once 'bit the nose off a woman
who dared to look at her man. Bit the nose clean off her face'. In
Carr's play, Synge's grotesque image is taken to its most extreme
conclusion.

She does the same with the image [in *Playboy*] of Jimmy Farrell's
dog which we are told was left 'hanging from the licence and [. . .]
it screeching and wriggling three hours at the butt of a string', by
presenting an horrendously grotesque version in *By the Bog of Cats*.
Here Hester recalls finding young James Cassidy 'strychnined to
the eyeballs [. . .] and his dog in his arms'. She accuses Xavier
Cassidy, the victim's father, of lacing his son's dog with the lethal
poison, in the sure knowledge that the boy would enfold the af-
flicted creature thus making contact with the strychnine, which
was intended for him. Hester suspects that Cassidy used the dog
in order to eliminate a weak and ineffectual male offspring. Just as
the vengeful Medea 'anointed' the dress and the coronet, gifts for
Jason's new bride, with such a deadly poison that 'all who touch
her will expire in agony',[3] so too does Cassidy deliberately smear
strychnine on his son's dog, fully cognizant of what that poison
does. '[. . .] a tayspoonful is all it takes, and ya'd the dog showered
in it. Burnt his hands clean away'. The playfulness of Synge's
grotesque is absent in these examples, and the perversion of 'normal' female, and fatherly behaviour, no longer provokes congenial
laughter in the shock of these mutated accounts.

In her study of Synge's plays Toni O'Brien Johnson shows how
the playwright explores the grotesque through a mixture of comedy,
incongruity, and ugliness, and by utilizing the fool motif. If Synge's
'fools' are those perceived as such by the 'official community' for
choosing to place themselves outside the established social struc-
tures, Hester Swane, like her mother before her, is Carr's version.
She goes beyond Synge's models however, and possesses even wider
mythic associations and possibilities. Hester is not only rejected as
an outsider—an itinerant—but feared also, as a woman in possession of 'a black art thing'. When outlining Synge's use of the literary fool Johnson highlights three important aspects. The fool is
closer to nature than the 'insiders', and is instinctive, vital and impulsive. The fool is irrational, which leads others, on the one hand
to admire his/her visionary ability to see into the heart of things,

3. Euripedes, *Medea and Other Plays*, trans. Philip Vellacott (London: Penguin, 1963), 41.

but on the other, to fear this as madness, and thus reject him/her. Finally, Johnson notes that the fool 'remains an outsider'.[4] Although coined as a description of Synge's early twentieth century outsiders, this account fits perfectly the character of Hester Swane conjured into existence almost a hundred years later.

Hester's bond with nature is symbolized in the opening moments by the lone figure dragging the dead swan, across the raw and corrugated landscape. It is emphasized throughout the play by her inability to settle in either house or caravan, and by her choice to occupy the liminal space between the two. Big Josie Swane, who 'hung around for no wan', had prepared her infant daughter Hester for a life in tune with nature, by choosing the black swan as a surrogate mother for the child she knew she would one day abandon. The ritual of placing the newborn baby in the swan's lair, and repeating the exercise for three consecutive nights, creates a bond which can only be broken by death. As the play draws to a close, Hester, anticipating her own impending fate, gives in to her vital instinctive side and burns down the house and stables, letting the bog 'have it back' which is 'what the tinkers do'. Her final impulsive act of union with nature is to slit her young daughter's throat, and then kill herself with the same knife, still warm and wet with her child's blood. Carr has taken the grotesque possibilities in the fool/outsider figure to a new and powerfully subversive level.

That Hester Swane possesses the second feature of O'Brien Johnson's 'fool' model, and is a visionary, a 'truth-teller',[5] is evident early in the play when Catwoman recognizes this quality as 'the best thing about ya'. Although Catwoman can find little to praise in the stubborn and turbulent Hester, she is aware that unlike others 'who manage to stay a step or two ahead of the pigsty truth of themselves', Hester faces her demons, and ultimately overcomes them. Frank McGuinness has pinpointed the paradox inherent in this, noting that while 'tragedy is so often caused by a fatal lack of self-knowledge, Carr's characters die from a fatal excess of self-knowledge'.[6] This irrational side to Hester Swane is probably what attracted young Kilbride to her in the first place. However, the urge towards land and respectability, coupled with the horrible guilt for his part in, and revulsion at her part in her brother's murder, turn him from her to a world that she can never inhabit. When the lure of her unconventional irrationality ceases to attract him he begins, like the others, to suspect her, and to question himself for having

4. Toni O'Brien Johnson, *Synge: The Medieval and the Grotesque* (Gerrards Cross: Colin Smythe, 1982), 118.
5. Ibid.
6. Frank McGuinness, Introduction, *The Dazzling Dark: New Irish Plays* (London: Faber & Faber, 1996), ix–x.

stayed with her for so long. He joins ranks with the 'settled' community when he expresses their belief that it is time Hester, the outsider, 'moved onto another haltin' site'.

This brings us to the third point in relation to the literary fool. She/he remains an outsider. Social assimilation, anathema to Synge's outsiders, is savagely rejected by Hester Swane. Synge's plays, as already observed, generally end with the departure of the outsider. Timmy's final prophetic words, presaging the drowning of the blind couple, in *The Well of the Saints*, offer a diegetic, off-stage possibility only. Nora's choice in *The Shadow of the Glen* does not ignore the attendant dangers, and Patch Darcy's fate hangs over that play as a constant reminder of the elemental forces, which are destructive as well as alluring. While death is always around the corner for Synge's departing outsiders, it is never mimetically enacted. Carr's historical placing allows for the gross note to be acted out on stage. Hester Swane, refusing to vacate the space, makes the choice that Synge had hinted at for his blind protagonists in *The Well*, and for Nora in *The Shadow*, as Carr expands the dramatic possibilities of the fool figure, by presenting onstage, Synge's off-stage suggestion.

By the Bog of Cats is set in a Beckettian no-man's-land and Patrick Mason's 1998 Abbey production chose to incorporate the house, which represents the settled community, and the caravan, which symbolizes Hester's tinker heritage, as offstage extensions of designer Monica Frawley's bleak stepped landscape of partially-cut, snow-covered bog. This decision effectively highlighted Hester's anomalous status, as the space she chooses to occupy is the liminal region between the two, the bog itself, which is a magnet for her, as the Belmont River is for the doomed heroine in [Carr's] *Portia Coughlan*. The cottage kitchen as the domesticated space of 'woman' has been entirely rejected by Hester who first shuns the house, and later obliterates it in her act of vengeance. Carr's troubled characters choose to roam the vast expanses rather than succumb to the asphyxiation of confined spaces. The surreal landscape of *By the Bog of Cats* provides a realm where the grotesque can flourish.

The opening image of Hester trailing the corpse of a black swan, and leaving a track of blood in the snow immediately strikes the 'gross note' that Synge insisted on, only here it is more stark as the image is presented visually rather than in language. *By the Bog of Cats* opens with a vivid image of bloody death, and the prediction that more will follow before the cycle is complete. The Ghost Fancier's 'mistake', coupled with Catwoman's injunction to Hester to 'lave this place now or ya never will', prepare us for the bloody *dénouement*. The ritualistic death dance is the Rabelaisian climax, which is at once terrifying and jubilant. Hester's death at the end of the play is the carnivalesque enactment of its opposite, representing renewal in a return to the great nurturing womb of nature, giver of life, death and continuity.

The violent thrust in Carr's work is undisguised, and lends itself readily to grotesque treatment. A brother's corpse is weighted down and lowered into the murky depths of a lake. A man uses a cocked shotgun to grope a woman's body. A boy embraces a dog laced with strychnine and is burnt alive by the contact. Such grotesque descriptions of violence abound, and even Hester's early humane impulse to bury the dead swan is subverted in the violent ripping of the bird from the ice, which leaves half her underbelly intact, while creating the bloody trail of a split-open corpse in the white snow. This opening image anticipates the flesh-ripping violence with which the play will close. Hester's savage nature is never hidden, and she warns Caroline of her capabilities early on as she describes the two opposite poles to her own nature: One, decent and tolerant, and the other who 'could slice a knife down your face, carve ya up and not bat an eyelid'.

Such savagery emerges against those who take away what she holds most precious. Her brother Joseph, she believes, took her mother's love, and Carthage is about to take her home and her child. Swallowing her pride, Hester begs to be allowed to stay on the bog, and when Carthage refuses her, she feels she has no choice but to wage 'a vicious war' against him. Hester goes on the rampage, pouring diesel over everything they once shared and setting it alight.

The evocation of burning stables replete with howling animals at the beginning of Act Three may be viewed as a reworking of the traditional festive hell-burning. The farm represents the wages of sin, built up from the money taken from the murdered Joseph. This bloody deed has turned Hester's life into a living hell as she grapples with the guilt. Carthage too is haunted, having 'rose in the world on his [Joseph's] ashes'. Hester's reckless actions at this point symbolize an impulse to eradicate a personal hell, an impulse that reaches its climax in the death dance. The discordant sound of howling animals, tied in, and burning to death, is a perverse reversal of the earlier scene where father and daughter, Carthage and Josie, exit hand in hand, to 'check the calves', and 'count the cattle', which represent the life-blood of the farm. The incongruity between the homely, and its perverse violent opposite, enacts that clash of opposites which is at the heart of grotesque and carnivalesque imagery.

Hester's final act of violence is prompted by Carthage's decision to take Josie from her. Her efforts to say goodbye to her daughter prove futile, as the child refuses to be separated from her mother, and Hester refuses to sentence her daughter to the limbo she has lived in since her own mother's departure. The killing of her child, by far the most controversial aspect of the play, is ironically perpetrated without overt violence, but with love. Carr has subverted the very notion of violence itself, by couching it in gentle, protective, motherly terms.

The final death, her own, is presented ritualistically in the death dance. The aesthetic beauty of the description of Hester's heart, cut out of her body, and 'lying there on top of her chest like some dark feathered bird', introduces a romantic sensibility which clashes with the gross. The hybrid nature of Carr's aesthetic allows for towering grotesque moments, alongside stylized ritual, and the ultimate disruption of carnival itself, which is employed in the superb second act of *By the Bog of Cats*.

Of all of Carr's plays this is the one that most obviously employs the strategy of carnival to generate a deliberate travesty of the social order. The disruptive power of this act represents a sustained attack on the ritual of marriage, which is subverted on every level, as the misrule of carnival is given free reign. Michael D. Bristol identifies the traditional carnival personae including fools, clowns, giants, oversized puppets and effigies, and explains how 'each of these figures represents a variant on the central pattern of travesty and identity switching'.[7] All these ingredients are present in Act Two of Carr's play. The grotesque, rooted as it is in the medieval carnivalesque tradition, sits comfortably in this environment where the spectacle of Catwoman slurping wine from a saucer is perfectly acceptable. This vision can also contain the physical representation of the blood-soaked ghost of Joseph Swane who enters the space in search of company, and reveals the awful loneliness of his purgatorial existence.

The subversive intention is further exposed with the entrance of the bride and groom, and Caroline's uneasy admission that they have 'done the wrong thing'. Carr does not simply present a carnival festival, which the folk unthinkingly embrace and partake in. What she offers is a travesty of the tradition itself, where the 'true' bride Caroline is trapped in a parody of a marriage, which bears no relation to the fantasy of 'a big ballroom with a fountain of mermaids in the middle'. Defeated, she admits to the pretence, resolving to endure the day, which should have been the happiest in her life.

The carnival laughter, temporarily dampened by the veracity of

---

7. Michael D. Bristol, *Carnival and Theatre: Plebeian Culture and the Structure of Authority in Renaissance England* (London: Routledge, 1985), 66.

the 'unhappy couple', resumes with gusto as Mrs Kilbride enters, enacting her very surname by usurping the role of 'bride' for herself. 'Disguised' as the bride, she reverses expectations by refusing to part with her son, by assuming the central position beside the groom in the wedding photograph, and by suggesting an Oedipal bond—referring to her 'son' as her 'husband'. Outrageous and grotesque, such reversals sit comfortably within the carnival tradition.

Catwoman's return, linking arms with the doting Father Willow, introduces a wonderful 'clash of incompatibles'[8] reminiscent of Synge. Here we have the two traditions, Catholic and pagan, arm in arm, and planning a holiday in the sun together. The ambivalent laughter of carnival which is gay and triumphant, and at the same time mocking and deriding can accommodate the spectacle of a Catholic priest, whose adoration is directed not at the God of his church, but at the blind pagan prophetess, with mouse fur stuck between her teeth. That he is unsuited to his pastoral role is indicated in the clothing imagery. The ecclesiastical uniform—black suit and clerical collar—is, for Father Willow, but a festive costume, and the pyjamas that can be seen peeping 'from under his shirt and trousers', remind us that what he wears is a disguise, a carnival mask.

Toni O'Brien Johnson describes how, during the Festival of Fools in the Middle Ages, all things sacred were profaned.[9] Marina Carr's priest, a monument to carnivalesque reversal, epitomizes the sacrilegious. By keeping 'a gun in the tabernacle', and by wearing earplugs in the confession box, he embodies a burlesque subversion of both sacraments, mocking the doctrine of transubstantiation, and denying the possibility of absolution for the contrite. The ambivalent laughter reaches a climax when the priest cannot remember the grace before meals, and instead launches into an anecdote, expressing regret at his own unmarried predicament.

Hester's arrival could be said to represent that moment when the carnival goes out of control. * * * When carnival festivity ends, social order should be restored, but Carr's festival spirals out of control with the dissonant entrance of Hester. This 'bride-effigy' will be destroyed, as all festive effigies are, before deviant impulses are pacified and brought under control.

* * *

8. Johnson, 2.
9. Ibid, 15–30.

On Theater in Ireland

VICTOR MERRIMAN

[Postcolonialism and Irish Theater]†

The twentieth century saw remarkable historical transformations on the island of Ireland. Fully absorbed in the British Empire in 1900, by 2000 the Republic of Ireland was a sovereign state, a member of the European Union, and an 'economic success story'.

A longed-for independent Ireland was the focus of eighteenth and nineteenth century anti-colonial dreaming. By 2000, the benefits envisaged as the inevitable bounty of national self-determination appeared to have been achieved. It seemed as if the historical moment of the late nineteenth century, in which a longing for decolonization crystallized around a construct of the Irish nation, had been vindicated. At that time, anti-colonial nationalist consciousness elaborated itself across all areas of Irish experience, and the nation was announced as an achievable utopia, should the British depart.

Cultural production was central to the development of nationalist consciousness, and the National Theatre Society occupied a central position in staging—and critiquing—available social models. Gregory, Yeats, Synge and Shaw recognized that the social reality most likely to emerge post independence carried within its genes the inevitable frustration of republican ideals around liberty, equality and social solidarity. The cultural *cul de sac* engendered by this reality was keenly experienced across Irish society. Two significant playwrights, Sean O'Casey and Samuel Beckett, emigrated to Devon and to Paris respectively, and continued to critique the choices made in the Irish Free State with the relative freedom of the exile. Even as the new state's failures produced an unbearable level of economic migration, peaking during the 1950s, playwrights such as M.J. Molloy and John B. Keane depicted the brutalization of rural Ireland by poverty, emigration and late marriage in plays such as

---

† From "Poetry shite: A Postcolonial Reading of *Portia Coughlan* and *Hester Swayne*," from *The Theater of Marina Carr: "before rules was made."* Reprinted by permission of Carysfort Press.

The Wood of the Whispering and *Sive*. Brendan Behan's *The Quare Fellow* argued bluntly that 'the Free State didn't change anything more than the badges on the (prison) warders' caps'.

The economic caesura of 1958–1959 was accompanied by the retirement from active politics of Eamon de Valera, enabling a cultural caesura to come into being also.

Since that time, the state has pursued an outward looking economic policy, driven by the conviction that 'a small open economy' must be open above all else, to compensate for the disadvantages of being small. Officially, economic openness has meant 'attracting inward investment' from Europe and the USA. The state has accepted the technocratic copying of political and economic forms and conventions from the Anglo-American world as a necessary motor of change. This habit of what J.J. Lee refers to as 'the official mind' installs and legitimizes implication in the global capitalist order as the national destination: the escape route from nineteenth century imperialism turns out to lead directly to collusion with the imperialist project of the twenty-first century. Embracing the New World Order, in gestation since the early 1970s, means living within its neo-liberal ground rules. Those premises are rooted in individualism and the primary of economic narratives of reality and possibility. They are fundamentally incompatible with the ideals underpinning late nineteenth and early twentieth century Irish nationalist consciousness. They are openly at odds with the Enlightenment principles underpinning a republic of equal citizens. Contemporary Ireland faces every day a profound historical irony: the diverted teleology of the nation-state demands the abandonment of the egalitarian and communitarian aspirations of anti-colonial nationalism. Such a contradiction ensures an unsettled country.

Inevitably, accounts of Irish experience other than those authorized by the official mind emerge and attract public support. Such accounts appear in both unofficial and non-official forms throughout the twentieth century. Unofficial versions of Irish openness question the received wisdoms of the extremely conservative social order dominant in Independent Ireland. Challenges are mounted to the extraordinary control of the Catholic Church, not only during the 1960s and after, but even in the 1930s, when its compact with de Valera was such that drafts of the 1937 Constitution were proofed and commented upon by the Archbishop of Dublin, Dr. McQuaid. Alongside unofficial narratives and practices, non-official forms of Irish openness proliferate: all the branded products of the global marketplace are enthusiastically embraced, as are sporting, cultural and capitalist heroes. A generally uncritical openness to the world manifests not in liberation from imperial domination, but in the limit situations[1] of neo-colonial social relations. Measured against the yardstick of republicanism, which guarantees liberty and equality for, and solidarity among its citizens, Independent Ireland has not decolonized in any significant sense.

Independent Ireland is a neo-colonial state, and that reality must be acknowledged in any consideration of contemporary Irish theatre.[2] Contemporary theatre cannot usefully be approached as a set of post-colonial cultural practices, in the sense of chronological severance that 'post-colonial' commonly intends. This essay reads postcoloniality as practices and conditions which emerge and are experienced under colonial and neo-colonial conditions. The moment of postcoloniality is a critical occasion, when the capacity to think otherwise is fully engaged, even if the capacity to decolonize—to live otherwise—is not materially present. In such moments are nations, societies and utopias imaginable. At such moments, artists seek to engage the critical faculties of the dreaming public as they contemplate possible worlds.

If, following Yeats's death in 1939, the National Theatre experienced decades of aversion from the struggles of the nation, Irish drama emerged again in rural Ireland to critique 'the leadership of men who freed their nation, but who could never free their own souls and minds from the effects of having been born in slavery'.[3] The spiritual emptiness of the 1950s and its mutation in the first phase of 'new openness' from 1959 on frame Tom Murphy's *On the Outside* and *Famine*, and Brian Friel's *Philadelphia, Here I Come*. Twenty years on, the urban dramas of Billy Roche's *A Handful of Stars* (1988) and *Poor Beast in the Rain* (1989) and Dermot Bolger's *The Lament for Arthur Cleary* (1989), stage the 1980s as a reprise of the 1950s, accompanied—especially in Bolger—by the violent consequences of two decades of cultural 'openness'. As Irish culture globalizes, and the world wants to come and take a look at the Celtic Tiger, Donal O'Kelly's *Asylum! Asylum!* (1994) and *Farawayan* (1998) include Europe's Others in contemporary Irish dramas of neo-colonial discontent and postcolonial dreaming.

Irish drama's claim to social significance rests on the pledge that

---

1. In her 'Notes' to P. Freire, *Pedagogy of Hope* (Continuum, 1996), p. 205, Ana Maria Araújo Freire writes: 'For Freire, human beings, as beings endowed with consciousness have at least some awareness of their conditioning and their freedom. They meet with obstacles in their personal and social lives, and see them as obstructions to be overcome. Freire calls these obstructions or barriers "limit situations."

2. For a detailed discussion of terms such as neo-colonial and post-colonial, as they are applied here, see A. Ampka, 'Drama and the Language of Postcolonial Desire: Bernard Shaw's *Pygmalion*' and V. Merriman's 'Decolonisation Postponed: The Theatre of Tiger Trash', in *Irish University Review*, 29 (2) (Autumn/Winter 1999), 294–304, and 305–17 respectively.

3. M.J. Molloy, 'Preface' to *The Wood of the Whispering* in *Selected Plays of M.J. Molloy*, edited by Robert O'Driscoll (Catholic University of America Press, 1998), p. 111.

in acts of theatre something more than box office, or the aggrandis-
ement of an individual artist, is at stake. Theatre is part of a
broader cultural conversation about who we are, how we are in the
world and who and how we would like to be. Theatre is a powerful
means of constituting and invigorating community. The questioning stance of dramatic artists is essential to the development of critical citizenship, without which no social order can remain healthy.
When J.M. Synge released his 'playboy' into the civic space opened
up by a national theatre, he demonstrated the critical vigour and
political significance of performative images themselves. Far from
demanding space to express or enunciate a rarefied 'aesthetic' position, the theatre of Yeats, Gregory and Synge inaugurates a conversation with 'Ireland'. Their use of ambivalent narratives and images
of community to critique triumphant nationalism establishes in
Irish theatre the commitment of artists to an ethical vision. This
critical cultural project engaged with the figure of the Irish peasant
and the dynamics of rural community life, not only because of an
aversion to a 'filthy modern tide', but because of the ubiquity of the
idealized peasant and rural community as human and social models
in nationalist rhetoric and iconography. If the stage looked to the
West and at rural society, it was because that was where nationalist
ideology argued authentic Ireland was to be found.

The playwrights of the National Theatre Society staged the peasant in order to question the social claims of a nationalist monolith
bidding to replace colonial personnel, while maintaining intact the
social relations of colonialism. Irish theatre is thus created as a site
of public conversation on the type of social order emerging in anti-
colonial nationalism. Such founding principles are uniquely available as the principled basis to interrogate the neo-colonial
conditions of contemporary society, and to critique prevailing theatre practices.

Not all plays staged in Ireland at this time may be understood as
the products of postcolonial consciousness. Not all plays are culturally useful, in the sense that they enable spaces for transforma-
tive dreaming, for thinking otherwise. Yeats and Gregory, and Synge
exposed in dramatic fictions the co-existence of two worlds, a dra-
maturgical choice which makes it possible to stage liminal states in
which desires may be anticipated, even performed. Such dramas
are cultural openings which enable participants in theatre to coun-
tenance utopian projects such as decolonization. Such plays
achieve their effects by subjecting anything which appears to be
new, to posit an end to histories either public or personal, to critical questioning. The stance of the artists involved in conceiving
and realizing such works is an example of the kind of practices
which, following [Paulo] Freire, I describe and valorize as culturally

useful. The liminalities I detect in the early Abbey plays, in *The Wood of the Whispering*, in *The Lament for Arthur Cleary* and in Charlie O'Neill's *Rosie and Starwars* (1997), are profoundly the product of social relations in which being, becoming and belonging, are present always as states unresolved. In such dramas, questions of being, becoming and belonging are staged as processes emergent in contemporary experience. The struggles for actualization of the *dramatis personae* of these plays problematize accepted strategies for the narration of the past, the representation of present realities, and the enabling or closing down of dreams of the future.

The Wood of the Whispering, and *The Lament for Arthur Cleary* are dramas forged in the dark days of the 1950s and 1980s. *Rosie and Starwars* appeared at a time when there was a sense of things improving, and acts as a reminder that full citizenship remains to be experienced by many Irish people. Specifically, in this case travellers. Exploiting the symbolic space opened up by Mary Robinson's presidency, Calypso Productions made a bold attempt to undo and critique the theatrical and film text 'Traveller', with all its reductive connotations. *Rosie and Starwars*, in content, form, and exhibition practices, set out to include Irish travellers in public conversations about Ireland. Some years later, Tiger Ireland was resounding to the clamour of the propaganda for 'success', and was undergoing a series of social mutations. In a reflection on the dawn of the twenty-first century, Fergus Finlay remarks:

> Now we are rich beyond our wildest dreams [. . .] Rich to the point where poverty is beginning to be defined as the absence of a second car. We love to consume, to spend, to have [. . .] I couldn't help thinking, when the budget caused such a furore last month, that at last we were beginning to get a taste of what a society without values might look like. That may seem an overstatement, but it seems as if something has died along the way. To be told that the economy was the priority now, that community values had to take second place, and that this was official government policy—there was a rude awakening in that for a great many people who are concerned about the decline of civic life.[4]

Driven by the manifest boom of Tiger Ireland, the state installed the right to consume as the supreme right, the duty to consume as the primary duty. Citizenship is a key concept in republicanism, and a central promise of the libertarian rhetoric of nationalist anti-colonial struggle. For neo-liberal legislators, guaranteeing citizenship

---

4. Fergus Finlay, *Cork Examiner* 31 Dec. 1999.

comes with unpalatable trappings, such as social responsibility and commitments to egalitarianism and solidarity. In keeping with this political turn, the resurgent neocolonialism of Tiger Ireland manifests itself culturally in the pursuit of local quietism and international success. Finlay points out that national élites seek totems of their achievements in the currency of the international bourgeoisie. They also require of that which is identifiably 'Irish'—and this includes, especially, representations of the past, and of rural society—that it perform new cultural tasks, especially in the matter of domesticating wealth and consumption. The illusion of a new future can also be engendered by staging the past as a place we're all glad to have left behind. The past, and rural Ireland, is up for grabs again, and what is at stake is competing models of present and future.

In the shadow of the Celtic Tiger, Irish theatre demonstrates some confusion about how best to honour its historical responsibility to critique accepted versions of *us now*. Apart from Calypso Productions taking to the streets with *Féile Fáilte*, few were able or willing to confront the construction of *us* at the expense of *them*, in the shape of refugees and economic migrants. Mainstream Irish theatre returned instead to the past and to rural settings in order to interrogate the safer worlds of *us then*. Such a resort enables theatre to appeal to contemporary urban audiences without placing actual dramas of Ireland now on the stage. In averting the gaze from existing sites of social contradiction, such dramas harmonize with the neo-liberal project of social reconstruction. And so, myth, grotesque and derivativeness appear as distractions from the predicaments of the present. In the case of Martin McDonagh's plays, the past returned to is that of the stage itself. The hoard of variations on Oirishry accumulated over the years is raided again, as familiar 'pot boiler' dramaturgy yields its historical bounty—crowd pleasers.

Marina Carr's *Portia Coughlan* and *By the Bog of Cats* opt for worlds even more tightly sealed than in McDonagh's. Narrative energy is sought in the psychic disjunctions of narcissistic protagonists haunted by dead brothers. Content which appears to be quintessentially Irish is overlaid with tropes and conventions deriving from Greek cosmology filtered through the pedagogical systems of the Anglo-American world. *Portia Coughlan* and *By the Bog of Cats* propose a rural Ireland full of self loathing, and dogged not by the events of its own history, but by tropes from Shakespeare and Ancient Greece. The resources of the most successful Irish theatre companies have been deployed in the service of deeply problematic work, to the extent that their theatricality—their ability to operate as spectacle—overpowers engagement with their significance as dramatic art. It is necessary to question the meaning of these representations as constitutive events in the evolution of civil society.

* * *

MARY TROTTER

Translating Women into Irish Theatre History†

A century ago, one of the central goals of the Irish Literary Theatre, the Gaelic League, and other nationalist cultural organizations was to advance representations of Irish character which
would contest British stereotypes of the Irish people. The stage was
the logical site for this challenge, and a century later, many Irish
playwrights still seek to dramatize realistic Irish experiences. For
example, * * *, Roddy Doyle, Paul Mercier, and the other collaborators in the Passion Machine Theatre Company have explored the
experiences of, and, thus, have given a voice to, Dublin's young,
postmodern, male-dominated working class. Considering the history behind such initiatives, it seems doubly important to ask,
"Where are the women's voices in contemporary Irish theatre?"
This essay critiques when and how women's voices are heard in
contemporary Irish drama. . . . * * *

While women have played vital roles in the Irish dramatic movement over the past century as playwrights, actors, managers, editors, and critics, their involvement has often entailed a hard-fought
struggle. Practically, biases within the theatre community often
make it difficult for women to get employed in theatres—a typical
problem in theatre communities around the world, but one which
women like Garry Hynes and Pam Brighton are helping to change
in the Republic and in Northern Ireland.[1] Critically, writing by
women playwrights is routinely overlooked, ignored, or marginalized. Often written and/or performed by collaborative groups or in
smaller, independent spaces, plays by women frequently go under-
reviewed and unpublished. Too often, the absence of major productions translates into very short lives for dramas by women, with no
published versions of their plays and few, if any, international stagings of their work.[2]

---

† From *A Century of Irish Drama* (Stephen Watt, Eileen Morgan, and Shakir Mustafa, editors). Reprinted by permission of Indiana University Press.
1. Garry Hynes, a founder of the Druid Theatre Company in Galway, has directed at the
   Druid, the Abbey Theatre, and the RSC and directed on Broadway in the spring of 1999.
   She has also served as artistic director of both the Druid Theatre Company and the
   Abbey. Pam Brighton made her mark directing Charabanc productions and has directed
   for stage and television in Ireland, Canada, and England.
2. Women playwrights are harder to find in print than are their male counterparts, but they
   are out there. Anne Devlin, Christina Reid, and Marina Carr have plays published by
   Faber and Faber; Marie Jones has published plays with Nick Hern Books. Margaretta

While American audiences may equate contemporary Irish drama with the highly acclaimed and excellently marketed innovations of writers like Brian Friel, Connal Morrison, and Martin McDonagh, Irish women playwrights are also transforming Ireland's theatrical landscape, at least in performance, if not often enough in print, and they are doing so through a variety of methods. For example, Charabanc's collaborative pieces in the 1980s used historical research and ethnography to explore Northern Irish women's experiences throughout the twentieth century. Emma Donahue radicalizes Dublin stages with her portrayals of lesbian experience. And Patricia Burke Brogan's play, *Eclipsed* (1992), * * * dramatizes the silenced stories of a group of Magdalene women, misfits in their community who were forced into servitude as laundresses in a convent.

Each of these examples points to the familiar feminist strategy of placing female characters and their stories in the subject position of the drama, reclaiming an aspect of the Irish experience— women's—which has been alternately idealized and ignored in the Irish mainstream tradition. The nationalist dramatic tradition was founded on the premise that this tradition would seek to rid the theatre of the stage Irishman, but far less attention was paid to rewriting the long-suffering mother figure or the idealized Colleen. And from Yeats and Gregory's *Kathleen ni Houlihan* (1902) to McDonagh's virgin/whore "Girleen" in *The Lonesome West* (1997), Irish female characters have embodied the nation, the land, the desires or responsibilities of male characters, but rarely have they been authentic, complex, autonomous women.[3]

D'Arcy's work is collected in a Methuen series. Smaller Irish presses, like the Attic Press, Salmon Publishing, and the Gallery Press, have put several women playwrights into print, including Patricia Burke Brogan. *The Dazzling Dark: New Irish Plays*, edited by Frank McGuinness, includes plays by Marina Carr and Gina Moxley. *The Crack in the Emerald*, edited by David Grant, contains plays by Marina Carr and Marie Jones. While Charlotte Canning, Lizbeth Goodman, Elaine Aston, Michelene Wandor, and Sue-Ellen Case, among others, have performed invaluable work in recording the histories and theories of feminist theatre practice in Britain and the United States, a record of Irish feminist theatre practice has yet to be written.

3. Arguably, for much of the twentieth century, actual Irishwomen found themselves equally idealized or ignored by the gender pressures of Irish post-revolutionary politics. Women in the North and in the Republic found themselves cast into the very auxiliary roles in everyday life that were being portrayed on the stage. Although women had fought in the revolution, the conservative faction which rose to power after the civil war pushed many women out of the public sphere and back into the home. Those who remained in the public eye often manipulated the idealization of women's domestic roles. Maud Gonne, a violent revolutionary, took to wearing widow's weeds and using the last name of her husband, even though she had separated from John MacBride years before his death in the 1916 Easter Rising. Her husband was an alcoholic who abused her, but he also became one of the martyrs of the fight for independence, and the title "Mrs. Maud Gonne MacBride" gave her a credibility and a right to a public voice which would have been denied Gonne in Ireland's post-war climate.

For critical examinations of contemporary feminism in the Republic of Ireland, see Pat O'Conor, *Emerging Voices: Women in Contemporary Irish Society.* Northern Irish

To write women into Irish theatre history, women playwrights write *outside* of Irish theatre history, finding new subjects (real Irish women) and alternative forms (street performance, cross-gender casting, contiguous narratives) to break out of the male-centered traditions of Irish drama and to develop Ireland's increasingly heterogeneous theatre scene. Likewise, by referring to popular Irish performance forms like the Irish melodrama and the *ceilidh* [dances], they in fact broaden the mainstream memory of Irish drama beyond the horizons of the formal traditions founded and perpetuated by the Abbey Theatre. Rejecting a version of history is an effective way to advance a new tradition, and these writers are certainly enriching Ireland's theatrical future by rejecting elements of its mainstream theatrical past.[4]

Regrettably, such playwrights—in Ireland and around the world—often find themselves in an economic and artistic catch-22. Audiences, trained to understand and appreciate male discourses, are often reluctant to embrace feminist forms, or they regard dramas with female protagonists as the theatrical equivalent of "chick flicks," designed for a solely female clientele. Such an attitude can only change by increasing audiences' exposure to alternative, gynocentric forms, but most theatres are reluctant to risk productions that do not have an established audience base. Thus, theatre by and about women remains ghettoized to the point where some women playwrights shun the term "feminist"—or even "feminine"—in descriptions of their work for fear of such marginalization. In Ireland, feminist playwrights find themselves on the margin of a theatre on the margins.

But there is progress. * * * Marina Carr and Christina Reid—two successful, mainstream playwrights—have subverted one of the central tropes of Irish realism, a convention which I will call the "family memory play," to place women's experience in the narrative foreground. Usually, the family memory play's male protagonist, who narrates his story outside the frame of the action, recalls his childhood. In his remembering, he tries to reconcile his youthful desire for autonomy with his connections to family, history, and land. Female characters provide the protagonist with emotional support, a source of conflict, or a sexual interest, but the real attention in the family memory drama centers on the patrilineal relation-

women and feminism are thoughtfully analyzed in Begoña Aretxaga's *Shattering Silence: Women, Nationalism, and Political Subjectivity in Northern Ireland* and in Margaret Ward's "The Women's Movement in Ireland: Twenty Years On." Several essays on twentieth-century feminism in the Republic and the North can be found in Bradley and Valiulis's *Gender and Sexuality in Modern Ireland.*

4. For a thorough theoretical overview of the feminist use of alternative theatrical forms, see Elin Diamond, *Unmaking Mimesis: Essays on Feminism and Theatre.*

ships. Even avant-garde Irish dramas, like Yeats's *Purgatory* and Beckett's *Endgame*, focus on the trope of the patrilineal family memory, and the trope continues to be found in some of contemporary Irish drama's most famous plays. In Hugh Leonard's *Da*, for example, an Irish emigrant returns to his hometown to bury his foster father, whose ghost takes him on a journey through his childhood. He remembers his first attempt at heavy petting with a local girl, but his mother, while mentioned, never appears. The two formative characters for the boy were his foster father and his (father figure) male employer. In Brian Friel's *Philadelphia, Here I Come!*, a young man, Gar, spends his last night in his father's home (before emigrating to America) by remembering the significant moments of his youth, thus confronting the still-unresolved relationship with his father that ties him to home. And in Connall Morrison's adaptation of the Patrick Kavanagh novel *Tarry Flynn*, beautifully staged at the Abbey Theatre in 1997, the audience follows the everyday experiences of the hero until he decides to leave his rural community to become a writer. The play glosses over the fact that he leaves his mother and sister to run their struggling farm and abandons a woman he may have impregnated.

Brian Friel adapted the family memory play's patrilineal narrative somewhat in his 1990 drama *Dancing at Lughnasa*. In that play, the adult male protagonist/narrator—who is onstage but outside the frame of the story throughout the drama—recalls his youth as an illegitimate child in 1930s rural Ireland, where he grew up in a house with his mother and her four sisters. While Friel's play gives us five vivid, colorful, and sympathetically drawn female characters, we see these women through the eyes of a man who is nostalgically remembering their experiences through the lens of childhood experience. The women may seem the center of the story, but the male narrator is firmly in control of the narrative, and we see the women exclusively through his eyes.

Employing the form of the family memory play to explore Irish women's struggles for personal identities amid the weight of family ties and cultural forces, Carr and Reid's work may, at first glance, look like the family memory dramas of Leonard and Friel. But they actually appropriate that traditional form to make a distinctly matrilineal narrative, revealing a great deal about women's experience in Ireland while simultaneously subverting several of the stereotypical representations of women that are usually found in mainstream Irish drama.[5] In other words, these dramas reflect how Carr and

5. Matrilineal narratives that provide a feminist revisionist history by describing several generations of women have been used to great effect by a range of contemporary playwrights and performance artists in the United States. Some of the best examples include Glenda Dickerson and Breena Clarke's *Re/Membering Aunt Jemima: A Travelling Men-*

Reid have mastered a prominent dramatic form only to subvert it in ways that reveal Irish women's perspectives in contemporary Ireland. Elin Diamond has remarked that "feminists, in our different constituencies [. . .] with our different objects of analysis, want to intervene in symbolic systems, linguistic, theatrical, political, psychological—and intervention requires assuming a subject position, however provisional, and making truth claims, however flexible, concerning one's own representations".[6] While Reid's and Carr's reappropriations of Irish realism do little to radicalize an audience's understanding of gender or performance (their plays are, after all, predominantly realist, and, especially in the case of Carr's work, they lean more toward liberal than material or radical feminist ideology), they do show a way in which a form that is traditionally exclusive to women may be co-opted to provide a legitimate vehicle for expressing women's experience.[7] These reappropriations are not so much imitations—or even emulations—of preceding works but are rather kinds of translations of a traditionally male-centered Irish dramatic discourse.

Translation has been a key trope—and point of cultural critique—in Ireland throughout the twentieth century. In *Inventing Ireland*, Declan Kiberd discusses the political and cultural role of the act of translation in Ireland—the array of methods individuals use to reject the imposition of one language by carrying the spirit of their own language into the translation. He cites Walter Benjamin, who wrote:

> It is the task of the translator to release in his own language that pure language which is under the spell of another, to liberate the language imprisoned in a work in his recreation of that work. For the sake of pure language, he breaks through the decayed barriers of his own language.

Kiberd goes on to historicize his theory in terms of Irish writers who resisted colonialism during the Irish literary renaissance, "by writing their own history and then rewriting it. This would be a literal re-membering—not a making whole of what was never whole to begin with, but a gluing together of fragments in a dynamic recasting". Kiberd uses an example from theatre: the nonverbal

---

strual Show, Louella Dizon's *Till Voices Wake Us*, and Leeny Sacks's *The Poet and the Translator*. Each of these dramas, I would argue, plays not only with assumptions of history but also with theatrical preconceptions and representations of that history.

6. Elin Diamond, *Unmaking Mimesis: Essays on Feminism and Theatre* (New York: Routledge, 1997), vii.

7. Other contemporary female playwrights who write outside of the Abbey/realist tradition are Gina Moxley, Marie Jones, and Emma Donahue. It is noteworthy that even more so than in the United States and Britain, the farther a woman writer works outside the mainstream discourse, the harder it is to find records of her work.

courtship of Yolland and Maire in Friel's *Translations*. "[I]n a strict sense," he writes, "it embodies the achievement of the higher ideal underlying every act of translation, for in a language of silence which has no need of recasting is the hope of a privileged space in which resistance to all degrading systems may be possible."[8]

While Kiberd is correct that Yolland and Maire's transcendent love "escape[s] the entrapments of language, being contained between the lines rather than in them", he does not mention the noisy, non-verbal languages of the stage that are constantly at work throughout the play. In theatre, translation can function not only at the textual level but also at the semiotic level: traditional ways of reading performance can be upstaged by new acting styles, new stagings, new points of view. As [Tennessee Williams's] *Belle Reprieve* still attests, a casting choice can foreground or alter the interstice between the original and translated dramas as elegantly as any textual rewrite.[9]

Since before Douglas Hyde called for the "deanglicisation" of Irish literature and before Lady Gregory translated Irish epic and Molière's *The Imaginary Invalid* into Kiltartan dialect, translation of Irish and European classics into a contemporary Irish idiom has been an ideological tool in the nationalist community. Even Yeats's poetic, highly formal theatre required (and requires) actors with a deep familiarity with Irish dialect and Gaelic pronunciations. Along with a translation of language and dialect among nationalist theatre practitioners was a translation of representations, as playwrights and actors strove to replace the stage Irishman performance tropes with nobler representations of the national character. The tales of heroes like Cuchulain and Deirdre became emblems of Ireland's noble past and models for the national character: the melodramatic gestures of the London stage Irishman were translated into Willie and Frank Fay's understated Irish realism.

Ireland's contemporary crisis, especially the hunger strike in [Northern Ireland] Long Kesh Prison in 1980, inspired playwrights to turn to translation in a new way, adapting Greek classical dramas as metaphors for the contemporary troubles.[1] Tom Paulin's conversion of *Antigone* into a parable about partition and Seamus Heaney's

---

8. Declan Kiberd, *Inventing Ireland* (Cambridge: Harvard University Press, 1996) 627, 628, 629.

9. For the classic interpretation of *Belle Reprieve*, Bette Bourne, Paul Shaw, Peggy Shaw, and Lois Weaver's gender-bending reinterpretation of Tennessee Williams's *A Streetcar Named Desire*, see Sue-Ellen Case, "From Split Subject to Split Britches."

1. W. B. Worthen articulates the politics of the Field Day Theatre's translations of classical texts in his essay "Homeless Words: Field Day and the Politics of Translation." While Field Day plays like Tom Paulin's *The Riot Act: A Version of Sophocles' Antigone* and Seamus Heaney's *The Cure at Troy* explore the pathos of the Irish troubles, Worthen argues, they also subtly retrench the nationalist/unionist debate linguistically, semiotically, and ideologically. Other Field Day dramas, however, like Tom Kilroy's *Double Cross*, actually blur the binaries between nationality and identity in modern Ireland. Other excellent essays on the Irish translation of classical texts in the 1980s include Eamonn Hughes's

rewriting of Sophocles' *Philoctotes* as a drama of reconciliation in *The Cure at Troy* simultaneously addressed Ireland's current situation through ancient Greek "classics" while politicizing and interpreting them in new ways. As the twenty-first century—and the Irish dramatic movement's second century—begins, these dramas from the 1980s are well on their way to assuming a position as "classics" themselves in the Irish dramatic tradition; that is to say, the Field Day Theatre's position in theatre history is secure. Yet most of the women playwrights writing during that period, like those from other decades of this century, remain for the most part on the historical margins, outside the mainstream dramatic tradition. Part of Carr's and Reid's success and acceptance within mainstream Irish theatre practice stems from their keen ability to translate within both the textual languages of the Irish tradition and the semiotic languages of the realist stage, taking those traditionally patriarchal discourses and remembering them to make room for Irish women's lives.[2]

LIONEL PILKINGTON

The Abbey Theatre and the Irish State†

* * *

With the foundation of the Irish Free State in 1922, the ruling Cumann na nGaedheal party (the renamed pro-Treaty faction of Sinn Féin) was faced not just with the formidable task of administering a new state, but also with what it considered to be an urgent cultural requirement: the need to rein in Ireland's anarchic forces of political militancy. This is a point upon which a wide range of intellectuals found agreement. The Catholic primate, Cardinal Logue, lamented that 'the people of Ireland were running wild after visions, dreams and chimeras and turning the country upside down in the process',[1] and Yeats wrote to his friend Edmund Dulac that

---

"'To Define Your Dissent': The Plays and Polemics of the Field Day Theatre Company" and Anthony Roche's "Ireland's Antigones: Tragedy North and South." Elizabeth Cullingford examines another translation of a classic conflict into an Irish idiom in contemporary drama in "British Romans and Irish Carthaginians: Anticolonial Metaphor in Heaney, Friel, and McGuinness."

2. I am grateful to Christopher Murray who, in a discussion of this paper, pointed out how Paula Meehan's mythopoetic comedy *Mrs. Sweeney* re-frames the pastoral, heroic myth of Finn McCool in contemporary working-class Dublin, thus translating across time and class as well as across gender lines.

† From *The Cambridge Companion to 20th-Century Irish Drama*, S. Richards, editor. Reprinted with the permission of Cambridge University Press.

1. Quoted in Margaret O'Callaghan, "Language, Nationality and Cultural Identity in the Irish Free State, 1922–7: The *Irish Statesman* and the *Catholic Bulletin* Reappraised," *Irish Historical Studies* 24.94 (1984): 227.

'people are trying to found a new society . . . It seems to be the very moment for a form of drama to be played in a drawing room'.[2] A. E. (George Russell), writing in the ex-unionist *Irish Statesman*, argued that boycotts, strikes or political violence would never achieve Irish unity. What was most needed instead, Russell continued, was a programme of education towards a 'social order in which there will be a real sense of identity of interest among our citizens'.[3] For state-building to ensue in post-Treaty Ireland what was required, in other words, was a restoration of the proper distinction between the exaggerated role-playing of theatre and the decorums and conventions of civic and political life.

Sean O'Casey's exposure of the folly of any form of political militancy directed against the state in *The Shadow of a Gunman* (1923), *Juno and the Paycock* (1924) and *The Plough and the Stars* (1926) accounts (at least in part) for the popularity of these plays with Dublin's new middle-class elite. The lure of playing the part of a gunman for Davoren in *The Shadow of a Gunman*, the absurd role-playing of 'Captain' Boyle in *Juno and the Paycock* or Jack Clitheroe's obsession with military costume and rank in *The Plough and the Stars* constitute a mordant indictment of antistate militancy and, in each of these plays, the deleteriousness of a republican tradition of militancy is diagnosed in terms of a misplaced or misrecognized theatricality. Indeed, the pro-Treaty writer P.S. O'Hegarty was so impressed with this aspect of *The Shadow of a Gunman* and *Juno and the Paycock* that he argued that O'Casey's plays had achieved the apparently transcendental status of history-writing itself: a 'true historical perspective . . . that air of detachment and disillusionment which the historian aims at'.[4]

Cumann na nGaedheal's granting of an annual subsidy of £850 to the Abbey Theatre in August 1925 seems to be directly connected to the NTS's institutional support for the Irish Free State. Given the government's fiscal rectitude and its consistently conservative economic policies in the 1920s, and given that the Abbey Theatre was the first English-speaking national theatre in the world to receive state funding, Cumann na nGaedheal's support for the NTS was, by any standard, an extraordinary political decision. Yeats welcomed the announcement as an expression of the government's benevolence and altruism,[5] but it is more likely that the decision was motivated by a more pragmatic recognition of the role of the

2. Warwick Gould, John Kelly, and Deirdre Toomey, eds., *The Collected Letters of W. B. Yeats*, Vol. II (Oxford: Clarendon Press, 1997), 702.
3. *Irish Statesman* 15 Sept. 1923: 4.
4. Quoted in Robert Hogan and Richard Burnham, *The Years of O'Casey, 1921–1926: A Documentary History* (Gerrards Cross, Colin Smythe, 1992), 146.
5. *Irish Times* 10 Aug. 1925: 5.

NTS in establishing the state as the sole legitimate arena of political action. As the *Irish Times* put it, not only had the Abbey Theatre
'lifted Dublin from the status of a decaying provincial city to that of
one of Europe's intellectual and artistic capitals' but, 'more than
any other agency', it had managed to rid Ireland of 'superstitions
and prejudices that are the relics of a barbarous age'.[6] To this extent
it is also relevant that the cabinet members who so strongly supported the Abbey Theatre subsidy in the 1920s, such as Ernest
Blythe and Kevin O'Higgins, were also those associated with a leadership cadre within Cumann na nGaedheal which was increasingly
concerned with a rowing back from the revolutionary and insurrec-
tionary tendencies of some of their party colleagues.

Maintaining the stability of the Irish state and supporting the
Abbey Theatre, then, were mutually reinforcing activities. Again,
this was not simply because of the explicitly pro-Treaty sympathies
expressed by O'Casey's Dublin plays or, on several occasions, by the
theatre's directors themselves, but because of a widely shared assumption that cultural modernization in Ireland required its people
to recognize and respect the difference between theatre and politics. A letter from Yeats to his friend Professor H. J. C. Grierson illustrates this well. Writing in February 1926 about the protests
against *The Plough and the Stars* Yeats describes to Grierson one republican protester who, having taken to the stage during a performance of *The Plough and the Stars*, interrupted his demonstration to
cover the actress playing the part of Mollser (a character portrayed
in the final stages of tuberculosis) with a blanket. For Yeats the incident amounted to an epiphany since it exposed the republican enthusiast as so marked by cultural naïvety that he appeared unable
to recognize the distinction between O'Casey's fictional character
and the actress who was playing the part: 'She was not the actress
in his eyes but the consumptive girl' (*Letters*, 711). This, for Yeats,
was precisely the point. As in the 1890s, Ireland desperately required cultural education, and a national theatre was ideally suited
to this task. Transforming a 'mob' into 'a people' remained the essential project of the NTS in so far as it entailed recognizing a distinction between, on the one hand, an illegitimate theatricality
associated with superstition and insurgency and, on the other, a
politics sanctioned by the authority of the state. Theatregoing itself,
therefore, became a demonstration of an innate cultural sophistica-
tion—an automatic recognition, as it were, of the parameters of
constitutional politics. To this extent acknowledging the importance of a national theatre was in itself a subtle reinforcement of
the authority of the state.

6. *Irish Times* 26 Dec. 1925: 4.

The value of a national theatre institution for the process of Irish state-building also helps to explain why the Abbey Theatre continued to receive government support during almost two decades of Fianna Fáil administration from 1932 to 1948. Despite the association of the Abbey in the 1920s with a pro-Treaty political position and despite initial sharp exchanges between the government and the NTS directorate arising from an Abbey Theatre tour of 'controversial' plays to the United States in 1932–3, de Valera and Yeats very quickly achieved a good working relationship. This is all the more striking considering that many nationalist and Catholic intellectuals of the time expressed strong concern in relation to what they regarded as the anomaly of an Irish national theatre still dominated by a predominantly non-Catholic directorate. Such objections came to a head in August 1935 with the first Dublin performance of Sean O'Casey's *The Silver Tassie* and the protest resignation of Abbey Theatre director Brinsley MacNamara. MacNamara resigned because of the play's alleged anti-Catholicism (the second act of *The Silver Tassie* entails a parody of elements of the Mass), and during the autumn and winter of 1935 the government received numerous calls to terminate the NTS subsidy altogether and to introduce theatre censorship. Not only did the Fianna Fáil government not respond to these calls, however, but within a few years it increased the NTS subsidy. Against many popular objections, the ideological benefits of a national theatre for the Irish state appeared to have had an overruling effect.

For many decades after the 1920s Ireland's national theatre continued to lend an air of gravitas and bourgeois normality to the postindependence state. It did this by evoking an impression of consensus and national unity and also by reinforcing a distinction between political agency authorized in terms of the state and what was seen as the threatening illegitimacy of socialist or republican militancy. Within the context of a resurgence of IRA activities from the mid-1930s, both of these functions were now just as important to de Valera's Fianna Fáil government as they had been to the earlier administration of Cumann na nGaedheal. By the early 1940s the Abbey Theatre repertoire was, once again, dominated by plays which urge the need for an unequivocal allegiance to the state and for an abandonment of antistate republicanism. The bulk of the NTS repertoire in this period—that is, plays by George Shiels, T. C. Murray, Paul Vincent Carroll and Rutherford Mayne—have a familiar thematic emphasis: the urgent need to abandon superstition and antistate loyalties in the interests of modernity and good citizenship. George Shiels's *The Rugged Path* (1940) and *The Summit* (1941) (the former one of the longest running plays in the history of the Abbey Theatre) are cases in point. The narrative action of these plays deals explicitly with the issue of citizenship and its obligations in terms of the legal authority of the state and urges the audience to overcome Ireland's traditional taboo on colluding with the state by informing.

As a national institution, then, the Abbey Theatre's relationship with popular nationalism is fundamentally ambivalent in a manner very similar to that of the Irish state. Committed to the notion of a consensual Irish identity, the NTS nevertheless finds itself pitted repeatedly against the militancy of traditional republicanism upon which the state is founded. As in plays like Bryan MacMahon's *The Bugle in the Blood* (1949), Walter Macken's *Twilight of a Warrior* (1957) and John Purcell O'Donovan's *The Less We Are Together* (1957), the NTS repertoire reveals a widening gulf between traditional nationalist views, associated with the foundation of the state, and a modern contemporary world for whom such views appear no longer to be relevant. As Christopher Morash has recently pointed out in an essay on the Republic of Ireland Act of 1949, plays written for the Abbey Theatre in the late 1940s and 1950s show a distinctive 'post-utopian' quality.[7] Within this context Ernest Blythe's appointment as Managing Director of the Abbey in 1941, coupled with his strong and sometimes dogmatic promotion of the Irish language, remained one of the few ways in which the Abbey Theatre was able to overcome this contradiction and express to the nation an unequivocally nationalist identity.

Major social and political changes take place in Ireland in the 1950s and 1960s. Heralded by the landmark Whitaker Report of 1958, there is a new emphasis on the development of an export-based economy and the encouragement of multinational inward capital investment. The resultant economic growth of the late 1950s and 1960s also coincides with a massive expansion of the state in the areas of economic and social planning. The dismantling of economic autarky in Ireland and the slow removal of a paternalistic state apparatus did not mean the state had diminished in power, merely that its mechanisms for the implementation of social policy were beginning to change. Keynesian principles were now installed as the main items on Ireland's developmental and modernization agenda, and, as in the postwar British welfare state, there was now a much greater emphasis on personal pleasure and on individual consumption as the basis for political agency.

Broadly speaking, therefore, the legitimacy of the Irish state tends to be viewed from the 1950s in terms of its responsiveness to the requirements of the individual rather than (as had previously been the case) as a reflection of any dominant national philosophy

7. *Writing in the Republic*, ed. Ray Ryan (London: Macmillan, 2000), 71.

or ideological position. It is this critical change in the relationship between culture and economics which helps to explain what might otherwise appear a conundrum: the striking coincidence between a widespread impression of the Abbey Theatre's irrelevance in the 1950s and early 1960s and the simultaneous emergence of what has been described as Irish drama's 'second renaissance'.[8] The *Irish Times*'s astringent conclusion that the Abbey was 'not a national theatre'[9] roughly coincides with the first production of Brian Friel's *Philadelphia, Here I Come!* at the Gaiety Theatre in September 1964 Dublin, an event often credited as the starting point of contemporary Irish drama. The trouble was that while Irish economic and social life had changed, the Abbey Theatre had not. As late as 1965, for example, Blythe described the cultural work of the Abbey as 'a constructive influence on public affairs . . . by means of satirical treatments of the Northern Ireland problem . . . and the ventilation of issues to do with Church authority'.[1]

The resurgence of Irish drama as evident in new plays by Brian Friel, John B. Keane, Thomas Kilroy and Tom Murphy which takes place in the 1960s arises because of a general shift away from this more tendentious treatment of popular nationalism. For this younger generation of writers the inadequacy or inappropriateness of traditional nationalist verities tends to be rendered not satirically (as it had been in plays by Shiels, MacMahon, Macken and O'Donovan), but as an existential trauma. In *Philadelphia, Here I Come!* (1964), for example, Gar has no option except to emigrate because Donegal and Ireland are unable to provide any viable alternative to multinational capitalism. And yet emigration—as this play keeps plangently reminding us—will result in an inevitable loss of plenitude. Similarly, in Tom Murphy's *A Whistle in the Dark* (1961), the focus is not so much on the political folly of militant nationalism but on the way in which nationalist rhetoric exacerbates the torment of emigration. The relentless irony of Murphy's play is that in order to achieve an Irish nationalist identity, a west of Ireland family has to emigrate to England and act out the self-destructive stereotype of the 'Paddy'. Whereas the Abbey Theatre of the 1950s and early 1960s was dedicated to the enactment of key *issues* relating to the twenty-six-county Irish state, for younger dramatists such as Murphy and Friel the emphasis was on the experience of the individual within an economy dominated by its increasing dependence on multinational capitalism.

8. Christopher Murray, *Twentieth-Century Irish Drama: Mirror Up to Nation* (Manchester: Manchester UP, 1997), 162.
9. *Irish Times* 20 Feb. 1963: 7.
1. Ernest Blythe, *The Abbey Theatre* (Dublin: National Theatre Society Limited, 1965), n.p.

The opening of a newly rebuilt Abbey Theatre in 1966 and Blythe's retirement as Managing Director in 1967 led to a distinct change in the artistic policies of the NTS. With Tomás Mac Anna's championing of Brechtian dramaturgy at the Peacock Theatre and an Abbey Theatre project to bring theatre to working-class areas of Dublin, the NTS presented itself not only as a forum for national consensus, but also as self-consciously politically engaged and as a catalyst for social change. But this impression of a postnationalist horizon did not last for long, since these radical artistic developments also coincided with the reemergence of serious political conflict in Northern Ireland following the civil rights marches of 1968–9. Within the context of stringent antirepublican emergency legislation such as the 1972 Offences Against the State (Amendment) Act, a close alignment between the NTS and the policies of the twenty-six-county state was, once more, in evidence. From the early 1970s theatrical responses to the Northern Ireland conflict at the NTS have been remarkably unified in their tendency to view the Northern Ireland conflict exclusively outside of a political context. The treatment of the conflict varied from satire and farce (as in the 1970 revue *A State of Chassis*, Patrick Galvin's *We do it for Love* [1976] and Stewart Parker's *Catchpenny Twist* [1977]), to an impression of the conflict's tragic inevitability (as in Brian Friel's *The Freedom of the City* [1973]), to a more general concentration on the suffering of the individual (as in Graham Reid's *The Death of Humpty Dumpty* [1979] and *The Closed Door* [1980]). Not until the 1980s, with the performance at the NTS in 1983 of Friel's *Translations* and Frank McGuinness's *Observe the Sons of Ulster Marching Towards the Somme* (1985) and *Carthaginians* (1988), was there an attempt to engage with the cultural and historical dimensions of the conflict, but even these plays are marked by their unambiguous lack of sympathy for republican or nationalist opposition to British rule in Northern Ireland.

Ireland's national theatre movement reflects, therefore, a long and close association with a form of politics organized exclusively in terms of the authority of the state. There are, as we have seen, particular historical reasons for this. At the beginning of the twentieth century the cultural significance of the NTS (and its precursors the Irish Literary Theatre, the Irish National Dramatic Society and the Irish National Theatre Society Limited) lay partly in its demonstration of a longed-for modernity, and was perceived by nationalists, and by some southern Irish unionists as well, as performing a vital role in the struggle for political independence or limited devolution. Though the sectarian aspects of modernization were bitterly disputed and gave rise to some notorious theatre controversies, the presence of a national theatre institution in Dublin was regarded generally as positive proof of Ireland's cultural and social advancement and thus of the need for some form of Irish political independence. The foundation of the twenty-six-county Irish Free State in 1923 in a context in which republican anti-Treaty militants disputed the legitimacy and authority of the state gave this modernizing function an added momentum.

Indeed, a history of the Abbey Theatre in the postindependence period suggests that the primary function of the NTS was that of underlining the authority of the state in the face of a contesting tradition of nationalist and republican militancy. And though there is little evidence of any direct interference by the state in the choice of plays performed at the Abbey theatre and Peacock Theatre, and there is no formal mechanism of theatre censorship in Ireland, the historical and formal association of the NTS with the state has resulted in a perennial anxiety that a distance be established between the authority of the state and an unauthorized national tradition of militancy and insurgency. This has manifested itself in a certain thematic predictability in terms of the Abbey Theatre's treatment of issues relating to the Northern Ireland conflict and in relation to Ireland's colonial history.

JOAN FITZPATRICK DEAN

Pageants, Parades, and Performance Culture†

St. Patrick's Day parades now flourish in Ireland, but far richer indigenous theatrical traditions have long existed in Ireland outside the architectural spaces known as theaters. Paratheatrical events ("para" meaning "separate from or going beyond") include a wide range of spectacles: parades, processions, funerals, festivals, protest marches, sporting events, dramatic interludes, and political meetings. Pageantry employs theatrical elements such as costuming, rehearsal, choreography, music, props, and stylized or symbolic action and actors who take on another identity. Pageantry also shares with conventional drama theatricality—the implicit acknowledgement of the artifice of performance for spectators. Irish people, indeed most people, experience paratheatrical events from an early age and on a regular basis.

Unlike theater, however, pageantry rarely privileges the fixed language of a script. Theater history neglects such spectacles because of their ephemeral, collaborative, or unique nature (some are local-

† Reprinted by permission of the author.

ized and performed only once). If a script ever existed, it probably was not published. The press seldom reviews these events as theater because they are often performed outside theaters by non-professional actors. Nevertheless, pageants could attract thousands of participants and tens of thousands of spectators.

Paratheatrical events—pageants, commemorations, ceildhes, sporting events, and religious ceremonies such as Christenings, marriages, and funerals—form the very fabric of life. Irish paratheatrical traditions are especially rich for many reasons, including a long colonial history that marginalized performances of Irish identity. Political rallies such as Daniel O'Connell's monster meetings often partook of pageantry. In Gary Owens' formulation: "Every monster meeting was nothing less than a performance in three acts whose players and audiences shifted with each change of scenery."[1] Although paratheatrical spectacles may appear naïve or anodyne, the civil rights marches in Northern Ireland, Orange parades, and even Corpus Christi processions have provoked controversy and even violence.

Irish Protestants as well as Catholics still demonstrate their religious affiliations through ceremonial displays, some with venerable histories. The Orange parades, staged on the Twelfth of July to commemorate the 1690 victory of King William at the Battle of the Boyne, trace their origins to the eighteenth century.[2] Catholic pageantry surfaces in Christmas or Nativity plays, passion plays, First Communion processions, and celebration of saints' feast days. In Ireland and elsewhere, some of the earliest records of dramatic performance are associated with the Feast of Corpus Christi. Processions that carry the Eucharist, which Catholics believe is the body of Christ, through secular public spaces remain vibrant in Cork, the Glenties, and elsewhere in Ireland even in our century.

Like theater, paratheatrical events perform identity and consequently are especially important during periods of change. Pageantry exists throughout twentieth-century Ireland, but four periods stand out as investing considerable resources to create historical and mythological pageantry. These distinctively Irish paratheatrical events are constructed of symbolic displays and exemplify what Eric Hobsbawm called "the invention of tradition."

---

1. "Nationalism without Words: Symbolism and Ritual Behaviour in the Real 'Monster Meetings' of 1843–45," *Irish Popular Culture, 1650–1850,* eds. James S. Donnelly, Jr. and Kerby A. Miller (Dublin: Irish Academic Press, 1998), 247.
2. See *The Irish Parading Tradition: Following the Drum,* ed. T. G. Fraser (New York: St. Martin's Press, 2000).

Revival: 1890–1910

Several scholars describe the turn of the twentieth century as a heyday for pageantry.[3] By the late nineteenth century, Irish nationalists routinely sought out opportunities to display publicly their opposition to British rule. Nationalists answered the bombastic celebrations of hegemonic power, a royal visit for instance, with gleefully subversive pageants of resistance. In response to the Children's Treat staged during Queen Victoria's visit to Ireland, Inghinidhe na hÉireann (the Daughters of Erin) sponsored a Patriotic Children's Treat in 1900 that paraded some 20,000 children through Dublin's streets.[4]

Other parades incorporated *tableaux vivants*, or "living pictures," that used non-professionals in elaborate or exotic costumes, often posed and framed in painterly configurations. Early in the century, the Gaelic League "took over the traditional Lord Mayor's Procession in Dublin, mobilizing up to 500,000 people . . . to participate in symbolic *tableaux* that portrayed the moral lessons of Irish history."[5] Performed in a variety of venues (including theaters), *tableaux vivants* proved especially popular because a large number of ordinary people—amateur actors, seamstresses, set dressers, et al.—could participate in nationalist spectacles. Circumventing patent and copyright law, *tableaux vivants* were often staged as benefits or fund-raisers. The vogue for *tableaux vivants* also cut across class lines. The first Irish performance of Yeats's *The Countess Cathleen* was a series of *tableaux vivants* staged at the Vice-Regal Lodge in Dublin performed by the wives of some of the richest, most powerful men in Ireland.

Amateur theatrical companies, notably the faculty and pupils of St. Enda's School, staged mythological and historical pageants. Padraic Pearse's *The Boy Deeds of Cuchulainn* (1909) and other St. Enda's pageants blended Celtic bravery and Catholic sacrifice to construct an inspirational heroic past that schoolboys might recreate and inhabit.

Yet another brand of pageantry could be seen in Dublin on August 1, 1915 as the mourners at O'Donovan Rossa's funeral performed an elaborate nationalist spectacle. Carefully blocked, fully scripted, elaborately costumed, Rossa's funeral came with full mu-

---

3. See David Glassberg, *American Historical Pageantry: The Uses of Tradition in the Early Twentieth Century* (Chapel Hill: U of North Carolina P, 1990). In *Theatre, Sacrifice, Ritual: Exploring Forms of Political Theatre* (London: Routledge, 2005), Erika Fischer-Lichte examines the "retheatricalization" of events such as the Olympic Games and Max Reinhardt's Theatre of the Five Thousand.
4. Mary Trotter, *Ireland's National Theatres* (Syracuse, NY: Syracuse UP, 2001), 73–90.
5. John Hutchinson, *The Dynamics of Cultural Nationalism: The Gaelic Revival and the Creation of the Irish Nation State* (Boston: Allen and Unwin, 1987), 179.

sical accompaniment and Pearse's now-famous oration: "the fools, the fools, the fools! —They have left us our Fenian dead, and while Ireland holds these graves, Ireland unfree shall never be at peace." Not only was Pearse's speech published, but so were two commemorative programs.

One common factor among these paratheatrical events is the element of performativity. For many, the performative opportunity was irresistible. For Gaelic League members, speaking, reciting, or singing in Irish (often in competition) signaled their commitment to the language revival. Marginalized groups, especially Irish-speakers and women, demonstrated their identity and sought broader alliances and new members through public performance. The very act of preparation—rehearsing, set building, costume making—strengthened the bonds among them and enacted their ideals.

Pageantry in the Irish Free State, 1924–32

The Free State needed to construct a distinct Irish history that tempered perilous post–Civil War times and refuted the compelling but critical view of recent Irish history of O'Casey's Dublin trilogy. As R. F. Foster writes, in the newly created Free State "it was important to stress the supposed message of Irish history—which involved a necessary degree of deliberate amnesia . . . The real nature of pre-1916 Irish society had to be glossed over."[6] In the decade after Independence, the Aonach Tailteann, the historical pageantry of Dublin Civic Week in 1927 and 1929, and the 1932 Eucharistic Congress looked to paratheatrical events to define, create, and instill pride in Irish heritage.

The Free State reached back to ancient times to recover the Aonach Tailteann. Explicitly positioned as the revival of an authentically Irish tradition, the Tailteann Games were staged in 1924, 1928, and 1932. T. H. Nally announced the spirit of the games, which featured competitions in everything from hurling to opera: "It is surely something to be proud of to know that our country has played a great and noble part in the Past, not merely in leading all the nations of Europe in intellectual culture and the higher arts of civilization, but also in the no less important province of physical development."[7]

A similar spirit informed the civic week celebrations. In 1927 and again in 1929, the Dublin City Council sponsored two civic weeks that made extensive use of historical pageantry to instill

6. R. F. Foster, *Modern Ireland, 1600–1972* (London: Penguin, 1988), 535.
7. T. H. Nally, *The Aonach Tailteann and the Tailteann Games: Their Origin, History and Ancient Associations* (Dublin: Talbot, 1923), 7.

pride in Irish history in its citizens. As its first commissioner said, the first Dublin Civic Week aimed to "tell of the history of Dublin, its past glories and triumphs, its present greatness and its promise for the future."[8] Drawing on romanticized Irish histories from the nineteenth and early twentieth centuries, the civic week pageants were designed to be inspirational, educational, and accessible.

In 1927, the week began with a Historical Parade, a chronological panorama of the Irish past that freely mixed historical and mythological figures: Mesgedhra (first century King of Leinster), Conall Cearnach, Knights and Warriors of the Red Branch, Fionn and the Fianna, King Brian Boru, Strongbow and Eva, Dermot MacMurrough, Hugh O'Neill, O'Sullivan Beare, Eoghan Ruadh O'Neill, and Patrick Sarsfield, all attended by their supporters, kinsmen, warriors. The procession ended with the Irish Volunteers, not Eoin MacNeill's 1913 militia, but ones from 1782. Staged in Trinity College Park, the *Grand Pageant of Dublin History* ranged from the mythic times of Conaire Mor, through the coming of the Norsemen, Brian Boru, and the Normans, and culminated with the rise of the Irish Volunteers in the late eighteenth century. Yet another *Historical Pageant and Tableaux*, staged at the Mansion House, offered a special children's matinee. All of these pageants neglected, in fact sought to efface, Ireland's colonial status by eliding recent and nineteenth century events. As the protocol for the Historical Costume Ball specified, it might be "any epoch from 1000 B.C. to the end of the eighteenth century." This Irish history was mythic, Celtic, Norman, and eighteenth century, but the previous one hundred and thirty years were too near, too painful, too demoralizing.

In 1929, organizers drafted Micheál Mac Liammóir to create *The Ford of the Hurdles*. This three-hour extravaganza of Irish history staged at the Mansion House with elaborate period costumes, epic battle sequences, huge casts, and full orchestral accompaniment by Dr. J. F. Larchet. Mac Liammóir discounted "historical exactitude."[9] *The Ford of the Hurdles* also challenges the prevailing sense of this period as gloomy, drab, or enervated. Two early episodes, "The Rape of Dervogilla" (featuring Coralie Carmichael in a flapper-like saffron costume) and "The Judas of the Gael: how Diarmuid Mac Murchadha betrayed the Irish to Henry II" mark Mac Liammóir's modern, nationalist gloss on Irish history. Mac Liammóir cast himself as Robert Emmet, not least so he could render Emmet's speech from the dock. The last episode, "Easter, 1916:

8. Seamas Murphy, *Dublin Civic Week 1927: Official Handbook* (Dublin: Civic Week Council, 1927), 7.
9. Philip O'Leary, *Gaelic Prose in the Irish Free State, 1922–1939* (University Park, PA: Pennsylvania State UP, 2004), 605, n. 97.

The City at Dawn," brought audiences much closer to their own day by the end of this overtly nationalist celebration.

These pageants conflated myth and history to evoke a patriotism informed more by boosterism than historical sense. They bespeak a sentimental, sanitized reading of Irish history that remains popular with militant nationalists, songwriters, and Irish-Americans. Remarkably, these epic dramatizations of Irish history were predominantly secular, but they whetted an appetite for pageantry that served Ireland well when it hosted the Eucharistic Congress in 1932 and when it commemorated the Easter Rising in 1935.[1]

An Tóstal

One of the many Irish cultural enterprises that had its origins in the early 1950s, An Tóstal featured historio-religious spectacles with a strong patriotic flavor. The first two Tóstals, held in April 1953 and 1954, imbricated the religious celebrations of Easter, the political commemoration of the 1916 Easter Rising, and the cultural agenda of Bórd Fáilte (the Irish Tourist Board). In 1954, the opening parade included three central elements: a parade of the defense forces; the march of the thirty-two counties; and a festival of flowers on thirty floats representing Irish industry. Organized by the Gaelic League, the march of the thirty-two (not twenty-six) counties depicted historical figures associated with each county. In a style reminiscent of the 1927 Historical Parade, "Each Provincial contingent is led by a mythic Princess of the Province concerned, borne on an ancient war chariot, preceded by her Standard Bearer, and escorted by her warriors dressed in traditional garb."[2]

As advertised in the *Dublin Evening Mail*, the 1954 Tóstal's centerpiece was *"The Pageant of St. Patrick . . . Cast of 1,700—Massed Choir of 400 voices—Greatest Pageant ever produced in Ireland—Four episodes extending over two days."*[3] The Pageant would present four site-specific scenes: the arrival of St. Patrick at Drogheda on Holy Saturday; the lighting of the Pascal Fire and the conflict with the Druids at Slane on that night; a Gaelic festival in Navan on Easter Sunday; finally, St. Patrick's confrontation with the High King of Ireland, the Druids and the Brehons at the Royal Court of Tara, in which he "confounds Paganism, symbolised by his destruction of Crom Cruach and his 'sub Gods twelve.'" Unlike his 1929 pageant, Mac Liammóir's 1954 open-air extravaganza positioned the conversion of pagan Ireland to Catholicism as the pivotal event

1. See James Moran, *Staging the Easter Rising: 1916 as Theatre* (Cork: Cork University Press, 2005), 68–83.
2. *An Tóstal: National Opening Ceremonies* (Dublin: Bórd Fáilte Éireann, 1954), 5.
3. *Dublin Evening Mail*, 3 April 1954 3.

an tóstal

THE PAGEANT OF SAINT PATRICK

APRIL 17th–18th

Cast of 1,700—Massed Choir of 400 voices — Greatest Pageant ever produced in Ireland — Four episodes extending over two days.

HOLY SATURDAY, APRIL 17th

DROGHEDA : 2.30 — 4.30 p.m.
● The Landing of St. Patrick on the Banks of the Boyne ● Reception by Chiefs and People.

SLANE : 8.0 — 10.0 p.m.
● The lighting of the Paschal Fire in defiance of Paganism ● The arrest of St. Patrick.

EASTER SUNDAY, APRIL 18th

AN UAIMH (Navan) : Gaelic Festival 2.0 — 5.0 p.m.
● Traditional Sports (2.0 p.m.). ● Tableau Vivant (3.0 p.m.). ● Hurling Match (3.30 p.m.) — **Cork** (All-Ireland Champions) and **Wexford** (Oireachtas Champions).

HILL OF TARA : 8.0 — 10.0 p.m.
Patrick, Champion of Christianity, confronts the High King of Ireland, the Druids and the Brehons at the Royal Court of Tara and confounds Paganism, symbolised by his destruction of Crom Cruach and his " sub Gods twelve."

This Pageant will be re-enacted on the actual sites where these epoch-making events took place over 1,500 years ago.

● **PRICES OF ADMISSION**

HOLY SATURDAY : APRIL 17th
Drogheda : Grand Stand 6/-
Slane : Reserved Enclosure 2/-

EASTER SUNDAY : APRIL 18th
An Uaimh (Navan): Reserved Enclosure 1/- (Stand tickets available on ground).
Hill of Tara : Grand Stand 7/-. Reserved Enclosure 2/-.

● **TRANSPORT**

C.I.E. and G.N.R. are providing special train and bus services for the Pageant of St. Patrick on April 17th and 18th. Details of these services will be found in the Companies' advertisements in the public press or on application to:—C.I.E. Road Passenger Office, 59 Upr. O'Connell Street, Dublin, or G.N.R. District Traffic Manager, Amien Street, Dublin.

● **ADVANCE BOOKING**

Messrs. Clery & Co., O'Connell Street.

Messrs. Brown Thomas Ltd., Grafton Street.

Messrs. Elvery's, O'Connell Street.

For details of travel and other arrangements from centres other than Dublin apply to:—Tostal House, 7/8, Mount St. Crescent, **Dublin**; Phone 61991. Pageant Headquarters, Beechmount House, **Navan**; Phone Navan 103. I.T.A. Bureau, 17, Queen's Arcade, **Belfast**; Phone 28338; or any C.I.E., G.N.R. or U.T.A. Office.

Issued by An Bord Fáilte

in Irish history. When Anew McMaster stepped off his boat as St. Patrick, unscripted spectators rushed to kiss the hem of his garment.

So impressed were the organizers that they decided to consolidate *The Pageant of St. Patrick* for six performances at Croke Park, the Dublin home of the Gaelic Athletic Association (GAA), for following year. Mac Liammóir's narration, recorded and broadcast over loud speakers, guided the choreographed movements of the participants, more than 800 of who came from the sodalities and confraternities at Our Lady of Good Counsel in Drimnagh. Mac Liammóir's recollection is of "an open-air pageant play about St. Patrick written by myself with Anew McMaster as the Saint surrounded by hordes of monks, druids, clowns, dancers, worshippers of the sun, and royal personages at Tara, their teeth, during most of the performances, chattering like castanets in a smart north-east gale."[4]

In its early years An Tóstal looked to historical and mythological pageantry to re-write Irish history yet again. Celebrating a nation whose defining moment was its conversion to Catholicism, *The Pageant of St. Patrick* offered an edifying spectacle with thousands in supporting roles. In 1966, Ireland commemorated the fiftieth anniversary of the Easter Rising with another pageant at Croke Park, *Aiseirí (Resurrection)*, one narrated by Mac Liammóir as the "Voice of History."

Macnas

The Irish group best known for the past two decades for pageantry is Galway-based arts company, Macnas, which means "joyful abandonment" in Irish. Macnas uses a demotic dramaturgy in parades and plays to address localized as well as national and even global concerns from a uniquely Galwegian perspective. Macnas intends to take theater out of theaters and integrate it to the community by appropriating public spaces, enlisting large numbers of volunteers, and amusing all they encounter with aggressively anti-elitist entertainment.

Macnas established its reputation in Ireland with parades and festivals. The annual Macnas parade in the Galway Arts Festival recruits hundreds of volunteers to produce a cleverly-themed spectacular grounded in Galway life. Macnas's productions routinely comment on topical events—sometimes overtly, as in the installation of a giant cigarette stubbed out on a Galway roundabout for

---

4. Micheál Mac Liammóir, *Theatre in Ireland* (Dublin: Three Candles, 1950, rev. 1964), 73.

Quit Smoking Day, but more often obliquely, as when the 2004 parade wryly commented on global warming with Martha Reeves' "Heat Wave" blasting from an elaborate tropical float. After Galway residents endured a ban on drinking tap water for more than four months, the 2007 Macnas parade featured the escape of a huge green cryptosporidium from its cage on a circus wagon. The final float dragged behind it hundreds of empty plastic water bottles in what looked like a mobile sculpture by Carl Andre.[5]

In the 1990s, Macnas performed a trilogy of highly choreographed narrative spectacles drawn from Irish mythology: *The Tain, Buile Shuibne/Sweeney,* and *Balor,* all credited to Padraic Breathnach. Recovering Irish legend to suggest its immediacy for audiences, Macnas' brilliant interpretation of *The Tain* (1992), which negotiated the Irish/English-language challenge by performing without dialogue, could be read as an analogue for the Troubles in Northern Ireland. With brother pitted against brother in a senseless, violent struggle, Macnas' Cuchulainn could not have been further from Pearse's 1909 boy hero.

The communal and collaborative energies that created historical and mythological pageantry in twentieth century Ireland depended on large numbers of non-professionals to create anti-celebrity, anti-elitist spectacles. By tapping ritual and including improvisation and audience interaction, they often staged fantasies parading as histories.

The impulse to perform identity by participating in an original, rather than canonical, work undergirds many of these paratheatrical events. The Daughters of Erin and Gaelic Leaguers seized agency by staging *tableaux vivants* or performing in the *feisanna.* The vast number of people involved in acting, singing, costuming, designing, and staging assured that these pageants were more likely to survive in human memory than in theater history. Paratheatrical events provided a vehicle to express identity and even a measure of celebrity to ordinary people—many of whom were otherwise precluded from such performative displays. Moreover, by creating their own pageants, the Daughters of Erin as well as Macnas implicitly reject published, canonical texts as inadequate to express their vision.

Parades and processions often dissolve the barrier that the proscenium arch and fourth wall use to separate audience from art. Unlike the early Abbey (most modern theaters, in fact) that demanded a disciplined audience that would sit in silence in a dark-

---

5. YouTube.com may make images of the Twelfth of July parades and Macnas' spectacles available.

ened room out of respect for the playwright's art, and unlike a realistic dramaturgy that sealed off theater from its ritual origins, pageantry elicited high levels of performativity from participant and patron alike. The sheer scale of pageants, sometimes involving thousands of participants, sets them off from the quotidian and argues for the grandeur of what they celebrate.

Chronology

1899   Irish Literary Theatre produces its first season in Dublin after earlier years of activity in London, with W. B. Yeats's *The Countess Cathleen* and Edward Martyn's *The Heather Field* at the Antient Concert Rooms

       Beltaine published as journal of the Irish Literary Theatre

       Yeats publishes "An Irish National Theatre" in *Dome*, a British journal

       Nationalist newspaper *United Ireland* founded

       Douglas Hyde, *A Literary History of Ireland*, work of scholarship published

       Irish Texts Society founded for recovery of Irish-language history

       Somerville and Ross, *Some Adventures of an Irish RM* published

       Oscar Wilde, *The Importance of Being Earnest* first performed

       Yeats poems, *The Wind Among the Reeds* written

1900   Unification of the Irish Parliamentary Party, previously split over issues surrounding Charles Stewart Parnell, under the leadership of the pro-Parnell John Redmond

       Inghinidhe na hÉireann (Daughters of Erin) founded after successful organizations of children's pageants

       Cumann na nGaedhael (Society of the Gaels), Gaelic cultural organization, by Arthur Griffith

       The Leader, Catholic cultural publication, founded

       James Joyce reads paper "Drama and Life" endorsing European modernist ideas

       Final visit of Queen Victoria to Ireland

1901   Death of Victoria and ascension of Edward VII

       Hyde, *Casadh-an-tSúgáin* (*Twisting of the Rope*) produced in Irish by Irish Literary Theatre Society

1902   Irish National Theatre Society established

       Yeats and Gregory, *Cathleen ni Houlihan*, performed by Frank Fay's National Dramatic company with Maude Gonne in the lead

       Gregory prose saga *Cuchulain of Muirthemne*

1903   Wyndham Land Act reforms property law and aids tenant ownership of Irish farmland

Creation of the Irish Theatre Society, with Yeats as President, and inaugural tour of England

George Moore stories *The Untilled Field*

Orange Order (Unionist) founded by T. H. Sloan

1904   J. M. Synge, *Riders to the Sea* produced by the National Theatre Society

Irish National Theatre Society lead actors Dudley Digges and Maire Quinn lead company to produce its work for the first time in America in St. Louis

Abbey Theatre opens in December at Mechanic's Hall on Abbey Street, under a Lady Gregory patent and on the English patron A. E. F. Horniman's subsidy; first program is *On Baile's Strand*, *Cathleen Ni Houlihan*, and *Spreading the News*

1905   Bernard Shaw's *John Bull's Other Island* rejected by Abbey

D. P. Moran publishes strong Catholic nationalist polemic, *The Philosophy of Irish Ireland*

Synge, *In the Shadow of the Glen* and *The Well of the Saints*

Ulster Unionist Council of MPs formed to organize resistance to devolution and Home Rule in the form of a return to an Irish parliament in Dublin

1907   Synge's *Playboy of the Western World* theater riots

Sinn Féin League (Republican) founded by Arthur Griffith by merger of small nationalist groups

Gregory, *The Rising of the Moon*

Labor organized by James Larkin stages a dock strike and clashes with police in Belfast

1908   Irish Universities Act for Dublin and Belfast colleges

James Larkin organizes the Irish Transport Workers Union, which evolved as the Irish Transport and General Workers Union (ITGWU) into the strongest labor force in Ireland

Padraig Pearse opens St. Enda's School (Scoil Eanna) with Irish Gaelic, nationalist, and performing arts curriculum

1909   Death of Synge

Abbey performs Shaw's *The Shewing-Up of Blanco Posnet* in defiance of British censorship rulings

Fianna Éireann, precursor to Fianna Fail, founded as Irish youth organization by Bulmer Hobson and Con Markiewicz

1910   Death of Edward VII; because it did not close in respect, Horniman withdraws subsidy from Abbey Theatre

Close reelection of British Liberal Party requires them to

form a coalition with Irish Parliamentary Party of John Redmond and to commit to a Home Rule Bill

Edward Carson becomes leader of Irish Unionist Parliamentary Party

1911   Kuno Meyer, *Ancient Irish Poetry*

Padraig Pearse's students perform a passion play at the Abbey Theatre

Irish Women's Suffrage Federation founded

British Parliament ends House of Lords' veto power, a likely obstacle to Irish Home Rule, but allows power to delay legislation

1913   Establishment Ulster Volunteer Force, Irish Citizen Army, Irish Volunteers

Dublin labor strike by ITGWU leads to long labor lockout by management

Third Home Rule Bill set back twice by House of Lords

Unionist sentiment against Home Rule takes the form of nearly a quarter million signatures to the Solemn League and Covenant

Foundation of the militant Ulster Volunteer Force in Belfast against Home Rule and the Irish Citizen Army in Dublin as a trade union militia

1914   James Joyce stories, *Dubliners*

Irish Parliamentarian Party pledges support for England in World War I

Home Rule Bill is passed in Commons; related amending bills exempting Ulster are introduced by Lords; Britain declares war on Germany; Home Rule legislation is suspended during war

Split by Home Rule and nationalist supporters over whether to answer the British call for Irish volunteers in the war effort

Gun-running commences by both Unionist and Republican groups

Irish Republican Brotherhood contemplates wartime rising

1915   Padraig Pearse's eulogy over the grave of Jeremiah O'Donovan Rossa crystalizes nationalist sentiment

Gaelic League leadership shifts to nationalist militants

St. John Ervine, author of the play *The Orangeman*, becomes head of Abbey Theatre

Supreme Council of the Irish Republican Brotherhood (IRB) forms and commits to nationalist insurrection before end of World War I

1916   The Irish Volunteers, in both alliance and miscommunica-

tion with IRB and Irish Citizens Army, occupy the General
Post Office in Dublin on Easter Monday and issue the
Proclamation of the Irish Republic; they surrender after
five days; in May, imprisoned leaders are court-martialed
and executed, causing a great shift in public opinion toward support for independence

Ulster Unionist Council moves to comply with Home Rule
legislation if six Ulster counties are partitioned from the
Irish state

The Ulster Division of the British Army suffers devastating
losses at the Battle of the Somme, one of the largest and
longest battles of World War I

Lennox Robinson, *The Whiteheaded Boy*

Joyce novel *A Portrait of the Artist as a Young Man*

Ernest Augustus Boyd's study *Ireland's Literary Renaissance*

1917   An Irish Convention, solicited by British Prime Minister
Lloyd George, achieves participation but fails to reach
agreement on resolution of national identities of Ireland

Arthur Griffith retires as head of Sinn Féin and is succeeded by Éamon de Valera; Sinn Féin adopts independent
republic of Ireland as goal; members elected to the British
Parliament decline to participate

1918   Joyce play *Exiles*

Sinn Féin members are interned (held without charges),
often on claims of German collaboration

Armistice ends World War I on November 11; Sinn Féin receives enormous support in December general elections

1919   Sinn Féin elected representatives meet in Dublin as Dáil
Éireann, an alternative to British Parliament; they ratify a
declaration of independence and a provisional constitution,
and elect as President Éamon de Valera, recently escaped
from prison in England

Anglo-Irish War (through 1921) initiated by Irish volunteer
killings of two policemen of the Royal Irish Constabulary in
Soloheadbeg, County Tipperary; conflicts proliferate, and
Irish Volunteers evolve into Irish Republican Army (IRA)

1920   Government of Ireland Act by British Parliament attempts
to introduce peace by partition of Ulster Counties; is accepted in the north and rejected in the south

Martial law introduced in south and sectarian riots erupt in
Belfast

Veterans of British Army, "Black and Tans," and Auxiliaries,
arrive to reinforce Royal Irish Constabulary policemen

1921   Northern Ireland parliament elected as overwhelmingly
Unionist and opened by King George V

IRA and British army reach truce; Sinn Féin representatives in London sign Anglo-Irish Treaty accepting dominion status in place of full republican state and accepting the partition of Northern Ireland

1922   Anglo-Irish Treaty approved by Dáil Éireann and Arthur Griffith elected President to succeed de Valera; provision government installed in Dublin Castle on pledging the Oath of Allegiance to British monarchy

Sectarian violence continues in Northern Ireland

Anti-treaty republicans opposed to dominion status, partition, and the Oath of Allegiance occupy the Four Courts municipal building in Dublin

Provisional government attacks republicans in the Four Courts to begin the Irish Civil War (through 1923)

Joyce novel *Ulysses*

1923   De Valera suspends republican campaign in April and ends Civil War with "arms dumping," or public disarmament, in May

Yeats awarded Nobel Prize for Literature

Irish Free State admitted to United Nations

James Larkin returns from United States and organizes a new labor organization, the Workers' Union of Ireland

O'Casey, *The Shadow of a Gunman*

Dublin Magazine founded; featured articles, fiction, poetry, drama, and reviews by Irish writers through closing in 1958

Censorship of films legislation is adopted

1924   O'Casey, *Juno and the Paycock*

Corkery study of Gaelic culture *The Hidden Ireland*

Leinster House in Dublin becomes home to Irish government

1925   Abbey Theatre awarded annual subsidy by the Free State government

Boundary Commission, a condition of treaty, institutionalizes the existing partition border between North and South

Shaw Awarded Nobel Prize for Literature

Legislation prohibiting divorce enacted by Free State government

1926   O'Casey's *The Plough and the Stars* theater riots

Sinn Féin party split over abstention from Dáil Éireann, and de Valera and followers form Fianna Fáil party

Creation of 2RN radio network, predecessor of Radio Telefis Éireann (RTE)

1927   Creation of the national Electrical Supply Board

Assassination of the government Minister for Justice, Kevin O'Higgins, by anti-treaty militants; this leads to the Electoral Act requiring elected members of the Dáil to accept the oath of allegiance, which de Valera and elected Fianna Fáil followers accept

1928 Gate Theatre Company founded by Micheál mac Liammóir to bring modern European classics to the Dublin stage and launched with a production of Ibsen's *Peer Gynt*
O'Casey's *The Silver Tassie* rejected by Abbey, and he withdraws his work from the theater
Yeats poems *The Tower*

1929 Censorship of Publications Board created by government to prohibit sale of material deemed obscene; it remains in effect though largely inactive
Denis Johnston, *The Old Lady Says No!* rejected by Abbey and produced instead by the Gate Theatre Company
Elizabeth Bowen novel *The Last September*
Shannon River's first hydroelectric project opened near Limerick

1930 Irish Free State elected to the council of the League of Nations

1931 Frank O'Connor stories *Guests of the Nation*
Statute of Westminster enacted by British Parliament, giving greater autonomy to members of dominion including the Irish Free State

1932 Death of Lady Gregory
Fianna Fáil wins general election; de Valera becomes President; Oath of Allegiance abolished (1933)
International Eucharistic Congress convened in Dublin
Foundation of Army Comrades Association, or "Blueshirts," which will endorse fascist positions and be declared illegal in 1933
Stormont, seat of parliament, opens in East Belfast in Northern Ireland
Sean O'Faolain stories, *Midsummer Night Madness*

1933 Fine Gael party founded as parliamentary opposition to Fianna Fáil

1934 Samuel Beckett stories *More Pricks Than Kicks*

1935 Prohibition of importation of contraceptives
Orange Order marches in Northern Ireland, triggering prolonged rioting

1936 IRA declared illegal
First flight by Aer Lingus national airline from Dublin to Bristol

1937 New constitution of the Irish Free State ratified, identifying the state as "Éire," its leader as "Taoiseach," and claiming sovereignty over the island of Ireland

1938   Douglas Hyde becomes first president of Ireland under terms of new constitution

1939   Death of Yeats

Yeats, *The Death of Cuchulain*

Joyce, *Finnegans Wake*

Sean O'Casey autobiography, *I Knock at the Door*

IRA bombing campaign in England to end partition of Northern Ireland

Shannon Airport opened in west Ireland, near Limerick

Declaration of Irish Free State neutrality in World War II, termed in the south "The Emergency," while Northern Ireland joins English war effort

1940   *The Bell*, literary journal, founded as opposition to conservative social legislation

1941   Ernest Blythe becomes director of Abbey Theatre and advances culturally conservative agenda, including Irish-language theater

Heavy bombing of Belfast by Germany

1942   IRA mounts heavier campaign of attacks to protest partition

1943   Famous Éamon de Valera Christmas radio broadcast celebrating pastoral values of Irish state

1945   At the end of World War II, de Valera expresses condolences at the German embassy on the death of Adolf Hitler, and Winston Churchill denounces Irish neutrality during the war

1949   Ireland withdraws from British Commonwealth and declares status as independent Republic of Ireland

Ireland Act passed in Westminster, awarding greater protection to Northern Ireland constitutional status

1950   Industrial Development Authority (IDA) established to modernize economy, aid industrialization, and recruit foreign investment

1951   Abbey Theatre accidentally burned; company eventually moves in 1966 to quarters at the much larger, formerly commercial Queens Theatre Dublin

Free Presbyterian Church established by Ian Paisley, a leader of Unionist movements in Belfast into the next century

Beckett novel, *Molloy* (first of trilogy)

First Wexford Opera Festival, a center for ambitious international productions

1952   Bord Fáilte (Irish Tourist Board) created

1953   Pike Theatre opened in Dublin; launches program that tests boundaries of propriety

First production of Beckett's *Waiting for Godot* in Paris

1954   Brendan Behan, *The Quare Fellow*

Flags and Emblems Art in Northern Ireland limits display of tricolour of the Irish Republic

1955   *Waiting for Godot* produced in English in London

Ireland admitted to United Nations

1956   IRA "Border Campaign" against Northern Ireland through 1962 and internment is reintroduced on both sides of border

1957   Beckett, *Endgame*

First Dublin Theatre Festival

1958   Second Dublin Theatre Festival canceled after censorship disputes and playwright withdrawals of plays

Beckett, *Krapp's Last Tape*, written in English and produced in London

Behan, *The Hostage*

Aer Lingus introduces transatlantic service

The T. K. Whitaker "Economic Development" report and the Industrial Development Act advance economic expansion through foreign investment in Ireland

1959   Éamon de Valera retires as political leader to serve in the more ceremonial role of President of the Republic

1961   Radio Telefis Éireann (RTE) television network founded

First proposal for Ireland to join European Union rejected

1964   Brian Friel, *Philadelphia, Here I Come!*

Campaign for Social Justice founded in Northern Ireland to implement tactics like those of the American Civil Rights movement

1966   Opening of newly constructed Abbey Theatre

Bombing destruction by IRA of Nelson's Pillar, Dublin landmark named after the British naval commander, on the fiftieth anniversary year of the Easter 1916 rising

Ulster Constitution Defence Committee and Ulster Volunteer Force created to advance Union to Great Britain and to prevent concessions to Ireland

1967   Northern Ireland Civil Rights Association (NICRA) founded to seek reforms in voting rights, gerrymandering practices, and discrimination in hiring and housing policies through protest marches

1969   Democracy March from Derry to Belfast attacked by Protestant protesters; British military troops are deployed to Northern Ireland

Summer rioters clash with troops in Derry and Belfast

Beckett awarded Nobel Prize for Literature

1970   IRA splits into Provisional (unification of Ireland) and Official (Marxist class revolt)
        Creation of Social Democratic and Labor (SDLP) party as a centrist, anti-Unionist alternative to Republicanism

1971   First British soldier killed by provisional IRA; Social Democratic Labor Party (SDLP) withdraws from Stormont parliament in Northern Ireland to protest lack of effective inquiries into civilian deaths caused by soldiers

1972   "Bloody Sunday" riots in Derry

1973   Republic joins European Economic Community
        Friel's play *Freedom of the City*, on sectarian strife, premieres

1975   The first professional Irish theater company outside Dublin, the Druid Theatre Company, founded in Galway

1980   Field Day Theatre Company founded and launched with production of Friel's *Translations* in Derry Guildhall; the production later tours north and south Ireland
        Republican prisoners in Northern Ireland organize hunger strikes; ten strikers die in 1981

1983   Charabanc Theatre Company founded in Northern Ireland to produce improvisational works based on the oral histories of local workers

1985   Anglo-Irish Agreement allows role for Republic in negotiations in Northern Ireland

1990   Mary Robinson, Labour politician associated with reform and women's rights, elected President of Ireland

1992   Bishop of Galway Eamon Casey's case of illegitimate son epitomizes succession of scandals of sexual abuses and abuses of power by clergy and institutional cover-ups by Catholic Church hierarchy

1995   Seamus Heaney awarded Nobel Prize for Literature
        Referendum legalizes divorce in Republic of Ireland
        Beginning of extraordinary economic period of growth called "Celtic Tiger," after Asian Tiger model of economic growth through international finance and new technology

1997   Conor McPherson's *The Weir* opens at the Royal Court Upstairs in London

1998   David Trimble (Ulster Unionist Party) and John Hume (SDLP) share Nobel Peace Prize, while Gerry Adams (Sinn Féin) is not recognized
        Good Friday Agreement restores power-sharing with local legislation in Northern Ireland
        Marina Carr's *By the Bog of Cats* opens at Abbey Theatre as part of the Dublin Theatre Festival

1999   A series of tribunals and investigations of business and personal scandals of four-time Taoiseach (Prime Minister) Charles Haughey epitomizes the erosion of national confidence in political institutions

2002   Ireland adopts Euro monetary system, while Britain maintains sterling system

Disagreements over disarmament suspend Good Friday Agreement and local legislation in Northern Ireland, and revert to direct administration of Northern Ireland from London; local administration is later restored and "the peace process" continues through tense negotiations

Selected Bibliography

• indicates works included or excerpted in this Norton Critical Edition.

ON IRISH HISTORY

Bardon, Jonathan. *A History of Ulster*. Belfast: Blackstaff, 1985.
Bartlett, Thomas, ed. *Irish Studies: A General Introduction*. Totowa: Barnes and Noble, 1988.
Beckett, J. C. *The Making of Modern Ireland*. New York: Knopf, 1966.
Bew, Paul. *Ideology and the Irish Question: Ulster Unionism and Irish Nationalism 1912–1916*. Oxford: Clarendon, 1994.
Bottigheimer, Karl S. *Ireland and the Irish: A Short History*. New York: Columbia UP, 1982.
Boyce, D. George. *Nationalism in Ireland*. Baltimore: Johns Hopkins UP, 1982.
Brown, Terence. *Ireland: A Social and Cultural History, 1922–2002*. London: Harper Perennial, 2004.
Connolly, Claire, ed. *Theorizing Ireland*. London: Palgrave, 2003.
Edwards, R. Dudley. *A New History of Ireland*. Dublin: Gill and Macmillan, 1972.
Fallon, Brian: *An Age of Innocence: Irish Culture 1930–1960*. Dublin: Gill and Macmillan, 1998.
Ferriter, Diarmid. *The Transformation of Ireland*. Woodstock: Overlook Press, 2005.
Foster, John Wilson. *Recoveries: Neglected Episodes in Irish Cultural History 1860–1912*. Dublin: University College Dublin P, 2002.
Foster, R. F. *The Irish Story: Telling Tales and Making It Up in Ireland*. Oxford: Oxford UP, 2002.
———. *Modern Ireland, 1600–1972*. New York: Penguin, 1988.
Garvin, Tom. *The Birth of Irish Democracy*. New York: St. Martin's Press, 1996.
Gibbons, Luke. *Transformations in Irish Culture*. Notre Dame: Notre Dame UP, 1996.
Hutchinson, John. *The Dynamics of Cultural Nationalism: The Gaelic Revival and the Creation of the Irish Nation State*. London: Alien and Unwin, 1987.
Jackson, Alvin. *Ireland 1798–1998: Politics and War*. Oxford: Oxford UP, 1999.
Kee, Robert. *The Green Flag: A History of Irish Nationalism*. New York: Delacorte, 1972.
Kirby, Peadar, Luke Gibbons, and Michael Cronin, eds. *Reinventing Ireland: Culture, Society and the Global Economy*. London: Pluto Press, 2002.
Lee, J. J. *Ireland 1912–1985: Politics and History*. Cambridge: Cambridge UP, 1989.
Lyons, F. S. L. *Culture and Anarchy in Ireland, 1870–1939*. Oxford: Clarendon, 1979.
———. *Ireland Since the Famine*. Rev. ed. London: Fontana, 1973.
MacCurtain, Margaret, and Dhonnacha O Corráin, eds. *Women in Irish Society: The Historical Dimension*. London: Greenwood, 1979.
Moody, T. W., and F. X. Martin, eds. *The Course of Irish History*. Cork: Mercier Press, 1967.

O'Brien, Conor Cruise. *States of Ireland.* New York: Pantheon, 1972.

O'Gráda, Cormac. *A Rocky Road: The Irish Economy since the 1920s.* Manchester: Manchester UP, 1997.

O'Toole, Fintan. *The Ex-Isle of Erin: Images of a Global Ireland.* Dublin: New Island Books, 1997.

———. *The Lie of the Land: Irish Identities.* London: Verso, 1997.

Sweeney, Paul. *The Celtic Tiger: Ireland's Economic Miracle Explained.* Dublin: Oak Tree Press, 1998.

Valiulis, Maryann Gialanella, and Mary Dowd, eds. *Women and Irish History.* Dublin: Wolfhound Press, 1997.

Ward, Margaret. *Unmanageable Revolutionaries: Women and Irish Nationalism.* London: Pluto Press, 1989.

ON IRISH LITERARY HISTORY

• Bradley, Anthony, and Maryann Gialanella Valiulis, eds. *Gender and Sexuality in Modern Ireland.* Amherst: U Massachusetts P, 1998.

Brown, Malcolm. *Ireland's Literature: Selected Essays.* Dublin: Lilliput, 1988.

———. *The Politics of Irish Literature: From Thomas Davis to W. B. Yeats.* Seattle: U of Washington P, 1972.

Cairns, David, and Shaun Richards. *Writing Ireland: Colonialism, Nationalism, and Culture.* Manchester: Manchester UP, 1988.

Costello, Peter. *The Heart Grown Brutal: The Irish Revolution in Literature from Parnell to the Death of Yeats, 1891–1939.* Totowa, NJ: Rowman and Littlefield, 1977.

Dalsimer, Adele. *Visualizing Ireland: National Identity and the Pictorial Tradition.* London: Faber and Faber, 1993.

Deane, Seamus. *A Short History of Irish Literature.* Notre Dame, Ind.: Notre Dame UP, 1986.

Fallis, Richard. *The Irish Renaissance.* Syracuse: Syracuse UP, 1977.

Foster, John Wilson. *Colonial Consequences: Essays in Irish Literature and Culture.* Dublin: Lilliput, 1991.

Garratt, Robert F. *Modern Irish Poetry: Tradition and Continuity from Yeats to Heaney.* Berkeley: U California P, 1986.

Howarth, Herbert. *The Irish Writers, 1880–1940: Literature and Nationalism.* New York: Hill and Wang, 1959.

Imhof, Rudiger. *The Modern Irish Novel: Irish Novelists After 1945.* Dublin: Wolfhound Press, 2002.

Jeffares, A. Norman. *Anglo-Irish Literature.* New York: Schocken, 1982.

Kearney, Richard. *Transitions: Narratives in Modern Irish Culture.* Dublin: Wolfhound Press, 1988.

Kenner, Hugh. *A Colder Eye: The Modern Irish Writers.* New York: Knopf, 1985.

• Kiberd, Declan. *Inventing Ireland: The Literature of the Modern Nation.* London: Jonathan Cape/Random House, 1995.

———. *Irish Classics.* London: Granta, 2002.

Lloyd, David. *Anomalous States: Irish Writing and the Post-colonial Moment.* Durham: Duke UP, 1993.

Longley, Edna. *The Living Stream: Literature and Revisionism in Ireland.* Newcastle: Bloodaxe, 1994.

———. *Poetry and Posterity.* Newcastle: Bloodaxe, 2000.

Mercier, Vivian. *The Irish Comic Tradition.* New York: Oxford UP, 1962.

———. *Modern Irish Literature.* Oxford: Oxford UP, 1994.

O'Connor, Frank. *A Short History of Irish Literature: A Backward Look.* New York: Putnam, 1967.

O'Connor, Ulick. *All the Olympians: A Biographical Portrait of the Irish Literary Renaissance.* New York: Holt, 1984.

Paulin, Tom. *Ireland and the English Crisis.* Belfast: Bloodaxe, 1984.

Ryan, Ray, ed. *Writing in the Republic: Literature, Culture, Politics in the Republic of Ireland 1949–1999.* London: Macmillan, 2000.

Skelton, Robin. *Celtic Contraries: Selected Essays.* Syracuse: Syracuse UP, 1989.

Smyth, Gerry. *Decolonization and Criticism: The Construction of Irish Literature.* London: Pluto Press, 1998.

Tymoczko, Maria and Colin Ireland, eds. *Language and Tradition in Ireland.* Amherst: U Massachusetts P, 2003.

Watson, G. J. *Irish Identity and the Literary Revival: Synge, Yeats, Joyce, and O'Casey.* Washington, DC: Catholic University of America P, 1994.

ON IRISH DRAMA

Bell, Sam Hanna. *The Theatre in Ulster.* Dublin: Gill and Macmillan, 1972.

• Boland, Eavan, ed. *Irish Writers on Writing.* San Antonio: Trinity UP, 2007.

Edwards, Philip. *Threshold of a Nation: A Study in English and Irish Drama.* New York: Cambridge UP, 1979.

Ellis-Fermor, Una. *The Irish Dramatic Movement.* London: Methuen, 1939.

Dean, Joan Fitzpatrick. *Riot and Great Anger: Stage Censorship in Twentieth-Century Ireland.* Madison: U of Wisconsin P, 2004.

• Eglinton, John, W. B. Yeats, A. E., and W. Larminie. *Literary Ideals in England.* London: T. Fisher Unwin, 1899.

• Fay, Frank J. *Towards a National Theatre: The Dramatic Criticism of Frank J. Fay.* Ed. Robert Hogan. Dublin: Dolmen Press, 1970.

Fay, W. G., and Catherine Carswell. *The Fays of the Abbey Theatre.* London: Rich and Cowan, 1935.

Fitz-simon, Christopher. *The Abbey Theatre: Ireland's National Theatre—The First 100 Years.* London: Thames and Hudson, 2003.

———. *The Irish Theatre.* London: Thames and Hudson, 1983.

Flannery, James W. *Miss Annie F. Homiman and the Abbey Theatre.* Dublin: Dolmen Press, 1970.

Frazier, Adrian. *Behind the Scenes: Yeats, Horniman, and the Struggle for the Abbey Theatre.* Berkeley: U California P, 1990.

• Gregory, Lady. *Our Irish Theatre: A Chapter of Autobiography.* 1913; rpt. New York: Oxford UP, 1972.

• Grene, Nicholas. *The Politics of Irish Drama: Plays in Context from Boucicault to Friel.* New York: Cambridge UP, 1999.

Harrington, John P. *The Irish Play on the New York Stage.* Lexington: U Kentucky P, 1997.

———, and Elizabeth J. Mitchell. *Politics and Performance in Contemporary Northern Ireland.* Amherst: U Massachusetts P, 1999.

• Harris, Susan Cannon. *Gender and Modern Irish Drama.* Bloomington: Indiana UP, 2002.

Herr, Cheryl, ed. *For the Land They Loved: Irish Political Melodrama 1890–1925.* Syracuse: Syracuse UP, 1991.

Hogan, Robert. *After the Irish Renaissance: A Critical History of the Irish Drama Since "The Plough and the Stars."* Minneapolis: Minnesota UP, 1967.

———, ed. *Modern Irish Drama.* 4 vols. Dublin: Dolmen Press, 1975–79.

• ——— and Michael J. O'Neill, eds. *Joseph Holloway's Abbey Theatre: A Selection from His Unpublished Journal, "Impressions of a Dublin Playgoer."* Carbondale: Southern Illinois UP, 1967.

Hunt, Hugh. *The Abbey, Ireland's National Theatre.* Dublin: Gill and Macmillan, 1979.

———. *Theatre and Nationalism in Ireland.* Swansea: University College, 1974.

• Jordan, Eamonn, ed. *Theatre Stuff: Critical Essays on Contemporary Irish Theatre.* Dublin: Carysfort Press, 2000.

Kavanagh, Peter. *The Story of the Abbey Theatre*. New York: Devin-Adair, 1950.

Levitas, Ben. *The Theatre of Nation: Irish Drama and Cultural Nationalism 1890–1916*. Oxford: Clarendon, 2002.

McDonald, Ronan. *Tragedy in Irish Literature*. London: Palgrave, 2002.

Malone, Andrew E. *The Irish Drama*. London: Constable, 1929.

Matthews, P. J. *The Abbey Theatre, Sinn Féin, the Gaelic League, and the Cooperative Movement*. Cork: Cork UP, 2003.

Maxwell: D. E. S. *A Critical History of Modern Irish Drama 1890–1980*. Cambridge: Cambridge UP, 1984.

Mikhail, E. H., ed. *The Abbey Theatre: Interviews and Recollections*. London: Macmillan, 1988.

• Morash, Christopher. *A History of the Irish Theatre, 1601–2000*. New York: Cambridge UP, 2002.

Murray, Christopher. *Twentieth-Century Irish Drama: Mirror Up to Nation*. Manchester: Manchester UP, 1997.

O'Driscoll, Robert, ed. *Theatre and Nationalism in Twentieth-Century Ireland*. Toronto: Toronto UP, 1971.

O hAodha, Micheal. *Theatre in Ireland*. London: Blackwell, 1974.

Pilkington, Lionel. *Theatre and the State in 20th Century Ireland: Cultivating the People*. London: Routledge and Kegan Paul, 2001.

• Richards, Shaun, ed. *The Cambridge Companion to Twentieth-Century Irish Drama*. Cambridge: Cambridge UP, 2004.

———. *Twentieth-Century Irish Drama*. Cambridge: Cambridge UP, 2004.

• Richtarik, Marilynn J. *Acting Between the Lines: The Field Day Theatre Company and Irish Cultural Politics 1980–1984*. Washington, DC: The Catholic U of America P, 1995.

Robinson, Lennox. *Ireland's Abbey Theatre: A History, 1899–1951*. London: Sidgwick and Jackson, 1951.

• Roche, Anthony. *Contemporary Irish Drama: From Beckett to McGuinness*. New York: St. Martin's Press, 1995.

Schrank, Bernice, and William Demastes, eds. *Irish Playwrights 1880–1995: A Research and Production Sourcebook*. London: Greenwood Press, 1997.

Sihra, Melissa. *Women in Irish Drama: A Century of Authorship and Representation*. London: Palgrave, 2007.

Trotter, Mary. *Ireland's National Theaters: Political Performance and the Origins of the Irish Dramatic Movement*. Syracuse: Syracuse UP, 2001.

Watt, Stephen. *Joyce, O'Casey, and the Irish Popular Theater*. Syracuse: Syracuse UP, 1991.

• Watt, Stephen, Eileen Morgan, and Shakir Mustafa, eds. *A Century of Irish Drama: Widening the Stage*. Bloomington: Indiana UP, 2000.

Welch, Robert. *The Abbey Theatre 1899–1999: Form and Pressure*. Oxford: Oxford UP, 1999.

Worth, Katherine. *The Irish Drama of Europe from Yeats to Beckett*. Atlantic Highlands: Humanities Press, 1978.

• Yeats, W. B. *Explorations*. New York: Macmillan/Collier Books, 1973.

ON W. B. YEATS

• Brown, Terence. *The Life of W. B. Yeats: A Critical Biography*. Malden, Mass.: Blackwell Publishers Inc., 1999.

Cullingford, Elizabeth. *Yeats, Ireland and Fascism*. New York: New York UP, 1981.

Donoghue, Denis. *William Butler Yeats*. New York: Viking, 1971.

Ellis, Sylvia C. *The Plays of W. B. Yeats: Yeats and the Dancer*. London: Macmillan, 1995.

Ellmann, Richard. *Yeats: The Man and the Masks*. London: Macmillan, 1949.

• Foster, R. F. *W. B. Yeatss: A Life*—Vol. 1: *The Apprentice Mage, 1865–1914*; Vol. 2: *The Arch-Poet, 1915–1939*. New York: Oxford UP, 2003.

Hone, Joseph. *W. B. Yeats: 1865–1939*. New York: Macmillan, 1943.

Howes, Marjorie. *Yeats's Nations: Gender, Class, and Irishness*. Cambridge: Cambridge UP, 1996.

Jeffares, A. Norman and A. A. Knowland. *A Commentary on the Collected Plays of W. B. Yeats*. London: Macmillan, 1975.

Moore, James Rees. *Masks of Love and Death: Yeats as Dramatist*. Ithaca: Cornell UP, 1971.

O'Driscoll, Robert, and Lorna Reynolds, eds. *Yeats and the Theatre*. Niagara Falls: Maclean-Hunter Press, 1975.

Qamber, Akhtar. *Yeats and the Noh*. New York: Weatherhill, 1974.

Skelton, Robin, and Ann Saddlemyer, eds. *The World of W. B. Yeats*. Rev. ed. Seattle: U of Washington P, 1967.

Unterecker, John. *A Reader's Guide to William Butler Yeats*. New York: Farrar, Straus and Giroux, 1959.

Ure, Peter. *Yeats the Dramatist*. New York: Barnes and Noble, 1963.

Vendler, Helen Hennessy. *Yeats's Vision and the Later Plays*. Cambridge: Harvard UP, 1963.

Whitaker, Thomas R. *Swan and Shadow: Yeats's Dialogue with History*. Chapel Hill: U of North Carolina P, 1964.

• Yeats, W. B. *Essays and Introductions*. London: Macmillan, 1961.

ON LADY GREGORY

Adams, Hazard. *Lady Gregory*. Lewisburg: Bucknell UP, 1973.

Coxhead, Elizabeth. *J. M. Synge and Lady Gregory*. New York: London House, 1962.

Gregory, Ann. *Me and Nu: Childhood at Coole*. Gerrards Cross: Colin Smythe, 1970.

• Gregory, Lady. *Lady Gregory's Journals*, Coole Edition—Vol. 1: *Books One to Twenty-Nine, 10 October 1916–24 February 1925*; Vol. 2: *Books Thirty to Forty-Four, 21 February 1925–9 May 1932*. New York: Oxford UP, 1978.

• Hill, Judith. *Lady Gregory: An Irish Life*. Sparkford, UK: J. H. Haynes & Co., Ltd., 2005.

Kohfeldt, Mary Lou. *Lady Gregory: The Woman Behind the Irish Renaissance*. New York: Atheneum, 1985.

McDiarmid, Lucy, and Maureen Waters, eds. *Lady Gregory: Selected Writings*. London: Penguin, 1996.

Mikhail, E. H. *Lady Gregory: Interviews and Recollections*. London: Macmillan, 1977.

Napier, Taura. *Seeking a Country: Literary Autobiographies of Irish Women*. Lanham, MD: UP of America, 2001.

• Saddlemyer, Ann. *In Defense of Lady Gregory, Playwright*. Dublin: Dolmen Press, 1966.

———, ed. *Theatre Business: The Correspondence of the First Abbey Directors*. Gerrards Cross: Colin Smythe, 1982.

———, and Colin Smythe, eds. *Lady Gregory: Fifty Years After*. Totowa: Barnes and Noble, 1987.

ON J. M. SYNGE

Corkery, Daniel. *Synge and Anglo-Irish Literature: A Study*. 1931. New York: Russell and Russell, 1965.

• Frazier, Adrian. *Playboys of the Western World: Production Histories*. Dublin: Carysfort Press, 2004.

Gerstenberger, Donna. *John Millington Synge*. New York: Twayne, 1964.
Greene, David H., and Edward M. Stephens. *J. M. Synge, 1871–1909*. New York: Macmillan, 1959.
Harmon, Maurice, ed. *J. M. Synge Centenary Papers*. Dublin: Dolmen Press, 1971.
Kiberd, Declan. *Synge and the Irish Language*. London: Macmillan, 1979.
Kiely, David M. *John Millington Synge: A Biography*. New York, St. Martin's Press, 1994.
King, Mary C. *The Drama of J. M. Synge*. Syracuse: Syracuse UP, 1985.
McCormack, W. J. *Fool of the Family: A Life of J. M. Synge*. New York: NYU P, 2001.
Price, Alan. *Synge and Anglo-Irish Drama*. London: Methuen, 1961.
Saddlemyer, Ann. *J. M. Synge and Modern Comedy*. Dublin: Dolmen Press, 1968.
Skelton, Robin. *J. M. Synge and His World*. New York: Viking, 1971.
Stephens, Edward. *My Uncle John: Edward Stephen's Life of J. M. Synge*. Ed. Andrew Carpenter. London: Oxford UP, 1974.
Tóibín, Colm, ed. *Synge: A Celebration*. Dublin: Carysfort Press, 2005.
Whitaker, Thomas R., ed. *Twentieth-Century Interpretations of* The Playboy of the Western World. Englewood Cliffs: Prentice-Hall, 1969.

ON BERNARD SHAW

Bentley, Eric. *Bernard Shaw*. Rev. ed. London: Methuen, 1967.
Berst, Charles A. *Bernard Shaw and the Art of Drama*. Urbana: U of Illinois P, 1973.
Davis, Tracy C. *George Bernard Shaw and the Socialist Theatre*. Westport: Greenwood, 1994.
Ervine, St. John. *Bernard Shaw: His Life, Work and Friends*. New York: William Monroe, 1956.
Ganz, Arthur F. *George Bernard Shaw*. New York: Grove, 1983.
Gibbs, A. M. *Bernard Shaw: A Life*. Gainesville, FL: UP of Florida, 2005.
Greene, David H., and Dan Laurence, eds. *Bernard Shaw: The Matter with Ireland*. London: Rupert Hart-Davis, 1962.
Grene, Nicholas. *Bernard Shaw: A Critical View*. New York: St. Martin's, 1984.
Holroyd, Michael. *Bernard Shaw: The One-Volume Definitive Edition*. New York: Random House, 1998.
———. *Bernard Shaw*—Vol. I: *1856–1898, The Search for Love*; Vol. II: *1898–1918, The Pursuit of Power*; Vol. III: *1918–1950, The Lure of Fantasy*; Vol. IV: *1950–1991, The Last Laugh*. New York: Random House, 1988–1992.
———. ed. *The Genius of Shaw: A Symposium*. New York: Rinehart and Winston, 1979.
Kaufman, R. J., ed. *G. B. Shaw: A Collection of Critical Essays*. Englewood Cliffs: Prentice-Hall, 1965.

ON SEAN O'CASEY

Ayling, Ronald, ed. *Sean O'Casey*. London: Macmillan, 1969.
Benstock, Bernard. *Sean O'Casey*. Lewisburg: Bucknell UP, 1970.
• Fallon, Gabriel. *Sean O'Casey: The Man I Knew*. Boston: Little, Brown, 1965.
Greaves, C. Desmond. *Sean O'Casey: Politics and Art*. Atlantic Highlands, NJ: Humanities Press, 1979.
Hogan, Robert. *The Experiments of Sean O'Casey*. New York: St. Martin's Press, 1960.
Kenneally, Michael. *Portraying the Self: Sean O'Casey and the Art of Autobiography*. Gerrards Cross: Colin Smythe, 1988.

Kilroy, Thomas, ed. *Sean O'Casey: A Collection of Critical Essays.* Englewood Cliffs: Prentice-Hall, 1975.

McCann, Sean. *The World of Sean O'Casey.* London: New English Library, 1966.

Murray, Christopher. *A Faber Guide to Sean O'Casey.* London: Faber and Faber, 2000.

• ———. *Seán O'Casey, Writer at Work: A Biography.* Ithaca: McGill-Queen's UP, 2004.

O'Casey, Eileen. *Sean.* London: Macmillan, 1971.

O'Connor, Gary. *Sean O'Casey: A Life.* New York: Atheneum, 1988.

Schrank, Bernice. *Sean O'Casey: A Research and Production Sourcebook.* Westport, CT: Greenwood Press, 1996.

Stewart, Victoria. *About O'Casey: The Playwright and the Work.* London: Faber and Faber, 2003.

ON SAMUEL BECKETT

Bair, Deirdre. *Samuel Beckett: A Biography.* New York: Harcourt Brace Jovanovich, 1978.

Brater, Enoch. *Beckett at 80: Beckett in Context.* New York: Oxford UP, 1986.

Casanova, Pascale. *Samuel Beckett: Anatomy of a Literary Revolution.* Trans. Gregory Elliott. London: Verso, 2006.

Cohn, Ruby. *Just Play: Beckett's Theater.* Princeton: Princeton UP, 1980.

Cronin, Anthony. *Samuel Beckett: The Last Modernist.* London: Harper Collins, 1996.

Doll, Mary. *Beckett and Myth: An Archetypal Approach.* Syracuse: Syracuse UP, 1988.

Fletcher, John, and John Spurling. *Beckett: A Study of His Plays.* New York: Hill and Wang, 1972.

Gontarski, S. E. *The Intent of Undoing in Samuel Beckett's Dramatic Texts.* Bloomington: Indiana UP, 1985.

• Harmon, Maurice, ed. *No Author Better Served: The Correspondence of Samuel Beckett & Alan Schneider.* Cambridge: Harvard UP, 1998.

• Harrington, John P. *The Irish Beckett.* Syracuse: Syracuse UP, 1990.

Kalb, Jonathan. *Beckett in Performance.* Cambridge: Cambridge UP, 1989.

Kenner, Hugh. *A Reader's Guide to Samuel Beckett.* New York: Farrar, Straus, Giroux, 1973.

———. *Samuel Beckett: A Critical Study.* Rev. ed. Berkeley: U California P, 1968.

• Knowlson, James. *Damned to Fame: The Life of Samuel Beckett.* New York: Simon & Schuster, 1996.

———, ed. *The Theatrical Notebooks of Samuel Beckett.* Vol III: *Krapp's Last Tape.* London: Faber and Faber, 1994.

———, and Elizabeth Knowlson, eds. *Beckett Remembering Beckett: A Centenary Celebration.* New York: Arcade, 2006.

Knowlson, James, and John Pilling. *Frescoes of the Skull: The Later Prose and Drama of Samuel Beckett.* New York: Grove Press, 1980.

McMillan, Dougald, and Marthe Fehsenfeld. *Beckett in Theatre.* London: John Calder, 1988.

Mercier, Vivian. *Beckett/Beckett.* New York: Oxford UP, 1977.

O'Brien, Eoin. *The Beckett Country: Samuel Beckett's Ireland.* Monkstown, County Dublin: Black Cat Press, 1986.

Oppenheim, Lois. *Directing Beckett.* Ann Arbor, MI: U of Michigan P, 1994.

Pilling, John, ed. *The Cambridge Guide to Beckett.* Cambridge: Cambridge UP, 1994.

Simpson, Alan. *Beckett and Behan and a Theatre in Dublin.* London: Routledge and Kegan Paul, 1962.

Webb, Eugene. *The Plays of Samuel Beckett*. Seattle: U of Washington P, 1972.
Wilmer, S. E., ed. *Beckett in Dublin*. Dublin: Lilliput Press, 1992.
Worth, Katherine. *Samuel Beckett's Theatre: Life Journeys*. Oxford: Clarendon, 1999.

ON BRIAN FRIEL

Andrews, Elmer. *The Art of Brian Friel: Neither Reality No Dreams*. New York: Macmillan, 1995.
Corbett, Toby. *Brian Friel: Decoding the Language of the Tribe*. Dublin: Liffey Press, 2002.
Dantanus, Ulf. *Brian Friel: A Study*. London: Faber and Faber, 1988.
Deane, Seamus. *Celtic Revivals: Essays in Modern Irish Literature, 1880–1980*. Winston-Salem: Wake Forest UP, 1987.
———. Introduction to *Brian Friel: Selected Plays*. Washington, DC: Catholic UP, 1986.
Hickey, Des, and Gus Smith. *Flight From the Celtic Twilight*. Indianapolis: Bobbs-Merrill, 1973.
Kerwin, William, ed. *Brian Friel: A Casebook*. New York: Garland, 1997.
Maxwell, D. E. S. *Brian Friel*. Lewisburg: Bucknell UP, 1973.
• Murray, Christopher, ed. *Brian Friel: Essays, Diaries, Interviews 1964–1999*. London: Faber and Faber, 1999.
O'Brien, George. *Brian Friel*. Dublin: Gill and Macmillan, 1980.
———, ed. *Brian Friel: A Reference Guide 1962–1992*. New York: G. K. Hall, 1995.
O'Connor, Ulick. *Brian Friel: Commitment and Crisis—The Writer and Northern Ireland*. Dublin: Elo Press, 1989.
Peacock, Alan J., ed. *The Achievement of Brian Friel*. Gerrards Cross: Colin Smythe, 1993.
Pine, Richard. *The Diviner: The Art of Brian Friel*. Dublin: Lilliput Press, 1988.

ON CONOR MCPHERSON

Costa, Maddy. "Human Beings Are Animals." *Guardian* 13 Sept. 2006.
Grene, Nicholas. "Ireland in Two Minds: Martin McDonagh and Conor McPherson." *Yearbook of English Studies*. January 2005.
O'Toole, Fintan. "The Weir." *New York Daily News* 2 April 1999; rpt. *Critical Moments: Fintan O'Toole on Modern Irish Theatre*. Dublin: Carysfort Press, 2003.
Simon, John. "Blarney's Tone." *New York* 12 April 1999.
Wallace, Clare. "A Micronarrative Imperative: Conor McPherson's Dialogue Dramas." *Irish Studies Review* 14.1 (2006).
White, Victoria. "Telling Stories in the Dark." *Irish Times* 2 July 1998.
Wood, Gerald C. *Conor McPherson*. Dublin: Liffey Press, 2003.

ON MARINA CARR

Jordan, Eamonn. "Unmasking the Myths? Marina Carr's *By the Bog of Cats . . . .*" *Amid Our Troubles: Irish Versions of Greek Tragedy*. Ed. Marianne McDonald and J. Michael Walton. London: Methuen, 2002.
Leeney, Cathy. "Exiled at Home: Teresa Deevy and Marina Carr." *Cambridge Companion to Twentieth Century Irish Drama*. Ed. Shaun Richards. Cambridge: Cambridge UP, 2003.
• ———, and Anna McMullan, eds. *The Theatre of Marina Carr: "before rules was made."* Dublin: Carysfort Press, 2003.

McMullan, Anna. "Marina Carr's Unhomely Women." *Irish Theatre Magazine* 1.1 (1998).

O'Dwyer, Riana. "The Imagination of Women's Reality: Christina Reid and Marina Carr." *Theatre Stuff: Critical Essays on Contemporary Irish Theatre*. Ed. Eamonn Jordan. Dublin: Carysfort Press, 2000.

O'Toole, Fintan. "Arts at the Crossroads." *Irish Times* 9 June 2001.

———. "Portia Coughlin." *Irish Times* 2 April 1996; rpt. *Critical Moments: Fintan O'Toole on Modern Irish Theatre*. Dublin: Carysfort Press, 2003.

Wallace, Clare. "Tragic Destiny and Abjection in Marina Carr's *The Mai, Portia Coughlan,* and *By the Bog of Cats* . . . ." *Irish University Review* 31.2 (2001).